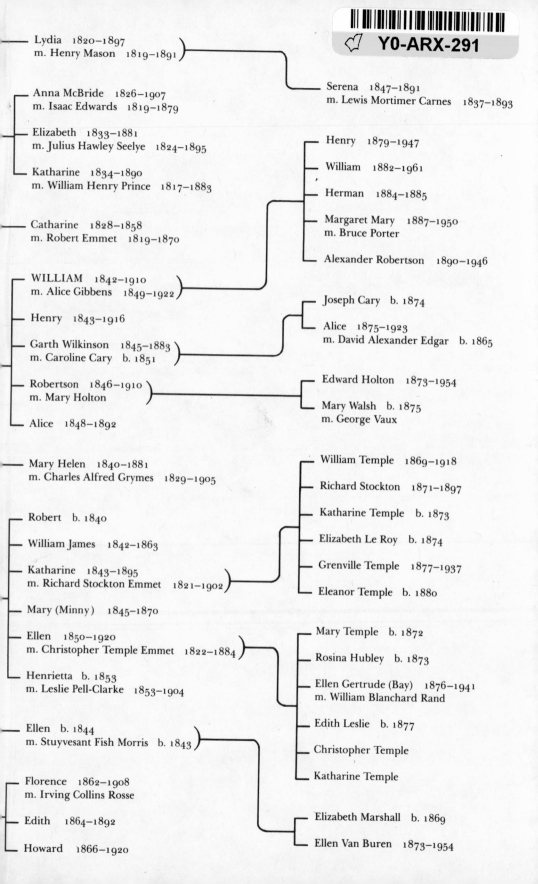

Lydia 1820–1897
m. Henry Mason 1819–1891

Serena 1847–1891
m. Lewis Mortimer Carnes 1837–1893

Anna McBride 1826–1907
m. Isaac Edwards 1819–1879

Elizabeth 1833–1881
m. Julius Hawley Seelye 1824–1895

Katharine 1834–1890
m. William Henry Prince 1817–1883

Henry 1879–1947

William 1882–1961

Herman 1884–1885

Margaret Mary 1887–1950
m. Bruce Porter

Alexander Robertson 1890–1946

Catharine 1828–1858
m. Robert Emmet 1819–1870

WILLIAM 1842–1910
m. Alice Gibbens 1849–1922

Henry 1843–1916

Garth Wilkinson 1845–1883
m. Caroline Cary b. 1851

Joseph Cary b. 1874

Alice 1875–1923
m. David Alexander Edgar b. 1865

Robertson 1846–1910
m. Mary Holton

Alice 1848–1892

Edward Holton 1873–1954

Mary Walsh b. 1875
m. George Vaux

Mary Helen 1840–1881
m. Charles Alfred Grymes 1829–1905

William Temple 1869–1918

Richard Stockton 1871–1897

Katharine Temple b. 1873

Elizabeth Le Roy b. 1874

Grenville Temple 1877–1937

Eleanor Temple b. 1880

Robert b. 1840

William James 1842–1863

Katharine 1843–1895
m. Richard Stockton Emmet 1821–1902

Mary (Minny) 1845–1870

Ellen 1850–1920
m. Christopher Temple Emmet 1822–1884

Henrietta b. 1853
m. Leslie Pell-Clarke 1853–1904

Mary Temple b. 1872

Rosina Hubley b. 1873

Ellen Gertrude (Bay) 1876–1941
m. William Blanchard Rand

Edith Leslie b. 1877

Christopher Temple

Katharine Temple

Ellen b. 1844
m. Stuyvesant Fish Morris b. 1843

Florence 1862–1908
m. Irving Collins Rosse

Edith 1864–1892

Howard 1866–1920

Elizabeth Marshall b. 1869

Ellen Van Buren 1873–1954

The Correspondence of

WILLIAM JAMES

This edition of the Correspondence of William James is sponsored by the American Council of Learned Societies.

The Correspondence *of*
William James

VOLUME 7

1890–1894

Edited by

Ignas K. Skrupskelis *and* Elizabeth M. Berkeley

with the assistance of
Wilma Bradbeer

University Press of Virginia
Charlottesville and London

THE UNIVERSITY PRESS OF VIRGINIA
Copyright © 1999 by the Rector and Visitors
of the University of Virginia

First published 1999

COMMITTEE ON
SCHOLARLY EDITIONS

AN APPROVED EDITION

MODERN LANGUAGE
ASSOCIATION OF AMERICA

Frontispiece: William James ca. 1894–95
(Photograph by Mrs. Montgomery Sears; by permission of the Houghton Library,
Harvard University)

Library of Congress Cataloging-in-Publication Data

(Revised for vol. 7)

James, William, 1842–1910.
The correspondence of William James.

Includes bibliographical references and index.
Contents: v. 1. William and Henry, 1861–1884.—v. 2. William and Henry,
1885–1896.—v. 3. William and Henry, 1897–1910.—v. 4. 1856–1877.—
v. 5. 1878–1884.—v. 6. 1885–1889.—v. 7. 1890–1894.
1. James, William, 1842–1910—Correspondence.
2. Philosophers—United States—Correspondence.
3. Psychologists—United States—Correspondence.
4. James, Henry, 1843–1916—Correspondence.
I. Skrupskelis, Ignas K., 1938–. II. Berkeley,
Elizabeth M. III. James, Henry, 1843–1916.
IV. Title.
B945.J24A4   1992   191 [B]   91-35923

ISBN 0-8139-1820-0

Printed in the United States of America

Contents

1890

1891

1892

1893

1894

Foreword

This is the seventh volume of the Critical Edition of *The Correspondence of William James* and is inclusive of correspondence written between 1890 and 1894. The first three volumes were devoted to the letters exchanged between the brothers William and Henry James. The subsequent volumes beginning with the fourth, published in 1995, will include all of the remaining correspondence of William James, arranged chronologically and having to do with members of his immediate and extended family as well as with friends and professional colleagues. This Critical Edition is projected to be completed in twelve volumes and will take the reader to 1910, the year in which William James died. Having completed nineteen volumes of *The Works of William James* in a Critical Edition, the editors and the editorial staff are pleased and privileged to continue the publication of an edition devoted to the correspondence of one of America's finest philosophers and writers, a person who stood four-square at the center of Euro-American thought for some fifty years.

The Editor of this edition is Ignas K. Skrupskelis, Professor Emeritus of Philosophy at the University of South Carolina and a lecturer at Vytautas Magnus University, Kaunas, Lithuania. Professor Skrupskelis is responsible for obtaining the letters and checking their legitimacy, place of origin, and chronology, for the annotations, and for the preparation of the index. His discussion of the letters is detailed in his Bibliographical Note, below. The Associate Editor is Elizabeth M. Berkeley, whose responsibilities include supervision of the transcription of the letters, textual editing, and seeing the copy through the press. The standards of transcription are detailed in the Note on the Editorial Method. She has been ably assisted in the preparation of this volume by Wilma Bradbeer, Judith Nelson, and Ann Goedde.

This edition is sponsored by the American Council of Learned Societies, to whom we are grateful in the persons of Stanley N. Katz, Steven C. Wheatley, and Hugh O'Neill.

Financial and advisory support for the edition has been provided by the National Endowment for the Humanities, specifically, Sheldon Hackney, Chairperson, and Daniel Jones, Program Officer. The support of the Endowment for the earlier edition of *The Works of William James* and for the present edition is a powerful testament to the importance of the American literary and philosophical tradition.

On behalf of the American Council of Learned Societies and the General Editor, we are deeply pleased and gratified to acknowledge a substantial award from The Andrew W. Mellon Foundation for the purpose of matching funds.

The editors are grateful to the University of Virginia for editorial office space in the Alderman Library, whose Reference Room staff has provided valuable assistance in locating source material pertinent to the project. We have received enthusiastic and caring support from Nancy C. Essig, Director of the University Press of Virginia, publisher of this edition. We express gratitude to the University of South Carolina, especially to George Terry, Vice President for Libraries and Collections, who assisted Professor Skrupskelis with office space in the Cooper Library.

Invaluable help was provided by the Reading Room staff of the Houghton Library of Harvard University, especially Melanie Wisner and Susan Halpert, and by the Curator of Manuscripts, Rodney Dennis, now retired, who gave permission to use that William James material subject to permission of the Houghton Library. We are indebted to Harley P. Holden, Curator of the Harvard Archives, for permission to use letters preserved in the Harvard University Archives.

Grateful acknowledgment is made to the following institutions for permission to publish letters from their collections: Bancroft Library, University of California, Berkeley; Manuscript Division, Rare Books and Special Collections, Princeton University Library; Smith College Archives; Beverly Historical Society and Charles W. Galloupe Memorial Society, Massachusetts; University Archives, Clark University; Rare Book and Manuscript Library, Columbia University; Wellesley College Archives; Department of Rare Books and Manuscripts, Boston Public Library; Special Collections and Archives, University of Massachusetts, Amherst; Beinecke Library, Yale University; Special Collections, University Libraries, University of Southern California; Library of Congress; College of Physicians of Philadelphia; Bodleian Library, University of Oxford; Massachusetts Historical Society; American Academy of Arts and Letters, New York City; Special Collections, Morris Library, Southern Illinois University, Carbondale;

Miss Porter's School Archives, Farmington, Connecticut; Harvard University Law School Library; Cornell University Library; Perkins School for the Blind, Watertown, Massachusetts; Bibliothèque publique et universitaire, Geneva; Schlesinger Archives of the History of Women, Radcliffe College; The Pierpont Morgan Library, MA 3564, New York City; John Hay Library, Brown University; Special Collections, Colby College Library; Bibliothèque de la Sorbonne, Paris; Manuscript and Archives Division, New York Public Library; Special Collections, Oberlin College Library; Master and Fellows of Trinity College, Cambridge; Cambridge University Library; Special Collections, Stanford University Libraries; Menninger Foundation, Topeka, Kansas.

We are indebted to the following institutions for access to letters in their collections: Ohio State University Library; Society for Psychical Research, New York City; Smithsonian Institution; Widener Library, Harvard University; Francis A. Countway Library of Medicine, Harvard University; University of Northern Iowa Library; Baker Library, Harvard Business School; University of California at Los Angeles; Huntington Library.

Among those to whom we owe thanks: W. W. Howells for special permission to publish the letter of 13 January 1891 from William Dean Howells to William James; J. F. Hornback and Natalie Koretz for assistance in locating the letters of Samuel Burns Weston and to Samuel L. Evans, Chairman of AFNA National Education and Research Fund, Philadelphia, for permission to publish the letters; Henry Holt and Company, Inc., for permission to publish the Henry Holt letters; Hilary Putnam, for permission to publish the letters of Charles Sanders Peirce; The Center for Dewey Studies, Southern Illinois University, Carbondale, for permission to publish the John Dewey letters; Carol M. Osborne for information about the family of Frank Duveneck; Leslie Perrin Wilson, Curator, Special Collections, Concord Free Public Library for biographical information about residents of Concord; Stuart Campbell, Archivist at Clark University, for his assistance to the editor; Charles Rice of the University of Virginia for checking the letters and passages in French; and William E. Jackson and J. Adelheid Synnatzschke-Cochran of the University of Virginia for their assistance in checking the letters and passages in German.

We are grateful to Harriet Furst Simon of The Center for Dewey Studies who reviewed the volume for the seal of the Committee on Scholarly Editions.

Important assistance was received from the James family: Henry James; Michael James; and Henry James Vaux, who generously provided the editors access to James's letters to Robertson James and Mary Holton James. In this regard we are deeply grateful to Roberta A. Sheehan, who shared her extensive collection of James memorabilia and her intimate knowledge of the extended James family.

· The General Editor is grateful to Patricia A. McDermott for her continuing research on this project and to Rex J. Zgarba, graduate assistant to the General Editor. The editors are grateful to the Advisory Committee for their support and to those persons who have given contributions to obtain matching funds, namely, Michael James, Steve Haken, John Lachs, Edward H. Madden, Donald McQuade, and Gerald E. Myers. Frederick H. Burkhardt, the General Editor of the *Works,* was a motivating and consulting person in the decision to go forward with the *Correspondence* project.

We are especially indebted to Robert Coles of Harvard University for his Introduction to this volume.

Alexander R. James, William James's grandson and literary executor until his death in 1995, gave the editors permission to publish materials on which he held copyright.

We thank Bay James, literary executrix of the James family papers, for her assistance to the editors.

Grateful acknowledgment is offered to the Rector and the Board of Visitors of the University of Virginia, who hold the copyright to the volumes in this edition.

John J. McDermott
Texas A&M University
General Editor

Introduction
ROBERT COLES

During the early 1890s (the time of the correspondence that follows) the William James who was a bright, sometimes moody, talented person of lucky and privileged circumstances, a physician, a college teacher, an essayist, a husband and a father, began a stride that would take him to the doors of history—when he died, in 1910, at the age of sixty-eight, he was the enormously respected, internationally renowned figure whom today's worlds of science and letters, both, continue to regard with admiration, with wonder, with the curiosity such emotions generate, hence the publication of these letters, a full century and more since they were written. No question, the appearance (in 1890) of James's two-volume *Principles of Psychology* launched his eminence, made him the subject of critical consideration, acclaim. Those books were not mere additions to an academic storehouse of scholarly texts—rather, they inaugurated an important new direction in America's cultural life.

Psychology was then a relatively obscure field of inquiry, much suspected and dismissed by the prevailing principalities and powers of most colleges and universities. In Germany and France psychologists had fared somewhat better—they were seen as laboratory scientists trying hard to explore the physical basis of the mind. James had studied physiology, knew well what his European colleagues were attempting to do, but he was also a philosopher, and a literate one at that—able to write in such a way that ordinary readers could grasp with relative ease his intended meaning. He understood well the complexities and obscurities of thought to which philosophy is heir, and he enjoyed coming to grips with them. But he was possessed of a clearheaded, urgent, inviting voice, whose rhythms attracted the interested attention of others—as a lecturer, a conversationalist, a letter writer, an essayist. That voice would make psychology an accessible part of the introspective life of thousands of late nineteenth-century Americans—a development hard for many of us today to imagine, because our thinking is so routinely, even reflexively psychological in nature.

History, then, is the great contextual arbiter—tells us at any moment in time what we are to contemplate, what we are to dismiss as irrelevant, unthinkable; and James became an instrument of that aspect of history. He persuaded the American literate, intellectual world of his time that psychological inquiry really mattered; that it enabled, generated philosophical wisdom; that the brain, so intent, with increasing success, on studying other organs of the body, and indeed, anything and everything outside it, ought to begin studying itself not only rigorously but imaginatively. Of course, he knew that his philosopher colleagues, not to mention novelists (such as his brother Henry) had always looked inward with great care and even brilliance—yet he also took note of the increasing mastery of the scientific method over matter, and though he was tempted (like so many of us, still) to spring our thinking and dreaming lives free of their bodily constraints—give "spirit" its own being—he was, again, an experienced laboratory scientist, and he brought to Harvard that kind of sensibility, even as he was more than tempted at times to hand over the details of such investigatory work to others.

The letters in this volume tell us a lot about this philosopher and literary essayist who dared embrace and enhance the life of psychology. Immersed as he was in an era's assumptions, and in his inevitable egoism, he could stand back as few of us can or will, take the longest possible view of things, including his own efforts: "It seems to me that Psychology is like Physics before Galileo's time—not a single elementary law yet caught in a glimpse of it. A great chance for some future psychologue to make a greater name than Newton's, but who then will read the books of this generation? Not many, I know. Meanwhile they must be written."

Such detachment doesn't always accompany high talent, genius. James lived with a sharply knowing sense of history—his letters constantly show him aware that what is may soon enough no longer be. He was hoping over one hundred years ago that women would be a full part of Harvard's intellectual life, as students and teachers, even as he realized how utopian (if not wild or crazy) such an idea was for others of prominence in Cambridge and elsewhere. At that time, after all, women weren't able to vote, and only a sustained struggle on their part would enable them to secure suffrage—and then only after the nation had gone to war on behalf of the "freedom" of others in Europe. As a matter of fact, a similar sequence of events happened a few decades later—women only became full-fledged Harvard students after the Second World War ended. No wonder in his last years James was studying war; he knew its ironic, positive consequences: nations are given much moral pause as all those casualties come home, hurt or dead—and so, once-fixed customs or attitudes begin to yield to a climate of introspection. Often, at such times, the prophets and seers who long ago argued in favor of such breakthrough changes are all too readily forgotten.

Nor was James's advocacy of women as desirable members of a university community his sole expression of rebelliousness. He clearly had little patience with faculty meetings, with the rules and regulations that various administrators wanted to impose on him and his colleagues, many of whom, he knew, were far more eager to be compliant than he. His stubbornly idiosyncratic, free-wheeling spirit keeps surging forth as he writes to his friends—yet he obviously loved teaching, for all its demands on his mind, his time, his energy. Moreover, he knew how to hold his tongue, even offer a graciousness and a spirit of humility and compliance not earnestly felt, when he dealt with his boss, Harvard's President Eliot. A professor of independent means, and, increasingly, a writer of great distinction and reputation, he nevertheless belonged to a college's faculty, and he realized that there were substantial reasons for him to be tactful and cooperative in his dealings with those "above" him in an institution that he himself described as the nation's leading university. After all, many of the letters in this volume have to do with a prominent faculty member's desire to bring another prominent colleague to his side—the eventually successful effort to secure a teaching position for the brilliant young German psychologist Hugo Münsterberg. Here, Harvard was taking a step toward its future as an internationally renowned research university, and Professor James revealed himself a skilled, insistent negotiator, adept at academic politics.

It is interesting to read James's explicit, demure self-portrayals, compare them with what, in fact, he was quite eager and willing to do. In an 1892 letter he declines to become president of a psychological society with this remark: "I am by nature so little of a man for societies, organizations, secretaryships, presidencies, powers, principalities, and politics (even the politics of science) that I can't bring myself to change them." Yet he could be a persistent, accomplished advocate for the very kind of change he claims others are better able to pursue. That is to say, he could be clearheaded about what needed to be done, articulate and persuasive in the pursuit of a particular institutional objective. Indeed, even as he regarded himself as an iconoclastic loner of sorts, he demonstrated a persistent, tireless, almost urgent sociability, and it is such a quality of mind that, finally, brought Münsterberg across the Atlantic and enabled the discipline of psychology to have a proper and substantial and increasingly autonomous position in the Harvard curriculum and intellectual scene.

In letter after letter James praised, pursued the European psychologist, and in letter after letter he also paved the way for an invitation to him, and later, for his welcome, and later still, for a satisfactory working situation that would, in the long run, turn a trial of teaching into a tenured stay. Part of James's effectiveness as a leader of others, a shaper of thought, opinion—and yes, of a major academic "principality"—had to do with the disarming charm of his professed humility, his incapacity with respect to social leadership. In fact, he had very clear and strong ideas about how a university ought to be run (and for whose benefit), and similarly with the professional societies to which he belonged. He was also, of course, compelling with words: in his letters he makes whatever case he has in mind to telling effect— he is even willing to turn the other cheek on occasion in response to unfriendly criticism or resistance to an idea, a proposal he has offered. Soon enough, those who have had doubts or reservations (or worse) begin to feel admiration for someone of such obvious, unyielding moral poise—a mix of displayed conviction and self-effacement; and soon enough, too, a measure of embarrassment, if not shame, descends upon the critic, the potential or actual adversary: this brilliant, wide-ranging writer and teacher who is so willing to renounce his own intellectual and political authority, even to embrace gratefully the demurrers others have directed his way, deserves a special kind of consideration, respect. The private person, the vulnerable one, the man who stands apart from institutional life—its dealings, if not bickering and scheming—proves to be no incompetent as his own kind of leader, even adversary.

Nevertheless, the academic life did not please James. He wrote of a "very stupid commencement" in a letter to his wife, and spoke of "another day of sterile tiresomeness" as his overall response to such a ceremony. In a long and revealing letter to Harvard's president he worried about "the risk of overwhelming the lives of men whose interest is more in learning than in administration." He made clear his disinterest in committee work, in university politics. He bluntly referred to "chairmen who like power"—those who headed the various departments in the faculty of arts and sciences. He called himself an "autodidact," made clear his enjoyment of teaching, obviously treasured the friendship of some of his colleagues, but chafed at those who run things, and like to run things—indeed, defined himself at their expense. For him, "power" had to do with reflection, with convictions earned against the gradient of doubt, and finally, with the effort at persuasion that words enable. By 1890 he had finished such an effort, a big-time one, in the form of his attempt to construct a broad canvas of psychology, yet in his letters he was still trying to get others straight on this or that aspect of the human mind's life, and really, he was exerting that kind of authority or power over his readers: a writer anxious even in his letters to make his views known in such a way that they become attractive, believable.

Above all, James wanted to reach his wife, convey to her his affectionate regard, of course, but also what was on his mind. Many of the letters in this volume were addressed to her, and they invite our consideration of the writer as a husband, a family man. Without question Alice and William were deeply in love, still, after a marriage that had brought them three sons and a daughter. The letters, obviously, tell of times of separation and thereby don't chronicle the everydayness of a lived life of togetherness, with its inevitable ups and downs. The latter moments assert themselves indirectly—a husband apologizing for not having been more attentive, for being so weighed down by the demands of his own life that he was distant while there, or literally not there, hence the need for a letter. Often, however, James's minor transgressions of mood or attention seem more in his mind than that of his wife, whose letters glow with a direct, affectionate simplicity, a lack of pretentiousness altogether exemplary and edifying. He is, in a sense, corresponding with his own stern, watchful conscience as much as with his wife, Alice. She seems quite understanding of him, but he can be given to self-doubt, if not self-accusation. His busy life, at times, becomes a third presence, and because of it, naturally, these letters, reveal a man who kept missing his mate ever so sorely, passionately, but who was also very much taken by his life as a scholar, teacher, writer—a man with an apparent and vigorous need to be with friends and colleagues, whether in person (the constant meals shared with such a range of individuals) or through the kind of "on record" communication of letters.

Today, of course, we casually pick up the phone, or get in a car, a plane, to be near our husbands, wives, in a matter of minutes, hours. A century ago, as these letters make ever so clear, both time and space were quite different. Back then William, in Cambridge, wrote to Alice in Chocorua as if an ocean separated them, and expected to read her response in a matter of days. Now the phone is at constant ready, and in a couple of hours one can make the drive from Irving Street in Cambridge to the mountains of New Hampshire. If there is much to be gained from such "progress," these letters prompt us to think about what has been lost. The sense of distance, of separation, of loss, even, can stir the heart, the moral imagination—and therefore the yearning, the ardor, the second thoughts, the inwardness, the re- morse of these letters, and too, the wonderful attentiveness to social detail, the narrative momentum (and sometimes urgency) that make us even now feel very much interested in what we are reading: grate- ful recipients of sustained reflective conversation meant to be taken seriously by another's eyes, head, heart. In contrast, all too often, our casual use of the phone, our heavy foot on the gas pedal, make for a different sense of what is possible—and so, ironically, the less con- centrated our attention, often enough to what we say to one another.

Indeed, as I read these husband-wife letters, and, some father-son ones, I remembered my own childhood. My father had come to the United States, to Massachusetts, from England, had subsequently met my mother, who came to Boston from Iowa. Back in the Yorkshire Midlands Dad's three sisters and one brother, not to mention his par- ents, pined for knowledge of his American life—and got it weekly, courtesy of a long letter he wrote every Sunday afternoon right after lunch. I remember him sitting down at his desk, taking out his foun- tain pen, making sure it was thoroughly supplied with ink, then filling up three or so pages with his descriptions of what had happened to him, to all of us in the family, during the past week; and as well, he would comment on world events, on what he had read (he was always immersed in the plot of one novel or another). When he had finished the letter, he would emerge from his study, hand it to our mother, who would read it carefully, and, likely as not, remark on something that had been mentioned, discussed by Dad. Then my brother Bill and I had a chance to read what our father had chosen to regard as significant enough to remark upon, and so doing, to experience a week a second time through someone else's memory and sensibility as both were brought to bear on those pieces of writing paper I can still see, with the commanding idiosyncratic script applied to them.

Soon enough, telephone conversation would threaten to make such letters unnecessary—but not for Dad. To be sure, he would sometimes pick up the phone and get to talk with someone in his family—but he never stopped his weekly letters, addressed (by name) to his parents, his sisters, and brother. When I was a college student, old enough to have some distance, literal and figurative, on my parents and their various interests, activities, I wondered aloud one Sunday, when home for lunch, why those letters were still being written—why, when there on the bulletin board, near the phone, was a list of Yorkshire telephone numbers. I can still hear Dad's brief, modest explanation: "The letters help me sort out my life—and so, I like to write them." That is what William was doing, sometimes, as he wrote to his beloved Alice: he was rendering an account, a chronicle, of how time was spent; but he was also picking and choosing among the moments of his very busy, active life, selecting certain thoughts and deeds for his own attention as well as that of his wife. No doubt when we talk on the phone we do likewise, but a letter can have a long life, is a potential part of an archive, as many who have written them have known—hence a certain heightened awareness, a sense of not only saying something, but putting it down, with a relative permanence as a possibility. My dad and mom saved the letters they received, even as his family in England saved every letter he sent to them. As I have read those letters again, in recent times, I have learned not only about family matters but a lot about a particular time and place (suburban Boston in the 1930s and 1940s) through the words of a particular witness.

So with James, as he tells of a Massachusetts trip (from Cambridge to Beverly), now a matter of a half-hour or so, but then a substantial part of a day's challenge, surely. "There is growing up an education which I suppose they have long had in england," he tells Alice in July of 1890—and then the concrete particularities: "of physical wholesomeness, good education, good manners, jollity, freedom, and good speech, which I'm sure didn't exist anywhere in this country 20 years ago." With those words he reveals a lot not only about the youths whom he met in a home to the north of Boston one summer, but his own values—his inclination to favor and applaud a relaxed, informal kind of decency as a necessary companion to intellectual achievement, lest the latter, cultivated relentlessly and single-mindedly, become a narrowing influence, as in Emerson's reminder, in his "American Scholar" lecture, that "character is higher than intellect." James had been spurred to pleasure and thought at the sight of young people who had about them a certain goodness of manner and being, even as they were bright, thoughtful; and he welcomed what he saw, heard—offered its essence to his wife in the course of reporting to her on his recent whereabouts.

Similarly, a summer later, when traveling south by train to North Carolina, William writes to Alice from a hotel in Danville, Virginia: "It was entertaining at the stations to see the great crowd of white & black, and the train was full of very decently dressed & clean black people, most of them young. Fearfully dirty town this, unswept, unpaved, ragged, base. Filthy dining room, but unexceptional bed in which I had a first rate sleep." The next day, in Asheville, North Carolina, he remembers time spent on the train "with the dear old niggers and dearer young niggeresses." He is not especially interested in their situation, however—he exults in the mountain views, and in his own rested state of mind. Yet he has given Alice a glimpse of "the American Scene," to use his brother Henry's phrase: the Reconstruction era South in its power to shape the thoughts (and assumptions) of those who came to it from the outside, never mind those who lived there all the time. Suddenly, this liberal-minded Yankee, this politically progressive teacher and writer who very much favored Jews as a presence at Harvard (and in general) at a time when many others of his background and occupation assumed a kind of anti-Semitism as a casual birthright, let alone a specific attitude, was taking note of people who were, really, utter strangers to him. For us the word *niggers* stands out—marks even this broad-minded, kindhearted man (who knew and corresponded with W. E. B. Du Bois, and sought his company in social circumstances as a full equal). He could take on Harvard on women and Jews, but people of color, with only a very few exceptions, lived in a world beyond his.

Not that other Yankees of the time were relatively indifferent, as he was, to the fate of such people. The abolitionists were a presence of no small proportion in Boston and its surrounding communities, and at Harvard. Families with surnames such as Shaw and Hallowell, prominent and very much part of the intellectual and social world James inhabited, had sent their sons south not only in defense of a nation undivided but out of a passionate idealism. As a matter of fact, the Union Club, where James often dined and wrote letters, was founded by those aristocratic Bostonians who led the well-known 54th Regiment of black soldiers south and who consequently experienced the disapproval if not the outright scorn of some of their Beacon Hill friends and neighbors (and fellow, fancy eating-club members), and so formed their own club, whose name indicated and honored their values. By the 1890s, alas, for the nation as a whole the situation of African Americans in the South had been all too decisively settled—they had become a voteless, impoverished people, utterly segregated, constantly humiliated, their lives even in jeopardy if they dared assert the most basic right of citizenship, the desire to cast a ballot in an election. James, in upper Dixie, lets none of that moral scandal wash over him. Thereby, yet again, we learn from what he writes and how he writes it, about him and others of his kind. Compassion, too, bows to history, to that of one's nation, but also that of one's family. Henry James Sr., William's father, was a wealthy New Yorker who had an enormous interest in theological and philosophical matters, and as the expression goes, worried Christianity hard— that is, kept trying to figure out how one ought to respond, in this life, to the teachings of Jesus, to the ethics of, say, his sermon on the mountain, his Galilean sayings as they got worked into his teaching, healing, preaching. But such an interest on a father's part, transmitted constantly to his children during the intensively introspective and valuable times of a family's life (at the dinner table, in the library or the parlor) did not get out of hand—prompt a behavioral self-scrutiny that would nudge those youngsters (and later those adults) toward a life of radical social or political action.

Closer to home, also, James wasn't always the fearless critic of bourgeois (or academic) conventionality or nearsightedness (and prejudice) that he sometimes could be. In April 1892, writing to his German friend Hugo Münsterberg, in anticipation of his coming American, and Harvard, visit (which, as mentioned, would become, eventually, a tenured stay) James becomes the domestic counselor in this way: "I advise you if you have a *good* servant, especially a good cook, to bring her with you. Our servants are the weakest spot of our civilization—mostly Irish, ill-trained, very independent, and able to ask enormous wages." Those are hardly the words of someone who is worrying over the conditions of working people who have just come to America and are trying hard to get a leg up as they make their own a country new to them. One detects, alas, a whiff of the smug condescension (and worse) offered Boston's newly arrived Irish of the middle and late nineteenth century by its earlier settlers who hailed from England or Scotland (an ironic matter, since a segment of the James family itself hailed from Ireland, though as part of that land's Protestant gentry). On the other hand, James could strike with fine impartiality at the very rich, including the top of the English. In June of 1891, he told his sister Alice, living in London, this: "The situation of Royalty in England seems to me so *trashy,* all fluff and plush, and gilt plaster, like one of Barnum's circus cars, with no real style or force. I always think of it as an annex to Mme. Tussaud's. The Prince of Wales with the everlasting *'tact with which he performs his duties'*(!) is simply nauseous to me—and I trust to you."

Here is a man of the nineteenth century speaking as if he were one of us, alive late in the twentieth century—he turns our attention to the sometimes preposterous Buckingham Palace, even as the people he collectively calls the "Irish" had their own good reasons to be unhappy with the English crown, and those who governed in its name. Like so many of us, James was both constrained by the world (and time) in which he lived, and moved to break free of it, see things with his own singular, morally awake vision. None of us can break completely free of the assumptions mandated by an era, and too, those connected to our class, our family's daily life, as it takes place in the company of others—those Irish maids, for instance, who had the nerve to require a decent living wage.

With the help of Jean Strouse a while back (1980) we have all been asked to think of William's sister, Alice—her nature, her interests, her sensibility. She died in 1892, so the pages that follow don't give us as much of the correspondence between her and her older brother that we might want to read—only the immensely moving last words, as it were, between these two, whose souls were similarly charged with moral and spiritual energy. I knew Jean Strouse when she was a Harvard undergraduate—she took Erik Erikson's course, in which I was a teaching assistant, and she was in my class. I well remember her brilliantly original mind—and we all owe her a great deal for bringing Alice James alive, bringing her to our attention, even as the few exchanges in this volume between her and her brother command our rapt, admiring attention. Dying, she elicits from William a profound moral seriousness—he, too, takes stock of his middle-aged life (he was fifty then), tells her that his "main interest" is now "that of seeing that the children turn out well," no small aspiration, and no small parental challenge, but a shift, one has to presume (how complete the author himself probably couldn't then know), from the implied, driving, careerist hopes of a younger man. Alice never tried to take on the world as her two older brothers did. Though blessed with their brilliant intuitiveness and sharply knowing intelligence, and too, their command of a lively, engaging manner of expression, a sense of the dramatic that she, like them, knew (in her letters) how to exploit narratively, she had never achieved that wider audience which a novelist or essayist can cultivate. She was her brothers' listener, and maybe, a living reminder to them of the sources of their life-long pain as well as their enormous, respective successes.

Shadowing all three of them were the younger two brothers, with their more evident trials and tribulations, unmodified by the startling intelligence, the brilliant way with words, the sixth sense, or second sight William and Henry and Alice had with respect to people and places. After a fashion, Garth Wilkinson ("Wilky") and Robertson ("Bob") had to put up not only with a family's inheritance (its biological and emotional and social roots) as it gets transmitted over the generations but with the breakthrough achievements of the two older brothers and the intellectual and spiritual link between them and Alice, the youngest of them all. It was as if Wilky and Bob were hemmed in. Wilky, actually, was the first of them to die (in 1883), but in his final moments he did not connect with either William or Henry the way Alice did. When she became fatally ill, one senses in her brother William's correspondence, a big part of him lay exposed, vulnerable, and so with his brother Henry ("Harry"). "Your name will be a mere legend amongst them," William writes to Alice, at once a declaration of loyalty and love, but also by implication an assertion of a larger-than-life significance for her—not to mention the one addressing her, as he makes clear with the parenthetical remark "until we all are legends." So they have become, of course, the three of them, and not only for William's four children, the only offspring the two brothers and one sister would tender the future of a new century.

William's description of Alice's dying days surely adds to that legendary side of Alice—her refusal to succumb to self-pity, or even the self-preoccupation that so commonly and understandably attends serious illness. As William puts it, in a letter to a friend, Mary Aspinwall Tappan, Alice's "soul was not subdued." To her last breath, almost, she turned her attention to others, spoke of the London world she had inhabited, concerned herself with the fate of her novelist brother's new venture as a playwright. No wonder William declares that "Harry is left rather disconsolate." He doesn't favor himself with any such observation, though surely Alice's departure was an "intimation of mortality" for him. In early March she had sent him this extraordinary telegram, worthy in its brief, metaphoric might, its penetrating dramatic power, of Emily Dickinson's similar affair of sorts with death, and of Tolstoy's, too (as in "The Death of Ivan Ilych" and "Master and Man"): "Tenderest love to all farewell Am going soon." Several months earlier, William had hurried to her bedside, not an easy task:

a crossing of the Atlantic by boat. No doubt during those days at sea he mulled over much: a family's melodrama, its morality play as it had been performed by a set of parents and their sons and their daughter over a spell of (nineteenth-century) time. William's melancholy journey across the ocean was but one of many that he had taken, would take in the course of his sixty-eight-year life—the last one, with his wife, Alice, and brother Henry, completed but days before he died.

Substantively the letters in this volume tell of a writer's struggle with the proofs of his important book; a husband's effort to stay in touch with his wife, and she with him, during times of separation; a professor's dealings with the university that employed him, and with those there with whom he taught; a person's desire to stay in touch with the numerous friends he seemed disposed to make and keep; a father's protective absorption in the day-to-day life of his children, and more broadly, in their larger (educational, vocational) destiny; a deeply reflective moralist's exchanges with those of his fellow thinkers who aren't conveniently nearby (for the lunches and dinners so often described in these pages); an emerging public intellectual's life (arguably, James was only America's second such person, after Emerson), his need to speak on various matters of the day; and not least, an inveterate traveler's account, entrusted to others, of what the various expeditions he took (alone or with his family) did to his mind and body, if not his soul—and especially, what a months-long sabbatical in Europe caused him to think and feel.

That extended stay in Switzerland and Italy and Germany, mostly, with a briefer time in France and England, reveals a lot—indeed, more about James the father and James the social observer than his local (American, Cantabrigian) correspondence offers, perhaps because travel abroad makes us think carefully about who we are (in contrast to the others we temporarily glimpse), and heightens our awareness of time and space, as we carry on our wayfaring days in the sure knowledge that a clock is ticking and that soon enough the "everydayness" (which the theologian and philosopher Søren Kierkegaard mentioned, and in our time, the philosophical novelist Walker Percy has vividly evoked) will return: the often deadening humdrum rituals and routines that bring us a sparing oblivion that precludes moral anxiety about this life's meaning and purpose. Moreover, while in Europe, William James the father, one gathers, was trapped: he had to assume certain responsibilities for his children (their living arrangements, their schooling) that were not otherwise borne by him—and so we catch vivid sight of him in this fatherly incarnation.

No question, James the traveler saw a lot, revisited old haunts, found himself glad at times to be connecting with the aged glories of a continent then far more an awesome presence to privileged, educated Americans than is now the case. But this vacation, in part meant to rest a hard-working professor's mind, or better, stir it to new reaches of contemplation, turned into a real disappointment, a dud: "I should not have brought the children, nor taken my year of absence but simply given myself a long vacation of 4 months, bringing Mrs James for perhaps two months, and gone back to work in Cambridge next year"—a letter to his friend Hugo Münsterberg in August of 1892. In that same month, to his wife, he writes of "horrid latin-race wickedness," while extolling in French the Germans and the English. Of course, such a letter to his wife, who was also in Europe, tells us not only about his racial attitudes but the state of his marriage, or maybe, of his own restless, peripatetic, volatile nature as it came to bear on that marriage. The volume of his overall correspondence, that is, has to do at least somewhat with a particular correspondent's desire to keep on the move, even when he *is* on the move, as an American abroad.

In Venice there is talk of a place that "reeks of vice and sin"—to the point of this comparison: "as no other place on earth seems to be." Such an unqualified broadside does at least supply some context for his sharply critical even contemptuous dismissal of faculty committees at Harvard—*their* not very attractive character. When he was moved to irritation or worse, he threw all caution to the wind. Indeed, as one reads this assault on Italy and its people, brother Henry comes to mind—the great pleasure he took in the same human and physical landscape. The two men now become antagonists, one finding beauty, inspiration, refinement, high culture where the other spots physical decay, bothersome inconvenience, and moral rot anywhere, everywhere on that historic peninsula of a country.

Then comes Germany, the promised land, and such a notable, even striking shift in mood and in message. In March of 1893, to his friend Dickinson Miller, James exults: "I love this Germany; I love to be again with a strong calm manly-voiced people around me." Then, to rub things in with respect to what (whom) he had just left behind, this parenthetical comment: "the poor Tuscans! Heaven help them." He goes on to say that "something in air, soil, *and people* [italics mine] intimately disagrees with me." In the same month, to another correspondent, his good friend Sarah Wyman Whitman, he declares that "Germany at bottom is better than all the Italies in the world, a race of adult male beings." Even as he wrote such paeans of praise, in the Austrian city of Linz, not far from the German border, and very much in the midst of a Germanic culture, a four-year-old boy, Adolph Hitler, was learning about what one of his biographers would call "a world of violence, cruelty."

At times James toyed with the idea of a spiritual afterlife: like ghosts, we somehow hover in space and through time, possessed of some consciousness—a distinctly self-enhancing fantasy best not spelled out too carefully. On the extremely slight chance that such is the case, one imagines a gathering of deeply regretful "souls," all too aware of history's revenge upon them for espousing what, alas, once seemed an evident kind of common sense. In that regard, I certainly remember the importance, a while ago, of the German language, a necessary part, of an education in physics, chemistry, biology—how hard it was for many to realize that the nation that had given so much knowledge and art to the world had become ruled by murderous thugs, who intimidated some relatively innocent and decent people, but also summoned the malice, the all too available meanness of mobs of individuals whom a William James, were he miraculously returned to the Third Reich of the 1930s and early 1940s, might well have described as possessed of a historically unprecedented amount of "vice and sins."

If James erred in his unqualified racial or ethnic generalizations, he could be tellingly, stunningly balanced with respect to individuals, their virtues and flaws of character—while at home, taking note of academic snobbishness, of a pedantry that kills language as well as the aesthetic and moral imagination, or in Europe, sizing up a Bernhard Berenson, who had exerted such an influence on the world of art history. In a letter to his dear friend and philosopher colleague Josiah Royce, written in March of 1893, James praises Berenson for his "noble gift of the gab, perceptions *dazu,* & learning." But he takes note of his "terrible moral defects," of "his constant habit of denunciation of the folly of everyone else." To another correspondent, Elizabeth Ellery Sedgwick Child, he throws an even more critical look at not only Berenson, the person, but those who come "to sit reverently" at his side, a "menagerie" he calls them, at one point—and then this refusal to pull punches: "These people are all eaten up with contempt for each other's blunders, blindnesses, perversities and ignorances. Art in their hands is a mere instrument for indulging self-pride and scorn of their fellow men, instead of being a smiling gift which one may attend to in the manner most natural to one, and let drop with no bad conscience if it happen not to appeal."

Such moral vehemence, directed at a particular individual, was not a regular aspect of James's writing life, even in his correspondence. True, he could be sardonic, even caustic, when contemplating his own professional life—the smugness and egoism, the small-mindedness that can turn faculty meetings, academic committees of governance into an exhausting tedium. But in that regard he was careful not to single out colleagues. Actually, his friend Josiah Royce, in deadpan irony, evokes such matters more candidly in a long letter sent to James, published here—a sad story of philosophers not exactly living up to the wisdom they profess in books and lecture halls when it comes to deciding on who will be responsible for what duty, obligation. This disparity between intellect and character constantly commanded James's attention—he was, in that regard, a true student of Emerson. Perhaps the lack of restraint that informs his critique of Berenson and his associates had to do with their safe distance from Cambridge, where he felt the need for a constant show of civility and restraint, lest his everyday working life be reduced to turmoil. Of course history, yet again, delivers its ironies—Berenson's legacy, *I Taiti,* is now itself a part of Harvard University. But James's vigorous dissent with respect to Berenson and those around him has to be contrasted with the adoring praise that art historian and dealer kept getting from Boston's Brahmins, Mrs. John Lowell Gardner especially, but also others who more than went along with her. Nor was James blind to Berenson's gifts—the issue, really, was a matter of "social ethics," a phrase favored by another Boston aristocrat, Richard Clarke Cabot: how ought one get on with others, no matter one's capability as a thinker?

James was a demanding idealist—and if he rails against art scholars, connoisseurs of the sightly and refined, for being ugly in their argumentative vanity, he does so out of a stern conviction that true beauty (at least of the human kind) has to be tested by life. In that regard he was rarely unwilling to arraign himself; he could hold himself wanting with respect to morally significant qualities of mind and heart. In July of 1893, writing to a friend, Frederic William Henry Myers, he calls himself "misanthropic, cold blooded, hollow-hearted, neurasthenic above all, and abstract." He tells his friend that he values his capacity for the "concrete," and confesses a hope that he will "get enlargement of view" through their relationship. Nor is such a self-directed broadside an unprecedented psychological moment in the life of someone otherwise quite contented with himself. In a letter to Grace Norton, written a half a year earlier (December of 1892) James worries about the emotional distancing that science can prompt—even in someone attending a concert or walking the corridors of a museum. In a devastating critique of cold, analytic scholarship he describes someone as caring not "as much for the pictures themselves as for the Science of them." Then he moves to the more general statement, laments: "But you can't keep science out—of anything, in these bad times. Love is dead, or at any rate seems weak and shallow wherever science has taken possession." For a moment, he at least seems to spare himself from this all too sweeping cultural generalization: "I am glad that, being incapable of anything like *scholarship* in any line, I still can take some pleasure from these pictures in the way of love."

Needless to say, he has already taken a swipe at himself in passing, even as he separates himself from those he has censured. But he won't let the matter rest there. A few sentences on he launches a major assault on his own kind, an intellectual's anti-intellectualism vented with gusto: "The professor is an oppressor to the artist, I fear." He adds this to the indictment: "What an awful trade that of professor is—paid to talk talk talk! I have seen artists growing pale and sick whilst I talked to them without being able to stop. And I loved them for not being able to love me any better. It would be an awful universe if *everything* could be converted into words words words."

Such confessional remarks tell us a lot about who William James was—tell us about the person, as opposed to the writer and thinker of consequence, the distinguished Harvard professor. There is in the above words (about words!) no small amount of modesty struggling against the gullibility of others, and maybe, the self-importance that is an occupational hazard of professorial (and authorial) distinction, success. Not a few big shots begin to believe what others think of them—with no reservations or qualifications on their part, never mind on the part of their followers, admirers. James stood on a platform, received the constant approval of others. Moreover, by the early 1890s, he was known across America, and across the continents as a most accomplished psychologist, a philosopher of great originality and compelling narrative capacity, and a uniquely independent-minded thinker whose mind ranged widely, deeply in the humanities and the sciences, both. All the more impressive, then, his persistent willingness to have some second thoughts about himself, his own kind—and share them with others.

He went further, took on critically an entire subject matter, a way of thinking, really: the beginning emergence of the social sciences as the dominant mode of social and introspective thinking—for some, a secular religion of sorts, vested with enormous authority. Early on James spotted the worst side of such a development—the over-wrought use of concepts and theories to explain anything, everything, when in fact they are simply speculations, or formulations awaiting further inquiry. He also realized how reductionist psychology (and sociology) can become in the literal-minded hands of theorists or those who hunger for certitudes. Here he is (exhilarating to some of us a century later) putting the matter boldly: "Yes, I *am* too unsystematic and loose! But in this case I permitted myself to remain so deliberately on account of the strong aversion with which I am filled for the humbugging pretense of exactitude in the way of definition of terms and description of states that has prevailed in psychological literature."

Those concerns were expressed (in November of 1892) to a colleague, James Ward, who had favorably reviewed James's *Briefer Course* in psychology. James was grateful for the kind words written on his behalf, and especially so because the reviewer, like him, had obvious reservations with respect to the direction academic psychology had taken. James refers to "the desperate character of all psychologizing"—a powerful, bracing call to arms: we are imposing an over-wrought language on the complex matter of human experience in such a way that we make fools of ourselves, or at least we do so if we compare our aggrandizing pedantry (which is immodestly oblivious to the embryonic nature of our explorations) to the telling capaciousness (with respect to life's ironies, ambiguities) of novelists such as George Eliot and Leo Tolstoy and Charles Dickens and Thomas Hardy and Anton Chekhov (who shared time with James), not to mention a certain American novelist who had taken up residence in England and was himself the younger brother, by a year, of a psychologist.

James was alert, early on, to academic "narrowness" (he used that word in a letter to Hugo Münsterberg in March of 1893). He saw what was happening not only to budding social scientists of his time but to the larger, secular world that was turning to them with more and more eagerness, if not hunger: tell us about ourselves in greater detail, for we are all that matters, and do so in the language of science, because that, finally is all that matters. The temptation was high, then, for young psychologists (and their compatriots in associated fields, such as sociology and anthropology) to hunker down, embed themselves in a technical language, ride the coat-tails, really, of the natural sciences, with their growing demonstrable prowess, and thereby enjoy an ever-expanding acceptance, even celebrity. Meanwhile, George Eliot, say, had offered the world *Middlemarch,* and Leo Tolstoy (who would die in the year 1910, the same year that James did), had given the world *War and Peace, Anna Karenina*—a "psychology," in such efforts, of enormous subtlety, unobtrusively and elegantly rendered through narrative exposition rather than through resort to the ponderous jargon James was reading in the various academic journals. Meanwhile, too (of all ironies), he himself was becoming a much sought-after writer, lecturer—a beneficiary, he knew, of the very cultural shifts he so clearly comprehended: the psychologist as a seer for those who had given up on looking heavenward, had turned to the god Science, and now wanted it to pay heed to *them,* their thoughts and dreams and personal experiences.

It is uncanny, actually, how prescient James was in his sense of the road ahead for psychology in America. In August of 1893, writing to William Baldwin, he worries about "therapism" or "therapomania"—the supposed healer who can't ever leave well-enough alone. How clearly I remember Anna Freud speaking of psychoanalysis as her father hoped it would turn out to be, in contrast to what had become its quite evident fate during the middle part of this century:

My father expected that with the help of his patients he would learn more and more about how the mind works. They were his teachers. He didn't think of psychoanalysis as a required "something" for everyone! I mean, now, in some circles, people talk of it as if you can't go through life without it, you can't bring up children well without having gone through it, or teach them, or be a doctor to them! I wish I was exaggerating when I talk like that! It is as if, for some people, all wisdom comes from only one direction—that of being an analysand! There is, you might say— some failure of common sense! It is not for me to answer why this has happened. [She had been asked.] I think we [in psychoanalysis] have been given far too much credit for knowing far too much about far too many things—and, I don't see too many of us willing to call a halt to all this! Of course, I admit, that would be one time we wouldn't be believed—if we asked people to stop expecting so much of us, believing so uncritically in our capabilities. Those are the times (how ironic!) that I do see doubt on people's faces—when I try to remind them that we are just beginning to understand how the mind works, and so it would be wrong to assume that we have answers and more answers for mothers and teachers and doctors and lawyers, and for everyone who has a "problem"! If I go further, and remind them, as I did in my last book [*Normality and Pathology in Childhood*] that we don't always come out right on our assumptions, or that all of us have gone down roads, and then had to stop and realize that we haven't traveled as far as we'd hoped, or expected—well, that doesn't go over very well. I fear that some people think we will disclose some great secret, and then there will be no further "problems" in life—and some people make psychoanalysis itself their life. My father saw that happening, and he spoke of the problem; he wrote about it. ("Analysis Terminable and Interminable," 1937)

There was more—an elderly, wise woman who had witnessed so very much in her life! Like James, she addressed teachers modestly in a series of lectures, tried to be of some clarifying help to them. Like James, she also grasped the desperate neediness of many who may be well-to-do and well educated, but who are ever so ready to toss aside all caution in the service of a version of "therapism" or "therapo-mania"—the conviction that certain psychological "procedures" or forms of "treatment" will bring about much more than the mere "understanding" Miss Freud (and her father) pursued. It was James who told Freud when the two met in Boston (1909) that "the future of psychology belongs to your work"—but little did either of them know what that "future" would bring, though it was James, actually, who foresaw its character rather more clearly than he would have been able to realize at the time.

Despite his aversion to "therapism," James was a physician who knew well how people suffer psychologically as well as physically—and like many healers, he himself knew plenty of emotional hurt. He is not loath in his letters (and not only in the ones addressed to his wife) to acknowledge moments and longer of low spirits, heaviness of heart, despondency. His moodiness (if not irascibility, crankiness) comes across in his communication with others, as does his effort to gain the upper hand over his sagging self. Perhaps the drivenness of his activity, the constant motion he sometimes seems to seek, and perhaps, too, the separations from his wife and children, surely not necessary but chosen out of some inner requirement, are evidence of the turmoil with which he struggled, a turmoil that craved expression, and found it in such action and movement (all those meetings and trips!), and in the relative isolation or seclusion that can characterize many encounters with many people, while on the run, as it were, from the sustained intimacy of a family's daily life. He keeps yearning for his wife in these letters—yet the reader of them wonders why many of those separations were necessary, and why they were so extended in duration.

At one point, in a letter to Frederic William Henry Myers (December 1893), James speaks of "a pretty bad spell," of "a new kind of melancholy" that had fallen upon him. He makes reference to visits with a "mind-curer"—no less than "eighteen sittings" devoted to treatment of his condition. We, today, wonder what took place during those meetings. Elsewhere he has recommended hypnosis to others, and he may well have had a sustained bout of it then. At the time, hypnosis was a major "instrument" of psychological inquiry, psychiatric treatment. The healer (whose background and credentials aren't described) was a woman, and James gives her great credit for his recovery—for instance, she restored his ability to sleep soundly. He claims (an interesting word) that she "revolutionized" his sister-in-law, and thereby our interest is even further piqued. He tells his colleague that "two other cases of brain trouble" also responded to that lady's interventions, of whatever nature. So James becomes her advocate, a fervent and uncritically optimistic one at that: "I should like to get this woman into a lunatic asylum for two months, and have every case of chronic delusional insanity in the house tried [another elusive, suggestive word!] by her."

James's correspondence at this time reveals that he was having a hard time returning to teaching after his sabbatical. He seemed to like the actual encounter with young people, the excitement of the lectures themselves, the affirmation (and consolation) that an attentive audience of intelligent, young people can offer a speaker who is putting himself as well as his "material" on the line. But he was more than wary (and weary) of other aspects of the professoriate. A year before his collapse, while in Florence (November of 1892) he had written to his protégé of sorts, Hugo Münsterberg, with respect to "committees of the faculty"—and the language was bitingly strong: "They [those committees] eat the very soul out of one with their tediousness & consumption of time. Keep clear of them and of the faculty as long as you can!" Such words are not out of keeping with James's larger role as a writer and researcher who very much became a public figure. He addressed the world rather than his Harvard colleagues—yet he did so as a professor in that institution: a bridge between it and others well outside it. Were he more comfortably, happily ensconced within that institution's "Yard," he might not have become a roving lecturer, a man attended by ordinary people, as it were, anxious to learn about what happens in the mind, and how to live a suitable, solid, useful life.

These letters, in their most substantial sum, become for us not only a source of biographical, historical, and cultural knowledge but an epistolary novel, with James, of course, the central character, but with others of great force and significance: his wife, Alice, needless to mention; his fellow and ever so distinguished academics, such as Münsterberg, Royce, Santayana; his various friends, with whom, at times, he could be both personally and intellectually quite forthcoming; and interestingly, to a much lesser extent, his brother Robertson and his sister. With brother Henry the correspondence was constant. Published in volumes 1–3 of this edition, the letters between William and Henry James display the affection that the brothers felt for each other. Separated by an ocean, they shared their lives, heart, mind, soul, each touched by the fire of genius—both of them so brilliant and gifted and thoughtful, both granted the power of persuasive expression, and both of them as intuitive, as psychologically alert and subtle, as the human mind makes it possible to be.

In this story, too, certain subplots incite particular interest: James's relationship to his philosopher friend Charles Sanders Peirce, for instance—a dramatic instance of two great intelligences in communication. The different fates of these two, actually, tells us quite a bit about what makes for "success" in this world. Peirce was enormously learned, and made spectacularly suggestive forays into the nature of human perception and communication—the essence of who (what) we are: the sentient creature who connects with others through language (the inward I become with another a mutually comprehending pair). In our time, no less distinguished a philosophical novelist and essayist than Walker Percy has looked constantly, admiringly, gratefully to Peirce for inspiration. Yet these letters reveal how vulnerable Peirce was, how excluded he was from the authority, the privileges of academic membership. A noticeable tension persists in Peirce's letters to James—who, in turn, is unfailingly gracious, generous. Peirce's letter of late December 1893 is especially instructive—and haunting: "You are widely known, and command the admiring credence of the public. I am unknown. I ask you, therefore, to write me a little note which I can print expressive of your interest in this publication. I am more sick of life than I can tell you." But tell him, he did; and James, surely aware of all the implicit envy and rivalry that he himself caused in this colleague whose ideas he much respected, could only try to be the attentive, considerate, utterly helpful person he so often was as a correspondent, not to mention a person.

Indeed, these letters can be vividly self-deprecating, surprisingly confessional. He would cut himself down, directly or by implication, in order to lessen the inevitable felt disparity between himself and others who looked up to him, looked jealously askance at him, because of who he had become. Even in a letter of recommendation for a young "candidate for any good opening in psychology" (March 1894) he is shrewdly informative but also extraordinarily broadminded, contextual, critically self-referential in his comments: "He is also a little imaginative about people and their relation to him—but what man eager and disappointed in a career, is not liable to be this, when thrown amongst those who can make or mar his destiny?" Once more he ever so politely yet trenchantly gets to the heart of things, points out what a fiercely, even murderously competitive world can do to us: rob us of our truthful selves, push us toward the false egoism of exaggeration and pretense—and from such a human possibility this powerfully prominent recommender chooses not to exclude himself.

William James, was, finally, yet another embodiment of American exceptionalism—the wonderfully idiosyncratic loner, blessed in so many ways, who is free to stand apart, even as he picks and chooses his way across a particular (intellectual) terrain. He wanted so hard, as he put it in 1891, "to keep psychology human for a while longer"— and those last four words, in a way, say so much about his apartness from others, his enormous historical detachment: he knew what, alas, had to happen, and why. He possessed such knowledge, wore it humbly, as if it had simply taken hold of him (a surprise, a gift) rather than become an assiduously acquired possession. He had, after all, as he repeatedly tells us in these letters, a most vulnerable psychological makeup. Often in personal pain, he seemed to marvel at his own exemplary survival, and too, his remarkable renown.

Fortunately for him, he had a most loving wife. Several of the letters to him from Alice Howe Gibbens James are, as a matter of fact, the most affecting in the collection. She was a psychological straight-shooter; her words are direct, unpretentious, and get wonderfully, sharply to the emotional point of things—and how contemporary, be it noted, some of her thinking: "The lack of you is like missing the air I breathe; and just how keen a want it is I think you will never imagine because you are a man and not a woman." (That, on Christmas Eve of 1893.)

Here James is, then, in all his informality, swept along by a passionate nature, stirred by a moral energy that never failed to assert itself. He can be, one moment, delightfully humorous—as when he mocks conventionality, yet again, through an assault on spelling (a predecessor, in that regard, to George Bernard Shaw and Flannery O'Connor). He can, in other moments, rise to heights of Christ-like tolerance, highmindedness—tell his friend Hugo Münsterberg to ignore mean-spirited criticism, academic pettiness, by refusing the temptation of anger, by turning the other cheek, by continuing his work, making it better and better. This was a principled man, indeed, one worthy of the praise sent him by, say, Oliver Wendell Holmes ("I have read your book—every word of it—with delight and admiration"). This was, too, a man of unrelenting good judgment, never deserted by common sense, immune, it seems, to the temptations of grandiosity: "How delicious the fact that you can't cram individuals under cut and dried heads of classification" (1890). In many ways, to be sure, he was imperfect. His wonderful quote from the response of Jonathan Edwards to the trustees of Princeton College, who had asked him to be president, was no doubt regarded by him as a self-description in its general statement of unworthiness. Yet there is the great charm of such a declared inadequacy—and so, no wonder we today look to Edwards, to James, in our great ethical hunger: their strikingly candid assertion of independence of mind and thought, their refusal of blandishments all too coveted by the rest of us, their loyalty, no matter the price, to certain beliefs and values, which they not only upheld, but tried to work into the rhythms of their daily lives.

I must conclude on a personal note. In these letters William James refers to his Emmet and Temple cousins—well, my wife, Jane Erin Hallowell Coles, through her maternal grandmother, was very much a member of those two families, which were so connected: they go back to Robert Emmet, he of Dublin's eighteenth-century Protestant ascendancy, who died (was executed) fighting for a free Ireland. When Jane was a girl, during the Second World War (her father away in the navy), she and her mother and brother stayed with "cousin

Billy" in his Cambridge home—with, that is, the Billy who figures in these letters. Billy was an artist, even as his father at one point here remarks upon a prelude to such an eventual occupation, a child's painting ways. Billy lived in his father's house on Irving Street, where Jane lived, too, as a six- and seven-year-old girl, and from which, like that giant of an earlier Cambridge world, she walked to a nearby place of learning, albeit a mere elementary school rather than mighty Harvard. I had heard of that house, of its artist resident, of its picture books and fun, fun, of the memories they inspired—and so, as I read these letters, kept seeing "95 Irving Street" on page after page, I was reminded once more of how wonderfully connected this life can sometimes be, how ironic, too, even as, thankfully, the William James who has crossed all generations, all boundaries of space and language, has thereby become an instructive, provocative, prophetic presence for all of us, his intellectually needy, morally thirsty heirs.

Bibliographical Note

Immediately after the death of William James in 1910, members of his family began the tedious work of collecting letters and preparing them for publication. The responsibility was shared by his widow, Alice Gibbens James, and his son Henry James. The family sought to retain control of James's reputation by presenting to the public its own version of his life and character. In his unpublished memoir of his mother, preserved at the Houghton Library, Henry notes that the attic of the house on Irving Street was crammed with papers and that in the evenings Alice would take down bundles of letters and papers, sort through them, and destroy what she thought should not be preserved. Although no records were kept of what was destroyed, she did make extracts of some of James's letters to her before destroying the originals. Henry's job was to contact his father's correspondents and ask them either to lend the originals or to provide transcripts.

The first to benefit from these efforts was the brother Henry James who included some William James letters in his autobiographical volumes, especially in *Notes of a Son and Brother* (1914). Henry James treated the letters with considerable freedom, but his versions are helpful because he sometimes provides complete names of persons obscurely alluded to in the letters. The son Henry James's labors, interrupted by the war, resulted in the publication of the two volumes of *The Letters of William James* (1920). The letters were heavily edited. Henry deleted mentions of what seemed to him unimportant details, softened or omitted harsh judgments made about living persons, normalized spelling and punctuation, and fleshed out numerous abbreviations. Some years later, Ralph Barton Perry made extensive use of the letters in *The Thought and Character of William James* (1935), but Perry had to make the letters fit his narrative and rarely included complete texts.

Somewhat fewer than 1,000 letters were published in this way, about ten percent of the surviving total. However, it must be repeated that the texts provided by the two Henry Jameses and by Perry are not reliable. There are significant omissions, and James's often slangy and informal epistolary style is normalized. This is unfortunate because James often used misspellings, abbreviations, slang expressions, and sloppy punctuation for humorous effect or to emphasize to recipients that the letters were written in great haste, in moments snatched from very busy days. Normalization often weakens the intended effect of the letters. In the present edition, the letters generally are reproduced as written, without corrections. For a detailed account of the methodology of transcription the Note on the Editorial Method should be consulted.

Family members were by no means the only ones publishing James's letters. Other recipients of the letters have included many of them in essays and books. Of the scholars who have published James letters two deserve special mention: Robert C. Le Clair, who published *The Letters of William James and Théodore Flournoy* (Madison: Univ. of Wisconsin Press, 1966), and the late Frederick J. Down Scott, who carried out an extensive search for unknown letters. Scott's work resulted in the publication of some 500 letters in *William James: Selected Unpublished Correspondence: 1885–1910* (Columbus: Ohio State Univ. Press, 1986). Scott also published a number of letters on several occasions in *San Jose Studies* and *The New Scholasticism*. Although he added much to our knowledge of James's correspondence, Scott did not remedy any of the defects in earlier publications because his work included only letters not previously published.

When Henry James began collecting his father's letters, some of the recipients permitted him to keep the originals. Others, who wished to retain the originals, allowed him to have transcripts made. Some letters unfortunately were returned to their owners without any detailed record kept of their contents. Through the efforts of the family, the bulk of James's correspondence, as well as other manuscripts, was saved and is now housed in the Houghton Library of Harvard University. The initial collection has grown through purchases and gifts from the estates of recipients. In addition to the Houghton Library, over one hundred institutional libraries in the United States, Canada, and Europe are known to have James letters. There are also numerous letters in the hands of private collectors, family members, and descendants of recipients.

As this volume goes to press, about 9,300 letters have been recorded, enough material for twenty large volumes. The present edition in twelve volumes will contain about seventy percent of the correspondence, while the remaining thirty percent will be calendared. Thus, every known letter will be either published in its entirety or listed with information about its provenance and a summary of its contents. Calendared letters will be indexed. It is virtually certain that as the edition progresses, additional letters will be found. Should they be located too late for inclusion in their proper place in the chronology, such letters will appear in an appendix to the last volume.

The decision as to which letters to publish and which to calendar is a matter of judgment. In the case of letters written by James, the decision is made more difficult by the fact that he rarely wrote dull letters, merely informational in content. In spite of his often proclaimed graphophobia, his letters generally are literary productions; even his ordinary business or social notes often have a sentence or two of literary decoration. Letters written at the same time and with similar content differ frequently in style and mood, producing different impressions. There is little duplication, and while letters often overlap, they rarely overlap completely. Of the letters that are primarily informational in content—letters describing his health, financial affairs, travels, and social activities—the ones calendared are those that in the judgment of the editors can be summarized with only a small loss of style and mood. Calendared also are routine refusals of invitations to lecture, acceptances or refusals of honors, and business correspondence with publishers.

Published in their entirety are philosophical letters, letters expressing religious, political, or social beliefs, letters in which he makes judgments about important figures or events or comments in detail about what he was reading, and letters detailing his professional activities and his literary plans. Also published are letters that because of their style and phrasing are judged of importance to biographers trying to estimate James's precise relations with members of his family or with his philosophical, literary, and scientific colleagues. The fact of prior publication was not taken into account in making decisions where James's letters are concerned.

Letters to James are treated differently and more severely. Prior publication is taken into account, affecting especially letters by Josiah Royce, Charles Renouvier, Théodore Flournoy, George Santayana, and Alice James. Because consideration of style plays a minor role in letters to James, some very readable letters are calendared. Selected are letters deemed to have a direct bearing upon James's intellectual development or to be of interest to James's biographers. For example, in his early years, he received considerable information about the state of psychology and physiology from Henry Pickering Bowditch and Granville Stanley Hall. In later years, Ferdinand Canning Scott Schiller, as well as many others, criticized in detail his philosophical ideas. These letters are included. Also included are letters that provide evidence of his reception and his reputation, or that convey information about James's friends and colleagues important from the point of view of James. Because many members of James's immediate family have drawn the attention of biographers, they are allowed to speak for themselves as much as possible.

For the purposes of this edition, only material actually sent to the intended recipient, either by means of the post or, in a few cases, by messenger, is counted as a letter. Among the papers of Charles Sanders Peirce at Harvard are numerous long drafts of letters addressed to William James. Many of these drafts, filled with symbols, diagrams, and intricate mathematical proofs, are incomplete, unsigned, and undated, but some appear to be complete letters signed by Peirce. While these drafts may be of interest to James scholars not only because they demonstrate Peirce's logical wizardry but also because they provide glimpses of his view of James as occasionally a hardhearted unbeliever unwilling to trust his feelings, they probably were never sent and in this edition are not counted as letters. Also not included are various notes and memoranda addressed to colleagues, friends, and students, which James wrote in books, notebooks, and on scraps of paper.

Letters are arranged chronologically by the date on which they were written. If a letter was written over several days, the first date is used. Letters that are dated only approximately are inserted either in their place in the chronology (if the date can be determined) or at the beginning of the month or year to which they are assigned. Letters to James are also placed by the date of writing since in most cases the date of receipt cannot be established. During James's time, letters mailed to Cambridge or Boston from places in the northeastern United States normally reached the addressee the next day; there are cases, however, of letters delivered on the same day. Letters mailed abroad arrived in about two weeks during James's early years. Gradually the time was reduced to about nine days, although much depended upon weather conditions encountered by steamers crossing the Atlantic.

James and his correspondents did not always date their letters. In many cases a more or less definite date can be assigned with reasonable certainty, a date at least definite enough to allow the publication of the item in approximately its proper place in the chronology. However, of the letters recorded to date, about ninety remain without even an approximate date. Most of the undated letters are routine social notes of no particular value. Undated letters will be either published or calendared in the final volume of this series.

The notes for the present volume are written from the point of view of William James. Of major importance in their preparation are Katharine Hastings's notes and correspondence concerning the genealogy of the James family, preserved at Houghton, and the genealogy prepared by her and published in the *New York Genealogical and Biographical Record* in 1924. Also preserved at Houghton is a genealogy of the Walsh family, prepared by William Walsh in 1903.

For purposes of annotation, each volume of letters is treated independently of the others. When a person is mentioned in only one letter in a volume, full biographical information is given in a note attached directly to the letter. When a person is mentioned in more than one letter, the information is given in the Biographical Register. In matters of spelling and transliteration of names, the *National Union Catalog* was followed. The notes also provide information about what is presently known concerning a recipient's or writer's surviving correspondence with William James and thus serve the additional function of referring to volumes in which the letters are to appear.

James himself as well as his wife, brothers, and sister are referred to by initials. Complete names are used for other members of the family. When the citation of a book includes a call number, in all cases the call number is that of the copy from James's library preserved at the Houghton Library.

The letters once published will provide a record of over fifty years of American cultural history from the perspective of an observer who had a vast range of interests and who was in the midst of most of the great events and movements of his time. University reform, the professionalization of philosophy, women's education, the development of modern psychology, psychical research, magazine and book publishing, unorthodox medical practices, the status of blacks in the United States, the pragmatism controversy, American imperialism, and other topics in literature, art, religion, and science are commented upon by James and his correspondents, American as well as European. Many of his correspondents were themselves eminent, and those who did not attain prominence are often interesting, for James, as has often been pointed out, had a talent for attracting colorful cranks.

I.K.S.

A Note on the Editorial Method

This Edition of the Correspondence of William James is intended for the general reader as well as the scholar. It follows that readability is given priority so long as it does not interfere with scholarly procedures. The letters are reproduced according to a system that may be described as modified diplomatic transcript, or clear text, which represents a faithful reproduction of the final text of the original except for the lineation and the positioning of inserted or marginal additions. All alterations in letters both *from* and *to* James are recorded in the Textual Apparatus. The letters are printed in chronological order; recipients and senders are identified.

The copy-text and provenance for each letter are given in an unnumbered note following the letter. In the case of letters dictated to family members, the name or initials of the amanuensis within parentheses follow the copy-text designation. The names of repositories are abbreviated according to the designations found in the *National Union Catalog.* Every effort has been made to find and print the original letters. Some letters, however, are known only from copies or entries in catalogs of manuscript dealers or published sources. In such cases, all known information about the letter and its source is supplied. A list of the abbreviations used in editing the letters is found on pp. lvii–lix.

Addresses and postal markings on envelopes (when preserved) and on postcards are printed immediately below the provenance line. Enclosures mentioned in letters are to be taken as no longer extant unless commented upon in the notes.

The principal objective of the editors is to provide complete and accurate texts of the letters. The capitalization, punctuation, and spelling of the original letters have been preserved. (Readers will note that James usually doubled the *c* in the various forms of the word *necessary.*) Although the utmost in readability would suggest the correction of inadvertent errors like *the the, restlessless* for *restlessness, thing* for *think,* and *that* for *than,* and the expansion of ampersands and of abbreviations like *wh.* to *which, do.* to *ditto,* and *A.K.* to *Aunt Kate,* the text will faithfully transcribe these on the theory that they have some interest as representing James's haste or else his assumption of informality as against formality. Missing opening or closing quotation marks and parentheses are supplied within inferior brackets, as are characters and words where needed for clarification and where authorial intent is not in question. Errors of commission are commented upon in the notes if clarification is indicated; [*sic*] is not used.

James's various idiosyncrasies in orthography are followed, whether or not consistent, such as his *tho* or *tho'.* His use of "reform" spellings such as *enuf* for *enough* is honored, as is his preference for minuscules in certain names and adjectives, such as *english, hegelian, greek,* and the like. James sometimes wrote contractions and possessives without apostrophes and abbreviations without periods; occasionally, he used dashes instead of periods at the ends of sentences. At times he followed the convention of placing an apostrophe before the final *s* in words like *your's.*

Silent editorial intervention in the holographs is limited to the resolution of certain forms of ambiguity. As with many writers, James's placement of punctuation in relation to quotation marks varied. His normal practice was to follow the standard American system of placing periods and commas inside quotation marks and colons and semicolons outside; at times, however, he violated his usual practice by placing punctuation inside or outside the quotation marks according to context as in the British system. The question of intent arises when James placed punctuation directly below the quotation marks. Often it is impossible to adjudicate whether the relative position of the punctuation is a shade in one direction or the other. In such cases the editors have followed James's usual and conventional practice in order to avoid what would eventually become misleadingly firm transcription into print of what are untranscribable ambiguities.

Another form of ambiguity involves the spacing of certain compounds and of some abbreviations. No question of intent can arise for some words—as when James occasionally spaced words like *together* as *to gether*—since he was by no means careful to link syllables, especially initial ones. All such anomalies are regularized since it is clear that authorial intent is not involved. Nevertheless, problems of intention do arise owing to this habit of James's when a legitimate question can be posed whether a division or a compounding was intended in certain words like *anyone* or *any one* and *everyone* or *every one.* Frequently his intention may be inferred from the incidence of a narrow space, when he intended the syllables to be linked, or of the normally wide space such as he was accustomed to use between two different words. Difficulties come when there is ambiguity in the spacing for words where he had a preference but might at random unthinkingly violate his custom either of separation or of linkage, such as may occur even with his usual *anyone* and *everyone*. Such textual ambiguities the editors have ordinarily resolved in favor of retaining James's usual practice whenever the spacing is in legitimate doubt whether as intended linkage or separation.

Similarly, whether James was or was not observing the contemporary though fading convention of separating such abbreviations as *didn't* to *did n't* or *wouldn't* to *would n't* is often in doubt. Without question his usual practice was not to separate, but on rare occasions convention would guide him. When the spacing is without ambiguity it is reproduced; when there is doubt, James's usual practice is followed.

James's hand is generally clear and offers few difficulties to the transcriber. He was likely, however, to form certain initial letters without much if any distinction between majuscule and minuscule, especially the letters *c* and *s*, and even *a, g, m,* and *n*. Where there is no question of intent, initial letters are transcribed as capital or lower case according to context and syntactical position, and no attempt is made to transcribe an obviously intended lowercase initial letter as a capital because of its formation. Problems do arise in distinguishing minuscule from majuscule, however, when the words in question are conceptual nouns, titles, names (including regional names), and certain adjectives (mentioned above) for which James might use either a capital or a lowercase. Occasional ambiguities also occur in punctuation as when a hastily formed comma is so shortened as to resemble a period. Once again, editorial interpretation of James's intention, based on context and his custom, must guide the transcription.

The procedure used in transcribing William James's holographs is followed in transcribing letters *to* James. While the handwriting of several of the correspondents presented a challenge, no serious difficulties were encountered. In instances of ambiguity, whether in the formation of characters or of punctuation marks, the writer is always given the benefit of the doubt.

Most of the letters in the *Correspondence* are recipients' copies or copies thereof. In those rare instances when a draft also exists, the recipient's copy is printed and the variants are recorded in the Textual Apparatus. Obvious typographical errors in copies of original letters are corrected without record; quotation marks enclosing extracts copied from original letters that are no longer extant are not reproduced. When there are letters bearing the same date, the letter *from* James precedes the letter *to* James. A letter misdated by the sender is printed in the correct chronological sequence and the correct date supplied within inferior brackets.

Each letter is prefaced by an editorial heading, giving the name of the recipient or sender. The formal elements of the letters have been standardized. The return address and date, occasionally written by James at the foot of a letter, are placed at the head and positioned flush right. Missing dates are supplied within inferior brackets by the editors. The salutation is positioned flush left; the closing and signature are positioned flush right. A letterhead imprinted on stationery is represented in print by small capitals. In the case of hotel stationery, only pertinent information such as the name of the hotel and the city and state are reproduced. Occasionally James stamped his address on his stationery. The stamp for his Cambridge address 'William James, | 95 Irving St. | Cambridge, Mass.' is represented by 'Cambridge' in small capitals, while the stamp for his Chocorua address 'William James, | Tamworth Iron Works, N.H.' is represented by 'Tamworth Iron Works, N.H.' in small capitals. To conserve space, the return address and date are printed on the same line, as are the closing and signature. Vertical lines indicating that the address and date or that the closing and signature were written on separate lines in the original are not used when these elements have been squeezed in or written around the margins of a letter; nor is a vertical line used between a printed letterhead and a handwritten date. Underlines, graphic embellishments, and flourishes, whether in the dateline or signature, are not reproduced. Quotation marks that appear at the beginning of successive lines of a quoted passage are not reproduced. James's occasional use of the archaic long *s*, typically when the consonant is doubled, has been normalized to the modern *s* in the present edition. Unindented paragraphs are printed with the conventional em indentation.

The parentheses and standard brackets in the letters are the writer's. Inferior brackets [ ] enclose editorial interpolation. Descriptions of the state of the manuscript, such as '*end of letter missing*', are italic within inferior brackets. Angle brackets 〈 〉 indicate material that is irrecoverable because the manuscript is torn or otherwise damaged. Text supplied within inferior brackets and angle brackets is obviously the responsibility of the editors.

Internal and terminal dashes, set closed-up, are one em; exceptionally long dashes or lines, used occasionally by James to indicate transition, are three ems. A series of dots or hyphens, indicating an incomplete thought or transition, is always the writer's, except in copies. In the body of the letter, words with single underlines are printed in italic; those with double underlines for emphasis are printed in small capitals (or large and small capitals, as the case may be). James's capital *A.M.* and *P.M.* are printed in small capitals.

When a letter in the hand of an amanuensis also contains text in James's hand, the autograph portion is signaled by '⌊*WJ's hand*⌉'. Text added by the sender either in the margins after a letter was completed or on the back of the envelope is printed in the position of a postscript; a note appended to a letter by someone other than the sender is reproduced in the notes. Annotations made by James on letters he received, as well as those made by recipients of James's letters, are printed in the notes. Markings made by archivists or others who have worked with the letters through the years are not noted. The presence or absence of page numberings is not recorded, nor are directions such as 'P.T.O.' or 'over.'

Whether in personal correspondence or in manuscripts intended for publication, William James was perennially conscious of his style and so had no compunction in deleting, interlining, and even writing over words to accommodate his choice. The development of any Jamesian sentence, therefore, has an interest all its own apart from its end product. In all cases of alterations, the final reading has been transcribed as representing the latest intention; the altered earlier readings are recorded in the Textual Apparatus. James seldom wasted space and frequently completed a letter by writing around the margins. Since these endings cannot be considered as alterations, they are not recorded in the Textual Apparatus. The position of text is recorded, however, when the addition was written on the back of an envelope. In revising his text, James occasionally misplaced a caret intended to indicate the position of an interlineation, duplicated punctuation when interlining, or neglected to reduce a capital after inserting a new word to begin a sentence. Such errors are corrected and the corrections noted in the listing of the alterations. The basic system for recording the apparatus is detailed in Fredson Bowers, "Transcription of Manuscripts: The Record of Variants," *Studies in*

Bibliography 29 (1976): 212–64. This system, with some emendations since 1976, is that used in the various volumes of *The Works of William James* for recording his alterations in manuscript. The chief characteristics of this system are spelled out in the headnote to the Textual Apparatus.

A special section of the apparatus treats hyphenated word-compounds. The first list shows those in the present text, with the form adopted, that were broken between lines in the copy-text and thus partake of the nature of emendations. The second lists the correct copy-text form of those broken between lines by the printer of the present edition. Consultation of the second list will enable any user to quote from the present text with correct hyphenation of the original letter.

This Note, with some modifications for the present volume, was written originally in collaboration with Fredson Bowers, consulting textual editor for the *Correspondence* until his death in 1991.

E.M.B.

Abbreviations

AGJ	Alice Gibbens James (wife)
AJ	Alice James (sister)
AL	Autograph Letter (in the hand of the sender)
ALS	Autograph Letter Signed (signed by sender)
AP	Autograph Postcard
APS	Autograph Postcard Signed
BBF	Jane Maher, *Biography of Broken Fortunes* (Hamden, Conn.: Archon Books, 1986)
BC	William James, *Psychology: Briefer Course* (Cambridge: Harvard Univ. Press, 1984)
C	Copy (handwritten)
CLSU	University of Southern California
CSmH	Huntington Library
CSP	Joseph Brent, *Charles Sanders Peirce: A Life* (Bloomington: Indiana Univ. Press, 1993)
CSt	Stanford University Libraries
CtY	Yale University
CU-B	University of California, Bancroft Library
DLAJ	Ruth Bernard Yeazell, *The Death and Letters of Alice James* (Berkeley: Univ. of California Press, 1981)
DLC	Library of Congress
DSI	Smithsonian Institution Library
ECR	William James, *Essays, Comments, and Reviews* (Cambridge: Harvard Univ. Press, 1987)
EPh	William James, *Essays in Philosophy* (Cambridge: Harvard Univ. Press, 1978)
EPR	William James, *Essays in Psychical Research* (Cambridge: Harvard Univ. Press, 1986)
EPs	William James, *Essays in Psychology* (Cambridge: Harvard Univ. Press, 1983)
GWJ	Garth Wilkinson James (brother)
HJ	Henry James (brother)
ICarbS	Southern Illinois University

LJR	*The Letters of Josiah Royce,* ed. John Clendenning (Chicago: Univ. of Chicago Press, 1970)
LWJ	*The Letters of William James,* ed. Henry James, 2 vols. (Boston: Atlantic Monthly Press, 1920)
MB	Boston Public Library
MBCo	Countway Library of Medicine
MCR	Radcliffe College
MeWC	Colby College
MH	Harvard University
MH-BA	Harvard University, Baker Library
MHi	Massachusetts Historical Society
MH-L	Harvard University, Law School Library
ML	William James, *Manuscript Lectures* (Cambridge: Harvard Univ. Press, 1988)
ML	Manuscript Letter (in the hand of an amanuensis)
MLS	Manuscript Letter Signed (signed by sender)
MNS	Smith College
MWC	Clark University
MWelC	Wellesley College
MU	University of Massachusetts
NIC	Cornell University
NjP	Princeton University
NN	New York Public Library
NNC	Columbia University
NNMor	Pierpont Morgan Library
OO	Oberlin College
OU	Ohio State University
PP	William James, *The Principles of Psychology,* 3 vols. (Cambridge: Harvard Univ. Press, 1981)
PPC	College of Physicians of Philadelphia
RJ	Robertson James (brother)
RPB	Brown University
SPR	Society for Psychical Research
SUC	*William James: Selected Unpublished Correspondence, 1885–1910,* ed. Frederick J. Down Scott (Columbus: Ohio State Univ. Press, 1986)
TC	Typed Copy
TCWJ	Ralph Barton Perry, *The Thought and Character of William James,* 2 vols. (Boston: Little, Brown, 1935)
TL	Typed Letter
TLS	Typed Letter Signed (signed by sender)
TT	William James, *Talks to Teachers on Psychology* (Cambridge: Harvard Univ. Press, 1983)

WB	William James, *The Will to Believe and Other Essays in Popular Philosophy* (Cambridge: Harvard Univ. Press, 1979)
WJ	William James
WJTF	*The Letters of William James and Théodore Flournoy*, ed. Robert C. Le Clair (Madison: Univ. of Wisconsin Press, 1966)

The Correspondence of William James

Volume 7
1890–1894

From Charles Augustus Strong

Matthäikirchstr. 11, | Berlin, W., Jan. 5, 1890.
My dear James:—

During the holiday recess I spent a week in Leipsic and heard some bits of psychological news that may interest you. But first I should like to tell you the errand on which I went there.

Perhaps you remember that when I wrote you last my mind was severely exercised over the practical question, whether I had better while abroad pay special attention to physiological & experimental psychology, or stick to my old trade of abstract philosophy.[1] Well, the conflict is now over, and I have come out into the daylight of clear conviction. I have decided to postpone philosophy indefinitely (except so much as comes involuntarily by the way), and go in with heart & soul for experimental psychology. I don't care if I have no more serious dealings with philosophy for five or ten years,—and yet it is the one thing that interests me. I have been led to this decision by two arguments.

When I called on Paulsen at the beginning of the semester, he told me there was a growing conviction in Germany (and what he said sounded like an echo of words I have read somewhere in Wundt) that the future philosopher must not be a philosopher merely, but also a scientific worker in some branch of the sciences, physical or historical. In an early lecture of his "Einleitung in die Philosophie," Paulsen defined Philosophy for us as "das einheitliche System aller Wissenschaften"—not a discipline apart from all others & working by a method peculiar to itself, but the science of sciences, critic of first principles & deducer of last conclusions.[2] No person therefore is fit for this business of summing-up who has not been drilled in the school of positive science and served his apprenticeship there. "Irgend wo, so möchte ich sagen, muss er mit den Füssen auf dem Boden stehen."

This gave me a dreadful feeling that I didn't anywhere "mit den Füssen auf dem Boden stehen" and that there was no hope for me philosophically till I should come to. I fell to thinking how best I might gain the experience & the discipline & the temper of the scientific worker; and I finally concluded that my only chance of salvation was psychology. This line of thought represents the first argument.

The second was suggested to me by a conversation with Prof. Ebbinghaus. He told me with as much emphasis as Paulsen that one must prepare for philosophy by working at science. The older philosophers (notably Descartes, Leibnitz, Kant) were also mathematicians & physicists, and came to the work of philosophizing with a broad basis of insight & fund of facts gained during their years of service as scientific men. But the modern *Philosophieprofessor* attempts to criticize their conclusions without having had their scientific experience, and both his negations & his positive constructions are in the air. This led me to see how little I know about the world, in a scientific way. For the ordinary man's conceptions of things, even of the commonest things, are inaccurate & largely symbolical; they are mere counters, though sufficient, it is true, for daily life & practice: but such conceptions are not enough for philosophy. The conceptions with which philosophy manipulates must be exact and scientific. This is especially true of ethics: no man ought to undertake to philosophize about morals till he has replaced our common-sense conceptions of idea, volition, impulse, pleasure & pain, by conceptions which are scientifically exact, i.e. until he has studied psychology. This was the second argument; and the two completely convinced me, and now I am in for a long course of physiological, pathological, & experimental psychology: übrigens interessieren mich diese Sachen ungemein.

I have had the pleasure during the last two months of meeting a number of very able men. One of them is Dr. Max Dessoir, Schriftführer der Gesellschaft für Exp., etc. He is only twenty-three years of age, but has already taken the difficult Dr.'s degree in Philosophy at Berlin. He is now spending a good deal of time on Nervous Physiology, Psychiatry, etc., with a view to taking an M.D. from some smaller University. He will thus be both Ph.D. and M.D., like his friend Münsterberg. Dessoir supports himself and his mother at the same time that he continues his studies, partly by tutoring & mainly (I imagine) by writing, e.g. he writes popular psychological articles for the papers; I recently read a very interesting article over his signature in the Wiener Neue Freie Presse on "Der Personlichkeitswechsel." He is also working at a book in two parts, the first a History of Psychology, the second entitled "Die Psychologie als selbständige Wissenschaft"; but it will be a year before any part of this book is published.[3] He intends when his studies are finished to *habilitieren als Privatdocent* here in Berlin.

I met him first in Hermann Munk's laboratory,[4] for he is taking the same as I the course on Nervenphysiologie. I spoke up one day and asked Munk if I might n't have a chance to experiment a little on frogs, and Dessoir at once said he would like to participate. Munk assented, and since then we have had a table to ourselves in one corner of the laboratory, and while Munk in his old coat is applying the electrodes to dog's brains at the other side of the room, Dessoir & I dissect out nerve-muscle-preparations, stimulate beheaded frogs & study their reflex motions, prepare dead ones for the Bell experiment,[5] etc. I have attended one meeting of the Gesellschaft für Experimental-Psychologie, and at Dessoir's suggestion think I will apply for admission to it. A singularly prepossessing, thoughtful, well-spoken set of laymen are its members. Dessoir read a brilliant paper on the different disciplines of psychology and the relations of each to hypnotism; I am to hear him finish it to-morrow night. He writes a very clear, easy, flexible style, for a German; he has a slightly Jewish look; I shouldn't wonder if he had French blood in his veins.

He advised me to go to Leipsic & call on Dr. Külpe, for the purpose of making inquiries about Wundt's laboratory, where I want in course of time to work; so I went. Dr. Külpe gave me an appointment at the laboratory & showed me through. It has been greatly enlarged since I visited it three years & a half ago, when MacDonald was in Leipsic,[6] and now consists of six rooms. There are sixteen persons in all working in it this semester, among whom five are Americans. I was shown some new pieces of apparatus—a new pendulum which vibrates at a snail's pace, and is used in solving problems connected with personal equation; and a myograph for the study of reaction-times—I didn't know they ever used myographs for the purpose, or anything but the Hipp chronoscope. Dr. Oswald Külpe is a young man of twenty-eight or so, is now in his third semester as Privat-docent, and seems to be Wundt's favorite pupil & right-hand man. I saw a good deal of him for several days & was a good deal impressed with his ability: a man with a fertile mind, well-balanced, with a taste for music & some humor, & all his answers wise & well-considered. He recommended me to call on Wundt, so call on Wundt I did, at 11 o'clock on Sunday morning. Wundt received me mildly & benignantly, as becomes a man who has just published a System of Philosophy;[7] he seemed to have aged since three years ago, & his hair was turning gray; he is in his 58th year, and is Rector of the University this semester, in which capacity he has so much to do that he cannot work for himself, on the *Völkerpsychologie* which is to be his next publication.[8] I look forward with expectation to hearing his courses & working in the Leipsic laboratory (where they say he shows himself every day) next Summer semester & the winter following.

I learned in Leipsic that Ebbinghaus has a Psychology in press which will shortly appear.[9] He will be forty the 24th of this month, and his pupils & admirers are going to make him a present, of what sort I have not heard. I am taking his *Übungen* this term, and find him overflowing with ideas and good humor, a man of superb vigor. I am working with Mead,[10] a man who took his Dr.'s degree at Harvard not long ago, over the Hipp Chronoscope, just to get an idea of the instrument; a Finlander is the third member of the party. This work, with *Anatomie* under Waldeyer[11] & *Gehirnanatomie* under Mendel,[12] fills what time I have left over from Munk.

Prof. Schurman writes me from Cornell that there is a chance of their expanding there in the line of philosophy, which means that they may found a chair of psychology & start a laboratory. If so, I shall have a good chance of the appointment, though I shall not under any circumstances return to America before a year from next fall.

Should any suggestions occur to you in regard to plan of study, places, subjects, which you think might be helpful to me, I should thank you very much for writing me them. It would interest me very much to hear the news from Harvard, but I do not wish to encroach upon your time.

I trust your health is good & your work going well, & beg you to believe me, mit schönem Grusse,

Ihr ergebenster | Charles A. Strong.

Prof. William James,
   Cambridge, Mass.

ALS: MH bMS Am 1092 (1050)

[1] See Strong's letter of 21 November 1889, *Correspondence*, 6:555–56.

[2] Friedrich Paulsen, *Einleitung in die Philosophie* (1892) (WJ 768.89); English translation with a preface by WJ, *Introduction to Philosophy*, trans. Frank Thilly (New York: Henry Holt, 1895) (WJ 350.68); WJ's preface reprinted in *EPh*. In his preface WJ states that he had heard about Paulsen's lectures at Berlin University from "young Americans," who brought back reports of the interest aroused in philosophy by these lectures, and notes that two years ago the lectures were published in book form (*EPh*, 90). The definition of philosophy quoted in this letter appears on p. 19 of the English translation; on p. 37 Paulsen quotes what he says is a similar definition given by Wilhelm Wundt.

[3] Perhaps Max Dessoir, *Geschichte der neueren deutschen Psychologie* (1894–).

[4] Hermann Munk (1839–1912), German physiologist.

[5] Charles Bell (1774–1842), British physiologist and anatomist, discovered that ani-

mals have both motor and sensory nerves. The experiment most likely involved the stimulation of the two kinds of nerves, resulting in twitching in the dead animal when the motor nerves were touched.

[6]Arthur MacDonald (1856–1936), American anthropologist, a graduate student in philosophy at Harvard in 1883–85, subsequently a student at several European universities.

[7]Wilhelm Wundt, *System der Philosophie* (1889) (WJ 796.59.6).

[8]Wilhelm Wundt, *Völkerpsychologie*, 2 vols. (1900–1909).

[9]Perhaps Hermann Ebbinghaus, *Grundzüge der Psychologie*, 2 vols. (1897–).

[10]George Herbert Mead.

[11]Wilhelm von Waldeyer-Hartz (1836–1921), German anatomist.

[12]Emanuel Mendel (1839–1907), German psychiatrist.

To Henry Holt

Jan. 15, 1890

My dear Holt:

All right then—we'll await the Spring for putting the book through the press.[1] As for Preble, I believe his Latin Grammar has a very good reputation here, but I will enquire. His character is all that can be desired—the incident which led to his leaving Cambridge being an absolutely insignificant thing in which he suffered great injustice.[2]

W.J.

TC: MH bMS Am 1092.1

[1]In his letter of 11 January 1890 (calendared) WJ suggested that he give Holt part of the manuscript of *Principles of Psychology*, to which Holt replied on 13 January (calendared) that as a matter of policy he never began typesetting a book while it was still unfinished.

[2]In his letter of 13 January 1890 (calendared) Holt asked WJ about the character of Henry Preble, author of *Handbook of Latin Writing* (1884). Preble had resigned from Harvard as of 14 December 1888 for reasons unknown, but the case is said to have received comment in the newspapers.

To William Mackintire Salter

Jan 28 [1890]

Dear Mack

Yrs. of 26th just in. By all means take "What can Ethics do for us," or your lecture of Jan 5 or s'thing susceptible of *impassioned* and popular treatment.[1] That's the way Adler made such a great hit.[2]— The note of *passion* which is never heard here.—Sanders Theatre is

hardly ever used now-a-days. It has n't been used this year & probably won't be. If it is to be filled by undisappointed people you
should speak to their hearts.

Terrible hurry.| Wm James

ALS: MH bMS Am 1092.9 (3668)

[1] Salter spoke on 27 March 1890 in Sanders Theatre on "What Ethics Can Do for
Us." The lecture of 5 January was not identified.

[2] Felix Adler spoke on "Ethics and Culture" on 9 January 1888; see *Correspondence*, 6:299.

To Samuel Burns Weston

Cambridge Feb 14. 90

My dear Weston,

Thanks for your very flattering request which I should gladly ac-
cede to *were it possible*—but it is n't.[1] I'm working for dear life to get
my psychology MSS into publishable shape for the summer, and every moment is precious. Why don't you ask Palmer for *any* ethical
article or lecture which he may have ready, on Spencer if possible.
I have a big fundamental article on Ethics in my brain—I don't know
whether it be worth anything or not—but I can't touch it until my
book is out, and probably not immediately then.[2]

I don't know why the ethical Record has stopped being sent to me,
I thought I was a subscriber. If that be the reason, let me know.
Margaret Gibbens bids me say that two copies of the last number (of
which receipt of price was acknowledged last Sunday) have not yet
come to her.

Long life to you!

Yours most truly| Wm James

ALS: Private

[1] Samuel Burns Weston was editor of the *Ethical Record*, the last issue of which is
dated July 1890, and managing editor of the *International Journal of Ethics*, the first
issue of which is dated October 1890.

[2] WJ, "The Moral Philosopher and the Moral Life," *International Journal of Ethics* 1
(April 1891): 330–54; included in *The Will to Believe* (1897).

To William Mackintire Salter

Cambr. Feb. 16 [1890]

My dear Mack

I advise you to write the second lecture and then see which of the two is the best. I suppose the 2nd one (I mean the 'What can Ethics do for us') will serve elsewhere, if you don't use it here. It is impossible for me to judge by titles which is best—it all depends on the treatment. The 'worth of life' suggest an oration—treatment rhetorical and hortatory, as it ought to be anyhow, in my opinion, for the Sanders theatre. The Ethics suggests a more reasoned treatment. The audience will probably stand reasoning—but *first-rate* oratory is a thing which no one can fail to be hit by. My advice is, write 'em both for the Sanders Theatre and pick out the most successful.

Either week you write of is as good as the others.

Love to all.

Yrs | W.J.

ALS: MH bMS Am 1092.9 (3670)

To William Mackintire Salter

Feb. 27 [1890]

Dear Mack,

Yours of 25th received. I think that the last week in march will be as favorable as the third, and will have the change made—nothing having yet been *announced*. Of course you ought to have everything most propitious to composing the best possible lecture.

I'm sorry Davidson should be so rambustious—your letter (of which I return Mary's copy) is only too good for the occasion.[1] Don't mind him, and he'll come round again all right. He passes from one such row to another and is none the worse for them.—Alice & I gave a dinner party last night to The Supreme Being and his wife,[2] The Craftses, the Wendells[3] and Jim Putnam. The most humiliating cookery & waitery you ever knew! It is at such times that one feels the benefit of having a religion—*even an ethical one*—to fall back on for refuge. Love to both Gibbenses[4] —

W.J.

ALS: MH bMS Am 1092.9 (3672)

[1] The reference seems to be to Thomas Davidson, "A Critique of Ethical Religion," *Ethical Record* 2 (January 1890): 230–34, in which Davidson claims that in Salter's *Ethi-*

cal Religion (1889) "the heart of a Christian saint and the head of a humanitarian positivist are trying to work themselves into harmony" (p. 230). Salter's reply appears on pp. 234–38.

[2] Charles William Eliot and his wife, Grace Hopkinson Eliot.

[3] Barrett Wendell and his wife, Edith Greenough Wendell.

[4] Reference is to Eliza Gibbens and Mary Salter.

To Charles Sanders Peirce

Cambridge March 16. [1890]

Dear Charles,

Nothing would please me better than to help stone Uncle Spencer, for of all extant quacks he's the worst—yet not exactly a quack either for he *feels* honest, and never would know that a critic had the better of him.   He's the *'Arry* of Philosophy![1]   But as for me, I can't touch pen to paper on the subject now, for I am terribly in arrears with an interminable mouse-parturition[2] of a book on psychology which must proceed to press in 6 weeks, and all my time and brains have to go to that.

I return your two columns which are very cleverly done, possibly a bit too interrogative and transcendentally suggestive to captivate the vulgar.   When are your own radical evolutionary speculations to see the light?

Always yours | Wm James

"He left a Spencer's name to other times, linked with one virtue and a thousand crimes."[3]   The one virtue is his belief in the universality of evolution—the 1000 crimes are his 5000 pages of absolute incompetence to work it out in detail.

ALS: MH bMS Am 1092.9 (3372)

[1] An 'arry' is someone who drops his h's and thereby shows himself to be lowbred. WJ uses the expression in his published accounts of Spencer; see *EPh*, 97.

[2] Probably from Horace, *Ars Poetica*, line 139.

[3] The concluding lines of Byron's "The Corsair," with 'Spencer' replacing 'Corsair'.

From Alice James

11, HAMILTON TERRACE, | LEAMINGTON. March 16th /90

My dear William

Thank you very much for sending Lilla's letters.   I have heard as yet nothing myself, for she will naturally wait until she can tell me a little more than the mere facts.   It is indeed a relief that the poor

dear man has emerged into day out of the night of his long bondage.[1]
Seen in his entirety what a curiously impressive & melancholy figure
he is! and what marvellous docility & self-control thro' those fifty
yrs. that he was entombed in that moral dungeon as effectively as
Bonnivard in Chillon—with the benignant Cousin Helen for inexorable turn-key![2] It seems to be a favourite joke of Providence to give
us these surprises, to take us down a bit by showing us what powerful
agents those, whom we have been in the habit of complacently considering the simple & the impotent, are in the human drama. But what
an interesting moment it is, when the familiar figures recede one by
one and are seen in the right perspective & live at last. I am entirely
overcome by that inspired document his Will, the embodiment of
"sweet reasonableness"—what jury could, or wd. break it?[3] I should
like to have the money in order to "cut up" better for my heirs, but
the 20 thousand wh. I have inherited from C. Helen & A. K. since I
have been in England has caused my income to be much less than it
was the first three years that I was here. I mention this, *not as a
lament,* but as a very droll illustration of the vanity of inheritances.
I am rolling in money, notwithstanding, and no Rothschild *feels* as
rich as I do, I sound too like a bloated capitalist wh. is always sustaining.

I was greatly distressed to hear of the children's illnesses What a
curious attack of Billy's, poor little man I hope it hasn't left him head-
achy. It has been a wretchedly sick winter here, not only the grippe
but illness of all kinds so that the doctors are almost dead, altho' there
are 40 of 'em. We have got off well in this house, Nurse alone having
a very mild attack. Alice must be well-nigh spent, give her my loving
sympathy. Also thank her for the Ethical Review & congratulations
on her brother-in law. I feel a reflected glory in being even so dis-
tantly connected with a man whose writings are forbidden in Russia![4]
If my brain allowed of the consumption of any other pabulum than
3 volume novels, I should ask to have the book sent, but don't do so
it would simply be a waste. Tell A. that the name Davidson made
me "vision" a waistcoat made out of a bath-towel surmounted by a
face with a space between the eyes wh. it seemed, by some freak of
Nature, an impropriety to look at, which ornamented a party one
evening at our house. I never saw the creature but once or twice
but that space, survives. Harry came on the 10th & spent the day.
He looked & seemed very well & cheerful. He is going to the Continent for the 'season'. He has 'lent' me his flat so probably Nurse &
I will go up for the 3rd Drawing Room. He is much & superfluously

distressed over my seclusion for it must be confessed that I have no power to seduce the Midland mind & my minute circle is dwindling and dwindling so as to be almost imperceptible.[5] I go for three & four weeks often without speaking to a soul but Nurse & Clarkey,[6] & then mayhap will come a half-hour of tabby-talk. I ought to have been started by Barnum. I am perfectly cheerful & content myself but you will admit that when there is naught but material suggestion 'tis dreary to suspend oneself and remain alone in the empyrean, so that I shall become more & more rudimentary and tax your indulgence further & further. This however has been a very gay week, for Mrs. Wm. Sidgwick came over from Rugby to tea one afternoon.[7] She is very anxious that I shd. let her bring the Henry S.'s who are coming to her at Easter, the inspiring motive to give me a hearing of *his* "flow"—"the most *flowing* talker in England" etc. The dear beings have no hyperaesthesia, but if Providence doesn't rescue me from that stammer by a whacking sick-headache I shall become a confirmed Atheist on the spot.

Revive Alice, who lately feared the infants were not precocious, by telling her that Father announces, in one of his early letters that none of the children "save Wm." show any intellectual taste[8]—"Just fancy that now!" and *Me* among the group—who all unconscious, constantly give birth to the profoundest subtleties and am "so *very* clever!" If you could only hear what small coin produces that desirable result amidst this grateful public you *wd.* laugh. One's head wd. be turned by having one's commonplaces so applauded if it were not neutralized by the perfect failure of all flights of fancy. Is it not a despairing moment when your lyrical gymnetics fall flat? it seems to permeate you with collapse, as if the bones had all become gelatinous, suddenly. Arm yourself against my dawn, wh. may at any moment cast you & Harry into obscurity, and take a hint from this "repartie qui annonce d l'àpropos et de la bonhomie + + + + + + 'Comment, Monsieur', s'ecria l'un d'eux, tout ébahi, 'vous êtes le frère de Mme la Marquise du Chatelet? vous appartenez, Monsieur, a cette femme si spirituelle si digne de tout éloge?'—'Oui Mons.' repondit l'Abbé de Breteuil, *'j'ai cet esprit-la.'*"[9] The other day a Miss Leppington who is the only bookish person I see,[10] brought me back Miss Jewett's pretty story, "Betty Leicester,"[11] saying she saw a great difference in the life at home but she insisted that it contained only elements that were suppressed in the Briton but nothing different in kind. This you may imagine was too much for me to remain passive under, so I insinuated that there was a flexibility in the Yankee of which there was no germ in the English mind, wh. *couldn't* play with anything that had been taken solemnly for a year or two. She pondered for a bit and resisted and then dear lady fell into the trap, turning herself into a document in the most obliging manner by naïvely asking "Do *you* think it is possible to take what is serious lightly?" She has a sister by the way who has as much grammar & as many syllables in her sentences, or rather paragraphs, as the Norton & Palfrey families rolled into one.[12] I wonder if it doesn't come from a Wesleyan descent keeping her remote from 'good form' wh. pens them in a dozen monosyllabic locutions articulated as imperfectly as possible. But let me stop for Heaven's sake if not for yours. My letters added to your work will bring you down with brain fag. Love of the best to all.

Yr. loving sister | A.J.

I meant to say how glad I was of yr. legacy, but it all seems so in the blue. I only wish our places were reversed if the will stands. I was very grateful for the "griminess" of Father's style the "raciness" wh. "belittles" while it "individualizes" shows genius. What started up the chirrup at this date?

ALS: MH bMS Am 1094 (1490)

[1] Henry Albert Wyckoff died on 23 February 1890.

[2] Helen Rodgers Wyckoff Perkins (1807–1887), sister of Henry Albert Wyckoff and widow of Leonard Perkins. Her mother and WJ's maternal grandmother were sisters. François de Bonnivard, a sixteenth-century Swiss rebel, is the central figure of Byron's "The Prisoner of Chillon."

[3] For the legal problems posed by the will of Henry Albert Wyckoff, see *Correspondence*, 2:158n.

[4] The *Ethical Record* 2 (January 1890): 246, with reference to Salter's *Ethical Religion*, noted: "The report has reached us that Mr. Salter's book has been prohibited in Russia."

[5] For HJ's view of his visit to AJ see *Correspondence*, 2:132. HJ was then living at 34 De Vere Gardens, London.

[6] Miss Clarke, AJ's landlady at the time.

[7] Mrs. William Carr Sidgwick, whose husband's brother was Henry Sidgwick.

[8] For AJ's reading of her father's old letters see *DLAJ*, 180.

[9] The anecdote concerns Gabrielle-Émilie Le Tonnelier de Breteuil, marquise du Chatelet (1706–1749), French mathematician and Voltaire's mistress, and her younger brother, Elisabeth-Théodore Le Tonnelier de Breteuil, a clergyman. AJ's source was not found.

[10] Probably Blanche Leppington, author of several essays in the *Contemporary Review*; see *Correspondence*, 6:611.

[11] Sarah Orne Jewett, *Betty Leicester* (1889).

[12] The family of John Gorham Palfrey (1796–1881), American author and statesman.

To Henry Holt

Cambridge, March 21, 90

My dear Holt:

Publishers are demons, there's no doubt about it.   How silly it is
to fly in the face of the accumulated wisdom of mankind, and think
just because one of them appears genial socially that the great natural
law is broken and that he is also a human being in his professional
capacity.   Fie upon such weakness!   I shall ne'er be guilty of it again.
I had thought I should expedite matters by getting the woodcuts
ready—and as I can't—*send* the Harvard Library books, and this next
week is vacation and I can accompany them I tho't you would vehe-
mently applaud the exhibition of energy on my part and let me get
through as much business as possible in the time.[1]   Later it will be
less convenient for me to go to N.Y.   It may delay things.   It may
result in the things having to be made here.   It is all on your "head".

As for the MS. I confess I don't know why you need the whole of
it en bloc in your own hands, before printing begins.   After this week
of recess I shall write a chapter which may take 3 weeks at the outside
and complete the book.   Some 1700 pp. of MS. will then be ready
for the printer without another touch from me.   There will remain
5 or 6 chapters, some of which need slight retouches and additions,
which can be added by me perfectly well in the intervals of correcting
proofs, thereby enabling the latter to begin about the first of May.
The *whole* work as I said will then be *written,* only those few chapters
not *revised*.   Time is so precious now that I don't see what possible
thing is risked by proceeding to press with the revised mass.   The
rest *could* be printed without revision, but it will be better to go over
it again.   Write and tell me what is your decree.   I want to get forward now with the least possible delay.

My visit to N.Y. was altogether for the sake of those woodcuts.   For
hygienic purposes just now I shall gain more by taking my week away
from the garish gas lights and excitements of the metropolis, and so,
my wife agreeing, I have decided after getting your note, to keep
New York till later and spend the week in exploring the wilderness
of Connecticut and Rhode Island.   That was the meaning of my telegram this P.M.   We will debit you with one dinner for some future day.
I find that I have lost the contract which you sent me last spring.   I
did not even examine it then.   Pray send another that I may see
what to do.

Yours always | Wm. James

Letterbook: NjP

[1] Holt refused to begin typesetting *Principles of Psychology* until the complete manuscript was in his hands; see letter of 15 January 1890.   He also declined WJ's proposal to bring to New York the Harvard Library books from which the illustrations for the book were to be taken.

From Pierre Janet

Paris 23 Mars 1890 | Rue Tronchet. 4.

Cher Monsieur James

L'article que vous avez eu l'amabilité d'écrire et de m'envoyer m'a fait le plus grand plaisir: il est d'abord très et même trop élogieux pour moi et ensuite il est un excellent résumé de mes idées.[1]   Vous avez eu raison de prendre la question d'une manière synthétique en commençant par la fin de mon livre pour en exposer d'abord les idées générales.   Cela est beaucoup plus clair comme exposition. Après bien des hésitations, je n'avais pas voulu prendre ce plan dans mon ouvrage pour bien mettre en relief la méthode expérimentale qui va des détails aux généralités, mais dans une exposition d'ensemble il est bon de renverser les choses.

Je ne serais peut être pas tout à fait d'accord avec vous sur quelques points de détail, mais ces questions sont si difficiles qu'il est déja heureux de l'entendre sur les grandes lignes.   Il reste toujours notre grand différend avec vous comme avec Mr Myers sur l'état constitutionnel et général des sujets hypnotisables.   J'aurais désiré, je vous l'avoue, une discussion plus complète sur ce point.   Je ne vois pas très bien comment vous pouvez admettre mes études sur les anesthésies (vous en citez un excellent exemple chez un medium) sur les desagrégations. etc. et ne pas admettre la conclusion qui en dérive. Si ces individus sont désagrégés, dédoublés, c'est qu'ils n'ont pas l'unité des personnes normales, c'est que leur synthèse psychique est affaiblie, modifiée, qu'ils sont sur ce point essentiel des anormaux, si vous ne voulez pas dire des malades.

Je voudrais vous dire ce que j'écrivais déja à Mr Myers.   Si vos sujets vous semblent être différents, donnez nous donc leur analyse psychologique pour que nous puissions apprécier l'importance de ces différences.   Par exemple, vous connaissez, dites-vous, une femme qui a un grand somnambulisme avec une foule de phénomènes caractéristiques et qui ne vous parait pas être hystérique.[2]   Soit, j'en serais enchanté, car cela serait une voie nouvelle à parcourir, mais vous comprenez bien que cette simple affirmation "elle n'est pas hystérique" ne m'apprend pas grand chose. Elle n'a pas de crises, cela importe peu, le somnambulisme les remplace; elle se promène et elle travaille, sans aucun doute, les nerveuses peuvent être très remuantes. Mais l'essentiel, vous ne me le dites pas. Quel est l'état psychologique de cette femme pendant la veille: (analyse exacte de tous les sens, avec des mesures, dessin du champ visuel, perception des couleurs et leur étendue dans le champ visuel, nombre des sensations simultanées . . . . . . ces sensibilités et en particulier le champ visuel se modifient elles à l'époque des régles. dans certaines *psychoses* hystériques que je vois en ce moment les gros symptomes sensoriels ne sont apparents qu'à cette époque. Cette femme a t'elle une hérédité nerveuse?—état des mouvements les yeux ouverts et les yeux fermés etc etc. ensuite analyse de tous ces phénomènes pendant l'état somnambulique etc. [(lvous savez tout cela mieux que moi) j'ajouterai encore: si la désagrégation ne se manifeste pas chez elle sous la forme hystérique (anesthésie, amnésie, paralysie convulsion, contracture.) ne se manifeste t'elle pas sous la forme neurasthénique qui est parallèle (distraction, doute, aboulie, impulsion, idée fixe.)?

enfin si vous ne trouvez aucune trace de tout cela et j'en doute fort quelle est la théorie psychologique, le schéma de son somnambulisme? Voila ce que je voudrais vous voir étudier. Je suis sur que vous nous feriez le dessus un travail remarquable, et j'espère bien qu'au lieu de l'opposer au mien il le compléterait et nous amenérait à une conception plus générale ce qui est le résultat le plus heureux des discussions. En ce moment d'ailleurs je suis engagé dans une étude qui, si elle aboutit à quelque chose, nous permettra déja d'étendre beaucoup la théorie de la désagrégation et de la rendre plus compréhensive. J'abandonne un peu mes amies les hystériques et je m'occupe de leurs cousins germains.

Je cherche à comprendre les maladies mentales que l'on rencontre chez les neurasthéniques et qui ont été baptisés de noms bien divers. Il me semble que tous ces accidents dérivent de la distraction comme tous les accidents hystériques dérivent de l'anesthésie. La folie du doute serait l'homologue de l'amnésie, la folie du contact serait l'homologue de l'aboulie et de la paralysie etc, mais tout cela est encore à l'état de rève.

Je voudrais bien pouvoir causer avec vous de nos recherches cela me serait très utile, mais quand nous reverrons nous?

Je vous remercie encore de votre aimable article et je suis

tout à vous | P. Janet

ALS: MH WJ 642.59

[1] WJ, "The Hidden Self," *Scribner's Magazine* 7 (March 1890): 361–73; reprinted in *EPs*. The article is based primarily upon Pierre Janet, *L'Automatisme psychologique* (1889) (WJ 642.59).

[2] Without naming her, WJ concluded his article with a reference to Leonora Piper as a nonhysterical woman who in her trances displays considerable knowledge about people she has never met (*EPs*, 268).

To Harry Norman Gardiner

Cambr. Mch 26. 90

Dear Sir,

The question asks for *vivid* hallucinations when *awake*.[1] This should exclude visions continued from dreams into the transition state; it should also exclude excessively fleeting visions hardly exteriorized, and the hearing of single words, or one's own name, which last is very common.

The best rule is to send an account of all such doubtful experiences on Schedule B, but not to put them down on A as either *yes* or *no*. The veridical hallucinations concerning which the question of the frequency in the community of all hallucinations like them arises, are all *vivid* and (relatively) *protracted*.

I enclose the schedules you ask for. If you know of anyone else who can help me, I should be thankful for his address.

Very truly yours | Wm James

ALS: MNS

[1] WJ was acting as the American agent for the Census of Hallucinations as announced by the International Congress of Physiological Psychology in 1889. For WJ's instructions to collectors and the several schedules, see *EPR*, 56–59.

From Granville Stanley Hall

CLARK UNIVERSITY, | WORCESTER, MASS. March 29. 90

My dear Professor James,

It is with great reluctance that I have deliberately advised our Miller here, who is, for his years, one of the brightest, best trained & most promising men I ever met in philosophy on the historico ethical non experimental psychological side, to apply for a Fellowship with you.[1]

He is a most lovable man personally & I thus sacrifice him because you can do so much better by him in his lines at Harvard than we can. The more you know him the more you will realize how sincere I am in the hope that in the philosophical field at large Harvard University & this may continue to supplement & not duplicate each others work.

[*Hall's hand*] Ever Yours | G. Stanley Hall

MLS: MH bMS Am 1092.9 (173)

[1] After graduating from the University of Pennsylvania in 1889, Dickinson Sergeant Miller spent a year as a graduate student at Clark University.

From Granville Stanley Hall

CLARK UNIVERSITY, | WORCESTER, MASS. April 1. 90.
My dear James,

How you pervert my meaning![1]   I am not assuming to be able to carry men beyond you, but we are fitting up 4 rooms at much expense & have 4 men solely for empirical study of physico-psychology, next year our arrangements will probably be complete.   This, as you know, is far more in this particular line than is now any where attempted.   What I mean by not duplicating would be therefore, when you have men with a strong tendency to the experimental, or we to the introspective, historical or ethical, for us to regard the departments of both institutions as if they were in one University so far as advising students as to their course goes.   Is not this plain & reasonable?   Of course one of us cannot do this without the cooperation of the other & I should greatly value as full & frank a statement of your own feelings on this important matter as I am giving you.   It is not impossible that your cooperation with this plan (& by yours I mean that of Royce & Palmer as well & of course in an entirely informal, unofficial & personal way such as that in which I write) may have its bearings on our own development here in this department.   Will you not let me hear from you a little more fully on this matter?

Ever Yours, | G. Stanley Hall.

MLS: MH bMS Am 1092.9 (174)

[1] The matter was precipitated by Hall's letter of 29 March 1890 and WJ's reply, which is not known.

To Alice James

Newport April 2$^{\underline{d}}$ 1890

Dearest Alice,

We (that is, I who dictate and she who holds the pen) were much pleased to get your letter three days ago, as well as the one which preceded it by a month or less.   I am glad to have been the first bearer of news to you of Henry's death.[1]   I had supposed you would hear from Lilla as soon as we did.   Hereafter I will send you immediately everything she writes.   Not one syllable as yet has come from N.Y. since that first announcement.   I wish it might all come to pass but it seems almost too good to be true.   At any rate the first thing will have to be a game of bluff between the two opposing lawyers. We are heartily sorry that your late inheritances have not even repaired the shrinkage of your original estate.   I suppose the latter is chiefly along of the C.B. & Q. which at last has begun to advance its rate again.[2]   Mrs Harry Russell called on us the other day and after speaking much of you, in reply to questions about her father, said he was feeling a great deal easier in mind of late since the railroad prospects were so fair.[3]

We are both heartily glad to hear that Harry goes to the Continent and you to London.   A little less London season for him, and a little more for you will surely be a better distribution of things.   I suppose you will move up early in May and I hope the change of base will be effected without injury from the Enemy.

As for ourselves, the April recess of seven days began last night, so down here we came, for the first two days of it, the remaining five being as yet undecided on.   I have been sticking very close to business and need a recreation and she is tagging along.   We have had a great deal of activity at home of late.   The Salters arriving from Chicago and he giving a Sanders Theatre address *What Can Ethics do for Us?*   And another in Boston a day later.[4]   We had a reception after the lecture in Cambridge and are beginning to feel like pillars of society.   I believe I told you of my new title and 4000 dollars salary.[5]   The height of human greatness in my line is now reached and no more flights can tempt me.   If we only get a good cook we shall aim at filling the place of the Gurneys(!) and give a dinner party every week.   Our attempts so far, it must be confessed, have fallen a little short of the model aimed at, owing to the treachery of the cook rather than to any defects in the posts.   Enough about us! except to add that the children are extremely well again and the spring is opening bravely.

Newport is unchanged save in poor Aunt Mary's failing faculties. Her mind is practically quite gone as far as engaging in conversation goes, though she looks well and laughs and has no impairment of speech but her memory is a chaos.   She asked last night if you were living with your husband and this morning had forgotten that either you or Harry were in Europe.   She also expressed surprise that we should be living in Cambridge.   When Mr Tweedy said after break-fast that he was going to *vote,* she said "What *boat* are you going in?" [*WJ's hand*]—as if a boat were as natural an after bkfst equipage as anything else.

A carriage is imminent to take us to see a portrait which Daisy Waring is making of Mr. Tweedy.   They are all artists now!   So Alice goes to change her dress and I put on my spectacles & finish this single handed.   Mr. Tweedy is as youthful as ever—rides a tricycle and takes gymnastic exercises.   But the evenings of talk here are as dull as ever.—

3.30 P.M.   We've just had a nap and Alice is lying on the bed read-ing the beautiful Mrs Deland's novel in the Atlantic.[6]   When in the world is the Tragic muse going to be ended?[7]   I long to read *that.* Elly Temple was at Cambridge the other day—entirely renovated as to her melancholy and certainly a most charming person.   What she ought to do now is to take her daughters abroad for a couple of years. But she says she has no money to do it.   Mrs. Dibblee, with whom she lived in Cambridge, wants very much to hire our house next year, so Alice & I have been talking to day of the possibility of she & the children being taken and left by me in Germany this next winter I to take my leave of absence the second year & spend that winter with them in france.   Castles in the air!

Heaven bless you!   W.J.

MLS (AGJ): MH bMS Am 1092.9 (1149)

  [1] Henry Albert Wyckoff.

  [2] Reference is to stocks of the Chicago, Burlington, and Quincy Railroad.

  [3] The father of Mary Hathaway Forbes Russell was John Murray Forbes, a railroad builder.

  [4] On 28 March 1890 Salter spoke in Pierce Hall, Boston, on "Reforms Good Men Might Agree About."

  [5] In November 1889 WJ's title at Harvard was changed to that of Professor of Psy-chology.

[6] Margaret Wade Deland (1857–1945), American author. Her novel *Sidney* was serialized in the *Atlantic Monthly* from January to October 1890 (vols. 65–66).

[7] HJ, *The Tragic Muse*, in *Atlantic Monthly*, January 1889–May 1890 (vols. 63–65).

From Henry Holt

Apl 2/90

My dear James:

If "publishers are [not] demons," it is a striking instance of long-suffering. I have illustrations here made years ago for manuscript that has never appeared.

Your letter makes plain what I took for granted—that your MS. will not be ready as early as May 1.

Of course you "dont know why [I] need the whole of [the MS.] before printing begins." It's not in your line to know. If you were gradually being converted into a demon, however, by the disappointments occasioned by authors, you would know all about it. I *never* began printing an instalment of a MS., so far as I can remember, without having to stop work before the book was finished, thus forcing the printer to put away the apparatus in place for it, and giving him excuses (which they always avail themselves of to the full) for dilly-dallying with the rest of the work when it came, and eventually getting out the work later and after vastly more friction than would have been the case if it had not been begun till the MS. was all ready. I remember Whitney—one of the most systematic and promptest of men, feeling very much hurt when I once urged these considerations on him, and telling me that I ought to know him well enough to feel safe that it wouldnt be the case with *him*.[1] I gave in to him, but it *was* the case, and the printers were out of copy two or three times and raised the devil by the delays they then permitted themselves.

I am now printing a book which the author concluded (as I expect you to, if you are not cautioned) to withdraw for revision, and he is returning it in instalments, expecting the printers to take out their cases and put them back whenever it suits him. I have simply had to order the work stopped until we get the MS. complete.

One of the things that makes me a demon, is to have to go over this weary explanation again and again.

I'm glad that you "want to get forward now with the least possible delay." To accomplish that, believe that I do too; put some faith in my experience; and complete your MS. before doing anything else.

My demoniacal character has not been developed so much by authors failing to look at contracts and losing them, as by the other thing; so I'm angelic enough to send you duplicates, of which please sign both and return us one.

I have just seen a contract signed by you to give us that MS. June 12/80 and yet, you, you, you, Brute (2 syllables) revile me for being a demon!.

I'm awfully sorry, all the same, that you're not coming here & to dine with us.   But that all must be in due time.

Yours Ever | H. Holt.

Professional Demon which being correctly interpreted meaneth Δαίμων

Letterbook: NjP

[1] William Dwight Whitney (1827–1894), American linguist.   Several of his dictionaries and grammars were published by Henry Holt.

To Henry Holt

Cambridge April 5, 1890

My dear Holt:

Your letter awaits me on my return from Newport.   Poor publisher, poor fellow, poor human being, ex-demon!   How those vermin of authors must have caused you to suffer in your time to wring from you such a tirade!   Well, it has been very instructive to me to grasp the publishers point of view.   Your fatal error however has been in not perceiving that I was an entirely *different kind* of author from any of those whom you had been in the habit of meeting, and that *celerity,* celerity incarnate, is the motive and result of all my plans and deeds.   It is not fair to throw that former contract into my face, when you know or ought to know that when the ten years or a little more from the time of its signature had elapsed I wrote to you that you must get another man to write this book for you, and that, as things were then going, I didn't see how I could ever finish it.

I would return these contracts signed, herewith, but for two points. First the provision that the author "shall prepare" matter for new editions "whenever called on" by publishers.   I should naturally hope to do that, but certainly can't pledge myself.   And as the text stands it seems to me useless, for no penalty is attached to my disobedience in case I fail to comply.   Shall we strike it out?—Secondly, I find in the former contract a MS. addition to the effect that on publi-

cation you deliver me 20 copies free of charge.   That seems fair
enough.   I was calculating the other day that I should have in all to
give away at least 75 copies of the book, most of them to professors
here and abroad.   As this helps your interest in the work as well as
mine the 20 copies (or even more) provision seems fair.
    Let me know about these points and I will sign.
Yours always | Wm. James

TC: MH bMS Am 1092.1

From Granville Stanley Hall

CLARK UNIVERSITY, | WORCESTER, MASS. April 7. 90

My dear James,
    Your note is certainly satisfactory & even gratifying, except your
supposition that we may want you to turn away all men who want
Experimental Psychology.[1]   No such thought ever entered my head.
All I wanted to know is given in your note, which I think is in every
way fair & just, at least to everyone except yourself.   It distresses me
to know that you have even moments of discouragement.   To this
you have no right.   You started this whole movement yourself & are
the very best man in my opinion, in the world at the present time in
your own lines & I only fear that you are working too hard on your
book.   The cause of Psychology in this country is more dependent
upon you & your safe delivery of that book than upon anything
else whatever.
    I wish I might see you in Boston some day soon.
Ever Yours, | G S. Hall

MLS: MH bMS Am 1092.9 (175)

[1] WJ's note is not known; see letter from Hall of 29 March 1890.

To Henry Holt

Cambr. Apl 8. 90

My dear Holt
    Here goes a copy of the contract signed by me.   I add as you sug-
gest, the clause about 20 copies; and I leave the clause about new
matter for new editions; but I warn you clearly that I shall only consent to furnish such new matter in case it involves no great sacrifice.[1]
I can easily imagine myself engrossed in some other work hereafter,

and having grown into such a state of disgust for my old psychology book as to find the rehandling of it an intellectually impossible task. In that case I should calmly fold my arms and say "the book has had its day—let it be republished if at all as an historical monument, not as a sham exhibition of my present opinions." There comes a time in all books when [*typed copy*] a man can't tinker them; he must write a new work altogether.

I also enclose blanks and thank you for your 'enterprise' at the Century Club.[2]

Ever truly yours, | Wm. James.

[*WJ's hand*] Your copy found again![3]

AL: NjP; TC: MH bMS Am 1092.1

[1] In his letter of 7 April 1890 (calendared) Holt gave WJ permission to include a provision in the new contract stating that WJ would receive twenty free copies of the *Principles of Psychology;* additional free copies would be available if they were to be used for advertising and not as "little personal amenities." The new contract required WJ to prepare revised editions, but Holt assured WJ that no penalties were attached to this proviso.

[2] In his letter of 7 April 1890 (calendared) Holt noted that he spent the evening filling out the Census of Hallucinations questionnaire instead of going to the Century Club.

[3] A reference to WJ's remarks, deleted in the letter, concerning the copy of the contract sent to him by Holt that he thought he had destroyed. For the deleted passage see entry 21.3 in the Textual Apparatus.

To Henry Holt

Cambridge May 7. [1890]

My dear Holt

If you will look at our contract I think you will see that it has yet over three weeks to run. I shall however be through in less than two, and as I am anxious, on every account, not to lose a single day, I don't see why we shouldn't be beginning already to decide on the page. The ms., to my great regret, is panning out bigger than I thought it would. I fear there will be no less than about 460,000 words, which would require 575 words on a page to make a book of 800 pp. I cant possibly cut this thing down, as it all belongs together; and I trust this bulk will not unfit it for the "series."[1] It is a disappointment to me not to have made a smaller book, that having been my aim all along.

My calculation isn't *close,* as the pages are very irregularly written, & there are many notes, internal headings etc. But I feel pretty confident now, that taking the "Mind" page, or the page of Ladd's Physiol. Psych.[2] (strange to say they contain each just about the same no. of words (460) although the Mind p. is so much smaller- and handsomer-looking to my eye) my book will hardly fall inside of a 1000 of 'em! What shall be done? Two vols? or publish outside of the series?—or what? let me know please, forthwith. It is only this A.M. that I have been able to make the calculation with any definiteness, owing to the broken up condition of the MS. hitherto.

Meanwhile I send you some of the first sheets, to be used if you wish to make experiments.

Always yours | Wm James

ALS: NjP

[1] *Principles of Psychology* appeared as part of Holt's American Science Series. Published in two volumes, the book contains some 550,000 words, counting 400 words on each of its 1,378 pages.

[2] George Trumbull Ladd, *Elements of Physiological Psychology* (1887) (WJ 448.17). WJ's review is reprinted in *ECR*.

To Katharine Peabody Loring

Cambr. May 7. 90

My dear Katherine

You are a blessing, and your letter is very interesting. I send Schedule B as required;[1] and I thank you enormously for the trouble you have taken. You say in your own case: "I was conscious of the presence." Was this presence a *distinctly exteriorized vision,* or an 'impression,' or what? And was the voice an *external voice*? The distinction is rather important.

In great haste | Yours always | Wm James

All well with us! I hope you're all the same.

ALS: Beverly Historical Society and Charles W. Galloupe Memorial Society

[1] Reference is to the Census of Hallucinations; for the schedule see *EPR*, 58–59.

To Henry Holt

Cambridge, May 9, 1890.

My dear Holt,—I was in hopes that you would propose to break away from the famous "Series" and publish the book independently, in two volumes. An abridgement could then be prepared for the Series. If there be anything which I loathe it is a mean overgrown page in small type, and I think the author's feelings ought to go for a good deal in the case of the enormous *rat* which his ten years gestation has brought forth.

In any event, I dread the summer and next year, with two new courses to teach, and, I fear, no vacation.   What I wrote you, if you remember, was to send you the "heft" of the MS. by May 1st, the rest to be done in the intervals of proof-correcting.   You however insisted on having the entire MS. in your hands before anything should be done.   It seems to me that this delay is, *now* at any rate, absurd. There is certainly less than two weeks' work on the MS. undone. And every day got behind us now means a day of travel and vacation for me next September.   I really think, considering the sort of risk I am running by the delay, that I must *insist* on getting to press now as soon as the page is decided on.

No one could be more disgusted than I at the sight of the book. *No* subject is worth being treated of in 1000 pages!   Had I ten years more, I could rewrite it in 500; but as it stands it is this or nothing— a loathsome, distended, tumefied, bloated, dropsical mass, testifying to nothing but two facts: *1st,* that there is no such thing as a *science* of psychology, and *2nd,* that W. J. is an incapable.

Yours provided you hurry up things,

Wm. James.

LWJ: 1:293–94

From Charles Augustus Strong

　　　　　　　Hotel Victoria, | Freiburg im Breisgau, | May 13, 1890. My dear Prof. James:—

I have some time to spare this morning & think I will write you a late answer to your much appreciated letter of Jan. 27th.

Till the first of March we fully expected to spend the present semester in Leipsic, but Mrs. S.'s health had been so poor during the winter & we heard such bad stories of the Leipsic climate that we made up our minds to come here, to the neighborhood of the Black Forest, & live as much as possible in the woods.   I have no cause to regret our decision so far as my studies are concerned; for the advantages here in the lines at which I am working at present are excellent. I hear Zoology under the famous Weismann;[1] dissect brains ad lib. in the laboratory of the comparative anatomist Wiedersheim;[2] do a little practical work in physiology under von Kries;[3] attend Emming-haus's psychiatrical clinic[4] & study the psychology of maniacs & mel-ancholics (we had a fine maniac woman, the other day, who screamed & cursed & smashed a chair against the wall); & last not least spend two hours a week experimenting with Dr Münsterberg.

I find him interesting intellectually & personally most agreeable. He reminds me a good deal of Schurman: he has the same physique, the same strong nerves & power of work; he is like him a universal devourer & producer. He lectures & experiments all day, talks bril-liantly in the evening, & then works at his desk till three or four in the morning, writing from fourteen to sixteen printed pages at a sit-ting. Like Schurman he has a *motorischen sprachapparat* that functions with surprising ease and copiousness; he told me himself that stu-dents call him the Kuno Fischer of Freiburg.[5] He spends little or no time preparing for his classes, & lectures well; he thinks of giving Psychology next semester, & will not prepare at all; *er wollte sich an-heischig machen, über irgend ein Kapitel der Psychologie einen einstündigen Vortrag zu halten ohne jegliche Vorbereitung.* He is not without some relish of satisfaction at the brilliancy of his own performances—in this respect unlike Schurman, whose self-unconsciousness is beauti-ful. He is deeper, more trenchant & more of a philosopher than Schurman; though how unerring his judgment is in *Principienfragen,* I have not yet made out. That is often the weak point of these brilliant productive men: they can make serious blunders on points of abstract theory. I fear that Dessoir, for instance, with all his learning, fecun-dity, & skill in exposition, is but a mediocre reasoner. Dr Mün-sterberg is certainly much his superior in this respect. He is younger than I, it made me blue to hear it. He is a popular Docent; he gave last semester a *publicum* on Hypnotism, a catching subject to be sure, that had three hundred auditors. I am listening to his *Einleitung in die Philosophie,* a course of philosophical encyclopaedia. Like Ebb-inghaus, Jodl of Prague the *Ethiker,*[6] & others, he is at work on a Psychology, in which he intends to mention the entire literature at the close of each chapter, e.g. all the psychological articles in Mind & the other periodicals, etc.[7] The experiments we began last Saturday are on the quantitative aspect of Association, & suggested by some carried on in Wundt's laboratory last winter by a Mr. Scripture. The subject sits behind a screen, and receives two perceptions simultane-ously, an auditive one in the form of a spoken word, & a visual one administered by means of a camera. He then announces what first enters his head.   Dr. M. thinks the results will throw light on the mechanism of Association, & help to settle the status of the *berüchtigte Apperceptionstheorie.*

What do you think of Ebbinghaus's new *Zeitschrift*?[8] I asked Dr M., who is to have a paper in the next issue, whether it did not represent a certain *Gegensatz* to Wundt.   He replied that Wundt was asked to collaborate, but declined; and added that Wundt has treated the *Bestrebungen* of the younger generation with so little sympathy & has made his polemics so personal as to have many enemies.   Then, too, his scientific position is so ambiguous on some points as to inspire the younger men with a certain distrust; I remember Ebbinghaus mentioning in this connection Wundt's attempt to mediate between nativism & empiricism,[9] & his equivocal theory of apperception, at once in harmony & at war with a consistent parallelism.

As for parallelism, it seems to me we don't need to wait for a great metaphysical theory to absorb the doctrine & relieve it of its one-sidedness: I mean we have the metaphysical theory already.   At least I heard hints of one in Paulsen's lectures, & haven't the least doubt that this cautious thinker could supply you with one that would be entirely satisfactory.   I have been trying of late to think the matter out, & should like, if I can without wearying you, to develope briefly the metaphysical consequences that seem to me to follow from the doctrine of parallelism.

You object that parallelism deprives spiritual facts of all voice in directing the affairs of the world, & degrades them to the level of *epiphenomena.* This is certainly the way Münsterberg puts the matter. He says that a consistent spiritualistic theory, a theory maintaining that spiritual facts are the reality & the condition for the appearance of physical facts, not vice versa, is simply impossible.   He says that the true condition for the appearance of spiritual facts lies in the nervous facts they accompany, & that it is impossible to explain spiritual facts as the effects of preceding spiritual facts: for while our thoughts & fancies might be explained as effects of previous perceptions, it would be impossible to give a purely psychical explanation of 1) the reappearance of consciousness after sleep or a period of unconsciousness, and 2) the origin of entirely new perceptions. These events can only be explained as the concomitants of brain-states upon which they are dependent.   In short, only the *physical* chain is continuous, the *psychical* chain is interrupted; there is in truth no psychical *chain,* for many of the links are missing; & it is therefore impossible to construe psychical events as forming a closed causal sequence. *Physical* events can be understood entirely by themselves because they are always the effects of other physical events; but *psychical* events cannot be understood by themselves, but only when taken in connection with physical i.e. nervous events.

As against this view, I believe that a consistent spiritualistic theory *is* possible, and just because the psychical chain *is* continuous. If we include in the psychical chain only states of clear consciousness, of course it appears interrupted; but there are other psychical states besides these, there are subconscious or practically unconscious states which are nevertheless psychical. There is the greatest significance in the fact that consciousness is capable of *degrees*. Our perceptions are not characterized by the same degree of clearness throughout their length & breadth; but there is a point in the middle which we see clearly, & from that point it shades off in every direction to unconsciousness. The parts of our perceptions to which we do not attend are for us as if they did not exist; yet they are none the less parts of our perceptions. Now, vast regions of our psychical life lie in this dim subconscious condition: our multitudinous memories while we do not think of them; the subterranean motives & preferences that govern our actions to a large extent; the sides of our sensations & perceptions that do not interest us, etc. The proof that these "submerged" memories & motives are psychically real consists in the fact that they codetermine our conscious thoughts & acts. What you once called "the psychologist's fallacy" depends for its possibility on the existence of subconscious states, that is on there being more in a man's psychical states than he is conscious of.[10] It would be interesting to know what is the nature of the "submerged" consciousness of Léonie, about whom I read in your suggestive paper in Scribner's, while she is in her normal waking state.[11] Are they developed, wide-awake consciousnesses like her normal one, or are they only fields of subconscious thought & action? In either case, they are psychical states as much as those of clear consciousness.

Of course it is theoretically possible to say (with Riehl) that mind & consciousness are the same thing, & that what is not conscious is simply nervous. But this leaves the mind a fragmentary thing, with unaccountable ragged edges, a sort of thing that we reject as incredible when reasoning about material objects. We are unwilling to believe that the walls of this room, the pictures, books, chairs, etc., all suddenly cease to exist the moment we close our eyes, or that they exist only as far as we see them: the same way with the mind. Because I am not at all conscious of the intensity of a sensation, it does

not follow that the sensation has no intensity; & its intensity is not
necessarily the intensity I believe it to have.   If the mind has any
proper form & shape, it must be more than present consciousness.
If a memory can lose 50% of its conscious distinctness without ceasing
to be a psychical fact, it can lose 99% or even 99.999 . . . . %.   But
you must know Höffding's excellent chapter on "das Unbewusste."[12]

Well, granted that we are at liberty to fill out the *lacunae* of our
conscious states with psychical elements of a subconscious sort: the
chain becomes continuous, & it becomes theoretically possible to explain any psychical event by previous events likewise psychical.
Apply this to the passage of a person from sleep to waking.   Psychical
elements that exist subconsciously during sleep are "aggregated" to
form the consciousness of the person awake.   This is parallel to what
goes on in the brain: the nervous system is *un appareil d'énergie latente;*
the nervous energy that is potential during sleep is transformed into
actual energy when the person wakes; if we could translate this process into psychical language, we should have a psychological explanation of the passage from sleep to waking.

It is more difficult to show how new perceptions could be explained
without transcending the psychical chain.   Yet I think not impossible.   One indispensable thing is to recognize that the individual
minds are not separated from each other by impenetrable walls; that
in truth there are not many minds, but only one mind & in it various
more tightly knotted complexes of ideas which are the individual
minds.   Thus the action of one mind upon another, or rather the
action of the minds of my axis-cylinders upon the minds of my nerve-
cells, cannot be ruled out as *apriori* impossible.   The proofs that the
relations of individual minds must be thus conceived are the following: 1) the body is a cell-state, each cell is an individual, phylogeneti-
cally all cells were originally alike, the mind of the entire organism is
simply the total mind of the cells; 2) if you cut a fresh-water polyp
or an angleworm in two, both pieces continue to live, i.e. to have
minds: this is the division of a mind in two; 3) the earliest reproduction i.e. fission is simply the cutting of an individual in two; 4) even
in human reproduction we have at bottom the separation of a new
individual from the parent.   This seems in flat contradiction to the
unity of consciousness; it is simply in contradiction to our present
way of construing that unity.

No, minds are not absolute, incorrigible individuals, monads; they
are but parts or phases of one mind, which is as diffused & all-
pervasive as matter.   I mean wherever you have material motion you

have some form however simple of psychical life. Certain extremely complicated physico-chemical processes are accompanied by what we know in ourselves as conscious perception & thought; but we cannot reasonably say that all simpler physico-chemical processes are unaccompanied by psychical life. It is more reasonable to assume that the kind of psychical life which accompanies any form of material motion is directly proportioned in its simplicity to the simplicity of that motion. So that the physical processes represented by the impact of light-rays upon the retina & the transmission of the resulting nerve-impulses to the brain are accompanied by some very simple form of psychical life; & this, it seems to me, is what explains the rise of our new perceptions. But, it will be said, psychical events so absurdly simple as we should have to assume the impact of light-rays & the transmission of nerve-impulses to be are not at all competent to account for such a great new astounding psychical event as a perception. Here it is we must remember that the nervous system is *un appareil d'énergie latente*. This is the same thing as to say that the nerve-impulses are not the total cause of the perception, but, like the spark that ignites the gunpowder, only the occasion of it. Perceptions do not come into our minds from without; they are only the tune that physical events play upon our minds as upon an instrument. What explains our perceptions is the inherited & acquired predispositions of the nerve-cells in the cortex. The subconscious states that form the psychical concomitant to the states of these highly organized brain-cells, these subconscious states are the true causal antecedent of any perception that arises. These psychical predispositions exist all the while subconsciously & codetermine all our thoughts & acts. Thus the rise of a new perception is explained in the same manner as the passage from sleep to waking. And neither one nor the other is explicable psychologically, indeed the application of the category of cause & effect to our psychical life is impossible & absurd, except on the assumption that the psychical realm includes subconscious as well as clear-conscious states.

Grant that the psychical realm is thus constituted, that it has a causality of its own quite distinct from though parallel to that of matter: we may then reasonably assume that psychical events are not à la Münsterberg dependent upon physical, but at all events that the two kinds are coequal. The theory that regards the two as only two different faces of a third unknowable reality seems to me epistemologically absurd. Since we know psychical phenomena directly, physical phenomena only through the medium of psychical, it is reasonable to assume that psychical phenomena are the only reality & that physical phenomena are only the way they appear when viewed from without. Our brains are only our minds viewed *ab extra;* & our task becomes, on the one hand to push the physiology & chemistry of the brain so far that we may know clearly what brain-events are, on the other hand so to conceive our psychical life that it may be credible that our brain-activities are the outer view of it.

On this theory mind is the only reality, mind alone has a voice in directing the affairs of the world, & if there is any *epiphenomenon,* it is matter. You cannot consider this theory materialistic. Deterministic it doubtless is; but there is no antagonism between determinism & moral choice, and a free-will theory which requires more will go away empty-handed.

I hope I have at last put my position in a clear light; I am sorry it has taken so much space.

I enjoy Freiburg very much; I cannot say "we", because Mrs. Strong has not yet come with her maid from Meran, Tirol, where we spent the vacation & whence I hastened on in advance of her. We are looking forward expectantly to seeing Prof. & Mrs. Schurman here.[13] They are at present in Paris, but are coming here the middle of June to remain at least a fortnight.

With kind regards to Mrs. James & yourself,

Very sincerely yours, | C. A. Strong.

Professor Wm James,

   Cambridge,

     Mass.

P.S. By the way, I have had an offer of an associate professorship at Brown University: what do you think of the institution? It is for the fall of 1891. I am corresponding with Pres. Stanley Hall, & should like best almost any appointment at Clark.

ALS: MH bMS Am 1092 (1051)

[1] August Weismann (1834–1914), German zoologist.

[2] Robert Ernst Eduard Wiedersheim (1848–1923), German comparative anatomist.

[3] Johannes von Kries (1853–1929), German physiologist.

[4] Hermann Emminghaus (1845–1904), German psychiatrist.

[5] Kuno Fischer (1824–1907), German historian of philosophy.

[6] Friedrich Jodl (1849–1914), professor of philosophy at Prague and Vienna.

[7] Münsterberg's book was not identified. He was then publishing his *Beiträge zur experimentellen Psychologie* in four parts (1889–92) (WJ 757.62).

[8] Hermann Ebbinghaus was editor of the *Zeitschrift für Psychologie und Physiologie der Sinnesorgane* (1890–).

[9] Reference is to different theories of the perception of space; for the terms see *EPs*, 72.

[10] For WJ on the psychologist's fallacy see *PP*, 195–96.

[11] Léonie or Madame B. is one of the mental patients described by Pierre Janet in *L'Automatisme psychologique* and discussed by WJ in "The Hidden Self." For the case see *PP*, 365–67.

[12] Chapter 3 on "The Conscious and the Unconscious" of Höffding's *Psychologie in Umrissen* (1887).

[13] Barbara Forrest Munro Schurman (d. 1930), wife of Jacob Gould Schurman.

To Granville Stanley Hall

95 Irving St, May 16 [1890]

My dear Hall,

I am shocked to hear of the stunning blow that has fallen on you, & must send you a word of sympathy.[1] Yet, death for death, who could wish a better one? I hardly know whether the little girl going too makes it worse or better. That such big things can happen so easily gives one a strange suspicion that our instinctive ways of feeling about things are wrong and that if we knew reality even this might seem light and benign. But I can express nothing but my heartfelt pity, my dear old friend, and pray that erelong you will find yourself again *zurecht*. I am sorry that I can never see her again.

Bless you! | Wm James

ALS: MWC

[1] While Hall was away, on 15 May 1890 his wife, Cornelia Fisher Hall, and eight-year-old daughter, Julia Fisher Hall, died from asphyxiation.

To Alice Howe Gibbens James

Cambridge May 17. [May 16, 1890] | 5.45 AM.

Darling Alice

Your two letters yesterday were a shower-bath of delight—rose-water and Veilchenduft! How nice everything sounds and what a blessing to have such a place. How changed art thou from last year. I'm glad that you like "Brown," and glad that the cow is so well. I wish that the horses might prove so equally.

Tweedy has n't yet come, and I confess I am rather glad, for it has been a very busy time. I wrote yesterday again from ½ past 5 to ½ past six, and have no question now but that by Monday the big job will be done.   You can't tell how queer it makes me feel.   From the theoretical point of view also things are smoothing out famously, so that as you said one time, I think it will have a sort of 'stride.'

Margaret is addressing my census-blanks, applications for which are pouring in at a great rate in consequence of my circular letter to the newspapers.[1]   It is a great relief to me and she doesn't seem to dislike it.   Your mother is very sweet.   They went to dine at the Ross's yesterday, and seem to have enjoyed themselves.[2]   I dined with Chubb at Taussigs and then heard Chubb talk to the Finance Club.[3] He is a perfectly charming fellow, but his talk although first rate in manner, struck me as rather lacking in solidity of grasp of the facts of life.—The spanish woman was here yesterday, but didn't get into the Library.   I was too absorbed to see what she was about, Ellen and your Mother looked after her.   The house upstairs looks very clean. I sleep with my door open into your room, and a sacred presence just flown seems to float there through the darkling listening air. Give kisses to all!   It has rained here pretty steadily.   Cambridge looked really beautiful yesterday in its steam bath.   Margaret had a bad headache until the afternoon yesterday.

Love to both of you!   W.J.

ALS: MH bMS Am 1092.9 (1712)

Address: Mrs. William James | Tamworth Iron Works | N.H.

Postmarks: <B>OSTON MAY 1<6> 1890   TAMWOR<TH IRON> WORKS N.H. MAY 16

[1] For WJ's letter on the Census of Hallucinations see *EPR*, 59–60.

[2] Reference is to Denman Waldo Ross.

[3] According to the *Harvard Crimson*, 15 May 1890, Percival Chubb, described as a member of the Fabian Society, spoke on 15 May on "Contemporary Socialism in England."

To Henry Holt

Cambr. May 18, 1890.

My dear Holt:

The Hamilton of whom you speak is perhaps an old fogy who wrote a book 10 or 12 years ago called "The Human Mind".[1]   He is correct, not cranky, well educated in the ante-evolutionary way, but a nullity both in matter and manner.   Logic being a perfectly cut and dried subject, he might treat that well.

My MS. is now finished and occupies (418 + 2552 =) 2970 pp., many of them pages of print.[2]   It will hardly go into 1000 pp. of the usual 8vo size. I base my calculation on the fact that it took just 90 pp. of my MS. to cover 30 of the Journal of Speculative Philosophy when my chapter on Taine appeared therein, which is now to be reprinted with hardly any addition or change.[3]

I expect to ship it to you tomorrow or next day with the list of woodcuts carefully made out and the books from which the photographs are to be made.[4] I shall then wash my hands of all farther responsibility except for the proofs, which I trust will be furnished at the utmost rate of velocity which the printing office can command. I shall be ready to give my whole time to correcting them from tomorrow on until they are done.

Yours truly | Wm. James

TC: MH bMS Am 1092.1

[1] Edward John Hamilton (1834–1918), Irish-born philosopher and Presbyterian clergyman, active in the United States, *The Human Mind* (1883).

[2] Since the manuscript of *Principles of Psychology* is not known, it can only be surmised that WJ did a good deal of cutting and pasting, using parts of articles already published and cutting pages from books. Some of the books that WJ quoted in *Principles* and preserved at the Houghton Library are missing pages or parts of pages.

[3] WJ, "The Perception of Time," *Journal of Speculative Philosophy* 20 (October 1886): 374–407, chap. 15 of *Principles of Psychology*. 'Taine' is probably the copyist's error for 'Time'.

[4] For a possible source of the books see the letter to Holt of 21 March 1890.

To Alice Howe Gibbens James

Sunday P.M. May 17 [18]. 90 | 9.50 P.M.

Beloved Alice

The job is done! All but some paging and ½ a dozen little footnotes the work is completed and as I see it as a unit, I feel as if it might be rather a vigorous and richly colored chunk—for that kind of thing at least!

I woke yesterday at 2, and with coffee wrote from 4 A.M. to 6 P.M. with great success and then went in to Ellen Dixey's to dinner where I sat beside a Mrs Bradley, broad church episcopalian clergymaness from Philadelphia, née Hinkley of Boston, a very charming woman indeed.[1] I spoke to no one else but Ellen. All ugly and unknown people the funniest party I ever see. The champagne I drank made me *dizzy* (not that I drank too much) and this A.M. I woke with a nausea which has lasted all day. I spent the day nevertheless at my writing table, and did the job, as I said before; and at seven Chubb & I went to dine with Charles Norton and passed a very pleasant two hours, the nausea departing with the ingestion of a certain quantity of *meat*. Edwin Mead is here talking with Chubb.[2] I have been writing notes, after talking a little and giving them a fire. Mead was at Hall's wife's funeral, and reports that H. himself seems to stand very well the shock.

How I wish I had you here for the next fortnight. No matter. *You* shall have *me* now in a way in which you have not had me for a long time, now that this big job is rolled off my shoulders like Christians memorable pack.[3]

Bob spent last night here. Much better than when he last went through.

Love to all. | W.J.

ALS: MH bMS Am 1092.9 (1714)

[1] Susan Hinckley Bradley (b. 1851), an artist, wife of Leverett Bradley (1846–1902), an Episcopalian clergyman.

[2] Edwin Doak Mead (1849–1937), American reformer and author.

[3] Christian, the central character in John Bunyan, *The Pilgrim's Progress*, carried a burden on his back, which dropped off at the sight of the cross.

To Christine Ladd Franklin

Cambridge May 19 [1890]

Dear Mrs. Franklin,

Here is your document at last, since you wish it back. It is simpler than I tho't and I need not have sent for it.[1]

Congratulate me! I have this day finished the manuscript of a "Principles of Psychology" which ought to be out in September, and which has been sticking to me like an old man of the sea for the last 8 or 9 years.[2] I feel like a barrel with its hoops gone! and shall grow young again.

As for your logical papers you can perhaps now understand why I have not read them. I have not passed 5 minutes since last August which was not in some way connected with that infernal Manuscript. I mean now to begin to read something, but am quite brain fagged at present, and am anyhow absolutely non-mathematical and non-higher-logical, so I'd better wait for a more propitious moment for your articles. I have found some of the C.L.F. abstracts in Hall's Journal very good.[3]

Poor Hall! what a blow! A friend who was at the funeral tells me that he bears up very well.

With respects to your husband, believe me

ever truly yours | Wm James

ALS: NNC

[1] In his letter of 29 April 1890 (calendared) WJ asked Christine Ladd Franklin to return his letter on illusions of motion. The letter is possibly that of 3 February 1889; see *Correspondence*, 6:462–63.

[2] Reference is to the old man in *Arabian Nights* who clung to the back of Sinbad.

[3] In the April 1890 (vol. 3) issue of the *American Journal of Psychology* there are four abstracts by Christine Ladd Franklin of journal articles on vision.

To Alice Howe Gibbens James

Cambridge, May 22. 90. | 5.45 P.M.

Dearest Alice,

I sat up till 2 last night putting the finishing touches on the MS. which now goes to Holt in irreproachable shape, woodcuts and all. I insured it for $1000.00 in giving it to the express people this A.M.. That will make them extra careful at a cost of $1.50. This morning a great feeling of weariness came over me at 10 o'clock and I was taking down a vol. of Tennyson, intending to doze off in my chair, when "Frank" arrived with the books from Hooper's and it took me a couple of hours to get them in.[1] The shelves have sucked them up like a great sponge and hardly show any difference. Margaret didn't know that there were any new books when she came in. This is something of a disappointment; but in spite of it, the addition to the library is a very valuable one. Royce came in ere I ended—then a Miss Calkins from Wellesley who wants to study Psychology next year, then Dr. Dunbar who wants to become a mesmerizer,[2] until now I wearily go to the club dinner, and thence to Hodgson's to get some more Hall.-blanks.[3] Margaret has been a great help to me with these. Tomorrow I shall go into town & order the lawn mower etc. How I wish that you were here. Your letter came this P.M. Yes, as for Gifford, he's not the man for all summer. Margaret isn't going till Saturday.

Good bye! Ugh! How I wish you were here to night instead of Margaret! T'would rest me so. Why is it we never can be together alone? Margaret is a perfect trump, only not my wife.

Thine   Wm.

She takes 150 dollars to her mother, and the stove lining.   The Franke's also paid a long visit to day.[4]   The great objection to being at home alone is that you are interrupted every 2 minutes by the doorbell.

It has grown very cold.

ALS: MH bMS Am 1092.9 (1717)

[1] WJ received many books from the library of Ephraim Whitman Gurney through Gurney's brother-in-law, Edward William Hooper.   Frank was not identified.

[2] The only physician named Dunbar listed in Boston and Cambridge directories for the period is Eugene Fillmore Dunbar (1851–1896), an 1880 graduate of the Harvard Medical School.

[3] Census of Hallucinations questionnaires.

[4] Kuno Francke (1855–1930), professor of Germanic languages at Harvard, and his wife, Katharine Gilbert Francke.

To Charles William Eliot

95 Irving St, May 23. 90

Dear President

Miss Calkins, teacher of Psychology etc at Wellesley College, who has next year "off" for study wishes to come here, and asks what I can do for her.   As I don't teach in the Annex and have such a heavy lot of teaching to carry next year anyhow that I shall be lucky if I get safely through,[1] I have had to tell her that I can do nothing for her, unless it were possible that she should attend my Phil 20a Course,[2] which at the same time I told her was probably *im*possible.   I write now to ask your opinion.   The instruction in that course (so far as it consists of lectures etc.) has always been given at my own house:— this year and probably next, in the evening.   Do you see any objection, *under those circumstances,* to her being present?   According to the report of Prof. & Mrs. Palmer she is a woman of exceptional intellectual capacity.—I of course shall not ask any laboratory privileges for her.

Since you have been interested in the progress of my everlasting book, I rejoice to inform you that the manuscript, drawings, and everything pertaining to the creature went off yesterday A.M. to the Publishers.   It will undoubtedly appear before October.   I am much relieved, and feel like a barrel without any hoops.   Having got rid of this thing, I now feel as if I might fall to and *learn* something about Psychology, and even other matters.

Always sincerely yours | Wm James

ALS: MH Archives

[1] The Annex or Women's Annex, as it was generally known, eventually became Radcliffe College.

[2] Philosophy 20a: Psychological Seminary, which in 1890–91 dealt with pleasure and pain.

To Mary Whiton Calkins

95 Irving St | Cambridge May 24 [1890]

Dear Miss Calkins

The President writes to me that he "sees no way to do anything for" you "not even in Philosophy 20a."

It seems very hard. But he has to keep guard all along the line, and I suppose that laxity would soon produce an involuntary and unintended occupation of a great many of these higher courses by women. When the Corporation move in that direction, if they ever do move, they mean to move openly and thoroughly.

I can only say now that if you do come to Cambridge, I shall be most happy to help you over difficulties and give you advice. Had I double my present strength, I should also enjoy giving you some instruction free of all duties and taxes, but I don't dare to propose any such thing, with as much work as I have, and so little ability to do it.

Believe in my sincere regret for this action of our authorities. Can't you get to Worcester almost as easily as to Cambridge? Stanley Hall's Psychological department ought to be the best in the world.

Sincerely yours | Wm James

ALS: MWelC

To Alice Howe Gibbens James

Cambr. May 24. 90.

Beloved Child-Wife,

How I long to see you! After my lecture yesterday P.M. I went into town for some errands (amongst them a second hand lawn-mower which seemed to be in good condition enough and cost 5.00 instead of 8). Then I came home very weary and lit a fire and had a delicious 2 hours all by myself thinking of the big *étape* of my life which now lay behind me (I mean that infernal book done) and of the possibilities that the future yielded of reading and living and loving out

from the shadow of that interminable black cloud.   Chief of all did
I melt *almost* to tears in thinking of my child-friend-wife who threw
in her lot with mine so many years ago, and whose confidence, so
rudely tried, has at last through one thing and another, struggled
along, ever gathering encouragement as one baby after another appeared, then the country place, then this noble house, and now at
last *the book*, which proclaims me really an efficient man—and last
not least 'the 2nd Messiah' about to be![1]   Do you remember the
promise I made in the boat on Lake Placid that night, to support you
by the proceeds of its sales?[2]   Even that may come to pass, my beauteous bride!   At any rate, darling, it does give me some comfort to
think that I don't live *wholly* in prospects, aspirations, & phrases, but
now and then have some thing done to show for all the fuss.   The
joke of it is that I, who have always considered myself a thing of
glimpses, of discontinuity, of aperçus, with no power of doing a big
job, suddenly realize at the *end* of this task that it is the *biggest* book on
Psychology in any language except Wundt's[3] Rosmini's[4] and—Daniel
Greenleaf Thompson's![5]   Still if it burns up at the printing office, I
shan't *much* care, for I shan't ever write it again.

I read Tennyson, and a sort of hush and calm stole into me by the
light of the fire, to which I have long been unwonted.   'Tis the sort
of thing we shall have all the time next year abroad.   But all this
time think of the pity of my lot.   It makes [me] gnash my teeth at
the mockery of married life.   The one thing which it seems to insure
is that husband and wife shall not be together.   With your mother
and Margaret I can be, but not with you!   That is postponed for
another year.   I can take no "trip" with you, either, this summer, on
account of the proofs (unless indeed we might go for a sunday up to
the mountains together!)   I would *command* you to come down here
on Monday, save that I fear you would be disconsolate again with the
infernality of the meals.   It only costs five dollars for you to come
and go back again, however.   So think it over!   I lecture on Monday,
so can't meet you at the train.   But do you come out and let yourself
in with Margaret's key, and I will come home from lunch and either
find *you*, or a letter from you at 3 o'clock, telling me what you think.

Ansel Bourne is coming Tuesday.   He may be not hypnotizable.
But if his case opens up, there may be several days of work over him,
which will keep me here.   I fear also that the starting of the book-
proofs may keep me here all next week.   I don't want to go to the
country till they are all under way in a routine fashion.   Fagged as I
now am and desiring mental simplification, it would be such a sweet

boon to me to have you here and avoid the social complications of these breakfasts with the neighbors, if you would only come and take things innocently not expecting to have a very luxurious time yourself. I confess that the thought of going to the country for rest and instanteously being confronted by Gifford, Fraulein, Andrew, the demands of the boys, etc etc, and getting at you only in their presence, seems a sort of ghastly farce—under the particular psychic conditions which always accompany my release from Cambridge at the end of the year. Afterwards, when I am a little toned up, it is another matter altogether.—Margaret has gone to the Childs to breakfast, I am waiting for her return when I shall go to the Holly tree Inn.[6] [*end of letter missing*]

AL incomplete: MH bMS Am 1092.9 (1718)

[1] AGJ was expecting their last child, Alexander Robertson.

[2] Since WJ signed the contract for *Principles of Psychology* in 1878, the same year that he and AGJ honeymooned near Lake Placid in Keene Valley, his promise likely was made in 1878.

[3] Wilhelm Wundt, *Grundzüge der physiologischen Psychologie*. WJ was familiar with both the one-volume first edition (1874) (WJ 796.59.2) and the two-volume second edition (1880) (WJ 796.59.4), as well as with later editions. For WJ's review of the first edition see *ECR*.

[4] Antonio Rosmini-Serbati (1797–1855), Italian philosopher, *Psychology*, 3 vols. (1884–88). WJ's review of the second volume is reprinted in *ECR*.

[5] Daniel Greenleaf Thompson (1850–1897), American author, *A System of Psychology*, 2 vols. (1884).

[6] The Holly Tree Coffee Rooms at 20 Brattle St., Cambridge.

To Alice Howe Gibbens James

Home, Sunday P.M. [May 25, 1890] | 4.30

Beloved Wife,

How I must have wrung your tender heart to make that appeal to you to come down when Lucy Russell is there![1] I quite forgot it when I was writing, I don't see how I came to do so. Of course you can't leave her. I was feeling badly yesterday on account of the intolerable interruptions that have made life almost impossible all the week. Ever since Wednesday I have been trying to clear away my table of the enormous mass of unanswered letters (hallucinatory & other) which have accumulated on it, but have been able to make no headway whatever on acc! of the incessant interruptions. Last night, however, I slept well, and after spending an hour at the Child's bkfst., succeeded in having a clear morning's work and did a big job in the way of correspondance. Dined with Royce, where I was followed up after dinner by Guy Waring, who brought me back here and has sat and talked till ½ an hour ago.[2] A nice fellow! even if he does prevent a nap! I feel ever so much better than I did yesterday. But you can imagine the sense of impotence and rage which filled me when I suddenly tho't that I had forgotten the barley.   I put it down on paper, carried it in to Boston meant to get it at Metcalf's,[3] read it more than once in town and as usual came out without it. One box goes by mail this morning. The rest can go later. I will register a letter tomorrow with some money which you can get on Tuesday. The swig is $233.36. I have sent 50 to Snider, and will send a June 1st check to Mrs. Möller.[4] I have paid for my spectacles etc. The day is super-beautiful here and I trust it is with you. I am ashamed to say how much I love the big rooms in this house. It all seems so square and fine. I am now going in to Boston to make arrangements with Hodgson and Prince for Ansel Bourne. I will try to get through the week as well as possible without you, and come up as fast as I can.

Ever thy W.J.

Yesterday a *very* intellectual young woman called and talked with a pleasant voice for 3 hours and twenty minutes without stopping. Such are my interruptions.   Kiss the dear children & give my love to Miss Russell. Say "He wishes he were there to help entertain you." So I do were other things equal.

ALS: MH bMS Am 1092.9 (1748)

[1] Lucy Russell was not identified.   For another reference to her see *Correspondence*, 2:85.

[2] Guy Waring (originally George E. Waring) (b. 1859), son of George Edwin Waring and brother of Daisy Waring.   Waring graduated from Harvard in 1882 and for a time raised cattle on a ranch in the state of Washington.   After a visit to Boston in 1891 he returned to Washington, where he lived in a log cabin.

[3] Theodore Metcalf & Co., apothecaries.

[4] WJ perhaps was paying tailoring bills; see the Biographical Register.

To Alice Howe Gibbens James

Cambr. May 26. [1890] 7. P.M.

Beloved Spouse—I am just back from Boston to get the Bryonia.[1] I mailed it there. I am very sorry for these bad colds—just the opposite of what you went up for—I thought all colds would stop by magic. Thank you for your blessed letter. Of course you can't come. And possibly I may get up there by Friday or Saturday. I have galvanized myself the last few days, and slept well, and feel very differently from when I wrote you that doleful appeal. But enough of *me*! Poor Miss Timmins is dead. I went in yesterday P.M. with Royce after taking tea with him and rang at the Brimmer's door in vain. R. then went to Mrs Whitman's to inquire. She said that "Gemma" had turned the corner the previous night, and that they were all jubilant and jocose in consequence. To day Geo. Dorr tells me this.[2] I went to Somerville this P.M. Kitty has been badly excited & suicidal for a month past, now refuses food and is fed forcibly—looks hardly recognizable, poor soul, and is, I trust, sinking.[3] They are pursuing the sodden Asylum routine of stomach pump etc. By Heaven I trust that the Doctors will catch it at the day of judgment for their besotted incompetence and authority combined. I gave Cowles a piece of my mind; but I fancy it made no practical impression.[4] The routine is for the sake of protecting themselves against possible future accusations of negligence. The best good of the patient is the last thing thought of. Ansel B. arrives to morrow forenoon and I take him to Hodgson's room. I sent you $100.00 to day in a registered letter which you ought to get simultaneously with this. The students have begun to come, so I say good night.[5] Heaven bless both you and the fruit.

W.J.

ALS: MH bMS Am 1092.9 (1719)

Address: Mrs. William James | Tamworth Iron Works | N.H.

Postmarks: BOSTON, MASS. MAY 27 1890 TAMWORTH IRON WORKS N.H. MAY 27

[1] A medication made from a plant of the genus Bryonia, sometimes used as a purgative.

[2] Gemma Timmins died on the morning of 26 May 1890.

[3] Reference is to Katharine Prince, a patient at the McLean Asylum in Somerville, Mass.

[4] Edward Cowles (1837–1919), psychiatrist at the McLean Asylum.

[5] Philosophy 20a: Questions in Psychology, which met in WJ's home.

To Alice Howe Gibbens James

95 Irving St. | May 27. [1890] 3.45 P.M.

Beloved!

No letter from you by the 3 o'clock mail. Possibly none at all to day. God's will be done! Here is this empty house, clean, sweet, roomy & handsome—A perfect fit for the two of us, and only one of us here to live in it. What a mockery marriage is, even worse than

Tolstoi makes it out.[1]   I bade farewell to Philosophy 20a last night.
On the whole it has been a good course.   I bkfstd. with Grace N. &
have been spending the rest of the morning at Hodgson's room with
Ansel Bourne.   He proves a dear old uncle of a fellow, as good as he
can be.   He has told us his memoirs pretty completely.   He could n't
do any automatic writing; but after our sausage and sourkrout lun-
cheon, he went off beautifully into the hypnotic trance.   Of course
at the first sitting I only tried to make suggestions which should pave
the way for something deeper next time.   But the first step is gained
in proving him a good subject.   I must now hurry off to the faculty.
There are endless jobs to do during these days—not the least of them
being the hallucination correspondance, which Margaret helped me
over when she was here.

    I have n't had time to write a word to Harry or Alice yet.   I can't
get away till Monday now, on acc! of Ansel B. who can give us the
remaining days of this week, but no more at present.   He goes home
at night—much the best arrangement.   Kiss dear Harry & Billy and
Baby.   How does the pony go?   Bless the Parker boys.[2]   *Make both
Harry and Billy write to me,* telling me how they like the horse, the
Parkers, Mr. Gifford and everything.

Love to *both* of you[3]   W.J.

    I wrote notes, both to the Brimmer's and to Mrs Whitman this A.M.

ALS: MH bMS Am 1092.9 (1720)

    [1] As his views became more ascetic, Tolstoi came to believe in celibacy as an ideal of
perfection.   The subject of marriage is central in his *Kreutzer Sonata* (1889), which
was being discussed in the United States in the spring of 1890 and is the story of a
husband who murders his wife.   Isabel F. Hapgood, whom Tolstoi expected to translate the story into English, gave a detailed summary of the plot in the *Nation* 50 (17
April 1890): 313–15, but argued that it was too realistic for translation.
    [2] Gurdon Saltanstall Parker and his brother Stanley Brampton Parker (b. 1881).
Stanley graduated from the Lawrence Scientific School in 1903 and became a landscape architect in Cambridge.
    [3] AGJ was pregnant with Alexander Robertson and the '*both*' could be an allusion
to this.

To Alice Howe Gibbens James

Wednesday [May 28, 1890] 4.15
Darling one,   Coming out in the horsecar I was longing for your
presence, oh! so intently and saying I *must* have her again here in the
plenitude of her sweetness when I found your white letter and your
blue one on the mat, and fortunately read the blue one first.   The

white one was indeed mad, reminding me of the worst moments of last year; but how glad I am that the blue one followed it so quick! *I* am really the gentle one of the family; for when I get mad altho I get more excitedly so so than you, 'tis always with myself, you with other people.   I suppose I intercepted the barley card; as it contained nothing but the order for the barley,[1] I presume I didn't notice whether it was for Margaret or for me.   I'm glad you've got it, after all.   Briggs seems to have got through all his work; and the house looks splendid in the fine afternoon light.

Ansel B. has told us all about his escapade—in the ordinary trance, too.   A grand success!   It is to continue to morrow, and will doubtless be more complete.   Aren't you glad?

Love again | W.J.

Don't let yourself get mad again   I had forgotten that you had already sent the check to Snider,   He has sent back the receipt and my later check for 80 doll[ar]s with a polite note.   I will pay Mrs. Möller.   She doesn't answer the note I sent her some days ago.

Remember that madness expressed in a letter, you incomparably dear one, lasts for 24 hours.   It is just as if you went on scolding for that length of time, so always send a postscript on blue paper after it.   How I love you for it all, darling!

W.J

ALS: MH bMS Am 1092.9 (1722)
[1] See letter to AGJ of 25 May 1890.

To Mary Whiton Calkins

95 Irving St, Cambr. May 29 [1890]

Dear Miss Calkins

I have been attacking the President again on the subject you know of.[1]   He tells me that the overseers are so sensitive on the subject that he dares take no liberties.   He received such a "tremendous wigging" from them a few years ago for winking at just this thing, that he is forced now to be strict.   They are at present in hot water about it at the medical school he himself being for the admission of women.

I think that in justice to him you should know these facts.

I am none the less regretfully

Yours | Wm James

ALS: MWelC
[1] See letter to Charles William Eliot of 23 May 1890.

To Alice Howe Gibbens James

Jim Putnam's office[1] | May 29th. [1890] 5.15 P.M.

Dearest Alice

4 hours of Ansel Bourne—then writing long letter to Weir Mitchell, then to P.O. then lunch then to John Homans's[2] and here where I'm waiting for Jim to arrive, to see whether I may not engage him for to morrow's work. The case doesn't develope. It is just a split off dejected tired fragment of Ansel Bourne calling itself Brown and re-membering nothing either before or after the Norristown escapade.[3] I think we shall get through with him to morrow, for the present.— I am incessantly revolving what *we* ought to do. I think on the whole that I ought not to ask you to go down but to go up myself on Mon-day. I can doubtless do it, altho I don't hear a word from Holt. I have no end of little things to do, but its best to cut 'em short. I must come down again the following Saturday. If you think you by coming down could spend several days here with any pleasure it would cost no more than my going up, and might be a little better on the whole as regards my duties here. But I feel as if I should thereby be shirking my duties towards Gifford & the family. How do you stand him? You write no more about him. I've paid the water tap. Here comes Jim!

W.J.

Let me know before monday what you think is best. I long to see the country. But I also long to see you by yourself, and I have much work here. If you come you can settle up the doctor business. Take care of yourself, dearest, this time!

W.J.

ALS: MH bMS Am 1092.9 (1723)

[1] 106 Marlboro St., Boston.

[2] John Homans (1836–1903), a physician in Boston.

[3] Ansel Bourne, a case of multiple personality, had lived for a time in Norristown, Pa., under the name of A. J. Brown.

To Henry Holt

Cambridge, June 3 '90

My dear Holt:

I go today to Tamworth Iron Works, N.H. whither, save for such intermissions as I shall notify you of, when I temporarily return to Cambridge, my proofs should hereafter be sent.

It is now a month or more since I sent you the opening pages of my MS. with a statement of excellent reasons why I wished to insist on getting the work immediately under way. It is a fortnight since the entire Ms. was forwarded.

Under these conditions I feel no farther responsibility whatever about having the thing published by October. I shall take the vacation which I shall sorely need in September, in the form of a journey somewhither, no matter in what condition of forwardness the proofs may be at the time. After the beginning of the college year my duties will be so unusually heavy that the proofs must take whatever spare time they can get. I won't even promise to touch them at all until the following summer. I say this that there may be no misunderstanding on your part as to what you have a right to expect of me, and that you may govern your present treatment of the MS. accordingly.

Very truly yours, | Wm. James

TC: MH bMS Am 1092.1

To William Noyes

CAMBRIDGE June 3. [1890]

My dear Noyes

Mitchell writes that he is about shutting up shop for the season and has nothing to propose about Bourne, so Hodgson and I go down Saturday to finish up matters with him (if we can) at his home in R.I.[1]

I have telegraphed him to send you if possible his photograph, and the bills for store-stock which he bought when there. I also send you copies of a couple of Mitchell's documents, and Hodgson's report of my second seance with him.[2] (We have no copy of the latter so you will take care of it, nicht wahr?) You observe that at one time he says the Hotel is opposite the City Hall, and at another near the Depôt, or as it seems to remain in my memory "opposite" the Depôt. This last however may be a confusion with N.Y. in my mind. I am afraid that you may have trouble with the boarding house. He *thinks* the number was 1115 Filbert St.; but he was wrong about the number of the Norristown store (255 instead of 252—see Dʳ Hinsdale's document p. 6, which however may itself be wrong)[3] and he calls the proprietor Read instead of Earle, Read being the surgeon's name. If they won't show the Hotel Register, Weir Mitchells influence may get it. If you find the boarding house, the photograph will help identification of their boarder by the landladies. I very much hope that you and Prince between you may have time and inclination to "work up" these clues as thoroughly as possible. I realize now how slight they are.—Thanks for your very well taken notes.

Always truly yours | Wm James

I go to N.H. to morrow, and get back here Friday for a few days more. Please send what you get to Hodgson

ALS: MH bMS Am 1092.9 (3363)

[1] The last session with Ansel Bourne took place on 7 June 1890 in Greene, R.I.

[2] In his "A Case of Double Consciousness," *Proceedings of the Society for Psychical Research* (English) 7 (July 1891): 221–57, Richard Hodgson provides transcripts of the sessions involving WJ and Ansel Bourne.

[3] Guy Hinsdale (1858–1948), American physician.

To Henry Holt

Tamworth Iron Works, N.H. | June 5/90

My beloved Holt:

I'm truly glad to find that you are still in so merry a humor over the delay.[1] My solicitude to get ahead fast has been wholly due to what I supposed were my responsibilities to your interests. For myself, now that the Ms. is once done, the longer it is withheld from the hands of my own students the better. For delay means ready-made stuff to lecture on, whilst publication means so much more work in providing new material. I hold therefore strictly to what I said in my last, about reserving the month of September and making no pledges for next year; and you can take your measures accordingly.

The mysteries of your trade are unknown to me, but I confess it surprises me that the time of nearly three men for a fortnight should need to be employed in counting the number of words in a Ms. before a specimen page can be chosen. The total number is pretty certainly between 1000 and 1200 pp. of the size of that of Mind or of the J. of Spec. Phil. (I forget now just how many words that means) and I should think that the size of page which would be good on the estimate of 1000 could not be so very bad on the estimate of 1200. But of course you know this part of the business best; and indeed it may have more to do with forcasting the price than determining the page.

I'm sorry the manuscript is so bad. We can't all furnish copy like John Fiske's. This is the sort of stuff I have always furnished to the printers, and I have never yet heard any murmurs from them, or found that the proofs suffered from the copy's illegibility.

I suppose my dear old Joker, that you'll consider me 'cocky' again. I'm sorry that the contrition you predict has not yet over-taken me. I confess, to tell the truth, that I have been put out at your *manner* in all this business. A little definite preliminary statement of what you expected would have saved all misunderstanding. But never a word in advance about anything, only a broadside of sarcasms and jeers over each new step which you leave to my unaided genius to take. I love you dearly as a human being, my dear H. H., but as a publisher I can't say that I enjoy your ways, nor find myself exactly at home in the strange atmosphere of blended business and sarcasm which seems to be your element. Keep prose for business correspondence—prose and exact explanation: and reserve sarcasm for less practical and better hours. I know that your heart is in the right place all the same, and shall ever remain,

Your loving | W.J.

TC: MH bMS Am 1092.1

[1] Holt's response to WJ's letter of 3 June 1890 is not known.

To Henry Lee Higginson

95 Irving St, June 11. [1890]

My dear Henry,

I couldn't shake hands wi' you last night at Sever Hall, and was not asked to meet you at White's.[1] But you can guess how I felt. To their dying day those men will remember your noble and simple appearance before them and the words you spoke. The best thing about this university is the chance these fellows get of meeting one man after another in Sever Hall who stands for something in the world outside and who gives them a glimpse of an example & makes one of those personal impressions that abide. I'm sure you hit the mark last night. And I'm sure the field will do all the good, & more than all the good, you can possibly hope from it.

Yours ever | Wm James

No answer called for!

ALS: MH MS Am 1821 (56)

[1] According to the *Harvard Crimson*, 11 June 1890, Henry Lee Higginson addressed the students on 10 June at the presentation of a new athletic field to Harvard, to be

called Soldiers' Field in memory of Higginson's six friends who died in the Civil War. The reception was at the home of John Williams White, who was then chairman of Harvard's committee on athletics.

To Grace Norton

TAMWORTH IRON WORKS, | N.H. June 26. [1890]

My dear Miss Norton

Alice recognizes the glass thingumbob as a piece of our property sent back by Mrs. Hildreth,[1] & the piece broken out is "all right," so pray trouble yourself no more about it; but give it "storage," if you will and thereby increase the debt to you of the James family. I am sorry I couldn't accept your invitation to dine with Leslie Stephen, whom I fain would meet again.[2] I have asked him up here; but he says that his stay is so short that he must cling to Cambridge. Perhaps 'tis just as well for him—I fear he might find it here *tant soit peu* "slow."

Our recreation this morning has been picking the stones out of a new harrowed field. As there are some 30 or 40 of them of all sizes to a square foot, the labor makes up in quantity what it lacks in quality of charm.—I have just read Harry's novel, and rejoice exceedingly at the manifestation of plenitude of power.[3] It is an exquisitely humane and harmonious thing. The length and minuteness are an essential part of the whole matter; but I hope that he will not go in for that sort of minuteness again. The reader can't be expected to have the leisure of mind which it requires *very* often in his life. Still, as it now stands, it is an exquisite thing. I hope it will be appreciated. My proofs come so irregularly that I may have after all to go back to Cambridge for a few weeks. I hope that Miss Anne A. still is comfortable.[4] How beautiful the weather keeps.

Ever affectionately yours | Wm James

ALS: MH bMS Am 1092.9 (3341)

[1] Achsah Beulah Colburn Hildreth, wife of John Lewis Hildreth (1838–1925), a physician in Cambridge. Prior to their move to Irving Street the Jameses rented the house at 18 Garden St. from the Hildreths.

[2] Sir Leslie Stephen (1832–1904), British essayist, editor, and critic. Correspondence with WJ is known from 1884 to 1902.

[3] HJ, *The Tragic Muse* (1890). For WJ's comments to HJ see *Correspondence*, 2: 142–43.

[4] Anne Ashburner.

To Charles William Eliot

TAMWORTH IRON WORKS, | N.H. July 2. 90

Dear President,

Mr. Benjamin I. Gilman writes me that he and Paine are already making application to you to authorize his course of 12 lectures on the theory of Music to be given in some way before the University next year. I had been intending to bring the matter before your attention in the Fall, but since that is already done, I write now to say that I wish very much that the lectures might be given.

Mr. Gilman studied Psychology with us two years as a graduate, and is a most accomplished man, whose only serious defect is lack of worldly ambition and a rather too high a standard of perfection in his work. He is now going to be married and must bestir himself for a position, so that the first defect will be in the way of being remedied.[1] I have no doubt that his course of lectures will be extremely solid and instructive. He has been for five years working at a book on Aestheticks treated in an experimental & psychological way, and he ought to be ready to publish but still postpones, in order to be more complete.[2] I am quite sure that if you can see your way to letting him lecture (whether with or without pay) that the course would be a most desirable addition to our bill of fare.

Very truly yours | Wm James

President Eliot, Cambridge

ALS: MH Archives

[1] Benjamin Ives Gilman married Cornelia Moore Dunbar in September 1892.
[2] The book was not published.

To Hugo Münsterberg

Harvard University | Cambridge (Mass.) | U.S. of A. July 2. '90

Dear Dr. Münsterberg

This will be handed you by Mr. Edward Delabarre who has been studying Philosophy with us for two years. He is especially interested in Psychology, has an uncommonly clear head, and independent character, and if he should fix himself in Freiburg for a time, I am persuaded that you will find him not only a most agreeable student to teach, but a most helpful collaborator in experimental work, for which he has an excellent aptitude. I wish I could have given him more training in that line. He got out a couple of very good

little optical things when he was with me, which have been published
in the American Journal of Psychology, and of which he only received
from me the general idea.[1]   Any kindness which you may show to
Mr. Delabarre will be warmly appreciated by me.

I wish we might have seen a little more of each other in Paris last
summer.   I need hardly say that I am immensely interested in your
masterly Beiträge, which seem to me to promise more for Psychology
than the work of any one man who has yet appeared.[2]   Only you
mustn't stop!

Yours, with great respect   Wm James

ALS: MB

[1] For Delabarre's contributions to the *American Journal of Psychology* see *PP,* 673, 717.
[2] See letter of 13 May 1890, note 7.

To Alice Howe Gibbens James

Monday, July 7th 1890 | 4 P.M.

My darling Alice,

My visit to Beverly went off most successfully, altho when I got
there I was rather alarmed to find the house occupied by three
couples of exquisite youths and maidens who seemed in the highest
heaven of animal spirits, game playing and general romping, to the
tune of which my own heart threatened but little to respond.   However, I thawed out, for they were most charming creatures, and Mrs.
W. said she had asked me then because she wanted me just to see
how charming they could be.[1]   They appear to be her favorite nose-
gay amongst the young; and truly their tone was *sweet.**   There is
growing up an education which I suppose they have long had in
england of physical wholesomeness, good education, good manners,
jollity, freedom, and good speech, which I'm sure didn't exist anywhere in this country 20 years ago.   The weather was superb, the
shore and house delightful, Mr. Whitman returned from a salmon
fishing trip early Sunday morning, and impressed me very favorably,
and if any one is to be *pitied* it is he rather than her.   She can't be
easy to live with, such a tiptoe thoroughbred!   My heart is made
calmer by the visit; though I *admire* her more than I ever did, as I
see more of the solidity of her ability in every direction, and the
underlying genuineness of her temperament as a worker.   She isn't
half thorough[2] her career yet, and we ought both to be glad to keep
near her as she pursues it.   You have no call to be jealous, my darling

darling generous-hearted wife, for she is as remote from me *personally* as Sarah Bernhardt would be were she here.[3]   But *we* are both members of the same spiritual body of which she is another member, and the members ought to recognize each other.   We were driven all over the coast yesterday P.M., and called on the Lorings, the Rockwells, the Brimmers, and Mrs. Lodge's sister Mrs. How.[4]   We also went into the Gurney's place which is *the* place, of those away from the sea. I got out and looked for his grave but couldn't find it.   It looked strangely majestic, in its lonely sternness in the sunset, with the tangled richness of the moorland round about.   Its windows are boarded up and it is left alone.   It is a subject for a poem.   We all came up this morning together, she going to her studio, where I presently called to see a little picture she had been painting of Gemma Timmins, as she looked in some tableaux or something, as a Fra Angelico Angel—a sweet sweet little thing—and also her portrait of Mr. Brimmer, really a grand bit of work, much her best in that line.—I spent a couple of hours with Hodgson; came out here to the bank; went to the Club which makes all the difference in Cambridge;[5] and found here no proofs, but a lot of hallucination letters, most of which I enclose for Margaret's noble treatment; and the enclosed clipping announcing poor Aunt Margaret's death.[6]   Fortunately the funeral is to day, so that I am exempted from going on.   I shall write to Lilla & propose that she pay us a visit sometime in the summer. I have had a nap, and coming down, find your letter with its enclosures.   Bob is inimitable!   So are you, with your dear headaches, and your tears.   Upon my word, I'm growing to love my possessions *really*.   Entering the boy's bedroom just now to deposit my trunk tray on their bed I was myself moved *almost* to tears, the place was so redolent of their brown-skinned goodness.   Farewell!   I slept splendidly last night, and probably shall to night.   I promised whilst at Hodgsons to visit a doctor and his wife from Baltimore with tip-top psychic narratives, at the Adams house to night;[7] but in consequence of the note you enclose from Miss Whitwell, I think I will send Hodgson alone to the Adams House and call on that virgin.   Adieu.   Cambridge seems awfully stale.   Love to Margy.   Kisses to the 3 offsprings.   Regards to Hubbard.   Gruss to Fräulein.

W.J.

2nd tho'ts—its no use sending hall. letters to Margaret, since she has no B schedules.

[*]Their names were Holkar Abbot (artist)[8]—Gardner teacher at the Groton school and owner of the yacht mayflower;[9] Cushing (se-

nior and artist)[10] the eldest fairchild girl, Powell Mason's daughter,[11] and one of the Lockwood girls.[12]

ALS: MH bMS Am 1092.9 (1727)

[1] Sarah Wyman Whitman.

[2] A slip for 'through'.

[3] Sarah Bernhardt (1844–1923), French actress.

[4] Mary Greenwood Lodge (Mrs. James Lodge), associated with Sarah Wyman Whitman in a circle of literary women, and her sister, Alice Greenwood Howe.

[5] The Colonial Club, located at 20 Quincy St., the former home of the Jameses in Cambridge; see also *Correspondence*, 2:140n.

[6] Margaret Ruth Lawrence Walsh (1822–1890), mother of Elizabeth Robertson Walsh.

[7] Henry Adams owned a house in Beverly Farms, Mass., but was in Washington, D.C. at the time.

[8] Probably Holker Abbott (b. 1858), who compiled several volumes of verses for the Tavern Club, a Boston dining club that had many artists as members.

[9] William Amory Gardner (1863–1930), a teacher of classics at the Groton School, Groton, Mass., nephew of Isabella Stewart Gardner (1840–1924), American socialite and patron of art. The yacht *Mayflower* won the America's Cup in 1886, but no evidence of Gardner involvement was found up to the time of this letter.

[10] Howard Gardiner Cushing graduated from Harvard in 1891. WJ is referring to his approaching senior year at Harvard.

[11] William Powell Mason (1835–1901), a lawyer and businessman, whose daughter was Fanny Peabody Mason (b. 1864).

[12] Florence Bayard Lockwood (1842–1898), American author, had two daughters: Florence Bayard, who married Christopher Grant La Farge (1862–1938), American artist and illustrator; and Frances, who married Henry Wharton of Philadelphia.

To James Sully

Cambridge, July 8, 90.

My dear Sully:—surely two such laborers can drop honorific titles— I am much flattered by your letter, and especially glad to hear that you are working your book over again—not that it needs it in my eyes—but it shows that you are still "energizing" at the old tasks. I learned that you were in still another way last week when I got a proof from the Editor of Brain of your paper on Attention with request for comment.[1] I agreed with it so entirely that I could say nothing hostile, and had no time for mere compliments, so have contributed nothing.

My book ought to be out in October, but the printers are dawdling fearfully with the proofs and I fear it may not be out till the new year. I'm sorry to say that my MS. table of titles of Chapters is in the country. But I will copy it and send it to you when I go back. It is a very different affair from yours—each of us is pushed fatally along in his own orbit, and mine has resolved itself into a mixture of critical discussion of Principles on the one hand and raw physiological facts on the other, with almost none of the descriptive psychologizing in the old sense, in which your book abounds to such good purpose. I had marked a whole page-full of places of passages in your book which I meant to quote, but as the writing proceeded I found that I could not weave in quotations from other authors in anything like the abundance which I originally had in mind, so at present your book is hardly used at all.[2]

It seems to me that Psychology is like Physics before Galileo's time.—Not a single *elementary* law yet caught a glimpse of. A great chance for some future psychologue to make a greater name than Newton's, but who then will read the books of this generation? Not many, I trow. Meanwhile they must be written. I will send you mine as soon as it appears, and I hope you'll do the same by me.[3] I should have sent you many things in these last years, but knew that you had moved, without knowing whither.

Cordially yours, | Wm. James.

TC: MH bMS Am 1092.1

[1] James Sully, "The Psycho-Physical Process in Attention," *Brain* 13 (October 1890): 145–64. WJ mentioned the article in a footnote in *Principles of Psychology* (*PP*, 422). The editor of *Brain* at the time was Armand de Watteville (b. 1846).

[2] In *Principles of Psychology* WJ several times cites James Sully, *Outlines of Psychology* (1884) (WJ 584.51.2); *Illusions* (1881); and *Sensation and Intuition* (1874).

[3] Possibly an allusion to James Sully, *The Human Mind* (1892) (WJ 584.51). WJ's review is reprinted in *ECR*.

To Alice Howe Gibbens James

CAMBRIDGE July 8. [1890] | 9 P.M.

Dearest Alice

I am just in after an afternoon of running about with the thermometer over 90. The inside of this house is deliciously cool however.

Well, to begin with, no proofs! I dawdled a good deal of the morning at the Club reading room where I bkfstd.[1] with Farlow & Myers, and at the Library—came home and wrote letters till 2, went to dine at the Childs, having been nabbed by Henrietta in the College yard,[2] found them rather pale and perspiring, but with their hearts in the right place, Child insisting on opening that bottle of Champagne, then I went over to the Ashburners, seeing Theodora on the stoop. To us presently came grace Norton, and we joked a while. Miss Anne has been much more comfortable and getting stronger; but to day suffers much from the heat. Then I went in again to Hodgson's, and bo't a cravat & white waist coat, and ordered two cheviot shirts.[3] and went to find Mary Tappan but she was out, so I took a horse car, went to the Club and got some blackberries, and conversed with Cleveland Abbé the meteorologist and astronomer of Washington whom I used to know here 28 years ago.[4] Thence to Grace Norton's, (if you will allow the expression) where I sat for ½ an hour, until now when I come into the coolness and find Coggeshall with his lamp.

I omitted to say that thy letter arrived all right with its account of Gordon.[5] I should like to know what harry meant by "a perfect fool of a father." I'm getting to like those boys more and more!

Now I must mail this and get to bed as early as may be, for I woke early and got no P.M. nap. The time flies here as usual with nothing to show for it.

Blessings on your head! If any accident happens, you know there is Miss Tibbets for a nurse.[6]

Love to Margy.

W.J.

ALS: MH bMS Am 1092.9 (1728)

[1] See letter of 7 July 1890.
[2] Henrietta Child.
[3] Boston directories do not list a haberdasher named Hodgson. Perhaps WJ went to Boston to call on Richard Hodgson and do some shopping.
[4] Cleveland Abbe (1838–1916), American meteorologist, a student at the Lawrence Scientific School in 1860–64.
[5] Perhaps Gurdon Saltanstall Parker.
[6] Miss Tibbets was not identified. AGJ was pregnant with Alexander Robertson James.

To Alice Howe Gibbens James

CAMBRIDGE July 9. 90

Beloved Weibsbild,

This A.M. when no proofs came my heart rather exalted, for says I to myself they fool me so much that I'm bound to make no sacrifices at all for 'em, but can just go back to Tamworth and correct them as is most convenient to me, not neccessarily sitting up at night to do it, but waiting if I like till the following A.M. I did not notice that a certain long envelope which I supposed to be an hallucination blank returned was from H. H. & Co, & contained the enclosed letter, which practically seals my doom.[1] Staying here is by no means the easy matter in reality which it seems from afar. The Club is too expensive to be resorted to often combining the bad qualities of both cheap and dear restaurants, viz. small portions and large cost.[2] To day my bkfst & lunch have cost together $1.20. Truly they were unusually heavy, as I had hardly any tea last night, and woke at 2. But I've felt astonishingly well in spite of it. What I think I shall do is to order ice, and eggs, bread, and berries from Beane[3] and get my own bkfsts by having the gas put on the house again, screw up the awning, and taking one meal a day at the Club, sponge on friends for the third. If the book gets really printed by August 15th "or earlier," it will be worth any amount of inconvenience. I can go up for one Sabbath *at least* between now & then, and you can come down here, altho I confess now that I *am* here, and see the sallowness and emptiness and feel the heat, the notion of your passing a fortnight with me seems much less rational than it did.

What a good letter from Harry. A note of physical enjoyment which I haven't heard in him in years. It is what I've been urging him to do all these years. But to see the Tyrol etc. in Co. with the *Curtises!* Great Gods!!![4]

I have no doubt that what you say of the fence *is* the best thing, so have it done. How I ever could have spoken to you thus, I cannot see. You seem to me such a white souled thing from here! white souled and white bodied! I have written to Mrs. P. about the Salters but she is supposed not to sit till Richardson has had her.[5] He wants to sit with me alone without Mrs. D. and I think we can arrange that soon. Mrs. P. is off in the country somewhere. Bob was in this A.M. full of delight with Ring's place.[6] I have been almost all day (barring a horse car ride to Hodgson's for a moment) executing hallucination correspondence. H. is to send Margaret a lot of blanks and I will forward to her the applications after this, thanking her wondrously in advance. She too is a white souled being! I forgot to write you that on Monday night I went to Miss Whitwell's whom I found with a *most* superstitious friend on the tarred and gravelled roof of the house cooling themselves in a tangle of electric wires, and heard the greatest lot of rubbish uttered by this woman. They are including the Keeley motor now amongst the supernatural properties of the Universe.[7] Poor May Whitwell, she's a dear thing notwithstanding! I must now write a letter or two, water the lawn, and see if I can get to Mary Tappans in time for tea. I fear I can't. That's the trouble of th[i]s life. *Always* belated for meals! I've had a splendid nap this P.M. however. it is now 5.

Ever thy | Wm

I enclose a sweet little poem which mrs. Whitman asked me to send to you. This also is one of her accomplishments!

ALS: MH bMS Am 1092.9 (1729)

[1] Probably the letter of 8 July 1890 from Vogelius (calendared), describing steps taken to insure completion of typesetting by 15 August.

[2] See letter of 7 July 1890.

[3] Enoch Beane & Co., provision dealers in Cambridge.

[4] For HJ's letter of 23 June 1890 see *Correspondence*, 2:140–42. In his first "clear holiday" abroad in years, HJ attended the passion play at Oberammergau and took numerous walks. His companions were Ariana Randolph Wormeley Curtis (1833–1922), American author, and her husband, Daniel Sargent Curtis (1825–1908).

[5] Probably William Lambert Richardson (1842–1932), American obstetrician, a member of the Society for Psychical Research. One letter is known (1881).

[6] Allen Mott Ring, a physician, operated a sanatorium in Arlington Heights, Mass.

[7] John Ernst Worrell Keely (1827–1898), American inventor and impostor, claimed in 1872 to have discovered "etheric vibration," a hitherto unknown energy, which led to his invention of the "perfect engine," a source of power without cost. For several decades he was in the news in connection with the "Keely Motor Company" and charges of fraud.

To Ellen James Temple Emmet Hunter

CAMBRIDGE July 13. 90

My dear darling Elly,

Your letter is an extravagant payment for my Religio-Philosophical Journal,[1] but Religion and Philosophy *are* good investments, though the vulgar ignore the fact. And so I forgot the name of your daughters, did I? Well, I never meant to; but I can see now clearly the psychological grounds for the oblivion. Explain to the dear delightful darlings that the contents of that article which I sent them so transported my mind back into the twilight of the past—that mysterious and innocent time when I used to practice on yourself and Henrietta in the manner depicted by the gifted writer, that I forgot the last quarter of a century—it was as if it were not—and the world became filled with pure Temples again.[2] God keep them, dead and living, old and young, forevermore!

I find I am becoming a lachrymose ass, which will never do. But dear old Elly, certain past things won't die, and I thank God for it;

and so, as this unexpected turn takes me, I must finish my letter. God bless you, and good bye!

W.J.

I am staying here all alone—more's the pity—for a few weeks, correcting proofs.

ALS: MH bMS Am 1092.9 (1067)

Address: Mrs. Temple Emmet | c/o Leslie Pell Clarke Esq | Springfield Centre | Otsego Co | N.Y

Postmarks: BOSTON MASS. JUL 13 90   CHERRY VALLEY N.Y. JUL 1<4>   <SPR>INGFIELD CEN<TER> JUL <14>

[1] The *Religio-Philosophical Journal*, edited by John Curtis Bundy, was devoted to spiritualism.

[2] Writing to AGJ on 14 July 1890 WJ refers to the article he sent to the Emmet girls as the "kissing article." It was not identified.

To Alice Howe Gibbens James

Sunday July 13. '90 | 5.20 P.M.

Darling of my heart,

Here I've been, but for the lunch which your dear Mother cooked for me and a solid hour-long nap after it, at my desk all day. I had some hopes of getting to Bob's at Arlington Heights this P.M., but they are quenched, I may get there this evening.[1] The proofs are hot and heavy, and I find that attending to them makes my head sodden. It is a kind of steady ocular attention to which I am not used. I think you *will* have to come down for a week or ten days anyhow some time, I don't think I can stick it out alone. Coggeshall is very little of a complication in the house, as he gets up at ½ past 4, goes into town at ½ past 7, and is away (so far) all day. The weather is cool and bright—decided drought on!—I am sleeping very well again and shall exist I suppose in this way and count the days until my task is done—not failing to get up, I trust, for a couple of Sundays of the time.

I quite agree with your most sensible, not to say paedagogical letter of yesterday, that it will be better to get my own lunches than my own breakfasts—in fact I had gravitated to the same conclusion myself. It has been a sweet boon to have your mother here cooking to day, only I fear that it has used her up, so that she has given up her projected visit to town in consequence, and is staying in her room. Now, to revert to yourself what do you mean by saying that there is no second Messiah?[2] Is it the expression of a passing impatience with his inertness, or an opinion based on facts?   I wish when you write such things you would let me know whether they are serious or jocose, because the practical turn they give to one's thoughts, if serious, is very great.   This house is a very good place for a Messiah to be born in—it seems delicious just at this moment—and the pecuniary Bewusstsein is lightened today by the appearance of $476 of June rents collected by Plumb, which gives us an additional 119 dollars apiece.   I will send you up a hundred of it by your Mar.   It seems likely too that there will be some sort of a balance left over after the building charges have been paid by the award.[3]   If only Henry W's will stands,[4] we can have 2 Messiahs as easily as one.— How, darling, are your dear veinules? your dear—*legs*?   I seem to myself to have been snatched away from you as one is snatched by death—irrevocably and with no chance for last words promises or explanations.   But all will go smoothly again, if we are patient.   I am experiencing in these days the tenderest *friendship* for you, o Comrade of my heart.   This is the best fruit of love, as it survives and strengthens on the years, whilst love does not.   What haven't you been to me?   And how I've been feeling it of late.   How I wish it were you moving upstairs at the moment instead of your dear mother—thee I should have to be writing this letter!   Our neighbors are sweet.   I've only been to G.N.s once.   Last night I supped with the Royce's.   He is back, very fat, from a western trip, which he enjoyed.   She is much better than her words, in every respect.[5]   She discoursed of sonnets and played on the piano to me—2 beautiful things.   Then I walked with Royce to Lowell's and went in alone, finding both invalids extended on long chairs on the piazza, and apparently not sorry for a call.[6]   I didn't stay long, but it was pleasant and friendly, and altogether in this loneliness with those direful massive *proofs* of my past, I feel pensive and like haveing old time human relations with all mankind, as a reaction against the atrocity of the other thing.

I must now haste to catch the 6.30 mail to take my proofs to N.Y. I will dress and get a car for Arlington & try to scale the heights. Kiss the dear boys, & 1000000 for thyself from

W.J

ALS: MH bMS Am 1092.9 (1732)

[1] See letter of 9 July 1890, note 6.

[2] The "second Messiah" is a running joke concerning AGJ's pregnancy with Alexander Robertson James.

[3] Reference is to insurance payments in connection with the fire of 24 April 1890 in Syracuse that damaged the James property; see *Correspondence*, 2:138.

[4] Henry Albert Wyckoff.

[5] Katharine Head Royce.

[6] James Russell Lowell was suffering from what he called the first illness of his life. The second invalid was probably his daughter, Mabel Lowell Burnett (1847–1898), who was then living with her widowed father.

To Alice Howe Gibbens James

CAMBRIDGE July 14. 90

Beloved Alice,

To day at 3 arrived your terse letter of Friday, and at 3.45 by the hand of Margaret your flowing one of Sunday etc. Thanks for both and for the *loving* character of the last—bless your heart. At last, darling I am experiencing the blessing of possessing in you no longer a crude green contentless beloved, but an *old friend,* full of rich tearful associations, stage upon stage deep-piled with memories, stratum under stratum of coloring, manifold of aspect as the changing year, tried, seasoned and found sound, brown and red and gold and ivory, etc etc—all thronging upon me when I think of you, and worth all the craziness of 12 years ago 20 times over, containing that as an element of poignant and pious sacredness to hold all the rest together. I assure you that nothing can take the place of *age* in the life of the heart. Yesterday I was writing a jocose letter to Elly Temple, telling her that the reason why I forgot that her daughter's name was Emmet was because that kissing article carried me back to the time when I used to practice it on her and Henrietta, and made me entirely forget the intervening years, and think the world full of pure Temples again as then,[1] when I suddenly found myself caught by a sobbing fit the like of which *some* day I shall have when I think of you, but not yet for I have not known you long enough—but dear, the time is ripening fast, for I have lately been having an approach to just that sort of inestimable emotion at the thought of thee. Some day you must come down and stay with me.

It is 9.45 P.M. I am just back from Boston with the Salters who wrote to your Mother to day that they were going to the Parker House, so I went to the Provincetown boat-landing & met them, and took them to dinner at Vercelli's, and here they are.

A famous lot of proof this A.M., which read well.   I got through at 2.30.   If it would only go that way every day, it would be splendid.

Charley Möring the idiot is dead, and his mother entirely prostrated by the loss Charley Bowen tells me.[2]

No news! no nothing.   I paid Cobb, Bates & Yerxa's bill this P.M.[3]

Kiss the dear Boys.   Love to Hubbard.   Grüsse to Fraulein.   1000 kisses to the "baby"   1000000 to yourself.

W.J.

ALS: MH bMS Am 1092.9 (1733)

[1] See letter to Ellen Hunter of 13 July 1890.

[2] Charles Stuart Bowen (b. 1850) was the son of Francis Bowen (1811–1890), American philosopher and professor at Harvard.

[3] Cobb, Bates & Yerxa, grocers and tea dealers in Cambridge.

To Alice Howe Gibbens James

CAMBRIDGE July 15. 90

Beloved Alice

Your letter of yesterday came this P.M. duly just as I had called a halt on the proofs and dressed to go to see Theodore Lyman at Brookline.[1]—I will write to the Toronto people as soon as *I get time*— I don't know when that will be at this rate.   I've got to go to Higginson's simultaneously for their address and for the mortgage note of Lepper's which is there, and to which I want to make them add a release.[2]

It has been a piping day, thermometer at 95° but with a breeze, drought hard set in, daily threatenings of rain which melt away again. We have had a most harmonious family—your mother at the currants Mrs Gourlay at the wash, Salter at the "Minds," etc in the Library, Margaret in high spirits and I at the proofs.   It is real fun now to make such plu[n]ges into the bowels of the book with every 24 hours now.   But as you say, it seems queer to have them all about me but you.   No matter; it is *infinitely* better up there than here.   The Salters can't possibly get up to morrow.   It will be Thursday.   I should have sent you the cash in a Registered letter yesterday, but I didn't know you wanted it till too late, and this A.M. I was too busy over proofs to get to the Square.   I hope that Thursday won't be too late.   I beg your pardon about taking the change from Robertson—I thought that was what you told me to do.[3]—By the way, our lawn-mower has never arrived at Brocks.[4]   It was sent with a tag to their address.

When you come to West Ossipee to meet your mother, if you do, please see about it & make them send a "tracer."—If you're not going, tell me and I will write.

I found poor Lyman "starched stiff." His devoted wife has to move his legs arms, head, everything for him, yet although his face has a fixed expression, it is a pleasant one, and his mind seems as cheerful & bright as ever it was.[5] Brookline looked superb, and the Lyman's place was by no means the least superb feature. When I was there Arthur Lyman & wife, Duveneck's babys adoptive parents came in, and I saw them for the first time.[6] I came whizzing home on the Electric cars—a most beautiful ride—all new, how I wished that you were by my side.—I then went to Hodgsons, came out & dined alone at the Club[,] Chaplin, Farlow, & Bartlett being on the piazza thereof, and coming here I find the house dark & empty— your mother, I imagine, has gone to bed, and the Salters' out for a car ride and dinner. I must, ere I mail this, write several notes and look up some Blodgett letters for Hodgson.[7]—I wish the soc. for P. R. had no American Branch on the whole.[8] You see I go down on Friday to the Morses for the night[9]—They were urgent that Sunday, and it will cool me off.

Your ever loving | W.J.

I will attend to all your errands to morrow—no matter what be-comes of the proofs. I've already got most of the things.

ALS: MH bMS Am 1092.9 (1734)

[1] Theodore Lyman (1833–1897), American zoologist and congressman.

[2] WJ purchased the Chocorua property from Adam Leppere; see *Correspondence*, 2:51–52n.

[3] There were several tradesmen in Cambridge named Robertson.

[4] Perhaps Brock Brothers, located in Brattle Street, Cambridge, dealers in stoves.

[5] Theodore Lyman was paralyzed for some time prior to his death. His wife was Elizabeth Russell Lyman.

[6] Francis Boott Duveneck, son of Elizabeth Boott Duveneck (1846–1888) and Frank Duveneck, was brought up by Boston businessman Arthur Theodore Lyman (1832–1915) and his wife, Ella Lowell Lyman, at their estate in Waltham, Mass., after the death of Elizabeth Duveneck, to whom the Lymans were related.

[7] The case involved efforts by Elizabeth Wild Blodgett to communicate with her dead sister, Hannah Wild, through the mediumship of Leonora Piper. For the case see *Correspondence*, 6:419–20n.

[8] In January 1890 the American Society for Psychical Research ceased to exist as an independent organization and became the American Branch of the English Society for Psychical Research.

[9] The Morses owned a house in Beverly, Mass.

To Frances Rollins Morse

95 Irving St. July 15 [1890]

My dear Fanny

I will come Friday P.M. by the 4.15 train, unless you should prefer to have me over Sunday, which from the point of view of the proofs might be a better arrangement.   They are falling thicker than the autumn leaves on Vallombrosa brooks "where the Etrurian shades high-overarched imbow'r" etc.[1]   But imbowered in your shady piazza I might be screened from them for a Sabbath morn.   Pray let me know in time and believe me with heartfelt thanks

Yours affectionately | Wm James

ALS: MH bMS AM 1092.9 (3204)

[1] From John Milton, *Paradise Lost*, bk. 1, lines 303–4.

To Frederic William Henry Myers

CAMBRIDGE July 15—90

My dear Myers,

I scribble you a line because it suddenly is borne in upon me that I must have written, in my little story about Mrs. Piper, that in the incident of her failure to read for Mrs. Blodgett the dead sisters letter, I had sent her the original sealed letter itself.[1] I did not; I kept that, and sent her a couple of articles of apparel one of them a glove, the other some head gear which Mrs. B. furnished me withal.   Pray make the correction & oblige yours truly &c.   At this time last year I was just reaching London from Scotland.   Now I'm all alone stewing in the heat here and correcting the proofs all day long of my "Principles of Psychology," of which I trust to send you a copy in Nov.—worse luck to it, I 'spise it now!   Let me congratulate Mrs. Myers on her new-brother-in-law.   I hope the Sister will keep him subjugated.   I'm more sorry than ever now that I did not have the privilege of her acquaintance next spring.   Surely *you*, the *père de famille*, were not the "best man" Myers of which the cable speaks?[2]

My proofs come in at the rate of 80 pp. to read a day, so I have no eyesight for anything else—I haven't even looked at the last Proceedings.   Hodgson keeps well; but the Treasury is low.   I am going to see if anything can be done, but its "flogging a dead horse."   Goodbye—with warm regards to both you & Mrs. Myers.

W.J.

Please "remember me" to your brother too.

ALS: MH bMS Am 1092.9 (3307)

[1] WJ is referring to his contribution to "A Record of Observations of Certain Phenomena of Trance," *Proceedings of the Society for Psychical Research* 6 (December 1890): 436–659, consisting of an introduction by Myers and accounts of Mrs. Piper by Oliver Joseph Lodge, Walter Leaf, and WJ; WJ's part is reprinted in *EPR*. The published text includes WJ's correction (*EPR*, 86). For the Blodgett case see letter to AGJ of 15 July 1890.

[2] On 12 July 1890 Sir Henry Morton Stanley married Dorothy Tennant, sister of Eveleen Tennant Myers. The *New York Times*, 13 July 1890, listed Myers as a member of the wedding party but not as the best man; see also letter from Myers of 26 July 1890. WJ's remark about not meeting Dorothy Tennant "next spring" is confusing. He was in Europe in July and August 1889 and perhaps means that he did not meet her then.

To Alice Howe Gibbens James

CAMBRIDGE July 16. 90 | 4. P.M.

Beloved Alice

The P.O. seems to be getting scandalously irregular   I have written every day, and mailed in midnight box or general Boston P.O. and yet you say in your letter which came ½ an hour ago that you rec'd nothing yesterday.   Well! you will have rec'd it to day I suppose.— As for the dear second Messiah, we shall have to wait, and all will be in due time revealed.[1]   I haven't myself the slightest doubt of his advent; and I'll try to do my duty by him when he's here.

Another hot day!   No proofs, so I went to town in the A.M. and ordered another black coat & vest.   Mine are getting shabby and I might as well order this now as in the fall.   I will send you a couple of books, as well as $50 cash, by the Salters who go to morrow.

Your mother and Aunt Nanny are cooling off up stairs.   Mary nauseated but making jelly in the kitchen with Mrs. Gourlay.   I have been writing a lot of letters (taking advantage of the holiday in the proofs)   I send Harry a preparation of Iron which tastes good and will make him eat more as well.   Keep it up for 3 weeks unless it disagrees with bowels or head   Dose ½ to 1 teaspoonful.—I'm glad Mary Tappan thinks me beautiful.   She seemed so to me when she came in.   I am going to dine at the Union Club with Chamberlin at 6.30[2]—Adieu!   I love you in spite of all, and will send another line by the Salters to morrow.   How I miss those boys!

W.J.

ALS: MH bMS Am 1092.9 (1736)

[1] Reference is to the approaching birth of Alexander Robertson James; see letter to AGJ of 13 July 1890.

[2]The Union Club, founded by men who opposed secession, was one of Boston's more prestigious clubs.

To Alice Howe Gibbens James

CAMBRIDGE July 20. 90 | 8. P.M.

Beloved Wifelein,

Another day. It took me till six P.M. ere I got through with yesterday's proofs. Luckily none came this morning. I am feeling rather nervous—having taken to waking early again, and must now go in (after ¼ of an hour promised to Grace Norton) to the Boston P.O. No matter! the book gets on right fast, and it seems to me to read pretty well when once it gets into the page-shape. I have been flirting with Mrs. Whitman by sending her a spicy sheet a couple of times.[1] She asks for "more." The "run" of the thing however is hopelessly dry and unfitted for human perusal. I have supped with the Royce's—He goes up to Bar Harbor to morrow, and then to North Conway to the Merrimans—in all 3–4 weeks. I both bkfstd. & lunched at the Ashburner's—Chas Norton was there at lunch. Yesterday I sent off a letter to you by the Child's—but they left in such confusion that I dare say that even if they will have seen you before this comes to you, they will have forgotten the letter. There was little in it. Your own yesterday was grateful & comforting indeed. I am glad you [are] enjoying mary so—the bright tone of your letter showed it. I found Mack very nice when here.—But ah! darling I do so want you to come! The upper room this P.M. with the golden shafts stealing through the blinds looked like your natural framework. You must manage it for next Monday—I say monday rather than Saturday because Sunday hitherto has been a bad day for proofs, and Monday a good one—but it makes little difference which, so long as you come and stay a week or ten days. The work is very continuous—and I think that my head begins to feel it.

Good bye, my blessed darling.

Ever thy Wm.

Of course write to Lilla now, if you feel like it—258 4th Avenue, N.Y.

We have got just a little bit of rain out of the change of weather.

ALS: MH bMS Am 1092.9 (1738)

[1]WJ was sending proof sheets of *Principles of Psychology;* see letter to Sarah Whitman of 24 July 1890.

To Alice Howe Gibbens James

CAMBRIDGE July 21. 90 | 9.15 P.M.

Beloved Wifelein.

Here I am again at the table after coming out from dining at Vercelli's with Duveneck. I stuck tight to the proofs till 5.45 finishing 22 galleys and a lot of page and took 'em in to mail, and meeting D. in the street we adjourned to V.'s. Poor D! he's a rudimentary form of mentality. But I like him thoroughly all the same. I have no news to tell, how can I when the proofs and the mail bound my horizon. Your mother came back this P.M. but I've hardly seen her. The light is out in her room, so I think she has probably gone to bed. To my great horror this A.M. on returning from bkfst. at the Club[1] where I had been treating Coggeshall I found a lot of wagons and workmen breaking ground on the lot opposite us, corner of Kirkland and Irving St. Wm Ellis was on hand seeing that the "restrictions" were observed.[2] I suppose there's no help for this they are going to put up 6 or 7 brick dwellings 18 feet wide—not particularly bad, of the sort. But what I fear is that it may make the rest of the land go badly in that quarter. I have just been to see Fox, but the house seems empty. We are in the hands of God! Your letter and bulky enclosures came duly this P.M. I can't read Miss Amanda Jones for a while.[3] Plumb writes of a rotten beam discovered, going across the back of our stores, so rotten th<at> "the walls seem to have been upheld by nothing but Divine Providence." It probably wont cost much; and we shall have a surplus, I imagine from the Insurance award,[4] but them stores have practically been all rebuilt now since we came into possession.—Coggeshall has just come in and gone to bed—a bitter, stealthy sort of a fellow, with all his virtues. I'm very glad we never risked him as a tutor.—I am sorry that old Beelee has a headache. Kiss him for me and it. Tell him that on the corner of Kirkland Place and Kirkland Street (living in the Peirce's house) I meet often that young fair and chubby-faced Harry Lewis who always asks me when Billy James is coming home.[5] The fair-faced McVare girl is gone.[6] I asked him whether she wasn't the best of all. He said "she's *almost* the best." I asked if she was better than B.J.—He said "Oh! I guess she isn't!" Tell Billy and Harry that I miss them very much and care for them much more than I ever did. They'll grow more and more decent all the while now, thank Heaven, and the good bringing up they're getting—God bless 'em! I ought to be writing them letters every day—but I simply *can't*—too much to do.—

I hope you have been at the work of sending hall.-blanks to the applicants whose letters were in the big Epicure envelope in my valise. They're getting fearfully into arrears.   I send a few more with this

Every thy loving   Dad.

ALS: MH bMS Am 1092.9 (1739)

[1] See letter of 7 July 1890.

[2] William Rogers Ellis was a member of the Cambridge city government.

[3] Amanda Theodosia Jones (1835–1914), American inventor, author, and spiritualist medium.   One letter is known (1895).

[4] See letter to AGJ of 13 July 1890, note 3.

[5] The 1890 Cambridge directory lists Mrs. R. H. Lewis at 4 Kirkland Place, the former home of Benjamin Peirce (1809–1880), father of Charles Sanders Peirce. Harry Lewis was not identified.

[6] Silas Marcus Macvane, who lived at 34 Kirkland St., had three daughters, Edith Elizabeth (b. 1874), Emily Dora (b. 1876), and Dorothy Alice (b. 1884).   WJ misspelled their last name.

To Alice Howe Gibbens James

CAMBRIDGE July 22 [1890] | 7.30 P.M.

Beloved Lieschen

My head feels like boiled mush over the proofs, part of to day's batch of which I am taking in to the P.O. and myself to get some dinner.   I bkfstd. at the Club, and then went to the Bank and to my tailor's Schonhofs[1] and to the rubber stamp-makers in town where I got my green stamp turned to black.   I suppose thou liks't better.

Your letter came duly this P.M.   I hope and trust that Billy's illness doesn't signify anything; as for Harry's hand, it is lucky it was no worse, after such an accident.   I hear nothing, think nothing do nothing.   I don't even sleep as I ought; and solace myself by reading at night Howells's Shadow of a Dream.[2]   That man is gaining all sorts of flexibility.   But to me theres the most curious unmasculinity about his intellectual temperament—I like and admire him all the same. Our whirligig lawn sprinkler is outside fizzling away to counteract the drouth.   Your mother is just back from S. Weymouth where she's engaged the Jackson's for Aug. 4th.   That makes it best that you come here on Saturday—only in that way you miss your mother. The 11.10 train is the best from west Ossipee is the one to take.[3]   It gets to Boston at 4.15.   Come out straight—it is so much better to meet you *in the house* than in public, don't you think so?—so much stronger a shock!—I will write of it again to morrow—You meanwhile decide which day is best for *you* Saturday or Monday. I can wait. I suppose that if you want to stay beyond the 4th, which comes on the following Monday, the Jacksons might be postponed for a day or two.

Love to all! | W.J.

ALS: MH bMS Am 1092.9 (1740)

[1] Boston and Cambridge directories have no listing for a tailor named Schonhof. WJ probably visited his tailor and Carl Schoenhof, who was a dealer in foreign books at 144 Tremont St., Boston.

[2] William Dean Howells, *The Shadow of a Dream* (1890).

[3] West Ossipee was the railroad stop nearest Chocorua.

To Alice James

CAMBRIDGE July 23. 90

Dearest Alice—I snatch a breathing space between two batches of proofs to send you a word which I have long meant to write, and which I ought to have sent you long ago had I been physically able to get to it. I don't mean any particular word, but just something in the way of a letter. Your Figaros,[1] Parises[2] and Punches[3] come raining down on us with regularity, and lately a post-card explaining why you didn't write. I suppose the "chairing" is over now on acc! of the bad weather which we hear of as so unremitting in the British Isles. Moreover I was told by K. Loring in Beverly a fortnight ago that an ulcerated tooth had been causing you misery. I hope that *that* could be attended to before the effects grew very bad. Your teeth at least ought to be *"indolent."*—Here what we suffer from is drouth—day after day now of the most delicious coolness with sky and clouds of the most delicious colour, yet never a drop of rain, so that the country is on the point of losing millions. I, as you doubtless know, found it neccessary to come here a couple of weeks since and correct my proofs. The printers are bent on overwhelming me and making me cry mercy now, (I having complained of slowness at first) so that every mail, four times a day, is apt to bring a big bundle. I have stood it so far, but its bad for head and stch. I carry the last ones in at night to mail in the Boston P.O. and often don't get at my dinner till 9 o'clock My bkfsts. I usually take in our old home in Quincy St, whose bran new bright surface together with certain structural alterations have entirely wiped away all old associations.[4] The outlook from the windows however is the same, only the trees about the back and sides have grown and closed in the view. I have it pretty much to myself there just now—Jim Myers being the only person whom I am likely ever to meet; and I confess it is pleasant to have that spot again recognizing my tread. Its walls are saturated with my groans and tears, as well as with yours! But the new wallpapers lie close, and let none of them transpire.—Charley Moering died suddenly about a month ago, a complete idiot I believe. I heard that his mother had taken to her bed, utterly prostrated by the loss, and I suppose by the cessation of the strain under which she had so long lived. This morning I learn that she died yesterday—I know not of what, unless it be a broken heart. *There's* a tragedy for some morbid novelist to work up!—Ann Ashburner is distinctly better, though they all, including Chas. Norton, are spending the summer in Cambridge on her account. The Childs have gone up to Chocorua, leaving the Prof. & Frank here. Frank is a severe moralist in spectacles 6 feet 3 in height but very thin, regaining his health and strength again, and devoted to horticulture and landscape gardening. He stays here now to take a course in surveying in the summer school. I spent a couple of nights at Mrs. Whitman's who improves year by year, and is on the whole the best woman in Boston now, I imagine, and one night at the morses on two different occasions lately. Fanny is there and dry looking, said by her bro.' Harry[5] to be not very well and always overworking herself, Mr. M. penurious Mrs. M. affectionately enthusing, Mary & her Husband like two turtle-doves still[6]—in short the whole family less modified by time than any collection of people you can easily find. Harry alone has changed—much for the better! Fanny still thinks too much about her being a plague spot on the face of nature. I saw the outside of your old house—it was much more pleasing than the last time I was there in the bleak november.[7] I saw Mrs. How,[8] the Rockwells' the Brimmer's and the Lorings.—I got a touching letter from Lilla yesterday about herself. I suppose she will have written to you to the same effect. How well that girl writes! I should like to see more of her, but I'm afraid I can't. She won't come to us in the summer, and in winter the work draws blood so that it is no time for guests. Mary Tappan is spending the summer so far in Boston on account of her Father. His "little red house" burnt down the other day, and he has come to Boston for the first time in untold years, and finds it so new and interesting a place that he stays on and she stays so that he may come to her house every afternoon and evening.[9] I have been there once—he is a very presentable and not old gentleman, with a certain weakness of character suggested by his speech. Mary wears *well.*—But here comes the postman with the proofs, which I've just opened—40 pages in galley and 56 of page-proof! I ought to get it all mailed to night—it's now half past 3—but of course I can't. Anyhow, no more dalliance with the likes of *you*! So good bye, and may Heaven lend you still more patience for the weather and the tooth.

I'm so glad Harry is enjoying the Tyrol. He ought to get more of that salubrious element. How *good* the Tragic Muse is! He can rest his reputation on that.

Adieu.

Mille baisers! | W.J.

The first sheet proved to be the last—of my big paper.[10]

ALS: MH bMS Am 1092.9 (1150)

[1] The *Figaro* was a French satirical newspaper.
[2] The magazine was not identified.
[3] *Punch* is a satirical magazine published in England.
[4] See letter to AGJ of 7 July 1890.
[5] Henry Lee Morse (1852–1929), a physician, brother of Frances Rollins Morse.
[6] Mary Lee Morse Elliot and her husband, John Wheelock Elliot.
[7] AJ owned a house in Manchester, Mass., near Beverly.
[8] Probably Alice Greenwood Howe.
[9] The red house was a farmhouse on the Tappan property in Lenox, Mass. Nathaniel Hawthorne and his family once lived there, renting the farmhouse from the Tappans.
[10] WJ began the letter on stationery of one size and finished it on paper of another size.

To Sarah Wyman Whitman

COLONIAL CLUB | CAMBRIDGE. July 24. 90

My dear Mrs. Whitman

How good a way to begin the day, with a letter from you, and a composition of yours to correct!

To take the latter first, I trembled a little when, after looking over the printed document I found you beginning so sympathetically to stroke down Mr. Jay, but you made it all right ere the end.[1] Since the movement is on foot, it is time that rational people like yourself should get an influence in it. I doubt whether the earth supports a more genuine enemy of all that the Catholic Church *inwardly* stands for than I do—*écrasez l'infâme* is the only way I can feel about it. But the concrete Catholics, including the common priests, in this country, are an entirely different matter. Their wish to educate their own, and to do what proselytizing they can, is natural enough; so is their wish to get state money. "Destroying American Institutions" is a widely different matter; and instead of this vague phrase I should like to hear one specification laid down of an "institution" which they are now threatening. The only way to resist them is absolute firmness and impartiality, and continuing in the line which you point out, bless your 'art! Down with demagogism!—this document is not quite free therefrom.

As for the style, I see in it nothing but what is admirable. A *pedant* might object (near the end) to a *drop* of (even Huguenot) blood *beating high;* but how can *I* object to anything from *your* pen?

And now 10,000 thanks for your kind words about the proofs. The pages I sent you are probably the most *continuously* amusing in the book—though occasionally there is a passing gleam elsewhere. If there is aught of good in the style it is the result of ceaseless toil in re-writing. Everything comes out wrong with me at first; but when once objectified in a crude shape, I can torture and poke and scrape and pat it till it offends me no more.—I take you at your word and send you some more sheets—only, to get something pithy and real, I go back to some practical remarks at the end of a chapter on Habit, composed with a view of benefitting the *young*[2]—May they accordingly be an inspiration to *you!*

Most of the book is altogether unreadable from any human point of view, as I feel only too well in my deluge of proofs. My dear wife will come down next week (I think) to help me through. Thank you once more, and believe me with warm regards to your husband

Yours always   Wm James

You make no mention of a note I sent you from the Morse's—but of course you got it all the same.

ALS: MH bMS Am 1092.9 (3899)

[1] In 1885 the Third Plenary Council of Baltimore required every Roman Catholic pastor to establish a parochial school, bringing to a head questions concerning the place of Catholics in American life and revivifying polemics dating back to the Reformation. Supporters of the public school system viewed parochial schools as a threat to a fundamental American institution. In an address to the National Education Association in July 1889, John Jay (1817–1894), American lawyer and diplomat, attacked the attempts by Catholics to establish their own educational system, viewing such efforts as a war against the public schools (see for example his letter to the *New York Times*, 5 March 1890). Jay's talk on "Denominational Schools" was reprinted in Boston, but the date of the reprinting is not known. What document prompted Sarah Whitman's comments in July 1890 was not discovered.

[2] WJ concludes "Habit," chap. 4 in *Principles of Psychology*, with several pages of "ethical implications and pedagogic maxims."

To Alice Howe Gibbens James

CAMBRIDGE July 25. [1890] | 3. P.M.

Beloved Lieschen,

Harry's letter was indeed delightful. Dost think now that he regards thee as a[1]   I can't help thinking the Husted letter about the
coral etc., a hoax—it is too lightly and charmingly written to be true.[2]
I will send Harry's back by your mother to morrow.   The rain came
down last night but in no very torrential amount.   Still the drought
is broken, and more rain may come.   I hope it's so with you as well.—
I am delighted over the fence, and that you look on it and say it
seems good in your sight.   It will seem still better in mine!   When
shall I ever get up there again?   No matter I'm to have *you* here
next week, and that is a heap better, all alone to ourselves (—and
Coggeshall!).   Bring with you when you come, all the Psychic
research-documents, in their cases.   Also Ladd's Physiological Psychol. and, the "Agent's" bank-book if it is still there.   I don't find it
here.   Above all bring a loving heart and a tranquil mind.   I deserve
them.   It is sweltering hot again, after the rain.   The only proof that
came this A.M. was a small quantity at eleven that I was through with
by one.   I am in the 2nd vol.   But that rascal of a Münsterberg has
been doing some exp^{ts} (rec'd this A.M.) which seem to "knock" a pretty
little theory of mine about Association.   I will print it still, pretending
I haven't seen the experiments.[3]   There ought to be laws prohibiting
the testing of theories by experiments.

I know there'll be so much proof by the coming Postman that I get
this ready now, in order not to be belated again to night.   Adieu!   I
yearn for those boys as well as for you.

W.J.

ALS: MH bMS Am 1092.9 (1742)

[1] The space following was left blank.   In his letter of 23 June 1890 HJ wrote in
reference to AGJ: "I hope Alice has time to lie on the grass" (*Correspondence*, 2:142).
See letter of 9 July 1890.

[2] Husted was not identified.

[3] Hugo Münsterberg, "Die Association successiver Vorstellungen," *Zeitschrift für Psychologie und Physiologie der Sinnesorgane*, vol. 1, no. 2 (1889): 99–120.   WJ refers to
Münsterberg's experiments in a footnote, *PP*, 1191n.

To Alice Howe Gibbens James

CAMBRIDGE July 25 [1890] | 8.30 P.M.

Dearest Alice;

Your two letters of yesterday come to me like a thunderclap this P.M. Poor little Billy! It suggested to me nothing but the grippe again. But I went to Driver (walcott being away) to see what it might suggest to him. He said it was a regular typical influenza attack with nervous symptoms. Pretty good for little Billy to have 3 attacks all to himself, whilst I have none. Kiss him—twill very likely be over ere this gets there. Meanwhile the D.^r says spray his nose inside with what I send in another package in the bottle, and if he is bad to morrow night, begin with antipyrin at 4 oclock and at 6 and 8 repeat the dose if neccessary (don't let him expect it)—but don't give more than three doses.

No proofs at 3. so it was handy to run to the doctor. I ran to McNamee's too, and saw the little stone which they had just begun to cut. I think it will look well enough. Born and died left out. *Poor* little Humster![1] How I should like to hold him in my arms once more. He's gone, and it is with me exactly as if he had not been. That awful time. I mean those years!

It seems odd that the Jackson's should be the *vital* element of our summer, to which your interests and mine must be sacrificed. You can't accelerate them, but you have the best of reasons for postponing them; and then, if they can't accept the later date you offer, you are not to blame. Unless indeed they might come on the 4th with *you not there.* But I suppose that wouldn't do. You and your mother must settle it together. Of course I *can* go without you here but I don't think I owe it to the Jackson's nor do you. Here goes for town with a considerable batch of 5 P.M. proof.———

Yours ever   W.J.

ALS: MH bMS Am 1092.9 (1743)

[1] Herman James.

From Frederic William Henry Myers

LECKHAMPTON HOUSE, | CAMBRIDGE. July 26/90

My dear James

1.   I am so *delighted* to hear that your Psychology is coming out! I shall get the book up from beginning to end, & then feel that I am a 'professed Psychologist.'

By the way, did you ever send Royce's book to H. S. as you promised?[1]   I do not happen to have heard him talk of it.

2.   I will see that the correction is made *re* Blodgett.[2]   Mʳˢ Blodgett's little sister deserves to be had in remembrance as having been the first person to do a thing wʰ ought to be as much a matter of course as making one's will.   I had arranged something of the kind with E.G.[3]—but now that the subject has turned up I may as well send *you* a closed letter,—containing a few sentences, wʰ you might try Phinuit or other 'controls' with if I 'pop over' first.

3.   We like Stanley very much—he is a gentle, childlike soul,—innocent & loveable—Of course I was not his best man;—it was the Comte d'Aarche, sent by the King of the Belgians.[4]   I suppose the Stanleys will be in Boston this winter, as he is to lecture in the States,—so of course they will be delighted if you will make their acquaintance.

4.   And that reminds me that I ventured to give a note to you to the Hon. Everard Feilding, son of Lord Denbigh, a Catholic Earl of very old family.[5]   Feilding is a *very* nice fellow, & deeply interested in SPR.

5.   We are getting lots more evidence of various kinds.   Richet has just been staying with me,—much stirred (tho' this is private as yet) by some *spiritualistic* phenomena in Russia with no paid medium,—very good evidence.

We have also got a capital English case *à la Piper*—but don't know as yet whether it will develop.   Miss Wingfield also most marvelous;[6]—much to tell you.

6.   The Piper report—(very long—) to come out about Nov.;[7] but we *must* have a full *medical* report from America,—field of vision & all the rest of it.   IF she keeps really *well*, we *hope* to invite her over here again.

7.   Whatever you *dont* read, you *must* read the Duvanel case in appendix to my article in Proc XVI.[8]   In fact *all* the cases wʰ I there give are, I think, excellent.   We shall be very glad of pabulum from

America.   Watseka wonder, or what not![9]   Dont let us go *too* slow, although we *have* eternity before us!

How *very* nice it will be to see you again!   My Wife sends warmest regards.   She is not satisfied with her picture of you[10]—can't make up her mind to send one—I sent you (to some *ironworks* from w.̣ you dated a letter to Pearsall Smith)[11] a good reproduction in the 'Lady's Pictorial' July 12/90 of a photograph of hers of Leo.[12]

Yours ever aff.   F W H Myers.

ALS: MH bMS Am 1092.9 (411)

[1] Reference is probably to *The Religious Aspect of Philosophy* (1885), the only philosophical book by Josiah Royce published by 1890.   The recipient was probably Henry Sidgwick.

[2] See letter to Myers of 15 July 1890.

[3] Edmund Gurney.

[4] See letter to Myers of 15 July 1890.   Leopold II (1835–1909), king of Belgium, was one of the financial backers of Stanley's explorations, which led to Belgian colonization of the Congo.   Leopold's emissary to the wedding was not identified; some newspapers give his name as d'Aroche.

[5] Everard Feilding (1867–1936), British lawyer and psychical researcher, was a son of Rudolph William Basil, 8th earl of Denbigh (1823–1892).   For Feilding's visit see *Correspondence*, 2:166.

[6] Telepathy experiments involving the Misses K. and M. Wingfield are reported in *Phantasms of the Living*, ed. Edmund Gurney and others (London: Society for Psychical Research, 1886) (Phil 7068.86.20*B), 1:34, and elsewhere.   For WJ's reference to them see *EPR*, 123.

[7] See letter to Myers of 15 July 1890.

[8] Frederic William Henry Myers, "A Defense of Phantasms of the Dead," *Proceedings of the Society for Psychical Research*, vol. 6, no. 16 (31 January 1890): 314–57.   On pp. 343–49 appear documents concerning August Duvanel, whose 1887 death in Switzerland was reported through automatic writing by a Swiss governess in Vilnius, Lithuania, within hours of its occurrence.

[9] For the case of Lurancy Vennum, known as the Watseka Wonder, a case of multiple personality, see *PP*, 375–77.

[10] Eveleen Tennant Myers was a photographer.

[11] The town of Chocorua was at one time known as Tamworth Iron Works, and WJ used Tamworth as the return address until late 1890.

[12] Leopold Hamilton Myers (1881–1944), a writer, son of Frederic Myers.   The *Lady's Pictorial* was published in London.   The issue was not seen.

To Mary Whiton Calkins

95 Irving St. Cambridge | July 30. 90

Dear Miss Calkins,

I thank you for your 3 schedules, and hope that the A-one will turn up in due time, filled.[1] The veridical dream seems important.

I am heartily glad to hear what you say about the Corporation etc.[2] It is flagitious that you should be kept out.—Enough to make dynamiters of you and all women.[3] I hope and trust that your application will break the barrier. I will do what I can.

Sincerely yours | Wm James

ALS: MWelC

[1] Reference is to the Census of Hallucinations.

[2] The governing body of Harvard, consisting of the President and Fellows of Harvard College, was commonly known as the Corporation.

[3] For a note on the use of dynamite in political struggles see *Correspondence*, 2:7n.

To Alice Howe Gibbens James

CAMBRIDGE July 30. 90 | 3.45.

Beloved!

As I dozed in my big brown chair in expectation of both your letter and the proofs by the 3.30 mail, the letter came but not the proofs. The letter, a double sheeter, was much richer and more impassioned in tone than I am accustomed to receive from you and has uplifted me accordingly. I am truly sorry to hear that Billy's cold still sits on his chest. Kiss him; and tell him that if he or Harry hear anything like a great big moth or beetle bumping against the mosquito nets of their rooms in the darkness, it is the spirit of their Dad taking flight through the drear night watches, when his body is asleep and striving in vain to get back to his dear children from whom he is so cruelly cut off.—As for you, dear Child, I was n't "rubbing in" your "unloveliness" of *last October,* when I said I dreaded to have you come to Cambridge and repent it.[1] I dreaded it überhaupt; viz. that you should regret it, for I have had many high thoughts to communicate to you. A sort of coming of age has come over me with these weeks, as if I were shuffling off an old epoch of my life and entering with hope and spirit a new one. I have thought of our past together in such a tear-welling & romantic way, as if it were all a history of youth on which we could already look back from afar and love its innocence.

I don't like you to be so far off when I have such thoughts, for we must advance into the future together; and I confess your seeming disinclination to move hitherwards (until the letter of today!) has made me feel a little sad. I haven't duly realized how bad Billy was; But your saying you couldn't let things "go as you please" there (with your mother mary and Margaret to look after them!) and the apparently supreme importance of the Jackson engagement, have made me resolve to urge you no longer, but to leave the matter entirely to you. All I can say is that if you do come, we can do many useful things, & many pleasant things together. Get the Hall plastering, & the floors attended to, and the fence under way. I take you to the stacks in the Library, to the excellent Comic Opera at the Museum, to the fall of Babylon etc.[2]—How *are* you, dearest one? I mean how is the little visitant, and the little varicosities, and all the little impediments to comfort? Pray, darling, tell me about them on paper, just as if you were lisping in my ear. My bowels *do* yearn after you! they do, they do.

I got in to the Parker House roast beef yesterday at 7, and at 7.50 took train for Medford to see my blind man, whose circular in Enclose.[3] Had a very instructive conversation with him in many ways. He is of a superior intelligence and thinks the blind ought not to be segregated and taught together and treated as a distinct class in the community; but should tumble in and make their living with no quarter shown. He hardly seems to think the loss of sight a deprivation! He is the man of whom his wife wrote that queer hallucination of a corpse in pepper and salt clothing sliding under the door etc.—I walked most of the way into Boston along the horse car track through the warm blanket of the foggy night, and it was midnight ere I got here. But I slept soundly until nearly seven and feel to day perfectly well again. I shall see to it hereafter that my meals are straight. I have bkfstd. this A.M at the Ashburner's, and lunched at the Club. Only two hours work on proofs so far! I wish I could tell in advance when they were coming and when not. Probably there'll be a big batch at 5—but then most of them will have to go over till to morrow. I am going on to an early dinner this evening, coute que coûte and either to the fall of Babylon or the Museum after it.

Poor Mack and Mary! What you say of their bust is touching.[4] I confess, poor as my own mental images are, the only motive I could ever have for getting a likeness of a dead one, would be that of ménager-ing a pleasant surprise many many years hence.—I have been feeling of late more and more the absolute neccessity of taking *your* likeness—myself!

Good bye. I enclose H.P.B's letter.[5] Why did n't you open it first yourself.

Love to all. | W.J.

ALS: MH bMS Am 1092.9 (1746)

[1] AGJ had been pregnant also in October 1889. That pregnancy ended in a miscarriage.

[2] The Boston Museum presented an obscure play, *Fauvette*, adapted by American journalist and author Roswell Martin Field (1851–1919) and American composer Benjamin Edward Woolf (1836–1901). The Oakland Garden offered the "magnificent spectacle" of *The Fall of Babylon*, presented by American showmen Phineas Taylor Barnum and James Anthony Bailey (1847–1906).

[3] An error for 'is enclosed'. No circular was found with the letter. In other writings WJ states that the blind man was named Perry.

[4] The Salters apparently were unhappy with a memorial to their daughter Eliza Salter, who had died in December 1889 at the age of two.

[5] Henry Pickering Bowditch.

To Alice Howe Gibbens James

CAMBRIDGE July 31. 90 | 8.30 PM.

Beloved

Your apparently telepathic letter about my sickness arrived this afternoon at 5. Don't fret! I'm well again and the work is going on so fast that I think I shall surely be back on your hands before the end of next week. All day at it to day, and about 40 pp. of galley still unread to go over till to morrow. I bkfstd. at the Ashburners and had meant to get in to the Boston Museum to night[1] but found at 6.30 that I hadn't cash for both dinner and ticket and so turned off to Grace Norton's, so as to go with a better conscience to morrow night. I shall buy a ticket now for to morrow, on my way in to the Boston P.O. I deserve some passive recreation. These social ties are alternately a comfort and a curse. One gets so entangled that one never arrives anywhere. For a week now I've been plotting an evening's amusement, but it's not yet achieved. Last night I was caught by the Shady Hill norton family who carried me up to dine with them just as I was starting for Oakland Garden.[2] Eliot had just arrived from N.Y. and is going to be married in Sept.[3] The "dinner" consisted, (5 of us being present) of 3 poached eggs, one small slice of salmon and two warmed-over mutton chops, bread, cake and tea. I ate one egg, one chop & part of the salmon. I don't know how the others felt; but Margaret[4] & Charles said most beamingly as I left, that they hoped I would "come and dine again soon." I think its all very well not to be profuse of apologies for scanty fare, but there's such a thing as making dignity ridiculous, and overdoing the silence-business—Grace showed the cloven hoof this afternoon in a way that "let me in" to the way you feel about her. The cold manner I mean in which she spoke of the Childs as if she'd once for all resolved to know nothing of their interior. I never caught her at it so before; it absolves me from all sense of obligation to her; and makes me quite indignant.—Something more than the *stupidity* for which in her I have always had such tender indulgence. We have had two sweltering days. Last night at half past eleven under the jaundiced moon-hid sky, I ran out under the apple tree in a state of nature, (after playing the hose on the grass as long as I could) and Coggeshall and Royce played them over me. Very jolly and free—a thing you can't do in term time!—I arose at four and something, read Rudyard Kipling till seven, and have been at proofs hammer and tongs all day long with no nap. I shall keep up my hygiene now—I will run down to Beverly for a night again—Wendell Holmes perhaps[5]—to N. Weymouth at the Putnams, and to Wayland. Now I go to the P.O. Heaven bless you. I wish I could hear your dreams! I'll send you $50.00 cash to morrow. I sent the Atlantic which is chock full of good reading. Read Holmes's poem aloud to the boys[6]—or let Mack read it to the circle: It's prodigious, the verse-making organ in that man's brain. Good night.

W.J.

ALS: MH bMS Am 1092.9 (1747)

[1] For the performance see previous letter.

[2] Shady Hill was the name of the Norton estate in Cambridge. WJ's house at 95 Irving St. was built on land that had been part of the estate. The Oakland Garden presented *The Fall of Babylon;* see previous letter.

[3] Eliot Norton married Margaret Palmer Meyer on 2 September 1890.

[4] Margaret Norton was the daughter of Charles Eliot Norton and often kept house for her widowed father.

[5] Oliver Wendell Holmes, Jr., owned a summer home at Beverly Farms, Mass.

[6] Oliver Wendell Holmes, Sr., "The Broomstick Train; or, The Return of the Witches," *Atlantic Monthly* 66 (August 1890): 246–48.

To Sarah Wyman Whitman

                                        Cambridge Aug 1. 90
My dear Mrs. Whitman
   You must be altogether parched and dried up with thirst for
"proofs" by this time; and indeed after your so handsome reception
of the earlier batch, I ought to be ashamed at sending you no more.
But the plain truth is that although I have never for a moment forgotten you or your needs and requirements, I actually haven't met with
a page, in all the last fortnight of correcting, that seemed in the least
degree worthy of your royal highness'es perusal. The book, I grieve
to say, except in gossipy parts of the second vol. about instinct and
the like which are too newspapery to send, is an irredeemable waste
of dulness from the human and literary point of view. Occasionally
a gleam, of course, a sentence, a paragraph*. But it dies away; and
for the rest

               "—boundless and bare
   The lone and level sand stretches far away."[1]

   I am pretty well tired out with the heat and my ceaseless application of 8, 9, 10 hours a day, and I write mainly to say this: that negotiations with the Holmes's have been consummated the fruit of which
is that I am to go to Beverly to pass Sunday night with them,[2] and
that I shall make bold on Monday morning, ¾ of an hour before the
10.27 train leaves, to ask if you are "at home," and (if not spurned
from the door as always happens at Mount Vernon St.)[3] to make my
party-call. I'm sure that if you are at home you won't have the heart
to spurn me, after I have taken all this trouble to notify you of my approach!
                              Ever sincerely yours | Wm James
   *—For example, the note which I enclose from to day's lesson
ALS: MH bMS Am 1092.9 (3900)

   [1] From "Ozymandias," a sonnet by Percy Bysshe Shelley.
   [2] The letter of 1 August 1890 from Oliver Wendell Holmes, Jr., inviting WJ is calendared. WJ noted on the letter, perhaps when sending it to AGJ, that the invitation
is the result of a "hint" made to Fanny Holmes.
   [3] Sarah Wyman Whitman lived at 77 Mount Vernon St., Boston.

From Charles Augustus Strong

Bad-Nauheim, Hessen, | August 1, 1890.

My dear James,—

Many thanks for your interesting letter of June 30th, as well as for those programmes, which filled Münsterberg & me with admiration & wonder. M. has been amusing himself counting up the number of psychological laboratories that are either in operation or projected in the United States—I think we counted 8 in all—& comparing our enterprise & enlightenment with the benighted state of things in Germany. He has several times asked me what I should think of his emigrating to America, whether he could secure a good position there, etc. He is dissatisfied with the slowness with which one rises in Germany, & regrets having settled in Freiburg.

This is the last epistle I can write you from Germany for a long time to come. We are resting at this quiet watering-place preparatory to our ocean voyage, & expect to sail from Southampton by the Augusta Victoria August 8th.

I wish I knew what you think of Clark University. My appointment there is of course only for the year, but if the place suits me I shall do my best to stay. They have a great deal of time at Clark; I have only to lecture or conduct a seminary in Greek philosophy once a week, & hope to spend half my time upon psychology, which I should be loth to drop at this stage of the proceedings. I wish I could divide my time in this way for four or five years to come between physiological psychology with its subsidiary sciences and the history of philosophy.

As to the graduate students, don't you think that many men e.g. in philosophy & psychology will be tempted to divide their time between Europe & Clark? Not even Wundt's laboratory affords such facilities as they have at Worcester, & there is no other equal to Wundt's.

You ask about Mr Rockefeller.[1] I wish I thought there was any hope of interesting him in the Harvard laboratory; it would give me great satisfaction to do so, if it were only in gratitude for benefits I have myself received. But though he is a man of uncommon refinement, he is not a man of intellectual interests, & I question whether his enthusiasm could be roused for so abstract a discipline as physiological psychology. He makes many gifts, but I think they are exclusively to religious & humanitarian enterprises, or for education in the broadest sense.

Münsterberg's radical positivism I have found very stimulating & interesting if not altogether convincing. He is pretty clear-sighted & consistent, but his system is very weak at points. When he does not content himself with recognizing the parallelism between physical & psychical phenomena, but interprets it in the sense of a one-sided dependence of the psychical upon the physical, he propounds nothing less than a metaphysical dogma, & a pretty unfounded one at that. I told him this, & it made him wince. He merely asked, Do I represent it so? There is nothing more painful to a denouncer of metaphysics than to be shown that he is metaphysicking himself. But M. is a good fellow, & very square, & I have learned a lot from him.

I am glad you are willing to regard the parallelism business as a possible alternative, and to shake hands over it "provided it be included in an over-lapping religious metaphysics."[2] But has the proviso really anything to do with the question whether or no parallelism itself is a fact? Hesitating over parallelism for fear it may not be unitable with a moral synthesis of the universe is the same thing, only much more refined, as rejecting evolution because it is inconsistent with the inspiration of the Bible. No; one must decide for or against parallelism in view of the immediate evidence, & leave the universe to look out for itself. Our moral demands are very right & proper in their place, but they must keep silent till science has finished its work. It is a pity the intellectual world should be divided into two camps, of men who are so interested in the empirical facts that they don't care about the moral result, & men who are so anxious about the moral result that they are not just to the empirical facts.

I am glad we shall be so near Cambridge this next year, & hope to drop in upon you often there as well as to see you often in Worcester.

With the very best regards to Mrs. James & yourself, I am ever

Sincerely yours, | Charles A. Strong.

I had a fine letter from Santayana, the other day, from Avila; & was delighted to find that he & I are perfectly agreed as to the foundation of ethics,—consequences.

ALS: MH bMS Am 1092 (1052)

[1] John Davison Rockefeller (1839–1937), industrialist and philanthropist, was Strong's father-in-law. Correspondence is known from 1909.

[2] WJ and Strong engaged in an extensive discussion of psychophysical parallelism in their letters of 1889, which are included in volume 6 of the *Correspondence*. The quotation appears to be from an unknown letter by WJ.

To Alice Howe Gibbens James

CAMBRIDGE Aug 3. 90 | 10.30 A.M.

Beloved Weibsbild

Since getting your letter of yesterday, you can hardly conceive of the inward happiness I feel. Far better for you to have waited till now than to have come to me ahead of the Jackson's and had to scutttle back etc. Besides, it is much better for me that you should be in at the finish of these proofs, where we can wind up things here together than in the middle. So come down Wednesday or Thursday, (letting me know which) and we will have the greatest week together that we have ever had yet, or that *any* two hearts that beat as one have ever yet had. I fully expected a tremenjus batch of proofs to day, but on going down with Frank Child and Dick N.[1] to the P.O. there were none there; but there'll be enough to morrow to make up for it. And I'm afraid since It will be near noon ere I get back from Beverly that I shall have to pay for it. No matter I have plenty of tinkering work to do to day—psychics table of contents etc. so the time won't be wasted. When you come down, we must do the Index *together*. But oh! *do* be friendly! you're *so* nice when you are. Since you wrote indecisively to Mrs. Merriman, won't you now accept. We shall be free by the 15th and I'm sure it will do us both a lot of good to go. After witnessing, a month ago Mrs Whitman's mode of taking life, I said to myself "that's the right way to get most out of it, and Alice and I must chuck in, and enter every opening hereafter. It is the way to keep young." So pray say you'll go! and of course write to her promptly. I reenclose her note. What pretty writing, by the way!—Read Vogelius's note and the compliment of the proof reader![2] That *is* a compliment worth having—an old case-hardened box-tortoise like that sitting up after hours *aus lauter Wonne!*—I found yestermorn that Theodora couldn't go to the operetta, so I proposed to mrs. Royce who gave me a rump-steak which I extravagantly devoured, for my reward, and accepted with joy. T'was a charming little piece to which you also must go;[3] and little Mrs. R. is the most harmless little thing at bottom, much like Mrs. Tweedy—in voice a lion, in action a lamb. But she *du* abhor Josiah. It is too bad! He was working away under the gaslight, after having written a rare good article about Frank Abbot's last book,[4] at another about Fremont,[5] and with his features all shining with perspiration and genius, and vague in expression with stress of work, he was a homely goodly sight. Very fat withal!—I've done something very bad about Theodora. I ought to have written to you long since to ask her to go up for a few days of rest—but day after day I forgot it when it came to write. I proposed it to her, and I know that it would have been a boon. It is now too late. But we must do it in Sept. She goes this week to Ashfield.

Farewell! Bring down the bank-book if you find it; whatever library books there may be; all the hallucination material *except blanks*—also yourself!

"Come back to me beloved, or I die!"

I send some epitaphs for the boys. Keep the slip.

Aff<u>ly</u>: WILLIAM JAMES[6]

AL: MH bMS Am 1092.9 (1753)

[1] Francis Sedgwick Child and Richard Norton.

[2] The letter from Vogelius of 1 August 1890 is calendared. Vogelius notes that Theodore F. Neu, the chief proofreader, is so interested in the book that he stays after hours to read it himself.

[3] For the operetta see letter to AGJ of 30 July 1890.

[4] Josiah Royce, "Dr. Abbot's 'Way out of Agnosticism,'" *International Journal of Ethics* 1 (October 1890): 98–113. This review of Francis Ellingwood Abbot's *The Way out of Agnosticism* (1890) gave rise to a heated controversy to which references will be found in later letters.

[5] Josiah Royce, "Frémont," *Atlantic Monthly* 66 (October 1890): 548–57. In this article, written shortly after the death of American explorer and politician John Charles Frémont (1813–1890), as well as in other historical writings, Royce examined critically Frémont's part in the American conquest of California. According to Royce, Frémont "possessed all the qualities of genius except ability" (p. 548).

[6] WJ used a stamp rather than signing this letter.

From Sarah Wyman Whitman

[August 3, 1890]

My dear Mr James, You will smile when I say that the first moment I have had to write (as a matter of pleasure) comes in the train on my return from New York!

I went thither yesterday because the sudden departure of my dear Mr Schuyler made me want to make one last pilgrimage to his shrine: & thinking the funeral was to be today.[1] It was delayed for certain reasons: but I am glad glad I went, for every reason: and especially because it gave me a quiet morning with them in his quiet presence, such as could only have been had today. I dont know whether you knew him: a really brilliant man: witty, profound & original, intellectually: wearing a charming mask, under which was a fiery heart. Homme du monde, to a degree almost continental. Yet with a transcendental faith and a touch of asceticism in his life.—Ah. I cared so much for him: and I like to feel that he died as he did, the last news of him that he had "sailed with the Squadron": and the great sea under his feet—I am sure that I get further & further from the Eastern point of view wherein the Each is merged in the All.— for so far as I can trace the results of the best living of this life it goes to develope & strengthen the fibre and flavor of the individual—the more consummate and supreme the experience, the more distinct and single the creature. Is not this true? And Habit[2] —regarding which your pages say the best word at every time—habit provides a scaffolding, a mode, an hypothesis, from which the person can work & play freely: and finally fly serenely into new conditions, & a less straightened air.———

You were very good to take time to sustain the school question:[3] which has indeed to be much looked after just now—& since then I am afraid you have worked at great odds with this scorching heat. I have had a difficult houseful of people: and haven't thought much about the temperature, physical: having to maintain the proper heat, moral, in vacuo! Did M[rs] James come down? If she did not I hope she will later, when it may be possible to offer the hospitality of Old Place.

Meanwhile I would like some more proof, when it suits the author.

Faithfully | SW

In some way you missed a brief answer to your letter from the Morses'. A letter to tell you my thanks.[4]

ALS: MH bMS Am 1092.9 (684)

[1] George Lee Schuyler (1811–1890), New York businessman and yachtsman, father of Georgina Schuyler, died suddenly on a yacht on 31 July. His funeral took place in New York City on 4 August.

[2] WJ underlined the word 'Habit' and in the margin wrote: 'I sent her the proofs of the end of that chapter'.

[3] See letter to Sarah Wyman Whitman of 24 July 1890.

[4] On the verso of the fourth page of this letter WJ wrote to AGJ: 'This is the next phase of my flirtation with Mrs. W.—just come this Sunday A.M.—You may say she's artificial, and an upstart, and what you like—but she has the real bottom thing in her, and in the long run I bet on her against the whole field, and I love her dearly—there!' On the same page WJ later wrote: 'This chaff must have been written as I sent the letter to my wife. ['In' *del.*] The ['T' *ov.* 't'] summer of 1890, I *spent at [*ov.* 'sent it'] Cambridge alone, correcting the proofs of my long Psychology | W. J. | Nov 4. 1904'.

To Alice Howe Gibbens James

CAMBRIDGE Aug 4. 90

Dearest Lieschen

It is 9. P.M. & I've done a stack of proof albeit I did n't get back from Beverly till 12 o'clock. The Old Doctor was particularly nice.[1] As for Fanny, how could I ever—?[2] I came home on the 10.15 train with parson Hall who is staying at the Morses'—why does *he* marry Fanny?[3]—and made him get the Kreutzer Sonata etc etc.[4] Dined at Club at 2.[5] Am sitting in the heat in my pajamas, famished again— and must run in to eat & to post.

Your letter to day was terse and simple. But what matters it when I am so soon to fold you in my arms? I can hardly await the day.

Kiss those dear children three. I long to see them.

W.J.

ALS: MH bMS Am 1092.9 (1754)

[1] Oliver Wendell Holmes, Sr.

[2] WJ is probably alluding to his admiration for Fanny Holmes; see *Correspondence*, 4:135.

[3] The reference is to Frances Rollins Morse. Perhaps WJ meant to write 'why does *he* not marry Fanny?'.

[4] Reference is to the story by Tolstoi; see letter to AGJ of 27 May 1890, note 1.

[5] See letter of 7 July 1890.

To George Bucknam Dorr

CAMBRIDGE Aug. 12. 90

My dear George

Hallelujah! John Fiske informs me that he has got a check of 3000 from Mr. Slater for the great cause. As usual, the race is to the slow. Obesity and inertia come in first. Long may they live! I refer to the Committee—I don't know whether Mr Slater is obese or not— Fiske *is*.[1]

This sets me nicely afloat, and is not a dollar more than I can well make use of. I feel, however, a little mean under the circumstances at keeping the money of those fashionable ladies, and should like with your permission to send back the 100 from Mrs. Fields and Miss Jewett. I enclose a check for the purpose which I pray you to en-dorse properly and explain to them the mysterious ways of Provi-dence, and the everlasting gratitude of W.J. I will myself return 100 dollars to that blessed Mrs. Whitman, who will probably refuse to take it back; in which case I will keep it, as she is an old friend, etc. But I hardly know the other two ladies, and moreover Miss Jewett makes her living just as I do.

The psychology is now done, all but the Index, and a sacred peace descends. By next Monday I shall be at Chocorua again, able to see a little of my family, and doomed to get up my new courses of lectures for next year. I hope you are all well and happy. Please give my love to your father and mother, and believe me always yours

Wm James

It suddenly occurs to me that it was twenty-five apiece which these dear ladies gave—my list is in the country—Such is my confidence in you that I send you a *blank* check, to be filled up with the proper amount. Pray notify me, so that I may keep my accounts straight.

WJ.

ALS: MH bMS Am 1092.1

[1] The Harvard Treasurer's Report for 1890–91, accounting for funds paid to 1 August 1891, shows that a total of $4,300 was collected for the Psychology Department, including the $3,000 from Slater. Edmund Tweedy, listed as "a friend," gave $500 (see *Correspondence*, 2:148n), while Sarah Wyman Whitman and others, mostly WJ's social acquaintances, gave either $100 or $50. Neither Sarah Orne Jewett nor Annie Adams Fields is listed. John Fiske was then chairman of the visiting committee on philosophy. News traveled slowly since Fiske had received the gift by 4 July 1890 (see *The Letters of John Fiske*, ed. Ethel F. Fisk [New York: Macmillan, 1940], 579).

To Alice James

CAMBRIDGE Aug. 13. 90

My poor dear Alice,

To day, following on the news from Katherine of two days since, comes a card from you of July 29th and one from your nurse of August 2 with your "naughty" message about our giving 3 cheers when you "vanish." You are indeed naughty—and too stoical. To think of saying nothing of your sufferings yourself. My heart has all been twisted up into a knot about you since seeing Katherine.[1] But as you've weathered so many capes, you'll probably weather this one too, and be a leader of society yet. Katherine is surely a good friend to have, to call upon from so far. It is lucky she's on hand—you might otherwise have *me* coming!—Grace Norton read me the letter in the Nation some nights ago and I saw unmistakeable inward evidence of its source.[2] When you get over this "spell" you must continue to contribute, now that you've made the plunge. I am entirely certain that you've got a book inside of you about England, which will come out yet.   Perhaps its the source of all your recent trouble. My book has come out—that is the last proofs are corrected, and nothing but the index to do.   I'll send you a copy when it appears. I've worked like a whole gang of niggers for 6 weeks past, and accomplished the feat of correcting 1400 pp. of proof.   Harry's letter from Vallombrosa has a *tone* which nothing but mingling with Nature can give.[3]   He ought to do some of it every year.—Good night, my poor dear Sister.   This is only a word to express my sympathy.   I enclose a letter rec'd from Jae Walsh the other day.   The thing to do about *that* matter is not to think of it at all.[4]

Yrs ever | W.J.

Remember me to Nurse Broadfield.[5]

ALS: MH bMS Am 1092.9 (1151)

[1] AJ had a serious breakdown on 2 August 1890, and in response Katharine Loring was leaving for England.   WJ's farewell letter to Katharine Loring of 13 August 1890 is calendared.   For a note on AJ's condition at this time see *Correspondence*, 2:147n.

[2] In the letter signed "Invalid," which appeared in *Nation* 51 (17 July 1890): 51, AJ describes an American woman trying to rent a room from AJ's landlady.   When told that an invalid lived in the house, the American replied that since her thirteen-year-old daughter liked to run and scream it was just as well that no rooms were available.

[3] For HJ's letter of 23 July 1890 see *Correspondence*, 2:144–45.

[4] Reference is to the will of Henry Albert Wyckoff; see *Correspondence*, 2:158n.

[5] In *DLAJ* AJ's nurse is identified as Emily Ann Bradfield.

To William Dean Howells

Tamworth Iron Works N.H. | Aug 27. 90

My dear Howells,

You've done it this time and no mistake!   I've had a little leisure for reading this summer, and have just read, first your Shadow of a Dream, and next your Hazard of New Fortunes, & can hardly recollect a novel that has taken hold of me like the latter.[1]   Some compensations go with being a mature man, do they not?   You could n't possibly have done so solid a piece of work as that 10 years ago, could you?   The steady unflagging flow of it, is something wonderful. Never a weak note, the number of characters, each intensely individual, the observation of detail, the everlasting wit and humor, and beneath all the bass accompaniment of the human problem, the entire americanness of it, all make it a very great book, and one which will last when we shall have melted into the infinite azure.　Ah! my dear Howells, its worth something to be able to write such a book, and it is so peculiarly *yours* too, flavored with your idiosyncracy. Congratulate your wife on having brought up such a husband.　*My* wife had been raving about it ever since it came out, but I could n't read it till I got the larger printed copy, and naturally couldn't credit all she said.　But it makes one love as well as admire you, and so o'er-shadows the equally exquisite, though slighter shadow of a dream that I have no adjectives left for that.　I hope the summer is speeding well with all of you.　I have been in Cambridge six weeks and corrected 1400 pp. of proof.　The year which shall have witnessed the apparition of your Hazard of N. F. of Harry's Tragic Muse, and of *my* Psychology, will indeed be a memorable one in American Literature!!　Believe me, with warm regards to Mrs. Howells,

Yours ever affectionately, | Wm James

The book is so d――d *humane*!

ALS: MH bMS Am 1092.9 (1017)

[1] William Dean Howells, *A Hazard of New Fortunes* (1890).　For additional comments on the book see *Correspondence*, 2:146.

To Hugo Münsterberg

TAMWORTH IRON WORKS | N.H. August 27. 90

Dear D! Münsterberg

Your welcome letter & the 3rd "Heft" of your Beiträge both arrived yesterday,[1] and I beg you to receive for both my thanks.　As regards young Delabarre, he is a *silent* fellow, but I think a very clear headed and solid one, and I fancy that you will be pleased with his work.　I am glad you can put him at some muscular sense experiments, and I am sure he will find it a most inspiring thing to work with a man in whose hands things are as plastic as they are in yours: If one has not a natural taste for experimenting, the habit of it must be formed when young, and kept up assiduously.　I am sorry to say that I have not done for Delabarre (or for any one) what I ought to have done in this respect; for I naturally hate experimental work myself, and all my circumstances conspired (during the important years of my life) to prevent me from getting into a routine of it, so that now it is always the duty that gets postponed.　There are plenty of others, to keep my time as fully employed as my working powers permit!—I wish that you could have stayed longer in Paris; it turned out very agreeable. But I am truly rejoiced that there is some prospect of your paying us a visit here, and I hope it may be soon. I have already read your 3rd Heft with avidity. Unfortunately it reached me too late late to be used in the appropriate chapter of my psychology, of which I finished the proofs a fortnight ago. The same is true of your little paper on association, which I received just a fortnight ago in the Zeitschrift, and which entirely knocks the bottom out from under a little speculation of my own about association-paths in the brain. I mention it in a note, but could not other-wise consider it.² I must say that you seem to me to be doing more to open out new vistas in Psychology than anyone to day, and your fertility in ideas and sagacity in making distinctions are only equalled by the promptitude with which you devise experiments, and the energy with which you fall to work at them. Moreover, you handle things with such a broad light touch in writing about them, that it is a constant pleasure to read what you say.

Most of your compatriots suffocate one under details which have no importance, and one suffers terribly from the lack of perspective, of proper subordination of parts, in their style. With you there is absolutely no pedantry. The details are given only so far as they are connected with the idea. As for your great idea, that of the all-importance of the muscular sense for comparison and relating thought, I am as yet by no means convinced. It is obviously one of those things that must be tested in many directions experimentally, and criticised from many points of view, by others besides yourself. You will have to defend it, as the attacks come out! But it will certainly be the stimulus to a large amount of psychological work, and it *may* triumph. It has knocked all my ideas *auseinander;* for I have been led, for reasons which I give in my book, to ascribe little or no importance to the muscular sense; and I find that a good deal of revision is going on in my own thought on this subject. If I get at any experimental work this year, it must certainly be connected with this subject.

I look with great eagerness to your larger book.³ I'm inclined to think that a manual of psychology must be an extraordinarily difficult task—all existing ones have such flagrant defects. The truth is that Psychology is yet seeking her first principles, and is in the condition of Physics before Galileo or Newton. Nerve physiology has some laws, even of a quasi elementary sort; but of a law connecting body and mind, or indeed of what is the *elementary fact* of mind, we have not at present even the beginning of an hypothesis which is valuable.

Meanwhile *all* books are valuable if they have any freshness in them at all; and nothing would please me so much as to think that you could find any suggestiveness in any part of mine. Of course I will send you a copy when it appears in September. With renewed thanks for your kind letter, believe me

always cordially yours | Wm James

ALS: MH bMS Am 1092.9 (3263); MB⁴

[1] See letter of 13 May 1890, note 7.

[2] See letter of 25 July 1890, 3 P.M.

[3] No such book by Münsterberg was found. WJ may be relying on information supplied by Charles Augustus Strong; see letter of 13 May 1890.

[4] The first part of the autograph letter (through 'ideas' at 89.11) is preserved in the Houghton Library at Harvard; the rest, in the Boston Public Library.

To Alice Howe Gibbens James

GLEN HOUSE | WHITE MOUNTAINS, N.H. Wednesday Sept 3. 1890 | 7.
P.M.

Beloved,

I reached this sublimish, mountaineous and sylvan place an hour and a half ago, since when have had my hair cut, seen Brown taken care of, and read some Descartes. We gallopped nearly all the way last night, the Merriman Horses being good 'uns, and each of the four being excited by the other 3. We took the upper road which goes off by the mill beyond Hommond's some distance.[1] You and I went along it once part way—it is good all the way, no longer than the other, though hillier, and vastly prettier. A great discovery. The Merriman's kept up to their own high standard, and I left 'em this AM. at 10 and came slowly, Brown having refused his breakfast, to Jackson which I reached at a little before 12, put the horse up at the hotel, and finding Wigglesworth just down there with his wagon, went up to his house to dinner. He has a fine house and a really magnificent view. His wife seemed a very plain, ladylike and modest person, and he was the same dear old boy.[2]—I have been to tea since the last sheet—seeing the people go in made me follow, and I fell into the hands of the only Harvard waiter, a disciple of Shaler, who bro't me eggs, smoked Halibut, potatoes, griddle cakes, and beer.— The ride hither from Jackson was effected in 2½ hours, 12 miles. I went over it some years ago when we were at Lawrences what time I came round by way of Shelburne.[3] Mt. Washington is glorious, and the breath of the everlasting forest all along here is the real old thing.

I did wish you were along. I shouldn't wonder if I burst into verse some day. Some things can only be expressed in verse. I have never known which things they were, nor by what phrases to express them. But as I cam along on brown, and smelt the forest, it occurred to me that the rapturous mystery and imperishable freshness of nature in one verse, of the heart of woman in another, and of the fact that there *is* something about verse which can't go into prose in a third, would be a good *subject*. How to express it, what meter, phrases etc. remain to be discovered!—The heart-of-woman-part of it was *you*. What a queer way to leave you! What was it all about? How did it originate? Who began first? Etc. etc.? All I know is that your level look into truth, your tender sensibility to discord, your absolute charity to me, and your valiant and unegotistic path of life, are things which, the mount[4] I turn my back upon you, loom up much higher than Mount Washington has done it this afternoon. Darling in all seriousness you have lifted me up out of lonely hell. I think that if you look at what I am now, & at what I was when you took me you can realize that fact—not as I realize it, but still enough to know that for it I can never cease to be grateful. You have redeemed my life from destruction and crowned me with loving kindness & tender mercy, and my fortunes are eternally linked with yours.—That poem will begin a new career for us.—I am going to bed early as my valise must start to Jefferson at 6.45 to morrow.—Adieu, angel! and give my love to all your family, especially to your dear Mother.

Ever thy | Wm.

ALS: MH bMS Am 1092.9 (1755)

[1] Hommond was not identified.

[2] Edward Wigglesworth (1840–1896), a physician, lecturer at the Harvard Medical School. His wife was Sarah Frothingham Wigglesworth.

[3] In September 1886 WJ was in Shelburne, N.H., while the family was in Jaffrey, N.H., on a farm owned by Frederick J. Lawrence (1851–1929).

[4] A slip for 'moment'.

To Sarah Wyman Whitman

Tamworth Iron Works | Sept. 9. 90.

My dear Mrs Whitman,

I find your most amiable letter of the 31st. on my return home from a week on horseback in the mountains. I thank you now for the hundred far more than before—better one that was dead and is alive again than seventy and seven that went not astray! (Do I quote rightly?) It shall be particularly well used. You write of destroying *two* checks—can it be that all that facetiousness on Chapman's part and mine was called forth by you in pure wantonness? I prefer to think that you have now made a slip of the pen.—I still dream of you. The other night it was your three sisters whose acquaintance I made in a strange antique italian city. One of them was a singularly attractive person, though unlike you in every other respect. I asked which was the oldest of the family, as it was impossible to tell by their looks. "Oh!" she said, "of course *the Spider!*" by which surprising name I immediately understood *you* to be meant, believing it to refer to the gracility, so to speak, of your configuration, rather than to any moral analogy. Now how do you interpret *that* dream?

But no matter for dreams—take realities. I have seen more than ever before of the Merrimans. She is a reality if ever there was one, and I must say I think her an extraordinarily fine woman. She is a good friend to you, too, as of course you by this time know. An interesting household in every respect!—Our own affairs go smoothly. I got some of the breath of the everlasting forest last week, which seems to me an essential ingredient of the year, only one ought to have a good deal more of it. I am grinding away at Descartes etc for next year,[1] and "the book" is a thing of the past, thank Heaven. As you may well believe, what you write about "life-stuff" etc is full enough of significance for me. But you have on the whole found your career and I have not; hence a certain pensive sadness in the mood in which I read your words, to be dispelled perhaps ere very long, for it is barely possible that I am going through a sort of crisis and turning point of life. But I won't write of that! The good Bryce! on the whole as *satisfactory* a creature as one can know. I wrote to ask him here if he were to be in the neighborhood. But he has made no reply.[2]—Thanks once more, and warm good wishes to you both, in which my Alice joins,

Yours always   W.J.

ALS: MH bMS Am 1092.9 (3901)

[1] In 1890–91 WJ taught Philosophy 10: Descartes, Spinoza, and Leibnitz. His notes for the course are included in *ML.*

[2] James Bryce was touring the United States and Canada at the time.

To Alice Howe Gibbens James

Monday night, | Sept 22 90
Beloved—This is only to say ere I go to bed, that the moment I have
you at a distance the unutterable excellence of your character
clutches me round the heart! I went with harry to Brown's who was
rather reassuring.[1] Poor good little harry! He is full of mature responsibilities. He said he did n't care for the fall of Babylon,[2] he had
so many duties to attend to, boys, butterflies, Brown etc., etc.—Well,
good night. The trunks are back, the house looks nice. I've got
from Royce just the book I want to begin my course with,[3] so everything promises well. But good bye one more summer! alas! alas!
The open horse cars seem already at an end.[4] They symbolize every
thing that is good. Good night!

AL: MH bMS Am 1092.9 (1757)

[1] George Henry Browne, who with Edgar Hamilton Nichols, operated a private
school for boys at 8 Garden St.
[2] See letter to AGJ of 30 July 1890.
[3] Probably Philosophy 10; see letter of 9 September 1890.
[4] The horse cars were closed in during the winter.

To Alexander McKenzie

TAMWORTH IRON WORKS | N.H. Sept 22. 90[1]
Dear Dr. Mackenzie,
I feel much touched by your thoughtful regard for me, and shall
be much interested in reading the little book you have sent. I don't
know whether, if unconverted, I can give you a very articulate account of the reasons why not, but we shall see. These things are
always excessively complex. I confess that in my own case it has so
far been the Bible itself, both old Testament and New, which has
seemed to me the document most fatal to the claims of the traditional
christian theology. All changes in theology have had their source
and authority in ways of reading the Bible. The merely humanistic
way which comes so natural to men of this generation hangs together
with a way of looking at things with which the christian scheme
of Salvation is (I may say almost invincibly) incongruous. And the
Bible-text lends itself so unconstrainedly to the humanistic interpre-

tation, that anything beyond that seems artificial.—I am of course a most convinced *Theist,* as you know.

Thanking you again, I am always yours

Wm James

ALS: CtY

[1] The date of the letter and the addressee are uncertain. WJ dated the letter clearly, but he was not in Chocorua on 22 September, indicating error as to either time or place. The letter probably is addressed to Alexander McKenzie (1830–1914), a Congregational clergyman in Cambridge, who as a member of the visiting committee for philosophy had visited WJ's classes. After one such visit in May 1889, WJ held a theological discussion with him (see *Correspondence,* 6:474). Alexander McKenzie had a son, Kenneth McKenzie (1870–1949), then an undergraduate at Harvard, later a professor of Italian in several universities, including Yale. One may conjecture that it was this Kenneth, one of many Kenneth McKenzies active at this time, who deposited at Yale the letter addressed to his father. In *SUC,* 68, Frederick J. Down Scott identifies the recipient as Kenneth Mackenzie (1853–1943), a clergyman in Westport, Conn., but this seems unlikely since WJ's remark "as you know" indicates that he knew the addressee. Alexander McKenzie published many sermons, both individually and in collections, and the little book mentioned in the letter was not identified. He is the author of *Christ Himself,* copyrighted in 1891, but its date of publication was not established.

To Alice Howe Gibbens James

Sept 23. [1890] | 9 P.M.

Dearest Alice

A rather disorderly day, but I have found the right lines of reading and so am safe for my Descartes course. Harry gives no very lucid account of his exam.[n] either to me or to you, but he seems to be admitted to the 2nd. class, & will probably scrape along.[1] He played football on the Common this P.M.—I have seen in one way or another many people. Strong was here to day, and several students. I met Lowell and Child walking. Isn't Elly Temple's letter nice? I wish you would write, asking her if she can't stop here on her way "out." Send me back the letter & I'll send it to Harry. Cambridge looks lovely; but what place doesn't at this time o' year? Love to pickerel William!—and to all. A student has been here for more than an hour, and has "riled me up," so I can't write more.

Thine | W.J.

ALS: MH bMS Am 1092.9 (1758)

[1] See letter to AGJ of 22 September 1890.

To Alice Howe Gibbens James

Cambr. Sept 24 [1890] | 7.10 P.M.

Dearest Alice,

Harry has started school and seems in good condition. The weather is splendid & is so I suppose with you. Your letter & Bill's came duly—Billy writes a better looking letter than Harry, even now. You know there is some of that larger linen paper in one of the table's side drawers. You had better use that for me. The day has been full of interruptions—students mainly—but I have got a good many things cleared for action, altho' the reading rather lags behind. I must go in a few minutes to a faculty committee meeting which cuts it off at that end. The candidates for Graduate Psychology are so far only 4 in number and not very well prepared to take the course— I don't just know what will come of it.[1]—As you see, this letter refuses to run in the line of sentiment—the business spirit with its ferocity & worry holds me as its prey—even as I have been writing the last few lines a student has come in with an insoluble consultation about his courses and he is sitting waiting for me to get done & discuss it on the way to University Hall. So I will stop. *Solid* love nevertheless,

W.J.

I sent you $50.00 in a registered letter this A.M.

ALS: MH bMS Am 1092.9 (1759)

[1] Philosophy 20a: Psychological Seminary, dealing with pleasure and pain. The final enrollment for this course was not established. In 1889–90 the graduate psychology course attracted six students.

To Alice Howe Gibbens James

CAMBRIDGE Sept. 26. 90 | 5.20 P.M.

Beloved—the weather is warm and rainy, and I am writing with one eye on the open window to see the posman, who ought to bring by this delivery the letter which he bro't neither yesterday nor at 3 to day. I have been much preoccupied since I have been at home with my leçon d'ouverture in the Descartes course. The truth is I don't give myself time enough in advance to prepare things, and the reading or rather skimming of too many books during the past week has hardly got me to the point of a composition. But no matter, it will go off somehow, as so many things have done before! After to morrow, I have the text of the author to fall back upon, and then the "sailing" will be comparatively "plain."

We get along well enough domestically. Harry seems healthy and happy, tho the school work has hardly definitely begun. I am calling him in now out of the rain. It would be absurd to have any 3rd person here to take care of him. There is absolutely nothing to do. Ellen washes windows etc. has a male visitor every night—

9.30 Interrupted by harry coming in, by your letter & then by darkness. Went thereupon out for a constitutional, picking up Royce on the way but it rained so hard that we got no farther than the Scientific school whence I returned & sat at his dinner table whilst he told me of his new formulation of teleology & mechanism—very extensive and very fine. A great book will come out of this course which Royce has been giving for so many years.

Met my would be psychologists this A.M.—29 in number.[1] Royce has 48 in his corresponding course and 18 in his Kant to my 6 in Descartes.[2] But I care not at all for that, and the relief of having small numbers is to me great.

Came in at 7 to tea fresh mackerel for the 3rd time to day, and not tired of it yet. Found that Sawin had left my books from Holt. They are good looking vols. on the whole apart from the raw cut edges etc, and I am sorry to say that fingering of them has kept me from settling down to my work for to morrow. So I'll haste to bed now so as to have a good long morning ere my lecture.

It was a boon to get your letter. I began to think that you might be sick, when the 3 o'clock-post failed to bring it. Mary shall be welcome to morrow.

Good night. Heaven bless you! & love to all.

W.J.

ALS: MH bMS Am 1092.9 (1761)

[1] In 1890–91 WJ taught Philosophy 2: Psychology, with twenty-eight students, at 12 noon on Mondays, Wednesdays, and Fridays. The text was the just-published *Principles of Psychology*.

[2] Josiah Royce had forty-four students in Philosophy 3: Cosmology, eighteen in Philosophy 12: The Movement of German Thought from 1770 to 1830.

To Alice Howe Gibbens James

Sunday 4.30 P.M. Sept 28. 90

Beloved Wife,

Your mother and Mary arrived yesterday whilst I was taking my nap. The former will have written to Margaret a full account. It was pleasant to see them, for the loneliness was rather austere. I wish you were all here, but don't come down till work is done. Your letter was *sweet*—and so are you. Having got off my historical introduction to the Descartes course yesterday (badly enough I must confess) I *slep* both afternoon and night, and to day was able to write to Elly Temple and Harry[1] and several other parties. It is always disconsolate work, this beginning of a new college year; and I suppose it will get worse and worse, because as my standard of goodness in philosophic instruction grows, my performances will give me less and less satisfaction. But I think I fully recognize that my moral task hereafter must be the suppression of everything that flows from this sense of my own inefficiency. How delicious does the repose and innocence of country life seem from the midst of it! I am glad you find it delicious too. But this struggle and failure is the higher thing, and we must take the other only as an occasional bath.

Statt der lebendigen Natur
Du Gott den Menschen schuf hinein,

We must put up for a while longer with the Thiergeripp & Todtenbein of philosophy.[2]

Royce seems in great heart as usual. They have had printed his really admirable address at the St. Paul Harvard Club.[3] His frémont article in the Atlantic is very readable—in fact the A. is all readable, and I will send it to you as soon as I get through. I find that the copies of my book which I shall have to give away will cost (with postage) about $450.00. Add to that a couple of hundred for extra proof correcting, and it is evident that we shall never "catch up" on that job either by sales alone. The gifts, however, will ultimately bring in a return in other ways, so we need n't fash ourselves. I enclose a most graceful letter of thanks from Theodora. I hadn't the heart to withhold one from either her or Grace Norton. I am now going out with a copy in each hand, for President Eliot *respectiv* G. H. Palmer. No news of Kitty Prince yet. I may possibly get there on Tuesday.—Harry has plenty of work before him, and I am glad of it, for it may get him into rapid habits. I imagine that his teaching both these summers has been very poor. He has taken all day to do 15

lines of Caesar which he had done a year ago.   I'm glad he is in a
school with harsher incentives and stiffer ideals.

Good bye angel

I think of you morning noon & night.

Kiss old billy goat

Wm James

ALS: MH bMS Am 1092.9 (1762)

[1] For the letter to HJ of 28 September 1890 see *Correspondence*, 2:149–50.

[2] Johann Wolfgang von Goethe, *Faust*, lines 414–16.   WJ quotes the text in *Pragmatism* (1907) (*Pragmatism* [Cambridge: Harvard Univ. Press, 1975], 24).

[3] Royce addressed the Harvard alumni on graduate studies and the three-year undergraduate course at Harvard.   His address was published as a pamphlet, *Professor Josiah Royce before the Harvard Club of Minnesota* (1890).

To Alice Howe Gibbens James

CAMBRIDGE Sept 30. [1890] | 8 P.M.

Beloved!   No time for anything these days so once more I must be
brief.   Mary who had been in town all day come out an hour ago
with your letter which she had got from Mack, and I thank you for
it.   You are particularly sweet in the letter line during these days.   I
will attend to the business with Temple to morrow.   Mary and your
Mother are very loveable, bless 'em.   Harry is quite overburdened
with the length of his lessons at home, but I imagine that he will
settle down into something brisker and briefer.   He has no time to
write to you, poor little fellow.   Mary's voice is now audible from
above, drilling him in something or other.   I gave an interesting lesson in Descartes to day and probably the usual feeling of comfort in
teaching will reach its average in a week or two as I get warmed up.
Surely I never before felt as *remote* from my work as I have been
feeling this year.   I can't get rid of my graduates, and I guess I can
swing 'em.   Royce begins to morrow night to give his Damenphilosophie in Sever Hall.[1]   Santayana has dropped his course in Lotze as
only 3 rather poor undergraduates offered themselves for it.[2]   As his
work thus becomes so light, I can fall back on his services again in
case I should find myself overburdened at the end of the year.   I met
Mrs. Child this afternoon with Frank—when I asked if he had finished his engineering work in Stockbridge they smiled constrainedly
and said it would take too long to explain.   I am sorry, for it evidently
has come to grief.   No other news in any quarter.   I sent the new
Rudyard K. to *Margaret* in order not to seem *hoggish*.   Only hogs send

things to their own wives, as you well know.   By sending to others
we buy ourselves *los*.   Mack brings news of your having a very bad
cold again.   I am excessively sorry.   And how is the infant's.   I paid
the bank to day, am refusing to pay Thayer's bill,[3] am negotiating for
coal, getting floors treated etc etc.

Kiss dear old William and Peggy, & believe me

ever thy | W.J.

ALS: MH bMS Am 1092.9 (1763)

[1] Josiah Royce gave a course of twelve public lectures on the "history and problems
of philosophy" on Wednesday evenings.   The lectures, prepared at the request of
Mary Gray Ward Dorr, were repeated several times to audiences of women, explaining
WJ's reference to them as "Damenphilosophie."   They were published as *The Spirit
of Modern Philosophy* (1892) and dedicated to Mary Dorr.

[2] George Santayana did not give Philosophy 13: Contemporary Systems in
1890–91.

[3] There were several tradesmen named Thayer.   When building the house at 95
Irving St., WJ expressed his displeasure in several letters with the work of the painter
Thayer and his men (see the index to *Correspondence*, vol. 6).   Perhaps the dispute
was still ongoing a year later.

To Alice Howe Gibbens James

CAMBRIDGE Oct. 1 [1890] | 6 P.M.

Dearest Alice,

No letter from you today—an unopened one from Margaret lies
in the hall your Mother & Mary having gone to Boston after bkfst.
and not being yet back.   I will trust that all is well.—With me the
same hurry continues.   The weather is beautiful and warm, and last
night I slept so well that I went to Palmer's lecture at 2 this P.M. to
keep my touch on the course which I am to continue.[1]   I shall have
to do this about once a week.   The bank yielded up its secrets and
we have 55 dollars left over from all outstanding checks.   The unpaid bills at this end are

My blk coat & vest	50.00
Shirts &c.	17.50
Taxes	390
Small bills	5
	462.50
Walcott's bill	50
	512.50
Painting (say)	10.
	522.50

As there will be no money from Syracuse till the 8th of next month, and as that will be a small amount on acc! of taxes we seem to be worse off than ever. Only we need n't be too discouraged, for we *got* behind by spending on the house—I don't know just how much. Still the next few months will be a tight time for us, beyond a doubt. Dec 1st ought to bring me $1000 from the College. No time for a word more. I've so many business notes to write and *must* start for Royce's lecture after tea.[2]

God bless you! I had no time to get to Temples this P.M.

AL: MH bMS Am 1092.9 (1764)

[1] WJ is referring to Philosophy 1: General Introduction to Philosophy, which had an enrollment of about 200 and was taught by Palmer, James, and Santayana. In 1890–91 WJ was responsible for the metaphysics portion. His notes are included in *ML*.

[2] See letter to AGJ of 30 September 1890.

To Mary Whiton Calkins

CAMBRIDGE Oct 3. 90

Dear Miss Calkins

I was about to write to you to day anyhow to express my gladness. My students 4 in number seem of divergent tendencies and I don't know just what will come of the course.[1] Having published my two rather fat tomes, I shan't lecture, but the thing will probably resolve itself into advice and possibly some experimentation. Our evening meetings have been provisionally fixed for Thursdays at 7.15. Will you please come if you can, next Thursday at seven so as to have a little talk in advance, or rather come at ½ past six and take tea.

Sincerely yours | Wm James

ALS: MWelC

[1] According to Harvard Corporation Records, Mary Whiton Calkins was given permission on 1 October 1890 to attend classes taught by James and Royce. The course was Philosophy 20a: Psychological Seminary.

To Alice Howe Gibbens James

CAMBRIDGE Oct 3. 90 | 7. P.M.

My own darling Alice,

Your letters are the brightest element in my days, and the one of this afternoon proved no exception. I'm glad you like the psychology's looks. I think, all but the raw edges, that it is a decidedly hand-some pair of volumes. It is certainly well *printed*. To day has been sultry again. Harry has ended his school with a B mark which means (on Browne's marking) only an average merit but still it is encouraging. I went to Temple's who was affable, and your mother will take all the plants with her. I trust they will be no trouble about getting them in on such short notice. I'm glad your aunt has bo't the dear hill place, though from the point of view of the boom, I should as lief it were some richer and more fashionable new yorker.[1]—I lunched at Grace Norton's with Eliot and his wife and Mrs. Higginson.[2] The latter was very nice. Mrs. Eliot has a de-lightful manner of speech, and is a "sweet" little slip of a thing, alto-gether. Browne's school bill has come in. 100 dollars. What is to become of us I don't know. But you shall see no more temper fits from me (*unless you are foolish yourself*) for I have achieved a moral victory over my low spirits and tendency to complain whilst I have been here these days, that is positive and will help me hereafter. I have actually by steady force of will kept it down and at last got it under for a while, & mean to fight it out on that line for the rest of my life, for I see that that is my particular mission in the world. It is raining and every thing promises well for a good evening of read-ing. Your mother will carry this and other news as well. I would give anything to have you here, but don't hurry down for my sake. It will be all the nicer when it comes, for being delayed. I do hope that the little freight is well, and that all your other little physical anomalies and complications are flourishing not too unkindly to their proprietress.[3] I wish I could nightly administer massage.

Good night, Angel! | W.J.

What you say is true of Royce's article "hideous good humor."[4] R. *is* a sort of a monster and goblin. One's salvation is not to get think-ing of him in that way, or it will grow on one to the exclusion of every other aspect as it has done with Hall. His voice and leisurely wal-lowing along in his own style were very unpleasant to me the other night at his lecture.[5]

Take good care of your dear Mother whom I am seeing off. And tell Margaret that she shall be very welcome for her own sake if she comes down only I think there is no need of it for Harry's sake.

ALS: MH bMS Am 1092.9 (1766)

[1] AGJ's aunt was not identified.

[2] Probably Ida Agassiz Higginson.

[3] Reference is to AGJ's pregnancy.

⁴ Probably the review of Francis Ellingwood Abbot; see letter to AGJ of 3 August 1890.
⁵ See letter to AGJ of 30 September 1890.

To Alice Howe Gibbens James

CAMBRIDGE Oct. 6. 90

Dearest Alice,

Your two letters to day are "too sweet for anything." Illness *does* soften the heart! But what a queer condition for you to be in, and why have you said nothing of it before? I hope it will soon be over, & have done you no harm. I should think you would be tired of having your aunt stay on so long with her worries. As Margaret didn't indicate her choice of seat for Concerts, I have asked for a seat in the upper gallery, that being my favorite place, and the lower gallery seats being probably by this time all taken up, as they are preferred by the sociable people.¹ I suppose, as usual, that I have done wrong. Running about all day and committee all the afternoon. Went to Atkinson after supper. All he meant was a genial hope for the possible day when he may be able to afford a horse. Naturally he can't afford one now.² I have put an advertisement in the Crimson which may unearth a buyer.³ Fletcher's friend can't be induced.⁴ I entirely agree in the sale of Captain, tho' he may bring very little. But we need the cash now more than anything; so send both horses down on Wednesday addressed not to Isburgh but to me (I enclose tags) and have me *telegraphed*.⁵ I can then decide whether to order Isburgh to send for them both or have Brown bro't out here. I trust you got my telegram of this P.M. in time to head of[f] the sending of Brown alone to morrow.

We must now begin seriously to retrench. And if we buy *nothing* for 6 months we shall go a long way towards catching up. It can be done. On[c]e a level start on some fine quarter day,⁶ and we can keep even, I think, on 5,500 a year which we now enjoy. I am willing to sink the gentleman for 6 months and you can't very well play the lady now.

Poor Child has an englishman come to him with an introduction from old Geo. Ashburner—a man whom A. *had never seen*.⁷ Child not only lunches him but considers it his duty to take him a driving through the suburbs of Boston on Wednesday! I have him to tea to morrow night, with Jim Putnam. A long letter from Jim this A.M. about the brain. He says "I am amazed to see how well you have covered the ground in your 1st Chapter."[8] Jastrow's letter will please you. I met Palmer when going to Atkinson's, who burst into the loudest praises of my book of which he had read the 1st quarter. Meanwhile I don't get hold of the students very well with it, but I think I shall before the year ends. Harry has smoothed himself out the last two days & has his old peaceful face on him again. I put him through quite a decent french lesson this P.M. Farlow presented me with a big dish of Mushrooms at the committee meeting which I can have for tea to morrow night.

Love to Billy and the Baby & all.

Ever thy | William.

Horses freight to be paid at this end. Every week now tells on the price at Auction, and they should be at Isburgh's on Thursday— wherefore Wednesday should see them started.

ALS: MH bMS Am 1092.9 (1768)

[1] WJ is probably referring to tickets for the Boston Symphony concerts in Sanders Theatre.

[2] Perhaps Edward Lincoln Atkinson (1865–1902), an 1890 graduate of Harvard, later a clergyman. Atkinson had served as tutor to WJ's children for one summer. One letter is known (1899).

[3] The following appeared in the *Crimson,* 7 October 1890: "For sale—A good saddle horse, sound and gentle. For particulars apply to William James, 95 Irving St."

[4] Fletcher was not identified.

[5] Isburgh & Co., carriage dealers in Boston, held horse auctions every Saturday.

[6] WJ's Harvard salary was paid quarterly.

[7] Some of the Ashburners who were related to Grace and Anne Ashburner lived in Britain. For a possible George Ashburner see *Correspondence,* 4:470. The guest is probably the man referred to as "Elliot the scotchman" in the letter to AGJ of 7 October 1890 (calendared).

[8] Chapter 1 of *Principles of Psychology* deals with the "Scope of Psychology," while chap. 2 is on the "Functions of the Brain."

To William Torrey Harris

CAMBRIDGE Oct 9. '90

Could you, WITHOUT TAKING TROUBLE give me the reference to your article in the J. of Spec. Phil. on the ontological proof of God?[1] My Journals are unbound and I shrink from the search, but if you give me the vol & page I can easily get the right one.

Many thanks for your kind words about my book.

AP: CLSU

Address: D: Wm T. Harris | Commissioner of Education | Washington | D.C.
Postmark: BOSTON MASS OCT 10 1890

[1] William Torrey Harris, "Faith and Knowledge: Kant's Refutation of the Ontological Proof of the Being of God," *Journal of Speculative Philosophy* 15 (October 1881): 404–28.

From Granville Stanley Hall

CLARK UNIVERSITY, | WORCESTER, MASS. Oct. 14 [1890]
My Dear James,

At last I have found an hour to glance at your magnificent book, & must before all congratulate you on what yon Lotze called the highest human felicity—successful delivery at one birth of a legitimate & noble expression of one's knowledge, apercus, & whole personality, a joy only possible to the philosophers.   Now we have you sure & even death cannot rob us of you & every one that reads the book will rejoice that you have lived & put yourself down.   In this country & England, & I hope elsewhere by translation, psychology will take a distinct step on & up.   You ring in your own personality so richly I fancy there will be but very few dull pages, even where you are most metaphysical.

I am going to try & form a little weekly circle here to read it—all too rapidly—200 pages per meeting—& then I *may* write you my further impressions or perhaps we can talk it over.

Hastily & most sincerely yrs | G Stanley Hall.
ALS: MH bMS Am 1092.9 (176)

To Sarah Wyman Whitman

95 Irving St, Oct 15. 1890
My dear Mrs. Whitman,

It does me good to hear from you, and to come in contact with the spirit with which you "chuck" yourself at life.   It is medicinal in a way which it would probably both surprise and please you to know, and helps to make me ashamed of those pusillanimities and self-contempts which are the bane of my temperament and against which I have to carry on my life long struggle.   Enough!   As for you, beat Sargent,[1] play round Chamberlain, extract the goodness and wisdom of Bryce,[2] absorb the autumn colours of the land and sea, mix the crimson and the opal fire in the glass, charm everyone you come in contact with by your humanity and amiability, in short *continue,* and we shall have plenty to talk about at the next (but for that, tedious) dinner at which it may be my blessing to be placed by your side! Also enough!—You will probably erelong be receiving the stalwart Stanley and his accomplished bride. I am reading with great delight his book.[3] How delicious is the fact that you can't cram individuals under cut and dried heads of classification. Stanley is a genus all to himself, and on the whole I like him right well, with his indescribable mixture of the battering ram and the orator, of hardness and sentiment, egotism and justice, domineeringness and democratic feeling, callousness to others' insides, yet kindliness, and all his other odd contradictions. He is probably on the whole an innocent. At any rate it does me a lot of good to read about his heroic adventures.

As for "detail," of which you write, it is the ever mounting sea which is certain to engulph one, soul & body. You have a genius to cope with it—But again enough!—

Naturally I "purr" like your cat at the handsome words you let fall about the Psychology. Go on! But remember that you can do so just as well without reading it: I shan't know the difference. Seriously, your determination to read that fatal book is the one flaw in an otherwise noble nature. I wish that I had never written it.

I hope to get my wife and the rest of the family down from N.H. this week, though it does seem a sin to abandon the feast of light, colour, and purity, for the turbid town.

Goodnight!

Yours faithfully | Wm James

ALS: MH bMS Am 1092.9 (3903)

[1] In her letter of 12 October 1890 (calendared), Sarah Wyman Whitman noted that John Singer Sargent has "been on the shore, painting a portrait a day, which has made me feel as if I were laced to mortal combat."

[2] In her letter of 12 October 1890 (calendared) Sarah Whitman expressed regret that WJ had not called while James Bryce was there and noted that Bryce "will furnish a solvent for the statements of W. Chamberlain, of which we have had many of late." The newspapers of the day do not mention any W. Chamberlain who fits the context. Joseph Chamberlain (1836–1916), English Conservative statesman, toured the United States some months before Bryce and perhaps the 'W' is an error.

[3] Sir Henry Morton Stanley, *In Darkest Africa* (1890). Stanley and his wife were on a lecture tour of the United States.

To Christine Ladd Franklin

CAMBRIDGE [October 16, 1890][1]

Dear Mrs. Franklin,

I thank you for your most appreciative note. My book is too long for any one to read, but if you read anything I wish it might be last Chapter of all.[2] It needed re-writing, but I had no time. I should like to know, however, from you particularly, whether it seems to you that I have given any sort of hitch forward in that Chapter to the old quarrel over the existence of a priori propositions and neccessary truth.

I had read the two reviews you sent me from the Nation, and suspected their authorship.[3] Your reviews are really useful. Did you also write the review of M. Ch. Henry's work in last week's number?[4]

Always sincerely yours | Wm James

ALS: NNC

[1] The dating is approximate, based on WJ's remark that the *Nation* of 9 October 1890 was that of last week.

[2] Chapter 28, "Necessary Truths and the Effects of Experience" in *Principles of Psychology*.

[3] Reviews in the *Nation* are unsigned and authorship sometimes cannot be established. Among possibilities because of their subject matter are reviews of E. E. Constance Jones, *Elements of Logic as a Science of Propositions* (1890), in *Nation* 51 (18 September 1890): 234; and Thomas Preston, *The Theory of Light* (1890), *Nation* 51 (2 October 1890): 273.

[4] Two books by Charles Henry (1859–1926), French physiologist and librarian, are reviewed in the *Nation* 51 (9 October 1890): 290–92, under the title "Psychophysics." The review is not by Christine Ladd Franklin.

From Horace Howard Furness

WALLINGFORD | DELAWARE COUNTY | PENNSYLVANIA 19 October 1890.

Dear James (why the d——l do you hold me out at arms length with your 'Mr'? Ha' we not rin about the braes of 'Ross' and pu'd the 'Berrys' fair?[1] and then to 'Mr' me! Fie!) It doesn't need a Hamlet to tell us that the 'times are out of joint' if such a man as Hodgson fails to find his vantage ground.[2] But the cruel spite of it is that in this particular instance I am not the one who is born to set them right,— nor is the Seybert Commission. Old Seybert (now with God or otherwise) gave us $50,000—to found a Professor's Chair.[3] After paying this Professors salary we were to use any surplus funds in investigating Spiritualism. At six percent we get exactly $3000—every dollar whereof has to go to the Professor. 'A double million magnifying gas microscope of hextra power' to quote Sam Weller,[4] cannot disclose to us any surplus funds. To investigate Spiritualism was, as we lawyers would term it, a 'condition consequent' in our acceptance of the gift, and no less did noblesse oblige likewise—Hence our investigation. Hence our Report.[5] Although the funds for both were taken fm the Seybert legacy—every dollar was returned to it. So that it is now intact, and the Professorship, which is absolutely obligatory, continues. Excuse me for boring you with all this, my dear, but I want you to see how hopelessly we stand, as far as any help for that superexcellent Hodgson is concerned. Heigho! I'm awfully sorry. I'd so gladly help if I could. Why, oh why wasn't I born rich instead of handsome!

The spirits are to blame for the whole of it. If they'd only shown me the smallest white of their eyes I'd have followed like a sleuth hound (whatever frightful variety of the canine tribe that may be) to the day of my death. But Mrs Piper broke my heart—I think I've never had a seeance since. She fell into line with all the rest. Ask a medium a question containing a probability and an improbability and just as sure as the Devil reigns in this world, she'll take the improbability. E'en so did la belle Piper. Her French Dr. said I was fond of books[6] 'Ay, what kind of books—very large ones or commonsized?' 'Very large ones' was the answer. 'Are they printed books or are they Account books, ruled for £, s, d?['] I asked 'Ruled for £, s, d.' was the instantaneous & confident reply fm M. le Docteur; and so it went on till in the end I figured as the owner of enormous cotton mills in England, the occupant of a noble mansion, in the midst of a noble park, with wife and children gambolling on the lawn! And her trance was feigned! I carried her some gay nasturtiums, and as they stood by her side in a little glass I called her attention to them in the most natural way & she forgot herself, turned her head & opened her eyes & looked at them—I should have had a lovely time with her, if there hadn't been a tinge of sadness which always creeps over you when you come face to face with deceit.

It now flashes over me that I have told you all this before. I cry you pardon, tis the forgetfulness of age.

Only one word more & I am done. I feel quite convinced that Hypnotism is destined, in classic phrase, to knock the bottom out of Spiritualism. Dieseits we may know, jenseits never.

Thanks for remembring my boys. The elder, Horace jr, became enamoured of Astronomy—studied it prodigiously hard, at the University here, sent a contribution to an Astronomical Journal of two printed pages of ghastly fractions and exuberant square roots, built a charming Observatory near the house here, with a fine five inch refractor, and then caught sight of an earthly star, fell desperately in love with it and married it.[7]   She is a charming girl in every way and they are both in perpetual apparition at the zenith of happiness & know no nadir.

The second, Willie, is studying most bravely at the Medical school here & bids fair to graduate next year among the very best in his class.[8] They have all been spending the summer in Europe.

And now tell me about your little girl in whom I shall always take an interest—sometime or other I'll tell you why—I can't now.

Like the man who said he had such trouble in settling his brother's estate that he was almost sorry his brother died, you'll be almost sorry you ever wrote to me, if it entails in you such a screed as this—It shan't be repeated—only remember that whether I am garrulous or silent I am

Yours faithfully | Horace Howard Furness

ALS: MH bMS Am 1092 (283)

[1] Hannah V. Ross and the sisters Helen C. and Gertrude Berry were mediums investigated by WJ and Furness. See *EPR*, 393, 402–5, and the index to *Correspondence*, vol. 6.

[2] In a letter now lost, WJ probably asked for money to pay the salary of Richard Hodgson as secretary of the American Branch of the Society for Psychical Research.

[3] The endowment was to support a professor of philosophy at the University of Pennsylvania.

[4] Sam Weller is Samuel Pickwick's valet in Charles Dickens, *Pickwick Papers*.

[5] *Preliminary Report of the Commission Appointed by the University of Pennsylvania to Investigate Modern Spiritualism* (1887).

[6] Dr. Phinuit.

[7] Horace Howard Furness, Jr. (1865–1930), author, editor of Shakespeare, married Louise Brooks Winsor on 3 May 1890. He was an 1888 graduate of Harvard.

[8] William Henry Furness III (1866–1920), American physician and writer, graduated from Harvard in 1888. WJ had used him in some hypnotic demonstrations; see *Correspondence*, 6:121.

To Simon Newcomb

CAMBRIDGE Oct 22. 90

Dear Prof. Newcomb

Thanks for your note. It is flattering to have anyone *react* on one's book, especially when the reacter is a man like you. I have never seen your articles in the Independent, nor can I get them here.[1] But I agree with you that a lot of the discussion that goes on is logomachy from not defining terms. I think that "materialism" is very well kept with the vague meaning (said to be ascribed to it by Comte) of "the explanation of the higher by the lower."[2] But of course one may define it as one will; and I, so far as I can remember, have abstained from using the term at all in my book. I think the word "freedom" is deplorable from its ambiguity. Once you speak of "indeterminism" you have a clear objective issue before you, about which it seems to me that there is the most serious issue that philosophy contains, no less than that between monism and pluralism überhaupt. I stand out for pluralism against the whole line. As for mental states that are not states of consciousness, I don't know what can be meant by them. Brain-states I know, and states of consciousness I know, but something that is more than a brain-state yet less than a state of consciousness I know nothing about, nor do I see the use of discussing its existence. I am sick of the subject of psychology for a while and shall lie fallow for a year.

Yours always truly | Wm James

ALS: DLC

[1] Simon Newcomb (1835–1909), American astronomer, "Modern Scientific Materialism," *Independent* 32 (9 December 1880): 1; (23 December 1880): 1; (30 December 1880): 3; 33 (13 January 1881): 3; (27 January 1881): 1–2. Correspondence is known from 1886 and 1890.

[2] French philosopher Auguste Comte (1798–1857), originator of positivism, defines materialism in this sense in his *Discours sur l'ensemble du positivisme* (1848). According to Comte, materialism "degrades the higher subjects of thought by confounding them with the lower" (*A General View of Positivism*, trans. J. H. Bridges [New York: Speller, 1957], 54). For WJ's use of this definition see *Pragmatism* (Cambridge: Harvard Univ. Press, 1975), 49.

From Oliver Wendell Holmes, Jr.

Court House Boston | November 10. 1890

Dear Bill

I have read your book—every word of it—with delight and admiration.   I think it a noble work and dont doubt that it will give you a reputation of the kind that our generation most values, here and in Europe.   Some of the chapters are schemes of all possible *belles lettres* in scientific form ∴ yet preserving the esprit and richness of empirical writing.

I highly appreciate your distrust of neat dilemmas as exhausting truth—although in one instance—your dealing with free will—you dont carry me—even by the suggestion that the baby is a very little one.[1]   I hope we should agree that one's opinion on that question can not rationally affect conduct a whit—that as I once wrote in an article for ingenuous youth "a part of man's destiny and the means by which the inevitable comes to pass is striving"—

I might pick out a hundred passages to praise—but will only refer to II. 453,[2] because it falls in with what I have so often thought as to materialism in general—The phenomenon to be explained is *given*. Your explanation may enlarge your notion of matter by showing that when tied in a certain knot it can wag its tail or die at the stake (which Hegel never can persuade me that a syllogism can do—)   But it doesnt degrade man except on the assumption that matter is something you know all about beforehand as inferior and incapable of all the fine things which you forget for the moment to be the *datum*. Apropos of II. 406, 407[3]—a lady told me some years ago that her child which in some way I forget had never had any preliminary practice at all, up and walked when the time came—I hope to be at the Club on Friday if my health remains better than it has been[4]—

Meantime accept my congratulations—

Yours ever | O W Holmes Jr.

ALS: MH bMS Am 1092 (392)

[1] In Frederick Marryat, *Mr Midshipman Easy* (1836), a woman defends her character in spite of having had an illegitimate child by saying that the baby was a very little one. WJ uses the episode in "The Sentiment of Rationality" (1879); see *EPh*, 37.

[2] *PP*, 1068–69.

[3] *PP*, 1025–26.   WJ suggests that when their nerve centers are sufficiently developed, infants who have not been allowed to get on their feet and practice walking will walk as well as they would have had they been allowed to learn walking in the usual way.

⁴The history of what was referred to simply as the Club is given in a letter by Thomas Sergeant Perry to WJ's son, Henry James, 11 July 1920 (bMS Am 1092.10 [134]). The Club, which usually met on Fridays, was formed in 1870 and included among the original members WJ, HJ, and Oliver Wendell Holmes, Jr.

To Silas Weir Mitchell

95 Irving St, Cambridge | Nov 12 [1890]

My poor dear Mitchell,

What a fantastically conscientious fellow you are. *Can* you suppose that I meant to inflict the *reading* of those awful tomes upon you? Save us from our friends, indeed, were that the case. I only sent 'em as a tribute, and "book of reference," with perhaps the hope of an hour of reading "with the thumb" on some day when you should be confined to the house after a spree!

Can Philadelphians take life so earnestly?

Always yours | Wm James

ALS: PPC

From George Croom Robertson

31, KENSINGTON PARK GARDENS. | NOTTING HILL, LONDON, W.
12/11/90.

This is only to say that, nearly a month after receiving your welcome announcement, I am still without copy of the *mag. opus*. I read of it as about everywhere—America, France, &c. &c.—save here. I suppose the hitch lies, for me in London, with the desired English publisher. Anyway, I think it as well to let you know that at this late date I am still out in the cold of unenlightenment.—Something of Baldwin's the other day in *Science* tells me—what I hardly needed to be told—that you ride hard the 'Kinaesthetic' nag.¹ I had a word about that quadruped in last *Mind* apropos of Münsterberg.² Deign to cast eye thereon.—I hope all goes well with you (& yours). Am trying unassisted the whole of my Coll. work, again, this winter: thus far *es geht*, at least *so ziemlich*.—What are your prospects now hitherward? The print load being shuffled off,—nay, rather, gracefully deposited and delivered, to mankind—are you not to be free next year to cross the water at leisure?

G C Robertson

APS: MH bMS Am 1092.9 (525)
Address: Professor W.ᵐ James | 18 Garden Street | Cambridge | Mass. | U.S.A.
Postmarks: PADDINGTON. W NO 12 90   NEW YORK NOV 19 90   BOSTON NOV 2<0> 90

¹James Mark Baldwin, "Origin of Right or Left Handedness," *Science* 16 (31 October 1890): 247–48.   While claiming that there are feelings of innervation, Baldwin refers to WJ and his "kinaesthetic memories . . . that sword with which he decapitates so many points of evidence in his 'Principles of Psychology.'"   For WJ's reply see letter to Baldwin of 7 December 1890.

²George Croom Robertson, "Münsterberg on 'Muscular Sense' and 'Time-Sense,'" *Mind* 15 (October 1890): 524–36.

From Thomas Davidson

New York: Nov.ʳ 19ᵗʰ 1890

My dear William,

I went home and read your last chapter, and am both delighted & instructed by it.¹   What a sense of humor there is in it!   But that is the least important thing about it.   It is most interesting to see you driven, so to speak, back to the position of Aristotle: that our knowledge, in so far as it is scientific (τέχνη and ἐπιστήμη), is a subordination of the sensibly given (αἰσθητά) to principles whose *locus* (τόπος) is the mind itself.   You will find all your doctrine of "Kind's Kind" (εἶδος εἰδῶν) at full length in the old Greek.   That doctrine led me years ago to my definition of Philosophy, as "an attempt to reduce all concepts to concepts that, as forming the very conditions of intelligence, are self-evident."   I have often said that all systems of mythology & theology are only so many attempts to find in the world an expression for an "innate" idea, the idea of God.   We do not *find* God in the world: we insist upon using the world to give us the consciousness, or, more properly perhaps, the "phantasm" of God, so that we may grasp Him in His reality.   Reality is but ideality reflected back from the phenomenal world.

Your book confirms me in my conviction that what we need more than anything else at the present day is a comprehensive view of those native contents or components of the mind, of which you have given three such striking examples.   They would form *quae in mundo quærunda sunt*.   This would give us a true Metaphysics, as well as a true *Physics*.

You, who read Plotinus in your youth, must know that he made a vigorous attempt in this direction.   Here is a passage: "The soul, being, in its nature, that which is, and being of the higher essence in the things that are, when it finds anything akin to it, or any trace of kinship, it rejoices & is deeply moved, *referring that thing to itself, and remembering itself & the things of itself.*"[2] Here 'remembering' means 'becoming conscious of.' Of course, we could do much better now than he was able to do, burdened, as he was, with the authority of Plato.

But, after all, Aristotle remains the "maestro di color che sanno,"[3] & the longer I live, the more I am convinced that the root of the matter was in him. It would interest you to read what Martineau says of him in the introduction to his "Types of Ethical Theory."[4] I see you do not quote Trendelenburg, the most considerable Aristotelian of modern times. And yet you would have found much in him to your purpose & liking. In a chapter headed *Die Gegenstände* à priori *aus der Bewegung und Die Materie,* he writes (*ad init.*)

"Im Vorhergehendem ist dem Geiste eine *ursprüngliche zeugende Thätigkeit* zugesprochen worden, das Gegenbild der äußern Bewegung, die Vermittlerin aller Auffassung. Da sie eine geistige Thätigkeit ist, so liegt die Weise wie sie wirkt, und das Gebilde das sie hervorbringt, d. h. *die mathematische Welt* der Einsicht offen." &c &c (Logische Untersuchungen, B. I. 236).[5]

You see I want to turn your powerful mind in the direction of Aristotle. With your preparation in the school of psychology, you are now in a position to do work that perhaps no other living man can do. I wish I could see more of you!

Don't forget my message to Hodgson. With love to all that ever bore the name of Gibbens, I am

Yours ever, | Thomas Davidson

ALS: MH bMS Am 1092.9 (123)

[1] See letter of 16 October 1890.

[2] The quotation is not from the *Enneads* of Plotinus and may be from some other Neoplatonic author.

[3] Dante, *Divine Comedy, Inferno,* canto 4, line 131.

[4] James Martineau (1805–1900), English Unitarian clergyman, *Types of Ethical Theory* (1885) (WJ 553.78.2).

[5] Adolf Trendelenburg (1844–1941), German philosopher, *Logische Untersuchungen,* 2d ed., 2 vols. (Leipzig: Hirzel, 1862), 1:233. The quoted text is not on p. 236 in the first edition (1840).

To Alice James

Nov 26. 90 | (Wednesday 6. P.M)

Dearest Sister

Jae for some unaccountable reason never telegraphed me on monday as I charged him to, what the result of the trial was, so I feared another postponement.[1]   To day however Lilla writes, incidentally to another matter that "the surrogate, without a single witness on our side having been presented decided 'Mr. Wyckoff's competency to make a will has been fully established,' and dismissed the application."

Lilla adds: "I cant help thinking Mrs W. will not resign a rod of her real estate without another struggle, yet if our lawyers are right it will only be a throwing away of her money."[2]

I congratulate you most heartily.   The division of the money will take place at the latest before June, Jae told me.   The farther move, on the real estate namely, will probably consume additional time.   I would n't speculate much upon that, but take it at[3] a gift from the sky when it comes.   The three thousand dollars which I received are most opportune, enabling me to pay off part of my house debt at a particularly needful time.

I have just been entertaining at lunch Hamilton Aidé,[4] & Jephson,[5] with seven Cambridgers, including T. S. Perry, Lowell, Agassiz, Chas Norton, Jas. B. Thayer, Denman Ross & Chaplin.   It was jolly enough—but I can't afford such things anyhow, and they give too much trouble to Alice & the 2 wenches.—Jephson is an uncommonly simple straightforward fellow.—But on the whole, *damn* the british tourist, is all that I can say.

You ought to order a bottle of champagne now, and drink it to the salvation of Henry Wyckoff's soul.   He went through *purgatory* ere he died.

If I were you, I would seriously try *hypnotism* which might do you good.   D̠r̲ Lloyd Tuckey has written what seems to me a very creditable book on its therapeutic effects.[6]   Myers if asked could give Harry his London address.

Bless you,   W.J.

ALS: MH bMS Am 1092.9 (1152)

[1] Jae: James William Walsh, Jr.

[2] Sarah J. Wyckoff, a businesswoman, wife of Albert Wyckoff (1840–ca. 1899), a nephew of Henry Albert Wyckoff.   For information about Sarah Wyckoff see *Correspondence*, 2:444.

[3] A slip for 'as'.

[4] Hamilton Aïdé (1826–1906), British novelist and poet.

[5] Probably Arthur Jermy Mountenay Jephson (1858–1908), British explorer who accompanied Stanley on some of his African explorations. Stanley was on a lecture tour of the United States, with Jephson as a member of his retinue.

[6] Charles Lloyd Tuckey, *Psycho-Therapeutics* (1890).

To Carl Stumpf

CAMBRIDGE Dec 1. 90

My dear Stumpf

It gave me the greatest pleasure to get your letter to day. There is a solidity of heartiness, so to call it, in the tone of your letters, of which you of course are not aware yourself as a peculiar quality, but which *is* altogether personal, and which makes me especially rejoice in the possession of you as a friend and correspondent. It is partly *deutsch;* but not all the *Deutschen* have it; so I make the most of it. Besides, so far off, you are the ideal *homo* or *vir,* and when you speak kindly, as now of my book, it is as if I were being approved by "the Absolute!"—an Absolute moreover who can write a Tonpsychologie![1] The second volume is still on my shelf waiting to have its leaves cut. It is the great trial of my life to have to move so slowly from point to point, and postpone what I most want to do till the things I least want are finished. I know that I shall learn endless things from that volume, but as I am giving this year a course in metaphysics[2] and one in the History of Phil. neither of which I have ever given before, all psychological reading is at a standstill.[3]—The publication of my two volumes has cleared my mind for *receiving;* and I feel now as if I might *learn* something about psychology, had I plenty of time to give to it. But life seems sometimes to consist of pure interruptions; and day after day often passes here without my finding an hour in which to *read.* *Sonst,* things go well, wife, children & self all in good health etc, etc.—I am sending a card of introduction to you to an old pupil of mine, D[r] F. Coggeshall, who has lately gone to Munich with his newly married bride,[4] to continue his medical studies. They will be perfect strangers in Munich, and I thought that an acquaintance with your wife might possibly make a great difference to Mrs. C. C. himself is a heroic fellow, widely cultivated, excessively conscientious, and who has had a hard struggle with poverty all his life. He lacks social ease somewhat, but is a good fellow through &

through, and any kindness which you & Frau Stumpf may show them will be appreciated by me.

Best wishes for Christmas & the New Year!

Yours ever,   Wm James

ALS: MH bMS Am 1092.9 (3784)

[1] Carl Stumpf, *Tonpsychologie*, 2 vols. (1883–90) (WJ 783.89).

[2] WJ is referring to his segment of Philosophy 1; see letter to AGJ of 1 October 1890.

[3] WJ is referring to Philosophy 10: Descartes, Spinoza, Leibnitz.

[4] Frederic Coggeshall married Louisa Canfield on 15 October 1890.

To James Mark Baldwin

CAMBRIDGE Dec 7. '90

Dear Mr. Baldwin,

I am afraid that the readers of Science may not be as deeply interested in our debate as we are, so I send you my remarks on your last letter in the shape of a private communication.[1]   And to save trouble I will paste your text in, and say what I have to say in the shape of notes thereupon.[2]   I confess that I find a certain difficulty in being sure that I catch your reasoning.   To me the alternative is this: Are certain sorts of stimuli (objects at a certain distance felt by the eye) natively correlated with paths leading to the right hand? or are the paths *natively* indifferent, and is the choice of the right hand for response to such stimuli due to reminiscences (explicit or implicit) of former experiences in which the right hand showed itself most fit to react upon them?   If the latter view be adopted then another alternative comes up, thus: Are the reminiscences those of "afferent" or of "efferent" experiences?

The fact that all movement was inhibited when the stimulus was too far away, looks as if reminiscence had something to do with it, for I *suppose* (and you will know whether I am right) that *originally* the child would have been excited to grasping movements of both hands, by objects presented beyond reaching distance.   He has now learned the uselessness of this, we will suppose; and similarly must have learned for a certain range of distance the superior usefulness of the right hand, we will say.   In your words,

> The new element must represent the influence of former ex
> perience.   I see no way to avoid this alternative.   This is what
> I meant by "memories," merely some kind of a conscious modi-

fication which alters future re-actions. A purely physical modification would not suffice, for it would have its full force also in cases which involved no effort. Now, we may hold that such "memories" are exclusively of afferent nerve processes, or that they involve also a conscious modification due to efferent nerve processes. If the former, we may attribute them to the greater "promptitude, security, and ease" of right-hand movements, as Professor James suggests, or to former movements of the eyes, involved in the visual estimation of distance (which I am astonished he does not suggest.)* The first alternative, which Professor James asks my ground for rejecting, is inadequate for the following reasons. If such memories of afferent processes be of movements with effort, they are already right-handed, and the question is only thrown farther back;†

*Of course the present eye adaptation must be the cue which calls up the memories of the arm movement whichever they be.

†I don't see the force of this objection. The right hand we must admit to be natively the cleverer. Grant then both hands set in movement by a stimulus so far away that it is reached with difficulty, and it will inevitably happen that in continuing the movements the child will feel its right hand *succeeding* oftener than the left. This "success" is unquestionably realized in various pleasant afferent feelings and the absence of unpleasant ones (sympathetic contractions elsewhere etc whether efferent feelings be present or no). It seems to me that *some* sort of right-handed achievement "already," is an essential element in every *possible* explanation by reminiscences, of the facts observed.—You continue:

but, if they be of effortless movements, then their motor influence would be perfectly indifferent, as I said in my former letter.

For effortless read "easy," and I suppose it can be admitted that, either hand reaching the goal promptly, no discriminative memories of the right hand's superiority would be stored up, and both hands might continue to be used.

My experiments show this. If there had been differences in "promptitude," etc., the child certainly would have shown preference for the right hand in effortless* movements during the latter six months of the first year. But, on the contrary, it was only

when making violent effort that there was any preference at all.†
Even after she developed such preference in cases of effort, the
use of her hands when no effort was required continued to be
quite indifferent. Does not this indicate that the traces left by
former afferent processes of the same sense are not sufficient?‡

*[WJ underlined 'effortless' in Baldwin's text] not so for the reason
just given
†Because only then had the right hand's native superiority manifested itself in former trials.
‡[WJ underlined 'not sufficient' in Baldwin's text] not sufficient,
merely, for choice of right hand where either hand had previously
done the work with success.

Moreover, in the absence of all feeling of the efferent current
what could sensations of "promptitude," etc., be but the consciousness of better adaptation and co-ordination of movements?
But at this stage of life all the child's movements are so ataxic*
that there seems to be no practical difference between the two
hands in regard to the lack of the tactile delicacy in which pathological cases show motor ataxy to consist.

*[WJ underlined 'ataxic' in Baldwin's text] My view is just this, that
the right hand is natively less "ataxic" than the left, and, having
proved itself so, is thereafter chosen more than the left. The ataxia
is originally not a fact of sensibility but of motor coordination. The
experiences of "failure," however, of retarded reaching the goal and
grasping, and continued contractions, which lead to the left hand
being inhibited when the eyes see a object 14 inches off, are sensible experiences.

If we seek for the needed "memory" among the sensations of
eye-movements in the case where the stimulus is weaker (more
distant), it is possible that we may find an afferent element which
brings up the intensity of the hand-memories to the necessary
pitch. There may be a connection between the centres for feelings of eye-movement and feelings of hand movement, so that
their united "dynamogenic" influence is the same as the high
intensity of the color stimulus.

It would not have occurred to me that the stimulus needed to be *more intense*, for the right hand to be chosen. It happened, indeed, to be so in your observations with the colours, and I noticed it as a remarkable fact. A certain sort of stimulus produces a certain sort of reaction, there is a specialized native adaptation of movement to visual sensation—that was what the observations on colour seemed to me to show. By analogy there *might* be a similar native specialized adaptation of right-handed movement to a certain range of accomodation and convergence, whether more or less intense. It actually is *less* intense in the case we deal with.

But, while freely admitting such a possibility, it only pushes the question farther back again; for how do we know that these eye-memories do not involve consciousness of the efferent process which innervates the eye-centre? And, besides this, there is another element in the hypothesis that afferent elements from other senses may furnish the "kinaesthetic co-efficient" for a given voluntary movement; namely, that such activities of the other senses invoked took place along with movements of the attention, which might, and probably do, contribute an efferent element to consciousness. This possibility I have never seen anywhere recognized.*

But in this case my experiments show conclusively that eye-movement memories did not re-enforce the intensity of the arm-movement memories; for, when the distance was more than fourteen inches, the re-action was inhibited altogether. The distance of the stimulus as apprehended by the eye, therefore, instead of giving the increased motor excitement which we require, rather diminishes it, and makes the need for some other explanation all the more imperative.

It appears, therefore, that the element needed in consciousness to explain the facts cited in my former letter is some kind of a difference in sensation corresponding to the outgo of the nervous current into the right arm, be it as vague, subconscious, and unworthy of the name of "memory" as you please; that is, I still think that my experiments support the traditional doctrine. On any other theory, right-handedness would have been developed independently of effort.†

J. MARK BALDWIN

Toronto, Ont., Nov. 18.

*[*WJ* bracketed Baldwin's paragraph] All this seems over subtle and *I* don't need it. You have been misled my[3] my quoting the bright colours into supposing that I required an *intenser* stimulus everywhere, for the discharge of the right hand.

†[*WJ* underlined 'independently of effort' *in Baldwin's text*] Not so, as I think you must admit, if by effort be meant retardation & difficulty of execution owing to an original ataxy which is least in the right arm!

Admitting the experience hypothesis, (which I adopt from you now, since I have made no observations and your sense of what is likely in this regard seems to me to have great weight) the way I represent the matter to myself is thus: The child originally responds to *all* optical excitements which strike his attention by bounding up & down and moving both arms. Erelong the movement becomes one of grasping with both. Some graspings prove easy and the original bilateral mechanism continues for a while associated with these. Others are protracted, and the superior native efficiency of the right hand in reaching the goal here, acts so as to inhibit the left hand altogether when the stimulus suggests a case of this kind.—Others again never succeed, the object being beyond range altogether, & all movements are inhibited for these at last.

Although I have made every possible concession to the experience theory, as adopted by you, I must say that the notion of a specialized native-impulsiveness for the right hand when certain distances appeal to the eye lingers in my mind as that of a natural possibility. Surely the similar native impulsiveness when bright colours appeal is a suggestive analogy. In neither case however, should it ever have occurred to me to resort to *efferent* memories. They seem quite superfluous; nor do I understand why *you* should so cling to things confessedly impossible to isolate by introspection, devoid of significance in speculative regard, and apparently only tending uselessly to increase, if they should exist, the complication of our machinery.

I am taking a terrible vengeance on you by sending you this long letter. But you began! I will promise to make no reply if you write [*end of letter missing*]

AL incomplete: Bodleian Library, University of Oxford

[1] For Baldwin's first letter to *Science* see letter from Robertson of 12 November 1890. WJ replied in "Origin of Right-Handedness," *Science* 16 (14 November 1890): 275 (reprinted in *ECR*). Baldwin responded in *Science* 16 (28 November 1890): 302–3. The quotations from Baldwin are from the second letter.

[2] Baldwin's printed text is published in extracts below. WJ's annotations are printed as footnotes to the extracts; the footnote symbols were supplied by the editors.
[3] A slip for 'by'.

To Sarah Wyman Whitman

95 Irving St, | Cambridge, Dec 7. 90

My dear Mrs. Whitman,

I have been at my desk since 9 o'clock this morning—'tis now 5.30—trying (with a perceptible effect) to reduce the arrears of my business correspondence for the week. And shall I not also correspond with you?—relatively to the window business, and tell you more clearly than I did not to come out without notification beforehand, so that I may be sure to be at home?

Was that Edward Silsbee, *quantum mutatus?*[1] It didn't dawn upon me till after I had left the house. Poor old fellow! I wish I had known it in time, I should have said something to him. He too seemed to have forgotten me—naturally enough, for we have seldom met, but he always made on me a great impression.

I must send you for a Christmas present the rummiest little book by one Furneaux Jordan on "Character" etc.[2] He divides the human race into "shrews" and "non-shrews." If a woman's husband jumps on her so that she has to be carried to the hospital, *she* is a shrew (= "active unimpassioned temperament") he a non-shrew (= "reflective(!) impassioned temperament") She has scanty hair & eyebrows, a clear skin, and a round back, inclining to "fleshiness;" he has plenty of hair, a flat back, pigment on his skin, and is probably lean, etc etc. It is very entertaining reading though it does n't *fit*, so far as my observation goes. I, *e.g*, am a shrew with a straight back. What are you? His classification is incomplete and breaks down ere it comes to my circle of acquaintance. In general it must be said that all these classifications are provisional. Haven't I seen *my* ideal of perfection in feminine character gradually develope (as I became better acquainted with the truth) into the ability to transact a maximum amount and variety of *business* in the smallest possible number of years, with the past forgotten, and the attention always partially turned towards the "next" item? Is this the classic ideal? No, but it is and always will be that of yours most faithfully

Wm James

ALS: MH bMS Am 1092.9 (3904)

[1] Edward A. Silsbee (1826–1900), American sea captain and manuscript collector, and most likely the same person as an E. A. Silsbee from Salem, Mass., who in about 1860 corresponded with Ralph Waldo Emerson concerning Herbert Spencer. WJ may have met Silsbee on some of his visits to Concord.

[2] Furneaux Jordan (also John Furneaux Jordan), surgeon and writer. On p. 1 of his book *Character as Seen in Body and Parentage* (London: Kegan Paul, Trench, Trübner, 1890), Jordan states that while working in hospitals he noticed that injuries suffered by women at the hands of their husbands differed from those that women received in accidents. Jordan argued that some men, upon marrying women of certain "anatomical combination," found "life arid and burdensome" and eventually turned to "violence and folly" (p. 4).

To Thomas Davidson

CAMBRIDGE Dec 13. 90

My dear Davidson

I have just seen Hodgson who gives an account of what seems to have been a very enthusiastic meeting, and shows me your proposed circular telling me with some disappointment, which I confess that I share, that you seem rather to be forming an independent N.Y. organization.[1]

I beg you to do nothing conclusive until you have carefully weighed the following reasons. They seem to me conclusive against doing anything which would weaken rather than strengthen the already too weak organization which we possess:

1.) The only society worth lifting one's finger for must be one for *investigation of cases*, not for theoretic discussion, *for facts*, and not yet for *philosophy*. The *name* "*S.P.R*" has been sadly discredited by certain literary & spiritualistic societies in Western Cities.

2) Investigation demands someone who will give his whole time to what is mainly drudgery. Hodgson now gives all his time & employs a clerk in addition. The correspondence is enormous, and its fruits have hardly begun to be published as yet.

2) Suppose that in N.Y. you could find a worker of the sort required, it would be sheer waste of his power to work *independently* of Hodgson—they ought to share their materials and divide their labor. The pecuniary saving of their working in common would be very great. The great use of the english Society in my eyes is that it is a central bureau in charge of proved experts, towards which all threads converge, thereby providing for a maximum of facts behind conclusions.

3) A *separate society* in N.Y would thus be extravagant, relatively impotent, and carry no prestige. It would be a sort of fire in the rear, competing with us for evidence, & interfering in other ways, and cheapening the name of all Soc? for P.R., which name heaven knows is not now exalted.

4) But you don't mean a separate society of course. You mean I suppose, a Branch coordinate with what you suppose to be the Boston branch, and founded as a concession to local pride, with a view to rousing more N.Y. enthusiasm.

5) To this, I say, "there *is* now no Boston branch." When the *American* S.P.R. was founded, local branches were formed in N.Y., Philadelphia & Boston—(the Society was organized in *Philadelphia,* as a matter of History). The Philadelphia Branch died first, then the N.Y.B., and a year ago the Boston B. died, leaving its members all over the country to join the London S.P.R. if they would. The London Council simply continued to keep their *Office* in Boston. I am sure they would be too happy to move it and Hodgson to N.Y., if some one else there proved a genuine investigator, or if money were forthcoming. Even if H. were to keep headquarters in Boston, he could spend ½ his time in N.Y. if the local interest, as testified by pecuniary aid, proved adequate. You must remember that *every* considerable donation which we have had since the beginning has been from Boston, with one exception from Philadelphia.

6) If the N. Yorkers are willing to give money there is one way, and only one, in which *at present* it seems to me to be likely to do much scientific good, and that [is] in paying for experimental or observational work to be done by Hodgson on people at a distance, covering, *inter alia,* his travelling expenses.

7) It seems to me quite absurd, when our existing organization just as it stands, is crippled for this (its *most* important) work, for lack of funds, to rally a crowd of people to the cause, and then divert their funds into any other channel.

I trust therefore, in conclusion, that your committee will not think of recommending anything but an enlargement of the american Branch as it stands, and a disbursement of donation thereto. You can then secondarily organize meetings in N.Y., look out for topics of investigation, and eventually, if you can, get the office thither, as it ought to be at the focus of interest, which *at present* decidedly is Boston. But don't for Heavens sake, get people to subscribe the precious dollars, and then go to work to reduplicate machinery which already costs far too much, I mean that of printing, clerk-hire postage, circulars and the like.   You couldn't inflict a worse blow on the cause.   And I must say I think it is *due* to the English S.P.R., which has been constantly growing in reputation and has stuck to its mission through good and bad report, until it is just about weathering the dangers of infancy, to divert "psychic" interest away from its channel, which is so infinitely more *effective* than any newly improvised one can possibly be.

Please read this letter to your committee.   I cannot but think that what I say ought to carry a good deal of weight.   I care nothing myself for either Boston or New York, but I do care to make Psychic Research *effective*.   For that, there is but one way, strengthen the existing organization!   By work & contributions to its Proceedings, if possible; if not thus, then by money to extend its field of experimental work in America.

Too busy for more! beloved Tommaso!

Yours ever   W.J.

ALS: MH bMS Am 1092.9 (866)

Address: Professor T. Davidson | 239 West 105th Street | New York | N.Y.

Postmark: BOSTON. MASS DEC 13 1890

[1] Calendared under the date of December 1890 are an undated note from WJ to Davidson and an undated draft in Davidson's hand of a circular.   According to the latter, a meeting was held on 8 December at 46 East 21st St., New York City, to consider the establishment in New York of a "sub-branch" of the Society for Psychical Research.   At this meeting a committee was appointed to negotiate with Richard Hodgson as secretary of the American Branch of the Society for Psychical Research and to report back at a meeting on 22 December.   In his note WJ states that he has asked Hodgson not to approve the circular because it seems to involve the establishment of a separate organization.   A report of the 8 December meeting appears in the *New York Times* of 9 December 1890.   Among those present at the meeting, which took place at the home of Dr. M. L. Holbrook, were Richard Hodgson, Thomas Davidson, Nicholas Murray Butler, and James Hervey Hyslop.   Nothing came of the 1890 meetings, but in about 1907 the society was reorganized and moved to New York under Hyslop's leadership.

From William Leonard Worcester

Little Rock Dec. 24, 1890

Professor William James:

Dear Sir:

I return your article on dizziness, in which I have been much interested.[1]   I once thought of writing something on the subject myself, but desisted when I found that you had covered all my ground.   I am greatly obliged to you for it.

At the risk of being tedious, I will try to make my meaning clearer than I seem to have succeeded in doing in my previous letter.   In what I said on the subject of sensation, I had special reference to what you say on pp. 172–3 of Vol I., and p. 231 of the same volume.[2] If I hear the sound V, for instance, and am able to imitate it accurately, that seems to me proof that I have had the sensations of all its elements, as I could not reproduce what I had not heard.   When I hear the sound and think "that is V," or "that is F + voice," the *mental states* are different, no doubt, but I see no reason, in what you say, to think that the difference is in the sensations.   Why should I judge them to be the same, if the difference is really "greater than that between the states to which two different surds (sounds?) will give rise"?   The difference seems to me to be, not in the sensation, but in the judgments which I make in regard to the sensation; and which I can make just as well in two successive moments, in regard to the same sound heard only once.   Would you say, in that case, that I remembered two totally different sensations?

On page 231 you say: "The grass out of the window now looks to me of the same green in the sun as in the shade."   Now I will not attempt to say what your sensations are, but I am certain that it does not look so to me.   Perhaps a little clearer example will be a sheet of paper, part of which is in clear sunlight, part receives the light through a prism, and part is in shadow.   I *judge* it all to be white paper, but I am perfectly aware that some of it *looks* red, some orange, some yellow &c., and some gray.   The object which I *infer* is white paper, but what I *see* is patches of different colors, of various shapes. When you say that my sensations change in the successive moments in which I think "that is a sheet of white paper," "that shadow" is grey," "that is the light from a prism,["] it seems to me that you impart into the sensations my judgments about them.   That is what I had in mind in what I said about the "psychologist's fallacy."   It is entirely true that we may "get the same object" by different sensations—sensations, even, received through different organs—and I find no difficulty in admitting that native mental states, occurring at different times are in all respects identical, but to say that no element of our thought ever recurs would, it seems to me, be going too far, and as far as my consciousness goes, it seems to me there is as good evidence of the identity of sensations as of any mental states.

As to the emotions, I presume the only conclusive evidence would be that to be drawn from cases in which there was absence of in[stan] taneous and visceral sensations.   One argument against your view, to my mind, is that we may have the same reactions in different emotions.   When a person "weeps for joy," the motor processes, so far as I have been able to discover, are the same as when he weeps from sorrow, but the feeling is very different.   Whether or not there is some other muscular action which makes sorrow sorrowful, it seems to me it can't be the weeping.   I dont know that it is pertinent to ask why spasm of the diaphragm in sobbing should be so much more distressful than in laughing if it were satisfactorily proved to be so, but it seems to me the presumption is against it.   Another spasm of the diaphragm—hiccup—is not associated with any form of emotion. Pallor, tremor and tumultuous action of the heart may be signs of rage or excessive joy as well as of fear.   Physical disgust, if extreme, may produce nausea, but nausea may exist without any emotion of disgust.   Terror may cause faintness, but faintness may come on without terror, or any other strong emotion.   Of course it may be said that in these cases we do not have the precise combination of sensations which constitutes the emotion, but as far as they go they appear to favor the view that the connection of motion and emotion is not a necessary one.

As to what you say about the "itching and scratching" illustration, there is something in your distinction, but, on thinking it over, I incline to put [it] in a somewhat different way from you.   With some diffidence I venture the suggestion that the relation of emotion to the pleasurable and painful element in sensation is analogous to that of perception to the element of sensation by which we perceive the qualities of objects. To carry the original illustration a little farther— I feel an itching sensation, which at once arouses the tendency to scratch.   If, now, I find that the itching is due to the biting of a flea, the perception may be accompanied by an emotion, as, for instance, a feeling of resentment, which will set in motion the muscles appropriate to his capture and destruction (I suppose, on your hypothesis, abstinence from such movements should develop a feeling of benevolence toward the flea).   Or, supposing a man kicks my shin, the immediate result is a painful sensation and an impulse to withdraw the injured member; the indirect result, if he were not too big, might be a feeling of anger, and, as the student told Abernathy, the setting in motion of the flexors and extensors of my right arm, or, on the other

hand, an emotion of fear, and the inauguration of movement calculated to take my whole body out of harm's way. Of course, the connection between the sensation and emotion is often a good deal more
indirect than in these cases, but there is, I suppose, always a sensation
at the bottom of every emotion, and I confess that this hypothesis is
more satisfactory to my mind than one which makes mental states
which, without being very intense, are perfectly clear in my consciousness dependent on sensations which I cannot, in many cases,
by the closest attention, bring directly into consciousness.

Finally, as far as this point is concerned, I would submit that the
line of argument which you take on pp. 143–4 of Vol. I is applicable
to this case.[3]   Whether you intended what you say there to apply
merely to sensations or to emotions as well I don't know, but I do not
see why it is not quite as applicable to the latter as to the former.

I am glad that you agree with me in regard to the relations of
imagination to volition. It is an aspect of the matter of which I don't
remember ever to have seen much notice taken in discussions of the
subject, although everybody recognizes it in practice. I would not
find any fault with the way you state the relations of conduct to belief
in your letter. It is rather different from the way you put it in the
passage in italics at the bottom of p. 321, Vol II.[4] Of course, in matters of practice, the surest way to convince a man that a belief is
erroneous is often to get him to act on it. As to the ethical bearings
of the subject, of course, a man must often act on uncertainties, and
so doing does not necessarily involve insincerity. What I called in
question was your apparently recommending such a course as a
means of determining one's belief. Perhaps a concrete example will
make my meaning clear. Would you think it justifiable for an atheist
to become a clergyman for the purpose of bringing about a change
in his beliefs?

The whole section on the relations of belief and will is rather unsatisfactory to me. I cannot take it as an adequate account of my state
of mind when, for instance, I become convinced that my father's last
illness must be fatal, to say that I "looked at the object and consented
to its existence, espoused it, said 'it shall be my reality'."[5] I believed
it, not because I chose to, but because I must. To have had all my
ideas of prognosis in regard to such cases overturned would not have
distressed me in the least.

I do not ask for any answer to the foregoing, which I have written
as much to clear up my own ideas as to influence yours. There is,

however, one point on which I do not remember that you touch, on which I should like your opinion. I judge that you agree with Byron, that

> "Man, being reasonable, must get drunk:
> The best of life is but intoxication."[6]

using the term, of course, in its wide sense. What I should like to know is, whether, in your opinion, any degree of alcoholic intoxication strengthens a man's power of voluntary attention, or reinforces his ideals against his propencities.

Thanking you again for the pamphlet and your letter, I am very truly yours

W. L. Worcester.[7]

ALS: MH bMS Am 1092 (1183)

[1] WJ, "The Sense of Dizziness in Deaf-Mutes," *American Journal of Otology* 4 (October 1882): 239–54; reprinted in *EPs*.

[2] *PP*, 173–74, 225–26.

[3] *PP*, 145–46.

[4] *PP*, 948–49.

[5] *PP*, 948.

[6] From Byron's *Don Juan*, canto 2, stanza 179.

[7] Found with this letter is a large envelope on which WJ wrote the following note: 'D͏ʳ Worcester of Little Rock criticising my Psychology | Dec 24. 1890'.

To Sarah Wyman Whitman

95 Irving St, Dec 25. 1890

My dear Mrs Whitman

I had cherished a small hope of getting into town this Christmas Thursday and trying your door-bell in the afternoon, but things have blocked my way. I can't withstand the temptation, however, of wafting you the "compliments of the season" and wishing both you and Mr. Whitman a merry Christmas and plenty of them to come. Here it is fairly merry, since the children have shown no "reaction" yet, and it is four o'clock P.M.

The youngest child, you may not be aware, is of the masculine persuasion, and only three days old.[1] Alice is extremely well and happy in the contemplation of his ferocious little person and the management of his education, whilst I feel comparatively homeless and thrown upon the world again for support.—This is not an *appeal*, however! So with a repeated merry Christmas, and a blessing, I am always yours faithfully

Wm James

I am in the middle of an essay on "the essentials of an ethical Universe" wherein I prove to the satisfaction of all truth-loving persons that were the world reduced to a rock with two guinea pigs upon it, provided they retained some sort of sentimental regard for each other and were capable of being disappointed in each others conduct, it would still be a moral world.[2]—And would it not?—But that requires more paper!

ALS: MH bMS Am 1092.9 (3905)

[1] Alexander Robertson James, at first named Francis Tweedy, was born on 22 December 1890.

[2] Reference is to "The Moral Philosopher and the Moral Life."

From Charles Carroll Everett

53 GARDEN STREET, | CAMBRIDGE. [January 1891]

My dear James.

I have read your two volumes with great delight, and, I hope, profit. How was it possible for you to accomplish the 1300 or more pages without a single Homeric nod, with every where ingenuity and freshness of thought, vividness of style, and the free use of the results of an extent of reading which to me is marvellous.

Of course, I should have no right to call myself a student of philosophy—in however humble a way—if I did not here and there—not to say more or less all along, find points often minor that suggest argument if not dissent. These, however, were not of a nature to disturb the enjoyment of the book. As a theologian I enjoyed your demolition of materialistic theories. Especially do I recall with satisfaction the discussion of the automaton view, & your last chapter, though, as I name these, others claim equal regard.

I call your attention to a typographical error, p 642—12th line from top [sequence][1]

P 484—3[d] fr bottom, you say "we have already traced" etc.—Is that possibly a reference to a discussion written earlier, but standing later in the book—or have I over-looked something, which the index does not recognize?[2]

I wish if ever you have hypnotic experiments, at which it would not be an intrusion, I could sometime have an opportunity to witness.

Yours very truly—with renewed thanks | C. C. Everett.

P.S.—In congratulating you upon this child of the brain, I must not forget the other, which doubtless seems to you the more important object of congratulations.[3] I hope the child may prove as stout and as intelligent as the book. You will accept our best wishes for you and yours.

ALS: MH bMS Am 1092 (179)

[1] The first printing of *The Principles of Psychology*, 2 vols. (New York: Holt, 1890), 2:642, has "sequnce." The correct spelling appears in later printings (*PP*, 1238, line 2).

[2] In later printings of *Principles of Psychology*, "we shall have to trace" replaces "we have already traced" (*PP*, 1097, line 13).

[3] Reference is to Alexander Robertson James.

To Sarah Wyman Whitman

Jan 2. [1891] 6 P.M.

Dear Mrs Whitman

I succeeded in seeing your peacocks at the Brimmers after leaving your house. I consider them a most satisfactory and manly piece of work, strong and sober and beautiful at the same time, and I should think that one might like them all the better after a hundred years familiarity—I had but five minutes, with the varlet waiting for me to get through.

I enjoyed your lunch very much—but such things are not what they once were! How amused you must have been at my question about "Miss Rotch." I've seen her over and over again since that long bygone day when she became Mrs. Sargent,[1] and it only shows what vague and addled brains inhabit the skull of yours most everlastingly

W.J.

—Not addled when I perceive your peacocks! You ought truly to be happy at such a success.

ALS: MH bMS Am 1092.9 (3906)

[1] Aimée Rotch Sargent (d. 1918) was the wife of Winthrop Henry Sargent, son of Henry Sargent (1770–1845), an artist.

To Jacob Gould Schurman

CAMBRIDGE Jan 4. 1891

My dear Schurman

Prosit Neujahr! and all sorts of congratulations on the success of your plans.   You must be a happy man, even if you are thereby bowed down with new responsibilites.   I grieve to say that I can't promise you a "contribution" for any definite date, as nothing is astir inside of me just now except a paper on Ethics which I have been wrestling with to day & which is destined for the Int. J. of Ethics.[1]

As for Wolf, I have never seen him, and know naught of him.[2]   A letter from him lately about some small question or other, struck me as written by one who was not a man of the world.

Always yours truly | Wm James

ALS: MH bMS Am 1092.9 (3705)

[1] "The Moral Philosopher and the Moral Life."

[2] Wolf was not identified.

To Parke Godwin

Cambridge, Mass. Jan 9, 1890 [1891][1]

Dear Mr. Godwin,

I have been too busy to do more than read your letter and enclosure until now.   You write as if you still had as much blood in your veins as in the early '50s, when I can remember how you used to sit in a certain chair in father's study at 58 W. 14th St, twirling your spectacles in your hand.[2]   Thanks once more for all the good you say of my book.   Thanks, too for your compact classification of the elements of experience.   I agree to feeling as a separate thing, it gives all the terms the subjects and predicates of discourse.   And I am struck at the neatness of the antithesis which your formula draws between knowledge and action, as respectively reversing ends and means.—I will keep the thing and use it some day—meanwhile thanks from yours always

W.J.

TC: MH bMS Am 1092.1

[1] The letter is known only from a typed copy, and it is not known whether the dating error was made by WJ or the copyist.

[2] The James family moved to 58 W. 14th St., New York City, in 1848 and stayed there until their departure for Europe in 1855.

To James Mark Baldwin

CAMBRIDGE Jan 11. 91[1]

Dear Prof. Baldwin

I am rather used up with overwork (trying to write something, along with my other duties) and am answering your interesting letter along with arrears of correspondence which have accumulated, so you will pardon me if I am short.

I can*not* think at this moment of any 'cat and kitten' analogies, but perhaps that is because I cannot think at all.[2]   If any occur to me later, I will let you know.   You are evidently in a fertile vein about the motor discharge and I hope that something will come of it.   I don't see yet all the implications of your *high potential* ideas, so will await their development ere I speak again.   I *do* believe that some kind of an intellectual school of psychology is needed, to rectify the raw philistinism of the Stanley Hall School.   Jastrow's little notice of your volume in Hall's Journal I thought simply scandalous when it appeared.[3]   I haven't even had time yet to read your last paper in Science.[4]   I will do so soon.

Yours ever, | W.J

ALS: Bodleian Library, University of Oxford

[1] In view of the fact that nothing was found fitting WJ's remark about Baldwin's last paper in *Science*, it is possible that the letter is misdated.   But Baldwin accepted WJ's dating when publishing the letter in his autobiography, *Between Two Wars*, 2 vols. (Boston: Stratford, 1926), 2:204.

[2] For the cat-and-kitten analogy see James Mark Baldwin, *Mental Development in the Child and the Race* (New York: Macmillan, 1895), 79n.   The reference occurs in connection with Baldwin's discussion of the origin of right-handedness, based in part upon his papers in *Science* and upon correspondence with WJ.

[3] Joseph Jastrow, notice of James Mark Baldwin, *Handbook of Psychology: Senses and Intellect* (1889) (WJ 406.49.2), in *American Journal of Psychology* 2 (August 1889): 669–70.   Jastrow found no reason justifying the publication of the book.

[4] Nothing fitting WJ's remark was found.   Baldwin published "Suggestion in Infancy," *Science* 17 (27 February 1891): 113–17, and "Infant's Movements," *Science* 19 (8 January 1892): 15–16, but both are too late assuming WJ's date to be correct.

From George Holmes Howison

Berkeley, | Jan 12. 1891.

My dear James,

Forgive me, forgive me, (if you *can!*) for so long neglecting to acknowledge the great gift you made me weeks & weeks ago, of the two costly volumes that sum up your life industry to their date. I had seen by the public prints that the book was to appear, & forthwith set it down among my "references" under the course on Psychology. But I fear none of my students have tackled it. Nor do I know when I shall ever manage the time necessary to read, in a proper & consecutive manner, its 1500 & odd pages. Of course I am already familiar with its doctrines, thro' its *disjecta membra,* as you have sent them forth from time to time; and, equally of course, you can hardly expect me to consent to them,—that is, to the characteristic ones. But your work excites my astonished admiration in spite of this. Only, how *could* you put down in cold & permanent print those bagatelle diatribes about "Hegelism," & what not? It truly seems to me they are unworthy of the book and of you.—I hear from Mezes[1] that there is a recent addition to your household. *Glück Auf!* to the little one, & most respectful & cordial & honoring regards to the mother,

From your always admiring friend   G. H. Howison.

ALS: MH bMS Am 1092.9 (254)

[1] Sidney Edward Mezes (1863–1931), American educator. Correspondence is known from 1906.

From Frederic William Henry Myers

Jan. 12, '90 [1891] Leckhampton House.
My dear James:

I have read Vol. I and part of Vol. II of your Psychology with deep interest, and much admiration—I am extremely glad that you have written this big and good book; and I trust that it will become both bigger and better in many a future edition. A few remarks suggest themselves.

I   The get-up of the book, while of course largely due to the native acumen of the writer, is also largely due to your far-sighted purview,—as compared with, say, Spencer, Ward, Bain, Sully, a purview extending not only over the German psychological field but also over our specifically *psychical* inquiries, which constantly enrich your descriptions with important facts.

II   I believe that with a view (a) to the good of mankind (b) even to your own ultimate fame, it is essential that a main part of your energy shall henceforth be devoted to these S.P.R. inquiries. As a professional psychologist you can work them in with admittedly orthodox speculation far more easily than (say) a physiologist like

Richet.   You can take things in your psychological stride at which the physiological horse will shy for many a year to come.

I therefore consider it as an immense boon to you to have to work at the American S.P.R. and to keep Hodgson there.   I do not [*illeg.*] your efforts;[1]—I don't mind your having to speak constantly at meetings, to interview informants, to write letters, etc., etc.   You may not *like* it but I am sure it is the right thing!   And far more important than teaching students ordinary text-book facts.   Don't kill yourself,—lay as many golden eggs as you can;—but never mind if the S.P.R. does give you a great deal of trouble.   It is out of that trouble that your main usefulness and fame will spring.

III   Not one single member of our small group (Richet and I count up less than twenty in all the world)—the group who are going for *the* discovery of this century, viz., scientific proof of man's survival;—not one single member, I say, is on the whole so well situated as you for the successful pushing of the inquiry.

Remember that in spite of our individual inferiority to Darwin, our collective work is far more important than Darwin's;—more important in so far as the evolution of a boundless spiritual future is more important than the evolution of a finite terrene past.

IV   I am trying to review your book; probably for our proceedings, but possibly for Frothingham, who asked me for something.[2] (See an article of mine now in print for XIXth Century, which I suppose will be out soon, "Science and a Future Life")[3]

V   I index a list of misprints in Vol. I some mere defects of printing and none important.

VI   It may amuse you to see a list of the few persons who (as Richet[,] Schrenck and I concluded) are both earnestly and intelligently interested in psychical research.

America	England	France	Germany	Russia
W. James	H. Sidgwick	Richet	Schrenck-	Aksakoff(?)[10]
Hodgson	Mrs. Sidgwick	Danex(?)[7]	Notzing	
	Crookes	Pierre Janet	Dessoir	
	Wallace[4]		(on the verge	
	Lodge		Hertz[8]—	
	F.W.H.M.		electrician—	
	Leif[5]		Münsterberg	
	Podmore[6]		Moll)[9]	

(Say 16—among these, Wallace, myself, Pierre Janet partly hostile, others like Podmore and Arthur Balfour are as earnestly and as intelligently interested as men can be; but have no time for inquiry.)

VII   The physical movements in houses of private gentlemen and [*illeg.*] his mediumship, still go on and develop.   We shall prob. have an article in next Proc. by him.[11]

VIII   Is it at all settled *when* you come to Europe again?   Any chance of your being able to turn up in Paris next Xmas to discuss Congress in 1892?[12]   We all count on you greatly for that Congress.

IX   My wife is now definitely dissatisfied with her portrait of you, and prefers to wait for another chance; as she feels that she *ought* to make a really good thing of you.

Yours always, | F. W. H. Myers.

X   P.S. One more Piper question—On talking over E. G. control in America we none of us felt sure how much weight you think we should attribute to control's mentioned as Miss "Fryer".   Do you think Mrs. P. could have heard of the communications from Ely to Miss F.?[13]

TC: MH bMS Am 1092.9 (413)

[1] In the absence of the original letter, portions marked by the unknown copyist as illegible cannot be reconstructed.

[2] The review of *Principles of Psychology* by Myers appeared in *Proceedings of the Society for Psychical Research* 7 (April 1891): 111–33.   Frothingham was not identified.

[3] Frederic William Henry Myers, "Science and a Future Life," *Nineteenth Century* 29 (April 1891): 628–47.

[4] Alfred Russel Wallace (1823–1913), English naturalist and investigator of spiritualism.   Correspondence is known from 1886.

[5] Walter Leaf.

[6] Frank Podmore (1856–1910), British psychical researcher.

[7] Xavier Dariex, French psychical researcher, editor of the *Annales des Sciences Psychiques*.

[8] Heinrich Rudolf Hertz (1857–1894), German physicist.   Hertz was a member of the Society for Psychical Research.

[9] Albert Moll (1862–1939), German psychiatrist.

[10] Aleksandr Nikolaevich Aksakov (1832–1903), Russian psychical researcher.

[11] No such article was found.

[12] The Second International Congress of Experimental Psychology was held in London in August 1892.   At the Congress, Henry Sidgwick presented the final report on the Census of Hallucinations, and perhaps Myers wanted WJ to take part in the drafting of the report.   WJ did not attend, although he was in Europe.

[13] Leonora Piper was in England from November 1889 to February 1890 when she gave many sittings, including some to Ada Goodrich Freer (1857–1931), British psychical researcher and folklore collector, who may be Miss F.   The episodes men-

tioned by Myers were not found in the numerous published Piper reports.   WJ sent Myers's letter on to Richard Hodgson.   A copy of a WJ note at the end of the letter reads: 'Dear H. | Read and return.   Myers is the stuff out of which world-renewers are made.   What a despot! | W.J.'

From James Ward

SELWYN GARDENS, | CAMBRIDGE 12 Jany 1891

Dear Prof. James,

Many thanks for your two bulky volumes: they have been continually refreshing my soul & stirring me up ever since I got them.   I don't think I am overmuch given to hero-worship but certainly you have been my one hero this Xmas-vacation.   The geniality, the incisiveness the trenchant vigour of your work mark you out as—well, as unique among psychologists.

I have just begun to lecture again upon psychology, after an interval of three years.   Your book will thus naturally be continually in my hands & in the hands of our more advanced students; so that I expect by degrees to find myself at home in it & perhaps, if I find it does not bore you or effront you too much, I shall venture to ask for enlightenment on sundry points.

At this moment the thing in your book that impresses me the most is your exposition of Will: there is a real "heave ahead" in this.   The thing that puzzles me the most is your treatment of the causal relation of Mind & Body.   I happened to be busy with this question as a question in metaphysics when your book came; but up to present I can't say you have resolved my difficulties nor can I as yet acquiesce in your proposal—as matter of method—to stick to common-sense so long as we are only psychologists.   But this is an old difference between us: I think I wrote to you about it once before a propos of your article on Automatism in *Mind*.[1]   Finally your *penchant* for "spiritualism" in the new sense amazes me.

Ten years ago you raised my hopes by saying you might come here to rest your eyes.   I trust your eyes are better, but is there still no chance of your coming?   I thought Am^n professors all had a sabbatic year.   I sh^d be fearfully delighted to see you

Yours sincerely   J. Ward

ALS: MH bMS Am 1092.9 (650)

[1] WJ, "Are We Automata?" *Mind* 4 (January 1879): 1–22; reprinted in *EPs*.   Ward's letter is not known.

To Parke Godwin

Jan 13, 91

Dear Mr. Godwin,

I am extremely sorry to hear of Mrs. Godwin's distressing situation.[1] As for the medical aspects of it, I can have no opinion. Until very lately all cases of intra-cranial trouble had to be left absolutely to nature. Lately they have been very bold in trepanning and operating on the brain where the lesion seemed to be a tumor, or other source of *irritation*, as evidenced by spasms, frets etc. In cases of simple paralysis, however, surgery would seem of no avail. Mrs G's Doctor or Doctors would of course be "up" in all these novelties, as I am not.

"Act" of thought does express the unity! And I did say too little about the *great* subject of signification!

I wish indeed that I might suggest something in Mrs. Godwin's case. How piteous it must be if speech is much impaired.

With warm regards and sympathy I am ever yours

Wm James

TC: MH bMS Am 1092.1

[1] Fanny Bryant Godwin (d. 1893). Her obituary notice in the *New York Times*, 24 June 1893, states that her death came as a surprise.

From William Dean Howells

184 COMMONWEALTH AVENUE. Jan. 13, 1891.

My dear James:

I must hail and congratulate you upon the boy who has come to live with you. I hope he will grow up heir of his father's delightful wisdom by which I am profitting, as much as a lower (metaphysical) animal may, in the *Psychology*. Has a philosopher any right to be so human, so charming? It is a serious question. I am always so browbeaten by the more pert of you scientifickers, that I hardly know what to make of drawing easy breath in reading your book.

My wife joins me in good wishes and hopes that all you and Mrs James expect of the boy will come to pass.

Yours ever, | W. D. Howells.

I did send the little book to H. J., for I wanted him to know what Winny had done, but tell him not to write of it; that is a burden which we did not mean to put on our friends.[1] It is cruel.

ALS: MH bMS Am 1092.9 (238)

[1] Reference is to Winifred Howells (1863–1889), daughter of William Dean Howells, and the privately printed memorial volume containing her poems.

To George Holmes Howison

CAMBRIDGE Jan 20. 91

My poor dear darling Howison,

Your letter is received and wrings my heart with its friendliness and animosity combined. But don't think me more frivolous than I am—"those bagatelle diatribes about Hegelism" etc are *not* reprinted in this book, not a single syllable of them! I make some jokes about Caird on a certain page, but Caird already forgives me, and writes that I am sophisticated by Hegel myself.[1] If you carefully ponder the *note* on that same page or the next one (vol I, p. 370) you will see the real inwardness of my whole feeling about the matter.[2] I am not as low as I seem, and some day (D.v.) may get out another and a more "metaphysical" book, which will steal all your hegelian thunder *except* the dialectical method, and show me to be a true child of the gospel.

Heartily & everlastingly yours, | Wm James

ALS: MH bMS Am 1092.9 (1031)

Address: Professor Howison | Berkeley | Calefornia
Postmark: BOSTON. MASS. JAN 20 1891

[1] In *PP*, 349, WJ quotes Edward Caird and comments that "this dynamic (I had almost written dynamitic) way of representing knowledge has the merit of not being tame." Caird's letter is not known.

[2] In *PP*, 350n, WJ states that he is willing to discuss the possibility of the transcendental ego on general speculative grounds.

To Mary Whiton Calkins

CAMBRIDGE Jan 27. 91

My dear Miss Calkins,

I have been pining for your society, and should have written to you to day even without your note. Please name any day of next week except Tuesday on which you may come between 11 and 12 forenoon and go to the laboratory with me & sup your fill of brains, returning hither for lunch at ½ past one, when you may also meet with Mrs. James.

I should say this week, only I am tired and going to Newport for a couple of days, and the sheep's heads likewise must be ordered in advance.

Most truly yours | Wm James

unnoticed till the note was writ—excuse the slovenly appearance.[1]

ALS: MWelC

[1] The reference is to WJ's false start of 'My d', deleted at the head of an otherwise blank fourth page.

To Frederic William Henry Myers

Newport R.I. | Jan 30. '91

My dear Myers,

Your letter of the 12th came duly, but not till now have I had leisure to write you a line of reply.   Verily you are of the stuff of which world changers are made.   What a despot for P.R.!   I always feel guilty in your presence, and am on the whole glad that the broad blue ocean rolls between us for most of the days of the year, although I should be glad to have it intermit occasionally, on days when I feel particularly larky and indifferent, when I might meet you without being bowed down with shame.   To speak seriously, however, I agree in what you say that the position I am now in (Professorship, book published & all) does give me a very good pedestal for carrying on psychical research *effectively,* or rather for disseminating its results effectively.   I find however that *narratives* are a weariness, and I must confess that the *reading* of narratives for which I have no personal responsibility is almost intolerable to me.   Those that come to me at first hand, incidentally to the Census, I get interested in.   Others much less so; and I imagine my case is a very common case.   One page of experimental "θ"-work will "carry" more than a hundred of Phantasms of the Living.[1]   I shall stick to my share of the latter however; and expect in the summer recess to work up the results already gained in an article for Scribner's Magazine, which will be the basis for more publicity and advertizing and bring in another bundle of Schedules to report on at the Congress.[2]   Of course I wholly agree with you in regard to the *ultimate* future of the business, and fame which will be the portion of him who may succeed in naturalizing it as a branch of legitimate science.   I think it quite on the cards that you, with your singular tenacity of purpose, and wide look at all the intellectual relations of the thing may live to be the ultra-Darwin yourself.   Only the facts are *so* discontinuous so far that possibly all our generation can do may be to get 'em called facts.   I'm a bad fellow to investigate on account of my bad memory for anecdotes and other disjointed details.   Teaching of students will have to fill most of my time I foresee; but of course my weather eye will remain open upon the occult world.

Our "Branch" you see has tided over its difficulties temporarily; and by raising its fee will enter upon the new year with a certain momentum.   You'll have to bleed, though, ere the end, devoted creatures that you are, over there!

I thank you most heartily for your kind words about my book, and am touched by your faithful eye to the errata.   The vols. were run through the press in less than seven weeks, and the proof-reading suffered.   My friend G Stanley Hall, leader of American Psychology, has written that the book is the most complete piece of self-evisceration since Marie Bashkirtseff's diary.[3]   Don't you think that's rather unkind?   But in this age of nerves, all philosophizing is really s'thing of that sort.   I finished yesterday the writing of an address on Ethics which I have to give at Yale College;[4] and on the way hither in the cars, I read the last half of Rudyard Kipling's "The Light that Faded"—finding the latter indecently true to Nature, but recognizing after all that my Ethics and his novel were the same sort of thing.[5] All literary men are sacrifices.   "Les festins humains qu'ils servent à leurs fêtes, ressemblent la plupart a ceux des pélicans," etc etc. Enough!   I am very eager to hear just what the physical phenomena are of which you're at last convinced, and hope that we shan't be kept waiting too long.

Yours ever,   W.J.

I mustn't forget your questions: I.) I come to Europe again, (D.v.) in July 1892.   II. It is MOST improbable that name was ever mentioned to Mrs. Piper.   It is however *possible* that Mrs Dorr may have mentioned it, and afterwards forgotten the fact.   The most likely thing is that she got it out of my mind or Hodgson's.

ALS: MH bMS Am 1092.9 (3308)

[1] Reference is to Edmund Gurney, *Phantasms of the Living.*

[2] The *Scribner's Magazine* article was not published.   A year later WJ published "What Psychical Research Has Accomplished," *Forum* 13 (August 1892): 727–42; reprinted in *EPR* and in part in *The Will to Believe* (1897).   For the Congress and the Census of Hallucinations see letter from Myers of 12 January 1891, note 12.

[3] Granville Stanley Hall, review of *Principles of Psychology* in *American Journal of Psychology* 3 (February 1891): 578–91.   On p. 585 Hall refers to the diary of Maria Konstantinova Bashkirtseva (1860–1884), Ukrainian artist and author, while making

the point that in his book WJ says a great deal about himself. Usually, according to Hall, authors disappear in their work. The word 'self-evisceration' is WJ's. For WJ's reading of Bashkirtseva see *The Varieties of Religious Experience* (Cambridge: Harvard Univ. Press, 1985), 439.

⁴"The Moral Philosopher and the Moral Life."

⁵WJ read Rudyard Kipling, "The Light that Failed," in *Lippincott's Monthly Magazine* 47 (January 1891): 1–97. This version is shorter and has a happy ending, while the book version, published in March 1891, is longer and has a sad ending. For other comments on the book see *Correspondence*, 2:174–75.

To Henry Holt

Feb. [3] 91

My dear Holt,

Thanks for the advertizing of H. J. & Maude.¹

As for the shorter course, don't expect it before the middle of next winter. I promise it then; but at present I have other things on hand.

I can't go into detail about the Educational Review. I suppose the fault is less with the edit<ing> than with the subject, which must perforce deal with mighty and aspiring generalities, & puerile concretes with nothing between to fill the gap. Harris and the schoolmarm! No. 2 was worth its price for the German Emperor's address.² He is the liveliest spectacle now on exhibition anywhere, and though not a Carlyle I thank God for him. If a country arranges itself for an Emperor, let them *have one!* He takes himself *au sériux.*— Haven't the ladies found a philosopher yet to do their center penance with?

Ever yours | Wm. James

Will you kindly order 3 more copies of my Psychology sent to me, and charge.

TC: MH bMS Am 1092.1

¹Writing to Holt on 1 February 1891 (calendared), WJ suggested that since Holt was preparing a new printing of *Principles of Psychology* he might add an advertisement on the fly leaf for the *Literary Remains of the Late Henry James* and for John Edward Maude's *Foundations of Ethics* (1887), both edited by WJ. Holt agreed and in volume two of the second printing of *Principles* (February 1891) an advertisement for the two books replaced the listing of works in the American Science Series that usually faced the title page.

²The first number of the *Educational Review,* published by Henry Holt, is dated January 1891. Included is William Torrey Harris's "Fruitful Lines of Investigation in Psychology" (pp. 8–14). The second number, February 1891, includes an address by William II (1859–1941), emperor of Germany, to the Commission on School Reform (pp. 200–208).

To Jacob Gould Schurman

CAMBRIDGE Feb. 7. 91

My dear Schurman,

Stanley Hall is, I fancy, growing more and more sot in his parti pris of barbariousness, and I don't see the use therefore of surrendering to him the whole psychological field.   Don't you think that a sort of synthetic report of the *outcome* of the year's literature in Psychology, Ethics, etc would be a good feature of your magazine?   I should like to be responsible for the psychology-part.[1]   It wouldn't be of the nature of a summary of the various papers, but rather an exposé of the way the various problems had been affected by the year's work. Think over the matter and let me know of dates and pages etc. if it seems to you good.

I tremble for you with your task.   Hang Hall! what a precious ally he would be, were he not a crank!

Yours always | Wm James

ALS: MH bMS Am 1092.9 (3706)

[1] The first issue of the *Philosophical Review,* edited by Jacob Gould Schurman, is dated January 1892.   WJ contributed numerous reviews until 1894 when he transferred his allegiance to the new *Psychological Review.*   His reviews are reprinted in *ECR.*

To W. E. B. Du Bois

95 Irving St. Cambr. | Feb 9th 1891

Dear Mr DuBois,

Won't you come to a philosophical supper on Saturday, Feb 14th, at half past seven o'clock?[1]

Yours truly | William James

ML (AGJ): MU

[1] William Edward Burghardt Du Bois (1868–1963), American black leader, educator, and historian, then a student at Harvard.   Correspondence is known from 1891 to 1907.

To Sarah Wyman Whitman

Feb. 10. '91

My dear Mrs Whitman

R.K. has *entrails.*   Never did a rain-shower do such complete work as in that musical little composition.   I see no need however of the goat's blood on his boots.—The story sings in the memory.[1] I am touched by your copying the poem for me. I knew it already, but did not think of the title when you named it. It fills the ear and mouth. He has all the major effects at his disposition. And I confidently prophecy that all the delicacies and harmonies will come when he's an older man.

I came back from Yale College this P.M. Not one soul made a syllable of allusion to my "Address"; and no wonder, for as I delivered the poor thing, I perceived that it was a skeleton with all the flesh plucked off it so as to fit within the hour.[2]

But no matter! I suppose you have seen Mr. Tiffany's window in the College Library.[3] If not, you must not fail to stop over between two trains the next time you go to N.Y. Luscious, luscious, luscious! My first impressions are never worth anything, but it is the freest treatment of glass I ever saw.

Good night! from yours most devotedly,

Wm James

ALS: MH bMS Am 1092.9 (3908)

[1] Reference is to an unidentified work by Rudyard Kipling.

[2] WJ addressed the Yale Philosophical Club on 9 February 1891 on "The Moral Philosopher and the Moral Life."

[3] Sarah Whitman also worked with stained glass.

To Jacob Gould Schurman

CAMBRIDGE Feb. 11. 91

My dear Schurman

All right! I'll begin to take notes after a while. I can't have anything before the Jan. no. at the earliest—perhaps not then.[1]

Youre a regular angel about my book, taking it so seriously and praising it so much. I didn't know there was such a man. Of course its value lies in *suggestions* only—and there can be no other service done at present in the so called Science of "Psychology."

I was at New Haven yesterday talking to Ladd, and we discussed your Professorship of Psychol. Why not aim at the best thing and import Munsterberg on a 5 years contract to see how it would work? I should go in for a genius "every time" were I a college president or any one with appointing power?

Always yours | Wm James

ALS: MH bMS Am 1092.9 (3707)

[1] Reference is to reviews for the *Philosophical Review;* see letter of 7 February 1891.

To James Mark Baldwin

CAMBRIDGE March 7. 1891

Dear Mr. Baldwin,

Mr. Tracy must run the gauntlet of a committee with many candidates for every fellowship.[1] Let him send all the credentials he can muster. I hope he will be able to come, fellowship or no-fellowship.

Hume was here two years and endeared himself to us all by his genial and manly character. He is very expert in the Green-Caird-Young way of thought,[2] I only hope it won't stand in the way of his attending to particulars. His fight with you for the professorship seemed to me rather amusing at the time, and made me glad that appointments here were not in the hands of the politicians.[3] However if the politicians would make places for *all* academic candidates, as they did in this instance, perhaps the quality of the contests might be condoned. Hume was under a misapprehension about the printing of an essay which he wrote for me on sensation. I had told him that I *might* print it, if suitable, but it turned out too heterogenous with my own stuff.[4]

I was much interested in your last baby-article.[5] My wife has often put her babies to sle[e]p by flaring up the gas upon them, but equally well by suddenly turning it down. She thinks the hypnotic effect comes from any sudden *change*. I admire your energy over the creatures: I don't think anything could lure me to put my baby to sleep more than one day at a time.

Very truly yours | Wm James

ALS: Bodleian Library, University of Oxford

[1] No suitable Tracy appears in lists of Harvard students for 1891–92 and he was not identified. At the time Baldwin was teaching at the University of Toronto.

[2] George Paxton Young (1818–1889), Canadian clergyman, professor of logic, metaphysics, and ethics at the University of Toronto.

[3] See *Correspondence*, 6:527–29.

[4] See *Correspondence*, 6:529n. Probably WJ had mentioned the possibility of including Hume's paper on sensation in *Principles of Psychology*.

[5] James Mark Baldwin, "Suggestion in Infancy," *Science* 17 (27 February 1891): 113–17.

To David Ferrier

Harvard University March 7. '91

Dear D.ʳ Ferrier,

My friend and former pupil D.ʳ Frederic Coggeshall is about to go to London where, as he will doubtless explain to you, he wishes to find almost any kind of work in which his biological and medical education will stand him in stead. As he has no friends in your country, I have taken the liberty of addressing him to you as a starting point. I should not have thought of this were he not a man of quite exceptional endowments morally, and attainments intellectually, thorough and conscientious in the extreme, and possessed of exceptional powers of work. You will perhaps advise him, even if you can do nothing else; and in any case you will earn the gratitude of yours most sincerely

Wm James

ALS: MH bMS Am 1092.1

To Samuel Burns Weston

CAMBRIDGE March 12. '91

My dear Weston,

I return the corrected proof, and much good may it do the Journal![1] I also send two dollars, being my long delayed subscription for the year: I don't *think* I've paid before. I am recreant to my own moral principles in sending you this money. I ought not to do it until you've agreed to have the Journal stitched instead of clamped with those hell-born wires which make all reading impossible.[2] For a Journal of Ethics such barbarism ought not to be! Pray reform it! Allow the pages to open!—even if it costs several cents more a number.

About the note: "Address at Yale etc"—I think it be must remain.[3] The whole *composition* was aimed at one hour's talk to an audience. It would have been very differently written if I had started it for an article, and it is unfair to the author not to have the conditions of composition known. Uberhaupt, I can't help suspecting that the dread which our american editors have of letting it be known that articles were originally lectures is a superstition. A lecture is always composed so as to be more readable. Addresses in the english maga-

zines I am sure are the things first read.   What essays can have been
more successful than Huxley's[4] Cliffords,[5] and Tyndalls?   Pray let the
note stand, and oblige yours always

Wm James

ALS: Private

[1] Reference is to "The Moral Philosopher and the Moral Life."

[2] For WJ's protest against the use of wire in bindings see his "The Steel-Wire-Bind-
ing Nuisance," *Nation* 55 (17 November 1892): 374; reprinted in *ECR*.

[3] A note that "The Moral Philosopher and the Moral Life" was delivered as an address at Yale appears in the *International Journal of Ethics* 1 (April 1891): 330.

[4] Thomas Henry Huxley (1825–1895), English biologist and essayist.

[5] William Kingdon Clifford (1845–1879), British mathematician and philosopher.

To Helen Bigelow Merriman

95 Irving St, | March 21. [1891]

My dear Mrs. Merriman

I have at last read your beautiful article.[1]   I don't know how trans-
parent it will be to the common herd—it is too original to be very
popular, I am afraid.   Indeed I think that the title shows a certain
inaptitude on the author's part for making herself exactly popular—
too much inside of her subject to feel how it looks and sounds from
the outside, for who of the Andover Review's reader's ever heard of
"*the school of 1830*" by that name?   *I* never did!   But you are most
originally and deeply inside of your subject, and see it out of your
own living eyes, giving the reader the sense of new ways of getting at
deep mysteries.   The analogy, however, which lights up so much for
you because you have lived so intimately with it, may not be so immediately clear to every one else.   Of one thing I am sure, however, and
that is that the article will be read over many times by those whom
it strikes.   There is a mysterious pithiness and pregnancy about these
things which are written from original intuition, which makes one
feel that he has not exhausted their significance, so one puts them
carefully aside and after an interval reads them again.   I have a number of articles which I treat in this way, and I know that such will be
the fate of this.   Not so much with me perhaps, for I think it is all
tolerably clear to me, but with others.

Pray continue!

With warm regards to both of you, believe me always cordially
yours

Wm James

ALS: MHi

[1] Helen Bigelow Merriman, "Some Philosophical Aspects of the School of 1830," *Andover Review* 15 (March 1891): 263–80. The School of 1830 is her name for what is also known as the Barbizon School of French artists.

To Thomas Sergeant Perry

CAMBRIDGE March 23. 1891

Dear Thos.

I have read every word in your book about the Greek philosophers, and can't refrain from expressing my high satisfaction with the manner in which 'tis done.[1] It could n't be better for the purpose, Plato especially. Readable, light, varied, and full of accurate information. Many of your sentences I have used in my lectures. It was a good test for I read half a dozen other accounts simultaneously, always with an eye to practical use, and yours had no appearance of insolidity, altho so much lighter and more agreeable to read than the more technical accounts. Keep on! One thing has struck me about your book. When a thing is as big as that it takes a rather heroic reader to go at it at all. Does not *such* a reader want the originals? In other words, is there need of "popular" books on that scale? Make your roman literature short & bright.[2]

Yrs ever | W.J.

ALS: American Academy and Institute of Arts and Letters

[1] Thomas Sergeant Perry, *A History of Greek Literature* (1890).
[2] No such book was published.

To George Santayana

95 Irving St, March 29. '91

My dear Santayana

I didn't say what I felt last night about your review, which I have read again carefully.[1] It is a beautiful composition, and though I say it who should not (in view of the complimentary epithets which you lavish) it seems to me wonderfully *just*. It is a great honour to me, and I thank you most heartily.

Yours always | Wm James

ALS: ICarbs

[1] George Santayana, unsigned review of *Principles of Psychology* in *Atlantic Monthly* 67 (April 1891): 552–56.

To Samuel Burns Weston

Cambr. April 2. 91

My dear Weston

Thanks for the $48.00. That is really *grossartig!* For an ethical journal, and even before the Journal itself arrives! Well who can say that the world does n't make progress?

There is so bad a misprint—more shame to me—on the 13th line from the top of p. 338 that I very much wish you might stick a slip to that effect in the rest of the edition and add it to the next number. It should read "though *He* made" etc—not "though *we* made."[1] I find my article very ineffective as I read it. It covers too much ground to give any point its full emphasis and value. Its composition was very difficult, because of the neccessity of coming back from every opening and lopping off inevitable digressions and expansions. The result is a skeleton of which few readers will see [*end of letter missing*]

AL incomplete: Private

[1] The text was corrected in *Will to Believe;* see *WB*, 148.

To Paul Henry Hanus

95 Irving St. | Cambridge, April 6, '91.

My dear Sir:

I am happy to learn from President Eliot that you are to be the incumbent of the new chair of pedagogy here.[1]

I write to ask what your preference is as to some 12 or 15 lectures on pedagogical psychology which the committee on the new department of work has adopted. Shall you or shall I be responsible for giving them. I am quite willing to sacrifice myself, but even more willing to be relieved. I should wait till you are on the ground and could know some of the other conditions which will meet you here before asking you such a question, and probably they can be left open anyhow until you come. But if you decidedly would *like* those lectures—I not knowing just what pedagogic psychology means except the habit, association, apperception, and attention chapters of common psychology—we could print your name forthwith on the forthcoming list of studies for next year as giving that course, and it would enable you to step without faculty discussion or explanation into the "philosophical department" where of course we should like to have you.

Pray understand that it is not *important* that you should answer this question now. If you prefer, you can wait till next fall. I only give you the chance of settling it now, if you like to.

Hoping, ere long to make your acquaintance, I am

Very truly yours, | Wm. James

Professor Hanus.

Paul Henry Hanus, *Adventuring in Education* (Cambridge: Harvard Univ. Press, 1937), 120–21.

[1] Eliot's letter appointing Hanus Assistant Professor of the History and Art of Teaching is dated 25 March 1891. His salary was $2,000 a year. Hanus's appointment marks the beginning of teacher training at Harvard. To WJ's question about who should give the lectures on pedagogical psychology, Hanus replied that WJ should give them. These lectures, often repeated and revised, became *Talks to Teachers on Psychology* (1899).

To Charles William Eliot

Apl. 7. 1891

Dear President,

Since speaking to you the other day about a Psychological Laboratory-assistant I have reviewed the situation, with an unhesitatingly affirmative conclusion.

I believe we ought to have some routine definite practical exercises, in addition to the present brain dissections, given to every man in the non-elementary psychology. The first year must be one of trial, and I can't set down on paper now the complete list of exercises, but I fancy if the class numbers over twenty five that with these and other duties I can fill an assistant's time pretty well for 3 hours a day five days in the week for all but the last 4 or 5 weeks in the year.

A certain Nichols of Clark who has shown marked ability and originality in the psychological direction is desirous of coming, and will, I think, make a good man, especially as he is a natural "tinker," which I am not.

Will you please think the matter over, & let me know, at your early convenience, the result, stating pay and room-privilege, which will be important factors if Nichols is the man to be negotiated with.

Very truly yours | Wm James

ALS: MH Archives

To William Dean Howells

95 Irving St, April 12. 1891

My dear Howells

You made me what seemed at the time a most reckless invitation at the Child's one day—you probably remember it. It seemed to me improper then to take it up. But it has lain rankling in my mind ever since; & now, as the spring weather makes a young man's fancy lightly turn away from the metaphysical husks on which he has fed exclusively all winter to some more human reading, I say to myself why should n't I have a copy from the Author himself of Silas Lapham and of the Minister's Charge, which by this time are almost the only things of yours which I have never possessed?[1] Take this as thou wilt!

I was very much pleased to see how good a notice you wrote of poor T.S.P.[2] To me his book seems a very good and human piece of work as far as I have read it. The Plato Chapter is as good as can be for the purpose. Hoping you're all well.

Yrs ever | Wm James

ALS: MH bMS Am 1092.9 (1018)

[1] William Dean Howells, *The Rise of Silas Lapham* (1885); *The Minister's Charge* (1886).

[2] An unsigned review by Howells of Perry's *History of Greek Literature* appeared in *Atlantic Monthly* 67 (April 1891): 557–60.

From James Mark Baldwin

24 Wilcox St TORONTO, CANADA, Apl 13 1891

Dear Prof. James,

I am glad my "review" was not in the main mistaken as to your point of view.[1] If I am ever anxious to avoid mistaken interpretations it is in notices. And I am greatly pleased that you thought it worth while to notice my minor points of criticism. I shall jot down below a note or two on your marjinal readings.

1) Why not use *feeling* for both the generic & the affective (purely)? as the English writers do ie. Bain, Spencer. Then *all* consciousness is *feeling* & *some* is *also knowledge* (about). "Thought" is so commonly confined to the *discursive,* that it seems too bad to break up the unanimity. Under our difference in terminology, however, there is a real difference of doctrine & I think your use of "thought" minimizes an error, i.e.

2) You hold that all feeling (or thought) has an object, is presentative (vorstellen); if I believed that I should be willing also to call it all thought. But I am not convinced—despite your eloquent pleading—I think your doctrine of space perception (& Ward's) begs everything; & tho' I speak with less confidence about space, yet as to "painful quality" "warmth" &c being at first objective I am sure you are wrong. I think we begin with experience wh. is neither subjective nor objective—what may be called *simple-reality feeling*, NOT BELIEF, as you make it. Part of this experience we learn to objectivize (knowledge) & always do objectivize, other part we do not objectivize (pain) except by reflection. What is the object of the *ought* feeling, or of the higher *aesthetic* feelings? or rather that part of these feelings which transcends the particular fact which calls them out?

3) What you find obscure on p. 365 of my article, may be illustrated. A child sees a strange man & calls him father: *felt* experience *from* (not *of*) similarity. Child's father's image is all the child has. But when he learns the existence of other men & that this *felt experience* above may or may not happen, it becomes a feeling *of* something, of the relation of similarity, & is based upon knowledge. The feeling before was *of* nothing: it can not be simply of the father, for it is different from the feeling of the father. There is no object corresponding to this new element of feeling until the child gets 2 objects between which a relation of similarity is discerned. Is my meaning still obscure? Im afraid so! Try diagrams (circle = consciousness)

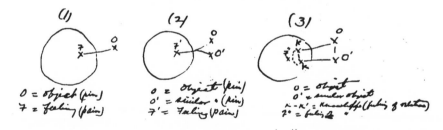

In (1) & (2) there is no object *in consciousness* at all, the simple pain is *all;* & the second pain tho' arising from actual differences in the two successive stimulations is not a feeling *of* that difference until the reproduced pain is held in union with the present pain: & this "holding in union" is knowledge (about).

4) *Apperception* = "reactive spontaneity *überhaupt*", selective, emphasizing, unifying, &c, &c. "Attention" would do if by it we mean not only reaction—its usual meaning—but also all that takes place

in the content of consciousness in consequence of the reaction.   To me it seems better to make apperception generic, to use attention for the fact of reaction & more special words, knowledge, thought, &c for the *fruits* of reaction.   Wundt is wrong in making apperception essentially voluntary thus shutting out reflex attention which is in my view non-voluntary, mechanical.   Don't you need some general word to gather up & present solidly attention plus the fruits of attention— its outcome for mental theory?   Can we not oppose an *apperception-concept* to the *association-concept*?

5)   To *whose observation* does the "frozen block" of the "specious present" "move along as a fact-rule"?   The self, as a part of the present object, is *frozen in*.

I think Hall's review of you will—or has—only heightened the discredit into which his "movement" is falling.[2]   I know of no competent men, outside of his own pupils, who have any patience with his arrogance.   The reference, in my article on your book, to "certain physiologizers" (p. 367) is meant for Hall & Jastrow—& I hope it's plain enough to be understood.[3]   Hall's attitude is positively demorilizing to all the best impulses of young American thought & life.   I for one find it impossible to water my scientific & agnostic propensities & let my ethical & *educational* obligations dry up.

Yours faithfully | J. Mark Baldwin

ALS: MH bMS Am 1092 (28)

[1] James Mark Baldwin, review of *Principles of Psychology* in *Educational Review* 1 (April 1891): 357–71; reprinted in Baldwin's *Fragments in Philosophy and Science* (1902).

[2] See letter of 30 January 1891.

[3] Baldwin writes of the "bold assumptions and crude philistinism of the kind of physiologizing now asserting itself in the name of psychology in certain educational circles in America" (p. 367).

From Charles Augustus Strong

Buckingham Hotel, | New York, Apr. 14, 1891.
My dear Prof. James:—

I want to tell you how much I have enjoyed your splendid article in the last number of the Int. Journal of Ethics.   It is long since I have read anything so masterly, or that so "went to the spot."   Your account, in the V.(?) section, of the historical process by which the ideals are weeded out, & the received morality evolved, seems to me especially fine.[1]

As a result of my own reflections I have come to conclusions quite similar to yours (though I could never have expressed them half so well), and I agree with you fully in giving to obligation a purely human basis. But I cannot see why a *demand,* as such, is sacred. I should rather say that what is primarily sacred is people's *well-being,* not what it enters into their poor benighted heads to demand. I cannot believe that the child's demand for the moon, or the debauchee's for sensual pleasure are, originally & in themselves, just as sacred as the mothers good wishes for her child, or the saint's aspiration for holiness. I cannot consider that the sacrifice of the former is a "butchery." I should say that the sacredness of demands does not exist at this stage, but only appears when the demand is considered in its reference to the *lasting well-being* of all concerned. Perhaps "well-being" seems to you vague, but it is easy to fill it out with soul-moving states drawn from experience. If you ask *why* such states are good, I answer, not because they are demanded, but because they *satisfy*—satisfy both the subject & those who look on. If you think this low & utilitarian, I answer that to base obligation upon the genuine & lasting well-being of all concerned is both more rational & more moving than to base it upon the mere fact of a demand, without reference to the rationality of the latter. Demands are such fearfully subjective, capricious, happy-go-lucky affairs; but well-being is something deeply founded in people's unconscious natures, & the rules it prescribes constitute a power above our conscious selves. So that I should say a demand is not sacred in itself, but only in proportion as it ministers to the well-being of all concerned. In so far as the subject recognizes well-being as such, at the time & afterward, I recognize the state in question as (in so far) sacred.

Now please don't be severe upon me for this effusion; I have read precious few ethical treatises, & I may be making a great fool of myself. But I thought I would hazard the criticism.

I am taking life easy, and hope to be equal to some solid work next fall. With kind regards,

Yours, | Charles A. Strong.

ALS: MH bMS Am 1092 (1054)

[1] WJ's "Moral Philosopher and Moral Life" is divided into five sections, but none of them is primarily historical.

To William Mackintire Salter

CAMBRIDGE April 24 [1891]
My dear Mackintire

The disappointments of Philosophy!   I had flattered myself that the living truths embodied in my article would make any rational being, especially you, say yea! yea![1] Well, I must begin the task again that is all.   But not now!   I will spare both you and myself.   The *fundamental* point is of course what I call the "superstition" of an abstract right.   I can't help believing that gradually everyone who thinks of it long enough will agree that it is *meaningless* to say that I "ought" to do what neither I myself nor any other living thing in the Universe wants to have done.   If there be a thing now not *anywhere* demanded, it can carry *no* obligation.

As for God, that is less elementary.   All I contend for is that *if* there be such a demander he becomes one of the factors of rights and wrongs, and the most important one *to those who believe in his existence*.   Because they would naturally conceive of him as both *eternal* and exceedingly *comprehensive* and *urgent* in his demands, and from the side of the demander these are the *only* marks of imperativeness in demands.   From the side of the *demandee* the most imperative demands are those to which he happens most to respond.   *If* posterity's demands are by any thinker responded to as much as god's, the God can be of no consequence in the ethics *of that thinker.* You can define your God, too, so as to make him of small consequence in the system; as by proclaiming him passionless and needing nothing.   Your ethics will change then with your theology.   The sort of God *I* was postulating was supposed to be a tremendous demander, and needer of our acquiescence.—The gist of it all is that ethics presupposes a certain state of *facts*.   How those facts have come to be *made*, we know not.   Only metaphysics can answer that question; but surely ethics begins *after* the fact.   Part of the fact *is* our *responsiveness to demands*.   I confess it surprises me that you should find a difficulty in admitting *in abstracto* that every demand *is* an obligation, to its own extent.   *It* feels the obligation, even if the demandee rejects it, so the obliga[tion] is actually imposed and there.

—Well, I lied when I said I was n't going to begin again!   If you answer this, I'll promise not to reply.   When my article appeared it looked insignificant.   But nothing is insignificant which is worth contradicting; so your letter, though I grieve at the hardness of your

heart, has set up my spirits about the essay.   So I thank you heartily.
Love to poor dear old Mary.

Yrs ever | W.J.

ALS: MH bMS Am 1092.9 (3694)

[1] Reference is to "The Moral Philosopher and the Moral Life."

To Carl Stumpf

CAMBRIDGE April 25. 91

My dear Stumpf

I am perplexed about translations of my book.   Herr Cossmann, whom I imagine to have been inspired by you, has sent me a specimen of his ability in the shape of the first chapter.   There are two or three mistakes in the sense, but the German seems to me free and readable.   Meanwhile Costenoble the Jena publisher wishes for my authority to publish a translation, and says that he is in correspondence with Prof. v. Giżycki on the subject.   I have written to Giżycki urging delay till the abridged edition comes out, and also advising him to consult with you on the subject.[1]   I don't know whom he has in mind as translator; but I think (and have told him so) that Mr. Cossmann has the "right of way" in the matter, and should not be interfered with.   His translation ought, however, to be looked over by someone completely familiar with english, as he *may* make mistakes in the sense.   Will you kindly tell me something more about him. My book is so unclassic in form, that I confess it seems not altogether right to inflict the whole of it on a foreign nation with whom my country is at peace.   Yet on the other hand I can see that the unconventionality and excursiveness of the style may have something to do with making it more readable than most of its rivals.   I write with great difficulty, and aim at brevity, hating too many words.   Yet although I may succeed with my *sentences,* I don't succeed with my *pages,* of which there are far too many.   I send with this a letter to Herr Cossmann, which I wish you would kindly read before sending to him, and between yourself, Gizycki, him & Costenoble, come to some conclusion as to what is best to do.   I will follow your advice.

Alas! I haven't yet had a chance to look into your second volume.[2] But vacation comes in 2 months, and ere the summer is gone I shall have read every word.   Next year, by way of variety, I am to be allowed to teach nothing but Psychology, and hope to be able to do some reading on that profoundly unsatisfactory subject.

Warm regards to both of you!

Yours ever | Wm James

ALS: MH bMS Am 1092.9 (3785)

[1] No German translations of *Principles of Psychology* and *Psychology: Briefer Course* were published at this time.

[2] Reference is to Stumpf's *Tonpsychologie*.

From James Sully

East Heath Road | Hampstead, | London. N. W. | 25 April/91

My dear James,

I have read your two volumes & written a longish notice of them for "Mind".[1] They have given me plenty of intellectual stimulus, a vast deal of uncommon pleasure, & have not infrequently provoked the combative instinct of the critic. I need not apologize to *you* for saying that I have traversed a good many of your ideas. This is I know how so energetic a thinker would like to be treated. I only hope I may have succeeded in my review in clearly showing that the deepest impression produced by your book is a genuine admiration of its vitality, its go, its rich fruitage of far-reaching ideas.

Meanwhile I am plodding away with my humbler effort, & am just sending a batch of M.S. to the printer. The book will be largely a new one,[2] & I shall issue it under a new title as a longer course side by side with the "Outlines" which still sells well on your side as well as on mine. There is a pretty competition just now among text-books in psychology. You are doing your best to make the old-country imputations unnecessary, & now Höffding is translated into English & issued in attractively cheap form.[3] Well, I will gladly say 'Prosit!' to them all. The more the merrier perhaps, & at least the better. It is good to have many aspects of so big a subject presented side by side.

Wishing you plenty of health for pursuing your vigorous research.

Believe me, | Yours very sincerely | J. Sully

My book will be out in October, I trust. I will not forget to send you a copy. I propose reducing the "Outlines" by cutting out most at least of the small-type-parags, but leaving the few practical applications. I trust in this way to make it a popular introduction to the subject. If from your experience or knowledge you can suggest anything on this head which would be likely to make the elementary work more suitable as a first-grade class book for American students, I shall be greatly obliged to you.   Ladd, I see has brought out a smaller edition of his "Physiological Psychology."[4]   It looks as if the student in the future might have an "embarras de richesse" in the matter of text-books.

ALS: MH bMS Am 1092 (1122)

[1] James Sully, review of *Principles of Psychology* in *Mind* 16 (July 1891): 393–404.
[2] James Sully, *The Human Mind: A Text-Book of Psychology* (1892), in two volumes (WJ 584.51).
[3] Harald Höffding, *Outlines of Psychology* (1891), translated by Mary E. Lowndes.
[4] George Trumbull Ladd, *Outlines of Physiological Psychology* (1891).

To Frederic William Henry Myers

95 Irving St, Cambr. May 5 1891
My dear Myers,

I have read your XIXth Century article, and today your remarks prompted by my book in the just arrived Proceedings no XVIII.   I think the article very masterly from the point of view of composition, and very impressive indeed from the point of view of content—in fact a most weighty production.   I don't even see how the "scientist" can help becoming grave at the considerations you present.   Each of your successive manifestations gets more solid-sounding, and it may be that the crown which comes to recognized leaders of new eras of thought will descend upon your brow sooner than you ever hoped it might.   Surely no one has ever discussed these facts as *broadly* as you—it amounts to an entirely new attitude and point of view and if that doesn't mean "epoch-making," what does?—Marillier's story is very interesting—conditions similar to crystal-gazing, I should say![1]

I am infinitely obliged to you for making so much of my book and bowed down with admiration at you for being able to read it.   Your comments are most suggestive—but I wait for the undifferentiated clairvoyant sense to be made more clear.   The ordinary facial perception of the blind is indubitably in the ear, in most subjects—read the interesting case of Mr. Steeley in the Religio-Philosophical Journal for May 2.[2]   I got Mr. Perry (the hero of the pepper & salt vision) to do some experiments which showed that he was dependent on his ears in a way which he did not realize himself.   I am glad that you are beginning to print American cases.[3]   It will help the cause here.

It is a slow hunt! But perseverance will tell. The Proceedings are already stately.

Good luck to all of you.

Yours ever | W.J.

ALS: MH bMS Am 1092.9 (3309)

[1] Léon Marillier, "Apparitions of the Virgin in Dordogne," *Proceedings of the Society for Psychical Research* 7 (April 1891): 100–110.

[2] The *Religio-Philosophical Journal*, n.s., 2 (2 May 1891): 774–75, reprints a letter from H. F. Steeley, of Rushsylvania. The blind author of the letter claims that he is aware of his surroundings not through his face but through his acute sense of hearing and therefore cannot move about when his ears are stopped up.

[3] A number of American cases are included in Eleanor Mildred Balfour Sidgwick, "On the Evidence for Clairvoyance," *Proceedings of the Society for Psychical Research* 7 (April 1891): 30–99.

To Samuel Porter

Cambridge May 6. [1891]

Professor Porter

Dear Sir;

It seems natural to be consulting you about matters psychological again.[1] Do you know of any cases, or records of cases, in which *not-deaf* children have been brought up so as not to acquire speech? And do you know whether or no such children were afterwards particularly hard to teach to speak? The only cases I know of are the wolf-children in India, who remained mutes. It occurs to me that there may have been children confined to the company of deaf mute parents, who may not have been taught speech until after the usual age, and that you may possibly know of such cases.

Do you think it worth while for me to write to Graham Bell for information?[2]

Were the *successfully* taught deaf mutes, like Mrs Bell[3] & Miss Lippit,[4] & Miss Brooks of Boston,[5] taught to articulate at a very *early* age?

Hoping this will find you well, and not trouble you too much,—it has important theoretic bearings in my mind, I am very truly yours

Wm James

ALS: Miss Porter's School, Farmington, Conn.

[1] WJ had consulted Porter on the sense of dizziness in deaf-mutes; see *EPs*, 134.

[2] Alexander Graham Bell (1847–1922), Scottish-born inventor and educator of the deaf.

[3] Mabel Gardiner Hubbard Bell (d. 1923), wife of Alexander Graham Bell. She became deaf at the age of five.

[4] Jeannie Lippitt, a student of Alexander Graham Bell, was the daughter of Henry Lippitt (1818–1891), businessman and governor of Rhode Island.
[5] Miss Brooks was not identified.

From John Dewey

15 Forest Ave | Ann Arbor Mich | 6 May 91

Dear Professor James:

I wish to thank you for the kindness & frankness with which you wrote me about my Leibniz.[1]   I assure you that your words have anything but 'forwardness' to me and that coming from you they have given me great encouragement.   I know in a good deal of my work that I have shown more zeal than discretion, but I have always believed that for a man to give himself away is one of the best methods for him to get rid of himself.   The public can always protect itself effectually enough.

I must protest against the imputation of considering you a barbarian—or if I do consider you one then I believe that the chief function of civilization is to produce barbarians,—unless civilization means sophistication.   On my side, I presume to think that I am more of a Yankee and less of a "philosopher" than sometimes may appear.

I wrote Messrs. Holt & Co a brief not[e] upon receiving your psychology from them, and should have been glad to express to you personally not only my enjoyment of it, but my great indebtedness to you for such portions of the book as had previously appeared. The whole book greatly deepened my indebtedness.   I am not going to burden you with my reflections or criticisms, but I cannot suppress my own secret longing that you had at least worked out the suggestion you throw out on Page 304 of vol I.[2]   If I understand at all what Hegel is driving at, that is a much better statement of the real core of Hegel than what you criticize later on as Hegelianism.   Take out your "*postulated*" 'matter' '& thinker', let 'matter' (i.e. the physical world) be the organization of the *content* of sciousness up to a certain point, & the thinker be a still further unified organization [*not* a *unifying* organ as per Green] and that is good enough Hegel for me.   And if this point of view had been worked out, would you have needed any 'special' activity of attention, or any 'special' act of will?   The fundamental fact would then be the tendency towards a maximum content of sciousness, and within this growing organization of sciousness effort &c could find their place.   At the risk, after all, of burdening you, it seems to me that on page 369 (I) you virtually fall into the meshes of the "psychological fallacy"[3] (Let me say that I think the discovery & express formulation of this *alone* would have marked any book as 'epoch-making') I surrender Green to your tender mercies, but the unity of Hegel's self (& what Caird is driving it)[4] is not a unity in the stream as such, but of the *function* of this stream—the unity of the world (content) which it bears or reports. It may seem strange to call this unity Self, but while Kant undoubtedly tried to make *an* agent out of this (and Green follows him) Hegel's agent (or Self) is simply the universe doing business on its own account. But I must forbear. But Hegel seems to me intensely modern in his spirit, whatever his garb, and I don't like to see him dressed up as Scholasticus Redivivus—although of course his friends, the professed Hegelians, are mainly responsible for that.

I hope you won't regret your letter when you find that it emboldened me to send you a copy of my Ethics as well as to write the above.[5]

Mr. Delabarre emphasized matters somewhat when he said he had a call here. Our present instructor, Mr Tufts, used to know him and wrote him a personal letter which was supposed to have no official character at all.[6]   From the tone of Mr. Delabarre's reply, I judged that he didn't care for a place here anyway, as he wanted to study longer. The work will not be specially heavy next year, the present instructor's work being divided, one taking the text-book work in logic & psychology, the other the work in history of philosophy & physiol. psychology, I am anxious to develop the latter branch here. I have written to Mr. Mead about the latter position,[7] & it was for that I had Mr. Delabarre in mind. In case there should be any hitch, on either side, with Mead I should be glad if you would let me know if any good man for such a combination comes into your mind. Thanking you again for your information regarding men, as well as for your letter,

Sincerely yours | John Dewey.

Would it horrify you, if I stated that your theory of emotions (where you seem to me to have completely made out your case) is good Hegelianism? Although of course, Hegel gets at it in a very different way. But according to Hegel a man can't feel his own feelings unless they go around, as it were, through his body.

ALS: MH bMS Am 1092.9 (128)

[1] John Dewey, *Leibniz's New Essays Concerning the Human Understanding* (1888).
[2] *PP,* 290–91.

[3] *PP,* 349; see also letter of 20 January 1891.

[4] A slip for 'driving at'.

[5] John Dewey, *Outlines of a Critical Theory of Ethics* (1891).

[6] James Hayden Tufts (1862–1942), American philosopher, one of Dewey's collaborators, then teaching with Dewey at the University of Michigan. Correspondence is known from 1905 and 1906.

[7] George Herbert Mead began teaching at the University of Michigan in the fall of 1891.

To William Dean Howells

95 Irving St. Cambridge, May 8. [1891]

My dear Howells

Surely never before did a work on mental Science get so judged at the court of letters.[1] I only wish you were not a friend of the family, so that my astonished eyes might read it as a tribute wrested by invincible evidence from an originally reluctant judge. It is a great deal too handsome for the book, that is all I can say.—I don't know what just reminds me that in the hurry of the book's final preparation for the press, *your* account of the symptoms of the naughty Bartley Hubbard's intoxication, which I had all marked to be quoted in a certain place, was accidentally left out.[2] My vols are so much the poorer.—The *deles* in this proof make me feel the space-relations under which you write—they take it out of the editorial departments! I have made bold to suggest a change in the erasures, egotistically sacrificing some of your text to mine. It seems to me that my extract hardly has a raison d'être without the lines scored out. But manage this as you will!

Your everlastingly obliged | Wm James

What an able fellow Weir Mitchell is![3]

ALS: MH bMS Am 1092.9 (1016)

[1] Howells reviewed *Principles of Psychology* in *Harper's New Monthly Magazine* 83 (July 1891): 314–16, focusing on its merits as literature.

[2] Bartley Hubbard is a character in several novels of William Dean Howells. In chaps. 24 and 25 of *A Modern Instance* (1882) Hubbard got drunk after being locked out by his wife.

[3] Silas Weir Mitchell, *A Psalm of Deaths and Other Poems* (1890). Howells wrote a notice of Mitchell's book for *Harper's New Monthly Magazine* 83 (July 1891): 316.

From John Dewey

15 Forest Ave.|Ann Arbor. May 10, 91
My dear Professor James

Your hearty note regarding the Ethics was very welcome to me.
The book has received a little of what is called "favorable comment"
as well as more or less of the reverse but so far as reported you are
the first man to see the point—and that I suppose is the dearest thing
to a writer.   The present preceptual structure is so great, and such
a weighty thing, both in theory & in practice, that I don't anticipate
any succ[e]ss for the book, but when one man like yourself expresses
what you wrote me, the book has already succeeded.

But unless a man is already living in the gospel & not under the
law, as you express it, words thrown at him are idle wind. He doesn't
understand what you mean, & he wouldn't believe you meant it, if
he did understand.   The hope seems to be with the rising generation—at least, most of them seem to be feeling for some relief from
the present load.   Many of my students, I find, are fairly hungering.
They almost jump at any opportunity to get out from under the
load & to believe in their own lives.   Pardon the somewhat confessional character of this note, but the man who has seen the point
arouses the confessional attitude.

I have had, since writing Professor Palmer, a long account of Nichols from himself.   Your account & his own fit entirely—very eager &
intense & great original capacity I judge, but still hampered by a one-
sided training.   I'm afraid he couldn't handle the history of philosophy very intelligently.   His sense for historic & human values seems
rather embryonic yet, tho' I think in the right atmosphere it would
develop rapidly.   It seems a pity, for the sake of his students, when
they come to get places that Hall can't give his men a chance at more
sides of philosophy.   Aside from the fact that we are not able to limit
a man's work to physiological psychology, I should distrust somewhat a man even for that, whose training had been exclusive. I think
a man's attitude towards what the world has previously thought
ought to be somewhat different than that of a "scientist" towards a curiosity.

Sincerely yours | John Dewey

I don't know that I told you that I have had a class of four graduates going through your psychology this year, & how much we have
all enjoyed it. I'm sure you would be greatly gratified if you could

see what a stimulus to mental freedom, as well as what a purveyor of methods & materials your book has been to us.

ALS: MH bMS Am 1092.9 (129)

To Alice Howe Gibbens James

Chocorua, ½ past 4 | Sunday afternoon | May 11. 1891[1]
Beloved Wife, I sit writing this in your mother's window through which the soft warm air is flowing. Not an insect; and the lake shore clad in the tenderest most vapory browns & yellows and emerald greens, the trees being as yet only in bud. The little place has a domestic expression all its own. But the drouth is bad.—Yesterday was a hazy smoky drouthy sky with no shadows cast, and not a breath of air. Instead of feeling most the sweetness of the country, I felt the sadness of the dead little empty house. On entering this room, I seemed to feel Aunt Kate as she last sat here; and in the Salter's room the little dead Eliza; and in your room I felt as I might if I had outlived you all, and was visiting amongst your relics; and a heavy fullness of heart and throat that were good things to have after my fury & hurry at home, filled me all the day. I went to bed at 9.30 and got up at eight 30, after a night the like of which for quiet I haven't had this year.—Whilst I was washing I heard a step in the house, which on being challenged proved to be Jim Chadwick, up here to see about his house. His road is just a building, and his h—
At this point the aforesaid J. C. came in on me again and now at 6.30 we are back from a walk over the hill to see Ross, who, together with his wife is sick o' the grip, so that I'll go to morrow P.M. and have a better chance at business. [Every one here has the grip] Ross has already got the berries etc in fine shape, and put in 2 good elms, one near the spring. This A.M. I drove to Hammond's with Chadwick. To morrow I'll go to Pollard's.[2] I dined with Nickerson,[3] and Hamner,[4] and go now with Chad^k to sup at the Bowditch's who are all here for a week.[5]

I wondered all last evening how my wife was enjoying her dinner at the Ames's all by herself.

Adieu: love to all, | W.J.

ALS: MH bMS Am 1092.9 (1775)

[1] Sunday was 10 May in 1891.
[2] The Pollards were a Chocorua family.

[3] Nickerson is most likely John Henry Nickerson, but there were other Nickersons in Chocorua.

[4] An error for 'Hammer'. Emil C. Hammer (d. 1894), Danish-born manufacturer and art collector, was the Danish consul in Boston.

[5] Charles Pickering Bowditch (1842–1921), brother of Henry Pickering Bowditch, was a trustee and archaeologist. His wife was Cornelia Livingstone Rockwell Bowditch and they had four children. The Bowditches had a summer home in Chocorua. One letter (1887) is known.

To Théodore Flournoy

CAMBRIDGE May 31. 1891

My dear Mr. Flournoy

I received the Journal de Genève a week ago, with your review of my psychology in it, and I need hardly say that it afforded me very acute pleasure. Unrestricted and unqualified praise is after all the real thing which authors crave, and the adjectives need not fear to make themselves too superlative! It is easier, however, to be a "noble et forte personalité" in a book, than in the bosom of one's family; and it is perhaps well that you wrote your review of the book before you had acquired a greater degree of intimacy with its author! But, joking and modesty apart, the review pleased me more than any other which I have yet seen, because, in spite of its being untechnical and avoiding every detail, I seemed to feel that you had better than anyone else caught the "point of view" of my lengthy pages. I am the more sure of this since I have read your "Metaphysique et Psychologie."[1] When it arrived last Autumn I laid it aside for a propitious moment; and finally as my year got fuller and fuller of drudgery and reading for my lectures, it took its place in a pile of books destined to be read in the summer vacation. The last lecture took place 3 days ago; the blessed vacation has almost begun—we have but two weeks more, for examinations—and I have just finished your little book. It has really delighted me, no less by the extraordinary vitality of the style than by the admirable good sense of the matter. This is to be really "scientific" without being a bar[b]arian into the bargain, as so many of our "scientists" are! You have a great future as a writer; and I hope as a thinker, although as yet you have shown so little of your hand. It behoves all of us who on the whole agree in aims and methods to close up our ranks and give each other a helping hand, and perhaps our "School" will prevail!

Thanking you once more most heartily for your so cordial and all too flattering words, I am yours faithfully

Wm James

Pray keep on writing! I have been reading myself to sleep of late by means of Voltaire, and I assure you that your style does not suffer by the close comparison.

ALS: MH bMS AM 1505 (1)

[1] Théodore Flournoy, *Métaphysique et psychologie* (1890).

From John Dewey

Ann Arbor June 3, 91

My dear James

I have been putting off writing you day by day as theses &c piled up about me. Besides, although I had read your ethical article once & recommended it to my class to read, I wanted to read it again.[1] The article rejoiced me greatly—if possibly, two things more than others, then your statement that any desire, as such, constitutes a claim & any claim an obligation, and your discussion of rules. I was only sorry that the discussion of obligation, in particular, had not appeared before I wrote my Ethics. I think it is the best & simplest statement I have ever seen.

I should say that there is something back (& something ahead) of whatever freedom of sight & treatment there is in my ethics. I got it from Franklin Ford to whom I refer in the preface.[2] By some sort of instinct, & by the impossibility of my doing anything in particular, I was led into philosophy & into "idealism"—i.e. the conception of some organism comprehending both man's thought & the eternal world. Ford, who was a newspaper man (formerly Editor of Bradstreets in N.Y.)[3] with no previous philosophical training had been led by his newspaper experience to study, as a practical question the social bearings of intelligence & its distribution. That is to say, he was on a paper & wanted to inquire. The paper would not let him; the more he was stopped, the more his desire to inquire was aroused, until finally he was drawn into a study of the whole matter—especially as he found that it was not any one newspaper but rather the social structure which prevented freedom of inquiry. Well, he identified the question of inquiry with, in philosophical terms, the question of the relation of intelligence to the objective world—is the former free to move in relation to the latter or not? So he studied out the following questions (1) The conditions & effects of the distribution of intelligence especially with reference to inquiry, or the selling of truth as a business; (2) the present (or past) hindrances to its free play, in the way of class interests &c (3) the present conditions, in the railway, telegraph &c for effectively securing the freedom of intelligence—that is, its movement in the world of social fact, and (4) the resulting social organization.   That is, with inquiry as a *business,* the selling of truth for money, the *whole* would have a representative as well as the various classes—a representative whose belly interest moreover is identical with its truth interest.

Now I am simply reducing what was a wonderful personal experience to a crude bit of cataloging, but I hope it may arouse your interest in the man & his work.

What I have got out of it is first the perception of the tone or practical bearing of idealism—that philosophy has been the assertion of the unity of intelligence & the external world *in idea* or subjectively, while if true in idea it must finally secure the conditions of its objective expression.   And secondly I believe that a tremendous movement is impending when the intellectual forces which have been gathering since the Renascence & Reformation shall demand complete free movement, and, by getting their physical leverage in the telegraph & printing press, shall through free inquiry in a centralized way, demand the authority of all other so-called authorities.

It is impossible to convey what I mean in a page or two, but, as I am all the more anxious to see you & talk with you on this very account, I hope I may not have made you suspicious of me.   I shall have with me in the summer a number of Ford's own writings which will convey in an orderly & rational way.   I do not think that any one who, like yourself, has the intellectual interest developed, the thirst for inquiry with no special interest or precept or church or philosophy to "save," can fail of being interested both in his theoretical discovery and in his practical project.

Davidson has already gone to the Adirondacks—Keene Centre is his address—I got some circulars yesterday & have just sent one to Miss Child[4]   Mrs Dewey left for there last week and is putting up some kind of an abiding place against my coming on.[5]   I most heartily hope you will be there this summer.   The natural attractions are certainly great—and there are no artificial ones unless you call the philosophical lectures such.[6]   And they are evitable.   It is possible that we shall have a couple of your Cambridge men here next year in philosophy.   I have written to Mead offering him the instructorship in history of phil & phy. psy. and am just going to write Lloyd offering him the one in psychology & logic.

Sincerely yours | John Dewey

I hope Nichols will get a place somewhere. He seems a strong & earnest fellow &, it seems, is quite disappointed at not falling in here.

ALS: MH bMS Am 1092.9 (130)

[1] Reference is to "The Moral Philosopher and the Moral Life."

[2] Franklin Ford (1848–1918), American editor and reformer, sometimes credited with turning Dewey's attention to concrete social problems. Ford conceived the idea of conducting research and publishing its results in a new kind of newspaper. In the spring of 1892 Dewey and Ford were planning to publish *Thought News*, a newspaper devoted to all aspects of social life, but no issue was published.

[3] *Bradstreet's*, published in New York City, was devoted to trade and finance.

[4] Miss Child was not identified.

[5] Dewey's first wife was Alice Chipman Dewey (1857–1927), American educator.

[6] Reference is to the Summer School of the Culture Sciences organized by Thomas Davidson.

To Alice Howe Gibbens James

Chocorua, June 10 [1891] | 12.30

Dearest Alice,

Everything is surprisingly simplified this year, though the place looks rather melancholy with the grass grown tall all about it the little starved strawberry plants sharing their place with the sorrel, and the few splindly asparagus plants all gone to seed. The other plot of vegetables hardly show their tips as yet;—but as they had a frost 3 or 4 days ago, it is just as well perhaps that the garden was n't planted earlier. I have been on my feet all day and just come home from a bath with billy. Clancy is taking hold of the barn-cleaning very well—he evidently is a neat person and shocked by the ramshackle conditions of things there.[1] He slept in the Salter's room last night. The keys turned up in Andrew's room where I suspected that I had forgotten them. On looking at the guest-room, I am inclined to think (with you?) that the entrance through the closet is the best. But Alonzo Nickerson can't get out any studding till next Monday,[2] so its no use having Hammond come till next week.—There are surprisingly few mosquitoes.—I am going to send Clancy this P.M. to Moore's for the tub-trough etc,[3] whilst I go on Vic[4] to Hammond's, Piper's etc.[5]—To morrow Clancy and Maggie[6] must do a lot of fencing between our place and Albee's.[7] I feel very languid, and my ideas don't flow, so I will close now.—One set of ideas I've been having for the last twenty four hours are relative to the redoubled and clinched and re-corroborated nature of my tie to you—du Einzige!   I never knew you so lovable as you've been in the past week—since Tweedy got well.   I will return by 2 on Friday.

W.J.

After dinner: Good grub!   Clancy is grand on barn cleaning.   He is going over it with a feather duster.

ALS: MH bMS Am 1092.9 (1777)

[1] Clancy was not identified.

[2] Alonzo Nickerson was a workman in Chocorua.

[3] Moore's Store, operated by Fred Moore, was in the town of Chocorua and had pews on the porch where visitors could sit, smoke, and talk.

[4] Vic was one of WJ's horses.

[5] The Pipers were a Chocorua family, some of whose members at one time had owned a mill.

[6] Maggie was one of WJ's horses.

[7] John Albee (1833–1915), American author, one of WJ's neighbors in Chocorua.

To William Dean Howells

CAMBRIDGE June 12. 91

My dear Howells,

You are a sublime and immortal genius!   I have just read Silas Lapham and Lemuel Barker—strange that I should not have read them before, after hearing my wife rave about them so—and of all the perfect works of fiction they are the perfectest.[1]   The truth, in gross and in detail; the concreteness and solidity; the geniality, humanity, and unflagging humor; the steady way in which it keeps up without a dead paragraph; and especially the fidelity with which you stick to the ways of human Nature, with the ideal and the unideal inseparably beaten up together so that you never give them "clear,"— all make them a feast of delight, which if I mistake not, will last for all future time, or as long as novels *can* last.   Silas is the bigger total success because it deals with a more important story (I think you ought to have made young Corey *angrier* about Irene's mistake & its consequences)[2] but the *work* on the much obstructed Lemuel surely was never surpassed.   I hope his later life was happy!

Altogether *you* ought to be happy—you can fold your arms and write no more if you like.   I've just got your "criticism and fiction," which shall speedily be read.   And whilst in the midst of this note have rec'd from the Postman your clipping from Kate Field's Washington, the author of which I can't divine, but she's a blessed creature whoever she is.[3]

Yours ever | Wm James

ALS: MH bMS Am 1092.9 (1019)

[1] William Dean Howells, *The Rise of Silas Lapham* (1885); *The Minister's Charge or the Apprenticeship of Lemuel Barker* (1886).

[2] The plot of *The Rise of Silas Lapham* revolves around Tom Corey, who courts and eventually marries Penelope Lapham, while everyone, including Penelope and her sister Irene, had thought that he was courting Irene. Corey appears more puzzled than angry upon discovering that he has been misunderstood.

[3] See next letter.

To Mary Augusta Jordan

95 Irving S! Cambridge, [June 13, 1891][1]

My dear Miss Jordan,

I *might* have thought of your name from our hallucination-correspondence, but I didn't.[2] Your review is the most flattering one which my book has received, and pleases me most because you seem to have best grasped the *spirit,* or "caught the point,["] of my unwieldy undertaking.[3] You are human, and not technical; and if there is anything I should *like* to do, it is to keep Psychology human for a while longer.

I wish I could see the rest of what you wrote. Can't you send it to me, at the risk of appearing technical and not human? But what an odd channel in which to publish such a review! And how can you reconcile your conscience to not having sent me a copy of the thing yourself? It was by the merest chance that I heard of this.

I am about falling to on an abridgement in some 500 pp. which will sell better, and in some respects be clearer though probably less "human." Sully is to produce a newer, larger work in the fall.[4]

Well! Heaven bless you! If you ever come to these parts *don't fail* to let me and Mrs. James know of it.

Yours gratefully | Wm. James

ALS: MNS

[1] Dating is approximate and is based on the fact that WJ received the clipping of Mary Jordan's review of *Principles of Psychology* from William Dean Howells on 12 June 1891.

[2] WJ is mistaken in thinking that he had corresponded with Mary Jordan about the Census of Hallucinations; see letter to Jordan of 29 June 1891.

[3] *Kate Field's Washington* 7 (10 June 1891), 452.

[4] James Sully, *The Human Mind.*

To Alice James

CAMBRIDGE June 14, 1891

Dearest Alice,

Katherine's account of Sir A. Clarke's visit was received yesterday, and I write you one line to tell you how interested we have been. I wonder how old this heart defect can be. I can well understand how it must comfort you to have something solid in the pathological way to lean upon; for your sufferings are the same whatever the cause, and heart disease is a "morbid entity" whose name justifies you for anything in the ears of the outer world.—I would to Heaven I could do something more than philosophize about it—your state of late most have been pitiable indeed. The only thing I *can* do, as it would seem, is to send you home gossip, of which since my last writing, none has accumulated. A week ago I spent a night at Miss Lizzie Perkins's pretty little Alhambresque abode at Beverly and in the train and at the Depôt in the morning saw everyone.[1] Mrs. Morse looked extremely vigorous and brown. Mrs. Whitman took me to her studio to see her portrait of D.ʳ Holmes which is really admirable, and the best thing which she has done in that line, I fancy. I have spent two days at Chocorua, mostly hard at work on the place, and am now back over business here. Mrs. G. & billy are up there. The rest of them follow in a few days, and I in ten or twelve. Our summer has been *very* dry, and for a week very hot. It has its pleasantness. Our little Irving St. settlement looks handsome, and we form a colony of very sociable neighbors. Our front porches & piazzas looking towards the East are covered with richly dressed ladies about sundown—just now, with Alice and our dome-headed baby, two other mother's and their babies.— — —I suppose you're not above taking an interest in the Baccarat Scandal.[2] What an ignominious situation for a descendant of what were once called "Kings"—not to be able to play a game in a friend's house without all the Methodists & Baptists sending him manifestoes. To be insulted publicly before a crowd of spectators, and no power of redress, etc etc. It is the least dignified place in the Kingdom, with neither rights, duties nor privacy, and one would suppose that any individual with genuine personal pride would be so disgusted with it as to withdraw into private life where he might have some power and liberty. The situation of Royalty in England seems to me so *trashy*, all fluff and plush, and gilt plaster, like one of Barnum's circus cars, with no real style or force. I always think of it as an annex to Mme. Tussaud's.[3] The Prince of

Wales with the everlasting *"tact with which he performs his duties"*(!) is simply nauseous to me—and I trust to you. When "King" means that degree of insignificance it had better become an archeological name, and the country a democracy.

Oceans of sympathy, you poor dear girl, from your loving brother

W.J.

ALS: MH bMS Am 1092.9 (1153)

[1] Lizzie Perkins is possibly Elizabeth Perkins of Boston; see *Correspondence*, 6:253.

[2] Sir William Gordon-Cumming was accused of cheating at baccarat, with the primary loser being the future king of England, Edward VII (1841–1910), then Albert Edward, Prince of Wales. In a case that attracted much public notice, Sir Gordon-Cumming sued his accusers for libel and lost.

[3] Marie Tussaud (1760–1850), Swiss modeler in wax, established museums of wax figures of famous people.

To Sarah Wyman Whitman

95 Irving St June 17. 91

My dear Mrs. Whitman,

I am laid up with tonsillitis, which is not so very bad a case, but it comes on top of wakefulness and makes me so sure of being *non compos* on Saturday and Sunday, that I am going to decline your beautiful invitation. "Let me go, return me to the ground!"[1] I am at present no fit associate for your youth & beauty, nor for the likes of that with which you are surrounded. Would I could think I should be missed!!—Pray excuse the sordidness of these details, but I must give you my true reason. When the year's lecturing is done I always come tumbling down like a sail whose halyard is let go; and until I've had a fortnight of genuine rustication, with no talk and no fashions, I never can pick myself up again. I don't see what "you 'uns" do without ever a vacation to your name.—You must forgive me; and before the summer is over, I promise to come and see you even more than you desire.

Always faithfully yours | Wm James

I found the Art Museum not yet open on the Monday Morning when I left you, and have been unable to get there since.[2] I want to see your picture alongside of the New Yorkers.—Your Dr Holmes leaves a splendid impression behind. I believe it to be a great portrait. Isn't it your best, so far?

ALS: MH bMS Am 1092.9 (3909)

[1] From Tennyson's "Tithonus," line 72.

[2]The thirteenth exhibition of the Society of American Artists opened at the Museum of Fine Arts in Boston on 3 June 1891 and closed on 2 July. The account in the *Boston Evening Transcript* of 4 June 1891 emphasizes the work of John Singer Sargent; it does not mention Sarah Whitman.

To Sarah Wyman Whitman

95 Irving St, June 20. '91

My dear Mrs Whitman,

You *are* magnificent! Here comes your letter at 6 o'clock just as I am looking wearily out of the window for a change, and makes me feel like an aspiring youth again. But I can't go to Beverly to morrow, nor indeed leave my room, I fear, for I've had every kind of *-itis* that can afflict one's upper breathing channels, and although convalescent, am as weak as a blade of grass, and feel as antique as Methusalem. A fortnight hence I shall be like a young puppy-dog again, however, and shall turn up inevitably between two trains more than once ere the summer is over.

I've managed to get through Vol I of Scott's Journal in the last two days. The dear old boy! But who would not be "dear" who cd. have such a mass of doggrell running in his head all the time, and make a hundred thousand dollars a year just by letting his pen trickle?[1] Bless his dear old "unenlightened" soul all the same. The Scotch are the finest race in the world—except the baltimoreans and jews—and I think I *enjoyed* my 24 hours of Edinboro' two summers ago more than any 24 hours a city ever gave me.

Good bye!—I'm describing W.S.'s character when I ought to be describing yours—but you never give me a chance. When I get that task performed, we shall settle down to a solid basis, though probably all that will be in "the dim future." Meanwhile my love to all the Youth and Beauty (including your own) and best wishes for their happiness and freedom from influenzas of every description till the end of time.

Affectionately yours | W.J.

ALS: MH bMS Am 1092.9 (3910)

[1]Sir Walter Scott (1771–1832), Scottish novelist, *The Journal of Sir Walter Scott* (1890). Scott's many books sold well, but his financial dealings were complicated and he was usually in debt.

To Alice Howe Gibbens James

CAMBRIDGE June 22. 91 | 8.45 P.M.

Beloved Alice—I hope that you are now all serenely settled after a fairly comfortable & dry journey. I went to Jim Putnam who told me there was no *sommité* in Boston for such operations, but that Chadwick & Jack Eliot would be as good as any one. In case of his own wife he would have Chadwick, because Chadwick has been her Doctor already. Of Kelly he knew nothing particular.[1] I saw Chadwick who doesn't mean to be at Chocorua himself for more than a couple of days at a time, but who said that the operation required patience & care rather than any great skill of manpulation—he frequently performs it. Kelly he said was a young man, from whom much was hoped but who had had no very wide experience. He favored the idea of Chocorua, with Wally's doctor to look at her daily until he shd. return a week later.[2] But I must say that under the special circumstances, I should prefer, if he were to do the job, to be in Boston. There is plenty of time to discuss the pros & cons hereafter.—I will write to Mack to morrow. I then went to the Art Museum, some rather interesting N.Y. pictures,[3] with poor Mrs. W.'s rejected Sally Fairchild hanging outside. There I met Jack Elliott & Mary Morse. Thence to Hodgson's, and then out here. H. says that he thinks Mrs. Piper would be very glad to visit us this summer.— The house seems disconsolate, and I in the sere & yellow leaf—but also I feel that vacation has begun. I am back from the Club, where Chaplin talked on amusingly for an hour. The veal cutlets were less good than Bridget's.—I send this letter of Katherine's—poor Alice! Thank Margaret for her letter—the first I ever received from her, and momentous on that acc! She speaks of Peggy's fears. If she doesn't get over Toby, he will have to be given away without telling her that its on her acc! Heaven bless you, you all too perfect wife.

WJ.

ALS: MH bMS Am 1092.9 (1778)

[1] Kelly was not identified.

[2] Perhaps William Phillips Walley (1843–1891), a lawyer in Boston. No information about the surgery, where apparently Margaret Mary was a patient, was found.

[3] See letter of 17 June 1891.

To Alice Howe Gibbens James

CAMBRIDGE June 24. '91 | 6.30 P.M.

Dearest Alice

Your pathetic little letter came duly this P.M. It's no disasters in the future; its the long grass and "the passion of the past."[1] Moreover its the *completed* place—no more to do, and it looks so little.

Another day of sterile tiresomeness. Very stupid commencement—the little Jap Kosaki's being the only brilliant "part."[2] Pathetic little Scientific School dinner. Rand, Briggs[3] & letters have bro't me till now. Slept well last night, and within past 2 hours, the sick feeling has largely gone. Bkfst.ᵈ very pleasantly with Theodora. No more to say—must read a number of conditioned exam.ⁿ books etc. & mow lawn.

Good night! Bless you.

W.J.

Poor little Peggy. Its awful.

ALS: MH bMS Am 1092.9 (1779)

[1] From Tennyson's "The Ancient Sage," line 219.

[2] At the commencement on 24 June 1891 Nariaki Kozaki, a divinity student and later a teacher of theology in Japan, spoke on Christian thought in Japan.

[3] Briggs was probably one of WJ's builders. If so, they were discussing plans for Eliza Gibbens's house.

To Mary Gray Ward Dorr

Cambridge, June 29. 91

My dear Mrs. Dorr

This is to waft an affectionate good bye to you and yours. I hope we shall all meet again younger, stronger, better and more beautiful two years hence than we are now. We *can* if we'll only live rightly! I know that you three will; and I know that my wife will; but as for me and the children, there is more reason to doubt.

I am winding up my work here and leave to morrow for Chocorua. I've had the grip and am still very seedy in consequence. Yesterday I returned from a 24 hours visit to Mr. Tweedy at Newport. Mrs Tweedy died early last week—gradually losing mind and strength and painlessly falling asleep, at the age of eighty one or two.—I have just read that *most* interesting life of Laurence Oliphant, by that good hearted but incompetent little ninny the novelist of the same name.[1] You have probably read it; but if you haven't, please do so immediately. It enlarges singularly ones conceptions of human Nature. I am also now in the midst of his "Sympneumata"[2] and wish I had George here to talk it over with.[3]

Good bye! a happy voyage, and a safe return, and God bless you all, from yours affectionately

Wm James

ALS: MH bMS Am 1092.1

[1] Margaret Oliphant Wilson Oliphant (1828–1897), British novelist and writer, *Memoir of the Life of Laurence Oliphant and of Alice Oliphant, His Wife* (1891).

[2] Laurence Oliphant, *Sympneumata; or, Evolutionary Forces Now Active in Man* (1885).

[3] Reference is to George Bucknam Dorr.

To Mary Augusta Jordan

Cambridge June 29 1891

My dear Miss Jordan,

In returning your your manuscript, I must say in a more serious tone perhaps than before, how deeply touched I am by the fact all the agonies and wearinesses & disgusts of the composition should become effective in the fashion which you express.

I am only sorry to find that you are not professionally a philosopher. Had you been one, I fear that you would have been insensible to those qualities in the book which now seem to have struck you most—you would have taken it less broadly. Your colleague, Professor Gardner was good enough to write me of the book, that he feared there was much in it "which younger minds would wrest to their destruction,"[1] so I judge that the English and the Philosophical departments in Smith University do not harmonize as well as they ought to.—If you did n't send me any hallucinations, how is it that as soon as I read your name it sounded familiar to me and connected itself with Smith College?[2] But no matter; we must see each other erelong not as in a glass darkly but face to face.

Gratefully & truly yours | Wm James

ALS: MNS

[1] Harry Norman Gardiner.

[2] In his letter to Jordan of 13 June 1891, WJ referred to correspondence with her about the Census of Hallucinations, apparently in error.

To Charles William Eliot

Chocorua, N.H. | July 3. 1891

Dear Mr. Eliot

Before leaving home I got from the recorder of Corporation Votes a notice that I had been put on the Admin. B. of the graduate School again.[1] You had written me that my entrance into the Committee of freshman-advisers should relieve me of this, so I was *tant soit peu* disappointed. I don't think I'm lazy, but my working powers are below par, and I'm always quite used up at the end of the year, and thrice have had to go abroad to recuperate, very inconveniently. I will do the duties of these too committees, but ask that in compensation I be relieved from the Committee on Fellowships, and possibly from that on Instruction, although the work on the latter is very light. I may as well tell you now that my desire is to take my leave of absence a year from now, and take my family abroad.

My impression is that in the extraordinary scrupulousness and conscientiousness with which our machine is being organized now, we run the risk of overwhelming the lives of men whose interest is more in learning than in administration. There has been endless groaning last year. Time will doubtless make the organism run more rapidly, provided ever new committees don't arise. But the great remedy, it seems to me, would lie in giving more and more full powers to the various chairmen, and get as chairmen men who like power, and in return for executive service have their other duties abridged. Personally I believe that I am good for nothing in concrete practical affairs, and that my time is much better put into Science and teaching. As freshman adviser I imagine I might be of some use. I suppose you are hearing this sort of grumbling from various quarters. It is only for your slow rumination, and of course demands no reply.

In re Rand, the matter stands thus in my mind: If he is here, he will unquestionably be employed to do all the mark-work in Philosophy 1.[2] Being so employed in reality, it seems to me *unfair* that we shouldn't publish the fact, and let him gain what credit from it he may, especially since he has so long been employed without credit. It is a godsend to us to have him; and surely as easy to resist an unfair demand of his in the future as this fair demand now. I hope that on reflection the matter will seem to you even so!

Always faithfully yours | Wm James

ALS: MH Archives

[1] For the 1891–92 academic year WJ is listed among the freshman advisers and as

a member of the Committee on Instruction. His name does not appear on the list of members of the Administrative Board of the Graduate School.

[2] Philosophy 1: General Introduction to Philosophy was taught by Palmer, WJ, and Royce in 1891–92. Benjamin Rand is not listed in connection with philosophy courses for that year.

To Alice James

Chocorua N.H. | July 6. '91

Dearest Alice,

To night there comes another letter from Katherine telling everything about D.ᵣ Clark's visit, especially the tumor in your poor breast, and the pain which you have suffered there. I didn't myself see very well how such a heart-defect as you could now be having could account for anything like the "heft" of your symptoms and condition; and so far from being shocked, I am, although made more compassionate, yet (strange to say) rather relieved than shocked by this more tangible and immediately-menacing source of woe. Katherine describes you as being so too; and I don't wonder: Vague nervousness has a character of ill about it that is all its own, and in comparison with which any organic disease has a good side.

Of course if the tumor should turn out to be cancerous, that means, as all men know, a finite length of days; and then good bye to neurasthenia and neuralgia and headache, and weariness and palpitation and disgust all at one stroke—I should think you would be reconciled to the prospect with all its pluses and minuses! I know you've never cared for life, and to me now at the age of nearly fifty life and death seem singularly close together in all of us—and life a mere farce of frustration in all, so far as the realization of the innermost ideals go to which we are made respectively capable of feeling an affinity and responding. Your frustrations are only rather more flagrant than the rule; and you've been saved many forms of self-dissatisfaction and misery which appertain to such a multiplication of responsible relations to different people as I, for instance, have got into. Your fortitude, good spirits and unsentimentality have been simply unexampled in the midst of your physical woes; and when you're relieved from your post, just *that* bright note will remain behind, together with the inscrutable and mysterious character of the doom of nervous weakness which has chained you down for all these years. As for that, there's more in it than has ever been told to so-called Science. These inhibitions, these split-up selves, all these new facts that are gradually coming to light about our organization, these enlargements of the self in trance etc., are bringing me to turn for light in the direction of all sorts of despised spiritualistic and unscientific ideas. Father would find in me to day a much more receptive listener—all that philosophy has got to be brought in. And what a queer contradiction comes to the ordinary scientific argument against immortality (based on body being mind's condition and mind going *out* when body is gone) when one must believe (as now, in these neurotic cases) that some infernality in the body *prevents* really existing parts of the mind from coming to their effective rights at all, suppresses them and blots them out from participation in this world's experiences, although they are *there* all the time. When that which is *you* passes out of the body, I am sure that there will be an explosion of liberated force and life, till then eclipsed and kept down. I can hardly imagine *your* transition without a great oscillation of both "Worlds," as they regain their new equilibrium after the change! Everyone will feel the shock, but you yourself will be more surprised than anybody else.—It may seem odd for me to talk to you in this cool way about your end; but my dear little sister, if one has things present to one's mind, and I know they are present enough to *your* mind, why not speak them out? I am sure you appreciate that best.—How many times I have thought, in the past year, when my days were so full of strong and varied impressions and activities, of the long unchanging hours in bed which those days stood for with you, and wondered how you bore the slow-paced monotony at all, as you did! You can't tell how I've pitied you. But you *shall* come to your rights erelong. Meanwhile take things gently—look for the little good in each day as if life were to last a hundred years. Above all things save yourself from bodily pain, if it can be done: You've had too much of that. Take all the morphia (or other forms of opium if that disagrees) you want, and don't be afraid of becoming an opium-drunkard. What was opium created for except for such times as this? Beg the good Katherine (to whom *our* debt can never be extinguished) to write me a line every week, just to keep the currents flowing, and so farewell until I write again.

Your ever loving | W.J.

I was making the boys spell "parallel" yesterday, when Margaret Mary asked me what parallel meant. I held up my two forefingers and said "See, my fingers are now parallel." "Does it mean *dirty*?" the maid inquired.—I *had* been weeding the garden a while before.— Margaret Gibbens, who came back here yesterday after 10 days at

Randolph Coolidge's,[1] overheard two ladies talking in the cars about a third. "She's one of those people who think that the Church belongs to the poor people as well as to the rich" said one. "Yes,["] said the other "it's absurd in her. And yet from her point of view, you can see what she means by it." "But," replied the first, ["]how *can* the church belong to the poor in the same *way* in which it does to the rich, when the rich pay all the expenses of the clergyman and everything?"

I've been here just a week. All goes well, and the little place is sweet enough. But the number of different things and people to be responsible for makes the prospect of two passive summers abroad in 1892 & '3 appear just in the nick of time. I'm about settling down to my tedious summer's task of abridging and partly rewriting my Psychology.—God bless you all—you particularly. Tell Harry he hasn't written for 3 months or more.

W.J.

ALS: MH bMS Am 1092.9 (1154)

[1] Perhaps Joseph Randolph Coolidge (1862–1928), an architect, connected with Lee, Higginson and Co. In 1886 he married Mary Hamilton Hill.

To Hugo Münsterberg

Summer address:|Chocorua N.H.|July 8. 1891

Dear D.̲ Münsterberg,

I have just read Prof G. E. Müller's review of you in the G.G.A. and find it in many respects so brutal that I am impelled to send you a word of "consolation" if such a thing be possible.[1] German polemics in general are not distinguished by mansuetude; but there is something peculiarly hideous in the business when an established authority like Müller, instead of administering fatherly and kindly admonition to a youngster like yourself, shows a malign pleasure in knocking him down and jumping up and down upon his body. All your merits he passes by parenthetically as *selbstverständlich;* your sins he enlarges upon with unction. Don't mind it! Don't be angry! Turn the other cheek! Make no ill-mannered reply!—and great will be your credit and reward! Answer by continuing your work and making it more and more irreproachable. I can't myself agree in some of your theories. *A priori,* your muscular sense-theory of psychic measurements seems to me incredible in many ways. Your general mechanical weltanschauung is too abstract and simple for my mind.   But I find in you just what is lacking in this critique of Müller's, a sense for the perspective and proportion of things (so that for instance you *don't* make experiments and quote figures to the 1000th decimal, where a coarse qualitative result is all that the question needs).   Whose *theories* in Psychology have any *definitive* value to day?   No one's!   Their only use is to sharpen farther reflexion & observation.   The man who throws out most new ideas and immediately seeks to subject them to experimental control is the most useful psychologist, in the present state of the science.   *No one* has done this as yet as well as you.   If you are only *flexible* towards your theories, and as ingenious in testing them hereafter as you have been hitherto, I will back you to beat the whole army of your critics before you are forty years old.   Too much ambition and too much rashness are marks of a certain type of genius in its youth.   The *destiny* of that genius depends on its power or inability to assimilate and get good out of such criticisms as Müller's.   Get the good! forget the bad!— and Müller will live to feel ashamed of his tone.

I was very much grieved to learn from Delabarre lately that the doctors had found some weakness in your heart!   What a wasteful thing is nature, to produce a fellow like you, and then play such a trick with him!   Bah!—But I prefer to think that it will be no serious impediment, if you only go *piano piano*.   You will do the better work doubtless for doing it a little more slowly.—Not long ago I was dining with some old gentlemen, and one of them asked "What is the best assurance a man can have of a long an[d] active life?"   He was a doctor; and presently replied to his own question: "To be entirely broken down in health before one is 35!"—There is much truth in it; & though it applies more to nervous than to other diseases, we all can take our comfort in it.   *I* was entirely broken down before I was thirty.

Yours cordially | Wm James

Delabarre & Mackaye[2] write to me of you with great admiration and gratitude for all they have gained.

ALS: MH bMS Am 1092.9 (3264)

[1] The first three volumes of Münsterberg's *Beiträge zur experimentellen Psychologie* were reviewed by Georg Elias Müller in *Göttingische gelehrte Anzeigen*, 1 June 1891, 393–429.

[2] Possibly Donald Mackay.

To Henry Holt

Chocorua, N.H. | July 24, 1891

My dear Holt,

I expect to send you within ten days the Ms. of my "briefer course", boiled down to possibly 400 pp. By adding some twaddle about the senses, by leaving out all polemics and history, all bibliography and experimental details, all metaphysical subtleties and digressions, all quotations, all humor and pathos, all *interest* in short, and by blackening the tops of all the paragraphs, I think I have produced a tome of pedagogic classic which will enrich both you and me, if not the student's mind.

The difficulty is about when to correct the proofs. I've practically had no vacation so far, and won't touch them during August. I can start them September first up here. I can't rush them through in Cambridge as I did last year, but must do them leisurely to suit this northern mail and its hours. I *could* have them done by another man in Cambridge, if there were desperate hurry, but on the whole I should prefer to do them myself.

Write and propose something! The larger book seems to be a decided success—especially from the literary point of view. I begin to look down upon Mark Twain!

Yours ever, | Wm James

TC: MH bMS Am 1092.1

From Hugo Münsterberg

Freiburg i. B. 28 Juli 91.

Sehr verehrter Herr Professor!

Haben Sie tausend Dank für Ihren überaus liebenswürdigen und herzlichen Brief, der mir eine ausserordentliche Freude bereitete. Der Zufall machte es, dass Ihr Brief anlangte unmittelbar, nachdem ich Brief, Bild und Buch an Sie abgesandt hatte. Sollten Ihnen dieselben nicht in Ihren Sommeraufenthalt nachgeschickt sein, so kann ich den Inhalt meines neulichen Briefes dahin recapitulieren, dass Herr Delabarre sein Examen sehr gut bestanden hat, dass Sie meiner kleinen Studie über die Methoden der Psychologie Nachsicht gewähren mögen und dass Ihnen die Photographie unserer Laboratoriumsgruppe ergebenste Grüsse übermitteln möge.—Was den Hauptinhalt Ihres Briefes, die Müllersche Kritik, betrifft, so kann ich Ihnen versi-

chern, dass von einem tiefer gehenden Gefühl der Kränkung bei mir
keine Rede war; diese Sorte von Kritik ist für mich garnicht vorhan-
den; nichts läge mir ferner, als in gleichem Tone zu antworten.   Ich
werde im nächsten Heft meiner Beiträge mit ein paar Wörten einige
Einwendungen sachlich zurückweisen; den Jargon der Strassenjun-
gen mir aber dazu meinerseits anzueignen, widerstrebt meiner ganzen Natur.   Überdiess muss ich dem Autor dankbar sein, denn die
Kritik hat mir von so verschiednen Seiten Worte freundlicher Gesin-
nung eingetragen, dass ich mich nicht zu beklagen habe; selbst
Wundt, der mir ja sachlich recht scharf jetzt gegenübersteht, hat mir
geschrieben, dass er die Müllersche Kritik für "brutal" hält.   Leicht
habe ich es ja nicht, insofern meine Gegner durchweg einflussreich
sind und mit Erfolg mir die akademische Carrière sehr erschweren
werden; aber sollte ich selbst ewiger Privatdocent bleiben, so wird
dadurch mein ernster Wille, mit schwacher Kraft der Wissenschaft
zu dienen, keinen Augenblick erlahmen, und am Erfolg meiner Ge-
danken liegt mir unendlich mehr als an Titeln, Gehalt und Würden.
Überdies bin ich erst soeben 28 Jahre geworden—ich habe also Zeit,
geduldig zu warten, wer zuletzt lacht, ich oder jene.   Dass meine
Arbeiten schwere Mängel haben, weiss ich natürlich am meisten und
für jeden foerdernden Tadel bin ich dankbar; vor allem will ich jetzt
wesentlich langsamer arbeiten, zumal ich auch meiner Lieblingsbe-
schäftigung, der Poesie, jetzt mehr Platz in meiner Produktion ge-
währe.   Könnte die Gehässigkeit deutscher Kritiken mir aber je die
gute Laune rauben, so würde sie mir sicher sofort durch die Freude
zurückgegeben, die ich durch den Verkehr mit meinen Studenten
habe; dieses Zustroemen von Studenten zu meinem Laboratorium,
mehr als zu irgend einem anderen in Deutschland, ist mir mehr Kritik als irgend etwas anderes.   So kann ich denn mit gutem Gewissen
versichern, dass nichts in Haus und Heim, in äusserem und innerem
Leben mir das reinste Lebensbehagen trübt—zum Glück auch nicht
meine Gesundheit.   Die Nachricht von meinem "Herzleiden" ist auf
dem Weg über den Ocean nämlich übertrieben angewachsen.   Tat-
sächlich hatte der Artz nur constatiert, dass mein Herz etwas durch
Fett gedrückt wurde, weil ich zu viel Kuchen gegessen und zu viel
am Schreibtisch gesessen hatte; ich sollte deshalb den Sommer über
die Arbeit liegen lassen, täglich Bergesteigen, keine Süssigkeiten es-
sen,—das habe ich drei Monate lang gethan und jetzt bin ich deshalb
wieder gesund wie ein Fisch im Wasser, mit guter Zuversicht für die
nächsten fünfzig Jahre.

Und Sie, verehrter Herr? Bringt Ihnen der Sommeraufenthalt die gewünschte Erholung nach den Anstrengungen des Jahres? In kürze will Herr Caldwell von Ithaca Ihnen persönlich meine Grüsse bringen; auch Herr Mackay ist schon vor einigen Tagen nach bestandenem Examen abgereist. Herr Siebert lebt noch in Berlin; von seinen Plänen weiss ich nichts näheres.

Nehmen Sie noch einmal allerherrlichsten Dank und die Versicherung tiefster Verehrung

von Ihrem sehr e[r]gebenen | Hugo Münsterberg.

ALS: MH bMS Am 1092.9 (359)

From Katharine Peabody Loring

41, ARGYLL ROAD, | KENSINGTON, W. July 30 [1891]

Dear William,

Alice tried to *write* to you for three days, but had finally to take refuge in dictation.[1]

Since I wrote to you, Dr Baldwin made another inspiring visit, with no new result—Alice discussed her case, & her demise with him as if she were talking about Queen Elizabeth, & he as well as Sir Andrew must have thought "preparation" unnecessary.[2]

Dr Baldwin is convinced that the parent cancer is in the liver; a pain under the point of A's right shoulder blade strengthens his belief; although the pain there is occasional—he judged of the case, very much by Alice's appearance—an "earthy hue" in the complexion, which is really quite marked—sometimes more, sometimes less; when more I had supposed it to be biliousness. He said this cancer of the liver is, as a rule, painless. The pain in the breast wh. was so bad is mitigated greatly by the morphia, which is acting well—the sore-aches cannot be much helped, but Alice begs me to remember to tell you that she does not suffer all the time—& I assure you that we have much joking; as her letter to you proves.

Harry seems to be extraordinarily content at Kingstown.

Give my love to Alice & believe me

Always most sincerely, | Katharine P Loring.

ALS: MH bMS Am 1094 (1492)

[1] AJ's letter dated 30 July 1891 is calendared.
[2] Reference is to Sir Andrew Clark.

To Mary Whiton Calkins

Cambr. Aug. 12, 1891

My dear Miss Calkins,

I come here just in time for your note. The candy jars with loose covers let alcohol evaporate. Of course they are all right for Zn Cl. You might make the covers tight in some way unknown to me. My jars are 'museum jars' made by Whitall Tate & Co(?) of N.J.[1] and bo't somewhere near the foot of Milk St, on a corner. They are admirable for their purpose. But I should think your "butler-jars" would do.

How "earnest" you are about brains. I gave the last touch to day (with a brain before me) to a practical routine of rules for dissection of sheep's brains in my abridgement. The completed MS. goes to the publishers to morrow. I fear it won't fall much within 500 pp.[2] I had to write a lot of twaddle about the physiology of the senses for it. But on the whole, for its purpose, it is a better composed book than the big one was, and I suspect will interest the classes who may use it. It ou[gh]t to be out by Nov. 1. I am *tired* and am off day after to morrow, probably to N. Carolina, needing to be where all impressions are new.

Your thesis has been waiting here for me all this time. I hope you don't need it before October. I can't *look* at anything psychological for a fortnight. Then I shall *devour* it.

Good bye & bless you! | W.J.

Poor Lowell! a happy release![3]

ALS: MWelC

[1] Whitall Tatum Co., manufacturers of glassware for druggists, chemists, and perfumers, with one plant located in Milville, N.J.

[2] A section of chap. 7 is titled "Practical Dissection of Sheep's Brain," *Psychology: Briefer Course* (New York: Holt, 1892), 81–90 (*BC*, 79–88). The whole book ran to 478 printed pages.

[3] James Russell Lowell died early in the morning of 12 August 1891.

To Alice Howe Gibbens James

Cambr. Aug 12 [1891]

Beloved Alice—Another fearfully hot day, but I got on pretty well without my waistcoat and have laid out 5 in a pongee silk coat for the cars etc as I go South. I found a South Carolinian at Child's last night who told me that it was as short by rail fm. N.Y to Asheville as

from Savannah, so, with my pongee coat, I go![1] J.R.L. is dead, rest
his soul.[2] I'm glad he's so soon set free. He is to be buried on Friday from the Chapel and I must wait for that. These delays fritter
one's life away. I found Theodora at Ashfield,[3] & Child on his piazza
with Miss C.,[4] young Sedgwick,[5] Lanman[6] & the S. Carolinian, Manley. Bkfstd there this A.M.—Went in to see Bradley & Storer, who
had told me yesterday the deed couldn't be signed in time. [Like a
fiend, I left your mothers letter to them at Chocorua, but I telegraphed them.] She need n't be at all anxious about the money. If
I go before they get the deed from the Ballards I will leave the cash
either with Chas. Norton or Child, who will receive the deed and
mail it to her.[7] I will send both her and you the 87.50 from Plumb
this month, to morrow by registered letter.—Your letter came this
afternoon my dear girl. I can see how grave you are and I don't
wonder. But we'll just set our faces to the new task; and shape the
future according. I'm getting over my old invalidism, and with
health, one need fear nothing. Even a new fortune may be made.
Be cheerful! You'll see me come back to you robustious. I finished
the text of my book this P.M. at 5 and then went to see the dear old
Ashburner ladies. Anne was on the piazza better than she had been
in a year. Grace pale in her bedroom, but so "nice". Dear old
things. Sally was there, very sweet. Big dinner ($1.00) at Club, then
here. I enclose a fine letter from Munsterberg. Miller would probably like to hear it. Keep it safe. Our house looks so nice. Pierce
has taken admirable care of the grass, and it and the hedge & plants
look admirable.

Love to everyone. You'll grow in power over Mary.

Yours more than ever *six* times more, | W.J.

ALS: MH bMS Am 1092.9 (1785)

[1] WJ may have misheard the South Carolinian, who is John Matthews Manly, because the distance in a straight line from Savannah, Ga., to Asheville, N.C. is some 350
miles and from New York City to Asheville, nearly 800.

[2] James Russell Lowell.

[3] Ashfield, Mass., where Charles Eliot Norton and others in WJ's social circle had
summer homes.

[4] Miss C. is probably one of the three daughters of Francis James Child.

[5] Ellery Sedgwick.

[6] Charles Rockwell Lanman (1850–1941), American orientalist, professor at Harvard from 1880. One undated letter is known.

[7] Richards M. Bradley and John H. Storer, real estate brokers. Eliza Gibbens was
planning to build a house at 107 Irving St., and the transaction involved the lot.
The Ballards were not identified.

To Alice Howe Gibbens James

Cambr. Aug 14. 91 | 9.15 AM.

Beloved Alice,

I enclose the key of my dirty brown valise which I fear may get lost unless you tie it thereunto the valise is in the closet of my bedroom. My other valise and the MS. &c for Holt are off by Sawin. I wait for Lowell's funeral at 12 & take the 3.45 train to Newport, seeing Tweedy & going on to N.Y. by the boat. To morrow to Asheville by train, 30 hours a great rest. Write to me there daily until telegraphed,—"*Battery Park Hotel.*" The Pierce's are terribly subordinate beings and rather spoil the fun of being at home—but it is a splendid thing for them. As a background to them the house seems a palace. I supped pleasantly last night with Sally, Dick C.N.[1] & G. W. Curtis. Am going in now to get state room etc.

1.30 P.M.—Just in from Funeral—Chapel a steam bath densely crowded. Pall bearers & family made a fine appearance—Eliot, Norton, John Holmes,[2] Cranch, Curtis, Child, Howells, etc. Arthur Lawrence[3] & Philipps Brooks officiated. I will now write a good long letter to Harry.[4] I found there was no state room for to night, so I go by rail direct & give up the visit to Tweedy. I reach Asheville early Sunday A.M. Trip costs $33.00 including sleepers. I am much in the mood for it, and should be much more so still if thou *sola* went along.—Coggeshall came in yesterday, just back. He looked well fed, but is I fear an impracticable fellow. I wish I had never recommended him to Abbot. His case is an argument against ever contracting a big debt.[5] He owes $5000 and talks still about the need of finishing his education! He has been employed for 3 months on the London Times, getting up some statistical work on Ireland.

No other news! Now that our family is increasing I am going to cut all other ties & settle down to business on that basis—that is eschew vanities & keep myself healthy and rich for the sake of my brood. I regard the Asheville trip as strictly neccessary for health—I don't know when I've felt such an inward weariness, but it will soon yield to novel mountain scenery, and as soon as it does I shall return, to take things easy in Sept. I want not to hear of Psychology till October.

Another letter from Schmidkunz with a "Berichtingung" in the 4teljhrschft. I send the *1st 2 pages* of the letter to amuse you. He *is* an amusing kind of an ass. In the Berichtingung he quotes my confession about Mrs Piper, and says he hadn't noticed it and so thought I was a routine spirit.[6]

I enclose a memorandum for your mother. I wrote 540.95 on her check and gave it with mine for 3140 to C.E.N. She will receive the deed from Bradley & S. as soon as it is recorded.[7]

I have seen Briggs who tells me he has written to your mother and explained—5500 over all. He says she never gave him the Richardson specifications.[8] She had better make no contract till I return.

God bless you my own life-partner!

W.J.

ALS: MH bMS Am 1092.9 (1787)

[1] Charles Eliot Norton and his son, Richard Norton.

[2] John Holmes (1812–1899), brother of Oliver Wendell Holmes, Sr.

[3] William Lawrence (1850–1941), American clergyman, then dean of the Episcopal Theological School in Cambridge.

[4] The letter was not written. For WJ's letter to HJ of 20 August 1891 describing Lowell's death and funeral see *Correspondence*, 2:183–86.

[5] According to information in the Harvard Archives, Frederic Coggeshall's parents wanted him to attend Yale. When he chose Harvard, he had to finance his education himself. Abbot is perhaps Edwin Hale Abbot (1834–1927), American railroad builder, brother of Francis Ellingwood Abbot. One letter is known (1896). In 1888 WJ had asked Abbot to assist George Herbert Mead; see *Correspondence*, 6:606.

[6] Hans Schmidkunz discussed WJ's views in "Der Hypnotismus in der neuesten 'Psychologie,'" *Vierteljahrsschrift für wissenschaftliche Philosophie* 15 (1891): 210–15. He then published a correction, *Vierteljahrsschrift*, 15 (1891): 348–50, in which he quoted WJ on Leonora Piper (*PP*, 374–75) and psychical research (*PP*, 372–73, 377n).

[7] In his letter to AGJ of 13 August 1891 (calendared) WJ wrote: "I will leave the check with Charles Norton who can surely be trusted!" Reference is to the purchase of a lot by Eliza Gibbens through Bradley and Storer, real estate agents.

[8] Apparently Eliza Gibbens was planning to use the same builders as WJ. The reference to Richardson is perhaps to Henry Hobson Richardson (1838–1886), American architect, who had sketched plans for a house for WJ; see *Correspondence*, 2:3n.

To Alice Howe Gibbens James

WRIGHT'S HOTEL, | DANVILLE, VA, Aug 16 1891 | 7.30. A.M

Dearest Alice

After a charmingly cool (in my "ponjee" coat) though dirty ride, I stopped over here last night in order to get the scenery between here and Asheville by day. Young Manley the S. Carolinian whom I met at Child's turned up in my car and beguiled ½ the day. It was entertaining at the stations to see the great crowds of white & black, and the train was full of very decently dressed & clean black people, most of them young. Fearfully dirty town this, unswept unpaved, ragged, base. Filthy dining room, but unexceptionable bed in which I had a first rate sleep. Now to bkfst, and thence to train. Arrive at Asheville 6.30 this evening.

Be courageous you dear old burden bearer.

Thy | W.J.

Love to Harry & Silly Billy. Also to Peggy & Miller as well as to the adults each & all. Tell Mary if she holds the letter to her forehead she'll feel an irres[is]tible wave passing o'er her.

ALS: MH bMS Am 1092.9 (1789)

To Alice Howe Gibbens James

BATTERY PARK HOTEL, | ASHEVILLE, N.C., Monday Aug 17. 1891 | 6.
P.M.

Dearest Wifelein, I find that I have just missed the hour of the mail. But you will be reconciled when you learn that it has been through a three hours afternoon nap, or rather drowsihead so lethal that I just woke enough to know how delicious it was to go to sleep again. Howe'er it be with me in other ways, at any rate my old "bearings" are getting quite as much rest as a sea voyage would have given them, and that seems to be what the long revolving spindles and alxes of my being most required. All day long yesterday in the cars with the dear old niggers and dearer young niggeresses, through scenery hardly worth mentioning until the last three hours or so, when it became pretty good; cool enough when the train kept going but very warm when it stopt, brought us to this charming little mushroom town at 5.30 o'clock. An electric car bro't me up to this really delicious hotel, with its amphitheatric mountain view spread out before the windows of my excellent bedroom, and piazzas very extensive from which to enjoy the same. I got lbs. of dirt off in a bath, & fell in at the supper table with a brother of Wm. T. Harris (late of Concord[)], who has a kaolin (white clay for porcelain) mine in the neigborhood and who told me a good deal.[1] I went to bed at 10 and slept deliciously. This A.M. after bkfst. I went to a hill-top some 3 miles off to get a view, but the heat was so extreme that I began to wonder whether I had better do any more mountain climbing in this region. I got into the woods near the top and managed to dry off in my shirt tail; and got down with less perspiration. The sky is over cast, the view hazy, the thermometer only 78, and so long as one sits still the air feels light an comfortable. But the moment one begins to move at all the perspiration begins. The air is very neutral and inert, makes no appeal to you at all, is quite toneless etc. I suppose on the whole that that is a good thing. After dinner went of[2] stairs and in a state of nudity, slept as aforesaid my three hours, with Howells's little Criticism & Fiction in my hand.[3]—The tone of this house is charmingly quiet. The guests seem gentlemen and ladies, I suppose they are the best sort of Southern people. I find less manners amongst them than I expected. They are not sociable, at any rate, and evidently not used to talking much with strangers. I have noticed this ever since leaving Washington. It is a sign of imperfect civilization. Here is enough egotism for one sitting! I picture you in your dear little Chocorua framework, and at this particular moment should most like to have a glimpse of young Tweedy, and to lay my hand on the top of his head. It seems very far away. Has Toby stayed? & does Peggy get on better?[4] I expect a letter from you in an hour and a half, so will await it before saying more.

Tuesday 17. 8.30 A.M.[5] Terrible hot night & showery morning. Strong impulse to go to Adirondacks straight. But being so near to the mountains here I decide to try M^t. Mitchell the highest, and have made a bargain to be carried to the foot in co. with a young N. Carolinian in the hotel.—No letter from you, yet.

W.J.

We start immediately

W.J

ALS: MH bMS Am 1092.9 (1790)

Address: Mrs. W. James | Chocorua | N.H.

Postmarks: ROAN MOUNTAIN AUG 24 JOHNSON CITY TENN. AUG 24 CHOCORUA

[1] Charles Joseph Harris (1853–1944), American manufacturer and politician.

[2] A slip for 'up'.

[3] William Dean Howells, *Criticism and Fiction* (1891).

[4] Apparently Margaret Mary had difficulties with one of the pets; see letter of 22 June 1891.

[5] Tuesday was 18 August in 1891.

From Shadworth Hollway Hodgson

St Mary's. West Malvern. | Worcestershire | Aug. 19. 1891.
Dear James

I am remorseful at owing you a letter for so long, which shall be something more than a mere reply, as my last was, to your kind present of your *Principles of Psychology*. I have long ago finished reading it, and have found it the most valuable & instructive book on the subject that I ever came across. This is chiefly because you make us see the reality of things, the real common-sense of the questions & problems at issue, while you go into full details on the moot points, and argue the whole out with the utmost fairness. I think the points which struck me most were two, your speculation of the tissues covering the joints being the real seat or rather origin of the so-called muscular sensations of motor directions; and that of the emotions being primarily and essentially due, owing, that is, their specially *emotive* character, to their being a record of organic or systemic disturbances, and depending on the sympathetic or ganglionic system of nerves for their incorporation into the general cerebral system. I state these things I am aware very loosely and inaccurately, and by no means do justice to your exposition of them, but you will know what I mean to point to. I have not the knowledge necessary to a really independent opinion on them, nor in fact do they directly affect my position in philosophy; though supposing you to be right on both points I should welcome it as a decided advance in clearing up the subject of the dependence of consciousness on the organism & specially the nerve-system.

By the way, I must say I think your whole book contributes powerfully to the support of the so-called conscious automaton theory. The more you explain, the less room do you leave for transcendental agency, since none of your explanations make any use of the latter. It is like an article in a Creed which we may believe if we please, because beyond the reach of positive disproof. This is logical in the case of a religious creed, because (to quote from a revered but antiquated authority—the old Eton Latin Grammar) "*Fides* Religionis nostræ *fundamentum* habetur."[1] I think you will acknowledge, if ever I complete my long-worked at big book, that I can make quite as good use of my hypothesis of Matter being the only positively known real condition of consciousness, I mean in the direction of Religion & Morals, as has ever yet been made of the hypothesis of an immaterial soul or transcendental Ego.[2]

Few things have given me greater pleasure than your kind mention of me among those four or five stars of high magnitudes, at the end of your Preface, especially followed up as it was by such frequent & full citation from my poor writings. I have certainly never before found myself in such distinguished company. But my dear fellow, the impression I have *really* made on you must be small indeed! My fundamental position you entirely ignore, & without mentioning it adopt unhesitatingly, in your Preface, and obviously throughout the whole book, the opposite and old traditional view of the relation between philosophical & psychological enquiry. My view is, that this relation itself, including of course the scope & limits of psychology, must be learnt from a previous philosophical analysis of experience in the widest sense. The old view I take to be, that the positive sciences come first, discover all the laws, & truths of every sort, they can, and then, whatever they find insoluble, including all their own false starts, that they dub "*metaphysics*", and relegate to philosophy. Much in the same sort of way as the old materialistic atheists used to push God out of this, out of that, out of Matter altogether, and leave him hovering in dim uncertainty outside the whole dominion of Laws of Nature. God forbid that philosophy should share his unenviable position!

You will have heard that *Mind* is to pass out of Croom Robertson's Editorship in January next, & into the hands of a Cambridge (England) syndicate, with G. F. Stout as Editor; and indeed seen it in the July N⁰ of *Mind* itself.[3] I am sorry. Sorry personally to miss Robertson as the editor, & very dubious about the philosophical character which may be maintained under the new management. I think Robertson may well be proud of the *monumentum* which in the First Series he has erected for himself.

I am finishing this letter on the 21ˢᵗ having been unavoidably interrupted meantime.

Ever sincerely yours | Shadworth H. Hodgson.

After middle or end of October, 45 Conduit Street London again.

ALS: MH bMS Am 1092.9 (208)

[1] The *Eton Latin Grammar*, described in some editions as an introduction to Latin for use in Eton College, appeared in numerous editions dating back to the 1780s.

[2] Hodgson labored on his *Metaphysic of Experience* (1898) for some twenty years. It is likely that it is this book which is referred to in various letters as the "metaphysician."

[3] *Mind* 16 (July 1891): 448, carried a notice that Robertson was to retire after the October number and publication of an index. The 1892 *Mind* was published as new series, volume 1.

To Alice James

.   Roan Mountain Hotel | Sunday Aug 23. 1891
Dearest Sister,   You will doubtless ere getting this have heard letters
both to Katherine and Harry,[1] written lately on this journey.   I reserve a word to you from the higher altitudes.   I walked up here
yesterday, and this peaceful sunny morning, with the billowy
mountain-world spread out all round and beneath, the air is as round
edged and balmy (in spite of its vitality) as if we were on the plain
instead of at a height of 6300-odd feet.   Very different from the
Mount Washington air!
     I got your admirable, inspired & inspiring letter before I left home.
It is good to hear you speak of this year as one of the best of your
life.   It is good to hear you speak of life and death from a standpoint
so unshaken and serene, with what one of the Adirondack guides
spoke of as such "heaven-up-histedness" in the point of view.   A letter from Harry, received only a few days later, confirmed me in this
impression.[2]   He says he is less "anxious" about you than at any former time, and I think we ought all to be so together now.   Poor
Lowell's disease was cancer.   He never knew what it was, and in the
shape of positive pain, suffered comparatively little, although he had
no end of various discomforts.   Now that he is gone, he seems a
much more unique and rare individual than before.   What a pity it
is always so.   I do hope that you will leave some notes on life &
english life which Harry can work in hereafter, so as to make the best
book he ever wrote.   Charles Norton, I see, receives the bequest of
Lowell's manuscripts etc.   The way that man gets his name stuck to
every greatness is fabulous—Dante, Goethe, Carlyle, Ruskin, Fitzgerald, Chauncey Wright,[3] and now Lowell![4]   His name will dominate
all the literary History of this epoch.   100 years hence, the Revue
des 2 Mondes will publish an article entitled "La Vie de l'Esprit aux
Etats unis vers la fin du XIXme Siècle; Etude sur Charles Norton."
He is our *"foyer de lumières"*; and the worst of it is that he does all the
chores therewith connected, and practically fills the position rather
better, than if he were the genuine article.—The poor Miss Ashburners are fading out patiently cheerfully & touchingly.   The brains are
still young, but the bodily machines are breaking down, and it looks
now much as if Grace would precede Anne.—*I* appear to be tougher
physically and capable of more continuous head work than in many
a long year.   The psychology turns out to be a much "bigger" book
than I thought it was; and reviews in the technical periodicals (I

am given to understand) are erelong to inform the world of its true greatness. Sully has already done nobly in Mind. The Journal of Mental Science-review of which Katherine writes, I haven't yet seen.[5] The Revue Philosophique is to publish in November a 30 pp. *article* (not a 'review') entitled "la Psychologie de W.J."[6] If the shorter edition captures the market, as I have a certain degree of confidence that it will, both in England and america, I shall make several hundred dollars a year by it. Our children grow lovelier every year and more confidence-inspiring. The baby is the most promising of the lot. I wish you could pass your hand over the broad downy dome of his cranium. It is prodigious. Their mother grows better & better every year,—not only as wife but as "lady-friend"—and the intimacy of our union is creditable to both parties. <But I> must [not] send you three sheets. God bless you, dearest sister.

Your loving   W.J.

ALS: MH bMS Am 1092.9 (1155)

¹ For the letter of 20 August 1891 to HJ see *Correspondence*, 2:183–86.
² For HJ's letter of 31 July 1891 see *Correspondence*, 2:180–83.
³ Chauncey Wright (1830–1875), American philosopher.
⁴ Norton wrote about or edited works and letters by all of those mentioned except FitzGerald. But he knew Edward FitzGerald (1809–1883), British poet, and in his essays often quoted FitzGerald's translation of the *Rubáiyát of Omar Khayyám*.
⁵ An unsigned review of *Principles of Psychology* in the *Journal of Mental Science* 37 (July 1891): 428–34. According to the reviewer the book gives an impression of its author as an "honest, simple, kindly man" of great "ingenuity and perspicuity."
⁶ Léon Marillier, "La Psychologie de William James," *Revue Philosophique* 34 (November 1892): 449–70; (December 1892): 603–27; 35 (January 1893): 1–32; (February 1893): 145–83.

To Alice Howe Gibbens James

Monday Aug 23 (or 24?) [1891]¹ | Roan M! Station Tennessee | 8.30
A.M.

Darling Wife—How I wonder how you all are. I spent a most inspiring 24 hours on the balmy mountain top & drove down yesterday afternoon in a shower of rain, behind the two valiant little mules who are wont to haul their six passengers and luggage every other day up 4000 feet 12 miles. I am now in the thick of Southernism—two regular specimens talking away at me and with me all the time. It knocks the prejudices in one every which way, and for this reason I'm glad I came as well as for the mountains and general change. I just scribble this line ere the mail leaves by the venemous little R. R.

which a couple of hours later I shall take in the opposite direction to Cranberry, thence by stage to Linnville where we sleep, after which a 4 hours ride to Blowing rock, a sanitary place just beginning to be a resort, 4000 ft. high and the home of the family of that wonderful and fascinatingly horrible Miss Carter whom Margaret may remember calling on me one morning for 3 hours 2 years ago in June. I met her sister last winter at the University of Pennsylvania.[2]

Farewell. W.J.

ALS: MH bMS Am 1092.9 (1791)

[1] Monday was 24 August 1891.

[2] Marion Hamilton Carter (1865–1937), a journalist, was born in Philadelphia but at various times lived in Blowing Rock, N.C., and New York City. Her sister was Kathleen Carter, who in 1892 married John Percy Moore (1869–1965), a zoologist then teaching at the University of Pennsylvania. Numerous letters from Marion Carter to WJ are known from 1903 to 1910.

To Ellen James Temple Emmet Hunter

Roan Mountain Station | Tennessee, Aug 24. 1891

Dearest Ellen,

Our correspondence seems to follow a law of long periods of repose, but you mustn't think, because you have had no return to your last letter and photograph, that you have been "off my mind." On the contrary, you have been "on" it every day from then till now, only no propitious opportunity has arisen for my assuring you of the fact.—You may wonder at the date of this letter, so let me immediately proceed to explain that since the College term ended I have been "feverishly" absorbed with finishing a "briefer course" of psychology, which I only got free from 10 days ago, and then felt so wearied that I had to come where nothing would meet me that I had ever seen or heard or tasted or smelt before. There *are* times when one feels like that inside, as you may possibly know. But up to the final decision to try things down here, I had hopes of going to the Adirondacks and of taking in Springfield Centre by the way,[1] and would n't write to you until I knew whether to announce my coming or not. On the final day my inward weariness proved too elaborate, and I bought a ticket for Asheville. I have been trying to get a chance to send you this line every day for a week, but have been travelling and knocking about so that this is the first opportunity that has occurred. I have been up several beautiful mountains on foot, am steeped in southern lingo etc., & am refreshed as a new born babe and ready to start for home again on Wednesday, and take up the customary thread of life. The forests here are beautiful, the accommodations fair, and in some places charming, and the people very cô-te-ous; but in the valley, the weather is too hot, and early June or late September are the proper times to come.—Now enough of *me*, let's turn to *you*. You may be already Mrs. Hunter for aught I know, and considering your maturity, I hope you are![2] I approve of his photograph decidedly, and only wish I had one anything like as good-looking to send him in return. May every felicity envelope you both. And don't, my dear Elly, let maternal sentimentalism (or sentiment) stand too much in the way of connubial freedom. As a husband myself, I realize that the supreme quality in a wife is to have no relatives. The more valuable they are as human beings the worse they are for the poor man's frailty. Send the girls to me to take care of, if you like—you've no idea how lovely Rosina seemed to me last winter—but don't take them *all* with you on the honeymoon! This is impertinence, I know, but you'll excuse it. If there is any one whom I want to be happy after this, it is you, my beloved.

It was a great disappointment to me to give up the N.Y. trip, but it was laid upon me as a sort of medical duty to myself to come down here, although the *traction* was all the other way. I should like so to see Henrietta again; and the *place*, not to speak of Leslie—how by the way does he use the poor thing now? [Remind her that in case of a final crash she knows where she can always find a home, permanent or temporary as she prefers.]—My own brood flourish, my book seems to be a great success, and next year (D.v.) we all go abroad.— Of poor Alice I hear the worst (or rather for her the best) news. They are sure she can't live many months and she is happier in the prospect than she has been for a long time. Miss Loring, for a mercy, is with her, and will stay. Believe me, dear old Elly, with tenderest love, and greetings to Henrietta & Leslie, and best wishes to Mr. Hunter

yours ever   W. James.

Lots of love to the girls also.

ALS: MH bMS Am 1092.9 (1070)

[1] Apparently, Ellen Hunter was then visiting her sister, Henrietta Pell-Clarke, in Springfield Center, N.Y.

[2] Ellen Emmet married George Hunter on 1 September 1891 in Pelham, N.Y. There are hints that it was not a happy marriage.

To Alice Howe Gibbens James

ESEEOLA INN | LINVILLE, N.C. Tuesday 25? Aug 189[1]
Dearest—I have struck it rich in this little paradise *in posse*—cool,
high, exquisite new neat hotel—roads laid out and macadamized and
not a loafer or a blot of every kind on the fair face of nature.   I
scribble this line at 8 AM. ere the stage starts to let you know where &
how I am.   I postpone blowing rock for a day, so as to go up "Grandfather" M! and take a long ride on horse back with the manager of
the concern—a Tech-graduate who, I imagine, supposes that I may
"write it up."[1]   Virgin forest all round filled with azalea and rhododendron, alas, not now in flower.
　　To blowing rock to morrow!
　　Farewell.   Millions of blessings & kisses to *thee*!

Love to all! | W.J.

ALS: MH bMS Am 1092.9 (1792)

[1] The manager was Hugh MacRae, an 1885 graduate of the Massachusetts Institute
of Technology.   WJ did write up the resort; see his "A Charming North Carolina
Resort," *New York Evening Post*, 3 September 1891; reprinted in *ECR*.

To Ellen James Temple Emmet Hunter

Chocorua N.H. | Aug 30. 1891

My dearest Elly,
　　On getting back here, I find your piteous letter to Alice.   You will
have had my letter from N.C. ere this.   I was not destroyed in the
accident, being in the first train after it the other way.[1]   A lonesome
and pathetic thing, with no newspaper capitals or wide reverberating
flourishes of excitement and publicity about it, as it actually happens.
The victims in fact left quite to themselves for a long time!—I forgot
down there that the portrait was only a loan—here it is none the
worse for wear.   It is "a fine figure of a man," as I observed when
Mr. Tweedy showed it to me—but nothing Elly, to you as a woman.[2]—
I find on getting back that our two maid servants and one man servant have taken advantage of my being away, to leave.   After a week
of chaos and "self-help," order was restored last night.   I'm glad I
was away!
　　Lots of accumulated "mail-matter" to answer!   Bless you all.

W.J.

ALS: MH bMS Am 1092.9 (1071)

[1] A Western North Carolina Railroad train from Salisbury, N.C., to Asheville fell off a ninety-foot-high bridge at about one in the morning of 27 August 1891, killing some twenty passengers and several members of the crew. Everyone in the Pullman car was killed. It was believed that two tramps, who had been put off a train earlier, had damaged the rails in revenge.

[2] The portrait was not identified.

To John Jay Chapman

Chocorua N.H. | Sept 4, 1891

My dear Chapman

You are a heroic student, as well as correspondent. That my psychology should be read by so many of the carnal minded world's people is the greatest thing in its favor. I thank you very much for the account of your feelings in your hand, which do not seem to depart from a usual type.[1] But I wish I knew why some people lose altogether their sense of the lost limb so quickly, whilst others keep it indefinitely long. My father kept the feeling of his foot for more than 50 years. Your account is so clear that it will be good to quote.

As for ether and the pure emotion of cognition, that also is a good contribution to a dark subject. I suspect myself that the experience in question is not as *contentless,* however, as one might think. In my own case in all intoxications I get an insight into a certain inexpressible genus of relation among things which seems extraordinarily pregnant of truth, & which I believe, with sufficient pains, can some day be expressed. I fancy it will then be fairly definite and discussable. Its *terms* vary according to the momentary associations, and will as you say be different in a mathematician and in a business man etc. But the scheme of relations which the terms hold towards each other is analogous in all cases. It has to do with the contradiction between two opposite species, which is removed by the perception that one species takes up the other into itself by being also the genus of both.—I will keep what you say for later use—I'm sure that more is yet to come of these experiences.

As for will, freedom and the like, ask Mrs. Chapman. A young husband has neither will nor freedom.[2] I relish your jibe about the baked beans and the beef, but still remain—for ethical reasons!—in my minority of almost one among the philosophers as champion of indeterminism.

I have just finished an abridgement of the book—about 450 pp. I think—which will be simpler, clearer, & more readable, and (I trust) a pecuniary success.   I have been secluded all summer and seen none of the fashionable world.   I hope that you haven't had to pass a great deal of the summer in N.Y.

With most cordial regards to Mrs. Chapman, believe me always yours

Wm James

ALS: MH bMS Am 1854 (877)

[1] In January 1887 Chapman thrashed a man he believed posed a threat to the "happiness" of his future wife.   Horrified by his action, Chapman burned his left hand, which had to be amputated. The target of this jealous rage was Percival Lowell (1855–1916), American traveler and astronomer.

[2] Chapman married Minna Timmins on 2 July 1889.

To Charles William Eliot

95 Irving St | Cambridge Sept 11. 91

Dear President,

I am suddenly summoned to London where my sister is in a very alarming condition.[1]   Had it been a week earlier I could probably have begun the term duly.   As it is, I can hardly get back before the 8th or 9th of October.   As my work is arranged this year it will be a very slight loss.   My part of Phil 1 comes in the middle of the year.[2] My assistant, Nichols and Mr. Miller (Walker fellow, who took Phil. 2. last year) will meet the men in that course on Oct 1, & answer questions, and Nichols will start them in my text book and have recitations till I come.[3]   Miller will meet the graduate students.   I have given him a list of things to be read, to distribute amongst them, so they need not be idle either.   The only serious drawback of my absence will be that I can't meet the freshmen immediately—I am now on their committee of advisers.   I am of course notifying Bartlett.

I trust that the peculiar nature of the call will excuse me in the eyes of the President and fellows.   I came down fm. N.H. to day and have taken passage in the Eider for to morrow.

Faithfully yours | Wm James

ALS: MH Archives

[1] WJ departed for his brief visit to England on 12 September 1891, sailing from Hoboken, N.J., on the *Eider*.

[2] In 1891–92 Philosophy 1: General Introduction to Philosophy was taught by Palmer, WJ, and Royce, with WJ responsible for the middle segment on psychology.

[3] In 1891–92 Philosophy 2: Psychology was taught by WJ. The text was *Principles of Psychology.*

To Alice Howe Gibbens James

On the train 6.30 AM. | Sept. 12. 91
Oh my Alice, if you could know the thoughts that have been filling me—thoughts of you lying bathed in your sweetness like a baby bee drowned in the honey of its cell! I had no time last night to write at length. The coat I wrote you about is probably not at Chocorua but at my tailor's in Boston—worse luck to it—he ought to have sent it out.[1] Royce drove in with me and was *delightful.* He is going to lecture twice a week on Psychology at a sort of normal school which Mrs. Hemenway is getting up.[2] He will be paid $1500, he says, which with Annex,[3] ethical lectures to ladies etc gives him an assured income for the year of $5500, which ought to make them feel very comfortable. Your mothers lot is begun—the whole place looked very nice.—I saw Fox. He said that he had written to Hodgdon telling him to send the whole bill to him, so we can't attack them on that score. I will mail Fox a check of $15.00 from N.Y. Margaret had better write to the Paines explaining things. The Merrimans sail on the 15th, I believe—so it is probably too late to communicate with them. Jim Putnam ought either to be invited or apologized to.[4] I promised old Piper $4.00 for the wharf he built, which ought to be paid.[5] Tell Billy to remember about the bolt for kitchen door—the screws are in the barn.—Lamp chimneys in my closet.—We are arriving in N.Y. the weather is effulgent and I will reserve the rest of this for a later moment.
—10.30. I've been to the Steamer which is a beauty & I have a first rate state room all to myself. I have breakfasted, bo't a pair of gloves, had my silk hat ironed etc. and am scribbling in Jae Walsh's Office he being at Stock exchange. I must hurry back to ship lest I be left—all Broadway is impassable.—My spirits are high and I am going to make of this a successful thing, and forget all remorse etc. It seems absurd the way I have talked to you the last few days—but no matter.—Jae is her[e] so I close Heaven bless you.
W.J.
Kiss all the dear children including Margy & Miller. Billy made me a solemn promise that he would stand by you against his grandmother in case of conflict.

I sent mileage ticket last night.—Remember Express box from Hubbard at Hotel.[6]

Dont get up too soon!

ALS: MH bMS Am 1092.9 (1794)

[1] In his letter to AGJ of 11 September 1891 (calendared) WJ asked her to pick out and save his "*good* black diagonal coat & vest amongst the clothes in the ice house."

[2] Mary Porter Tileston Hemenway (1820–1894), American educator and philanthropist, established the Boston Normal School of Gymnastics in 1889. It was there that Royce probably lectured, but since she established several similar institutions, error is possible.

[3] The Annex, the nucleus of the future Radcliffe College, was the common name for the program associated with Harvard that offered college instruction to women.

[4] No information about the incident was found. Jabez Fox was a near neighbor on Irving Street, but John Knowles Paine lived elsewhere in Cambridge. The Merrimans were connected with Worcester and Chocorua, while James Jackson Putnam lived in Boston. Hodgdon was not identified. It is of course possible that WJ is taking note of several unconnected social obligations.

[5] The reference is to construction on Chocorua Lake. There were Pipers living in Chocorua but Old Piper was not identified.

[6] Perhaps J. H. Hubbard, an apothecary. But there is a possiblity that the reference is to the tutor of that name.

To Alice Howe Gibbens James

                                        Southampton [September] 20 1891

Mrs James
W Ossipee MA
    Fine voyage all well

                                                            William

Cablegram: MH bMS Am 1092.9 (1795)

To Carl Stumpf

        34 De Vere Gardens | London W | England | Sept 21. 1891
My dear Stumpf

Do not be too much surprised by this superscription—I am only here for a week, having been suddenly called over by the alarming illness of my only sister, and being obliged to return on Tuesday* of next week to go on with my professorial duties. On the ship, coming over, I finished the second volume of your Tonpsychologie which one frustration after another has prevented my attacking at all until about three weeks ago. And truly it is not a morsel to be taken up when

one's mind is occupied with other things, but a book to be studied
with all the liberty of one's attention. You have done a monumental
piece of work, which will be a model to all time of the way in which
general views and the minute study of details can be combined. My
interest in the reading lay more with the general views, for although
I know a little more of music than I did when I was with you at Prag
I am still an exiled spirit kept outside the walls of that paradise. Of
course for you, & for such readers as are truly worthy of you, the
culmination of the work will be the aesthetical part, and as the only
effects you can there treat will be simple effects, I do not despair, by
the time the next volumes are out, of being able to some degree to
"catch on" to their significance also. But my powers of "Analyse und
heraushören" will always, I fear, be minimal. The way in which you
squeeze the last drops of formulable truth out of the facts is admirable, but of course your strong point is your incorruptible critical
clear headedness. It is certainly not the clear headedness of a purely
and drily logical mind which always seems negative and shallow, but
that of a mind whose dissatisfaction with vague and facile formulas
proceeds from its own sense of the presence of profounder sources
of truth. What a strange thing an intellectual *atmosphere* is! To
many of your "popular scientist" readers you must seem displeasingly
cold-blooded, but it was a constant delight to me to feel the firm and
close knit *texture* of your thought. It is a strange fact—for your positive and constructive ideas seem to have no great similarity to mine—
that I feel you, perhaps more than any other psychologist whom I
read to day, to be a *gleichgesinnter Mensch* with myself. I am sure that
if fate had allowed us to grow up side by side we could have worked
out many things together—a thing now probably impossible even if
we *were* side by side, on account of the difficulties which increasing
age brings to the irresponsible interchange of unmatured ideas.—Of
one thing I am sure: the quality of your book will give it a *permanent*
place in the history of Psychology.

I am so overwhelmed with the thought of all things to do during
these few days—(I hope in the midst of it all to be able to run over
to Paris for 24 hours—) that I am in no mood for going into details
in regard to the book. Let me say that §28 particularly interested
me, especially the part about klangfarbe. After that, §22. In the
"Verschmelzung" business you have no doubt struck a fertile new
conception, and I am curious to see what its farther developments
will be. The positive manner in which you have struck the *Räumlich-
keit*-note, is also something quite new, and naturally pleases me very

much. I confess that what worries me most is the sense of similarity and the metaphysics thereto appertaining, concerning which I have found your previous writings most instructive. It seems to me an almost irresistible *postulate* that resemblance should be analyzable into partial identity. May we be here before one of the antinomies of the infinite—to be treated no differently from the others? Your whole doctrine of "Mehrheitslehre" and of existent sensations not discriminated is at variance with the formulas I have used in my book, and seems to me hard to keep clear of entanglement with psychic chemistry etc. I believe that there will be no satisfactory solution of that whole matter except on some *erkenntnistheoretische* Basis, which will succeed in clearing up the relations between the "state of mind" and its "object." This is an obscure matter about which I have aspirations to write something which shall do away with the contradictions which occur so much on the psychological plane. I mean no ontological theory of knowledge, but an analysis of the way in which we come to treat the *phenomenon* or datum of experience sometimes as a thing sometimes as a mental representation of a thing etc etc. But this is unintelligible ——!—Cossman writes that he prefers the abridgement of my book. It will doubtless sell well, being only ⅓ (or less) of the size of the big book, and without polemic and other dry matter. Confidentially, is he a man to be trusted. He strikes me as energetic & pushing, and asks for various cooperations from me (such as a new preface etc) but I fear to give any pledges until I know more of his quality. Cordial greetings to Frau Stumpf! I hope that you both are well.

Always yours   Wm. James

I haven't read your controversy with Wundt yet—I see it has reached the dangerous stage.[1] Poor Wundt—he is only a make-believe strong man in his powers of execution, but his *program* is so noble that I feel kindly towards him, & don't wonder at his having been irritated by the references in your book.

[*]6 hours later—my departure is on Saturday Oct 3rd.

ALS: MH bMS Am 1092.9 (3786)

[1] Wilhelm Wundt, "Über Vergleichungen von Tondistancen," *Philosophische Studien* 6 (1891): 605–40. Stumpf responded in "Wundt's Antikritik," *Zeitschrift für Psychologie und Physiologie der Sinnesorgane* 2 (1891): 226–93. Wundt was defending a student whose work Stumpf had criticized in his *Tonpsychologie*.

To Alice Howe Gibbens James

41, ARGYLL ROAD, | KENSINGTON W. Sept. 21. 91 | 6.30 P.M.
Dearest Alice

I write this in Alice's sitting room after a very successful visit of more than ½ an hour. Katherine says she was highly pleased, tho' made a little faint, when she announced to her half an hour previous to my arrival that I was about to come. It appears that some weeks ago it had been a serious question with her of writing to ask me to come over. So as far as that is concerned it is highly fortunate that I came, and I imagine that Katherine herself is pleased. Expecting to see alice badly changed, I was quite surprised to find her so little so in the face. Her voice is weak, but her manner was free from any appearance of nervous overexcitement. She talked about Harry's plays (concerning which he refuses to say a word to me) and which she considers very great.[1] She alluded constantly to her approaching end, saying when the play on Saturday night was spoken of, that it was then not only her "mortuary attractions" that had bro't me over etc. She can only lie in one position on the bed, seems to feed almost exclusively on poisons, and is of course in a profoundly miserable condition, although none of it showed to day. I confess that the liver cancer theory doesn't seem to me very solid, and my only hope is that heart-weakness, which seems increasing, may suddenly take her off some time before her breast tumor (which she made me touch) comes to the surface and goes through its loathesome course. Poor strange and wonderful little being that she is.

Well! enough of her for the present. The weather yesterday cleared beautifully ere we left southampton—the ride thence was exquisite and I had an hour of communing with the spirit of Old England from 5.30 to 6.30 in Kensington Gardens (Harry being out when I arrived) which I wouldn't have missed for anything. The impression was very deep—all the elements conspiring. I would give several thousand dollars to have had you there for just that one hour! Harry seems heartily glad to see me, although he is so busy with rehearsals etc. that I don't expect to have much of his society this week. I might as well be killed for a sheep as a lamb, so I have decided to stay for a fortnight and taken a berth in the Augusta-Victoria (Hamburg Southampton & a crack ship)[2] and shall (D.V.) be in Cambridge again on Saturday night the 10th or Sunday A.M. the 11th. After all, there were no berths to be had to day in the ships of other lines going at earlier dates. If we arrive on Saturday in time for an afternoon train, you must go to the extravagance of coming to meet me in a hack at the depôt just as you did from my first winter away. Of course I will telegraph you from N.Y.—Now that I'm here I mean to make a hearty thing of it, and not have a *divided* mind. The expense is to be tho't of as a bonne aubaine due to Henry Wyck-off and not bro't into relation with any other accounts. Thus is the conscience best appeased. London is such an old story to me that a mere external tourist life palls—I shall therefore work, see pictures & people so far as they promise to be profitable. I shall also go to Paris for several days.

(22nd. Harry's) I was interrupted last night at this point by Katherine coming in and presently afterwards dinner. K. seems very happy here on her own account, with much outward activity in the way of studying the antiquities as well as the social arrangements of London. To morrow A.M. she is to conduct me to some old church in the city. I kissed her, & need not say that I find her an admirable person. I shall never let your intuitions warp me from the living truth in that direction.[3] To day on sallying out I met her and she took me to the "Stores," where I got some of that gray paper for you to write on, and socks.[4] Since then (it is now seven) I have been just dawdling about the streets which at bottom *I*'m tired of, but which *you* would enjoy, oh *how* much! A few small purchases and much poking into bookstores, but no buying. Went to Croom Robertson's but he was in scotland—Called at Alice's but she was not in a state to be seen. Harry will momentarily come in, then we will dine, & go to the "Naval Exhibition."[5] Alice's has had a very successful photograph taken which I will take home. I sent you this AM. Harry's admirable characterization of Ibsen.[6] Keep the Review.—Heaven bless you. I am inwardly spoiled all the time, and as it were transfixed, with a kind of big persistent consciousness of YOU in the background. It divides my attention in the stupidest manner and spoils my life. Are you worth it?—You will be when I get back, I know.

W.J.

ALS: MH bMS Am 1092.9 (1796)

Address: Mrs. William James | Chocorua | (N.H.) | U.S. of A.

Postmarks: SOUTH KENSINGTON S.W. SP 22 91   NEW YO<RK> OCT 1 91   CHOCORUA N.H. OCT 2

[1] HJ's play was *The American.* WJ attended the opening on 26 September 1891. There are many references to this and other of HJ's theatrical ventures in vol. 2 of the *Correspondence.*

[2] WJ did not sail on the *Augusta Victoria.*

³There is little information about AGJ's views concerning the relations between Katharine Loring and AJ. For a possible text see *Correspondence*, 5:344.

⁴WJ probably means the so-called cooperative stores in London.

⁵WJ watched the naval exercises that began on 21 September 1891 and were designed to provide training in coastal defense.

⁶HJ, "On the Occasion of Hedda Gabler," *New Review* 4 (June 1891): 519–30. *Hedda Gabler*, a play by Norwegian playwright Henrik Ibsen (1828–1906), opened in London in April 1891.

To Alice Howe Gibbens James

34, DE VERE GARDENS. W. Sept 25. 1891

Beloved Wife,

Too nights ago, your letter of Sunday inclosing Rabier-Boirac,[1] and this A.M. that of the 15th, enclosing Ned's & Bob's. Bless you for all. The distance seems so much shorter than of yore! I have enjoyed myself in a quiet way—always with the old inner cry of "why aint *she* here?" London is pretty *banal* to me alone. The money goes like water, but I haven't *wasted* a cent, unless it be on a ticket to the Garrick theatre last night, where Robertson's "School" was enacted—terribly milk & watery affair.[2] I have seen Alice 3 times—it is hard to believe, from her animation, that she will not last long. That is the thing to be dreaded now—if her breast cancer becomes open etc., it will be a horrible time. She talks death incessantly, it seems to fill her with positive glee. I lunched pleasantly with Joe Clarke yesterday. He looks rather older & somewhat careworn, but represents himself as in comfortable conditions again pecuniarily. I walked with him some distance, and bo't a little silver cream-pot for Bessie Seelye.[3]—I am naturally much pleased by the Rabier Boirac proposition, & have written to the latter a long note. I have decided not to go to Paris, and have changed my berth to the City of Paris, which sails Wednesday the 30th and ought to be in N.Y. on the Thursday following at latest. Better three days more of you in this life, than three days more of Europe!—You who represent "Cathay"—![4] I suppose this won't make *you* sorry either.

In a couple of hours I start for Cambridge. Back to morrow in time for the play.[5] On Sunday lunch with Sully, and to Haslemere (Pearsall Smiths) for the night.

Bless the boys & bless you all. How I should "admire" to be at your side again.

1000000 Kisses! W.J.

ALS: MH bMS Am 1092.9 (1797)

[1] The plan by Émile Boirac to translate WJ's *Psychology: Briefer Course* was not carried out. The role of French philosopher Élie Rabier (b. 1846) was not established.

[2] Thomas William Robertson (1829–1871), British playwright. His *School* opened at the Garrick Theatre on 19 September 1891.

[3] A wedding gift for Elizabeth James Seelye Bixler (1862–1894), daughter of Julius Hawley Seelye, recently married to James Wilson Bixler, a clergyman.

[4] Perhaps an allusion to Tennyson's *Locksley Hall*, line 184: "Better fifty years of Europe than a cycle of Cathay."

[5] The opening of HJ's *American*.

To Alice James

On board City of Paris | Thursday [October 1, 1891] 9. AM. Darling sister—Everything opens auspiciously,—brilliant weather and just enough pitching to accustom us gradually to farther possibilities.[1] The vessel is enormous; and whatever we may have to complain of before we get in, we can't complain of *solitude* at any rate. The ship is like an enormous american hotel—very different from the gentlemanly Eider in which I came. The ventilation in my inside state room is perfect, and I have "contracted an alliance with one of my own species" there, since my chum is a young Harvard MD. We are due to arrive in N.Y. early Wednesday morning, according to the account I get.

It seems absurd for me to have come and whisked about so soon after such short interviews and such contracted opportunities for conversation—but after all it is but part of the general queerness of all the deeper things of life, for that is just the way I feel about my wife the moment my back is turned upon her—it seems as if in the past twelve years I had had no opportunity to have any particular talk with her about the innumerable things that are of most importance. Tis only a matter of degree. How *Harry* will miss *your* conversation when the opportunity for it is gone. Between us we promise you to try to work some of it into Philosophy and the Drama so that it shall become a part of the world's inheritance!—I go back to a life of which the main interest now is that of seeing that the children turn out well—insidious change in one's ambitions brought about by life's changing course. Your name will be a mere legend amongst them— until we are all legends.—So no more, my dear old Alice! Here is Queenstown harbor—God bless you forever & ever.

Your brother | W.J.

Let Katherine try hypnotic suggestion to relieve symptoms as they turn up. I am sure it will succeed, especially if begun when you are ready to go to sleep.

For Harry:

Don't forget tailor's bill, nor ½ crown to lift-boy. Also not to send me Mrs. Bell's "Game of Dinner openings"—I think the title was that.[2]

Love to both H. & Katherine! About the American I feel an absolutely tranquil mind.

ALS: MH bMS Am 1092.9 (1156)

Address: Miss James | 41 Argyll Road | London | W

Postmarks: QUEENSTOWN OC <1> 91   LOND<ON> W. OC 2 91

[1] WJ returned to the United States on the *City of Paris*, leaving Liverpool on 31 September 1891 and arriving in New York City on Wednesday evening, 7 October.

[2] Lady Florence Eveleen Eleanore Olliffe Bell (1851–1930), British writer, *Conversational Openings and Endings: Some Hints for Playing the Game of Small Talk and Other Society Pastimes.*

To William Noyes

95 Irving St. Oct 10. 1891

Just back from a suddenly forced trip to England, I find your letter of the 18th Sept. in the pile. *Very* interesting observations, which I will try to verify on myself. The whole subject of sense of direction is rather a puzzle from the fact that imaginary feelings of movement seem as vivid as real ones.

Wm James

APS: MH bMS Am 1092.9 (3356)

Address: D.ʳ Wm. Noyes | McLean Asylum | Somerville Mass

Postmark: BOSTON. MASS. OCT 11 1891

To Henry Holt

Cambridge Oct. 15, 91.

My dear Holt

I am glad to get at the proofs and get that job off my hands—it is hateful to have to go so often over one's own tracks.[1] I may not be able, with my college duties so heavy, to send back the proofs quite as promptly as either the printer or I should like, but of course I'll do my aller darnedest.

We have made no contract yet, and in surveying on the one hand my ruined estate, and on the other the fact that this work will surely be more lucrative than its predecessor, it seems to me fair to ask for slightly more liberal terms.   What I propose is that I should pay no extra-proof correction bill and that you should pay for the index, which I can easily have made here, but have no time to execute myself.   Otherwise the terms of the older contract will suffice, unless you have something better yet to propose.

Mr. Vogelius asks me for the addresses of the German & French translators.   Will you kindly give them to him?   The German one is[2] [*end of letter missing*]

TC incomplete: MH bMS Am 1092.1

[1] In his letter of 14 October 1891 (calendared) Joseph Vogelius informed WJ that the first batch of proof of *Psychology: Briefer Course* was sent yesterday.

[2] The French translator was Émile Boirac; the German, Paul Nikolaus Cossmann. Neither completed his task.

From Henry Holt

Stowe, Vt. Oct 17/91

Dear James:

It tries my faith in human nature to have one of its best exponents let an innocent and confiding publisher run on trusting in the general principle that precedent rules where action is taken without anything said to the contrary, and then bring him up with a round turn *in media res.*

A publisher is never admitted to have any rights against an author, however, so I'll tell you what I'll do.   If after the new book has been published two years, it has made my firm more profit than the old one did in it's first two years, I'll devote our excess pro rata with yours (if you have any) to returning the charge that will have been made against you for alterations and index.   It does not follow that you will make more profit if we do, or that we will if you do.   Such things cant run with absolute uniformity.   "Two years" will have to mean four semi-annual settlements.   We can't tell what the existing book has done at any day between them.

The fact is, however, that a greater apparent profit to the publisher from the new book may not be a greater real one, as it will need more pushing against competitors than the old one.   That was unique.

I expect to fight my dyspepsia here a fortnight longer; I hope more, if it isn't then overcome.

Yours Ever | H. Holt.

Letterbook: NjP

To Frances Rollins Morse

95 Irving St, | Cambridge Oct 19 [1891]

My dear Fanny,

I send you by express—being in despair of visiting your part of the town at any near date[1]—the photograph of Alice which she asked me to hand to you from her.   I'm glad I went over, if only to have as pleasant an image as will now abide with me of the *scene* of her last months.   All its circumstances are of the best, and with K.P.L. there, you can imagine how well she is taken care of.   She is positively exultant over the prospect of departure, and of course the only thing to be prayed for is that it should not be too long delayed.—This photog was taken a couple of months ago.

I hope that you and your mother are both well.   I trust to be able to get to your house *some* time ere the new year.

Much love! | Wm James

ALS: MH bMS Am 1092.9 (3206)

[1] Frances Morse lived at 12 Marlboro St., Boston.

From Carl Stumpf

München Georgenstr. 15 | 24. Oct. 91.

Mein lieber Freund James!

Verzeihen Sie, dass ich Ihren lieben langen Brief aus London, worin Sie mir so viele freundschaftliche und anerkennende Worte sagen, erst jetzt beantworte, obschon Sie auf eine rasche Antwort zu rechnen schienen.   Der Brief traf mich in den Vorbereitungen zu einem Wohnungswechsel, während zugleich zahlreiche Besuche der aus dem Gebirg heimkehrenden Collegen und die Correctur kleiner Arbeiten meine Zeit wegnahmen.   Nun ist dies alles glücklich überstanden und ich kann mich ein wenig mit Ihnen unterhalten, was mir viel mehr Vergnügen macht als die Unterhaltung mit dem—Collegen Wundt.

Also vorerst meinen innigen Dank für Ihre guten Worte über mein Buch. Wenn ich auch einen Teil davon auf Ihre persönliche Freundschaft zu mir schieben muss, so ist mir doch eben diese Freundschaft selbst ein hohes Gut, und Einiges bleibt doch auch für das Buch übrig. Sully hat es so verdriesslich rezensirt[1] und Wundt mich überhaupt so schlecht gemacht, dass ich für ein Lob aus solchem Munde heute doppelt empfänglich bin. Was Sie über die tiefinnere Verwandschaft unsrer geistigen Tendenzen sagen, ist mir aus der Seele gesprochen. Ich verstehe auch vollkom̃en die Einwendungen, die Sie gegen viele meiner Ansichten im Einzelnen zu machen haben, und empfinde deren Gewicht hinreichend, um mich auch in diesen Puncten, die uns trennen, in Sie hineinversetzen zu können. So besonders die Opposition gegen die unwahrgenom̃enen Empfindungen. Ich selbst würde sie vor 12 Jahren geleugnet haben; aber die Consequenz zahlreicher Einzelbetrachtungen scheint mir dahin zu führen, dass wir zwischen den eigentlich "unbewussten" Vorstellungen und den unbemerkten Teilen eines Complexes unterscheiden; die ersteren scheinen mir unannehmbar, die letzteren notwendig. Ich glaube nicht, dass es der "psychologische Fehlschluss" ist, der hieran die Schuld trägt, sondern nur bestim̃te Argumente im Einzelnen. Aber gewiss bedarf diese Sache einmal einer eingehenden prinzipiellen Untersuchung, die zu einer Verständigung führen *muss*. Wenn ich Sie recht verstehe, gibt es nach Ihnen überhaupt keine *Teile* in dem Vorstellungsinhalt; jeder ist eine absolut einfache Qualität. Alle "Zergliederung" ist statt einer wirklichen Zergliederung eine Entdeckung oder Production gänzlich *neuer* einfacher Qualitäten.

Die Consequenz davon scheint mir zu sein, dass es auch keine Classification gibt. *Nichts* wäre den einzelnen Erscheinungen gemeinsam; jeder allgemeine Begriff wäre selbst wieder eine neue einfache Qualität sui generis. Ist dies Ihre Meinung?

Auch Ihre Opposition gegen die "einfachen Ähnlichkeiten" kann ich würdigen, da auch diese Behauptung sich mir erst spät aufgedrängt hat, und da ich gewisse Schwierigkeiten selbst noch im̃er darin finde. Aber gerade von *Ihrem* Standpuncte scheint mir diese Annahme am wenigsten vermeidlich. Denn wenn es überhaupt keine Teile in den Empfindungen gibt, wie dürften wir dann "Ähnlichkeit" durch "teilweise Gleichheit oder Identität" definiren?—

Vielleicht würden wir mündlich besser und jedenfalls leichter hierüber discutiren. Ihr Schüler Delabarre, der mich kürzlich besuchte, machte mir Hoffnung, dass Sie im nächsten Jahre Ihre grossen Jahresferien halten würden; und davon wird, hoffe ich, auch ein Teilchen auf München entfallen. Der Schwager, den Sie in London besuchten, ist wol Herr Salter? Ich habe vor ihm die allergrösste Hochachtung und drücke ihm im Geiste die Hand, obschon mir die Überzeugung von einem allwaltenden νοῦς moralisch nicht *so* irrelevant scheint wie ihm. Gewiss bleibt jede Pflicht auch für den Atheisten die nämliche. Aber für die ganze Leben*stimung* ist doch ein Unterschied wie zwischen der Vorstellung des Firmaments als einer festen Decke und als eines unendlichen Raums, oder noch viel mehr Unterschied!—Ihrer Frau Schwester geht es hoffentlich wieder gut und Sie konnten beruhigt zurückkehren?

Cossmann betreffend, will ich Ihnen *ganz vertraulich* mitteilen, was mich veranlasste, den Verkehr mit ihm abzubrechen. Es fiel mir zufällig ein Collegien heft von ihm in die Hand, worin er die Ausführungen meiner Psychologie-Vorlesung, statt sie correct niederzuschreiben und dann darüber nachzudenken, sogleich während des Hörens mit Bemerkungen wie "läppisches Argument" u. dgl. begleitet hatte. Es war eine Anzahl beschimpfender Ausdrücke darin, die mir zeigten, dass ihm jede Pietät gegen mich, der ich ihm persönlich in jeder Weise zu seinen Arbeiten behilflich gewesen, fehlte. So lieb mir ein *kritischer* Schüler ist, so konnte ich es doch nicht mehr über mich gewinnen, mit einem jungen Menschen, dessen Kritik solche Formen annahm, persönlich zu verkehren. Ich schrieb ihm deshalb, dass ich mich gezwungen sehe, den persönl. Verkehr abzubrechen, ohne jedoch das Motiv namhaft zu machen, um jede Discussion abzuschneiden.

Dies zur Aufklärung *unter uns;* für Sie braucht es ja in keiner Weise bestimend zu werden. Ich glaube, dass er die Übersetzung gut besorgen wird, wenn ich auch über seinen deutschen *Stil* noch keine Ansicht habe. Aber Sie werden sie ja selbst durchsehen.

Ihr Mitgefühl mit dem "poor Wundt" kann ich leider nicht teilen und wundere mich fast darüber, da Sie ihn doch an verschiedenen Stellen Ihres Buches noch schlechter behandelt haben (z. B. ††277).[2] Und haben Sie nicht auch mit *mir* in dieser Sache Mitgefühl, dem die crasseste Unwissenheit und die abscheulichsten Tendenzen vorgeworfen werden? So wie ich Wundt *jetzt* kenne, reut es mich "erst recht" nicht, den Kampf mit ihm aufgenomen zu haben. Schwindel!—Aber wir wollen uns darob nicht böse werden.

Tausend herz! Grüsse v. Ihrem | C Stumpf

ALS: MH bMS Am 1092.9 (628)

[1] James Sully, review of Carl Stumpf, *Tonpsychologie*, vol. 2 (1890), in *Mind* 16 (April 1891): 274–80.

[2] According to WJ, Wundt's theory of space perception was the "flimsiest thing in the world" (*PP*, 906–7).

To Henry Holt

95 Irving St., Oct. 25, 91.

My dear Holt,

I enclose my receipt for your check, for which I am I trust duly grateful.   I also acknowledge hereby your last letter from Stowe, which is a model of the suaviter in modo and fortiter in re.   I am afraid that after the four semi-annual settlements, the amount of ciphering which will need to be done to fulfil the agreement which you propose will be more than the redistribution is worth to anyone. However since you propose it, let it stand, and see if either of us remembers it when the time comes!

My impression is that the proof corrections will be comparatively slight, after we get through all this wretched twaddle about the senses which I am correcting now, and which had to be put in to satisfy the market.   But *how* sorry I am we can't have a book of 350 pages!   The fact is that the subject can't possibly be treated concisely and interestingly at the same time.   And I think that as things go, the most interesting book will be the one that sells best.   When I got through the job last summer I had a rather distinct impression that this work would kill most of its competitors for the reason that they are all (except Taine) so uninterestingly written.[1]   We shall see.

I am curious for Baldwin's second vol.[2]   It will doubtless be better than his first one, he is such a growing man.   I acquire more and more respect for him.

Yours always | Wm. James

TC: MH bMS Am 1092.1

[1] Hippolyte-Adolphe Taine, *De l'intelligence* (1870) (WJ 684.41).   WJ used the English translation several times as a text in his psychology classes.

[2] James Mark Baldwin, *Handbook of Psychology: Feeling and Will* (1891) (WJ 406.49). Holt was Baldwin's publisher.

To Oliver Wendell Holmes, Jr.

CAMBRIDGE Oct 26. 91

My dear Wendell,

H's address is 34 De Vere Gardens W.

I was only wait[ing] to read all of your speeches again to write and thank you for them. They are simply magnificent; and the way you chuck yourself headlong at the topic, with summersault or dislocation as the result is a spectacle for the gods. Even that soul freezing atmosphere of Yale College does n't lower your oratorical temperature![1]

May you give us many more as good.

Thine ever | W.J.

ALS: MH-L

[1] Oliver Wendell Holmes, Jr., *Speeches* (1891), including a speech titled "Love of Honor," which Holmes delivered at Yale in 1886 on the occasion of receiving an honorary degree.

To Charles William Eliot

Oct 29. 81 [1891]

Dear President

I have unaccountably mislaid Droppers's letter about Ikeda which came a fortnight ago.*[1] The gist of it was that the Tokio people, altho' they have agreed to send money for the next three years to Ikeda in case he gets no scholarship here, will never understand the misunderstanding, should it come to their having to do so, but only remember the fact that whereas he had come to America with a pledge of $250 a year secured, the pledge had somehow not been kept. Droppers says that this will very seriously hurt the reputation of Harvard in Japan. Possibly the root of the "pledge" is Mr. Knepp, who appears to have preached a farewell sermon in which he distinctly and positively stated that there were 12 scholarships of $250 each for Japanese students (three scholarships for 4 years).[2] Of these Ikeda was supposed to be sure of one. He is the most perfect little gentleman, and now that there has been a misunderstanding says that the only scholarship he is willing to take will be an ordinary prize scholarship, which however it will be hard for him to attain on account of his slowness with English. Droppers is highly desirous that he should be *forced* out of the high toned attitude, the *practical result* of which will look ill over there.

Very truly yours | Wm James

*I have found it again & enclose it.

ALS: MH Archives

[1] In the upper corner of the first page WJ had written 'Ikeda', perhaps as a note to himself. Seihin Ikeda, a student from Japan, graduated from Harvard in 1895, and in later years lived in Tokyo. Garrett Droppers (1860–1927), American educator and diplomat, taught political economy in Japan. There are many references to Droppers in vol. 6 of the *Correspondence*.

[2] Arthur May Knapp (b. 1841), Unitarian clergyman and missionary to Japan, who in 1891 had returned from one of his many trips to Japan.

To Alice James

Cambridge Nov 1. 91

Dearest Alice,

I have received innumerable letters from Katherine since getting home, but such has been the drive of life, breathlessly hurrying from one thing to another from 6.30 AM. when I rise and go down to the furnace* till 11 P.M. when I put out my light, that until to night I have had no chance to send anything but a couple of brief words on business to Harry, which of course you will have seen. Katherine's last came simultaneously with a note from Harry two days ago, and told most excitingly of the visit of the Prince of Wales to the play and of his deigning to quote its words.[1] Don't you feel sorry now that you should ever have felt any secret or open pleasure at the loosening of the old bonds of loyalty between the people and their Prince? I do, and I think it will be a judgment on us if, in spite of this example the public doesn't catch on, or rather hold on. *I* can't for my life see why they shouldn't anyway, the play being so thoroughly good and curious to follow. I believe they *will,* and expect to hear the good news strengthen in the next fortnight.

The Salters and Peggy got back from the country last night, Mrs. G. follows, and we shall then be *au complet* for the winter, the Salters going to Philadelphia.[2] At last too, we are *au complet* in the kitchen, two very promising colored persons having arrived the day before yesterday. There is a sort of crisis in domestics the supply being very small, the wages enormous, the capacity zero. Poor Alice feels tired out with the long dreary interregnum. I long to get her to Europe, where she can *board.* I have no news in particular. Child & Howells were both here to day, Howells carrying some letters from Lowell to Chas. Norton, Child full of wrath at the refusal of the Corporation to drop the "Dudleian Lecture" which by an old bequest has to be delivered once in four years before the University on "the damnable errors, heresies, and superstitions of the Church of Rome." The institution has slumbered for 30 years because the income from the fund had shrunk so low. Now it is revived by this "non-sectarian University"[3] —Child was in his best wrathful-humorous vein. The Howells's are to board in N.Y. to be near their boy, who goes into the architect's office of McKim, White & Mead.[4] Bob is in N.Y. for a time, occupying a "hall bedroom" etc. I suppose he'll be back in Concord soon, and the change will have been good for him. Mary was here a couple of days since and returns to dine on Wednesday. She has seen Carrie this summer who is nursing her brother Ed on his deathbed. It seems that the eldest bro. Charlie died a year ago.[5] C. left his money to Carrie, and according to Mary Ed has made her his sole heir, so Mary says she is a rich woman. The boy Cary, Mary says, has been kept at home the past winter apparently doing nothing.[6] Mary has induced Carrie to get a tutor for him, and to send Alice to school at Utica.[7] She says that Carrie would be willing to have him go to College, only he seems insusceptible of being "fitted" therefor. Its a rather sad business. We have asked Carrie (when East with the children) to come and see us at Chocorua twice. Neither time could or would she come. If the end of our summer had not been so broken up, we should have invited the children alone this year, so as to learn to know them. But with such a mother what can they be? "Take a hole and pour iron round it" was the classic irish receipt for cannon-making. Take nothingness and pour blind maternal instinct & dead obstinacy round it, and you have Carrie. The trouble with the children is that they are now so old, that the mischief of their bad education or no-education is probably irretrievable. But I don't want to rile you up about them—this is the first news I have had from them in so long a time that it ran out of my pen. Ned has a pleasant room here, and is a really prepossessing young fellow.[8] Two of my colleagues have spoken to me of him as having attracted their attention.—The air here is filled with the election. No one seems to know which way Massachusetts will go.[9] It is a curious epoch of unstable equilibrium in our politics, but little by little Satan gets a looser hold. Boott looks in ever & anon—intensely eager about you & especially about Harry's play. Among the faithless faithful only he![10]   Alice, and Mary Gibbens send deathless love. & so do I!—to K.P.L. as well.

W.J.

*I prefer this—our man comes in the evening. Simon Hassett by the way came into this Library to hear all about you. He's the same intense eyed, over worked, pompous good creature that he ever was.

ALS: MH bMS Am 1092.9 (1157)

[1] For HJ's note of 21 October 1891 concerning the Prince of Wales see *Correspondence*, 2:191.

[2] As a leader in the Society for Ethical Culture, Salter went to Philadelphia to take over the group there after being asked to leave his post in Chicago because of his defense of the Haymarket anarchists and other radical views (see *Correspondence*, 6:286n). He returned to Chicago in 1896.

[3] The Dudleian Lectures were established in 1750, discontinued in 1857 in order to allow the fund to build up, and resumed in 1888. According to the *Boston Evening Transcript*, 19 May 1894, the lectures were to cover four topics in rotation: natural religion, revealed religion, corruption of the Church of Rome, and validity of Presbyterian ordination. The lecture in 1890 dealt with revealed religion and was delivered by John Joseph Keane (1839–1918), Irish-born Roman Catholic clergyman, then bishop of Richmond, Va. His lecture gave rise to protests that a Catholic should not be paid from the Dudley Fund.

[4] John Mead Howells (1868–1959), an architect, son of William Dean Howells, and a nephew of William Rutherford Mead, a member of the architectural firm of McKim, Mead, & White.

[5] No information about Ed Cary and Charles Cary was found.

[6] Joseph Cary James (b. 1874), son of GWJ.

[7] Alice James (later Alice James Edgar) (b. 1875), daughter of GWJ.

[8] Edward (Ned) Holton James was a freshman at Harvard in 1891–92.

[9] In the elections of 1891, a nonpresidential year, the Republicans won all the offices in Massachusetts except the governorship, which was won by the Democrats.

[10] From Milton's *Paradise Lost*, bk. 5, line 897.

To Mary Whiton Calkins

95 Irving St, Nov 6. 1891

My dear Miss Calkins,

I read your thesis at last, a week ago, and have but just found a moment in which to drop you a line about it. My laboratory knocks four hours daily out of my time and from 6.30 AM. till 11 PM. I have to *run*—hence the "unconscionable" delay.

The thesis has given me exquisite delight. The middle portion, with its classification and criticism gives the subject a real hitch ahead, and is luminous. It certainly ought to go to Schurman's Journal of

Philosophy,[1] & if you are too modest I will "introduce" it to him. The important pp. to have printed are 35 to 67. The end is only compilation, and the first 34 pp. are partly non-original and to my mind partly non-conclusive.* The middle is *solid,* and altogether original. So pray revise it and let me know. Whither shall I send it? I send this to Newton, thinking it may find you spending Sunday at home.

Yours most sincerely | Wm James

[*]Vide one or two pencil notes which I scratched.

ALS: MWelC

[1] Mary Whiton Calkins, "A Suggested Classification of Cases of Association," *Philosophical Review* 1 (July 1892): 389–402. The *Review* was edited by Schurman.

To Sarah Wyman Whitman

95 Irving St. | Nov 8. 91

My dear Mrs. Whitman

I send you Abbot's pamphlet, which was found almost immediately after you went away.[1] Read pp. 13 to 16, whatever else you read. But the whole thing is very good reading—it is so well written.

I happened accidentally to have just now in my hands a little-known book of Mark Twain's which I also send you for the sake of the story that begins on p. 30.[2] You may know it already. Longfellow ought to add it to his répertoire—it seems to contain the soul of Connecticut!

Do I not in showering this "reading matter" upon you, at last treat you "synthetically"?

You manifested the real goodness of your soul yesterday to yours ever

W.J.

ALS: MH bMS Am 1092.9 (3912)

Address: Mrs. Whitman | 77 M! Vernon S! | Boston | Mass

Postmark: BOSTON. MASS NOV 9 1891

[1] Francis Ellingwood Abbot, *Professor Royce's Libel: A Public Appeal for Redress to the Corporation and Overseers of Harvard University* (1891). Abbot was protesting against the harsh review by Royce of Abbot's *The Way Out of Agnosticism* (1890); see letter to AGJ of 3 August 1890, 10:30 A.M. For writings in the controversy besides those mentioned in the present text see Ignas K. Skrupskelis, "Annotated Bibliography of the Published Works of Josiah Royce," *Basic Writings of Josiah Royce,* ed. John J. McDermott, 2 vols. (Chicago: Univ. of Chicago Press, 1969), 2:1185–86.

[2] The story was not identified.

To Charles Sanders Peirce

CAMBRIDGE Nov. 12. 91

My dear Charles,

I have been somewhat amused and somewhat made sorry by your letter in the Nation about Abbot-Royce.[1] If you knew Royce as I do, and had seen the whole evolution of his side of the business as I have, you would see how simply comical is the notion of there being any element of intellectual rivalry with Abbot in his attitude. The animus of his article was *objectively philosophical;* but being a man of mass, he can't do a thing briefly or lightly, and "laid it on" thick enough to justify a sore feeling on Abbot's part. Abbot's view that its animus was personal persecution is however simply silly; and I am surprised that you should treat it as plausible.

In the negotiations which ensued, I heard of each step from Royce, and know for certain that what was foremost in his mind was his duty to the Journal. What Editor, launching a new Journal, would *not* seek: 1st to keep a controversy from trailing its length through several numbers (as Abbot began by insisting it should if any editorial rejoinder was to be made), & 2nd., to keep it decent in tone? Royce and Adler and Weston from every point of view would have been derelict as editors had they not tried to do this.[2] Such controversies make a Journal stink in the readers nostrils. They had Abbot's reply (more than twice as long as Royce's original article) in type, with two pages of rejoinder from Royce, exceedingly courteous and personally apologetic, and mainly consisting of passages from Abbot & Hegel.[3] Whilst Abbot was insisting that this rejoinder should appear in the following number to the one in which his reply was to appear, the latter came out. They then offered, finding how his temper grew, and that he was threatening to publish the thing as a pamphlet and bring the review into bad odour, to publish it *without reply* if he would use "parliamentary" language. This fact he omits from his address to the Corporation. The warning from Warner that if he published a pamphlet he must risk the consequences was an ordinary legal step,[4] designed first to make him pause and possibly cool off; second to put the Review in a good position if he should bring the action for libel which on his part he was more or less darkly threatening, since not treating his threatened pamphlet as libellous might be construed in court as implying that they admitted the original article to be so.

For my own part, Abbot's soreness is excusable, but his rabid personal tone is simply pathological. Instead of discussing Royce's review objectively he began immediately the sort of furious personal th[i]ng of which the appeal to the Corporation is a specimen.[5]   He never will discuss objectively.   I have tried my best to have rational discussion with him.   But when objection is made to any of his views, he stops the conversation by saying that he doesn't expect any of his contempories to understand him—Posterity however will "do him justice."   His philosophy surely must seem to *you* the scholastic rubbish which it seems to me and which it seemed to Royce.   Why not speak out one's mind about such rubbish, especially when paraded as the great American philosophy reared on the ruin of the Greek and the German philosophies?   He has been treated with respect it is true by some critics.   Renouvier wrote a long article about him, wholly unfavorable however, and ending with the words "triste signe, en-vérité, du delabrement moral de notre epoque!"[6]   It shows little delicacy in Abbot to quote in his own favor a vague introductory phrase from renouvier in which his book was lumped with Royce's and a couple of others as so many original & profound attempts etc, which R. would review in as many successive articles, when the entire special article about himself was damning.   I know nothing of his other critics abroad, his critics here have all been of the pigmy pattern—those at least which I have seen.

In short as a hyperaesthetic human being, Abbot deserves our pity at being so handled without gloves.   But as a philosopher I can see no ground for complaint on his part; what are philosophers here for but to fight with each other?   On the whole, I wish you had let the thing die away in silence, and not propagated a new series of undulations from the Nation's columns.

Always yours | Wm James

Abbot seems to me simply *insane* in all that touches on his philosophic or personal pretentions.   He ought never to be touched by a critic's hand—what good does it do?   Of course I agree that Royce's phrase "professional warning" sounded very pretentious.[7]

ALS: MH bMS Am 1092.9 (3370)

[1] Charles Sanders Peirce, "Abbot Against Royce," *Nation* 53 (12 November 1891): 372.

[2] Samuel Burns Weston was editor of the *International Journal of Ethics;* Royce and Felix Adler were on the editorial board.

[3] Both Abbot's reply and Royce's rejoinder are preserved in the Harvard Archives. Royce claimed that Abbot's theory was not original but was derived from Hegel.

[4] A letter from Joseph Bangs Warner, Royce's lawyer, is quoted by Abbot in *Royce's Libel*, 41.

[5] See previous letter.

[6] Charles Renouvier, "De quelques systèmes contemporaines de haute philosophie spéculative," *Critique Philosophique*, n.s., 3d year, vol. 2 (1887): 416–42.
  [7] Josiah Royce, "Dr. Abbot's 'Way Out of Agnosticism,'" 112.

To William Torrey Harris

Cambridge Nov 14. 1891

Dear D: Harris,

I naturally feel much flattered at your request, but it is quite impossible that I should comply with it. Writing is difficult in the extreme to me, and I have absolutely nothing to say about education that every teacher born of woman doesn't already know a great deal better than I do.

They are forcing me to give ten lectures here on "Topics of Psychology of interest to Teachers."[1] It is lamentable work!

Have you thought of Paul Hanus, our new Professor of Pedagogics, from Colorado? He is a sensible man, but I know nothing of his powers as a writer.

Truly yours | Wm James

ALS: CLSU

  [1] The first talk was given on 27 October 1891. For other dates and an account of the lectures see *TT,* 216–23, 234.

From Charles Sanders Peirce

CENTURY CLUB, | NO. 7 WEST FORTY-THIRD STREET. [November 14, 1891]

My dear Willie

I have your letter at the beginning of a busy day. It shall have my careful and affectionate attention. Reading it now hastily, it does not seem to touch my point, which is that when a man has been a sincere student of a subject for many years he ought to be held exempt from sweepingly contemptuous criticism, unless it be a case of undeniably flagrant incompetence. I consider that Abbot's position in *logic* is very strong and original, and the idea that his theory is derived from Hegel so extremely false as to be discreditable to Royce. This, however, I abstain from saying in my letter. I consider criticism such as Royce's, cruel, wicked, and injurious in several ways to the cause of speculative study. But against Royce as as philosopher I say nothing in my letter, though I really rank him no higher, certainly, than Abbot. His own theism is just as nugatory as Abbot's; but that is a fault it shares with all the greatest works of philosophers.

Abbots attitude toward the general results of science seems to me sensible, Royce's puerile.

Abbot you say is almost insane. I have never praised his good judgment publicly or privately; but if he is in such a state of mind, all the more reason for gentle treatment. Let us insist that sincere students shall treat one another with gentleness.

very faithfully | C. S. Peirce

ALS: MH bMS Am 1092 (664)

To William Noyes

CAMBRIDGE Nov. 16. 91

My dear Noyes,

Are you going to use your Hipp's chronoscope this winter?—And if not could you contemplate the possibility of lending it to Harvard College.

I explain:—I need to do a reaction time investigation, for which I have been hoping to use a chronoscopic invention of Ewalds which I ordered six months or more ago. It arrived a month since, but proves so delicate as to be practically useless, breaks down every few minutes. Believing in this, I didn't order a Hipp until three weeks or more ago. But I hear from Leipzig that the Swiss people are full of orders and that Külle[1] in Leipzig can't expect to get one from them before January. This I am convinced means that I shan't get anything before March or April, too late to begin the work this year.

If your Hipp is in good order, and you shan't want it, you will run no risk in lending it, for if anything untoward happens to it, I will simply make over to you the new one when it arrives, and keep yours.

Let me know if this seems feasable to you, and if it does I will go over in a coupé and bring the instrument here.

Truly yours | Wm James

ALS: MH bMS Am 1092.9 (3357)

[1] An error for 'Külpe'. The reference is to Oswald Külpe.

To Charles Sanders Peirce

CAMBRIDGE Nov. 16. '91

My dear Charles,

Your second letter crossed mine. It does honour to your head and heart, but doesn't convince me that Royce is not *now* the party sinned against. I echo your opinion that Philosophers ought to deal gently with each other's errors, though not as gently as novelists poets, and other artists ought, their works being pure *gifts* and the objections not being generally susceptible of reasoned proof, or getting it. I have myself always thought that *silence* was the proper treatment of a bad book, in any line; unless it happened to be popular, in which case it is perfectly fair to go for it—in fact one may need to. Abbot's books seem to me to fall under the treatment of silence—they seem to me incompetent in the extreme, and I can't well understand how you can speak of them with such respect. Royce pitched in, and is, as I personally *know*, sorry not only for the rumpus, but for Abbot's wounded feeling, which he didn't expect to be what it is. He has done little else but shower expressions of this upon Abbot, but the latter has insisted that he must swallow his expressions of opinion about the book as well. You say a hostile critic does n't usually mean to ruin his authors reputation, and quote yourself in rê Abbot & Royce. It depends on *how hostile he is;* and I contend that it is fair (as the established critical customs go) for a man to be as destructive as he can *provided he gives reasons*—which in a philosophic review are a matter of course. For the "pretentiousness" no reason was given, but will anyone question the appropriateness of that epithet in Abbot's case? It is a mere obvious descriptive term to apply the proof; but what I had in mind when I wrote it was simply the fact that Abbot's pamphlet was all you had to go on, and that that hardly was enough to qualify you as an "impartial" judge. Your *animus* was impartial enough I feel very sure.

Enough!

Yours always | Wm James

ALS: MH bMS Am 1092.9 (3371)

From Mary Elizabeth Litchfield[1]

2 Clinton Street | Cambridgeport. | Nov. 16$\underline{\text{th}}$ [1891]

Prof. James,

Dear Sir,

As you invited remarks, I avail myself of the opportunity.

For fifteen years I have been a teacher—teaching in private schools. My children now are girls varying in age from eleven to eighteen years of age. They come mostly from cultivated and many of them from fashionable families. They lack, perhaps more than anything, the power of concentration and the ability to do disagreeable, dull tasks without inward rebellion.

From my experience, I should say that the modern tendency in education is to provide interesting tasks to such an extent that the power of steady "grinding" so useful in study and in life is not brought out. Some teachers have told me that children taught in Kindergartens expected to be continually amused, & lacked concentration. Would the plan of "inhibition by substitution" if carried out too fully be likely to produce this result?[2] Or can you suggest the system most likely to produce concentration and to educate the will that there may be less inward rebellion at difficult tasks? Of course, we should all agree that to do things from a sense of duty—and to do them with the consent of all our powers whether we wish to or not—is one of the things we should learn in school or out.

Very truly yours | Mary E. Litchfield

ALS: MH bMS Am 1092.9 (4536)

[1] Mary Elizabeth Litchfield (b. 1854), American teacher and writer.

[2] For inhibition by substitution see *TT,* 112.

From Charles Sanders Peirce

CENTURY CLUB | 7 WEST FORTY-THIRD ST. 1891 Nov 17

My dear William:

I went to the Nation office and asked to see any reply to my letter & they showed me yours.[1] I am sorry you should see fit to sneer at my impartiality. That is more of the sort of thing I think reprehensible. I know the two men equally well. I was a classmate of Abbot's, but saw little of him, & his manners were always rather forbidding. I have been told Royce's manners are also bad; but I never felt it. Royce is about the only person who ever paid me a compliment in print. In the branch of philosophy which I have most studied, *logic*, I think on the whole better of Abbot, since things he sees that Royce does not are more rarely discerned. Yet his hard, dualistic style of reasoning I have criticised; and Royce is quite free from that. Therefore, in searching my consciousness, I cannot detect any more leaning to one side than to the other.

As to the conduct of the Editors of the Review, you adduce some new facts. These I wish to reflect further upon, before expressing myself. But your treatment of the principal question, that of the propriety of criticism like Royce's, I will say to you in secrecy that it seems to me a little sophistical. And sophistry upon a highly important question of right and wrong is hurtful and blamable. Such remarks I keep for the ear of my friend. It is not true (this is what I shall perhaps say publicly) that every attack of one philosopher upon the doctrine of another is an attempt to injure that man's reputation. I attacked Abbot's Scientific Theism when it appeared;[2] but Abbot himself saw nothing injurious in it. I wrote an adverse criticism upon Royce's Religion of Philosophy,[3] in which I set forth all the fine qualities of his intellect, praised his scholarship, and said that if he had failed it was with the Plato's and Pascal's to whom his genius allied him. Was that trying to ruin him? to take the bread out of his mouth? By the way, I wrote that criticism at the request of the editor of a review here. It was not mere criticism but partly discussion. One of the most studied things & one of the best reasoned I have ever done. It was warmly received at first; but after ten days it was returned to me with the statement that the editor had concluded it was not sufficiently favorable to Royce. Perhaps you will see in this evidence that I am somehow not impartial. Philosophy has not reached the position of an exact science where being in the wrong is somewhat of a reflection upon a man's competence. Even in physics, Magnus[4] does not come forward to warn the public that Tyndall is a fraud, or precisely stated, that he is 1$^{\underline{st}}$ ignorant, 2$^{\underline{nd}}$ blatant, 3$^{\underline{rd}}$ pretentious. In philosophy, unfortunately, we are all probably pretty far wrong so far, though we think we are approaching an issue from the woods. Plato, Aristotle, Aquinas, Descartes, Leibniz, Kant, Hegel, Mill, and all are generally acknowledged to have been radically wrong. That hardly affects our estimate of their merit as thinkers, of the usefulness of their thought. The same is true today. We can come to no agreement, however long and sincerely we study the subject. Under those circumstances, to say a man's philosophy is wrong is no more than to say he parts his hair on the wrong side. It does not go to injure him. Now Royce was plainly, overtly, trying to injure Abbot and take away his bread and butter. Anybody but a clammy Yankee (I am one & you are not) or one imbued with the spirit of New England ought to see that. He makes much of his bad taste in regard to style and capitals, etc. He repeatedly adverts to his pretentiousness. He practically accuses him of ignorance in philosophy. His *general tone*, which cannot be denied, is that of contempt. That there may be no mistake after *much* of this he at length says he "warns the public" against him! What can that mean? He *professionally* warns. That is, he plainly says Abbot ought not to be reckoned as among those who are to rank as serious students of philosophy. Finally, he says, he shows no mercy and asks none.

Now *will Royce say he did not mean this?*

very faithfully | C. S. Peirce

ALS: MH bMS Am 1092 (665)

[1] WJ, "Abbot Against Royce," *Nation* 53 (19 November 1891): 389–90; reprinted in *ECR*.

[2] Charles Sanders Peirce, "Dr. F. E. Abbot's Philosophy" (a review of his *Scientific Theism* [1885]), *Nation* 42 (11 February 1886): 135–36.

[3] Charles Sanders Peirce, "An American Plato: Review of Royce's *Religious Aspect of Philosophy*" in *Writings of C. S. Peirce: A Chronological Edition* (Bloomington: Indiana Univ. Press, 1993), 5:221–34.

[4] Heinrich Gustav Magnus (1802–1870), German physicist and chemist.

To Henry Rutgers Marshall

95 Irving St | Cambridge, Nov 18. 91

Dear Mr. Marshall,

I got your reprints of Pleasure & Pain etc duly, but not before I had cracked my brains over the articles in Mind's own pages.[1] You have certainly come to closer quarters with the question than any previous analyst, and your scheme seems to cover more facts than any other—in fact there is no other which seems to have been framed under such a pressure, from all sides, of the facts which it was bound to keep account of. Other writers give far more the impression of starting off "at a tangent." One thing occured to me as an objection of a rather radical sort when I was reading, but I did n't note it down, and it does n't come back to me now as I write.[2] It doubtless will erelong. The great trouble with the theory is its extremely abstract character. One doesn't represent to one's self at all just what is meant by your two energies and their relation. The formula *has*, however, to be ultra-vague—the "energy of the stimulus" especially must be kept vague, you can't mean a real numerical $\gtreqless$ relation, for the stimulus, numerically taken, may be vastly less than the reaction, & probably yet give pain. In the case of muscular reaction Matteucci[3] found the relation to be $^{27.000}/_1$ where the stimulus was a galvanic current applied to the motor nerve. What your formula means is evidently $\gtreqless$ than the normal ratio, which normal ratio must differ from one organ to another, and from one person to another of different habitual experience. Nevertheless the formula expresses a *real,* as distinguished from a merely *ideal* relation.

I regard it as one of those things which one must keep & use before one can know how much or how little there is in it. So far I can truly say that it is the deepest thing I know on the subject—the most scientific. It is hard reading—so very deficient in concrete illustrations.

One of my students offers a report of it to our "Seminary" next Wednesday evening.[4] Others have been reading it, and I wish that you might come to the discussion. Can you? I can put you up, and you might find it a lark—though I can't offer to "pay your travelling expenses."

If you can't *come,* can you at least let me have before next Wednesday evening an elucidation of a point which I have found obscure? From the passage on p. 352 it would seem that the pains of obstruction are *vascular* pains. Do you mean anything more definite by this than appears? It appears somewhat like an hypothesis because there *must be one*—a stop-gap to round out the form of the scheme. It is not fair to judge your theory definitively till one sees what it will do in the sphere of aesthetics proper. You apply it now only to simple pleasures & pains. The pleasures & pains that come from mutual furtherance & hindrance of processes might be conceived as pleasures of enhanced reactive energy and as pains of obstruction. Do you carry the thing all the way through on the same lines?

I hope I am not troubling you. The upshot of my reading this fall is to make me realize how few *ideas* there are in the literature of this subject, and how we still wait for an entrance to the method of treatment which is to prove really scientific. So far I confess you are ahead of anyone.

I do hope that you may come.

Very truly yours | Wm James

ALS: MNS

[1] Henry Rutgers Marshall, "The Physical Basis of Pleasure and Pain," *Mind* 16 (July 1891): 327–54; (October 1891): 470–97.

[2] Marshall wrote in the margin: 'Dr James told me at the time of my visit that he must have made a mistake of meaning as he wrote, for he could not find the objection by subsequent thought. RM.'

[3] Carlo Matteucci (1811–1868), Italian physiologist and physicist.

[4] Philosophy 20a: Psychological Seminary, with seventeen students enrolled.

To Alice James

CAMBRIDGE Sunday, Nov 22. 91

Dearest Alice,

Katherine's letter to Alice of the 11th, came to day just as the inward forces were summating themselves in me for a letter to you. She reports that you had been having a rather good spell—the bill of fare of poisons on which you seem fed is so unnatural a regimen that one outcome of it seems as likely as another in the way of comfort. It is lucky that they agree—especially the hyoscin and the spartein. It is a great mercy that I went and got the impression of you which I did—seeing you so well-*minded* has coloured all my imaginings of you with a cheerful tinge, which without the actual experience of your presence would probably have been replaced by most gloomy heart-contractions of wondering pity. Not that the pity is absent by any means; but the *interest in the play* which K. says you now feel to have prevented you from getting the "full good of" *me*, has left so robustious an impression on my mind of the essence of you that morbidness is no part of it. We are all in good shape for the winter—Alice quite hearty again, two good colored servants, children all well, Mrs Gibbens' house 3 doors away, growing in beauty as it matures, College work going well, etc etc etc. Theodora is in the parlor talking to Alice over the wood fire. Harry is sitting at one table in this Library reading under the lamp Baker's Wild Beasts and their ways,[1] whilst I write this at another. I am just in from walking over to Somerville to see Anna Meeker. I didn't see her once last year—I believe. She was out this evening, but the moist cloudy soft air was beautiful and as I entered the Norton estate the woods looked quite grand. The only excitement in our domestic circle is the Abbot Royce controversy into which I have been drawn (see the Nation) by Charles Peirce's letter. Warner is to publish s'thing in next weeks Nation.[2] Then Abbot himself will claim to be heard, and if I mistake

not the Nation won't get rid of *him* without a row.[3]   Godkin was recently thrown from a bucking horse and hurt—his head I believe—
but is all right again.—I don't well understand now the status of Harry's play. K. says it is "meeting with great approval." Does this mean
crowded houses?   A rumor came recently that Compton had announced his intention to keep it going till Christmas "at any cost."[4]
As this was spoken of as "plucky," it leaves me in doubt of the financial
success, which is I take it, at this stage, the great point.   But with
alterations never ending, I should think the whole thing would be
knocking a good year out of poor Harry's life.   I haven't yet got a
chance to read his "Chaperon" but it is spoken of as of his best.[5]

Oh the time! the time!   You have so much!   If human lots could
only be averaged!   On this sabbath afternoon I at last succeeded in
snatching a quarter of an hour for which I have waited two months, &
gave the bull terrier a bath.   "Naldire's dog soap" which I haven't
used for years, brought back all the old Bunch effluvium.   No dog
like Bunch![6]   Good night, dear child, and Heaven bless you.   Alice,
who now sits writing opposite sends her warmest love; and thanks
Katherine for her letter.   She bursts out with: ["]What a big void
there'll be for us when Alice is gone!   She stands for the wider sphere
of reference etc!"   True indeed! indeed.   Good night.

Yrs   W.J.

ALS: MH bMS Am 1092.9 (1158)

[1] Sir Samuel White Baker (1821–1893), British traveler, *Wild Beasts and Their Ways*
(1890).

[2] Joseph Bangs Warner's "The Suppression of Dr. Abbot's Reply," *Nation* 53 (26 November 1891): 408, includes text of Warner's letter to Abbot of 9 June 1891, warning
Abbot about possible consequences.

[3] Francis Ellingwood Abbot, "Mr. Warner's 'Evidence in Full,'" *Nation* 53 (3 December 1891): 426. The *Nation* published a note below Abbot's letter stating that it would
publish nothing else about the matter.

[4] Edward Compton (1854–1918), British actor and manager of Compton's Comedy
Company, which staged the dramatization of HJ's *American*.

[5] HJ, "Chaperon," *Atlantic Monthly* 68 (November 1891): 659–70; (December
1891): 721–35.

[6] For Bunch see *Correspondence*, 1:250.

From John Dewey

15 Forest Ave | Ann Arbor Mich. Nov 22, '91

My dear James

The unfortunate personal direction which the Abbott Royce controversy has assumed suggests one remark which fortunately is not personal. Both Mr Royce and Mr. Abbott profess to believe in the organic character of intelligence—which means (if it mean anything) that the individual *qua* individual is the organ or instrument of truth but not its author. If this is so, a book can only be one thing: a piece of news, an event in intelligence. The discussion of the book is then (*per* theory) an attempt to place the book as this piece of news, as a contribution to intelligence, just as the discussion of a political event is its placing in its outcome or relationships. And yet—and yet! Or is philosophy, at least idealistic philosophy, a Pickwick club where things are true in some special sense[1] —where the organic character of intelligence is True *as philosophy*, but not in specific action?

Excuse this pedagogic letter, but its origin is not pedagogic. It is the outcome of my own experience as subject & object—mainly object—of reviews. The book review seems at once to assume a form of a duel between the individuals (when the review is 'favorable' the standpoint is the same) Now from benighted holders of the exclusively individual theory of intelligence, from sensationalists, nothing different should be expected. But, alas, that the 'absolute intelligence' man should, after all, have the same belief as his theoretic opponent. If the organic theory of intelligence is true as theory isn't it time something was done to make it true as fact, that is as practice?

This inquiry has been bottled up in my mind so long that it now discharges at you as the most convenient target. Besides you at least have never joined the Pickwick Club.

Yours sincerely | John Dewey.

Mr Wm James
  Harvard Univ.

ALS: MH bMS Am 1092.9 (131)

[1] A reference to Charles Dickens, *Posthumous Papers of the Pickwick Club* (1836).

From Sarah Wyman Whitman

November 22 [1891]

I have just read your letter, dear Mr James, in re Royce, and felt a just satisfaction in it: for it does justice.   Indeed I think it quite a masterpiece of successful criticism, for in sustaining Royce it so admonishes him!

I read the Abbott pamphlet—able writing as you said: but weak in having to prove his points by contemporary adulation—and too personal for the dry air of philosophy.   Your letter will square up the matter I fancy.

But *did* you think that you were offering me a novelty in Great Men & the Environment?[1]   Did you not know O vain man that I read that essay as it fell from the printing press & have gone on quoting it ever since?   & thrust it boldly in the face of those who would make us not only the sport but the very *product* of circumstance?   You must be told this, for it is true.

And in all these days, & nights, I have not yet read one word of the books—eager as I am for the story of Imitation:[2] for I have been fairly in a state of siege with the press of affairs & of the demands which have come with other people's misfortunes.   Last of all this death of young Sam Dieter & his mother swept by yet one more storm of her destiny.[3]   These have been days which have heightened the realization of this strange scheme of human life that we live.   You will know what it is to feel the surge of this inner sea: the scope of this recognition.   At such times one seems to have part in every current of the outer air: in every face one passes in the common road—one lives out, *out, out* into the demands & needs of varying people and circumstances: one does not spare any effort.   And all the while one is aware of a deep central fire in which one's heart is hid & which would consume one if the heart were not indestructible.   It is all very wonderful—& more honored in silence than in speech: but I am glad to have a word with you.—

With greeting to all the household—whom I missed last Saturday at the studio—I am

Faithfully yours | SW

ALS: MH bMS Am 1092.9 (687)

[1] WJ, "Great Men, Great Thoughts, and the Environment," *Atlantic Monthly* 46 (October 1880): 441–59; reprinted in *The Will to Believe* (1897).

[2] She seems to be referring to the books WJ sent her; see letter of 8 November 1891.

[3] Sam Dieter was not identified.

From Charles Sanders Peirce

YOUNG'S HOTEL, | BOSTON, Nov 30 1891

My dear William

As it is doubtful whether I shall be able to get to see you, I will say that I think you assent to my plea for gentleness of criticism on partly wrong ground. A critical journal gives its readers to understand it will notice all books they would be pleased to know about, & is under contract to do so. It is bound to consider its readers first of all and to tell them about a book the *truth*. For *that reason* it is bound not to say a book is mere rubbish, when persons highly qualified to judge may regard it as valuable. As long as that is the case, it is *not* rubbish. (Hence when you tell me you think Abbot's books rubbish, your remark is about as forcible as if you were to inform me you thought Hamilton's Quaternions rubbish.)[1]   What competent men find helpful-to-them, is not rubbish. You may not find Hamilton's Quaternions helpful to you; and that certainly proves *something*.

In the second place, philosophy is nothing but a polite amusement. It has nothing to do with feeding, women, hunting, or any of our other passions; and therefore it is ridiculous to lose one's temper over it or to say anything calculated to wound another in connection with it. It is true we think it an elevating amusement, just as votaries of music or mathematics think of their pursuit. But it ceases to be so when made a vehicle of spleen.

In the third place, squabbles of philosophers are most unedifying to outsiders, and go to diminish the respect in which students are held, and to divert material assistance.

Those are my reasons for condemning brutal criticism in philosophy. First, it is unveracious; second, it is bad manners; third, it is imprudent.

very faithfully,   C. S. Peirce

If a critic indul<ges> in *unwarranted* criticism, he is to be justly blamed for all unhappy consequences. But if he is within his right, not. This corresponds to the legal doctrine & seems just.

ALS: MH bMS Am 1092.9 (666)

[1] Sir William Rowan Hamilton (1805–1865), British mathematician.

From Charles William Eliot

HARVARD UNIVERSITY, | CAMBRIDGE, December 1st, 1891.

Dear Dr. James,—

Mr. Rand has been appointed assistant with a salary of $500. a year. It remains for the Philosophical Department to get the corresponding amount of work from him.

So far as the College is concerned, I think your Psychology atones for the absence of laboratory instruction during the past ten years. Hereafter we can fortunately have both.

Very truly yours, | Charles W. Eliot

Professor William James.

TLS: MH bMS Am 1092.9 (147)

To Mary Whiton Calkins

95, IRVING STREET, | CAMBRIDGE, MASS. [December 15, 1891]

My dear Miss Calkins,

The *important* part to publish seemed to me the pages I indicated— but of course have an introduction if you will.[1]

As for continuous & momentary, I can't tell without the context. You You know what a heathen I am about the universal element etc. I want you when you strike, to *kill;* and my only objection to the first third of your paper is that it does not seem to me a *final* statement. Some day either you or I will make one!

But for Heavens sake don't leave out assimilation or reduplication or whatever you may call it. It is a special case which deserves a name. See how many associationist philosophers have tried to explain "contiguous Ass.ⁿ" by a preliminary awakening of the *same idea* from the past, to which the 'contiguous' ideas then are found adhering It seems to me you circumvent them nicely by representing this recall of the same as a special case of a complex process, and by giving it a name. *Don't* leave it out!

In haste yours faithfully | Wm James

ALS: MWelC

[1] See letter to Calkins of 6 November 1891.

To Mary Whiton Calkins

             95, IRVING STREET, | CAMBRIDGE, MASS. Dec. 20. 91
My dear Miss Calkins,

    I have just written to Schurman, in a way that will ensure his atten-
tion. I had done so already without saying who you were.

    Pray send me your 'sample sheets' etc. I think that your "examples"
of association are a grand idea, and should 'admire' to see some of
the quotations from Plato, Tennyson etc. I never thought of such
an exercise myself!—but I will crib it from you, and apply it as soon
as we come to the subject.

    I am sick of the association of ideas and all things connected with
psychology. The result of too unending an application to my own
text, of the 'briefer Course' of which the miserable proofs are not yet
finished! When they are I shall have to go right over the stuff with
the class again. Treadmill work seems preferable. I don't know
what delays Sully with his new and enlarged edition.[1]

                    Ever faithfully yours | Wm James
    Have you noticed the fearful blunder of 4th for 3rd ventricle in
the figure 37 of the Brain chapter which I sent you?[2]

ALS: MWelC

[1] Probably a reference to Sully's *Human Mind*.
[2] The published text refers to the third ventricle; see *BC*, 86. WJ probably sent
her a partial prepublication copy; see *BC*, 480–82.

To Edward Bradford Titchener

           95 Irving Street | Cambridge (Mass.) U.S. | Jan 3. 1892
My dear Sir,

    You are very obliging to take the trouble to write me about the
Hipp instrument, and I thank you heartily. When I wrote to Witmer
I had never used one, nor taken the study to puzzle it out exactly
in the books. I have postponed buying one because of the general
atmosphere of complaint that my mind had come to associate with
it. I have now borrowed one, and understand it thoroughly, and
shall use it until my new one comes. Your letter makes me more
sure of certain points.

    I wish I were 20 years younger and had the advantages of you
fellows! I am an "autodidact" in psychology, have no native aptitude

for experimental work, and begin to be responsible for a labortory at the age of nearly 50—a bad combination!

Whilst I am writing let me ask why in your article on the unlucky Münsterberg, you speak of me as applauding him wherever he runs counter to Wundt—I forget the exact words.[1] The only case of wh. I can think to which such a description would apply is in rê Innervationsgefühl. I have quoted him several times, for ideas that had no connexion with Wundt's, for his *results* on compound reaction-times, and for his ideas about association and muscular sense which ran counter to my own. It seems to me, when a youngster as full of ideas as M. and with so thoroughly healthy a tendency to test them by experiment, starts up, that his exuberances and excesses should be treated in a more paternal manner and not after the brutal fashion of G. E. Müller. I confess I was sorry to hear you speak with joy of his "annihilation"—the word not suggesting to the reader's mind a very ideal picture of the *Gemüthszustand* of psychologists.[2] I am curious to see what the quality of his work will be after these shocks.

Thanking you again I am very truly yours

Wm James

ALS: NIC

[1] Edward Bradford Titchener, "Dr. Münsterberg and Experimental Psychology," *Mind* 16 (October 1891): 521–34. In his closing remarks Titchener notes that WJ has welcomed Münsterberg's "anti-Wundtian doctrines with open arms."

[2] On p. 526n Titchener takes note of Georg Elias Müller's "annihilating criticism" of Münsterberg. For Müller's paper see letter to Münsterberg of 8 July 1891.

From Robertson James

Concord. Jany 12. [1892][1]

Dear Wm.

Is there to be no dividend of rent this month from Syracuse? Please let me know.

Old Channing, the poet who lives here and who refuses to speak with any one I had an opportunity of cornering the other day and he had a good deal to tell me about father.[2] He was very savage at first and said "No one knew your father—he wouldn't let any one know him. All people save one or two were quite alike to him. No one could talk to him for as soon as the occasion demanded he was away up above everything mortal. But he was the most generous man in America. I once took a poor devil to him when he lived in the Astor House in N.Y.—a poor chap who was without means but quite worthy of help. Your father paid for his outfit and paid his passage to the Sandwich Islands where it was promised that he could get employment. He did this without question and the way in which he did it has always made me remember him. I also knew of his taking a friendless girl out of the Street about that time in Boston— putting her beyond want and temptation and of other cases. I never saw any one quite like him. But he wouldn't ask any one to dine with him for fear of being bored. I never read his books and never wanted to. He had no right to use the extravagant language he did for there were those who believed him. I used to call him but myself never talked. His conversation would roll out as if there was no end to it. He had nothing to do with people in this world save one or two.["]

Old C himself never speaks to any one but Sanborn.[3] I had a long letter from Harry yesterday but there is no change in Alice's state.

Always yours | R.J.

ALS: MH bMS Am 1095.2 (22-24)

[1] The dating, though uncertain, was made with reference to AJ's health.

[2] William Ellery Channing (1817–1901), American poet, living in Concord.

[3] Franklin Benjamin Sanborn (1831–1917), American journalist and philanthropist. Correspondence is known from 1879 to 1886.

To Théodule Ribot

95 Irving Street, | Cambridge, Mass. | Jan. 22, 1892.
Dear Monsieur Ribot,

Thanks for your very considerate letter of the 10th. Pray do not on *my* account feel any chagrin about Marillier's delay. The poor fellow is doubtless overburdened (as we all are) for his strength, and I am only too happy to have so solid a review as he will probably make, at any *date*.[1]

You speak of Mind. I doubt whether its character will be much changed by Robertson's defection. The Revue Philosophique remains at the head! The new American "Philosophic Review" has a good editor, and will, I trust, develope into an important Journal.[2] There is a great fermentation commencing in this country in the line of philosophy and the higher education generally, and it is hard to say where it will end.—The strange thing to see is the almost entire cessation of psychological study in England.

With best wishes for the New Year, I am very sincerely yours

Wm. James.

You will ere this have received the abridgement of my Psychology which M. Boirac is, I believe, engaged already in translating for the french public.

TC: MH bMS Am 1092.1

[1] See letter to AJ of 23 August 1891, note 5.

[2] The *Philosophical Review* was edited by Jacob Gould Schurman.

To Alice Howe Gibbens James

Tweedy's Jan 28. 92

Beloved Alice,

I have had a very good 36 hours here, plenty of reading, a 2½ hours walk on the Cliffs yesterday in the magnificent wind, and a complete cessation of my feelings of fatigue.　Tweedy seems extremely well and contented—everything going like clockwork in the house, although Joanna the cook is dead and poor Eliza has had another attack of mental melancholy & has gone to boston to live with her sister.

My only trouble is, as usual, remorse, remorse for attacking you so about the chickens, and making the difficulties of of your nobly and successfully followed housekeeper's path, more difficult than ever. You *all* seem saintly to me, especially your mother & harry.

I will call on Miss Goodwin[1] and the Warings this afternoon, & tomorrow P.M. I will repair to Fall River, to be back with you by Saturday morning.

Heaven bless you! | W.J.

ALS: MH bMS Am 1092.9 (1800)

[1] Probably Juliet R. Goodwin, who was active in Newport's social life.

To Henry Holt

95 Irving St. Cambridge | Jan. 31, 92

My dear Holt:

I am to be at that infernal S.P.R. meeting on the 10th; but how long I can stay in N.Y. before or after that day I know not now.[1]　If

I stay it will be at the house of a cousin of mine in 25th St., and I shall be most happy to "break bread" with you on one of the other days, *en famille*. I will let you know as soon as my "plans are formed".

Always yours, | Wm. James

TC: MH bMS Am 1092.1

[1] WJ chaired a meeting of the New York section of the American Branch of the Society for Psychical Research on 10 February 1892, where he addressed an audience of some 400 primarily on the Census of Hallucinations.

To Henry Rutgers Marshall

CAMBRIDGE Jan 31. 92

My dear Marshall,

I have read your reply to Sidgwick with interest, though it seems to me that the case is insoluble in general terms and without making discriminations which (as you say) language has not provided for.[1] I found Sidgwick's article instructive, and as I use the words "desire" and "painful" have felt like subscribing to it. Most desires, like most volitions, lead immediately to action and the even incipient gratification seems to neutralize effectively whatever may be unpleasant in the desire, just as the sensation of an accomplished muscular contraction eclipses instantly the image which defined it to the mind as an object of volition. If the action is thwarted, we have an "uneasiness" which leads to "pain"—if the thwarting becomes strong or prolonged. But whenever there is a crescendo in the direction of prompt satisfaction, to my consciousness its pleasure is much stronger than the potential pain of the desire, in ordinary cases.

Delboeuf somewhere asks whether the beginnings of sexual desire are not pleasant. I suppose most men would say yes. Only after considerable thwarting will "pain" come in.

That is all I can say of the matter just now.

I thank you for your invitation to the Century.[2] I can't tell now how many hours I can spend in N.Y., but I will let you know in time.

Yours very truly | Wm James

Of course *send your rejoinder!*[3]

ALS: MNS

[1] In his "The Physical Basis of Pleasure and Pain," Marshall often refers to Henry Sidgwick's *Methods of Ethics*, 4th ed. (1890). Sidgwick commented on Marshall in "The Feeling-Tone of Desire and Aversion," *Mind*, n.s., 1 (January 1892): 94–101.

[2] The Century Club was a club in New York City.

[3] Henry Rutgers Marshall, "The Definition of Desire," *Mind*, n.s., 1 (July 1892): 400–403.

To Edward Bradford Titchener

CAMBRIDGE Feb. 1. '92

My dear Mr. Titchener

I thank you for your obliging letter of the 13th. *Ewald's* little chronoscope would seem on the whole to be a useful instrument if it were of better construction—as it is I can do nothing with it. When the new Hipp and the new fall hammer come,[1] we shall go on our way rejoicing. From your letter it would seem that the newly discovered constant error is in the older chronoscopes—whether in the newer ones or not *bleibt dahingestellt* for aught that you say.

As regards Wundt, it would be easier to talk than to write. What I last wrote you had reference exclusively to your implication that I applauded M——g so far as he ran against W——t, a most absurd idea. For W. himself, I admit that I was guilty of ignorance of most of his 3rd edition when I pub.^{d} my P. of P. After having read through both 1st & 2nd., it was perhaps natural to flinch from the 3rd.[2] in a world so crowded with new things that one can't read for lack of time. Külpe's articles on the Will first informed me of Wundt's conversion, less than a year ago, and then I look the matter up.[3] With all my gratitude to Wundt for inspiring me with his wide ideals of study, I must say that I think he is getting in his old age into very reprehensible ways. His infernal pretention to be *smooth, e.g.* to advance *without jolt,* makes him smear over everything. Surely if any name has been identified with the innervationsgefühl it is his. Why can't he then say when driven out of it, (it is the *rother faden* through all his psychology) that his view is *changed.* One would suppose from his present allusions to the subject that he had never believed in it, and that on the contrary Ferrier and others had. When a man pub.^{s} 3rd editions, he ought by chapter and verse to indicate in the preface where the reader will find changed views. I must say there is something in Wundts manner of late, in Külpe's way of assuming that he never believed in Innervationsgefuhle, in your article on M——g, and in your phrase now about my "hostility" to W., which strongly suggest to one that W. is feeling himself to be in a sort of pontifical position, from which all appearance of fallibility must be removed, and all reluctance in others to acknowledge which must be followed up and punished. If this is really so, it is shameful, and blots a noble career. Yet what can one think after the ignominious Stumpf-Wundt controversy, bad eno' on S's side, but wholly bad on W's.?

My life long complaint of W. is his pretention to be *smooth* and his haziness in fundamental ideas. Külpe has made "apperception" clear to me. Why couldn't W.? He hadn't made it clear to himself. If he had, he never would have chosen so bad a name for it. I think K's statement an admirable plea for our sense of inner spiritual activity.

As for Münsterberg, time only can show his importance for Psychology, and we must both wait. What charms me is his big free flexible quality—the quality of a big man full of ideas and inventions. I am prejudiced von Vornherein against most of his ideas and results. But a psychologists importance has nothing to do with his infallibility. It is his power as a ferment. Fechner's darling idea is rubbish,[4] Helmholtz has been completely wrong on fundamental matters. Wundt's space-theory is in my opinion *hinfällig,* and his other fundamental ideas vague. That doesn't prevent all these men from having been first-class influences in the progress of Psychology. I confess I should be glad to believe that the same could one day be said of Münsterberg.

But what a tirade! Being young and vigorous, you will doubtless be moved to some words of reply. Pray do so if you feel like it—I will leave you then with the last word.

Thanking you for your interest in my laboratory plans, I am very truly yours,

Wm James

ALS: NIC

[1] Possibly an instrument used in reaction-time experiments.

[2] Wilhelm Wundt, *Grundzüge der physiologischen Psychologie* (1874) (WJ 796.59.2); 2d ed., 2 vols. (1880) (WJ 796.59.4); 3d ed., 2 vols. (1887). The third edition is not known from WJ's library, but both volumes of the fourth edition (1893) were sold from his library.

[3] It is not clear whether WJ meant to write 'I looked the matter up' or 'I took the matter up'. Oswald Külpe, "Die Lehre vom Willen in der neueren Psychologie," *Philosophische Studien* 5 (1888): 179–244; (1889): 381–446. For WJ's view of Wundt see his "Professor Wundt and Feelings of Innervation," *Psychological Review* 1 (January 1894): 70–73; reprinted in *EPs*.

[4] Gustav Theodor Fechner (1801–1887), German philosopher, physicist, and psychologist. For a possible interpretation see *Correspondence*, 5:81.

From Henry Holt

Feb. 2, 1892.

Dear James.

The enclosed speaks for itself. I suppose that this chap represents quite a "party", and that it may be worth while to shape things a little to suit his views, as you can probably do without suppressing your own.[1]

Yours ever, | H. Holt.

Prof. William James.

Letterbook: NjP

[1] The enclosure, no longer extant, was probably an irate letter concerning *Psychology: Briefer Course*. The first and second printings contain a passage about the copulation of frogs and toads, "occasionally between males, often with dead females," that some readers found offensive (see *BC*, 97). In the third printing WJ toned down the sexually explicit description and wrote instead that "an immense waste of batrachian life . . . takes place from no other cause than the blind character of the sexual impulse in these creatures" (*BC*, 495). The protest received by Holt testifies to the popularity of the book as a text. The identical passage in *Principles of Psychology* (*PP*, 34–35) remained explicit.

From Henry Rutgers Marshall

CENTURY CLUB | 7 WEST FORTY-THIRD ST. 2 Feby—92

My dear Doctor

Thank you very much for yours of 31$^{\underline{st}}$ The case of sexual desire I would explain as I do that of hunger appetite. We do not in such cases "discriminate with sufficient care between the craving and the voluminous and vivid feelings coincident with the wide and vague active functioning which ensues" &c &c.[1] In retrospect the desire pain is overwhelmed by the revival of these other feelings.

It appears to me that the *desire* to move toward the loved object disappears with the moving: that a new desire arises after we have approached the object and when the movements to which it prompts become actual *that* desire disappears, and so on indefinitely.

Under such a view it is certainly erroneous to hold that the original desire continues through all the complex train or that any desire at all exists if the activities follow one another with no restraint whatever.

Hoping to see you on Wed^y of next week I am

Yours truly | Henry Rutgers Marshall

To Dr Wm James

ALS: MH bMS Am 1092 (548)

¹ The text appears in Marshall's "Definition of Desire," 401.

To William Noyes

CAMBRIDGE [February 6, 1892]

Bravo! This something like a discovery! I dare say that we might evolve something by conference together. Can't you come over and visit my laboratory any day, M.W.F. (9.30 to 11.30), & Thursday 4 to 6.30. Tuesday 8 to 10 PM.

W.J.

APS: MH bMS Am 1092.9 (3359)
Address: Dr William Noyes | McLean Asylum | Somerville | Mass
Postmark: CAMBRIDGE. BOSTON MASS FEB 6 92

To Mary Whiton Calkins

CAMBRIDGE Feb. 14. 92.

My dear Miss Calkins,

I hardly know what to advise, in my ignorance of just what Cornell gives, just what such a place as Freiburg would give, just what Paris might give. Munsterb. had a woman student a year ago, she figures in the collective photograph. Can't you postpone the decision till you know the facts better. Delabarre will be back from Paris in 6 weeks I believe, and can tell you just what Freiburg & Paris can do for you. Much is gained atmospherically by going abroad apart from any particular "advantages." A young fellow named Jankowich from Freiburg is here now¹—I expect to see him next Saturday night—he can supply information as to the lot of Woman there. We may ourselves go and settle in Freiburg next winter. Pray postpone your decision as to *where* you go as long as you can!

Don't read my chapters too often! You'll grow demented.

Yours ever | W.J.

ALS: MWelC

¹ Jankowich was not identified.

From Francis Lee Higginson[1]

Mentone | Feby 14. 92.

Dear Willy—

Did you ever read Ed. Hale's story of "my double & how he undid me"?[2]—You used to be my double do you remember how your good old mother tried to cross the street to kiss me or beat me for you, only Miss Alice wouldn't let her.

So you want to undo me & I suppose you will succeed—my only safety is in the little gap of 4000. miles that divide us.[3] When I come home next summer I will honour your drafts in a small way as you suggest to C. C. Jackson[4]—but out here it is a bother to arrange it all—if you haven't yet got the odd $25.—you speak of for the last case, send in to C.C.J. for it for my a/c.

D——d the old world Billy—Ameriky is good eno. for me. I am bored to death. I don't know whether I like hard work very much but I'll be hanged if I like complete idleness. I am too old & too stupid to study—so I read read read & walk—no one [to] talk to except my boy, & he is too young to talk back, he only asks questions, that he is an adept in.[5]

Have you a new cure for seasickness if so send it along—some of my family suffer.[6] Harry came to see us in London & was simply sp[l]endid—but he didn't come again. I thought he was much taken up with his "American" which was being acted—being a bachelor perhaps he was taken up with the very attractive actress who acted Claire[7]—in his place I should have been.

My love to you sweet William

Yr | F. L. Higginson

ALS: MH bMS Am 1092 (334)

[1] Francis Lee Higginson (1841–1925), American financier, brother of Henry Lee Higginson. Francis Higginson's acquaintance with WJ dates to the 1860s; see *Correspondence*, 4:44. Only the present letter is known.

[2] Edward Everett Hale (1822–1909), American clergyman and author, "My Double and How He Undid Me" (1859). One letter is known (1889).

[3] Menton is on the Mediterranean coast of France.

[4] Charles Cabot Jackson (1843–1926), American banker, who was for a time associated with Lee, Higginson and Co.

[5] Francis Lee Higginson (1877–1969), a banker, son of Francis Lee Higginson.

[6] For WJ on seasickness see *EPs*, 188–89.

[7] The role of Claire de Cintré, the heroine in *The American*, was played by Elizabeth Robins (1862–1952), American actress and author. One letter is known (1907).

To Hugo Münsterberg

95 Irving St. | Cambridge, Mass. Feb. 21. '92

Dear D.̲ Münsterberg,

Is it conceivable that, if you should be invited, you might agree to come and take charge of the Psychological Laboratory and the higher instruction in that subject in Harvard University for three years at a salary of say 3000 dollars (12000 Marks)?

This is a private question of my own, and not an inquiry on the part of our University authorities. My mind is in travail with plans for regenerating our philosophical department, and the importation of you has come to figure amongst the hypothetical elements of the case. I cannot of course go on with the combination till I know whether or not that particular feature is impossible. So pray tell me.

The situation is this: We are the best university in America, and we must lead in Psychology. I, at the age of 50, disliking laboratory work naturally, and accustomed to teach philosophy at large, altho I *could, tant bien que mal,* make the laboratory run, yet am certainly not the kind of stuff to make a first-rate director thereof. We could get younger men here who would be *safe* enough, but we need something more than a safe man, we need a man of genius if possible. Meanwhile there is no additional money at the disposal of our philosophical department, and if you were to come, it would be neccessary to raise money for 3 years expressly by appealing to friends of the cause. Such a thing might *possibly* succeed. After three years (if it did succeed), you would know us, we should know you, and it *might* be possible to make the arrangement permanent. You would have to contemplate, in deciding to accept such an invitation, the possibility of going back to Germany after an experiment of three years. Of course we should hope for permanence. Our university is one you need not be ashamed of. I got a fund of 4,300 dollars last year to start a laboratory, of which some 1600 still remain unspent. You would have an assistant (or two if needful) and of actual *teaching* would not be called to do more than 6 hours a week, or less.

Once more, this is a private question from me to you, and you will oblige me by not making it public. The scheme will require much labor to carry it into effect, and I cannot begin the work at all unless I have something definite to go upon on your side.

At your age and with your facility I am sure the language won't trouble you after the first year.

Faithfully yours, Wm James

Of course you understand that an affirmative answer to me now will not *pledge* you to say yes hereafter, in case additional details should then come up, which might make you change your mind.

P.S.   Whilst you are writing should you mind telling me whether the schools for boys in Freiburg are first-rate.   I shall probably go to Europe with my family for next winter, and have thought of Freiburg as an abode.   I have one boy now of twelve, and another of nine. Can the latter enter a gymnasium, or must he go to a lower school. Any practical *"Winke"* about the schools which you may be able to give me without taking too much trouble will put me under great obligations.

W.J.

ALS: MH bMS Am 1092.9 (3265); MB[1]

[1] The first six pages of this letter are preserved in the James Collection at the Houghton Library, the last two ('P.S. . . . W.J.') in the Boston Public Library.

To John White Chadwick[1]

95, IRVING STREET, | CAMBRIDGE, MASS. Feb. 23. 93 [1892][2]
Dear Mr. Chadwick

I am amused at your assumption that I may be a stranger to you, I who have followed your career with admiring eyes since those old divinity school days when I used to hear poor old C. C. Salter and May talk so incessantly about you.[3]

Well you've given a fine puff to my book, and I hope will have no reason to repent it.   I[t] is a fine sermon.   Only I am not so sure about "our *whole* self acting spontaneously" etc.   It is a deeper stratum of our self which kills the rest, and I don't wonder at the traditional interpretation of it as miraculous grace acting in us.

My wife begs her remembrances, and I am always sincerely yours
Wm James

ALS: RPB

[1] John White Chadwick (1840–1904), American clergyman.

[2] The year 1893 is an error.   The sermon in which WJ's book is mentioned, "The Price of Moral Freedom," was published in the middle of February 1892, and WJ probably told about the "puff" shortly thereafter.   The sermon was included in a collection of sermons by Chadwick, *Seeing and Being* (1893).

[3] Charles Christie Salter (1839–1870), a divinity student at Harvard in 1863–64. Scott in *SUC,* 567, identifies May as Joseph May (1836–1918), also a divinity student at Harvard.

To Christine Ladd Franklin

95, IRVING STREET, | CAMBRIDGE, MASS. March 3. 92

Dear Mrs. Franklin,

It gives me great pleasure to receive your letter which in business like and expeditious manner, I must answer point by point. I had no idea you were abroad, and on the whole congratulate you on the opportunity. I am myself to have my "sabbatical" next year, and take the family in July to Germany. Possibly your[1] and Professor Franklin will still be there.

Thank you for your continued indulgence as to the Psychology. The last chapter however is the one for which I mainly craved your approval as a logician & mathematician, and now it turns out to be the one which you chiefly disapprove![2] The unfathomable ways of woman! If I ever do revise the book you shall go in with the horopter. I didn't mention that because it seemed to me to have much more mathematical than psychological interest—in fact hardly any of the latter except what your illusion gave it.

I have a sort of terror of Müller as of all mathematically minded geniuses including yourself.[3] But I'm glad you & he are such good friends—of course we are going to have women in Harvard soon—göttingen mustn't be allowed to get ahead there. But which theory of Hering's do you mean—he has so many? Is it colour, space, contrast, what? I rather admire Hering all round. Helmholtz of course is much the greater man, and yet he probably has made more mistakes. I shall be greatly interested in your article, wherever it appears.[4]

I shall be delighted to read your Intuition and Reason in the MS., and to do what I can to recommend it.[5] Don't you want the Pop. Sci. M.?

Always faithfully yours | Wm James

ALS: NNC

[1] A slip for 'you'.

[2] See letter of 16 October 1890.

[3] Georg Elias Müller was then professor at Göttingen.

[4] Perhaps Christine Ladd Franklin, "A New Theory of Light Sensation," which she presented to the International Congress of Experimental Psychology in 1892 and which was published in the *International Congress of Experimental Psychology* (n.d.).

[5] Christine Ladd Franklin, "Intuition and Reason," *Monist* 3 (January 1893): 211–19.

From Alice James

London Mar 5 1892

William James
95 Irving St
Cambridge Mass
Tenderest love to all   farewell   Am going soon.

Alice

Cablegram: MH bMS AM 1092.9 (1494)

From Hugo Münsterberg

Freiburg i. B. 7 März 92.

Verehrter Herr Professor!

Verbindlichsten Dank für Ihren Brief, der mir ehrenvoll und in sachlicher wie persönlicher Hinsicht erfreulich ist. Sie werden vielleicht verwundert sein, wenn ich Ihnen sage, dass ich, wenn ein entsprechender officieller Ruf an mich ergeht, sehr wahrscheinlich gerne Folge leisten würde. Ich kann somit Ihre Anfrage im wesentlichen mit *ja* beantworten.

Keinenfalls würde ich länger als drei Jahre in Amerika bleiben, da ich jedenfalls Deutscher bleiben will und die ganze Angelegenheit nur wie eine grosse schoene lehrreiche Reise betrachten würde. Ich würde hier für drei Jahre Urlaub nehmen und während dieser Zeit trotz meiner amerikanischen Wirksamkeit Freiburger Professor bleiben (ich bin nämlich vor einigen Wochen hier zum Professor ernannt.) Das, was mich dazu triebe, Ihrer Aufforderung Folge zu leisten, wäre also neben dem Wunsche, Amerika kennen zu lernen, lediglich der Wunsch, der experimentellen Psychologie nach jeder Richtung mit bester Kraft zu dienen. Ich meine, dass drei Jahre in der Tat völlig ausreichten, um den experimentellen Unterricht zu organisieren. Bestimmend ist für mich dabei natürlich der grosse Ruf und die hohe Bedeutung, deren sich die Universität von Cambridge erfreut; für eine kleine Universität würde ich nicht Europa verlassen.

Die einzigen Bedenken, welche ich habe, sind die folgenden.

In erster Linie befürchte ich, dass ich zu ungeschickt in der englischen Sprache sein werde, da ich vorläufig vollkommen Anfänger in der Sprache bin. Ich nehme nun freilich an, dass ich erst zum

Herbst oder, was mir noch lieber wäre, erst zum nächsten Frühjahr
hinüber soll; bis dahin würde ich möglichst die Sprache studieren,
obgleich ich geringes Sprachtalent besitze und es zu einem fliessen-
den Sprechen wahrscheinlich niemals bringen werde.—Es kommt
hinzu, dass meine Wirksamkeit ja in erster Linie eine rein praktische
sein würde, ich also zusammenhängende Vorträge, wenigstens vielleicht im ersten Jahr, nicht zu halten brauchte. Bei dem praktischen
Unterricht im Experimentieren ist die Sprache ja nicht so wichtig.
Wenn Sie zufügen, dass dieser Unterricht nur 6 Stunden die Woche
beanspruchen würde, so können Sie versichert sein, dass es an mir
nicht fehlen soll, auch wenn der Unterricht 6 Stunden den Tag be-
trägt.

Mein zweites Bedenken—ich spreche ganz offen—betrifft die materiellen Verhältnisse. Hier in Deutschland gilt das Leben in Amerika für fürchterlich teuer, und Sie werden begreifen, dass ich den
Wunsch habe, bei dem amerikanischen Unternehmen nicht auch
noch grössere Summen zuzusetzen. Hier in dem billigen Freiburg
gebrauche ich jährlich etwa 10000 bis 12000 Mark (ich habe Frau
und zwei kleine Kinder); ich würde, um dieselbe Lebensführung in
Amerika fortzusetzen, dort zweifellos etwa 18000 Mark verbrauchen.
Sie schlagen mir nun ein jährliches Gehalt von 12000 Mk. vor; wenn
ich aus eigner Tasche ein paar tausend zusetze, würde ich damit also
auch auskommen. Nun kommt aber die Reise und der Umzug
hinzu, und ich muss befürchten, dass dadurch das Gehalt des ersten
Jahres vollkommen verbraucht wird. Endweder schicke ich meine
ganzen Moebel etc. hinüber, dann kostet der Transport Unsummen
oder ich kaufe dort neue, dann ist es erst recht teuer. (Oder würde
es sich empfehlen, dass ich für drei Jahre eine möblierte Wohnung
miete?) Dann kommt die teure "Überfahrt für uns alle mit Dienst-
boten hinzu, kurz ich fürchte die Reise und der Umzug hin und nach
drei Jahren zurück, wird mir mindestens 3000 Dollars kosten. Prof.
v. Holst, der von hier mit 7000 Doll. nach Chicago berufen ist, be-
kommt ausdrücklich 3000 D. extra für die Reise. Würden mir für
die drei Jahre im ganzen 12000 Dollars bewilligt (also 3000 für jedes
der drei Jahre und 3000 extra für Hin- und Rückfahrt mit Familie),
so wären meine materiellen Ansprüche vollkommen befriedigt. Jedenfalls soll die Sache an der materiellen Klippe nicht scheitern, und
zu denjenigen, die nach Amerika wollen um Gold anzuhäufen, ge-
höre ich wahrlich nicht; die wissenschaftliche Sache, die Hoffnung
auf einen grossen Wirkungskreis, der Wunsch tüchtig zu lehren und

tüchtig zu lernen ist es allein, der mich veranlassen könnte, mein ruhiges behagliches Leben hier für einige Jahre aufzugeben.

Sehr dankbar wäre ich Ihnen, wenn ich die officielle Berufung recht bald erhalten würde, damit das unbehagliche Stadium der Ungewissheit für mich recht kurz dauert. Ich würde mir dann natürlich noch eine kurze Bedenkzeit erbitten müssen, vor allem um den Rat der deutschen Collegen unter dem Gesichtspunkt zu erbitten, ob nicht die Unterbrechung meiner hiesigen Tätigkeit schädlich für mein Weiterkommen in Deutschland wäre. Schon jetzt glaubte ich im Vertrauen den Rat der mir nächststehenden Collegen erbitten zu dürfen; sie haben mir alle zugeredet, einen etwaigen Ruf für 3 Jahre ruhig anzunehmen.

Dass es mir, verehrter Herr Professor, eine ganz besondere Freude und Ehre sein würde, an Ihrer Seite und unter Ihrem Schutz zu wirken, bedarf kaum der Versicherung.

Was Ihre persönliche Anfrage betrifft, so bin ich zweifelhaft, ob ich Ihnen raten soll, den Winter in Freiburg zuzubringen. Freiburg ist im Sommer sehr genussreich, im Winter bietet es herzlich wenig. Die Schulen sind hier gut, aber nicht anders als in den meisten deutschen Städten. Mich würden Sie im nächsten Winter keinenfalls hier treffen; gleichviel ob ich im folgenden Frühjahr nach Amerika gehe oder nicht, in jedem Falle stand es schon lange bei mir fest, dass ich studienhalber um grössere Bibliotheken etc. zu benutzen, den Winter in Berlin und München zubringen wollte, zum Teil auch in Italien, da ich mit einer grösseren Untersuchung über den Ausdruck der Gemütsbewegungen beschäftigt, dort dazu Kunstwerke studieren will. Der Winter ist hier langweilig und gesellschaftlich unerfreulich. Ich würde Ihnen raten, vielleicht nach München zu gehn, wo Wissenschaft, Kunst und heiteres Leben sich glücklich vermischen; selbst Heidelberg scheint mir angenehmer als Freiburg, wenn auch natürlich im Sommer die Freiburger Naturschönheit, die mich seinerzeit herzog, den Kampf mit Heidelberg sehr wohl aufnehmen kann.

Nur einen Nachtrag noch: ich wäre gern bereit, einen Teil meiner Laboratoriumsapparate nach Cambridge mitzubringen und zur allgemeinen Verfügung zu stellen.

Ich wiederhole meinen herzlichsten Dank für Ihre ehrenvolle Anfrage und bitte Sie nur noch einmal am möglichste Beschleunigung, damit ich mich recht bald entscheiden kann; eine lange Ungewissheit in solchen entscheidenden Fragen ist gar zu lästig. Eventuell können wir ja den Telegraphen zu Hülfe nehmen.

Mit ergebenstem Gruss | in vorzüglichster Hochachtung | Ihr | Hugo
Münsterberg.

ALS: MH bMS Am 1092.9 (360)

To Charles William Eliot

95 Irving St | Cambr. March 21. 92

My dear President,

I wish very much that you were here in order to give a decision
about a matter of some importance to the James family. As it is, I
resolve to write to you and beg you to telegraph an answer at my expense.

Can I have leave to depart on the 25th of May?

I can sail on that date on a first rate Antwerp steamer and save
(from Boston to Switzerland) 200 dollars which I should have to pay
if I went by any other line. The other Antwerp steamers are unfit
to take until June 15th—a difference of three weeks.

I have carefully been over the matter with MacVane and Bendelari,[1] and find that what I should lose from College duties is two
lectures in Philosophy 2.[2] [My last meeting in Phil 20a falls on the
26th, & I can easily transfer that to the 23rd.] I may lose besides a
meeting or two of the Committee on Fellowships, and (possibly) an
honour examination. The examination in Phil 2., I should in any
event have no scruples about letting Nichols mark; and, to save appearances, he might perfectly well, if I went, give the last two lectures
of the course to the men.

Pray decide as you think best for the College discipline, and if you
telegraph "no" I shall say "Amen." The temptation to me to exchange three weeks of Cambridge (in the fagged state in which June
will find me) for three weeks of Switzerland, has been so strong that
I feel my own inability to look at my duty objectively, and would
rather leave the decision to you altogether.

If Palmer accepts the Chicago invitation,[3] it will probably oblige a
postponement of my leave of absence next year.[4] I have no idea how
the balance is inclining, but it is not easy to believe that he can turn
his back on the College Yard. When the final moment comes I suspect that he will stay. With so many possibilities in the air, the Loisette money, the Münsterberg idea, and the uncertainty about Palmer,
you will readily imagine that the inner life of the Philosophical department is in danger of being *momentarily* more interested in tempo-

ral than in eternal things!   They do distract one's attention a little, it must be confessed.   If Palmer should go, even without any Loisette money, I still think it will not be hard to make the department as efficient as it is now.

I trust that Mrs. Eliot and you are getting on the whole more recreation than labour out of your trip.   With cordial regards, believe me always faithfully yours

Wm James

ALS: MH Archives

[1] George Bendelari (1851–1927), Italian-born instructor; after 1895, a journalist. In 1891–92 he was chairman of the committee on changes of elective studies.

[2] See letter to Eliot of 11 September 1891.

[3] Palmer did not take a position at the newly founded University of Chicago.

[4] On the first page of the letter Charles Eliot wrote originally 'Yes. Go. If Palmer goes you probably cannot be spared'.   Then erasing 'probably . . . spared', he rewrote the last sentence as follows: 'If Palmer *accepts [ab. del. 'goes'], you will *postpone [ab. del. 'forego'] ['your le' del.] leave *of [intrl.] absence | Professor William James | Irving St | Cambridge | Mass'.

To Hugo Münsterberg

95, IRVING STREET, | CAMBRIDGE, MASS. March 23 '92
Dear Professor

First let me congratulate you on the possession of that well deserved title, and then let me say that I am extremely glad to hear what you say in your letter of the 7th about coming here.   I feared the answer would be negative.

I can well understand your desire to have so important a matter settled at the earliest possible date.   But we must all have a little patience.   The plan, as I explained to you in my letter is only *my* plan, so far.   Since new money will have to be raised from friends of the university (everything here in America proceeds by voluntary contributions) if the plan is to be a reality, that is the next step in order.   Naturally I couldn't go to work to raise money for a new Director of the Laboratory until I was sure that the Director would come if asked.   It will certainly now take a month before the money question is decided, and more than a month before the authorities of the University can invite you to come, for the President is now in California and will be absent several weeks.   The matter has not been brought in any shape before the "President and Fellows" (our governing body) yet—it is merely a dream of mine in which I ask you to play a non-resistent part, until other forces, more powerful than my will, come into play. I promise you that as soon as anything *is* definitively decided, I will immediately let you know by telegraph what it is. It seems to me incredible that with your German *Beredsamkeit* you should not soon me[1] master of English. But I believe that Victor Hugo could never learn English; so, whilst hoping for the best, am prepared for the worst! When I said six hours of instruction a week I meant (eventually) that number of regular *lectures* as a maximum. Of ordinary laboratory advice and consultation the hours would of course be *ad libitum*.

Yes, Cambridge is a dear place to live in. It must be to Freiburg fully in the proportion of 3 to 2. But of all those details we can talk later. I must first of all see about the money!

Cordially yours | Wm James

ALS: MH bMS Am 1092.9 (3266)

[1] A slip for 'be'.

To Charles William Eliot

Cambr. March 24. 92

Dear President,

I enclose you a letter just received from Münsterberg—I had hardly dared to hope for anything so favorable. His own mood about the three years is just right for us, since if he doesn't "assimilate" he can then retreat with no awkwardness on either side. But if he does, his feeling about going back may change and we may keep him. In either case his presence for three years will be invaluable for our psychological school. He will initiate a movement which can for a certain time be kept up after he is gone. The only alternatives to M. are vastly inferior ones. I have made a (to me) irresistible(!) sounding appeal to Loisette; and will let you know the fruit of it as soon as it arrives. If you then telegraph me your authorization to invite M., I can telegraph the essential fact to him (since he is so impatient) and the final contract can be negotiated through the mails. I think you need have no doubts whatever of M's superiority over any other nameable incumbent. He is only 27 or 8 years old and has started livelier discussions in Psychology than anyone living. Everyone *has* to read what he writes! Delabarre, who spent last winter with him, on being consulted when here a fortnight ago, thought he would be an admirable acquisition, and everyone speaks of his personal good nature and freedom from angles. Of course he has enemies. I myself am one of the strongest disbelievers in his theories about the muscular sense etc; but no one denies that he is a great "force". Royce entirely agrees with me about his superiority, for our needs, over any american candidate. The only doubt is about Loisette. If he doesn't inflame, the process of begging is likely to be a slow one, and I fear we may lose our chance!

The signs are that, altho Mrs. Palmer is eager to go to Chicago, P. is bound to stay. If M. is secured this will be an absolute certainty I know.[1]

Always truly yours | Wm James

President Eliot.

ALS: MH Archives

[1] On the letter Charles Eliot noted: 'I approve inviting Muntersberg at three thousand salary and six hundred travelling expenses each way. Consult Hooper & Walcott. Keep Santayana next year only.'

To Henry Lee Higginson

95 Irving Street, | Cambridge, March 26, 92.

PERSONAL.

My dear Henry:

If you ever look at my account with your house, you will see that I borrowed $500 last September and a couple of months ago 100 more. This looks bad; but it is really less bad than it seems; and as I contemplate moving upon your works once more, I think I ought to give you a complete account of our affairs.

I inherited last year from my queer old Cousin H. Wyckoff in N.Y. $2850, which was paid in in the summer. My mother-in-law and her daughter put into this house when I built it a sum which, with unpaid interest, amounted to $4354.08 cents in August last. With the above legacy and some of my income, I paid of this sum all but 750 dollars in September. So you see that though I have drawn upon you, I have also laid by in another way even more than I have drawn, and kept within my income after all.

But now comes a period of new expense. I must soon pay in that remaining 750 dollars; and as Mrs. Gibbens has just built a house for herself near by and is moving into it, I must carpet and otherwise furnish the rooms which she has occupied here whilst living with us. I understand that my share of my sister Alice's estate will amount to about $20,000 and will be paid in in the course of three months or less. The trouble with me pecuniarily all these years has been the fact that I have got overworked so often and required these infernally expensive trips of travel to get me on my feet again. (Don't you go for to get a "neurasthenic diathesis" like mine!) This year I have been in a fearfully fagged condition, and nothing will do for it now but to take my sabbatical year (which is two years overdue anyhow) and go to Europe with wife and kids for 15 months, leaving them a second year, if the boys seem well placed at school there, and going again to fetch them the third summer. If we rent both our Chocorua and our Cambridge houses well, this ought not to be so very extravagant a plan. My wife thinks even that we can economize. We shall see!

The result of it all is that I may have to borrow 1000 or 1200 dollars from you within the next couple of months to furnish the house completely for a tenant and to close up my Gibbens debt.

There will remain $6,500 to pay on this house (mortgaged to Cambridge Savings Bank for that amount) and I think that it will be better to devote the income of what remains to me of Alice's bequest to gradually paying off that, than to pay it with the principal all at once. I wish to keep Alice's bequest so far as possible intact and use the income for investment alone so far as possible. When it comes in, I want your advice about what is best to do.

Meanwhile, I beg you to send me 400 dollars on account of the debts above mentioned. As more becomes needed I will send for it, and pay for all I take out of Alice's legacy in a couple of months. I wish I could furnish the house with income but I can't! The legacy comes at a convenient time.

How lucky I am to have such a friend as you for a banker! Our April recess begins on Wednesday, April 6 and lasts a week. I *must* get away into the country. This latitude is always too cold. Can't you come along with me to the N. Carolina Mountains? I saw two splendid places there last Fall,—Linville and Blowing Rock—new summer resorts, fine roads and splendid scenery. I may possibly draw up some colleagues here for the trip. Pray say you can come!

Yours always, | Wm. James.

TC: MH bMS Am 1092.1

To Shadworth Hollway Hodgson

95, IRVING STREET, | CAMBRIDGE, MASS. March 28. 92

My dear Hodgson

The sight of your noble handwriting does my heart good. I am sorry that Sully should have given you any alarm about my health, which is I trust fundamentally good, although it has been overlaid by a superficies of brain-fag and consequential doleful dumps this winter. I imagine that all I need is a good solid holiday; and *that* I am about to take by bringing the whole family to the Continent. I wrote to Sully that once in Switzerland I should probably let the Congress go, since the buzz and excitement would do me less good than the "grassy slopes"; and the journey to England and back would be an extravagance.[1] Things look now, however, like an earlier start; and I *may* turn up during the C. after all. I shall have no "communication" to make. I shall be particularly glad to see you again

Gryon s/Bex, Switzerland,

July 13. 1892

My dear Hodgson, this letter is an illustration of the fact that unless one answers immediately, one is apt to answer very late, and of the farther fact that if you lay down a letter unfinished it may be weeks ere you "get round to it" again. This sheet lay on my table for some days and then it became impossible to finish it—but I bro't it with me to Europe as a monument of my intentions, and hurl it now at your head. I am amused as I read the phrase on p. 2. about getting a "solid holiday" by bringing the "whole family" to the Continent. The wear and tear of continuous exposure to infancy in the narrow quarters with which one has to put up in hotels is something not to be imagined without actual trial. But with the two boys soon to be domiciled in families to learn french, and certain perplexities decided which have harassed my mind, I fancy the solid holiday will soon begin. But I shall not get to England for the Congress. It costs too much, for one thing; and the grassy slopes are too delicious for another. I saw the menagerie, essentially, 3 summers ago, and though I would fain see some of the English *Men* this time, *you* particularly, yet I hold out against the temptation. Besides, I doubt whether I can leave the neighborhood of the "family" just yet. You write of inviting Pillon, he is the best of men, but of that cat-like french domesticity that I doubt whether he would dare to enter a foreign land. They buy their perfection in their own french line by a singular incapacity for everything else. I am glad that *you* will attend the Congress. Poor Robertson of course will not, and *überhaupt* will apparently attend few things any more. I never knew so sad a case of frustration. I had imagined that good and charming woman nursing him always and surviving him; but God disposes! He *has* a good monument in Mind; but he no doubt aspired to a more personal one, and his best monument will be in the hearts of those who know and love him as you and I do. Seldom has there been a braver, more human or more generous spirit—*hülfreich und frei*! I hope his disease may give him a little respite, now that his hard working responsibilities have ceased.

I have 15 months furlough on half pay, and *ought* to make a good thing of it. After the stubble of psychology on which I have spent a good deal of my working force for the last 10 years I have a sort of longing for erkenntnisstheorie, and even Cosmology, and the prospect of the possibility of a little unimpeded *reading* next winter is most sweet. We shall probably go to Paris or its immediate neighborhood, and put the boys to school there. *Then,* of course, I will pay a visit to London. I spent 10 days in Freiburg, and saw quite intimately Münsterberg whom I heartily rejoice to say that we have secured for Harvard—a charming human being and a genius for Psychological work, whether some of his theories be true or false. Riehl, there, was very friendly, but makes on me the impression of a somewhat melancholy and disappointed man.

Heaven speed your own work!

Always yours, | Wm James

Address me always:
c/o Baring Bros & Co
London E.C.

ALS: MH bMS Am 1092.9 (984)

[1] WJ did not attend the International Congress of Experimental Psychology, held in early August 1892 in London.

To Henry Pickering Bowditch

CAMBRIDGE April 2. 92

My dear Henry

I am under the painful neccessity of raising $10,000 for our psychological Department; and on calling this P.M. on J.J.P.[1] he suggested that if you had not seen your way yet to using the income of the Blake fund in the medical school, you might find this a good application of it.[2] The facts are these:

1. We must keep the supremacy in Psychology. It is a rather critical moment now, with all the big universities starting laboratories etc. & we must not fall behind.

2. *I* am not the proper man to be responsible for an experimental laboratory in a first class institution. To *you* that prop? needs no proof!

3. Münsterberg of Freiburg *is;* and, if appointed promptly, will come for three years at 3000 a year and a generous sum to cover travelling expenses to and fro. What needs to be *raised* is 10,000.

4. With him here we shall scoop everything; for although only 28 years old, he is a real genius and a charming fellow (by the account of everyone who has been with him, a fellow with no angles) in the bargain. Every psychologist *must* read what he writes, and he has made more stir than any one yet in that Science has succeeded in making in the same time.

With him here I shall have the best of consciences in falling back upon the more philosophical kind of study where my peculiar genius(?!) is most at home. It's no use for Harvard to invite some dwarfish safish, goodish man like several whom I could name. We ought to go for the biggest obtainable *genius* every time; and *most* lucky are we that this chance now offers. After this year I imagine that M. will no longer be obtainable. If he doesn't "assimilate," the three years contract enables a retreat without awkwardness to either side. If he does, he may be prevailed on to stay. In any case he will have organized things in the department, left an example and standard the effects of which will last. There is a probability that before the three years expire means will be forthcoming for a permanent professorship. Of that I can't speak more now, since the urgent thing is to get him secured quickly.

I don't just know what your medical school plan has been. But this is also in the line of neurological work which Mr. Blake designed; and I question much whether any more vital good could possibly be done for the university with the money than in acquiring the presence of a man of M's calibre, even for a short time. Remember B.-Séquard in the Medical School![3]

If you could give the income of your fund for 3 years, it would leave only 5500 to be begged *aliunde*—a great gain. I have just been

writing a lot of letters to people. Can you think of any one in particular whom it might be well to address?

Bless you! Bless *all* of you!

Your Grandfather | Wm James
M. is an M.D. as well as a PhD. Of course this plan must not be
talked about at present.

ALS: MH bMS Am 1092.9 (795)

[1] James Jackson Putnam.

[2] The only Blake fund found at Harvard is one established by Stanton Blake (1837–
1889), Boston businessman and philanthropist, who left $5,000 to Harvard in his will.
But this would provide income of about $200 a year and seems too small to have
attracted WJ.

[3] Charles Édouard Brown-Séquard was professor of the Physiology and Pathology
of the Nervous System at the Harvard Medical School in 1864–67.

To Josiah Royce

Wednesday A.M. [April 6, 1892][1]
My dear Royce

I send back Rod's book for which I have no room.[2]

My mind, slowly digesting the Loisette episode, feels as if the Professorship, with here-living to trade on it, ought to be too stiff a dose
to carry, & that we had better drop the idea of it altogether. Even
the Münsterberg fund rather makes my gorge rise, from such a quarter. He has *exploiter*-ed *us* so far, without a penny of return; and in
the inscrutable "*mélange*" of things, (as Walt Whitman says) probably
has some secret motive for doing so which will continue and grow
more rampant if he once acquires the position of a patron saint.

I mean therefore not to suggest again to him the donation of one
cent. The M——g plan, alas! is pretty sure to fail!

W.J.

ALS: MH bMS Am 1092.9 (3607)

[1] The dating, which is uncertain, was made with reference to the Münsterberg negotiations. It is not known when WJ departed for the trip (to New Hampshire)
mentioned in his letter of 5 April 1892 (calendared). He may have left on 6 April,
dashing off the note to Royce before leaving for the station. His "I have no room"
suggests that he was packing.

[2] Édouard Rod (1857–1910), Swiss-born novelist and critic. One letter is known
(1899).

To Clarence John Blake[1]

CAMBRIDGE April 11. 92

My dear Blake,

You plighted your troth last summer that you would send me an ordinary bill, just as if I were an ordinary human being, for services rendered & good done to my daughter. Tired of procrastination & exasperated by prevarication, I send you my check for what seems to me about the proper sum. I should gladly pay you in metaphysical services—perhaps when my mediumship gets more developed I may be able to do good to your family in a spiritual manner, but at present "lawful money of the U.S." seems more tangible.

I have lived in perplexities of a practical kind for the past 6 weeks, and they are not yet settled: The future of the psychological department, the possibility of a sabbatical year, the renting of our two places etc. etc. I prefer straitforward teaching as involving on the whole less wear and tear.

I hope that you are all well.

Gratefully yours | Wm James

My wife sends her best reme<m>brances.

ALS: MH bMS Am 1092.1

[1] Clarence John Blake (1843–1919), Boston inventor and physician, specializing in diseases of the ear.

To Charles William Eliot

95 Irving St. April 11. 92

Dear President,

Many thanks for your telegram[1] & letter from the Hotel Raymond, approving of Münsterberg's appointment. Your allusion to Santayana seemed to mean that M. should be paid out of current funds. Nevertheless, to make this more explicit, I telegraphed you on Sunday (I only got your telegram, which arrived here on Wednesday, on saturday night on my return from N.H.) to ask whether the appointment was unconditional or not. No answer to that telegram has been received, but your letter makes the point perfectly clear.

I shall continue however to try to raise the rest of the needed fund—so far I have only 700 dollars. Your decision leaves us plenty of time in which to do that. I will telegraph M. today that the main thing is secured; and after referring the matter to Hooper & Walcott, instruct the former how to address M. with his official letter. M's reference to six hours work was a misunderstanding which I have already cleared up in my reply. I had written to him that six hours of *lectures* was the maximum that could ever be asked of him.

I am sure that we shall have made a great *coup* in all this, and shall "scoop" all the other universities as far as experimental psychology goes. If Münsterberg isn't a first rate power in the full sense of the word, then I'm a—dutchman!

We have been having high jinks in your absence with that hoary sinner Loisette, who lectures by invitation of the Philosophical Club in the Sanders theatre Monday night on the improvement of the memory.[2] He stayed a couple of days with me, and saw things somewhat. But I prophecy that he will never give us his $100,000; and am disposed to believe that it is all brag anyhow, and he will get such pleasure by *exploiter*-ing the hopes which it will continue to awaken in the breasts of various institutions that he will never during his lifetime change it from a possibility into an actuality. He has not even committed himself as yet to a single dollar in favor of Münsterberg. You were very wise not to see him in New York!

Always truly yours | Wm James

ALS: MH Archives

[1] Eliot's telegram of 6 April 1892 (calendared) is the same as his annotation on WJ's letter of 24 March 1892.

[2] Marcus Dwight Larrowe lectured on "The Improvement of the Memory" at Sanders Theatre on 18 April 1892. The *Harvard Crimson*, 26 April 1892, published a letter from WJ (not recorded in WJ's bibliographies), saying in effect that "Professor Loisette" has written WJ and is willing to give his three lectures on memory training at Harvard in May, provided that 100 students sign up at $5.00 per student, the proceeds to benefit the Harvard Psychology Department. The same issue of the *Crimson* contains an advertisement for the lectures to be held in May. No indication that they were given was found.

To Hugo Münsterberg

95, IRVING STREET, | CAMBRIDGE, MASS. April 13 '92
My dear Colleague—soon, I trust, to be such!—I telegraphed you yesterday that all was *gelungen* and got your reply last night.[1] The facts are simply these: The President has written to me from California that you are to be invited at a salary of 3000 and an extra *600 each way* for travelling expenses. This is somewhat too little—but I think it will be almost enough, and I trust that the difference between

this allowance and what you proposed will in no wise induce you to change your mind. I wrote you a week ago that the money-question seemed likely to suffer shipwreck—and you may imagine my relief at this prompt solution of the difficulties. You will receive an official letter of invitation from our Treasurer (who is now in Washington) a week after you receive this.[2] I shall have a conference with him about the specification of your duties. Of course during the first year nothing will be expected of [you] but such *advanced* laboratory investigation and instruction as you may yourself wish to give. The laboratory exercises of the less advanced students will be supervised by D? Nichols, who has been my assistant this year, & who will (probably) have a second assistant under him. I am in a great hurry to day, and will write to you about a number of practical matters (house, furniture etc) next week. Meanwhile let me say that the price I am to pay from New York to Antwerp on the Friesland of the Red Star Line is only 460 dollars for a family of 2 adults, 4 children and a nurse. From New York to Boston (Cambridge is practically a quarter of Boston) the fare is only 5 dollars a head.

Believe me, with the greatest delight that our negotiations have succeeded so far,

Yours always | Wm James

ALS: MH bMS Am 1092.9 (3267)

[1] Münsterberg's telegram of 12 April 1892 is calendared.
[2] The treasurer was Edward William Hooper.

To Hugo Münsterberg

CAMBRIDGE April 19 '92
My dear Münsterberg (let us drop titles of ceremony hereafter) Your letter of the 8th reaches me this morning just as I am about to write to you. Our treasurer, Mr. Hooper, is just back from Washington, and informs me that your appointment must first be officially voted on by the "Corporation" of the University which meets on Monday the 25th. There is no reason whatever to expect any obstacle or delay after this, and I sincerely trust that your reply will be prompt & affirmative. You will before receiving this have learned just what the money-proposition is on our side, and I am glad to note from your present letter that your own hesitation (if there is any) will not be on *that* account. I think you ought to bind yourself for 3 years at least— of course not for more; though my own hope is that by the end of

that time you will have become an enthusiastic Yankee and have forgotten your mother-tongue! Then we may hope to keep you for a longer time.

We are now preparing our pamphlet of courses to be given next year. Naturally if you are coming we wish your name to figure therein, and it must be published by June first. You see therefore how desirable it is to get from you a prompt answer. I will telegraph you that an official invitation is on its way to you, as soon as the Corporation votes. After the neccessary delay, you will then please telegraph your own decision; and if it be affirmative we can immediately proceed to print your name.

I rather advise you to take a furnished house for the first year. Pack your own furniture so as to send for it in case you wish to at the end of that time, and get a certificate from a U.S. Consul that it has been in use for more than a year—I believe that it then comes in duty-free, otherwise not, with our infernal tariff laws. I advise you to arrive not later than September, so that you and Frau Münsterberg may get comfortably settled before the University-work begins, which it does always on the last Thursday of that month. I will begin immediately to see about what houses there may be in the market. There have been a number of very good furnished houses at high rents, but they are all taken with the exception of our own. I am kept in a very disagreeable uncertainty by my colleague Palmer, who is invited to the new Chicago University, but whose decision may be postponed for another six weeks or even more. If he *goes,* I cannot stay away next year; but even if I take my family to Europe, must return and assume some of his work. Meanwhile, trusting that he will stay, I have offered my house which is new and handsome (a better house than I can afford!) for 1600 dollars. So far no one has even inquired about it; and we *may* not go abroad at all. It may be however that we go, and that the house will be still unrented when you arrive. In that case you can have it (if you wish) for 1000 dollars. It is hard to get a good house, furnished, for less. Though I saw a house two days ago for 800 dollars, which was comfortable, though *shabby,* and in a very good situation. That is doubtless the cheapest house in Cambridge.

I have a neighbor who brought her furniture hither from Italy a few years ago. I will find out from her what the expense etc was, and write you next week about *un*furnished houses, of which there are plenty to be had. If *we* are not here when you arrive, it will give my *sister-in-law* great pleasure to furnish all possible help to Mrs.

Munsterberg in the way of making her acquainted with our ways of housekeeping etc.

I advise you if you have a *good* servant, especially a good cook, to bring her with you. Our servants are the weakest spot of our civilization—mostly Irish, ill-trained, very independent, and able to ask enormous wages. Five dollars a week is as little as one can now get a decent cook for. On the other hand our housekeeping is made easy by a number of mechanical arrangements which are possibly not yet so common in Germany. But if you have two faithful servants, bring them *mit!*

Hoping erelong to shake you by the hand, I am

always truly yours | Wm James

ALS: MH bMS Am 1092.9 (3268)

To Mary Whiton Calkins

CAMBRIDGE April 29. 92

Dear Miss Calkins,

I sent the package unpaid—so take back your stamps!

I am always amused when you tuck a stamp into one of your modest letters to me. Don't do so any more, pray. I care no more for postage stamps than I care for life!—With regard to M——berg, you may disclose the awful secret now, since the Corporation has regularly appointed him. All I fear is that he may relent at the last moment and sa[y] "no," and then where shall be[1] all be?

Yours ever faithfully | W.J.

ALS: MWelC

[1] A slip for 'we'.

To Mary Aspinwall Tappan

95 Irving St. Cambr. April 29. 92.

My dear Mary

Your kind letter about poor Alice came to day, and makes me do what I have long been on the *point* of doing—write a friendly word to you. Yes, Alice's death is a great release to her, she longed for it; and it is in a sense a release to all of us.[1] In spite of its terrific frustrations her life was a triumph all the same, as I now see it. Her particular burden was borne well. She never whimpered or complained of her sickness, and never seemed to turn her face towards it, but up to the very limit of her allowance attended to outer things. When I went to London in sept. to bid her good bye, she altogether refused to waste a minute in talking about her disease, and conversed only of the english people and Harry's play. So her soul was not subdued! I wish that mine might ever be as little so! Poor Harry is left rather disconsolate. He habitually stored up all sorts of things to tell her, and now he has no ear into which to pour their like. He says her talk was better than any one's he knew in London. Strange to say, altho practically bedridden for years, her mental atmosphere barring a little over vehemence was altogether that of the *grand monde,* and the information about both people and public affairs which she had the art of absorbing from the air was astonishing in amount.—

We are probably all going to Europe on the 25th of May—"Friesland," Antwerp. Both Alice and I need a "year off," and I hope we shall get it. Our winter abode is yet unknown. I wish you were going to stay and we could be near you. I wish anyhow we might meet this summer and talk things over. I[t] doesn't pay in this short life for good old friends to be non-existent for each other, and how can one write letters of friendship when letters of business fill every chink of time? I *do hope* we shall meet, my dear Mary. Both of us send you lots of love, and plenty to Ellen too.[2]

Yours ever, | W.J.

ALS: MH bMS Am 1092.9 (3812)

[1] AJ died on 6 March 1892.
[2] Ellen Tappan Dixey.

To Michael Anagnos

CAMBRIDGE April 30. 92

Dear Mr. Anagnos,

I should like to take some of my graduate students in Psychology to see Helen Keller if you think it good for the child and not to[o] inconvenient to you or any one else. I have a splendid lot of graduates this year.[1] If you smile upon this plan I wish you would name your most convenient time. On the whole, I suppose that Saturday afternoon would be ours, but other afternoons can be found. I doubt whether *most* of us could go in the the morning. We are 16 in number all told.

I shall also be glad to shake you by the hand again in memory of old times.

Always truly yours | Wm James

ALS: Perkins School for the Blind

[1] Philosophy 20a: Psychological Seminary had an official enrollment of seventeen, twelve being graduate students.

To Hugo Münsterberg

CAMBRIDGE May 3. 1892

My dear Münsterberg,

A telegram arrives from you "joyfully accepting the call."[1] *Gottlob!* I believe that this has been the best stroke I ever did for our University! Not that I deem you infallible, far from it; but I have the greatest confidence in your combined originality and sanity, and in the solidity of your future career—in spite of the Müllers and the Titcheners! It is an enormous relief to me to see the responsibility for Experimental psychology in Harvard transferred from my feeble and unworthy shoulders to those of a man as competent as you. I shall proceed immediately to proclaim the news, as an early ventilation and publication of it will decide many wavering students to come to us next year.

No more to day! I forgot in my last to say that nothing could please me more than the dedication to me of anything that you might write, and I am much gratified that you should have had the thought.

Go to work immediately upon English so that your ears and tongue, if possible, may be expert when you arrive. Greetings to your *gnädige Frau* from both myself and my wife.

Always truly yours   Wm James

ALS: MH bMS Am 1092.9 (3269)

[1] Münsterberg's telegram of 3 May 1892 is calendared.

From George Herbert Palmer

3 Mason St. | May 6, 1892

Dear James:

Mrs Palmer came home yesterday, a few days earlier than I anticipated. She brought no new data for the Chicago problem; & Harper also writes that he cannot be here for a fortnight. I do not see therefore why I should delay longer the announcement of a decision which was practically made up some time ago. Last night I telegraphed Harper that I declined, & tomorrow morning I shall put a note into the Crimson informing the College.[1]

To you I write first of all my friends, because your plans are so closely interlocked with mine & because you have been so generous in dealing with all the difficult arrangements of the last weeks. Because my delay has not been in my own interest, but in that of the University of Chicago, it must have been harder to be forbearing. I want to thank you for your kindness, & to say that it is your & Royce's presence here which justifies my refusing such an opportunity.

Cordially yours, | G. H. Palmer.

Please tell Royce. I have so many letters to write that I know he will excuse me from sending a special one to himself—

ALS: MH bMS Am 1092.9 (427)

[1] A letter by Palmer, headed "Professor Palmer to Remain at Harvard," appeared in the *Harvard Crimson* of 7 May 1892.

To Hugo Münsterberg

CAMBRIDGE May 15. 92

My dear Münsterberg,

I am now in receipt of three letters from you, one written just before, the other just after, your telegram accepting the place, and the third written on the 3 of May about Wadsworth, etc.

I have laughed most heartily at your psychological description of yourself in the last days of April, for I know just what the agonizing feeling of indecision is before one makes so important a venture. I believe that *writing that letter* cleared your mind of the cobwebs, and enabled you to say "yes" with relative ease! The letter will remain a valuable *document humain*. To us who live here, and find everything very tolerable and comfortable, the tragic aspect of the case does not present itself so vividly. But your fears about disappointing us by not picking up the english soon enough I believe are groundless. The German brain always manages, in a couple of years, to get along with a foreign tongue. Even if you should keep a foreign accent, and still make some mistakes, I think (judging by all the analogous precedents which we have) that you will be able in two years to lecture with comparative ease to *yourself.* Agassiz, who came here from Switzerland at about your age, soon became a most effective lecturer, the most generally popular lecturer we ever had. Hagen, from Königsberg, Professor of Entomology, who came here in middle life with no practice in English, has never lost his German accent, but is a most successful talker and teacher to the few students who specialize in his branch. I think you had better dismiss all anxiety on that score. But, in fairness to yourself, I think it would be well that you should give during the first year some popular lectures in your own tongue. With our very methodical organization here (which you will learn to understand when you get here) it will be hard to get continuous audiences for more than a few entirely public lectures—and the subject, etc., can best be chosen in consultation with your colleagues in the Philosophical Dep! after the year has begun.[1] No need to announce such a course now—the only courses which we announce *now* being the regular long one's which count for the several degrees.

Next, as regards the three years question.[2] I hope that that will not be a stumbling block. I have been to see our President this morning but he was out. I am sure that he will interpret that condition as applying merely to other *American* Universities. It is quite in the line of our precedents for a professor to bind himself in that way. But if you wish to reserve the liberty to return to Germany if called thither to a better place, I think that that will be accorded.* I will immediately get an assurance from the President, and let you know without delay. The delay in the telegram telling you that the official letter was on its way, was due to a delay in the meeting of the "Overseers" who had to "confirm" your appointment—there was no *opposition* at any stage of the proceedings.

Now as regards all the economical matters of which you write, it is our present intention to sail for Antwerp in the Friesland on May 25th, "with bag and baggage"; and you may imagine how busy we are in winding-up all sorts of affairs, and putting the house in order for a tenant. Very soon after reaching Europe we shall go to Freiburg; and there Mrs. Munsterberg and my wife, and you and I can have a complete talk about those details. I will, before I leave, ascertain all the latest facts about houses to let, furnished and unfurnished, and boarding houses; and give you the best advice I can. My present impression is that you would do wisely to "board" the first year, *pour mieux reconnaître le terrain.* It will be cheaper than "keeping house," although of course rather *narrow.* Your great source of suffering will be from our american furnaces, which keep our houses too hot in the winter. You, with your family, ought to live *well* on $5000 a year—*travelling*, however, is the most expensive of recreations, as you well know![3]

Most of the instruments you mention are not duplicated here.[4] We have a Hipp's Chronoscope, and a set of König tuning forks, however.[5] I will send you in a few days a complete list of our apparatus, so that you may order in time anything additional which you need, and our university will pay for it.

As for the second assistantship, I am delighted to hear that Mr. Wadsworth has done such good work with you. We have already, however, decided upon another man for the only place there can be, and it still remains doubtful whether that place can receive any pay.[6] Will you please tell Mr. Wadsworth, with my regards, that I am sorry to say that he had better renounce all hope of an assistantship in Harvard.

I shall send you, as soon as it is out, the announcement of our courses for next year. Your name is down simply for the Psychological Seminary and advanced laboratory work. The general course in Psychology ("Philosophy 2" so-called) is under D[r] Nichols. The students of this course will do regular laboratory exercises in one of the two laboratory rooms; and *as far as their work goes, D[r] N. will be autonomous.* You will find him a very obliging and *human* fellow, and I am sure you will get on well together. Of course this arrangement applies only to the year 1892–93.

I hope that, by the time this reaches you, the mental waves will have grown rather calm. I know that all difficulties will smooth out when the time to meet them arrives. For myself, I wish to say again that your acceptance of the place takes a perfect load off my mind. I had come to the settled conclusion that I was myself unfit to be director of our laboratory—a humiliating conclusion!—and the only thing to heal my wounded pride was a feeling that in stepping out myself I could simultaneously put in the best possible man and make the Harvard laboratory the unquestioned *first* in America. This you have enabled me to do! And I thank you again. I have passed a really *shameful* year myself, done so little work etc. The fact is, my brain is very fagged, and I ought to have gone to Europe a year ago instead of now. The neccessity of starting the Laboratory held me back; but the result has been that no investigation on my part has been done. I am by nature no experimentalist—an exclusively critical, logical, and literary mind. I am moreover a bad case of neurasthenia, so the quantity of my work is always deplorably small. I am deadly tired just now, and shall give my brain entire rest during the summer. After next year, I shall return with no responsibility for experimental psychology, and shall no doubt find (in Herbert Spencer's phrase) that the inner relations and the outer ones correspond more harmoniously.[7]

My wife sends cordial greetings and good wishes to yours. Believe me, in the hope of a speedy meeting, yours fraternally

Wm James

I took my class yesterday to one of our Massachusetts insane asylums. Your old friend Strong, who is just made instructor in Chicago University, and is visiting our laboratory, was of the party.[8] He seems very well, and was greatly pleased to read your letter before the decision, which I showed him.

*Of course we don't expect you to bind yourself against unforeseen emergencies at home, or disappointments here which might call you back to your Fatherland.

ALS: MH bMS Am 1092.9 (3270)

[1] In his letter of 30 April 1892 (calendared) Münsterberg had asked if he would be able to give public lectures in German, such as the lectures on hypnotism that he gave every week to some 300 students.

[2] In his letter of 30 April 1892 (calendared) Münsterberg indicated that he wanted to remain free to terminate his services at any time for either family or professional reasons.

[3] In his letter of 30 April 1892 (calendared) Münsterberg had asked whether he, his wife, two children, and a children's maid could live for $5,000 a year, stating that while they did not need luxury and he neither smoked nor drank, they would like to be able to afford some small excursions.

[4] In his letter of 30 April 1892 (calendared) Münsterberg listed the apparatus he planned to bring with him.

[5] Rudolph König (1832–1901), German-born writer on acoustics and instrument-maker for the study of acoustics.

[6] In his letter of 3 May 1892 (calendared) Münsterberg had proposed that William Scott Wadsworth be appointed as a second assistant. Wadsworth had studied science at Harvard, taking psychology with James and philosophy with Royce. Münsterberg based his recommendation on the fact that Wadsworth had done good work for him in Germany, where he had studied color harmony and other subjects. Wadsworth was in the process of choosing between medicine and psychology, however, and needed a quick answer. Wadsworth eventually chose medicine. Edgar Pierce was appointed as assistant in psychology.

[7] For Spencer's formula see *EPh*, 7–8.

[8] Charles Augustus Strong served as associate professor of psychology at the University of Chicago in 1892–95.

To Hugo Münsterberg

May 15th. [1892] 10 P.M.

My dear Münsterberg

I have just seen President Eliot who asks me to explain to you that the condition in Mr. Hooper's letter which binds you to Harvard for three years is intended only to apply to possible calls from other American Institutions. In case you desire to break your engagement with us for any other reasons you will be considered free to do so.

My own impression is that should another American Institution wish to steal you away from us after one year, and should you decidedly wish to go, the President would not insist on holding you fast by the terms of the appointment. In general our appointments are terminable at the will of the instructor.

I hope that this will quickly remove your only remaining scruple.

I wrote you a long letter this morning which you will probably get along with this.

Always truly yours | Wm James

ALS: MB

To Eleanor Mildred Sidgwick

Cambridge, May 15. '92

My dear Mrs. Sidgwick,

I got your letter with the provisional scheme of work on hallucinations long long ago, and how I came to let day succeed day without writing you even an acknowledgment is one of those things to explain which would be possible but hardly worth the pains to you of the reading. Let it pass to the account of my shame!

The plan seems to me a splendid one, and from the point of view of my own collapse, I don't see how it can fail to cover you with a certain sort of glory if it all gets worked up in definitive shape. The labor is enormous, as I can testify. *My* mistake was in not "keeping up" daily, or at least weekly, with the correspondence involved in all the schedules I received. In the midst of my other occupations, I was irregular, and let them go, keeping no systematic account of the correspondence, until now I fear the matter is irreparable, so far as the original Gurney-an percentage argument goes. But I have small hopes of that argument anyhow, as I believe you know; and there remains out of my labors a collection of some 600 positive cases of hallucination of every variety, which are more or less available for study. These, with all my other materials, I have passed over to Hodgson, with your MS., to see what he can do for your report before the end of July.[1] The cases are analytically indexed, so that the work of classification will be easy.

The importunity of the Editor of the Forum aiding, I have tried to make a certain compensation for being such a broken reed about the Halls. by "slinging" an article about the S.P.R. which will doubtless do good to its reputation, and (perhaps) to its pecuniary estate.[2] It is a general description and laudation of the Society and its work, intended to penetrate through the armor of the popular-science stratum of the human Intellect.

We sail, with bags, boys and babies, for Antwerp, in ten days. I ought to have taken my year-off a twelve month ago, but it was practically impossible; and the result has been a very unsatisfactory year, in which my cerebral machinery has "run rusty" and very little outward scientific effect accrued, although my hours have been steadily filled with occupation. I am enormously relieved at having negotiated an engagement between Harvard and Münsterberg of Freiburg, who will represent experimental Psychology for the next few years here in an adequate way, and leave me free for things for which I am not quite so unfit.

I will write again, to Myers probably, as soon as I reach Switzerland. Meanwhile forgive me if you can, and believe me with warm regards to your husband, yours very truly

Wm James

I trust that your new relations to Newnham will not be destructive to your scientific activity![3]

ALS: Cambridge University Library

Address: Mrs. Henry Sidgwick | Cambridge | England

Postmarks: BOSTON. MASS. MAY 15 1892   CAMBRIDGE MY 25 92

[1] Leaders of the Society for Psychical Research were preparing a report to the International Congress of Experimental Psychology on the Census of Hallucinations. For the American statistics see *EPR*, 63–64.

[2] WJ, "What Psychical Research Has Accomplished," *Forum* 13 (August 1892): 727–42; reprinted in *EPR*. For the financial arrangements see letter to Hodgson of 25 May 1892.

[3] Eleanor Sidgwick became principal of Newnham College, Cambridge.

To Richard Hodgson

GRAND UNION HOTEL | NEW YORK, May 25 1892 | 10.30 AM.
Dear H.—We came down by the boat last night, and after getting my brood safely on the Red Star Friesland, Jersey City, I came straight hither hoping to intercept you.[1]   I should have telegraphed last night or early this P.M.[2] but I had no time *then,* and saw no telegraph office this A.M.—

I have left in your room my hallucination-book, and sent all my *stock* to the office.   The last batch, which will be delivered there to day or to morrow (I left Salter to box it in the agony of getting away it was left till yesterday & then no time) contains two boxes of unan-a[l]lyzed cases—at least I think most of them are—and an index book of old American S.P.R. cases *with analysis* (mostly dreams), plus an envelope with some other cases.   The earlier instalment explains it-self.   The first couple of hundred cases of the analytic index were prepared by my student - - - Wood[3]—the rest by myself, mostly dic-tated to Mr. J. W Alger by me, as I read.[4]   He did a few alone.

In the smaller box now going to you are some uninteligable sched-ules A., which you will understand.[5]

My impression is that beyond the crude appearances, no *accurate analytic statistics* can be based on the A's, from the imperfection of the record.   The "yes" cases, many of which are "independent" (I only began later to note the schedule number at the end of the analysis so that many are without it) form a splendid basis for classification after Mrs. Sidgwicks method.   Her skeleton-paper with a note to me is enclosed in the first batch.   If you could work them over so as to fill in the blanks in time to send her the paper by the July congress—'twould be well!   Heaven help you anyhow: You'll be troubled with duplicates and ambiguities enough.   That the *number* seems suffi-cient for statistics, however, appears proved by the fact that both she and I have the same percentages.   (Vide her last "provisional re-port")[6]

I wrote an article of (I imagine) beneficial nature to the Forum on the S.P.R. instructing the Editor to forward *both proofs & check to you.* Give $50 to the Society from me, and send the rest to Lee Higgin-son & Co, 50 State Street on my account.   I would give more, only I have had to sell 1500 dollars worth of my small stock of bonds to pay up and get off.—So much spent beyond income, which is a bad thing—and Cambridge house as yet unrented.   Thaw (bless him) has taken Chocorua place.[7]   I'm glad Mrs. P. is "progressing."[8]

God (or the Unknowable) bless you!   I will write soon from 't other side.

My address meanwhile is c/o Baring Bros. London E.C.

Yours ever | W.J.

If you *can* get to Jersey City, come!   The steamer leaves at 3.30. Desbrosses St ferry is the most convenient

ALS: MH bMS Am 1092.9 (965)

[1] The *Friesland* sailed for Antwerp on 25 May 1892 at 4:30 in the afternoon.

[2] A slip for 'A.M.'

[3] Perhaps Frank Hoyt Wood (1864–1930), American educator, then a graduate student at Harvard.

[4] No information about J. W. Alger was found.

[5] See letter to Gardiner of 26 March 1890.

[6] A provisional report signed by Henry Sidgwick appeared in the *Proceedings of the Society for Psychical Research* 7 (July 1891): 259–64.   For other reports see *EPR*, 408–9.

[7] Thaw was not identified.

[8] Leonora Piper.

To Charles William Eliot

Steamer Friesland | May 25 1892

No time to call & say farewell & square accounts.   Escaped by "skin of teeth."—1) I shall see Munsterberg in June & advise him of all practical neccessities.   The "fund" in my hands has amounted to only a little over 4000 dollars, with a few names yet to hear from.[1]   It seems to me a case for the visiting committee.   At any rate *next year* is more than provided for!

The bursar tells me that 300 odd dollars, lab. fees for this year in Phil 2 and Phil 20, go to credit of lab. next year.   Nichols, who will be autonomous as regards Phil 2. asks to have these fees from that course made into his "appropriation" next year.   The request seems reasonable, as it makes that course independent of Münsterberg for that year.—I told him I would mention it to you.

I think 1000 the very least that the Corporation ought to give Nichols next year.   With lectures & lab. he will richly deserve it, and I expect him to do some creditable original work of his own.   I wish his paltry 250 for this past year could be augmented.

Farewell, and good fortune attend you and H.U.!   I expect to come back thoroughly rejuvenated, and to do better work than ever.

My address is Barings.

Faithfully yours | Wm James

ALS: MH Archives

¹ See letter to Dorr of 12 August 1890.

To Charles Sanders Peirce

[25 May 1892]¹

Dear Charles—It has been a great chagrin to me to have you here all this time without meeting or hearing you. I especially wanted to hear you on Continuity, and I hear of a godlike talk at Royce's. But Continuity will appear in Monist.² *Talks* can never come again!! "Was man von der minute ausgeschlagen, gibt keine Ewigkeit zurück."³—I have been so driven that even now we shall just escape by the skin of our teeth. Three lecture hours yesterday—and the house to be left without a scrap of paper lying about and every drawer empty for a tenant.

I meant to write you long ago to say how I enjoyed your last paper in the Monist.⁴ I believe in that sort of thing myself, but even if I didn't it would be a blessed piece of radicalism. Pray send it to Ch Renouvier, au Pontet, Avignon (Vancluse) France, and to J. Delboeuf Bᵈ Frère Orban, 32, Liège, Belgium. It will strengthen their hands.

I enclose you a scrap for Harper which you can send with your other "credentials."⁵ I very much wish you could get such a place, and do work regularly.

Ever fondly thine | W.J.

Will write to Harpers fm Steamer now b——

ALS: MH bMS Am 1092.9 (3373)

¹ Dated with reference to WJ's sailing date.

² Charles Sanders Peirce, "The Law of Mind," *Monist* 2 (July 1892): 533–59. In his diary for 21 May 1892 Francis Ellingwood Abbot noted that he heard Peirce lecture to twenty "graduates and friends"; see Brent, *CSP,* 218.

³ The concluding lines of Johann Christoph Friedrich von Schiller's poem "Resignation."

⁴ Charles Sanders Peirce, "The Doctrine of Necessity Examined," *Monist* 2 (April 1892): 321–37.

⁵ Peirce did not receive an appointment at the University of Chicago; see *Correspondence,* 2:218n.

To Charles Ritter

HÔTEL FÖHRENBACH | FREIBURG I.B. June 13. 1892
My dear old Friend,

Here I am in Europe again, this time with a wife, four children,
and any number of trunks (quantam mutatus ab 1859!) to stay 15
months, recover from cerebral fatigue, and give my boys next winter
a chance at either the french or the german language.[1] Can you
give me any advice which will help me through the summer? I start
from here in a week to seek in Switzerland a place where we can stay
quietly for a couple of months; and it occurs to me that you may be
able to tell me of some spot the knowledge of which will save me a
great deal of search. It must be rural, bea[u]tiful, neither too hot,
nor too cold, not too high (as I sleep badly in high places) not fashionable, yet not too primitive, and *cheap, dazu.* Do you know the exact
place?—if so, dahin, dahin O mein geliebter lass uns ziehn! You
see that my demands, both on the place, and on your friendliness
are modest!

Of course when the family is once settled I expect to do a certain
amount of walking of a moderate kind. One of the pleasantest
things that I look forward to this summer, is meeting you again. I
suppose you are still in Geneva, and I hope to find you as little
changed as you were when I revisited you thirteen years ago.[2]

Pray pardon my coming to you thus for help in my perplexity.
You must know Switzerland so well as to be able to suggest places
that otherwise I might never hear of. I said above, I start from here
in a week to explore, & my family will follow when I have found the
spot and made the bargain.

Believe me, as always, my dear old Ritter, your friend,

Wm James

I am also writing to Professor Flournoy, with whom I have corresponded, to see what *he* will say.

ALS: Bibliothèque publique et universitaire, Geneva

[1] The *Friesland* arrived in Antwerp on or before 7 June 1892, and the Jameses proceeded to Freiburg to meet Münsterberg.

[2] WJ was in Switzerland in the summer of 1880.

To George Croom Robertson

                Hotel Föhrenbach, Freiburg i/B | June 15, 1892
My dear Old Friend,—Your heart-rending letter of the 21st. of May
has just been put into my hands, forwarded from Cambridge. How
sorry I am, how sorry I am![1] And what a burden you both of you
have had to carry all these years. To think that even when I saw you
in London three years ago the shadow of this was over her, and that
I knew nothing about it! The way her radiant-kindly face used to
beam upon me during that gloomy winter that I passed in London
10 years ago has been, and always will be, one of the warmest spots
in this memory of mine which has its share of good things to look
back upon; and I wish you would tell her so. In particular I remember a visit you both made me in Bolton Street, giving me from that
moment onwards the sense of being at home in London. It is inex-
pressibly touching to me (and to my own dear wife) that in her ex-
tremity she should have thought of sending me a farewell. May *she*
fare well, whatever sphere of being may now take her up! But even
as I write, dear Robertson all may be over, and you left alone with
your own burdens and this vacuum. I had always thought of Mrs.
Robertson as continuing to be your nurse, and it is hard for me to
think of you without her support. But my dear fellow, in all the
darkness, "as of night eternal," that girdles us about, there must be
some ulterior significance in the fact that the hearts of onlookers are
so warmed when they see calamities such as yours have been, en-
dured with such a staunch and uncomplaining spirit. The experience of which *that* is an integral part cannot interiorly be as bad as it
outwardly seems. You of course know your own weaknesses, and
your own failures and disgusts; but I assure you that to others your
life has been a source of deepest inspiration—and more I cannot say.
    I am so sorry that both the Professorship and Mind must go!—
Was mich betrifft, I have been in Europe 10 days, with my family, on
furlough for a year. We are proceeding to Switzerland for the summer, and whether Germany or France shall take us for the winter is
not yet decided. I had decided against going to the London "Congress," but may at the last moment yield to the temptation and go
over. One of the chief motives will be to grasp you by the hand
again, though of course you will not be where the so-called Congress is.

Good bye, my dear old Robertson!   Warmest love to both of you from your friend

Wm James

My safest permanent address is Care of Baring Bros. & Co London E.C.

ALS: MH bMS Am 1092.9 (3551)

[1] In his letter to WJ of 21 May 1892 (calendared) Robertson had written that his wife had been suffering from breast cancer for some three years, which after a period of respite, had become acute.   Caroline Robertson died on 29 May 1892.

From George Croom Robertson

31 Kensington Park Gardens | London W. | 17. 6. 92

My dear James,

Tho' I put my London address (for identification) at top, it is at Malvern, where I am for a few days, that yours of the 15th has just reached me.   You will, I suppose, receive in due course the few lines which, only some 10 days after my own letter, I had to ask my brother to write to you.   On Sunday the 29th May, my beloved one left me. She suffered much till the very end: not, indeed (in the last days) in the former way of gnawing wearing pain, but yet with much physical distress of breathing &c.   The same high spirit, brave and calm and thoughtful, till the last 2 or 3 hours of semi-consciousness that led in the end.   Within an hour after death, the face lost all its traces of sore suffering and became transfigured with a semblance of radiant youth, greater almost than I had ever remembered of her.

Yes, it is hard to believe that all that love and righteousness do not somehow continue active in the personal form that gave them their blessed energy.   But not a hair's breadth would she depart from her line of truthfulness in her latest hours of speech.   Before her, she said, it seemed all blank: if she had no fear, she had also no light; and if she had no personal fear, she yet could not forget what a hopelessly cruel world the present one was for so many.   For herself, she had learnt much in this life, and if now she had the chance of other life she thought she might do better.

For me, I shall make a poorer job of it now than ever, without her—be it for longer or shorter.—I am to remain on at 31 K.P.G., with a nephew of hers (Treasury-clerk in London, son of Llewelyn Davies, & a scholarly man) as housemate from about September.[1] This was her heart's desire for me in the circumstances, and in the

circumstances I think I cannot do better. But the circumstances—
the circumstances!

I shall surely see you some time or other—and for more than a
glimpse—within your year. But I shall not be about in Congress-
time, if I am able to be away. My purpose, after return to K.P.G. on
20th is to remain not more than 3 weeks there and then go to Scotland till end of August at least.

My heart's thanks for all you say in your letter & also for the sympathy of your wife whom my lost one will now never see.

Write to me some lines.

Yrs affly | G C Robertson

ALS: MH bMS Am 1092.9 (528)

[1] John Llewelyn Davies (1826–1916), British theologian, was the husband of Mary
Crompton Davies (d. 1895), who was a sister of Caroline Robertson. Which of their
six sons was the housemate was not established.

To Alice Howe Gibbens James

GRAND HÔTEL NATIONAL | LUCERNE [June 19, 1892]

Sweetest and best of human beings—

I only need to be absent from you for ½ a day to "find my Self"
and know that its place is to stick like a thorn and its healing plaster
both in one upon your side. I left you in such a hasty impatient
unlovely way! But you will have forgiven me ere now, I know, and
blessed my departure. I suppose that you will have gone to the
Brookses, and hope that you will have made everything right with
Herr Förster.[1] I hope also that Tweedy and the other dear young
ones are gedeih-ing. Kiss them for me & apologize for my abrupt
Abfahrt. The R.R. trip passed very quickly—Munsterberg is really
delightful—at heart a perfect gentleman. We have talked shop
hardly at all—and I had a short nap and haven't felt fatigued by the
beständiges Gespräch. The Lake is magnificent, and I am sure that
the moment you strike Switzerland you will be so glad that you are
out of that damp hotel and dark Street. We had a lively shower after
arriving here, with a tremendous rainbow, and to morrow promises
to be fine, even if showery. It has rained until to day steadily for 8
or 10 days here. So I didn't start too late. To morrow I spend the
day with M. visiting three places on the lake shore where he says
board can be had *cheap*. Even if not good for July and August until
July it might [make] me a first-rate halting place. Oh the beauty!

and the delicious air. I left my keys in the thin brown delicate striped trowsers. Leave them there!

Good night, dearest dearest wife. You'll feel all right when the baby is out of danger. I fancy the food is the only trouble now. Kiss the boys and Peg.

W.J.

Write to poste restante Montreaux, or telegraph me if needful to this hotel. I will order them to forward.

ALS: MH bMS Am 1092.9 (1805)

[1] Herr Förster was not identified.

To Alice Howe Gibbens James

GRAND HÔTEL NATIONAL | LUCERNE Monday evening. | June 20(?) 92

Beloved Alice—

I have spent about the whole day on the Lake which makes it seem perfectly grotesque that you should remain in the Hotel Föhrenbach when such things are to be had for a less price. I telegraphed you this evening that I had found a place and asked you to say when you could come. The place was a pension at Hinter Meggen on the Lake where we can have 4 capital rooms in operatic scenery, balconies over the lake charming park-country, grass, trees, everything, for 35 francs daily for the party, everything included. I saw on Lake Zug a much cheaper place but very small rooms with wooden partitions and lake bathing not so near. To morrow I will visit 3 more places, one of which may be cheaper tho' no bathing. *Any* of them is good *enough;* the best more than good enough for any body; and my feeling now that I am here is that it is sheer madness to stay a day longer than you can help in that dark dismal town street.

I got your letter including Flournoy's for which many thanks. How disappointed I was at there being no sentimental effusion! I have felt so extraordinarily tender towards you.

Münsterberg is a brick I like him more and more—a beautiful nature on the whole, as distinguished from a heroic one.

I hope the baby is doing well again. At any rate, get him out of that hotel! The only feasable train to Lucern leaves at 1.02 and obliges you to spend one night *here.* Dont leave therefore till Wednesday—I may telegraph you to morrow to go to Zug via Zurich instead of to Lucerne. Once here, you can begin to get the unspeakable blessings of the Swiss country, and I can explore at my leisure the Rhone Valley for July and August. But this is a paradise, and one by no means dear. I want first of all to free you from Freiburg. Good night my own close darling. Kiss the dear boys, Peggy, Tweedy & all. I gave 10 Mks to the head waiter, & 5 to Fritz—Give 5 & 3 respectively to each—If you haven't enough cash to get away, F'bach will trust you surely on Brooks's guarantee. The handkerchiefs can be sent by post. You must change cars in Basel for Luzern—for Zurich I know not.

1000 kisses!

Your | Wm.

ALS: MH bMS Am 1092.9 (1801)

Address: Mrs. W. James | Hotel Föhrenbach | Freiburg i/B | Deutschland

Postmarks: LUZERN   AMBULANT 21. VI. 92   FREIBURG 21. 6. 92

To Alice Howe Gibbens James

GRAND HÔTEL NATIONAL | LUCERNE Tuesday June 21. 92 | 4. P.M.
Darling Alice,

No letter from you yet to day, but a telegram saying you will come on Thursday. Gottlob! I hope the baby is going on well with his new food etc. If he is, you will wish when you get here that you had come earlier. I saw three new places on the Lake this A.M. and have chosen one of them, since it was 30 francs instead of 35, smaller and more domestic than the place I had telegraphed about yesterday. They are all as good as they can be; and how they can give so much for the money I confess I don't understand. I want to see you every moment of the time, but I will not go to fetch you unless you telegraph me to do so, on acc! of the extra expense. If I can be of the least use, I charge you solemnly to telegraph. I can leave to morrow afternoon at 5 and be in Freiburg at 10. If you come without me, you must know that you change cars at Basel. There are two depots there, the Badische 1st and the Central 2nd and you stay in your car till you get to the 2nd or Central. *Make sure whether this is so!* The swiss cars are on a different model, and you will be more crowded. Münsterberg and I took 1st. class and found it just as full as 2nd— perhaps because of Sunday. No free baggage is allowed, so if you *could* pack one trunk to remain with Föhrenbach till further orders, it would be very good. I am intensely curious to hear from you, whether you are engaging the Munsterberg girl or not. Of course Fraulein comes now mit. I am sure that Tweedy will revive when once he gets into this country air.   I have only engaged for a week; and when you are once here we can visit other neighboring places together deliciously and better ourselves if you see best.   But I imagine the thing for me to do after a day or so is to go to Paris and decide that *most* momentous question of all.

Tell the boys that they can both swim, row, and fish here!   The water is, however, not very warm yet, so they must stay but a short time.

Good bye, my own heart's comrade.   Keep up your spirits—I believe that all will go well.   Kisses all round!

W.J.

I am writing to Barings about letters.   Tell Foh[r]enbach to forward as per enclosed picture which leave with him.

Your train arrives at 5.38 and you drive straight to the pension which is only two miles off—

ALS: MH bMS Am 1092.9 (1802)

Address: Mrs. James | Hotel Föhrenbach | Freiburg i/B | Deutschland

Postmarks: LUZERN 21. VI. 92.   FREIBURG 21. 6. 92

To Alice Howe Gibbens James

Hotel National [June 21, 1892] 7 o'clock

Dearest Wife—On coming in from a walk of a couple of hours all over this extraordinarily picturesque town, I find your letter enclosing Pillon's.   Its small size made my heart sick for I feared in you a sort of deadness, and I see that you are very tired and dispirited, poor darling.

Don't come a day before it is convenient.   My only motive for hurry was on your account, because I feel as if you were under a sort of a spell in that Fohrenbach house—you can't tell how dark and fatal it seems to me here.   The only good point of it seems to be Peggy's school.   But telegraph me if Thursday is inconvenient, & we will say Friday.   I can abundantly occupy myself here if the weather is fine—e.g. walk up the Righi.

Telegraphic address is

Pension Stutz

S! Niklausen

bei Luzern.

Why didn't you read Pillon's letter?   And what do you mean by Fraulein's not coming?   You ought to bring her.   I don't see how you can manage without her—but you know best. By my not going to meet you—her fare is paid. You'll need her on the long railroad journey if no where else—it lasts 5½ hours—there is a change of time by which a ½ hour is lost.

You see Pillon says Versailles or Sceaux! My, what trouble! The 1st of October is however a much better commencing time than the 1st of Sept. as at Freiburg. Pray ascertain exactly whether it is the 1st. of Sept.

All will come out right—you bet!

1000 kisses   W.J.

I have got a baby-wagon

ALS: MH bMS Am 1092.9 (1806)

To Charles William Eliot

Lucerne, June 22. '92

Dear President;

Before leaving Cambridge I sought you to say good-bye and hear any "last dying words" which you might have to pronounce, or instructions to give; but I failed to find you, and the time was too thick with the business of winding up things and packing, for me to make many attempts.—We have got safely over, have spent nearly two weeks at Freiburg, & are now to come for a time to a delicious little pension on this operatic lake, where for your money you get more than one can well understand to be possible. Later we shall settle in the Rhone Valley, I think.

I have seen a great deal of Münsterberg, who is a great deal of a human being in all sorts of ways. The questions he and his wife have asked about Cambridge, and the sort of trepidation they are in, would have amused you. He has just been to Strasburg to try on I know not how many suits of clothes "nach Amerikanischem Muster" which he brings with him, and the whole family has been vaccinated! He is undeniably vain, and of tremendous loquacity, and very *naif* in certain ways, but a thorough gentleman in all his feelings and impulses, and I feel that we shall have secured in him a *great* prize if only he gets along with our language. I confess that his present attainments are below what I supposed they would be. His students all adore him; and the sight of the quantity of work he has got through with experimentally in the laboratory, and of the ease with which he seems to handle it all, has been to me a real revelation of human power in that direction.   As a *teacher* of psychology, everyone here seems to agree that he is at present the best man in Germany. He is amiability and frankness incarnate, and has a very wide range of intellectual interests.   He is of a rich lumber-merchant's family in Dantzig which gave up the Jewish faith long ago, and have intermarried with Christians, so that he is registered now as a protestant. He looks very Jewish, however; and his wife, (whom we both like uncommonly) is an obvious jewess.

I am writing to the Treasurer's Office at his request to see whether the $600 promised him for travelling expenses can be advanced.   He is making a very heavy cash outlay to get off and it seems proper he should not be put to great inconvenience.   I hope you will further this, obviously reasonable, demand.   I wish I could have done more for the *fund* before I left.   Only $500 of it (so far as I know) have as yet been subscribed on condition of the whole being raised, so I suppose it is all good as far as it goes, though in my various begging letters I named $8000 as the entire sum I was trying to get.   I wish Royce might fall to and beg, whilst the cause is still warm.   I fear that when M. is once there people will deem the need less urgent.— To sum up regarding him, I am more than ever sure (subject to the doubt about his english) that we made a capital stroke in inviting him.

Nichols wished me to ask you ere I left whether the laboratory fees from last years Phil. 2, amounting to about $300.00 might not be made a special appropriation for Phil 2 next year.   As he has charge of that course, he would then be independent of M. in the disposition of the money.   I see no objection to this plan.   Nichols will be sure to spend money prudently, and will probably not spend the whole sum.   As he is a candidate for some independent appointment elsewhere, he naturally wants to show what he can do autonomously, and his pay was so incommensurate with his service last year that it seems fitting to be as generous to him as we can hereafter.

With cordial regards both to yourself and Mrs. Eliot, I am ever truly yours

Wm James

ALS: MH Archives

To Josiah Royce

Luzern, June 22 92
My dear Royce and verehrteste Herr College, Agreeably to the
promises I made on the eve of my departure I take pen in hand to
inform you of our prosperous voyage and safe arrival and to hope
that yourself and family are the same. We have been ten days in
the deliciously pretty little Freiburg (days for the most part rainy,
unfortunately) and I am now here as scout for a "pension" to bring
the family to, the weather having gloriously cleared up and Nature's
full orchestra going it on this extraordinarily operatic lake. I have
finally got a place where we pay 30 francs a day all told, and the brood
comes on to morrow. The fate of the children is not yet settled, and
future responsibilities weigh heavy on my mind—but of that I will
say nothing. No one ought to travel with children, who wishes also
to travel for his own pleasure: so much have the past weeks taught
two simple adult souls!—My great purpose in writing is to speak of
Munsterberg, whom I have seen a good deal of—he came on here
with me and we spent the whole of the next day scouring the shores
together for boarding places and talking all the time—so that I feel
as if I knew him pretty well. He is an extraordinarily engaging fellow, not of the heroic type, but of the sensitive and refined type, big,
inclined to softness and fatness, poor voice, vain, loquacious, personally rather formal and fastidious I think, desiring to please and to
shine, liberal of money, quick to forgive, painfully conscious of his
judaism, though baptized when a child, fond of travelling and of all
kinds of experience, interested in many intellectual directions, and
talking anything rather than "shop" when he gets out of harness. I
imagine him to be a man of the truest moral refinement and idealism,
with probably a certain superficiality in his cleverness, and lack of
the deeper metaphysical humor (such as the Harvard philosophical
department possesses in such unwonted measure). But he is *gentlemanly* through and through, so far as one can be a gentleman without
ferocity, and is a man to whom I should suppose one might easily
become deeply attached. It is in the Lab. that he appears at his best,
and that best is *very* good. His indefatigable love of experimental
labor has led him to an extraordinarily wide range of experience, he
has invented a lot of elegant and simple apparatus, his students all
seem delighted with him, and so far as I can make out, every one
recognizes him to be, as a *teacher,* far ahead of every one else in the
field, whatever they may think of his published results. His brain

never tires; he is essentially a man of big ideas in all directions, a real genius; and I feel more than ever, since I have been here, how great an addition he will be to our strength, *if only he gets along with our language*. *That,* I confess, is the doubtful point. He is much less advanced than I supposed he would be. Since the call came he has been studying from 7 to 9 every morning with a teacher, and from 11 to 12 Wadsworth coaches him in talking about the apparatus in the Laboratory. But he has never read much English. Wundt, he says, can hardly decipher English; Hering, you know, wrote me that *he* knew no English;—*we* apparently are the most cosmopolitan of peoples, and know all languages. With münsterberg's torrential flow of eloquence in his own tongue, he will have a fearful Hemmungs-gefühl when he tries ours. You must all try to help him out next year! I don't know how quickly he will learn, he is timid about trying now, and Cambridge will probably teem with anecdotes about him before he has been there a month. His wife, a charming straightfor-ward creature [*almost* as charming, though not *quite* as straight-forward, as your adorable Frau Gemahlin!] chucks herself into our language more boldly.

Riehl is a disappointed man with a morbid expression of contrac-tion on his face, whom I heard deliver a very well composed lecture on Hegel's Naturphilosophie, and with whom I spent two very agree-able evenings & had an afternoon's walk in the rain. He is extraordi-narily well read, and prompt of memory, talks like a man of the world, and we got on well together, though I confess I rather shrink from a long winter's *tête a tête* with one who is as sensitive as he evidently is. Wadsworth appears to have done good work with M.——berg, and not to have shown any deeper excentricities. I talked with him almost daily at table d'hôte. He is extraordinarily clever and percep-tive; but his point of view is that of steady contemptuous amusement at everything that can be mentioned, and although nothing insane came out, I found it wearisome enough. He says that he is now glad to go into medecine, and doesn't regret psychology a bit. *Tant mieux!*—Hodder has a good slim young wife, *very* unaffected and simple, who with better health would probably look handsome, as her features are large and calm. He is evidently in a tight place pecuniarily, but now that he is here, ought by hook or crook to stay, and work at philosophy, and not branch off to business or literature as he fears he must. He is two self reliant, and too ignorant of the complicated relations of this world. But he also is ideal in his make up, and ought to be helped to a good teaching place. He looks very pale and delicate—I didn't see him a great deal. The Baldwins were at Freiburg, B. a nice fellow in every way,[1] the Stewardson's were there,[2] and the John G. Brooks'es—too much social excitement for me just then, so I'm glad to be here for a while.

Well—I must end some time so let it be here. I find myself *lazy* beyond measure, and I had better let it work. I hope the year has ended well for you. Pray have half a dozen of the Courses of instruction and Philosophical Dep! Programs for next year sent me. Also some to Münsterberg.—And oh! I forgot—pray make thorough inquiries about board for him. I fancy they will be amiable people for the landlady to deal with. His brother's agent in N.Y. will meet him at the ship.[3] But if you could meet him at his arrival in Boston I think it would be a great relief. I have advised him to take the Shore line (since he does not take to the Providence Boat) and have recommended the Thorndike House as his first halting place. Perhaps you can do better. He sails late in August. Best love to you both.

W.J.

Give my love to Nichols if you see him, & say that I will write to him soon.

ALS: MH bMS Am 1092.9 (3608)

[1] James Mark Baldwin, who was touring European psychological laboratories, and his wife, Helen Green Baldwin.

[2] Possibly Langdon Cheeves Stewardson (1850–1930), American clergyman and educator.

[3] Münsterberg's brother was Otto Münsterberg.

To Carl Stumpf

Pension Stutz, Lucern, 24. 6. '92

My dear Stumpf

I have been in Europe with my whole family for nearly three weeks, but SO LAZY all the time that until this morning I have lacked energy to inform you of the fact. My purpose is to stay 15 months myself, and (if the boys' schooling goes well, and my wife is happy) to leave her with the children for a second year. But *where?*—that is the question. I don't want a big city, on the children's account. I don't want a small dull place on our own. I don't think it makes much difference, as far as the children are concerned, whether they absorb french teaching or german teaching during the time of their stay—they cant get both, and either will be equally useful to them hereafter. I mean that they shall *live* at home with us, while at

school. If my own taste were to decide, I should go to Munich—
but my two youngest children have a terribly catarrhal tendency, and
I hear such bad accounts of the Munich climate that I am afraid. I
suspect that Versailles will be our destination, with Paris close at hand
for the parents, and a certain amount of rusticity for the children.
But I should be very grateful to you for *any* advice whatever—I feel
quite lost sometimes, and wish I hadn't brought them at all. My
eldest boy (*aet.* 13) won't fit exactly into any German Gynasium, I
fear. I examined that at Freiburg i/B where we have spent 10 days.
It has a good reputation, but the latin is begun so early in Germany
and studied in so grammatical and practical a way, that whereas my
boy is hardly up to the *quarta* in that; in other things, he is in the
ober tertia, and I don't like to drop him into the *quarta* merely on
account of the latin. He will fit into a *lycée* better, if he can only get
far enough on with french before the 1st of October. Freiburg is a
sweet little town, but I dread the narrow social life, and absence of
Art etc. Is there any german place which you think perfect for a
man like me? Not Berlin, not Dresden, not Leipzig!

But I ought not to trouble you with our perplexities. My main
object in writing to you is to ask what your summer plans are, so that
I may know whether it will be possible to meet you. My family will
be here for at least 10 days longer, so you had better address me
here. *I* go, however, in two or three days to the lake of Geneva to
make a lot of inquiries, and we shall certainly be in Switzerland all
summer. I *hope* that you may possibly be coming this way. Are you
perhaps going to the Psychologists' Congress in London at the end
of July. I am *not;* the expense is too great; and although it will doubtless be amusing enough, it will do me more good after the cerebral
fatigue of last year to stagnate intellectually and use my legs in the
midst of this beautiful Nature, than to chatter and drink ale and wine
for several days with a lot of exciting and stimulating companions.
I hope all the same that the Congress will succeed; and since you
were not at the last one in Paris, I should think that you might find
it quite profitable to go to this one and see the psycho-zoo-logical
garden.

You will have heard of our calling Münsterberg to Harvard University. We have there now a first rate laboratory, and a lot of students,
and we ought to have the best experimental teacher; and when all is
said that can be said against Münsterberg (and much has been said
that is very unjust) it remains true that he is a great *force* in Psychol-

ogy, a wonderfully active thinker who tries to test all his ideas by experiments, and a man so amiable and liberal minded that he is sure to grow riper with the years. I have seen a good deal of him and like him thoroughly, I should think one might grow to love him very much. Meanwhile he is, by the unanimous confession of all his students, a *teacher* whom it is impossible to surpass. My only doubt is as to his ability to master the english language sufficiently, in a limited number of years. At present he is quite unprepared.—I also say[1] a good deal of Riehl at Freiburg. Both he and his wife treated us very kindly. He reads a lot, especially of english; but I fear he is a somewhat disappointed man, and his face wears a curious contraction which suggests melancholy or inner discord of some sort.

I have been too lazy to read Marty's review of my psychology until just now.[2] I shall write him a letter about it. It has been very instructive to me. Much of his criticism hits home; some of it (far the smaller part) is based on misunderstanding. My chief complaint is that he is too microscopic—*i.e.* doesn't sufficiently realize the general paedagogic attitude and intention of the book, and that he is too long. Who but *I* will care to read so long and minute a review?—I doubt whether *you* have read it all or ever will! But I feel honoured and touched that anyone should have studied the book so very seriously and thoroughly as to write such a review. Only germans are capable of such devotion!

Pray write soon, and say that you all are well, to yours always cordially

Wm James

ALS: MH bMS Am 1092.9 (3787)

[1] A slip for 'saw'.

[2] Anton Marty, review of *Principles of Psychology*, in *Zeitschrift für Psychologie und Physiologie der Sinnesorgane* 3 (1892): 297–333.

To Alice Howe Gibbens James

Aigle P.O. Thursday [June 30, 1892] 7.40—
Rapture at getting your postcards here, having hardly dared to hope them. The boy's problem will be no easy one. I saw Flournoy's man at Lausanne[1]—most things first rate except price, which would come (with lessons) to 550–600 a month—Also no bathing & not much comradry. I have a letter to a pastor at Ormont in the

Chateau d'Oex region and shall go thither to morrow, by stage.　I wish our possibility in Germany were not limited to the one town of Freiburg—it seems absurd—because the french language and Art u. Wesen of which the taste begins at Geneva is at bottom hateful to me! However we can speak of all that when I get to you again.　I feel so guilty leaving you alone to care care of those children, who I imagine find so little to do at the Pension that you all must be more than ready to come away.　I am a selfish beast—The lower end of this lake Leman is splendid for beauty, but terribly hot.　Write cards now to Aigle and to Bulle (Grisons).　I go to Chat. d'Oex day after to morrow and probably thence to Bulle.

W.J.

How bad about Tweedy's food.

APS: MH bMS Am 1092.9 (1807)

Address: Mrs. James | Luzern | Pension Stutz

Postmarks: AIGLE 1 VII 92　LUZERN 1 VII 92

[1] In his letter of 13 June 1892 (calendared) Flournoy recommended as one of several possibilities among his "best friends," a Professor David at Beaumont, near Lausanne.

To Alice Howe Gibbens James

Ormonts dessus | (Diablerets) | July 2. [1892] | 6 AM.

Sweet Wife

I seem the worst of criminals to be in this high spread out somewhat austere but pure and exquisitely modelled valley without the bride of my soul.　My quest for those boys seems no easy one.　The pastor here is a doubtful case.　They tell me that Chateau d'Oex is hot and full of English so instead of going there, I will go to Gryon now where there is a pastor and of which I hear the most contradictory accounts as an abode.　I have engaged a guide to carry my bag and start now after my chocolate—a walk of 4½ hours over the "col de la Croix."　I can go to morrow to Chateau d'Oeux if Gryon fails. If Gryon succeeds I will come to you directly and exchange views.　I long to see you and fear that the boys are eating both their heads and yours off with the monotony.

You are a good woman!　Don't write to Bulle!

Heaps of love to all of you.　I dreamed of Tweedy last night with his old *zugespitzt* smile.

The girl I saw at Aigle yesterday was *very* respectable looking, good dry swiss face, 25 years old, allways been with babies, now with a couturière, can give good references, etc.

Your loving | Wm.

ALS: MH bMS Am 1092.9 (1808)

To Alice Howe Gibbens James

G^D HÔTEL DU MUVERAN | VILLARS S/OLLON, LE 2 Juillet 1892
Beloved Wife—I have just sent you another startling telegram—too *short* for distinctness. Always this fatal *economy*, as I now realize it!! Things are coming slowly to a crisis. The village of Gryon was charming—the walk thither (only 3½ hours) delightfully exhilarating. The pastor was a decidedly promising man who could give the latin himself and get a *good* french instructor outside. But he couldn't admit the boys to his house or table till Aug. Yesterday at Ormonts I believe I told you that the pastor was away but his wife a nice woman said they could take the boys, & he would write me to Aigle about the lessons & terms. 450 fr. a month is the least total we can hope for. I walked from Gryon here in ¾ of an hour. For *us*, & Peg (& the little Menschen-Schifflein probably) *this* would be the place. You've no idea how charming it is. The immediate motive of my telegraphing you was the sight of the last rooms in the cheapest of the three hotels here (all there is in the way of board) which may be taken to morrow unless I engage them, and which we can put our family into for 38 fr. per day. One quickly gets at the possibilities in Switzerland: either Hotels of this type, clean and comfortable but with the terribly tiresome table d'hôte, and in the end tiresome every-way, or cheaper country houses where the rooms are so small that we should die in rainy weather. At Gryon I saw a chalet to let for 500 francs for the season. A cook can easily be got in the neighborhood, & the rooms were *very large*. It wd. be cheaper doubtless than boarding. But it is right on the village street, and Gryon strikes me as hot in the middle of the day.

You see how the seesaw goes! I imagine now that the first thing to do is to get you into the region, *somewhere*. Then we can decide. Everything is filling up at a tremendous rate, and we shall probably have to lie in wait for vacancies where we want to go. Once here, though, we can with little loss of time do *either* of the 3 or 4 only things which seem possible to us, and at any rate it will be a step towards bringing the creatures into the mountains where after all they have to come.

But there again! I couldn't have imagined the torture to which we were going to be put on the boys' account, or how the fullness of everything in the season was to make speed so neccessary. You *may* regret to leave the Lucerne region after all, if the end of things should turn out to be a German tutor. Hearing the hideous french vocalization around me at the table d'hote to day made me hate the idea of Paris.—*On the whole*, though, I feel as if the safest thing was for you to come as quick as possible.

On getting your telegram at Aigle I will telegraph you again, and this letter is only to let you understand the state of my mind to night.

I think of you, darling Alice, with steadfast tenderness—you with this new physical infirmity. I hope and pray that the relief continues, and that the spool has done no harm, burst through or anything!

Love to all, | W.J.

ALS: MH bMS Am 1092.9 (1809)

To Charles Ritter

Lucern, 4. 7. 92

My dear Ritter

I found the problem of education no simple one, and the result of my travels is that we are going to Gryon s/Bex in a day or two, where the pastor can take our boys into his family soon, and *we* can be in the immediate neighborhood. I had, with considerable reluctance to decide against M. Barblan's house, which (as you said) was a little gloomy;[1] and Morges seemed so hot, in comparison with some of the mountain places that I afterwards visited, that I wrote to M. Barblan that the balance had inclined elsewhere. I should have been too happy to put the boys with him on account of the association with you, but the material side carried the day!

I much enjoyed my little tour from which I returned last night. We leave for Gryon in a day or two.

How I did enjoy that incomparable volume of Lemaître![2] He makes criticism as fresh and as *refreshing* as original production— *almost*. And, not knowing a great deal of Voltaire, I say that his breadth of style and tremendous good sense are equal to V.'s.

You[3] can't tell you [how] good it was to see you again, my dear old comrade. When we get settled at Gryon—if we ever *do* get settled—

you must come and be with us for a week and let my wife make your acquaintance. She is now reading your volume of Lemaître. I wish I could spend the winter in Munich; but an implacable destiny seems to carry me towards Paris.

Always your friend | Wm James

ALS: Bibliothèque publique et universitaire, Geneva

[1] Barblan was not identified.
[2] Jules Lemaître (1853–1914), French critic.
[3] A slip for 'I'.

To Hugo Münsterberg

Pension Stutz, Luzern, 6. 7. 92

My dear Münsterberg [You mustn't "Professor" me any longer (now that you and I are colleagues) but rather adopt our English informality!] I only got your letter of the first, last night, on my arrival here from a week's trip to Geneva and the Rhone Valley region. We shall start tomorrow for Gryon (sur Bex) where I can probably get instruction for my boys in the pastor's family, as well as "board" for ourselves in a big chalet near by.

Destiny seems to be inevitably dragging us towards Paris. I am sorry, for I rather *hate* the french language etc., etc., although I am much more at home in it than in German. But I see that I must resign myself to a year without the satisfaction of my *Gemüth;* and trust that by simply amusing myself with externals I shall be able to return to Cambridge fat and good natured, and full of metaphysical originality!—You poor fellow, overburdened as you were during those last days, you ought not to have given up 48 hours to me & to the Lake of Lucerne! But I shall remember it in your favor as long as I live, and hope to repay you some summer in the U.S.A. A letter arrived yesterday from Mrs. Gibbens (my wife's mother) containing the following passage which is of interest to you. "Mr. Royce and Margie* have been energetic in getting a boarding place for the Münsterbergs—4 rooms, meals served in rooms, their own servant to wait, etc. Royce tho't $60 per week would be reasonable for Mr. & Mrs. M., 2 babies and maid. Margie objected to the price and we all sustained her in it. At 18 Sumner S! 4 rooms, good rooms, can be had their meals served as wished, etc., for 40 dollars. Mrs. Fox [a neighbor] says the cooking is excellent in that house[1]—bad style at the table but as the M.'s wont go to the table that makes no difference.

I do not believe (after hearing a great deal of talk) that they can find any place so well suited to their needs.   You see, in all the other houses the meals *cannot* be served in the rooms, & $48 at Mrs. Hewes's,[2] $50 at Mrs. Webb's are the prices.[3]   Mr. Royce has no authority from the M's to engage, and the rooms are to be reserved for two weeks only.   If the Münsterberg's lose them, it looks as if they would have to go to Boston for rooms."   I imagine that Royce will have already written to you about this.   I don't know the house in Sumner St, it can hardly be a *very* good *house;* but if Royce has not written to advise you, and if the price is an important thing, I think I should advice you to telegraph to "Gibbens Irving S! Cambridge Mass" to "engage Sumner S! board."   In Boston you will have to pay *much* higher prices.   Whatever the place may be you can probably endure it for one year, and the price is decidedly low.   I think it must be the house where some neighbors of ours once went for their meals during repairs of their kitchen (or something), and I imagine that the food *is* good.   The situation is very near our house.

It will please Mrs. Münsterberg to know that I have engaged a very promising *vaudoise* girl for the children and I think she will give us satisfaction.   She awaits us at Aigle where we shall arrive in 3 days.

Cordial regards from both of us!   I hope that Pyrmont will do Mrs. Münsterberg good, and that you will get quite as much entertainment as fatigue from your *Rundreise.*   I wrote immediately, upon your departure from here, to the President and Treasurer about paying your travelling expenses in advance, and you will doubtless soon receive the sum.

Pray take every opportunity now of *speaking* english!

My wife and babes hate to leave this place.   They have been very happy here.

Permanent address: c/o Baring, Bros. & Co., London E.C.

Always truly yours | Wm James

A very affectionate letter from Stumpf urges me to come to Munich.   How I wish I could!

W.J.

*(my sister-in-law)

ALS: MH bMS Am 1092.9 (3271)

[1] Susan E. Thayer Fox, wife of Jabez Fox.
[2] Perhaps Mrs. Eleanor B. Hewes at 11 Mason St., Cambridge.
[3] Mrs. Webb was not identified.

To Robertson James

Gryon, Switzerland, July 10. 92

My dear Bob,

Your Letter explaining about Plumb, Warner, Mary, yourself etc, came duly a week ago. Of course I knew your trouble was but a transient one, and I suppose you will prefer to continue receiving my share which will make Plumb more immediately responsible to you, and less likely to delay with any part of the remittance. I must say that such conduct as you report of Plumb in the way of not answering letters and telegrams has *never* occurred before. I believe him to have been uniformly as prompt as he could be, and he over and over again has advanced money out of his own pocket to make up Clary's, Hazer's and Lofties rents when they were tardy, rather than make me wait beyond the 10th. His holding back a certain amount of our money to pay Clary's notes, lest Clary should fail to do so, was all right, only he should have *explained* long before. If Plumb shows any symptoms of demoralization, I imagine the best agent to take will be William Cowie. But Plumb has shown himself so far simply *admirable,* and his natural gift as a mechanic has stood us in good stead in all repairs. I wish you would send me his letters—I want to see exactly how Clary's rent is coming out. I am mighty glad you went to Syracuse, and trust it will have an effect. As for the question of my making up to you any loss of rent from Clary, you are welcome to take it out of my share, if you think fit and right. But I deny the liability, as I shall deny your liability to me in case any of our tenants fail to pay up in full whilst you are corresponding with Plumb and deem it better to wait and give them a chance than to kick them out. Clary had been our tenant for 10 years or more and had paid us over $25,000 without ever a month's delay. His worst crime had been paying late in the month. When his debt rose to $400 you proposed to turn him out in spite of the facts that his reasons for being short seemed temporary, that Plumb & Plumb's counsellors advised trusting him, and that the empty shop would almost surely have bro't no rent till the 1st of May, as all leases begin then. To attempt to make rents a mathematical certainty, and to charge the agent with a deficit, when he has used his best judgment, is absurd from the business point of view. Nevertheless, you are welcome to the money if you think it right to take it. Only let me know just how the accounts stand.

How did Ned get through his exam:? and what does his mental

condition seem to be?   I shall be glad to see Mary and both of the young ones here if they come.   *Our* destiny seems driving us on to Paris for the winter, although I confess that I hate the idea of it.   But all German towns, for one reason or another, seem cut off; and the french school program fits Harry better than the German.   I suppose Mary will pass through Paris or stay there some time if she comes, and I will (D.v.) try to get her a lodging and make her comfortable if she arrives after we're settled.   We are in this high and picturesque alpine village to get teaching for the boys—a hard thing to find just now.   They will probably begin to morrow.   But the place is too steep for Alice & the two little ones, so *we* shall most likely move on after the boys are settled.   Switzerland is magnificent, from the Mountains down to the beds.   I vow it makes me respect the universe to find such a place in it.   But it's fearful travelling with children with such uncertainty of the future, and with *their* needs the whole pivot of the situation.   The small bedroom and huddle & clutter make me think of my insensibility to poor Mother's and Father's deserts when they dragged us after them in times gone by.

Keep addressing Barings.   I hope you'll have a first rate summer. Alice sends her love.

Yours always,   W.J.

Harry is still in Italy.   He expects to join us in 10 days or so.

W.J.

ALS: MH bMS Am 1092.9 (3138)

To George Croom Robertson

Gryon s/Bex Switzerland, 11. 7. 92

My poor dear Robertson,

It fairly stabs me to think that you have been waiting all this time for an acknowledgment of your letter of June 17th, and that I have not sent it.   Of course I got the letter duly, but because my essential response was in the former letter, and because I was on the eve of starting for Switzerland to find a settling place for the family, I did not answer *immediately;* and since then I have been zigzagging so wildly and writing under such difficulties (yet having much correspondance of a business sort to conduct both with America and here) that I have waited for a more propitious and settled moment to write to you, though I have *thought* of you often enough.   I imagined whilst writing to you before, that the end had probably come;—it was whilst we were at sea, and you have now been alone for a month and a half. As you say, the "circumstances" are depressing enough, and I can only hope that no attack of your own organic enemy has come to make them worse. With both of your responsible avocations gone and with the light at your hearth extinct, you might well be excused for becoming melancholy, and yet my dear Robertson I don't expect that of you, because you are of another sort. As far as Mind and the Professorship go there will be relief in letting responsibilities go for which one has n't strength. The dreadful thing in life is the *trying* to do work to which one feels one's self incompetent, and when one *sincerely gives up,* in the old religious fashion, then one can *erst* look round one and take things in. The fever, the fret, the ambition, and the sham!—they are the worst of all. But willingly to *be* simply, like the unnumbered herd, that must be peace.—But here I sermonize! I wish I could see you soon, and hear you talk, you best and friendliest of men. But of course you won't leave the Island, and I don't see how I can possibly leave the Continent until the Fall. Then, however, we shall meet. I brought my children abroad, meaning to "put them in a french or german school," but taking little thought in advance of the details of the process. I find their education unexpectedly become the whole pivot of the situation, and a very difficult puzzle to solve. Destiny seems to be driving us on to Paris, which on many accounts I hate; and I imagine that we shall settle there by the middle of September. I have had much trouble in finding a family to teach them french here, and from point to point have reached this Gryon, where we shall stay a fortnight, and the boys perhaps all summer. Travelling with 4 children, 2 quite young, is no holiday pastime.

You ask me, dear Robertson, to "tear up when read"—your letter. I have not done so, & I hope you won't insist, for I wish to keep it as a relic. I valued your wife's friendship deeply, and I am sorrier than words can tell that my own wife now can never meet her.

With warmest good wishes, believe me ever affectionately yours

Wm James

ALS: MH bMS Am 1092.9 (3552)

To Grace Ashburner

Gryon sur/Bex, Switzerland | July 13. 1892

My dear Miss Grace, or rather let me say my *dear Grace,* since what avails such long friendship and affection, if not that privilege of familiarity?—I have thought of you often and of the quiet place that harbors you, but have been too distracted as yet to write any letters but neccessary ones on business. We have been in Europe 5½ weeks and are only just beginning to see a ray of daylight on our path. How could Arthur, how could Madame Lucy, see us go off and not raise a more solemn word of warning?[1] It seems to me that the most solemn duty *I* can have in what remains to me of life will be to save my inexperienced fellow beings from ignorantly taking their little ones abroad when they go for their own refreshment. To combine novel anxieties of the most agonizing kind about your children's education, nocturnal and diurnal contact of the most intimate sort with their shrieks, their quarrels, their questions, their rollings about and tears, in short with all their emotional, intellectual and bodily functions, in what practically in these close quarters amounts to one room, to combine these things (I say) with *a holiday* for *onesself* is an idea worthy to emanate from a lunatic asylum. The wear and tear of a professorship for a year is not equal to one week of this sort of thing. But let me not complain! Since I am responsible for their being, I will launch them worthily upon life; and if a foreign education is required, they shall have it. Only why talk of "Sabbatical" years?— *there* is the hideous mockery! Alice, if she writes to you, will (after her feminine fashion) gloze over this aspect of our existence, because she has been more or less accustomed to it all these years and *on the whole does not dislike it(!!)*, but I for once will speak frankly and not disguise my sufferings. Here in this precipitous Alpine Village we occupy rooms in an empty house with a yellow plastered front and an iron balcony above the street. Up and down that street the cows, the goats, the natives and the tourists pass. The church roof and the pastor's house are across the way, dropped as it were 20 feet down the slope. Close beside us are populous houses either way, and others beside *them*. Yet on that iron balcony all the innermost mysteries of the James family are blazoned and bruited to the entire village. *Things* are dried there, quarrels, screams and squeals rise incessantly to Heaven, dressing and undressing are performed, punishments take place, recriminations, arguments, execrations, with a publicity after which, if there *were* reporters, we should never be able to show our faces again. And when I think of that cool spacious and quiet mansion lying untenanted in Irving St. with a place in it for everything, and everything in its place when *we* are there, I could almost weep for "the pity of it."[2] But we may get used to this as other travellers do—only Arthur and Lucy ought to have dropped some word of warning ere we came away!

Our destiny seems relentlessly driving us towards Paris, which on the whole I rather hate than otherwise, only the educational problem promises a better solution there. The boys meanwhile have got started on french lessons here, and though we must soon "move on" like a family of wandering Jews, we shall probably leave one behind in the pastor's family hard bye. The other boy we shall get into a family somewhere else, and then have none but Peg and the baby to cope with. Perhaps strength will be given us for that.

Switzerland meanwhile is an unmitigated blessing, from the mountains down to the bread and butter and the beds. The people, the arrangements, the earth, the air and the sky, are satisfactory to a degree hard to imagine beforehand. The[re] is an extraordinary absence of feminine beauty, but great kindliness, absolute honesty, fixed tariffs and prices for everything etc., etc., and of course absolutely clean hotels at prices which, though not the "dirt cheap" ones of former times are yet very cheap compared with the American standard. We stayed for 10 days at a pension on the Lake of Lucerne which was in all respects as beautiful and ideal as any scene on the operatic stage, yet we paid just about what the Childs pay at Nickerson's vile and filthy hotel at Chocorua. Of course we made the acquaintance of Cambridge people there whose acquaintance we had not made before—I mean the family of Joseph Henry Thayer of the Divinity School, whose daughter Miriam with her splendid playing and general grace and amiability was a proof of how much hidden wealth Cambridge contains. They were all very nice, except Mrs. T. who was charmless.[3]

But I have talked too much about ourselves and ought to talk about you. What can I do, however, my dear Grace, except express hopes? I know that you have had a hot summer, but I know little else. Have you borne it well? Have you had any relief from your miserable suffering state? or have you gone on as badly or worse than ever? Of course you can't answer these questions, but some day Theodora will. I devoutly trust that things have gone well and that you may even have been able to see some friends and in that way to get a little change. Your sister, to whom pray give the best love of both of us, is I suppose holding her own as bravely as ever, only I should like to know the fact, and that too Theodora will doubtless ere long acquaint us with. To the last named exemplary and delightful Being give also our best love; and with any amount of it of the tenderest quality for yourself believe me, always your affectionate

                                                          Wm James

Love to all the Childs, please and all the Nortons who may be within reach.[4]

ALS: MH bMS Am 1092.9 (725)

Address: Miss Grace Ashburner | Kirkland Street | Cambridge (Mass) | U.S. of A. | Amérique

Postmarks: GRYON 14 VII 92   NEW <YOR>K JUL 23 92   CAMBRIDGE BOSTON MASS JUL 24 92

[1] Arthur George Sedgwick and his wife, Lucy.

[2] From Shakespeare's *Othello*, act 4, sc. 1, line 191.

[3] Joseph Henry Thayer (1828–1901), professor of New Testament criticism at Harvard, whose wife was Martha Caldwell Thayer.   Their daughter, Miriam Stuart Thayer (b. 1866), in 1896 married Theodore William Richards (1868–1928), a chemist teaching at Harvard.

[4] On the back of the envelope Sara Norton wrote the following note: 'Thank you for this—We were all much entertained with it. | S.N.'

To Robertson James

                                                     Gryon 13. 7. 92

My dear Bob

Your letter of the 30th from Albany is a startler.   Plumb must have collapsed all of a sudden.   I pity the fellow, for he certainly began with the most honorable ambition and never has made the faintest slip till now, unless indeed he has misinformed me of late about Clary. Of course we must change our Agent; and I have already written to you that Cowie, so far as I knew, was the best man.   I liked his conduct for his clients the McCarthys when they bought our store through him.[1]   The only trouble is, he has more business than Plumb, and would not attend to the piddling mechanical details, which Plumb did in a very superior fashion.   He told me he had a partner who took care of the buildings—I forget his name.   All the Insurance policies are not with Hanchett, some being with one Stanley Bagg.[2]   Hazer is a bad tenant, and we have been waiting for a chance to get a better one in order to ship him.   He has no lease, and I hope he will soon go.   Loftie is slow, but always "good."   Alice says, "why doesn't Bob remain as agent himself."   But I should think, in spite of the economy, to you, for you might take the fee, that the agent would need to be on the spot, and be a professional.   Every month there are repairs, the tenants quarrel and encroach upon each other, etc. I wish, though, that you would send my dividends to L. H. & Co., instead of Mrs Gibbens. She would simply turn the money over to them.

I will telegraph to Ginty to pay you the rents if they have any cable-connexion in this alpine village.[3] In case they should not, I will mail him a letter. He is the best of all our tenants, but over exact in this instance, I must say. He will probably have paid you anyhow before this.

I feel better this AM. than any day yet, and shall swing off from the family and walk a bit ere long, which I doubt not will make me all right. The confusion and worry of close quarters with the children and their everlasting uproar and quarreling wear us both out.

I wrote you two days ago.

Affect[ly] W.J.

I need hardly say how glad I am that you took such prompt action, and recovered the money immediately.

P.S. later: I find that the postmaster here has no cable tariff so I simply write to Ginty.

ALS: MH bMS Am 1092.9 (3139)

[1] For the sale to McCarthy & Co. see *Correspondence*, 2:271n.

[2] Milton Waldo Hanchett (1822–1904) and Stanley Bagg (1831–1917), insurance agents in Syracuse.

[3] J. B. Ginty (1832–1895) was one of the James tenants at 215 South Salina, Syracuse.

To Elizabeth Glendower Evans

Gryon, Switzerland, 15. 7. 92

My dear Mrs. Evans,

I wanted to answer your sublime letter, received just before our departure on the spot, but the press of things made it impossible then, and you know how long under such circumstances it takes for the moment to come round again. We have been distracted with the natural lassitude always consequent upon the change, with the children living all the time as it were in one & the same bedroom with us, with inward perplexities about the educational problem and the future abode, and with my wildly zigzagging to and fro to find the proper place both for ourselves and the boys. We have come to a temporary rest in this precipitous alpine village, but although I start to morrow again to look for a better abode, many of our perplexities are already solved by the experience of 5 weeks and we begin to breathe more equably. Under these circumstances my fingers turn, as my thoughts have so often turned, to you and to that letter. My dear Mrs. Evans, you are one of the people that make the name of friendship into a reality in this world. If we were not already rolling in ill-gotten and shameless opulence, if we *needed* money to help us to any virtuous ends and you offered it, you may be sure that no miserable sentiment of pride would ever make us say no, just as I trust that you would love and trust us enough to let us help you if ever there came a time of need. But such a time is apparently not at hand for either of us yet, and I hope it won't be, so that *your* surplus may now go to someone in genuine want. *July 17th—Lausanne* There are enough! Meanwhile bless you for thinking of us!

I was interrupted at the word *want,* and have been dashing round ever since to find families to put the boys into. No easy task, one becomes so fastidious here that the crumpled rose leaf makes one say "no"—the fact being I suppose that one dreads to alienate the little critters after all. But Switzerland is *good,* in spite of lake steamers blowing up[1] and St. Gervais disasters[2]—good through and through, and calculated to make the worst pessimist respect the Universe.—I hope that your summer thus far has gone well in spite of "labour troubles" and presidential uproar—where you are I have not idea.

Believe me always affectionately yours, | William James

ALS: MCR

[1] A boiler explosion that occurred on 9 July 1892 on the *Mont Blanc,* a steamer on Lake of Geneva, resulted in some twenty-five deaths.

[2] In the early morning of 12 July 1892 a glacier destroyed the town of St. Gervais-les-bains, killing about 125 people.

To Eliza Putnam Webb Gibbens

Lausanne, 18. 7. 92

Dearest and Sweetest of mothers in law, Your letter enclosing Bob's, with your "account"—monument of your scrupulous fidelity was sent to me hither from Gryon by Alice, and it made me gnash my teeth afresh to think how abominably you have been treated first by me and then by Plumb. About 100 dollars were all the debts Alice and I could possibly think of—the overdrawn bank account was a blow from behind which however you didn't have to pay, fortunately. My own check book showed an exact balance, but the bank is always right and I always wrong so there was no excuse on my part. Plumb's collapse was entirely unexpected, he has been a model heretofore. And that the debts should have run up to 250 dollars, and you, unable to feed your own starving family, have had to borrow money to pay them, goes beyond all possible imagination. I can only prostrate myself and hope that the time will some day come when you treat me similarly and take your revenge.

I have been staying here in the delightfully clean Hotel Riche-mont to see whether we can get a more satisfactory settlement of ourselves. The great difficulty is the boys, and I suppose that what makes us find the difficulty so great is our own dread of leaving the interesting William, with his nocturnal terrors, etc to himself. I have seen several places any one of which at home we should have been too happy to find, but in each I see an obstacle—either the situation is not rural enough, or the house is gloomy, or the face of the man disagreeable, or the companions not the right age, or *something*. I think however to morrow that the inventory of possibilities will be complete and that I can go back and consult Alice. I walked to a couple of Places above the lake to day, and felt so mean in the delicious air with no rain, to see the Rhone valley filled with great curtains of it for the major part of the time and Alice immured there in her confusion. When I'm there I only add to it however, so I quieted my conscience with that thought. If we once get the boys fixed, everything will seem easy relatively. One element of the difficulty is the breadth of the possible combinations that offer themselves. Nothing being fixed, one floats in mere potentiality. I can't even yet reconcile myself to going to Paris, it makes me angry whenever I think of it, and yet on the whole it seems to promise most for the boys.

We have had a good deal of rain in the past week—I hope it isn't going to be a summer like the last, in which I believe that in the M^{ts} there were only 6 days with no rain. That is fatal! I am glad you are going to get so much good out of your new house this summer. It does seem a pity to build it and then go off. If you *do* go, pray don't forget to leave the key of our big house with Ellis for a possible tenant. Would he might come!—this year is bound to cap the climax of our extravagance, and I pray nightly for a tenant as well as for a favorable decision of the court in the case of Henry Wyckoff's residual estate. If the latter comes out all right my mind will be at peace and I will even bring you home some more cologne and handkerchiefs. Tell mack I have his letter and will write to Mr. Clarke as soon as the proof comes.[1] I should think the little book might go off well—it does fill a need, and its shortness is a great point in its favor. I do hope the Madison Place will go well, and not cost too much, but I advise him *not* to invite the M——berg's—it will be a terrible effort, and the M's will have plenty to occupy them in Cambridge during September, making near excursions and getting acquainted—I mean no one will *owe* it to them to invite them anywhere. How glad I am of the better news from that dear and good and strenous Mary! I am just now reading Lawrence Oliphant's Masollam, which she might like.[2] I find it very curious and interesting.

Don't worry over the splenetic character of our last letters. Tis but a little crisis which works off steam in that way. Switzerland is wonderfully *good*—no words for it! and the air is something sui generis for strength & sweetness.

God bless you all, especially you you dear Mother. Alice is gentleness incarnate.

Your loving son | William

I have written to Bob not to bother you with my money. Cowie the new agent is a capital man. I wrote to Bob to get him, before I knew of the crash in Plumb's affairs, if P. should again be so remiss.

ALS: MH bMS Am 1092.9 (1813)

[1] William Mackintire Salter, *First Steps in Philosophy* (1892). The book was published by Charles H. Kerr in Chicago, and Clarke is likely someone associated with the company.

[2] Laurence Oliphant, *Masollam: A Problem of the Period* (1886), a novel.

To Alice Howe Gibbens James

HOTEL RICHEMONT, LAUSANNE (SUISSE). Monday [July 18, 1892] 5.30
P.M.

Sweet Alice—I wrote to Stumpf, Myers and a couple of post cards to others last night, read Masollam and went to bed, after strolling about the town about sundown—it grows on one a good deal. This A.M. at 9.50 I went to Chexbres by train, saw the beautifully situated Hotel du Signal where they can give us (*without* the boys) good rooms for 35 *francs* a day, another hotel (not good) and the pastor whose name had been given me, but he told me he couldn't take a child. Thence down on foot to the lake shore where at Rivaz I took the train for Vevey, lunched on beer cheese & eggs and walked to la Chièsaz to see M. Cérésole, the pastor whose name the boys can't pronounce. Charming house & grounds and a nice couple (she a niece of old

Agassiz) with seven children, the youngest a boy of 10, the next a girl of 13. They could take either Harry or Bill letting him share the room of the 10 year old boy. Mrs. & the eldest son would give lessons (amateurishly?) Price about 200 fr. all told a month. I go after dinner to see a pastor here, the last on my list, but family highly spoken of. He was out when I called on Saturday. I confess that the thing that seduced me most on Saturday was the swiss widow of an australian professor, with 3 children, a boy of seven and 2 girls older. They all speak english like natives, but ditto french. She was so very wholesome a woman, her children so good looking her house so nice (but she leaves it for a month to go to S! Cergue on the Jura and would take her pensionnaire with her) that I thought of her as a good mother for the tender William. [She has cured her daughter of nocturnal terrors by homoeopathy]—Back by boat from Vevey, to find your dear letter. The governess! well, every one we meet seems to want to come with us. I admire her immensely, but wouldn't she be a white elephant, and she surely *couldn't* be as cheap as boarding a child. Moreover, Peg wants a younger companion. However, I see that I shall wind up my affairs in this region to morrow and get to your side very likely in the afternoon to talk over the situation once more. I felt so diabolically *mean* to be enjoying myself on the hillside this A.M. (I walked 3½ hours) under a cloudy sky with no rain and delicious air, whilst great curtains of rain filled the Rhône Valley, and I thought of you cooped up. But the bitter reflection came that were I with you I should only augment your distress and worry instead of relieving it, and then I felt meaner still. I have written to the Dolmateff (or whatever she is called) at Sepey and expect an answer to morrow. I am sorry you think the Villars hotel impossible—I tho't so at first. But there is very little else than that kind of thing on the one one[1] & the Saussaz kind of thing on the other, and the latter is just impossible for us in rainy weather. The Hotel du Pillon at Ormonts (Diablerets) is well situated and good, something intermediate, but I fear rather cramped quarters there. *Entweder* cramp *oder* 12 or 14 dollars a week!

Bless you, you angel W.J.

ALS: MH bMS Am 1092.9 (1828)

[1] Probably WJ meant to write 'on the one hand'.

To Théodore Flournoy

GRAND HÔTEL DE RICHE-MONT | LAUSANNE Tuesday, 17. [19] 7. 92[1]
My dear Flournoy—I hope you will let me follow our anglo-saxon
custom and drop titles of ceremony between such colleagues and
gleichgesinnten Menschen as we now are, you of course doing the
same—I have travelled and seen almost as much as Ulysses since I
left you on Saturday night exposed to the fury of the tempest, and
I only hope that you got safely home. Without going into details I
may say that I now know of several places in either of which my boys
would be well off. To morrow I go (I might have gone to day, with
a little more energy)—to Gryon to talk it all over with my wife, and
decide on the best combination. Meanwhile I cannot *now engage* the
rooms at Madame Cruchon's and must run the risk of losing them,
though I think they might very well be the best thing we could do
in August. Will you kindly say this to Madame Cruchon? My wife
writes that she is getting fonder and fonder of the mountains, in spite
of the rain, and does not wish to abandon that region. I will let you
know in a couple of days just what we shall have done. I meant to
have told you last time for the sake of M. Claparède that there is
now at Lucerne (Pension Stutz) a charming young American lady, an
admirable musician, who has a most elaborate system of chromatic
symbols accompanying sounds, letters of the alphabet, and names,
also a number diagram, of all of which she can probably give an
intelligible account. To a remark which I made, she said "my mind
must be like a sort of little Switzerland, for picturesqueness, compared with yours." She has had these things as long as she can remember.

Will you please present my best respects and regards to Madame
Flournoy, and believe me always truly yours

Wm James

For a week my address will be Gryon—if I go they will forward
letters

ALS: MH bMS Am 1505 (3)

[1] Tuesday was 19 July in 1892 and the 19 July date better fits WJ's movements.

To Alice Howe Gibbens James

G? HOTEL RICHE-MONT LAUSANNE Tuesday 19. 7. 1892
Beloved wife—The continued rain fills me with remorse and chagrin
for you, and yet I decide to hang on here, as all the threads of our
combination are not yet in my hands. I await an answer from Dolmateff, and a telegram or a letter from Harry.[1] I wrote a letter to
your angelic mother last night, and slept well. My sleep, which you
ask about, has been irregular, but it doesn't bother me *a bit*, since I
don't have to lecture off it. I went last evening and again this morning to a pasteur Thélin in the town, with a garden and rurality close
by. He has been strongly praised to me for his character, and personally he & his wife pleased me better than anyone I have met,
though their house is rather disorderly. They take other pupils (only
one english who goes shortly)—have a boy of 11 in whose room billy
would sleep. They prefer Billy to Harry, who would do well at
Cérésole's. He argues strongly against the french lycées which he
says are pure machines, and says the College Galliard here is better.
One of my other men, Rosselet, who spent 10 years at Paris, also
argued against them. They do but cram—not but that cramming
may not be a fairly good thing for a year or two of our little angels'
lives. A first-rate german american family here recommends the Hotel des Salines, 25 minutes drive away from Bex, as an admirable
abode. Mosquitoes present only at the end of August.
Combinations to choose from

Harry	*We*	*Billy*
Cérésole	— Here & at Vers chez les Blanc	— Thélin
Meylan	— H. du Pillon	— Dolmateff.

I shall certainly be with you tomorrow night, whatever the weather.
I feel relieved by the tone of your letter of yesterday. Peg seems to
be the really bad element in our lives just now, poor little darling,
and we the bad element in hers. I am *so* glad you could walk to
Villars again without bad consequences. It may be that that sort of
thing is really what you most want.

Love to you all | W.J.

ALS: MH bMS Am 1092.9 (1814)

[1] HJ's letter is not known. WJ was making arrangements to meet HJ at Domodos-
sola; see *Correspondence*, 2:223–24.

To Shadworth Hollway Hodgson

Hotel Richemont, Lausanne | 22. 7. 92

My dear Hodgson,

I am taking the great liberty of giving a card of introduction to you to my friend, and as it were *famulus,* Dickinson S. Miller of Philadelphia who (having just been appointed to teach philosophy in a small but good girl's college in Pennsylvania, Bryn Mawr by name) has come abroad for a year of additional study.   He is a darling young creature, with an extraordinarily economic and Humian intellect, but a rich aesthetic and humane character, and a perfect little gentleman withal.   I am extremely attached to him, and I am sure that you will become so if you get to know him.   He is a great admirer of your writings,—after which I need say no more, except perhaps this, that since he is poorer than a church mouse and writes me that he thinks of staying for the "Congress," if your room should end by going a begging (which it is to me inconceivable it should) and the spirit should then move you to invite him, it might be a deed of beneficence!

Ever thine | W.J.

ALS: MH bMS Am 1092.9 (985)

Address: S. H. Hodgson Esq | 45 Conduit St, Regent S! | London W | England

Postmarks: LA<USANN>E 23 VII 92   LON<DON> JY 25 92

To Henry James III

Hotel Richemont, 27. 7. 92

Dearest Harry,

Your post-card does the highest credit to your
  considerateness;
  patience;
  heroism; and
  magnamity

of character.   Your mother wept when she read it.   Now that your headache is over I hope that things will go well.   You must have had a dismal homesick time during it.   Poor Billy came back last evening for a visit, in very doleful dumps, poor fellow, with homesickness, but we hope he will be better to night.   He does n't like the victuals nor sleeping three in a room.[1]   The doctor did n't "panser" him till bedtime.   He is rather run down with his sores, but will I doubt not, enjoy his situation in a week. You my dear Harry, by your patience and self reliance, are a great comfort to us both. If your Uncle Harry comes in time to morrow we will go and see you about ½ past 6.—otherwise we will do it on Friday.

Your loving | W.J.

ALS: MH fMS Am 1092.4

[1] Son William was placed with Pastor Thélin.

To Alice Howe Gibbens James

Brig, Monday AM. [August 1, 1892]

Dearest Alice—I enclose the Hotel Bill which I found in my inside vest-pocket. It also occurred to me at 10 o'clock last night that we ought to have tried carbolated vaseline on poor Billy's skin, beginning with a few inches square to see how it worked. (Vaseline à l'acide phénique—faible). It might have allayed the itching, and why, oh *why*, didn't I think of it before? I hope your dear deserving head rested last night, but I fear it didn't, and I have a sort of conviction that it is aching to day. I spent a glorious time on the train, in that wonderful Rhône Valley so rich colored after the storm, and returned the devoutest thanks that my good angel had saved me from that temptation of the Evil one to go to London. Twould indeed have been the dog returning to his v——t, and the sow to her wallowing etc. Neither you nor Harry can understand the hollowness and in-nutrition of that sort of thing to me. What I *need* is to regain nervous *tone,* which brings health of soul with it, and that is what the blessed mountains and a moderate amount of solitude for a time can give. Tell Harry I am sorry to have given him so confused and ugly a day as he got yesterday, but he must remember that after two months of bedroom with Billy and peg, one grows explosive.[1]—And now darling, what shall I say of *you. Never* did you seem to me more noble commanding, more *on top,* than during the last few days. *Your* "nervous tone" is restored most beautifully, and if it is so under all you've been through, think what it will be after a month or two of real repose.—I am in the cheapest inn of the place, good bed with only one bug in it which I killed. Richard Feverel good, good.[2] Stone floors, walls 2 feet thick soaked with sin. Cobblestone streets, narrow, high stone houses, not a sprig of green, all that horrid latin-race wickedness and vileness sweating out of the look of things. That it should never occur to them to *want* any greenery or rusticity, shows a nature so different from ours.   Vivent les Allemands, les Anglais etc.—I bkfsd in Co. with a solitary English woman, of the lower orders, who has been in this hole since April because forsooth she can get German lessons at the Convent for *30 centimes* a lesson(!!).   It gives one an idea of frugality on both sides which America knows nothing of

I go now to the Post to get a place for Gletsch where it arrives this Evening—to morrow I will walk to Andermatt.

Let me know how billy is.   Love to all, including the dear brother,

W.J.

ALS: MH bMS Am 1092.9 (1815)

Address: Mrs. James | Hotel Riche-mont | à Lausanne

Postmarks: BRIGUE 1. VIII. 92   LAUSANNE 1. VIII. 92

[1] Writing to Grace Norton on 23 August 1892, HJ did not allude to WJ's explosion: "I was near William and his family in Switzerland rather than with them—as they were much dispersed" (*Henry James Letters*, ed. Leon Edel, 4 vols. [Cambridge: Belknap Press of Harvard Univ. Press, 1974–84], 3:394).

[2] George Meredith (1828–1909), British novelist, *The Ordeal of Richard Feveral* (1859).

To James Mark Baldwin

Pension Cruchon, | à Vers-chez-les-Blanc | (sur Lausanne) |
Switzerland | 9. 8. 92.

My dear Baldwin,

On returning from a 10-days trip *solus* to the Engadine, I find your letter of Aug 5. relative to an "extraordinary Congress in America next year," and containing the flattering suggestion that I should be its president.

You ask for an immediate reply.   I confess this gives me some embarassment, for I do not yet fully understand the plan.   Still, whatever it be, I don't see how I can possibly be "President" next year. All my plans are at present laid to continue in Europe with my family until the very last day of the vacation next summer, and I am by nature so little of a man for Societies, organizations, secretaryships, presidencies, powers, principalities, & politics (even the politics of Science) that I can't bring myself to change them.   So that to that part of your letter I must return a regretful but decided "no."   Either you or Stanley Hall would be a vastly more *efficient* president than I, even were I to be on the ground.

Next, as to the existence and organization of the proposed reunion. *Prima facie,* I can't say that it seems to me desirable to have the "International Congress" diminish the emphasis of its great meetings by intercalating extra meetings anywhere, though you who have been on the ground this summer may have seen reason to believe in good effects from more continuous intercourse. As a member of the *International Congress,* I should be rather opposed to this irregular offshoot. If, on the contrary, it is to be considered as a purely American affair, I think it ought to be referred to the newly constituted American Club of Psychologists of which you have doubtless received notice from Jastrow.[1] My own sentiment (which may, I confess, be entirely subjective) is that we Americans should do better to aim at the 1904 meeting. By that time, the beginnings which are so promising now with us will, I trust, have borne some rather solid fruit, and we might well expect to produce a somewhat startling impression of our activity on the foreigners who might come over. Just now we are hardly mature enough to offer them any very striking results. *I* say, therefore, *bide our time* and *claim* the 1904 meeting! I see no great use in the meeting you propose for next year, which will be neither genuinely American nor genuinely international. Aim at an american club pure & simple, and get all its members interested in working towards a great success at a meeting of the International Congress in America twelve years hence! Psychology, I opine, is at present hardly a massive enough subject to bear too frequent International assemblages. Hoping that this churlish sort of a response will not displease you too much, and feeling sure that my humble opinion will have very little practical effect on you more active men, I am ever faithfully yours,

Wm James

P.S. I have my boys in pastor's families near here learning french, but the winter abode is still unsettled. You tell me nothing of the Congress, but I expect to hear all about it from the Myerses who are to arrive here to morrow. I hope it was a great success. Poor M'berg writes me from Freiburg that he is down there with "gastric fever." I am sorry.

ALS: Bodleian Library, University of Oxford

[1] The founding meeting of the American Psychological Association was held on 8 July 1892, at the initiative of Granville Stanley Hall, with Joseph Jastrow acting as secretary. While WJ is listed as a charter member and sometimes, erroneously, as a participant on 8 July, it is generally believed that he was at best lukewarm about the project.

To Hugo Münsterberg

Vers chez les Blanc, sur Lausanne | 9. 8. 92.
My dear Münsterberg—I have but just received your letter from Freiburg of the 2nd August.   I am *excessively* grieved to hear of your illness.   That it should have come at just this particular moment is indeed a most unhappy stroke of fortune, for the visit to the London Congress would have been not only a most agreeable but also a most instructive experience for you, and the assembled psychologists ought certainly to have had the advantage of seeing the face and hearing the voice of one whose works have excited so much of their attention in recent years!   You speak of a gastric fever—an acute gastritis is a pretty serious thing, and I hope it is not that from which you have suffered.   But since you speak of being already convalescent, and of travelling away again soon I assume that all cause for anxiety must be over, and I only hope that you may never have a relapse.

I am using certain scraps of paper which are all that I can lay my hands on.   I only arrived here last night, and my wife who has the paper supply locked up is gone off on a walk.—It would appear from your letter that two of our epistles have gone astray.   I never received the letter you say you wrote me from Berlin, the last letter I had from you being at Lucerne, on the eve. of your departure from Freiburg.   You on the other hand appear never to have got a letter I wrote you from Lucerne (about the 8th of July?)[1] in which I advised you to telegraph to Mrs. Gibbens to take the rooms in Sumner Street for you.   I did this in consequence of a letter from her, and am glad to hear that Royce has already taken them.   I sent my letter to the care of your brother Otto in Danzig.—I hope you have already received the $600 for travelling expenses concerning which I wrote to President Eliot.   A letter from him of July 20th. says "There will of course be no difficulty in M's getting the $600."

As for ourselves, we are both feeling well, and I have had a certain amount of walking in these beautiful mountains, though less than I could wish.   I am just back from a flight of 8 days to the Engadin and Italian lakes, *solus.*   "The educational problem" is still *infernal*!   Our boys are at present in the families of 2 pastors, one at Lausanne, one near Vevey, learning french, and I think that in no case shall we go to Paris.   It looks as if we might stay hereabouts.   But I hanker after Germany; and having just heard of the Realgymnasium at Stuttgart with Willman at its head,[2] I am turning over the whole question again, and *may*, in a few days, run off to Stuttgart to see whether the place looks tempting for a winter abode. Had I foreseen this trouble, I should not have brought the children, nor taken my year of absence but simply given myself a long vacation of 4 months, bringing Mrs James for perhaps two months, and gone back to work in Cambridge next year. At present I envy you your prospect. I hear nothing from Nichols, and shall be sorry if he goes away to Cornell, for you will find him very useful if he stays.[3] If he does go, I should think that Mr. J. R. Angell would be the best man to appoint in his place. Angell is young, but *exceedingly* clear headed and practical, and made a more favorable impression on me last year than any student I have ever had, from the experimental point of view. As this is only a one year's appointment, we can hardly secure a better-known man. But I must leave that whole question to Royce, Nichols, you, and the President.

I hope that Mrs. Münsterberg is refreshed by her "Kur," that you will have no sea sickness, and that after the first shock of our American butter, bread, street pavements and various other things, you will begin to like the new life very well. You had better address me in case you write again before you leave (but I hardly think you will do so) "Pension Cruchon, Vers chez les Blanc, sur Lausanne, Schweitz.["]

Always heartily yours | Wm James

ALS: MB

[1] See letter of 6 July 1892.
[2] Willman was not identified. WJ may have been thinking of the well-known Otto Willmann (1839–1920), German educator, who was a professor at Prague.
[3] In 1892–93 Herbert Nichols taught Philosophy 2 at Harvard.

To Josiah Royce

10. 8. 92

Could you, as editor, launch a copy of the Int. J. of Ethics—the number containing my article on the Moral Philosopher etc (I can't recall the date), to the address of *Prof. Flournoy, Florissant 9, Genève, Switz.*?—I can think of no easier way of getting it to him. He is a most excellent fellow, with whom we find ourselves at this boarding house above Lausanne.—I hope all goes well with you and that next year's prospects loom large. M'berg just writes me that you have secured "board" for him in Sumner St. I am glad that that is settled. He is a dear lovable creature, and I *do* hope he may sometime learn

english. I haven't heard from Nichols, but M. says that he writes of
the Cornell appointment as not improbable. If he goes, either
Angell or Gilman would be my candidates, but you must settle it over
there.—We have our boys at last in pastor's families to learn french,
but the winter's prospects are still obscure, all on acc! of the direful
"educational problem." I have at last begun to "pick up" my normal
health & spirits. Mrs. J. very well. Love "von Haus zu Haus."

W.J.

Address *c. of Barings.*

APS: MH bMS Am 1092.9 (3609)

Address: Professor Royce | Irving Street | Cambridge (Mass.) | U.S. of A. | Amérique
Postmarks: LAUSANNE 10 VIII 92   NEW YORK AUG 20 92

To Alice Howe Gibbens James

Hotel d. Salines, Bex, Monday A.M. [August 15, 1892]—
We had a magnificent day yesterday, starting 6.30 from Hotel des
Diablerets over Col de la Croix to Gryon (the same walk I made with
Harry) a couple of hours with dinner at the Saussaz's, thence to les
Plans (with nearly an hour's nap on the grass by the way) and after
that to this place, some 7 hours in all. The Saussaz's were more
cordial than ever. I saw Frl. Hichbrunner who had been up the Cha-
mossaire the day before. She said that she spoke italian "même très
bien" and knew Florence well, didn't care where she lived. Is going
to Geneva to day, her missus having gone the day before. Got your
letter with enclosures, bless you. Am very glad about Slater, & appreciate the Merriman's agony. *That* business was bad![1]—F.W.H.M.
is a queer fellow—such intensity in his own line, or lines, I never
knew, but . . . . . Fl. is a brick. He leaves us to day, I am sorry to say.
I'm glad you give so good an acc! of Bill, who will, I hope, improve.
Switz! is good, good. Such a mass of goodness as we've seen! My
feet keep all right. Kiss Peg. Regards to Mrs. Flournoy.

W.J.

Tomorrow to Chamonix.

APS: MH bMS Am 1092.9 (1818)

Address: Madame James | à Vers chez les Blanc | sur Lausanne | Pension Cruchon
Postmark: BEX 15 VIII 92

[1] For similar remarks involving the Merrimans see letter of 12 September 1891.

To William Wilberforce Baldwin

Chamonix, Aug 18. 92

Dear Dr Baldwin,

I am taking the liberty of sending you *via* my brother Henry, this note of inquiry about Florence and its schools. You have been so extraordinarily kind to other members of the James family, that perhaps you will add to the debt by a short letter of written advice to me.

It looks rather as if Florence might be the line of least resistance in our search for winter quarters. I have long known of the Domangé school as having had a good reputation, but Henry tells me of a new English school which you had some part in promoting and which you think good. Therefore

1°. *Do* you still think it good?

2°. Is english the general language, and the boys mostly english?

3°. When does the term begin, and need one apply beforehand to get a boy in?

4°. Could you be the means of having a circular sent me?

5. Are the "sanitary" aspects of the building good?

I have two boys, one of 13 whom we shall *most likely* leave at Lausanne. The other, of ten, we shall certainly take to Florence if we go. What he *ought* to be getting is lots of either French or German? Mightn't Domangé's school be better for him by reason of the French?

Finally, one more question: How late is it safe to leave open the question of an apartment? Ought I to go to Fl. early in Sept. to be in time to get something sunny and heatable?—or might it be left till we all go, say Oct. 1st.?

Pray pardon this intrusive appeal—neccessity knows no law, and believe me your already most grateful

Wm James

Address: Pension Cruchon
    Vers-chez-les-Blanc
        sur Lausanne
            Suisse.

ALS: NNMor

To Alice Howe Gibbens James

Hotel du Mont Blanc | Chamoni<x>, Thursday, 18 Aug. 92 |
9.15 AM.

Dearest Alice—No letter from you this AM. at the P.O., so I write to
you instead.   You seem to me so spotlessly pure and quiet and unselfish where you are, so different from F. W. H. Myers whose desires
are so imperious, whose movements so impatient, and whose interests
at bottom so egoistic in their nature.   An unique individual for the
intensity of his life.   His poor brother is so different, and so subordi-
nated, but he has a beautiful conscientiousness and humbleness.[1]
Yesterday, as my card told you, we went up the Brévent, steep &
steady, but with a view which paid for all.   These Alps are absolutely
medicinal, and I can well understand the passion growing for higher,
higher, if the strength wd. only grow in proportion.   To day I feel
quite stale, and tho' the Myerses are ready to walk, we have agreed
to postpone anything till the P.M.   The weather is intensely hot, very
unusually so, and I suppose you get your share of it.   We shall leave
here sunday A.M. and I will spend that night in Geneva.   Have a card
or telegram for me at the Hotel de l'Ecu,[2] saying whether I can have
a bed in the pension.   If not, perhaps I must stay at the Richemont
till there is room and you can come down for another night.   "Regrets!"   How could there be.   I keep saying to myself, "if Alice were
only able to travel with me me and have her mind enlarged and her
soul uplifted by seeing all these delicious nooks, villages, streams, and
heights, how much better it would be for both of us.["]   But, as Bob
Temple used to say "it *mote* not be!"[3]   I have read hardly a thing
since I left except some of the delightful Anatole France[4] and Myers's
short but eloquent autobiography.[5]   In a remote and half conscious
way I think of next winter, and on the whole the Florence plan looks
good to me, tho' I imagine that the genius of the place will not be
very favorable to work, and I think we ought to think twice about
the cold for our younger children.   Loeser said that Mrs. Costello
was going to spend the winter there.   I am going now to write to
Loring, to Henry for Baldwin's address,[6] & to Harry & Billy.   You
can't tell what a pleasure it was to see Harry's so clear, handsome,
healthy and perfectly smiling face at the Cérésoles, who *are* a rather
superior family I think.   *He* will give us no anxiety, wherever he is.

Farewell, sweet sister of my soul!   W.J.

Warm greetings to the Flournoys, and kiss[es] to all the James's
principally to yourself.

P.S. I am forgetting to allude to Billy's heroic conduct in not asking to stay with you. Did he feed up, and get any better looking? Poor interesting little man—he *does* draw one's heart towards him. I am sure that the Thélin experience, if he does voluntarily stick to it, as now, will be worth vastly more to him than passive comfort by your side.

ALS: MH bMS Am 1092.9 (1819)

Address: Mrs. James | Pension Cruchon | Vers-chez-les Blanc | sur *Lausanne [*surrounding db. qts. del.*] | Suisse

Postmarks: CHAMONIX HAUTE-SAVOIE 18 AOUT 92   LAUSANNE 19. VIII. 92

[1] Arthur Thomas Myers.

[2] The James family had stayed at the Hôtel de l'Écu in Geneva in 1859.

[3] Robert Temple (b. 1840), one of WJ's Temple cousins, brother of Ellen James Temple Emmet Hunter among others.   For additional information see *Correspondence*, 4:619 and 6:14–16.

[4] Anatole France (1844–1924), French author.

[5] In 1893 (see letter of 9 July 1893) Frederic Myers printed several copies of his *Fragments of Inner Life* and distributed them to friends, including WJ.   Apparently, he also circulated the autobiography in manuscript.   After Myers's death his widow made great efforts to retrieve the copies; see *Correspondence*, 3:311n.   Eveleen Myers published an edited version of the autobiography in *Fragments of Prose and Poetry* (1904).

[6] William Wilberforce Baldwin.

To Margaret Mary James

Chamonix, Aug 18. [1892]

Sweet Peg![1]

Here is a kiss from your Dad, who is so far away. I hope that you are being a great comfort to your Mammy. Poor little Billy had to go back to school, but it was manly of him not to beg to stay at the Pension Cruchon. I hope the other girls and you are nice and having a nice time together. Blanche is a nice one.[2] Your Mammy writes that you play in the woods barefoot. That is good, for infancy.

With kisses to Tweedy and darling love to yourself I remain most affectionately yours

Wm James

ALS: MH bMS Am 1092.9 (2978)

[1] This letter, addressed to 'Miss Margaret Mary James', was enclosed in the letter of the same date to AGJ.

[2] Blanche (d. 1905), daughter of Théodore Flournoy.   She was several years older than Margaret Mary.

To James Mark Baldwin

Chamonix, August 20. [1892]

Yours of 12th just received here. You put on me—on one man—a somewhat absurd responsibility—absurd in the sense that a "Congress" whose being depends on one man's presence (and that man *such* a ½ man) confesses itself not founded in the eternal fitnesses and veracities. You, Hall or even Ladd would make better presidents. I vote for *you*. But let the potshards fight with the potshards. I stay here. I think we *have a right to claim* 1904.[1]

Bless you!

W.J.

TC: MH bMS Am 1092.1

[1] See letter to Baldwin of 9 August 1892.

To Hugo Münsterberg

Pension Cruchon | à Vers chez les Blanc | sur Lausanne | Aug 24. 92

My dear Münsterberg—if you call me "verehrter Herr Professor" any more, I shall refuse to speak to you when we meet, and send your letters back unread!!—So now you are warned!

On returning yesterday from a tramp through the mountains with F. W. H. and A. T. Myers I got your letter, and your card from the steamer. I meant to have sent you a card of adieu which you should have received on board, but I let the date pass by unperceived. How glad I am that you start with so smooth a sea. May it remain so to the end!

I am glad you got my letter after all, which I send to your brother's care,[1] but I am very sorry to have lost your letter from Berlin. When you get this, you will be housed in Sumner Street, and I can only hope that the shock of our bad streets and wooden houses will not be too great. Remember that the first weeks are always the lonely and unnatural ones, and that when work begins, your whole feeling towards America will change. I hope that Miss Gibbens will take you into my library and offer you the use of any books there which you may need. You will have a terribly hot week (we always do) the first week in September. After that it grows cool. With warmest regards and best wishes from both of us, to both of you, I am every truly yours

Wm James

ALS: MH bMS Am 1092.9 (3272)
[1] Otto Münsterberg.

To Théodore Flournoy

Pensione Villa Maggiore | Sept 19. 1892

My dear Flournoy,

Your most agreeable letter—one of those which one preserves to read in one's old age—came yesterday. I had only been waiting, to write to you, until our plans should be more definitively known. We are waiting now for a word from our friend the American doctor at Florence to know whether it is safe to take the baby there immediately.[1] If so we shall go. If not, I think we shall go to Alassio for two or three weeks. (A. is a watering place on the mediterranean near Genoa)—We were driven from Chateau d'Oex by the cold and wet after a week, but had a fine day on the Simplon, and have been at this place for eight days. The house is fine but very dirty and ill-kept, and the weather fine, but hot as hades. The lake is beautiful enough, but the town repulsive. I am glad to have got into such prosaic, practical, and commonplace relations with a place which for most people is as exclusively romantic as the Lago Maggiore. A delightful Swiss pension in the country at Canobbio near the head of the lake was full so we couldn't get into it, and this place is so bad as to table etc that we can't stay much longer. The material perfections of Switzerland seem quite ideal now that one has turned his back on them forever!—but I sincerely hope not forever.

I am *much* obliged to you for the paper by Secrétan,[2] and (unless you deny me the permission) I propose to keep it, and let you get a new one, which you can do more easily than I. It is much too oracular & brief, but its *pregnancy* is a good example of what an intellect gains by growing old: One says vast things simply. I read it stretched on the grass of Monte Motterone, the Righi of this region, just across the Lake, with all the kingdoms of the Earth stretched before me, and I realized how exactly a philosophic Weltansicht resembles that from the top of a mountain. You are driven, as you ascend, into a choice of fewer and fewer paths, and at last you end in two or three simple attitudes from each of which we see a great part of the Universe amazingly simplified and summarized, but nowhere the entire view at once. I entirely agree that Renouvier's system fails to satisfy, but it seems to me the classical and consistent expression of *one* of the great attitudes, that of insisting on logically intelligible formulas. If one goes beyond, one must abandon the hope of *formulas* altogether, which is what all pious sentimentalists do; and with them M. Secrétan, since he fails to give any articulate substitute for the "Criticism" he finds so unsatisfactory. Most philosophers give formulas, and inadmissible ones, as when Secrétan makes a *mémoire sans oubli* = duratio tota simul = eternity!

I have been reading with much interest the articles on the will by Fouillée in the Revue Phil. for June and August.[3] There are admirable descriptive pages, though the final philosophy fails to impress me much. I am in good condition now, and must try to do a little methodical work every day in Florence, in spite of the temptations to flânerie of the sort of life.

I did hope to have spent a few days in Geneva before crossing the Mountains! But perhaps for the holidays you and Madame Flournoy will cross them too and see us at Florence. The Vers chez les Blanc-days are something that neither she nor I will forget! You and I are strangely contrasted as regards our professorial responsibilities, you are becoming entangled in laboratory research and demonstration just as I am getting emancipated. As regards *demonstrations* I think you will not find much difficulty in concocting a program of classical observations on the senses etc. for students to verify;—it worked much more easily at Harvard than I supposed it would when we applied it to the whole class, and it improved the spirit of work very much. As regards *research,* I advise you not to take that duty too conscientiously, if you find that ideas and projects do not abound. As long as a man is working at anything, he must give up other things at which he might be working, and the best thing he can work at is usually the thing he does most spontaneously. You philosophize, according to your own account, more spontaneously than you work in the laboratory. So do I, and I always felt that the occupation of philosophizing was with me a valid excuse for neglecting laboratory work, since there is not time for both. Your work as a philosopher will be more *irreplaceable* than what results you might get in the laboratory out of the same number of hours. Some day I feel sure that you will find yourself impelled to publish some of your reflections. Until then, take note and read, and feel that your true destiny is on the way to its accomplishment! It seems to me that a great thing would be to add a new course to your instruction. Au revoir, my dear friend! My wife sends "a great deal of love" to yours, and says she will write to her as soon as we get settled. I also send my most cordial greetings to Madame Flournoy. Remember me also affectionately to those charming young *demoiselles* who will I am afraid, incontinently proceed to forget me.

Always affectionately yours | Wm James

ALS: MH bMS Am 1505 (4)

[1] In his letter to William Wilberforce Baldwin of 14 September 1892 (calendared) WJ asked about the quality of the milk in Florence.

[2] Charles Secrétan (1815–1895), Swiss philosophical writer.

[3] Alfred Fouillée, "Existence de la volonté," *Revue Philosophique* 33 (June 1892): 577–600; "Le Développement de la volonté," pt. 1, *Revue Philosophique* 34 (August 1892): 159–81.

To Charles William Eliot

Florence, Oct 1. 92

Dear President,

Prof. Münsterberg, at the end of a long letter in which he expresses his satisfaction with Cambridge, now that he is settled, says that the assistant question is still dark for him, etc.—He will have made you acquainted with his difficulties; and before now you will doubtless have seen Dr Nichols on the subject. So far as my understanding with Nichols went, he was to be autonomous in Phil 2; that is to say, Münsterberg was to have no authority in deciding how he should carry it on. Apart from this, I supposed that Münsterberg, as Director of the Laboratory, was to have entire authority, that *all* assistants were to be directly accountable to him, and that whatever work went on (except the exercises in Philosophy 2) must have his approval. I supposed, and suppose, that Nichols understands this as a matter of course. It was also understood between Nichols and me that the laboratory should have a third person as assistant. I think this was mentioned by me to you also. In its report to the Committee on Assistants answering the Committee's question, the dept of philosophy said that there would be work for two laboratory assistants of a manual sort, each six hours a week or more. I supposed that Nichols himself should give what Laboratory *demonstrations* might be required to Phil. 2, whilst the keeping the apparatus in order, the clerical work, etc, would fall to the assistant. I never doubted that this was also Nichols's view, though I can't remember any explicit conversation on the subject with him. It was never mentioned, nor did it ever occur to me, that N. should have an assistant subject to his orders alone, unless by some division of labor that should prove desirable to Münsterberg after work got started.   In other words there could be no question of *coordination* of N. with M. in the laboratory.   On the other hand I did not say or expect that M. should have a claim on N's services as a *manual* assistant.   But as a general helper, coadjutor interpreter etc., in the higher laboratory instruction I supposed he would have a right to claim some of Nichols's time.   It is hard to define such assistance in set terms in advance, and no attempt was made to do so; but the expectation was repeatedly expressed by me to Nichols (and never, that I remember, demurred to) that he was to do anything reasonably in his power to facilitate M's laboratory instruction.

I have no doubt that everything has solved itself *ambulando* by this time, without need of set stipulations.   Münsterberg appears to be the soul of amiability; and Nichols, whatever he may say or do at a given moment, is in the long run a thoroughly unselfish and helpful fellow, who would never stand and see things suffer for lack of his lending a hand.—He may be in poor nervous condition by this time, however, for want of summer change, and anxiety about money and the future.

I *do* hope the Laboratory will be a great success!   Münsterb., who has seen them all, writes that it is now the best equipped of all.   *I* am well set up by the vacation and ready for work again.   I often wish I were going back now!   My wife is also very well.   The fate of the children has been a great worry—some obstruction everywhere. At last we are here, and here I suppose we shall stay for the winter. There is a new boy's school (english!) said to be very good.

I hope that your summer and Mrs. Eliot's has been "crowned" with every benefit, and I send up my prayers for a prosperous academic year.

Always faithfully yours   Wm. James (c/o Barings)

ALS: MH Archives

To Hugo Münsterberg

16 Piazza dell Independenza | Firenze, Oct. 5. 92

My dear Münsterberg   (Still the word "verehrter" in your mode of address! *pray* address me as I address you—that is our custom!) Your truly monumental letter of Sept 17th. rejoiced my heart two days ago.   What a sickening time you must have had of it at first, but how quickly you appear to have got over it. I now must pray every night that you and Mrs. Munsterberg will not have a relapse. I think, however, that when work has once begun you will keep cheerful all the time. Our bread, our roads, our newspapers, *are* bad indeed. Eat *toast!* No need of having bad *matches* with us; and as for our watermelons anyone who speaks ill of them is my personal enemy! I remember well the house you are in. We thought of hiring it ourselves before the Mulfords came there. The rooms are pleasantly shaped, as I recollect them, and the garden then was very large, with a pleasant open field opposite. But the whole street has been spoiled in the last few years by the building of so many new cheap houses. It would have been pleasant indeed to think of you in *our* house, but I quite appreciate your feeling about a three years' lease. Our house, notwithstanding its size, is *very* easy to keep house in, owing to its convenient arrangement; and not very expensive to heat.

I wrote immediately upon getting your letter, to President Eliot and to Nichols, telling both of them what I understood the arrangement with Nichols to be.

1. N. to be autonomous class-room & lab. work in *Phil* 2.

2 *All* other laboratory work, by whomever performed, to be subject to your approval.

3. *All* laboratory assistants to be immediately subject to your orders.

4. N. to give lab. *instruction* in Phil. 2., but to have *manual* assistance in his laboratory-work there.

5. N. to yield you no *manual* assistance (unless voluntarily), but to be ready at all times to aid you in the instruction which you give, as interpreter, adviser etc. etc.

6. One or two young manual assistants to be appointed.

I feel sure that the whole thing will have smoothed itself out by this time. I know the unselfish character of Nichols, & his frankness; and knowing also your amiability, I don't see how there can be any friction between you. If there is, *the president* is the man to arbitrate.

I can write no more to day. We moved into this furnished apartment last night, having taken it for 6 months. Florence is pleasant, but the proper place for *children* is *home;* and my wife felt this morning very much as I think you must have felt when you first woke up in Cambridge. *No* conveniences in the house, and a man-cook with whom we communicate by naked Aryan roots without terminations. He seems nevertheless to catch our meaning even better than we do his!

Good success to you all! I am so glad you are pleased with the Laboratory.

Yours ever, | Wm James

ALS: MH bMS Am 1092.9 (3273)

To Charles Ritter

16 Piazza dell' Independenza | Firenze, Oct 5. 92

My dear Ritter,

We left Switzerland after all without getting to Geneva again, or seeing you. The week of bad weather which occurred early in September found us at Château d'Oex. We had meanwhile decided upon spending the winter in Florence; and, not knowing how long the cold and rain would last, we came down to Brieg and went over the Simplon on the very day on which the clearing occurred. I don't regret it much; for after 8 days on Lake Maggiore we came here and found that we had the pick of all the furnished apartments in town. Two days ago we moved into this one on the P.ª del' Indep.ª It is sunny, clean, and roomy, and if the boy's school turns out good, and the little children keep well, our winter indoors will probably be a happy one. *Out of doors* there can be no doubt of it, for Florence seems to me even more attractive than it was when I was here 18 years ago. We have taken our apartment for six months. I shall read philosophy, dabble a little in the history of art, and lead a very quiet winter.

But how sovereignly *good* is Switzerland! It meets all the major needs of body and soul as no other country does, in summer time. After the aesthetics, the morbidness, the corruptions of Italy, how I shall want again in *ihrem Thau gesund mich zu baden!* You have doubtless been shocked by Renan's death.[1] A true magician, but a man who caused legitimate disappointment by the form which his intellect finally found most congruous. He used the vocabulary of the moral and religious life too sweetly and freely for one whose thought refused to be *bound* by those ideals. Moral ideals go with refusals and sacrifices, & there is something shocking about the merely *musical* function they play in Renan's pages. So I call him *profoundly* superficial! But *what* an artist!—I am so sorry, my dear old Ritter, that you and my wife couldn't meet. Let us hope for next summer; and meanwhile let me pray that your winter may be full of happiness, and in particular that your *eyes* may remain in good condition.

Always truly and affectionately yours   Wm James

ALS: Bibliothèque publique et universitaire, Geneva

[1] Joseph-Ernest Renan died on 2 October 1892.

To James Sully

16 Piazza dell' Independenza, | Florence, Oct. 5, 92.

My dear Sully:

Your kind note is just received.

What a shock about poor Robertson![1]   I had not expected anything of this kind so soon, and it fills me with regret that the letter I had been meaning to write to him about this time should never have been written.   But now that it is over, I think we can call it a mercy.   The battle was lost for him, the rest of life however long could hardly have been anything but a history of endurance and resignation, and the sooner it's over the sooner to sleep.   Considering what the lamentations of some men would have been, the utter unquerulousness of Robertson in the conditions of the last ten years has been simply magnificent.   As Read says, he was *magnanimous,* a bright example to us all![2]   His monument, in the 14 volumes of Mind, is after all one to be satisfied with.[3]   God keep him!

I return Read's letter, with thanks.   Pray give *him* my remembrances (most cordial ones, when you next meet him).   You and I will surely meet ere I return, but I fear not in so good a place as the immortal Schweiz.   We have just moved into a furnished apartment (see dating of letter) where we expect to spend six months.   A letter addressed to Baring Bros. & Co's care will always get me.   My respects to Mrs. Sully, and hearty wishes that you may have a thoroughly satisfactory first year in poor R's old place.

Yours always, | W.J.

TC: MH bMS Am 1092.1

[1] George Croom Robertson died on 20 September 1892.

[2] Carveth Read (1848–1931), British philosopher. Correspondence with WJ is known from 1898 to 1909.

[3] Robertson edited sixteen volumes of *Mind.*

To William Mackintire Salter

16 Piazza dell' Independenza, Florence, Oct. 6, '92.
My dear Mack,

. . . So the magician Renan is no more! I don't know whether you were ever much subject to his spell. If so, you have a fine subject for Sunday lectures! The queer thing was that he so slowly worked his way to his natural mental attitude of irony and persiflage, on a basis of moral and religious material. He levitated at last to his true level of superficiality, emancipating himself from layer after layer of the inhibitions into which he was born, and finally using the old moral and religious vocabulary to produce merely musical and poetic effects. That moral and religious ideals, seriously taken, involve certain refusals and renunciations of freedom, R. seemed at last entirely to forget. On the whole, his sweetness and mere literary coquetry leave a displeasing impression, and the only way to handle him is not to take him heavily or seriously. The worst is, he was a *prig* in his ideals.—Excuse this—Much love from both to both!

Yours ever, | W.J.

TC incomplete: MH bMS Am 1092.9 (3673)

To Ellen James Temple Emmet Hunter

16 Piazza dell' Indipendenza, | Oct 9. 1892
My dear, dear Elly,

You know my tardiness and lethargy about writing letters, and can probably account for the long silence which has emanated from me to-you-ward without supposing death, insanity, or alienation of affection. I have tho't of you very often, and often been "on the point" of writing, but my nerveless hand has never actually grasped the pen till now. Invincible intellectual laziness took the place of the overstrained activity of the past two years the moment I got on the ship, and has faded away so slowly that it is only within the past month that I feel as if I had possession of my natural brains again. It seemed a good normal way of resting from fatigue, so I let it take its course, and think now that I was wise. I suppose I ought to give you some account of what we have been up to. It was after many misgivings that we decided to come for the whole year and bring the entire family, and I think now that the misgivings were fully justified. Children, even of Harry's age, don't enjoy travelling or sight seeing, or "promenading," which is the only sort of sport open to them. They have been sick a great deal, possibly from change of climate. The school question for the boys has, for one reason or another, proved insoluble in the way in which I had hoped to solve it, namely putting them into a french or German government school; and after a summer of anguish, perplexity and shilly-shallying in Switzerland, we have brought up, of all places in the world, in Florence, where they are to go to an *english* school, and learn perforce some *italian* (which they don't in the least need and will probably make no use of hereafter) but where at least *we* can be comparatively happy, and where they can play cricket and foot-ball in a regular way. Oh for a world where children could cease from troubling & babies be at rest! We have had the doctor for three of them since being here; and *did n't* I give you good advice when I told you to leave all yours at home for your own honeymoon year! Alice has led an exclusively nursery-existence since being abroad, and it isn't what she ought to have come for.—Don't think me an unnatural parent, Elly; I like the brats well, only a life *exclusively* occupied with making them contented is not just the change one craves for in one's sabbatical year. Besides, we have kept this tolerably well pent up from the Gibbens relatives, and it does one good to open the sluices to an ancient intimate like thee— "One in whose gentle bosom I, may bury all my heart of woes, like the care-burthened honey-fly, that hides his murmur in the rose" . . etc, etc.

Florence is delicious, we have a clean and sunny apartment, a man-cook with whom we converse in naked latin roots without terminations (and who strange to say seems to catch our meaning), a gigantic Bernese Governess of ungovernable appetite,[1] and, although there are no domestic conveniences of any sort whatever for housekeeping, we shall (if we don't freeze) probably pass a very happy winter, and one of which the *future* fruit for the children will be important. Our house in Cambridge isn't rented yet, and probably won't be. We saw Harry for a week at Lausanne. He was well and benignant, is working still at the drama, and I devoutly hope that some of his things may receive the glare of the footlights. Bob's father-in-law died in the Spring, less rich than was supposed, but still very comfortably off, and left something to all his grandchildren and to Mary.[2] She and her children, with Wilky's carrie and his children, are now in Europe, probably going to spend the winter in Dresden. I haven't seen any of them yet. Bob remains at home in Concord for the present, though I suppose he may come abroad in the Spring.—So much for the state of the facts about our side of the house.

And now for yours. Bert Dibblee, whom I occasionally met last year, has been my only informant concerning you, and of course he could tell me nothing but the names of certain localities where you had been.[3] The last news was of Pelham. Of course you may believe that we are both eager to hear something more authentic & first hand. So sit *right down now* (to wait 24 hours will be to wait 6 months!) and give a full account of yourself, Mr. Hunter, Kitty[4] & her tribe, Henrietta, and everyone else. *Don't* let us hear you say that this marriage is already unhappy, or that Mr. Hunter especially regards it as the crowning folly of his life! *Anything* but that! Treat him well, Elly, be submissive, don't insist on your own way in *Everything.* Give him a chance!—Cordiallest regards to him, and to you the old tap! i.e love, from both of us.—Address as above   Love to Kitty, Henrietta & all.

W.J.

ALS: MH bMS Am 1092.9 (1072)

Address: Mrs. George Hunter | c/o Richard S. Emmet Esq | Pelham, N.Y | Stati Uniti di America; forwarded to Box 101 | Southampton Long Island | U.S.A.

Postmarks: PELHAM N.Y. OCT 24 1892   NEW YORK OCT 22 92   NY 10-24-92

[1] Fräulein Hichbrunner.

[2] Edward Dwight Holton (1815–1892), a wealthy businessman and railroad promoter in Milwaukee.

[3] Albert James Dibblee (b. 1870), a lawyer, one of the children of Annie Meacham Dibblee.

[4] Katharine Temple Emmet.

To Grace Ashburner

16 Piazza dell Indipendenza | Florence, Oct 19. 92

My dear Grace,

It is needless to say that your long and delightful reply written by Theodora's self-effacing hand reached us duly, and that I have "been on the point" of writing to you again ever since. That "point," as you well know, is one to which somehow one seems long to cleave without jumping off. But at last here goes—irrevocably! I did not expect that in your condition you would be either so conscientious or so energetic as to send so immediate and full a return, and I must expressly stipulate, my dear old friend, that the sole condition upon which I write now is that you shall not feel that I expect a single word of answer. [Needless to say, however, how much any infringement of this condition on your part will be *enjoyed*.]

Well! Cold and wet drove us out of Switzerland the first week in September, though, as it turned out, we should have had a fine rest of the month if we had stayed. We crossed the Simplon to Pallanza on Lake Maggiore where we stayed ten days till the bad fare made us sick, and then came straight to Florence by the 21st. As almost no strangers had arrived, we had the pick of all the furnished apartments, most of which threatened great bleakness or gloominess for the winter, with their high ceilings, and *some* rooms in all of them lit from court or well. Our family seems to be of the maximum size for which apartments are made! We found but this one into all the rooms of which the sun can come either before- or afternoon. It is clean, and abundantly furnished with sofas & chairs, but not a "convenience for housekeeping" of any kind whatsoever. No oven in which to make maccaroni *au gratin,* no place to keep more than a weeks supply of charcoal, or I fear more than 3 or 4 days supply of wood for the fire when the cold weather comes, as come it will with a vengeance, from all accounts. I hope our children won't freeze! Harry and Billy started school at last 2 days ago, and glad I am to see them at it. In the immortal words of our townsman Rindge in his monumental inscription, "every man," and every boy, "should have an honest occupation."[1] What they need is comrades of their own age, & competitive play and work, rather than monuments of antiquity or landscape beauty. Animal, not vegetable or mineral life, is their element. The school is english, they'll get no more french or german there than at Nichols' and Brown's, and they'll have to begin Italian, I'm afraid, which will be pure interruption and leave not a rack behind after they've been home a year. Still one mustn't always grumble about one's children; and they are getting an amount of perception over here, and a freedom from prejudices about american things and ways which will certainly be of general service to their intelligence, and be worth more to them hereafter than their year would have been if spent in drill for the Harvard exams,—even if what they lose do amount to a whole year, which I much doubt. But I think it may be called certain that they shan't be kept abroad a *second* year!

For ourselves, Florence is delicious. I have a sort of organic protestation against certain things here, the toneless air in the streets which feels like used up indoor air, the "general debility" which pervades all ways and institutions, the worn out-faces, etc. etc. But the charming sunny manners, the old world picturesqueness wherever you cast your eye, and above all the magnificent remains of art redeem it all, and insidiously spin a charm round one which might well end by turning one into one of these mere northern loungers here for the rest of one's days, recreant to all one's native instincts. The stagnancy of the thermometer is the great thing. Day after day a changeless air, sometimes sun and sometimes shower, but no other difference except possibly from week to week the faintest possible progress in the direction of cold. It must be very good for one's nerves after our acrobatic climate. We have an excellent man-cook, the most faithful of beings, at 2½ dollars a week. He never goes out except to market, and understands, strange to say the naked latin roots without terminations in which we hold *un*sweet discourse with him. But on Dante and Charles Norton's ADMIRABLE "pony" I am getting up the lingo fast![2]

All this time I am saying nothing about you or your sister or the dear Childs, or the Norton's or any one. Of your own condition we have got very scanty news indeed since your letter, from Mrs Gibbens. Perhaps Theodore[3] will just sit down and write two pages—not a *letter,* if she is n't ready, but just two pages—to give some authentic account of how the fall finds you all, especially you. I hope the opium business and all has not given you additional trouble, and that the pain has not made worse havoc than before. When one thinks of your patience and good cheer, my dear dear Grace, through all of life, one feels grateful to the Higher Powers for the example. Please take the heartfelt love of both of us, give some to your dear Sister and to Theodora, and believe me ever your affectionate,

Wm James

Love, too, to the Nortons old & young, and to the Childs'

ALS: MH bMS Am 1092.9 (726)

Address: Miss Grace Ashburner | Kirkland S! | Cambridge | Mass | Stati Uniti di A.
Postmarks: FIRENZE 19 10 92   NEW YORK OCT 30 92   CAMBRIDGE BOSTON MA<SS>
OCT 31 92

[1] In 1887 Frederick H. Rindge gave several parcels of land to the City of Cambridge, with the condition that inscriptions specified by Rindge be placed on the buildings built on the lots. WJ is quoting the inscription on the Manual Training School building, which was several minutes walk from his house on one of several possible routes between the James house and Harvard.

[2] Probably Charles Eliot Norton, *Notes of Travel and Study in Italy* (1860).

[3] A slip for 'Theodora'.

To James Ward

16 Piazza dell Indipendenza | Florence, Nov. 1. 92

My dear Ward,

I must thank you for your very "handsome" review of my "Briefer Course" in the October Mind, which only reached me a few days since.[1] I ought to apologize or in some way "make it up" to you for giving out so much of your precious self on so unworthy an occasion, but it's all in the line of our trade, so I won't waste time on humility. Your heartily expressed objections give to the cordiality of the praise all the more solidity of flavor; and feeling as I do the desperate character of all psychologizing, that you should find any merit at all in the book is enough for the notice to seem to me in the main highly flattering.

Yes, I *am* too unsystematic & loose! But in this case I permitted myself to remain so deliberately, on account of the strong aversion with which I am filled for the humbugging pretense of exactitude in the way of definition of terms and description of states that has prevailed in psychological literature. What does a human being really learn from it all beyond what he knew already by the light of nature?—*But*—I doubtless have carried my reaction too far, so I won't defend myself. I admit that the best pedagogic order would be a general analysis followed by a detailed synthesis (only the analysis seems to me to be one of the things we need no book for) but when you contend for *genetic* treatment I must say that you seem to me unpractical. What *light* is shed by enumerating the *order* in which terms (themselves unexplained) make their appearance? For I shouldn't suppose that for *you* the namby-pamby baby-lore of M. B. Pérez would have any instructiveness, nor that even such careful genetic description as Sully's account of the growth of space perception in his last book, would really appear explanatory.[2] The real thing to aim at is a *causal* account; and I must say that that appears to lie (provisionally at least) in the region of the laws as yet unknown of the connexion of the mind with the body. There is *the* subject for a "Science" of psychology!

As for what you say of the relation of feeling to emotion and action, I will admit that what one may call *elementary* feeling may be an integral part of all consciousness. What you, Külpe, and lately Fouillée have written on that seems to me pretty conclusive.[3] Only in developed states, the elements grow so magnified out of all proportion to each other that the state is called by the name of one or the other exclusively. As I discussed the hedonistic contention, it was the doctrine that states of feeling in the developed sense are the only conceivable springs of action that I combatted. If you fall back on the germinal infinitesimal element of feeling, which all consciousness must have, to save psychological hedonism, it seems to me you have given up the case as commonly held, and raised another question altogether, of an interesting theoretic kind, it is true, and essential to psychology, but disconnected with the old historic battle. It is only in this transcendental sense that I should be disposed to admit that *thought of pleasure is* a pleasure. I have taken things too coarsely, however I dare say, so I bow my head. As regards the Self, I can't bow my head, and I feel really discouraged at the difference that subsists between us. It makes me suspect misunderstanding, especially since you protest against sensations knowing sensible qualities. It is surely the sensational "element" in a mental state by means of which that state knows a sensible fact.

But here we come upon elements vs. states, and the whole problem of synthesis, concerning which all that has been written (either by you or by me I feel like saying) is as nought. There can be no psychology worth the paper it is written on [*except* the science of the correlations of brain states with objects known] until something sound in epistemology is done.

Pray go ahead and do it!

Yours always, fraternally and teachably, | Wm James
P.S.

Your *boutade* on the S.P.R, since it touched others, I have just written a short note about to the Editor.[4]

ALS: MH bMS Am 1092.9 (3834)

[1] James Ward, review of *Psychology: Briefer Course* in *Mind,* n.s., 1 (October 1892): 531–39.

[2] Sully discusses the development of space perception in *The Human Mind;* see WJ's review of the book in *ECR,* 428–29.

[3] For a possible article by Külpe see *ML,* 211.

[4] WJ's letter, dated 24 October 1892, appeared in *Mind,* n.s., 2 (January 1893): 144, together with a rejoinder by Ward, dated 11 December 1892. Both are reprinted in *EPR.*

To Alice Howe Gibbens James

Albergo Croce d'Oro, Padova | Nov 2. '92
Beloved Wife,   It may seem mean after being in such vile spirits
when with you to write to you now when alone that I have rarely in
my life passed a day of greater contentment, but you wish to know
the truth and that is it.   The contentment doesn't come from your
absence, (far from it, for I've done little else but wish that you were
by my side) but from the extraordinary satisfaction which this place
yields to the eye.   It soothes it as stillness soothes the ear or lukewarm water the skin.   I surrender to Italy, and I should think that
a painter would almost go out of his skin to wander about from town
to town.   One wants to paint everything that one sees in a place like
this—as a *town* Florence can't hold a candle to it.   She has her galleries, her palaces and her bridges, but the rest is encumbrance, here it
is the entire town that speaks to one in the most charming unpretending way.   I spent 61 francs on the whole set of Arena Chapel
Giotto's.[1]   I understand G's eminence now.   It started the tears in
my eyes to see the way the little old fellow had gone to work with
such joyousness & spirit on that Place, and it is an honour to human
nature that so many people feel under his quaintness that he is a
moral painter.   No carriages in the streets, most of the houses with
arcades so as to make you see just what the old painters had in mind
in the architecture which they reproduce.

Sig. Ermacora was a shy and rather dingy man of about 30, looking
much less intelligent than he is.   The lady is a little weak sprig of a
thing who wrote a good deal very illegibly, but I gained nothing by
seeing it.   To night he calls for me again, introduces me to some of
his friends, and hopes to show me a little more.[2]

I think I must have another lick at Giotto to morrow forenoon and
then at 1 & something go to Venice.   It is absurd to hesitate when I
am so near, although I feel as if I ought to be at home with my
own children.—I telegraphed to day to your mother *not* to send the
overcoat!   15 francs.   Such submission to you does separation bring.
Kiss the dear boys.   Also the dear Peg, & get them to kiss you for

W.J.

ALS: MH bMS Am 1092.9 (1821)

[1] Most of the early work of Giotto is represented by the frescoes in the Capella degli
Scrovegni in Padua.

[2] Ermacora was experimenting with Maria Manzini, an automatic writer living in
Padua; see letter to Myers of 14 November 1892.

To Alice Howe Gibbens James

Hotel Britannia Venice | Nov 4. 92
Beloved wife. To think of finding oneself *accidentally* within 35 minutes of Venice!   I rose this AM. after a good night wrote 8 pp. to
Myers, bkfstd. and sallied forth once more to see my dear little Padua.
The weather was most exquisite.   Summer without heat—and in the
midst of November.   Saw glorious frescoes by Avanzi & Altichieri in
the Capella S. Giorgio,[1] and then the rather poor collection of pictures in the Museo Civico, and strolled till 12/30 when paid hotel bill
and took train.   Glorious day for Venice which I find the same mixture of squalor and gorgeousness as ever, only stro[n]ger looking both
ways than before.   Went to S. Zaccaria to see a John Bellini altar
piece that had struck me as the most *perfect* thing in Venice before,[2]
but they had moved it into a bad light, and it made hardly any impression on me at all—a good example of the capricious way in which
our minds act.   Other places being closed I have loafed about the
town & read Times in reading room of Hotel till now (6.30) & dressed
for table d'hôte of which bell has just rung so I must go down.   Begin
to feel a little tired, and Venice has n't the *purity* of the smaller places
to counteract it.—Last night with Ermacora & 5 friends for 2 hours,
I understood all the narratives they told in Italian to my surprise and
satisfaction.   Your post card came.   Others will be forwarded.
                                              Heaven bless you all! | W.

ALS: MH bMS Am 1092.9 (1822)

   [1] Jacopo Avanzi and Altichierro, fourteenth-century Italian painters.

   [2] Giovanni Bellini (ca. 1430–1516), Italian painter. WJ probably saw the altarpiece
in 1882, on HJ's recommendation; see *Correspondence*, 1:334.

To Alice Howe Gibbens James

Albergo Britannia Venice, Nov 5. '92 | 5.45 PM.
Darling Alice I got in a quarter of an hour ago after sightseeing the
whole day.   I slept late & sound and didn't get out till ½ past 9.
Spent 4½ hours in the Academy, which seems less stupendous to me
than it used to, & I am inclined to think, with Denman Ross, that
Venitian pictures don't wear quite as well as some others.   Lunched
at a pastry cook's and then found my way on foot to the Frari Church
where in the fading light I saw the great monuments on the walls.
Back partly on foot partly in steamer on Gd. Canal.   The days has
been foggy & cheerless but not cold, and I am glad at last to have

seen Venice in a work-aday atmosphere, colourless, prosaic and american. The Canal seemed on the whole richer to me than ever before
as I swiftly passed between its multitudinous ruins in the falling
night. On the whole I get a stronger idea of the *weight* which Venice
must have had in old times. But the place reeks of vice and sin as
no other place on earth seems to. Such cavernous houses for people
to live in, such swarms of people *all* dirty and poor living off each
others scabs & rags to all appearance. A wicked place! I bought a
pair of silver salt cellars (which are really good) for 55 frs. They will
do for a wedding present for somebody. I noted down a good many
things about paintings, but I doubt whether I can ever get up my
famous lecture. I went to the theatre last night, a roman tragedy of
which I found I could understand only isolated words, not even the
general sense. Discouraging. I stayed an hour, admiring the beautiful elocution of the chief actress, and think I shall go again to night,
as I don't feel at all tired, except as to the eyes.—I long to know how
you are getting on, all by yourself. I shall stay over to morrow, being
here, and probably go back on Monday, unless it seems really important that I should see more pictures. Dearest, I do love you, and
ever shall more and more.

Your | W.

ALS: MH bMS Am 1092.9 (1823)

From James Rowland Angell

Berlin. Potsdamerstrasse 123^{IV} | Nov. 6, '92.
My dear Prof. James:
   Nichol's article, which you so kindly sent, reached me in the midst
of the turmoil consequent to settling down in a new abode, and I
have been awaiting a period of comparative calm in which I could
both read and acknowledge it.[1] I am exceedingly obliged to you,
the more so that the library here contains no traces of the Phil. Review, although a horde of less important American publications are
accessible. Despite some obvious flaws in arrangement,—to say
nothing of the style—I think Nichols has at last succeeded in making
perfectly clear his fundamental notions and his reasons for the same.
Unless I greatly err, he has failed to comprehend with any justice the
position of what he would call the "old school", and for myself I
cannot help feeling that he has vastly overestimated the significance
of Goldscheider's somewhat tentative results. I wrote the latter opin-

ion to him recently and I was in some measure reassured to see in a notice of the article in the last number of "Mind" that the reviewer considered "that he has quite misconceived the purport of Gold-scheiders discoveries" or words almost identical.[2] I will not trust my memory for perfect verbal accuracy and anyway you have doubtless seen the paragraph.   But whether—as I think—he has failed to make his case, or not, he is unquestionably entitled to congratulation for the great ingenuity with which he has turned a new light on a great body of facts.   There is much of genuine suggestive worth in the whole article I think.   As for his excursions in the higher Aesthetics I have little to say.   On his own showing, if his theory represents the facts, the higher values of Aesthetics are obviously so elaborated and artificially evolved out of their original elements that any study of them with reference to scientific classification must proceed in a manner identical with that now employed, and our situation is exactly what it was before.

I have been reading the last day or so Wundt's last publication—a most excellent little critical essay on hy[p]notism.[3] He makes the subject the excuse for firing some hot shot into the Society for Psych. Research, and into some Berlin and Paris Societies which have pre-sumed to recognise work on hypnotic subjects as legitimate experi-mental psychology.   On the whole the tone is candid and fair and the essay seems to me a valuable contribution to the literature of the subject.   As one might anticipate, the outcome for him is the dis-carding of hypnotism from the ranks of experimental psychologic method, and accepting his definition of psychol. method—strict sci-entific method—the conclusion strikes me as valid.   At this point my own presumption floods my soul with a conviction of sin—doubtless you have read the article long since.   If not, a final word of presump-tion—I know you will find it exceedingly interesting.

I am very attractively situated here, the only drawback being the distance from the University.   The Hodders, after going to Paris for a week or two, came on here and are occupying the room next me. I should tell you more of them had I not heard Hodder say he had a letter to you half finished.   They are both very well and Miller also, who is this moment chatting with them through my door.   You would find a warm welcome if you could drop in on us.

Work in the University is somewhat disappointing owing to its ex-ceedingly elementary nature.   I am hearing Paulsen—who by the way is a charming lecturer—on Spinoza and on the principles of Ethics; Ebbinghaus in Logik & Erkenntniss Theorie, Lasson,[4] Dessoir and Döring[5] in Metaphysic, Aesthetics and phil. tendencies of the day respectively. I hear these fellows regularly and innumerable others from time to time and as the spirit moves. I look with great pleasure to having more time for work of my own than has hitherto been possible and I hope therefore, in addition to tidying up several ragged ends, to turn out some careful work. A long letter from Pierce speaks in highest terms of Münsterberg and the work. Bakewell has gone with young Higginson to Colorado and Japan for the year.[6] I am much surprised and have heard nothing from B—— in explanation. I found on arriving here that the Amer. Jour. Psych. had printed the matter Pierce and I sent.[7] It looks pretty well in type and I trust will strike you as creditable to the laboratory. A letter from my father incloses a clipping from Leland Stanford showing that my cousin is using your small book as text book[8]—The recent review of the latter in "Mind" by Ward does not strike me as very broad nor yet penetrating. Father also writes that Chicago has about 150 graduates and about 250 undergraduates in attendance—rather a comedown from 11000! I haven't heard from Harvard, but Michigan is overflowed and father says all the colleges are full.

My pen has run away from me tonight and I had not realised, until the end of this page came in sight, how much paper I had been covering. With many thanks again for Nichols paper and best of wishes for you all, I am

Faithfully Yours | James R. Angell.

ALS: MH bMS Am 1092 (15)

[1] Herbert Nichols, "The Origin of Pleasure and Pain," *Philosophical Review* 1 (July 1892): 403–32; (September 1892): 518–34.

[2] The phrase is taken from *Mind*, n.s., 1 (October 1892): 567, in its survey of periodical literature. Alfred Goldscheider (1858–1935), German physiologist, is one of the discoverers of specific points on the skin for specific sensations; see *PP*, 809.

[3] Wilhelm Wundt, *Hypnotismus und Suggestion* (1892).

[4] Adolf Lasson (1832–1917), German Hegelian philosopher, professor at Berlin.

[5] August Döring (1834–1912), German philosopher.

[6] Higginson was not identified.

[7] James Rowland Angell and Arthur Henry Pierce, "Experimental Research upon the Phenomena of Attention," *American Journal of Psychology* 4 (August 1892): 528–41.

[8] The father of James Rowland Angell was James Burrill Angell (1829–1916), American educator and diplomat, from 1871 president of the University of Michigan. One letter is known (1883). The cousin was Frank Angell.

To Alice Howe Gibbens James

Venice, Nov 7.? (Monday) [1892] | 6.30 P.M

Darling Alice

Your generous card has just reached me, and makes me feel free to stay, but on the whole I don't care for much more Venice, and as for Bologna, Ferrara etc. I'd rather wait to go with you. This selfish enjoyment palls, and the enjoyment itself is less keen at the end that[1] at the beginning of the week. Besides Venice is rotten through & through painters and all, most of them. So leave by the 2.5 train to morrow which brings me in at 11.15 P.M. Tell Raphael to go to bed, and take a snooze yourself but be alive to open the door when my ring wakes you at 11.30 if the train isn't late.

You can tell how moral and good you seem to me after this Venice, or how much my home is near you, mind cure & all.

W.J.

ALS: MH bMS Am 1092.9 (1824)

[1] A slip for 'than'.

From James Ward

TRINITY COLLEGE, | CAMBRIDGE. Nov. 10, 1892

My dear James,

I was fearfully glad to get your letter & find that I had not for ever alienated you by that "critical" notice. The fact is I did mean to wind up with a humble sentence or two but Stout, though I asked him specially to let me have the proof in page, printed the thing off as it was. I do feel it is great cheek in me to sit in judgment upon you, but—of course, I forgot that while I was at it. As you have let me off so mildly this time I think I may promise to show due gratitude for the future.

But don't suppose—indeed you can't suppose it—that I set up to teach you or anybody. I am all in a fog, God knows, but I only don't keep for ever saying so because the past is so hideously palpable.

I don't believe that anybody could have more serious misgivings as to the bulk of the opinions I have ventured to put out than I have myself. I spend a good deal of time refuting myself: & if there really were any chance of the said opinions finding general favour, I sh^d probably imitate Master Hartmann & anonymously demolish myself.[1]

You won't mistake this for cynicism. No, I honestly feel that the best thing I can do is to go on: even an erroneous view worked out will help things on by lessening the − though not by adding to the +.

One part of my craze is precisely this straining after exactitude that you say you cannot abide. True, there has been plenty of barren defining in the world—witness the scholastics—still I fancy a strong general presumption in favour of the attempt in psychology could be made out from the history of science as a whole. And a history of psychology—a "critical" history, let us say, would shew that "appropriate conceptions", to use Whewell's phrase,[2] have been the great want & the few that have been so far hammered out the great help & the great story.

I wont defend the genetic method if the procedure of Perez & Co is to be meant by it. All that I found puzzling in your exposition was the detail into which you carried your analysis without any subsequent synthesis. After such analysis, of course, synthesis would have entailed serious repetition. To avoid this I sh.^{d} vote for 1. An analysis after your model full enough to be impressive 2. A statement of clearly ascertained generalisations—Habit, Association, &c. 3. A synthesis in which Perception wd. precede Imagination & that precede Conception; & in which, in particular, Reasoning & Self.ess would come late. I have tried this plan myself in my lectures & perhaps that is why I believe in it.

The position that you (& Bradley) take up about Self (= Subject) is absolutely incomprehensible to me. I have poured over Bradley & cannot make him out. As to you I find it hard to believe that the same man has written such opposite & seemingly incompatible statements as some of yours on this topic are to me. I sh.^{d} apply to you the words of Goethe:—

Es sind zwei Menschen in dieser Brust u.s.w.

I shall some day perhaps play off James the psychologist against James the metaphysician, moralist & human.

In your letter to me, e.g., you say: "It is surely the sensational "element" in a mental state by means of which *that state knows a mental fact*". Now I can't understand this at all. If state A knows a fact (x) & state B knows a fact (y) either they have a common part or they haven't. If they have, isn't it that common part that enables you to say A & B are my states? And when the like can be said of a continuity of states A . . B . . . C . . . . D . . ., is not that common part the knower in *all* these states? And if it is common to all the states how—according to ordinary psychological theories of knowledge—can it be *known* in any? On the other hand if the conception of knowledge requires a knower as well as a known, is not this common & unknown part of all states the being that has them all, that is active in them all? But what a fool I am, to pester you with these raw giblets—my knowledge, I call it, my organic sensations it will seem to you. For verily temperament has much to do with these things: a "melancholiker" like me with a good stable base in that imposing viscus the liver is bound to make much of the "I" while a "sanguiniker" like you is impressed only by the "Me".

No doubt psychophysics is the business of the hour: *is,* whether it ought to be or not, & *will be,* spite of all the protests of me & those like me. But for all that I regard it as a needless & wasteful detour. And yet I say this, much as I might commend a canal as a model to a river. Nature is everywhere zigzagy, & the straightening out is artificial. Still however picturesque the course of knowledge in the making, all this turning aside from the straight & narrow way is—like sin—a thing to transcend & correct from the point of view of the ideal. And so I stick to my jeremiad & lament over transgressors. But it is an odd position for me who has worked for two years in physiological laboratories & of whom it has been said that he is "a physiologist spoiled".

My reference to the "S.P.R"—(those potent symbols of bygone glory, pity they couldn't squeeze a Q. in)—was no "boutade".[3] I think you a most arrogant set of people. You have spoiled two good words—psychical & spiritual & made us no wiser. I have always let you alone & always mean to; but then I expect to be let alone myself.

Are you likely to be coming to England in the summer. If so perhaps you would come to stay with us a little while if you can put up with cottage life for a bit: or I might meet you in Scotland or somewhere, where the atmosphere has less azote than here.

       Believe me ever truly & admiringly yours | James Ward

ALS: MH bMS Am 1092.9 (651)

[1] Eduard von Hartmann (1842–1906), German philosopher. His *Das Unbewusste vom Standpunkt der Physiologie und Descendenz Theorie* (1872) was published anonymously and is a critique of his own writings.

[2] William Whewell (1794–1866), British philosopher and historian of science, who held that the thinkers of the past generally failed because they lacked "appropriate conceptions"; see his *The Philosophy of the Inductive Sciences,* 2d ed. (London: Parker, 1847), 2:18–20.

[3] Ward is punning on the initials of the Society for Psychical Research and of the phrase *Senatus Populusque Romanus.*

To Eliza Putnam Webb Gibbens

Sunday | 16 P. dell I. Nov. 12 92[1]

Dearest Mother-in-law—

This is only a line (written whilst alice is dressing to go to lunch with the Rosses) to tell you how much I love you and live on your letters, and to express my joy at the Republican rout, for by Friday's Daily News (which came in this A.M.) it does seem a rout, and it is surely the greatest moral revolution we have had since Lincoln's election in 1860—& on the whole a quite similar phenomenon.[2] There is no great news to tell, except of a highly enjoyable week which I spent by myself in Padua, & Venice, finding alice children- & sewing-ridden as usual when I got back. I think she will yield to my importunities and take a second woman after this. Yesterday evening little Tweedy (who is wholly well again) frightened us almost as much as he scared himself, by emptying a camphor bottle over his face and up his nose. This AM., all right save a big catarrh in consequence. The weather keeps extraordinarily good, no rain to trouble us, and many brilliantly sunny days. No fires yet, in spite of occasional chilliness, and no colds till 2 days ago when the whole family save me caught them in bright warm weather. Thermometer hasn't gone below 58 Fahr. Alice and I poke into all the curiosity shops and give ourselves the air of millionaires. In Venice I actually bo't some pictures, for about 200 dollars. They have really good things for sale, but nothing for less than $800 or 1000 that one can fairly call so. These things will do to decorate some of our spacious walls with. I wish I had had several thousand dollars to buy pictures with in Venice. You spoke in your last letter about Nichols having pitched into Salter's book. Don't mind Nichols, who is at his worst when he gets on to metaphysics. The book is admirable for clearness, and goodness as far as it goes. Thank you for turning off our water—I suppose you didn't forget to empty the pipes inside the house. I am sorry you had so much trouble about my tax bill. I tho't the discount limit was Nov. 1. and so didn't write to Warner as promptly as I should have done. I am right glad the check from Holt is so big. This is really the first *profit* from the books.—I hope my telegram about the fur coat didn't scare you. I considered as the weeks wore on that we cd. get on without it. Everyone here talks so about the cold that when I sent for it, I thought it would be useful indoors, and be, in fact, my only chance to *use* it in my life. I calculate that my telegram reached you in time. Danion has been ill in Paris, with

pleurisy according to his account, and is without money or employment.[3] Much love to Margaret & thanks for her letter & other remittances. Love to Aunt Nanny—I do envy you in many respects!

Yours ever affectionately   W.J.

ALS: MH bMS Am 1092.9 (927a)

[1] Sunday was 13 November 1892.

[2] In the elections of 1892 Grover Cleveland, a Democrat running as the reform
candidate, won by a large majority. The Democrats also won both houses of Congress. The *Daily News* was published in London.

[3] Stanislaus Danion, instructor in French at Harvard in 1890–92.

To Frederic William Henry Myers

16 P.ª dell Indip. Nov 14. [1892]

My dear Myers,

Yours of 10th rec'd, bristling as usual with "points" and applications of the spur. This galled jade however will not wince. The
good years shall devour me, flesh and fell or ere I write a paper of
an expository and historical nature for that Chicago Congress.[1]
What we want is *facts*, not popular papers, it seems to me; and until
the facts thicken, papers may do more harm than good. "Professional" opinion won't be conciliated by popular expositions, but only
by S.P.R. Proceedings, & my feeling is that you and the Sidgwicks'
might as well save your thunder. I say nothing about your XIXth
Century paper,[2] because there are social considerations in England
with which intellectual progress is mixed, and of which I cannot
judge. [I can see it here at the Reading Room, but should also like
a copy *if you have 'em to waste.*] At any rate, as far as America is
concerned, I am not the man to do anything in the way of expository writing.

Of course I give Hodgson carte blanche as regards my resignation.
I am afraid that the thing may come to grief, through Coues.[3] And
quite apart from Coues, I doubt whether there exist in America material for a solid "Congress."

To the fraudulent medium black list, I should say "quite impossible." It is stooping too low, even if the terrific practical difficulties
and responsibilities were overcome.

Memorial to legislatures seems to me not bad. It amuses me, however, to see Bundy's mantle so gracefully adorning *your* shoulders!
Re-incarnation, not celestial immortality, is evidently the truth.—But
what would interest *me* would be a tracing of the subconscious psy-

chological processes by which the Cambridge hellenizing tory mind has evolved up to the higher level of that of the Illinois pioneer. Science, the great democratizer, did it! Science and scientific politics![4]—I know of no one else who is on the Congress or whom Hodgson could reach directly as regards resignation, etc. If you have a list, please send it to me.

I shall be delighted to see your proof on Sensory automatism.[5] Bakewell, I have just heard, went *via* California round the world. So you must, I suppose, not expect his contribution just now. I see no reason why you shouldn't *mention* the fact, however, if you need it, on my authority.[6]

Italy has given us good weather, and the pictures etc are a feast. The climate however suits me no better than of yore, makes me "nervous" as I haven't been in many years, and my eyes give me much trouble again, so you see every rose has its thorn.

Yours ever, | W.J.

I have of course no opinion about what the prophecy was in Ermacora's case. Prima facie (barring the sex-coincidence) it looks like the vegetative soul giving information.[7]

ALS: MH bMS Am 1092.9 (3310)

[1] The Congress Auxiliary, in conjunction with the World's Columbian Exposition held in Chicago in 1893, included a session on psychology. WJ is quoting William Shakespeare, *King Lear*, act 5, sc. 3, lines 24–25.

[2] See letter from Myers of 12 January 1891.

[3] Elliott Coues (1842–1899), American ornithologist, theosophist, and psychical researcher, was chairman of the Congress of Psychology of the Congress Auxiliary. The session at which he was the prominent speaker was devoted primarily to psychical research. The circumstances of WJ's resignation were not established.

[4] John Bundy died on 6 August 1892. WJ could be alluding to Bundy's many efforts to expose fraudulent mediums, a task which Myers also planned to pursue. Myers is the Cambridge Tory and Bundy, the Illinois pioneer.

[5] Myers was publishing a series of papers on "The Subliminal Consciousness," pt. 5 of which was on "Sensory Automatism and Induced Hallucinations," *Proceedings of the Society for Psychical Research* 8 (December 1892): 436–535.

[6] In his note to Myers of 19 November 1892 (calendared) WJ states that he is sending "Bakewell's observation," which Myers may still want to use. Myers includes Bakewell's narrative, a case of "persistent after-images," in *Proceedings*, 8:450–52.

[7] WJ called on Ermacora at the request of Myers (see *Correspondence*, 2:240) and seems to be answering questions posed by Myers in a letter now lost. Ermacora described the case of automatic writer Maria Manzini in his "Telepathic Dreams Experimentally Induced," *Proceedings of the Society for Psychical Research* 11 (July 1895): 235–308. Myers quotes Ermacora on Manzini in "The Subliminal Consciousness," *Proceedings* (June 1893): 9:68–70. Among the facts Manzini revealed under the guidance of her control was that her cousin had given birth to a girl, an event of which she herself was unaware.

To James Ward

16 P.ª dell' Indipendenza, Florence | Nov 15. 92

My dear Ward,

You are a man with a Soul, so creatures such as I must needs take delight in your existence, in spite of the hardness of your heart towards S's.P.R. and other humble and struggling forms of life, and of your sins generally. I mean seriously that your letter touches me and I should like just to say so. I don't wish renovare dolorem about the Self, but a passage in your letter shoots a gleam that looks as if there might really be misunderstanding. You say we need a part that is *common* in states A & B, to account for their identification as *my* states. I grant it; only whereas you give what seems to me the merely nominal definition of "Ego" to the common something, I attempt to determine it more concretely and really, by saying that it is the *actually experienced relation* which these states alike have to state *M* which *calls* them "mine." That common relation *constitutes* practically what we *mean* by being part of an ego; and I say: "What need of reduplicating it by an abstract ego as its *ground*?["] This is what you seem to me to do. So, if A & B both know a common object O, there is again something common to them. But what? Why what but the fact of that determinate relation to a third thing. No need of any *antecedent* commonness before the fact—no need, at any rate, for descriptive purposes!

Pardon my pertinacity, & believe me ever gratefully yours

Wm James

ALS: MH bMS Am 1092.9 (3835)

To Francis Boott

16 Piazza dell Indipendenza, | Florence, Nov 18. 92

My dear Mr. Boott,

For a month past I have risen from bed daily with a rousing determination to write to you, and slunk into it again nightly with a sense of defeated good-will. At last thank Heaven, here goes! All letters, during the past 10 days have had to be postponed to the finishing of a big german book, which being finished last night, the decks are clear. [I swear that's good English, though you'll call it Cockney.] We have been here now for just two months, in an apartment on the northerly side of this square or rather the north westerly side so that we get the morning sun in front and the afternoon sun on the back-rooms. As yet we have done without fires, because the lighting of one in one room will make the others seem so much colder than before. When we are forced to it, as we soon shall be will[1] will light as many as we can; and though every one talks as if the cold here were something quite awful, I have little doubt, the season of it being now so short, that we shall worry safely through. Someone has intro-duced of late years a portable sheet iron stove which they say does wonders very quickly and with very little fuel. You set it down in front of any fireplace on a sheet of zinc, run the pipe into the chimney and light it. In an hour it has warmed the largest room temporarily, and is cool enough to be taken into another room to warm that. We shall get a couple of these, and proceed. I find the climate here disagrees with me as much as before, makes me excessively "nervous" during the sirocco of which we have had a good deal. But I am sure that the stagnant thermometer, and lack of general meteorological excitement will by the end of the winter have done me a lot of good. The acrobatic climate of the U.S. involves a lot of wear and tear. The boys are at a school which seems really *good*. The language is En-glish, and they are not even trying to learn italian, but they are kept well "braced up" in their work. Alice and I both enjoy the city of Florence immensely, and the *delightful* ways and manners of all the people whom we have to deal with. Our italian is of the bottom-most-infernal quality; and the pathetic resignation of the natives to the like of it, which they get from all us foreigners, is a touching sight. Cen-turies of servitude have bred in them a spirit very different from that noble mirth & scorn with which the free anglo-saxon meets the at-tacks of outsiders on his mother tongue! We have made very few acquaintances, and to tell the truth I am rather shy of social entangle-ments, for I ought to be doing a lot of reading, and I find that with the monuments and exercise the days go by pretty fast. We have seen Duveneck, who was here only two days ago and said he had good accounts from you. He looks very stout, and is much troubled, as you of course know, about getting a piece of marble.[2] We have also seen Miss Huntington at the Villa Castellani—my first sight of that house hallowed by Lizzies memory,[3] and so much talk in the past. We have seen most of Mrs. Villari and Frank & Mary Loring. Mrs. V. seems boundlessly sociable and kindly, and has had much to ask and say of you. I like her very much. Whenever I go to Vieus-seux's[4] I think of you, but I find, counter to my expectation, that I don't go there a great deal, there being so much to read at home.

Mr. Vieusseux senior died the other day, by the bye. The business still goes on however.—I made a delightful trip to Padua and Venice 10 days ago, being away for 8 days. Italy *has* a charm! The very rottenness and worthlessness ends by corrupting you into sympathy with it; and the people are so truly gracious and amiable. Then *what* a language!—The Rantzau, Opera by Mascagni, has been making furore here.[5] We shall go to morrow night, I think, though tickets are 12 francs. To night I am asked to dine at D.ʳ Baldwin's in Co. with Chas G. Leland[6] & Mark Twain!—I get first rate news about my successor Münsterberg in the Psychol. Lab.—I hope you may meet him sometime, he is "so very human." I think of your regular peregrinations in the *dintorni* of H. U. & wish I might join you once a week. I think also of the *comforts* of our house. This house hasn't a comfort or a convenience, except our cook Raffaello, who is a perfect *monster* of faithfulness and conscientiousness. We were extraordinarily lucky to get such a man, who[se] only passion seems to be for his saucepans. He doesn't seem to have an acquaintance in the city, and he never leaves his work. Best of love to Mrs. Greenough & her daughters when you see them. Lots for yourself from both of us.

Yours ever.   W.J.

ALS: MH bMS Am 1092.9 (763)

Address: Francis Boott Esq | Cambridge | Mass | Stati Uniti di America

Postmark: CAMBRIDGE STA. BOSTON MASS DEC 92

[1] A slip for 'we'.

[2] Frank Duveneck was planning a memorial to Elizabeth Boott Duveneck.

[3] Elizabeth Boott Duveneck.

[4] The several Vieusseuxes were not identified.

[5] *I Rantzau* by Pietro Mascagni was first performed on 10 November 1892.

[6] Charles Godfrey Leland (1824–1903), American author.

To Hugo Münsterberg

16 Piazza dell' Indipendenza | Florence, Nov 24. 92

My dear Münsterberg

I am in your debt for two letters and the 4th part of your Beiträge. The first letter, of Oct 9th, was a fairly encyclopaedic document, with its Antrittsrede and list of subjects for possible investigation. I congratulate you heartily on the fact that your english goes so well. If you composed those remarks without assistance or correction, it shows that your progress has been very rapid, and that you have nothing to fear, for there are no mistakes. Nichols in fact wrote me sometime since that he thought you would be able to lecture without difficulty in six months. Well, I am delighted to find, from both of your letters, how well the University, and America in general, seem to agree with you. Your program of occupations in your last letter indicates what is called "a full life." The excitement of novelty won't last forever, so keep it up whilst the mood continues! Only I'm afraid that by springtime you may experience a sort of fatigue which you haven't been accustomed to feel in Germany. Overstimulation and depressive reaction are the great evils of our otherwise interesting & on the whole, it seems to me, beautiful climate. You are experiencing one great exemption, which if you stay much longer, you will hardly escape—I mean serving on various committees of the faculty. They eat the very soul out of one with their tediousness & consumption of time. Keep clear of them and of the faculty as long as you can! I am much pleased that you and Nichols have established a modus vivendi which is cordial. Nichols has noble mora<l> qualities, and he writes most enthusiastically of yours, so I have no fear<.> Mr[s]. Gibbens writes that you<r> relations with Mrs. Mulford are unpleasant, and that your house is infested by rats. How I do wish that you were now in ours! It is a singularly easy house for servants to take care of, and as Mrs. James will most likely stay away a second year, you could probably have it for *two* years at least. But regrets are wasteful when it is too late!

Your Beiträge came some weeks ago, but owing to occupation with other things, I didn't get to reading them till a few days ago. They are simply *charming;* and I don't see what your worst enemy can say, except with reference to the last few pages, which seem to me a speculation in rather too simplified a form. If your record of Harvard work at the end of this year results in a volume at all comparable with this, it will be magnificent. The Zeitausfullung, Gedächtniss Studien, Associations studien, & mitbewegungen interested me most. In the latter you quote me. The fact I had in mind when I explained Loeb's results as due to an automatic reversion to an infantile type, was the symmetrical movements of both arms which I had noticed in my own babies towards the end of their first year, when for many weeks together (I think) they manifested all emotional excitement by alternate flexions & extensions of the trunk, with symetrical rising and falling of both arms.[1] Their movements during the first months are certainly mostly unsymmetrical, according to my observation; and the period I noticed, of sym! movem[ts], is transient. I was too little explicit in my book. I suppose you would also class Loeb's results under the general head which includes your own observations. Your "law" seems to me highly plausible. As regards the pleasure-pain business, your frank distinction between *schmerz* and the *gefühl* which it awakens is important, and starts a new era of discussion. I can't help suspecting that the antithesis between mere extension and flexion is ultra-simple for man as now constituted, but I am willing to admit it as the original & fundamental distinction.—All I hope is that you may have more ideas & opportunities to work them out in this fashion! It is a great pity that Angell, Hodder, and Bakewell are not with you this year—they were three splendidly strong fellows out of whom you would infallibly have got good assistance, both in the way of discussion and criticism, and of experiment.

Our winter comes on well. The boys are contented at their school, and I am beginning to do a little serious reading. I have just got through Lasswitz's Gesch. d. Atomismus,[2] and am about to attack Wundt's system d. Philosophie. The pictures are delicious. Unfortunately I have no visual images whereby to enjoy them when my back is turned. One can buy old pictures here so easily, that I wish I had a little money to spend upon them. We have only lighted fires to day, the thermometer having hardly varied from 16° C. during the past month. Good bye! Pray give the best regards of both of us to your wife, be industrious and cheerful!, and believe always yours affectionately

Wm James

ALS: MH bMS Am 1092.9 (3274)

[1] For the views of Jacques Loeb and WJ's interpretation see *PP,* 1125–26n.
[2] Kurd Lasswitz, *Geschichte der Atomistik,* 2 vols. (1890).

To Alice Howe Gibbens James

Hotel Stella d'Oro | Padova, Wednesday [December 7, 1892]
Beloved Alice, I had a long letter to you in my mind yesterday evening, but I got into Darwin's room, and he opened upon the subject of Mrs. Piper so that the time flew. I then had to dress quickly so as not to keep the rest of the english party waiting, to go to the ball given by the municipality from which I did n't return till midnight, too late for the mail. Your letter came to me at dinner-time and gave me an idea of the virtue of your life. I am glad you went to Baldwin, but tremble at the boldness of a man who has confidence to order a complete change of regimen in so prompt a way. Of

course the effect of it will decide his farther opinion. I have naturally been full of remorses since I left, I do so little for you. In the
cars I had such a vision of your life history—when I first saw you
you were a form of beauty, now you are a "form of use." I know
darling Alice that when we begin to make excursions, this depressed
feeling you have about yourself will melt like snow in the sun. I have
all the variety, you all the monotony in this partnership. I'm glad,
however that you didn't come on here. It is cold, the hotel is very
poor & I have a bad room; and I find the town far less gemüthlich
looking under this clear hard sky than it was in the warmth and
softness of a month ago. Of the details of our celebration I will speak
when I return. The big solemnity in the Aula of the University takes
place this noon.[1] Hitherto there have only been preliminary skir-
mishes and introductions. A visit to the monuments yesterday noon
in barouches. Beautiful ball given by the municipality last night, to
the minister of public instruction, banquet to night, etc. I find Darwin a charming companion full of vivacity. The two other englan-
ders are rather heavy, tho one of them, Sir Joseph Fayrer, a medical
swell, lent me his shirt studs for the ball last night. There is, so far,
but little fraternization among the professors native and foreign. I
have slept splendidly both nights and feel hearty in the cold weather.
Love to you *all*, you angel-mother & brood.

W.J.

ALS: MH bMS Am 1092.9 (1825)

Address: Signora James | 16 P.ª dell Indipendenza | Firenze

Postmarks: PADOVA 7 12. –92   FIRENZE 8 12 92

[1] WJ was Harvard's delegate at the Galileo Festival at Padua, commemorating the
300th anniversary of the installation of Galileo as a professor at the University of Padua. WJ presented a scroll from Harvard and received an honorary doctorate. For
his account see "The Galileo Festival at Padua," *Nation* 56 (5 January 1893): 8–9;
reprinted in *ECR*.

To Alice Howe Gibbens James

Stella d'Oro, 8th. [December 1892] | 11 A.M.

Dearest Alice—Your postcard of yesterday and Mrs. Evans's letter
were found by me on my shoes at the door when I opened it to get
them ½ an hour ago. You see I sleep late, which means that I sleep
enough. I didn't get into bed till one, and then in a new room, a poor
fellow who broke his leg on the stairs having been put into my bed
during the dinner, and all my effects transferred.—I took a long walk

in the twilight with Ermacora and a young medium named Giarda around the outskirts of the town[1] and very lovely the sweet winter landsape looked.   Then to the big dinner down below, some 130 people as I reckoned, which was a great success, excellent food & service and very short speeches, the whole thing over by ½ past 8.— 5.30 P.M.   Interrupted at this point by Stone who rushed in saying that the Germans had a wreath 4 feet wide to deposit on the Galileo statue, and that the English must not fall behind so with the help of the hotel porter we ran to a wreath store, and the englishmen & I both bo't big tin laurel wreaths with white streamers on which with marvellous celerity they printed big gilt inscriptions.   Mine was "dalle Università dell' America del Nord."   A big procession of civic functionaries, schooboys, students, & professors then went through the town in the bright weather & deposited the wreaths.   Since then endless standing in the University & talking, with a final visit to the Museum of the War of 1859.   To night a banquet at which I shall *perhaps* have to speak—in french.   Then a big students' howl in the town Hall.—I doubt whether I get home before Saturday, but can't tell yet.   I am thoroughly enjoying it now—the sociability having increased.—Good bye—I must compose my *possible* speech & learn it by heart & dress before ½ past six, so the minutes are counted. Blessing on all your dear heads.

W.J.

ALS: MH bMS Am 1092.9 (1827)

[1] Giarda was not identified.

To Charles William Eliot

16 Piazza dell' Indipendenza | Florence, Dec. 10. 1892
Dear President,

On receiving your command to go to Padua, I immediately put myself in communication with the rector, and the consequence is that I am just back from a most enjoyable occasion.

They get up festivities most admirably in Italy.   The town and the University combined in the most graceful way, each giving a banquet, whilst the town had a great gala representation at the Opera, and the University a ball.   There were over twenty-five foreign delegates, and a very large number of Italians.   Not many of them wore robes or costumes, but those that did added much to the splendor.   Allen Marquand from Princeton and I were the only Americans present, and Marquand could only stay for one day. I got a big metallic laurel wreath to lay on Galileo's statue, with a long white streamer with "Dalle Università dell' America del Nord" in big gilt letters on it, since that was evidently the graceful thing to do. I had a very pleasant time with the English colleagues, Geo. Darwin, Sir Joseph Fayrer the medical swell, & Stone of the Ratcliffe Observatory.[1] Tisserand[2] and Förster,[3] the Berlin and Paris astronomers, were there. The hero of the occasion was Professor Ferraris, the rector (statistician) who did *all* the chores, never forgot a face or a name, spoke 4 languages simultaneously, didn't lose a second of time but instantaneously perceived the only right thing to do, and withal kept as jolly & amused as if he were a passive spectator. Some division of labor would doubtless have been better, but, granting the neccessity of a factotum, his performances were something unheard of for ability. In case we ever deal with italians, he is a man to be particularly remembered—Carlo F. Ferraris.

The addresses from many european Institutions were very elaborate and handsome, some of them richly bound and illuminated. Everything of that sort tells on a ceremonial occasion! Of course they gave us foreigners honorary degrees, mine being that of Litt. et. Phil. D.

The winter is passing pleasantly for all of us here, and the weather is very favorable. I am right glad to hear that you are pleased with Münsterberg, glad also to hear of a movement for adopting the Annex, and that Royce is full Professor. With best regards from both of us to both you & Mrs. Eliot, I am ever faithfully yours

Wm James

I subjoin a receipt for my expenses, which you might have paid by a check to the order of Mrs. E. P. Gibbens, Irving St.

ALS: MH Archives

[1] WJ misspelled the name of the Radcliffe Observatory.
[2] François-Félix Tisserand (1845–1896), French astronomer.
[3] Wilhelm Julius Foerster (1832–1921), German astronomer.

To Josiah Royce

16 Piazza dell Indipendenza, | Florence, Dec 18. 92

Beloved Josiah

Your letter of Oct 12 with "missent—Indian mail" stamped upon its envelope in big letters was handed in only 10 days ago, after I had long said in my heart that you were no true friend to leave me thus languishing so long in ignorance of all that was befalling in Irving S! and the country round about.   Its poetical hyperboles about the way I was missed made amends for everything, so I am not now writing to ask you for my diamonds back or to return my ringlet of your hair.   It was a beautiful and bully letter and filled the hearts of both of us with exceeding joy.   I have heard since then from the Gibbenses that you are made Professor—I fear at not more than $3000, but still it is a step ahead and I congratulate you most heartily thereupon.   What I most urgently wanted to hear from you was some estimate of Munsterberg, and when you say "he is an immense success" you may imagine how I am pleased.   He has his foibles, as who has not, but I have a strong impression that that youth will be a great man.   Moreover his naïveté & openness of nature make him very loveable.   I do hope that the english will go—of course there can be no question of the students liking him, when once he gets his communications open.   He has written me exhaustive letters, and seems to be outdoing even you in the amount of energizing which he puts forth.   May God have him in his holy keeping!

From the midst of my laziness here the news I get from Cambridge makes it seem like a little seething Florence of the XVth Century. Having all the time there is, to myself, I of course find I have no time for doing any particular duties, and the consequence is that the days go by without anything very serious accomplished.   But we live well and are comfortable by means of sheet-iron stoves which the clammy quality of the cold rather than its intensity seems to neccessitate, and Italianism is "striking in" to all of us to various degrees of depth, shallowest of all I fear in Peg and the baby.   When Gemüthlichkeit is banished from the world it will still survive in this dear and shabby old country; though I suppose the same sort of thing is really to be found in the East even more than in Italy, & that we shall seek it there when Italy has got as tram-roaded and modernized all over as Berlin.   It is a curious smell of the past, that lingers over everything, speech and manners as well as stone & stuffs!   I went to Padua last week to a Galileo-anniversary.   It was splendidly carried out, and great fun; and they gave all of us foreigners honorary degrees.   I rather like being a doctor of the University of Padua, and shall feel more at home than hitherto in the merchant of Venice.*   Allen Marquand was there, just returning from a very thorough hunting up of all the specimens of Della Robbia pottery in Italy, for a monograph which he is preparing.[1]   He didn't strike me as having any special sympathy with the aesthetic side of art, but I find that now a days the critical cataloguer regards the man whose interest in art is artistic as a most miserable and ignorant worm. Denman Ross seems to *me* a saint in this matter, with great love and acquaintance but little scholarship and humbug or conceit of knowledge. Mark Twain is here for the winter in a Villa outside the town, hard at work writing something or other. I have seen him a couple of times—a fine soft fibred little fellow with the perversest twang and drawl, but very human and good. I should think that one might grow very fond of him, & wish he'd come and live in Cambridge.—I am just beginning to wake up from the sort of mental palsy that has been over me for the past year, and to take a little "notice" in matters philosophical. I am now reading Wundt's curiously long winded "System" which in spite of his intolerable sleekness and way of *soaping* everything on to you by plausible transitions so as to mak<e> it run continuous, has every now and then a compendiously stated truth, or aperçu, which is nourishing and instructive. Come March, I will send you proposals for my work next year, to the "Cosmology" par<t> of which I am just beginning to wak<e> up.[2] Benn, of the history of Gre<ek> Philosophy, is here, a shy Irishma<n> (I should judge) with a queer manner whom I have only seen a couple of times, but with whom I shall probably later take some walks.[3] He seems a good and well informed fellow, much devoted to astronomy, and I have urged your works on his attention. He lent me the New World with your article in it which I read with admiration—would that belief would ensue![4] Perhaps I shall get straight. I have just been "penning" a notice of Renouvier's Principes de la Nature for Schurman.[5] Renouvier cannot be *true*—his world is so much *dust*. But that conception is a *zu überwinden des Moment* and he has given it i[t]s most energetic expression. There is a theodicy at the end, a speculation about this being a world fallen, which ought to interest you much from the point of view of your own Cosmology.—Münsterberg wrote me, and I forgot to remark on it in my reply, that Scripture wanted him to contribute to a new Yale Psychology review, but that he wished to publish in a vol. I confess it disgusts me to hear of each of these little separate College tin trumpets. What I should really like would be a philosophic *monthly* in America which would be all sufficing as the Rev. Phil. is in france. If it were a monthly M——'g could find room for all his contributions from the Lab. But I don't suppose that Scripture will combine with Schurman any more than Hall would, or for the matter of that, I don't know whether Sch. himself would wish it.—I hear that Mrs. Palmer is to go to Chicago.[6] Is this to end by drawing P. gradually thither, or not? I also hear that they have 250 graduates, which might well account for any amount of depletion elsewhere. Have you heard of their filling out Palmer's philosophic program at all? What are you working at? Is the Goethe work started? Is music raging round you both as of yore? How is Christopher and the younger ones? We heard last night the new opera by Mascagni 'I Rantzau' which has made a furore here and which I enjoyed hugely. How is Santayana, and what is he up to? You can't tell how thick the atmosphere of Cambridge seems over here? "Surcharged with vitality" in short. Write again when ever you can spare a fellow a ½ hour, and believe me with warmest regards from both of us to both of you,

Yours always   Wm James

Pray give love to Palmer, Nichols, Santayana, M——g, & all.

*I have written a letter to the Nation about it, which I commend to the attention of your gentle partner.

ALS: MH bMS Am 1092.9 (3610)

[1] Allan Marquand wrote extensively about the Della Robbia family, Florentine artists of the fifteenth century.

[2] In 1893–94 WJ took over Royce's course Philosophy 3: Cosmology, "a study of the fundamental conceptions of Natural Science, with special reference to theories of Evolution and Materialism." He taught the course regularly thereafter.

[3] Alfred William Benn (1843–1915), British scholar, author of several books on Greek philosophy.

[4] Josiah Royce, "The Implications of Self-Consciousness," *New World* 1 (1892): 289–310; reprinted in Royce's *Studies of Good and Evil* (1898).

[5] WJ, review of Charles Renouvier, *Les Principes de la nature*, 2d ed. (1892), *Philosophical Review* 2 (March 1893): 212–18; reprinted in *ECR*.

[6] Alice Palmer accepted an appointment as dean of women at the University of Chicago but by special arrangement continued to live in Cambridge.

To Carl Stumpf

18[1] Piazza dell Indipendenza | Florence, Dec 20. 92

My dear Stumpf,

I really cannot remember now whether I ever wrote to you since leaving Luzern, whether in particular I ever told you that we were coming to Florence, or whether to all the other crimes which my vice of unpardonable laziness has piled up for me to expiate in purgatory, the omission to give you any more information about my whereabouts in Europe has been added. I can only assure you that there is no one in Europe of whom I have *thought* more often (I find two blank post cards *addressed* to you in my portfolio now as I seek your last letter) and there is no one the loss of whose neighborhood I have so much regretted in coming to Italy. My plan is now to go to Munich alone by the end of April, and see you and take counsel with you about many things. But may not you yourself be meditating an "Italiänische Reise" during the Easter vacation? I sometimes think that you may turn up in Florence before I do in Munich. If you did we could revisit the monuments together and soften Philosophy with Art. Doesn't the idea tempt you at all. We are settled here in a furnished apartment, with an ultra conscientious and cheap man-cook, and save that our rooms are uncomfortably cold, the winter is passing pleasantly away. We could devise no entirely satisfactory school-plan for our boys, so tired of the problem we said "Old age has its rights as well as youth, let's make sure of a light & entertaining winter for ourselves, which shall be a real holiday, and go to florence.["] We have not regretted it. The city is both small and *important*, a very rare combination. You go from one end of it to another in an ordinary afternoon walk, and yet you feel as if in a *Weltstadt*. The streets are endlessly entertaining and the art-treasures divine. The boys are at a school which, though english, seems really good, and are kept hard at work, and I, after months of absolute intellectual lethargy am beginning to wake up again, and feel as if there might be some powers of production left in me yet. I suppose the lethargy was a wholesome reaction upon the fatigue which made me leave home. I hear excellent news of the way in which Münsterberg is taking hold of the work at Harvard, and he in turn seems delighted with the place. I don't know whether you have yet looked into the 4th Heft of his Beiträge, but they seem to me charming, and I don't see what fault his worst enemy can find there. He *is* rash, oversweeping and shallow in his generalizations;—but who is not, in Psychology? A psychologist's merit seems to me, in the *present* condition of that science, to consist much less in the *definitiveness* of his conclusions, than in his suggestiveness and fertility. Creatures like G. E. Müller are up so high on horseback on their mathematical & logical criticism of experimental methods that they make experimentation simply impossible. They are sterile themselves [I confess however that I have n't read M's. Theorie der Muskelcontraction];[2] and almost the entire upshot of the work of the exact school of Psychophysic experiment, including especially the work of Wundt's laboratory, tends to show that *no* experimentation can be exact enough to be of any value. The result will be to abandon experimentation altogether, as a false and fruitless direction of activity! I am now in the midst of Wundt's System der Philosophie, which interests me a good deal, though he irritates me more and more by his strange mania for appearing *smooth*. He oils his transitions and *soaps* all his conclusions on to you by plausible apriori introductions that make you sick. It is the subtlest sort of mental dishonesty, born rather in the sphere of an abominably false aesthetic ideal than in that of the will, but it is turning him fast into a humbug. Moreover, this everlasting search for *unoccupied ground* on which he may plant a new theory!—I went last week to Padua to a Galileo tercentenary at the University. I represented Harvard, and it was great fun. There were 6 german professors there. How I wish than[3] you had been among them!

I hope that you, Mrs. Stumpf, and the children are all well, and that the year's work is going bravely. How comes on Vol III of the T.psy.?[4] We both send to both of your our heartiest Christmas wishes, and beg you to believe me your sincere and faithful friend

Wm James

ALS: MH bMS Am 1092.9 (3788)

[1] A slip for '16'.
[2] Georg Elias Müller, *Theorie der Muscelkontraktion* (1891).
[3] A slip for 'that'.
[4] Only two volumes of the *Tonpsychologie* were published.

To Mary Sherwin Gibbens Salter

16 Pᵃ dell' Indip. Dec. 26. 92

My dearest Mary

Although it will arrive a little late, I can't help sending you a greeting for the New Year. Your letters to Alice have been meat & drink to both of us, and your grim grubbing in the roots of righteousness (with your anti slavery studies etc etc,) is in such contrast to our epicurean sucking in of picturesqueness passively from the atmosphere and feeling as good as possible about it, that nothing but the sense that every dog has his day, and that we shall take our turn for grubbiness, whilst you and Mack float passive on a summer sea of enjoyment some years hence, reconciles me to the existence of such inequalities of outward station in members of the same family as the present winter shows. I am beginning now to enjoy myself fearfully, eyes, legs brain etc all being in perfect equilibrium, so that I can read till midnight without being sleepy sleep till ½ past seven without being wakeful, walk all day if need be without getting tired, & in short do everything I please. Moreover, so unsociably are we made that the freedom from the door-bell which we enjoy here is something unspeakably delicious. To think, night after night, that one can sit till midnight under one's lamp with books, and be quite sure of no interruption. I begin now to count the days before my return, when it will end, alas! alas! Of course there are other sides to it. Reading with Alice, the two boys, Peggy, Tweedy, and the nurse all carrying on their various avocations and vociferations by the same one lamp, round the same small table, in one narrow (if high) room around a dreadful little sheet iron stove (—fortunately the chimney is open up which its pipe is thrust) is not exactly the same thing as me with Harry in the library at home, two lamps & two tables, Billy in your mother's room and the rest up stairs,—and yet for a certain part of the day it is the condition that has to prevail. But six weeks more of cold will make our other sitting room again available, and then all will be convenient once more. I am reading philosophy again with great zest in view of next year's work, only I wish that some law could be devised which would prevent people like Wundt from writing wishy washy "System der Philosophie" when they really have nothing of the least importance to say. The only things that excuse a book's existence are brevity, originality of matter, or great literary talent. Books that are both long, commonplace and dull should be ruthlessly suppressed. Every now and then we dip into the Renaissance period—I've just read the 1st. vol of Yriartes Caesar Borgia, a plastic enough subject treated with dulness.[1] I tell Alice that the career of that old villain of a pope shows how bad a thing family affection is when pushed to an extreme.[2] I am always accusing *your* family, you know, of having too much of it! Beware of counting in history as Borgias! Caesar himself doesn't appear to have had any too much however! If mack would get Machiavellis "Prince" and read it, he would not only be mightily interested, but could probably make a first rate Sunday lecture of it. Alice has been reading Villaris interesting book on M. which however, she says, is more of a compilation than the one on Savonarola.[3]—I can't imagine anything more fascinating than to get hold of Italian early enough in life to become *intimate* with italian literature and history. Nothing as personal and dramatic and highly spiced in the whole world, I should think! But we have come in just too late!

Heaven keep you both! I hope the ethical society will roll up like a snowball. Poor France just now! It makes one realize the blessings of our country and England, who have no pack of wolves thirsting for the very life of the Constitution.

Good bye! And a happy New Year to you and Mack!

Yours ever | W.J.

ALS: MH bMS Am 1092.9 (3648)

[1] Charles-Émile Yriarte (1832–1898), French historian, *Les Borgia* (1889).

[2] Cesare Borgia (ca. 1476–1507), Italian cardinal and soldier, was a son of Pope Alexander VI.

[3] Pasquale Villari, *The Life and Times of Niccolò Machiavelli,* trans. by Linda Villari (1888); *Life and Times of Savonarola,* trans. by Linda Villari (1888).

To Grace Norton

16 Piazza dell' Indipendenza | Florence, Dec 28. 92

My dear Grace,

I hope that my silence has not left you to think that I have forgotten all the ties of friendship. Far from it!—but have *you* never felt the rapture of day after day with no letter to write, nor the shrinking from breaking the spell by changing a limitless possibility of future outpouring into a shabby little actual scrawl? Remote, unwritten to and unheard from, you seem to me something ideal, off there in your inaccessible Cambridge palazzo, bathed in the angelic american light, occupying your mind with noble literature, pure, solitary, incontaminate,—a station from which the touch of this vulgar epistle will instantly bring you down, for you will have been imagining your poor correspondent in the same high and abstract fashion until what he says breaks the charm (as infallibly it must) and with the perception of his finiteness must also come a faint sense of discouragement as if *you* were finite too—for communications bring the communicants to a common level.—All of which sounds, my dear Grace, as if I were refraining from writing to you out of my well-known habit of "metaphysical politeness," or trying to make you think so—but I think I can trust you to see that all these elaborate conceits (which seem imitated from the choice italian manner and which I confess have flowed from my pen quite unpremeditatedly and somewhat to my own surprise) are nothing but a shabby cloak under which I am trying to hide my own palbable *laziness*—a laziness which even the higher affections can only render a little restless and uncomfortable, but not dispel.—However, it *is* dispelled at last, isn't it, so let me begin. You will have heard stray tidings of us from time to time, so I need give you no detailed account of our peregrinations or decisions. We had a delicious summer in Switzerland, that noble and medicinal country, and we have now got into first rate shape at Florence, although there is a menace of "sociability" commencing, which may take away that wonderful and unexampled sense of peace I have been enjoying of late in sitting under the lamp until midnight secure against any possible interruption and reading what things I pleased. I believe that last year in Cambridge I counted one single night in which I could sit and read passively till bedtime; and now that the days have begun to lengthen and the small end of the winter appears looking through the future, I begin to count them here as something unspeakably precious that may ne'er return. The boys are at an english school which, though certainly very good, gives them rather less in french and german than they would have at Brown's & Nichols's. Peg is having first-rate "opportunities" in the way of dancing, gynastics and other accomplishments of a bodily sort. We have a little shred of a half starved, but very cheerful, ex-ballet dancer who brings a poor little humble peering-eyed fiddler—"Maestro" she calls him,—three times a week to our big salon, and makes supple the limbs of Peg and the 2 infants of D! Baldwin by the most wonderful patience and diversity of exercises at 5 francs a lesson. When one thinks of the sort of lessons the children at cambridge get, and of the sort of price they pay, it makes one feel that geography is a tremendous frustrator of the so called laws of demand and supply. Alice and I lunched this noon with young Loeser, whose name you may remember some years ago in Cambridge. He is devoted to the scientific study of pictures, and I hope to gain some truth from him ere we leave. He is a dear good fellow. Baron Osten Sacken is also here—I forget whether you used to know him. The same quaint, cheerful, nervous, intelligent rather egotistic old bachelor that he used to be, who also runs to pictures in his old age, after the strictly entomological method, I fancy, this time, for I doubt whether he cares near as much for the pictures themselves as for the Science of them. But you can't keep science out—of anything, in these bad times. Love is dead, or at any rate seems weak and shallow wherever science has taken possession. I am glad that, being incapable of anything like *scholarship* in any line, I still can take some pleasure from these pictures in the way of love, particularly glad since some years ago I thought that my care for pictures had faded away with youth. But with better opportunities it has revived. Loeser describes Bôcher as *basking* in the presence of pictures, as if it were an amusing way of taking them, whereas it is the *true* way. Is Mr. Bôcher giving his lectures or talks again at your house?—Duveneck is here, but I have seen very little of him. The professor is an oppressor to the artist, I fear; and metaphysical politeness has kept me from pursuing him too much. What an awful trade that of professor is—paid to talk talk, talk! I have seen artists growing pale and sick whilst I talked to them without being able to stop. And I loved them for not being able to love me any better. It would be an awful universe if *everything* could be converted into words words words.

I have been so sorry to hear of the miserable condition of so many of your family circle this summer. Arthur's condition was especially tragic. Where is he now, and how? Poor Rupert's was no less so, except that he was in better condition to be a victim. I hope that by this time he will be none the worse for having gone through the trial. Pray give him my love. Give it also to your brother Charles, to Sally, Lily,[1] Dick,[2] Margaret[3] and all the dear creatures. Also to the other dears on both sides of the Kirkland street driveway.[4] I hope & trust that your winter is passing cheerfully and healthily away. With warm good wishes for a happy new year, and affectionate greetings from both of us, believe me always yours,

Wm James

ALS: MH bMS Am 1092.9 (3344)

[1] Elizabeth Gaskell (Lily) Norton (d. 1958), daughter of Charles Eliot Norton. Correspondence is known from 1895 to 1909.
[2] Richard Norton.
[3] Margaret Norton, daughter of Charles Eliot Norton.
[4] Grace Norton, Francis James Child, Theodora Sedgwick, and the Ashburner sisters lived on Kirkland Street, which is near Irving Street.

From George Herbert Palmer

Cambridge— | Dec. 28, 1892.

Dear James:

The coming of the New Year suggests some problems on which I should like to get your judgment.

Santayana & Nichols are appointed annually; & to my mind that means that we are each year to decide whether they can do our work better than any other available man. If we think we can strengthen our staff by changing them, fairness to our students will oblige us to do so.

Santayana is a good way from satisfactory. His subtle & beautiful mind has a strange lack of reality. The man is merely an amused observer, without stake in the world he inhabits. I doubt if he will ever wield an invigorating influence among our students. Yet I should retain him. His damaging peculiarities grow a little less each year. He is a scholar, has lines of his own, & in Esthetics & Scholastic Philosophy we could not replace him. Unless you have a decided opinion to the contrary, Royce & I shall recommend his re-election.

Nichols' case seems to me more doubtful, but here your opinion & that of Münsterberg should outweigh my vague impressions. Nichols' work is so different from mine that I know very well I am not competent to assess it. I hear his course in the Annex spoken of well. He is evidently very kind, very industrious, & very fertile in ideas. To me he does not seem a man of cool judgment. His narrow training frequently comes to the front. He is fussy & gossipy, quite capable of blundering badly, & little likely to convey to his students or the public the impression of being a man of weight. In view of traits like these I feel pretty well convinced that I should be unwilling to see him rise at any time to a position higher than that he holds at present. As an assistant I do not object to him, if you & Münsterberg want him. But when I have offered to find him a place elsewhere & have told him that at his years he ought not to stay on in a subordinate position, he has said that he wished to continue because he hoped to succeed Münsterberg. Is it not unfair to allow him to remain with this fancy? If we are clear that we should never want him for any higher work, ought we to continue him another year? I confess I think we ought not. He is not a Rand, but is far too good a person to spend his best years on us & then be told by us by & by that we have no further use for him. If we are clear that we shall not wish him permanently, I believe we had better make our change this year.

This is what I want you to think of, & to send me word as soon as possible. Of course if he goes, he needs time to find another place & we too need time to secure the best possible successor. You & Münsterberg must settle the matter. Münsterberg is tender-hearted & will let things drift; but I think he thoroughly distrusts Nichols' solidity & recognizes that some other man would give us better results. I hope, therefore, if you have any definite opinion, you will speak it out positively.

If you do not care to have Nichols go on, we must set about finding another man. Münsterberg talks of Witmer of the Univ. of Pa. but when I asked if he was better than Delabarre, he doubted if he was. I have no personal acquaintance with either of them. Possibly neither could be had. But we ought not to be hindered by doubts about the possibility of getting either from applying to the one that we judge is best. Delabarre, I believe, has property enough to make the small salary here a matter of little consequence. He is having at present pretty elementary teaching to attend to & no opportunity for original experimentation. It seems therefore not impossible that he might be willing to come, if you really consider him the man most likely to come to power & serviceableness here. But on these points we want to be sure, & on your judgment in the matter I must mainly rely.

Münsterberg is proving a great success. Everybody likes him. He strangely combines enthusiasm & sanity. Experimentalist as he is, he is no mere physiologue or nerve man; it is the classic problems of philosophy which fundamentally move him. I strongly hope he will remain after the end of his term.

I like to think of you in Florence, we enjoyed ourselves so much during three months there, at first on your Piazza & then keeping house on the Lung Arno Accagnoli. But nothing is quite so good as Venice—unless Boxford or the library of 3 Mason St.[1] Anywhere in Italy one can find rest & beauty. Certainly you will find them; & next year you will come back to us—who greatly miss you—thoroughly refreshed, I hope. We plod on, the Mid Years right ahead. During them I am going out to Chicago with Mrs Palmer, who has been at home since Oct. 15. She is now trying to raise an endowment for the Annex. I will enclose her circular & you can hand it to some Millionairess who wants to give away a substantial piece of her property.

Always yours, | G. H. Palmer

ALS: MH bMS Am 1092.9 (428)

[1] Palmer was born in Boxford, Mass., and until 1894 lived at 3 Mason St., Cambridge.

To Théodore Flournoy

16 Pᵃ dell' Indipendenza | Florence, Jan 3. 1893

My dear Flournoy,

Your letter of new-year's greeting was a most gratifying event yesterday. I had been thinking of you and of your family all the week, and "innervating" myself to write, but the muscular discharge fell short of accomplishment! I am sure you can forgive the weakness of an ultra-lazy man. Now that your letter supplies the stimulus, no effort is required—quite the reverse. Your hopes about the *beau so-leil de la Toscane,* etc, sound rather ironical in the midst of the cloudy skies we have been having for a month. But we have had no cold below the freezing point, and very little as low as that, and no such bad weather in general as seems to have prevailed north of the alps. The only inconvenience of our life is the small size of the living room in which the boys and their parents both have to huddle when they are all at home together, in the latter part of the day. But now that we are embarked on January and steering straight for Spring and Freedom, my spirits rise. They have also risen since a dinner, at which we had four friends on Sunday night, has proved that the resources of the establishment, glass, spoons, cook, & *bonne,* are adequate to a dinner party of six.[1] So that hereafter we may accept an invitation, without feeling that to return it will be an impossibility. The streets of Florence are everlastingly interesting, but the evolution of italian art is much too complicated for the successive steps in its evolution to be traced in any clear way. It seems as if a large number of men coordinately made most of the advances. I see here a couple of young men who are devoted to Italian painting in a streng-wissenschaftlich manner, their principal interest being the re-naming of all the pictures in the galleries. I have also another friend, who is an entomologist, blessed with a great memory for details and who has taken up Kunstgeschichte in an entomological manner.[2] Alongside of their severity there seems little room for a merely loving relation to the pictures. But the good thing about a work of art is that it tells all sorts of things to different spectators, of none of which things the artist ever knew a word.—You speak of Marillier's articles, of which the third was brought by the postman an hour ago. I fear that during eternity I can never indemnify him for the trouble my unfortunate volumes have given him. His exposition seems to me excellently clear and faithful, and the whole thing is an immense compliment to me, but I don't believe in such very long compte-rendus. They are neccessarily colorless and tame compared with the originals, and yet they are difficult reading. I should rather any day read a hundred pages of an original author than 30 pp. of a compte rendu. Then it grieves me to find that the Lord has hardened poor Marillier's heart against the reception of so many of my truths. In spite of the pains he has taken, I fear he will not be saved!   He *is* conscientious, though, is he not?—I have just read, all but the last 100 pp., Wundt's System der Philosophie.   That man can write more pages on any given theme than anyone who ever lived.   Intelligent too, and clear; but it's all surface and plausibility, and the success with which he escapes saying anything really decisive or important is astounding in a man who has done such an awful *quantity* of hard thinking and study.   I think that some machinery will have to be organized to *pay* men for not writing books, from whom there is reason to think that the world is threatened.   Wundt ought certainly to be pensioned off now—we have labored enough over his pages.   I should like to be present at your Kant-session with the Orientals.   Of course you have read that wonderful thing of Paulsen's "Was Kant uns sein kann" in the earlier years of the Viertelj'sch.?[3]   Don't take your laboratory too severely, or let it weigh on your soul.   Your two little contributions were well worth the year you spent.   Best love from both of us and wishes for the New Year to both you, Madame Flournoy & the children.   Peggy & Tweedy got the pretty Christmas cards & Peggy sends love and thanks.   Please give our cordial greetings also to Frl. Hünersdorf.

AL: MH bMS Am 1505 (6)

[1] For the guest list see next letter.

[2] For the art historians see letter to Grace Ashburner of 5 January 1893.   The entomologist is Carl Robert Osten-Sacken.

[3] Friedrich Paulsen, "Was uns Kant sein kann," *Vierteljarsschrift für wissenschaftliche Philosophie* 5 (1881): 1–96.

To Margaret Merrill Gibbens Gregor

Florence, Jan. 3, 1893.

Beloved Margaret,—A happy New Year to you all!   My immediate purpose in writing is to celebrate Alice's social greatness, and to do humble penance for the obstacles I have persistently thrown in her path.   By which I mean that the dinner which we gave on Sunday night, and which she with great equanimity got up, was a perfect success.   She began, according to her wont, after we had been in the apartment a fortnight, to say that we must give a dinner to the Villaris, etc.   If you could have seen the manner of our ménage at that time, you would have excused the terrible severity of the tones in which I rebuked her, and the copious eloquence in which I described

our past, present, and future life and circumstances and expressed
my doubts as to whether she ought not to inhabit an asylum rather
than an apartment. As time wore on we got a waitress, and added
dessert spoons, fruit knives, etc., etc., to our dining-room resources;
also got some silver polish, etc.; and Alice would keep returning to
the idea in a way which made *me*, I confess, act like the madman with
whose conversation at such times (dictated I must say by the highest
social responsibility) you are acquainted. At last she invited the Lorings, I. Ostensacken and Loeser for New Year's night; I groaning,
she smiling; I hopeless and abusive, she confident and defensive, of
our resources; I doing all I could to add to her burden and make
things impossible, she explaining to Raffaello in her inimitable Italian, drilling the handmaids, screening the direful lamp most successfully with three Japanese umbrellas after I contended that it was impossible to do so, procuring the only two little red petticoats in the
city to put on our two candles, making a bunch of flowers, so small
in the centre of a star of fern leaves that I bitterly laughed at it, look
exquisitely lovely—and then, with her beautiful countenance, which
always becomes transfigured in the presence of company, keeping the
conversation going till after eleven o'clock. I humbly prostrated myself before her after it was over,—for the table really looked sweet—
no human being would have believed it beforehand,—threw the
wood-ashes on my head, and swore that she should have the Villaris,
and the King of Italy if she wished and whenever she wished, and
that I would write to you in token of my shame. It will please your
mother to hear what a successful creature she is. Her diet is still
eccentric,—flying from one extreme of abstinence to another,—and
her sleep fitful and accidental in its times and seasons. She sits up
very late at night, and slumbers publicly when afternoon visitors
come in, upright in her chair, with the lamp shining full on her beautiful countenance from which all traces of struggle have disappeared
and [where] sleep reigns calmly victorious—at least she did this once
lately. . . .

P.S. On reading this to Alice she says she does n't see what call I
had to write it, and that as for my obstructing the dinner, I had n't
made it more impossible than I always make everything. This with
a sweet ironical smile which I can't give on paper. . . .

LWJ, 1:338–40

To Grace Ashburner

16 P.ª dell' Indipendenza, | Florence Jan. 5. 93.
My dear Grace,

This is a rather tardy New Years greeting, but better late than not at all, and you must look at the spirit rather than the date. Theodora's letter of Nov 1st has been long in my portfolio, and I ought to be writing to her, or to *have written* to her rather, but experience has taught me that she is not of a jealous disposition, so I follow the path of my higher inclination and address you, knowing that what I write will leak out, and the day not pass before she learns it all, so it will really be almost the same thing as if I wrote to her. The account she gave of the summer was no very cheerful one, with poor Arthur's terrible illness, Rupert's ditto, Geo. Curtis's death,[1] and all, on top of your and your sister's continued bad condition. What would you all do without her strength, devotion, and good spirits? A helpful character, indeed! Bless her! I have had no news of Arthur since her letter and am decidedly concerned to know how and where he is. Perhaps news will come from some other quarter before I get any reply to this. Inflammatory rheumatism is one of the most infernal calamities that can befal a human being, and particularly abominable, coming as it did so soon after they were "out of the woods," with Mrs. A's recovery.[2] Arthur may be in Italy now for aught I know.—not in Florence I know, or we should have met. The terrible reputation of Florence for cold is much exaggerated. We have been a little chilly in our bed rooms, but nothing to complain of, and in the sitting room and dining room we have little sheet iron stoves with their pipes thrust into the chimney, and removeable when visitors come, which keep us perfectly warm with their disagreeable quality of heat. So far little sunshine; but now that the solstice is past and we are steering towards February, the heart looks forward to the coming season with high hope. Even the galleries are not too cold to frequent, provided one stay not too many hours. *Then,* I admit one's feet feel pretty frozen. I have found some first rate acquaintances here from the point of view of art culture, Loeser, who graduated at Harvard five or six years ago, and Berenson who did the same. Both know all the pictures of Europe by heart, and love to make disciples. B. is a genius, Loeser not a genius but a dear good fellow and perfect gentleman. Both jews. B. has but just turned up, so his ministrations lie rather in the future. Besides this, there is a young italian named Costa, whose knowledge is fabulously exact and wide.[3] The chief industry of these men is in the first instance to change the names of all the painters to whom the several pictures are ascribed. I have no doubt that they are entirely right in doing so for the most part, and that the traditions and in general the administration of these galleries have been quite scandalous. Then, after a sound objective basis has been reached, some sort of historic philosophy of painting becomes possible. I live in hopes of growing into it, but am much afflicted in my efforts by having no visual memory whatever, so that I can't recall, when my back is turned, what a picture is like, on which I may have gazed with interest for a quarter of an hour. The best way to get over that is to buy lots of photographs. One can buy them now by the thousand; and the more recent ones are very good. But they cost a mint of money, and are only one example of the difficulty of economy when one is over here. I don't well know what people mean by coming abroad to economize. One is on a *buying* basis far more than at home. To economize, stay in your own house and don't entertain company—that is the best receipt I know!—In all this I say nothing of your health. What can I do but hope & surmise? I hope that you are comfortable, whether it be by the help of opium or not. To tolerate opium is one of the greatest constitutional advantages that one can have. But at best the days must pass slowly enough for one of your active nature, when the hours are prolonged by pain and one is forced to keep in bed. I wish your winter was to be as short as ours! Theodora has given a surprisingly good account of your sister's well being. Long may it continue! Pray give her, and take for yourself, giving to Theodora also, the tenderest love of both of us, and warmest wishes for a good new Year.

Yours ever affectionately, | Wm James

ALS: MH bMS Am 1092.9 (727)

¹ George William Curtis died on 31 August 1892.

² Mrs. A. is Lucy Tuckerman Sedgwick.

³ Enrico Costa, a Peruvian living in Italy, friend of Bernhard Berenson.

To Elizabeth Ellery Sedgwick Child

16 Pª dell' Indipendenza | Florence, Jan. 5. 93

Dear Mrs. Child,

I wrote to poor Miss Grace Ashburner this morning, and, try as I will not to be over precipitate in writing to your family and expressing my undying amity therefor, I can hold out no longer, but - - - - -

Jan 6.—At this point I was interrupted yesterday afternoon by a stream of visitors, who lasted till ½ past nine o'clock—Mrs. Costello, then Frank Loring, and then Mrs Glendower Evans and her sister. Mrs Costello used to be Miss Mary Smith of the Annex, that rare and radiant daughter of Pearsall Smith of Philadelphia towards whom I vainly tried to warp your strong hearted husband's affections when she breathed in our midst. She has grown older, more political, and harder since then, but is still very handsome, and is here, with her husband and babies left behind in England, in order to sit reverently at the feet of young Berenson, whose name as an undergraduate you may remember, and who is supposed to be the profoundest and most voluminous of the various connoisseurs of the history of art with which the age abounds. I saw him for the first time yesterday and found him very interesting. It is getting to be a perfect menagerie here in that direction, and Mrs. C. is the queerest organism of them all. Take, my dear Mrs. Child, a modern woman of athletic intellect, tough moral fibre, and good memory for a master's phrases, deprive her of all native sensibility to aesthetic effects, and animate her with ambition to be an art-prophet, and you get a wonderful result. These people are all eaten up with contempt for each other's blunders, blindnesses, perversities and ignorances. Art in their hands is a mere instrument for indulging self-pride and scorn of their fellow men, instead of being a smiling gift which one may attend to in the manner most natural to one, and let drop with no bad conscience if it happen not to appeal. The throes of the human spirit on its sublime path towards culture are amongst the more fantastic arrangements of this odd universe. The goal is peace, harmony and easy insight, the way is over rocks of wrangling, bitterness and every repulsive sort of difficulty and pedantry, and personal grotesquery. Yet it *is* the way, after all. In comparison with these people, Denman Ross seems an angel of light, with his free and easy capacity for loving and enjoying what he likes and lightly letting fall what he doesn't care for. Yet he began years ago as the most preposterous doctrinairian prig. Your born philistine (I *don't* mean Ross, quite the reverse!) is as a rule the the only person who ends by getting anywhere, namely because he has to work for it. Native aristocracy of intelligence and temperament are always left behind.—But instead of a letter I am writing a diatribe, for which that precious and beautiful Mrs. Costello is to blame. Mrs Glendower Evans (whom, I believe, you know) has not yet recovered from the fatigue with which she left home, and is urging Alice to accompany her for six weeks to Egypt. Alice wont go, being too much of a "stay at home body"—I wish she would! But it is not a case of duty to Mrs. Evans, who in her worst state of nervous exhaustion has about 10 times as much practical energy and efficiency as Alice herself, so I say nothing to make her have a bad conscience about refusing to go.—And now enough about these accidents which befel as I was beginning to write. The chief thing is to know how you all are and something about your biographies since we left, seven months ago. I hope that a letter may even now be on its way. From Theodora I have heard that poor dear little Susie had not been very well[1]—I hope the colder weather may have brought her up again. The same informant said she had not seen your venerable husband look as young in many days as he was at the end of the summer. I hope and trust that the gout hasn't got at him again. I used to find myself wishing that you could all come abroad for a year. But from this pinnacle from which I survey all the possibilities of a Harvard professor's life I see there are two sides to that. The girls of course would enjoy it, but the wonting oneself to vagrancy and the confined quarters to which one is condemned when travelling make middle aged people lose a good many weeks and months before they have made their natures over again so as to begin to enjoy life on the unusual basis. I did a good deal of yearning for my library in the first few months, but now I'm completely in the foreign mood. The contact one has with Italy is irredeemably superficial or rather external, however. And coming abroad makes more and more impossible that slow growth into some kind of intimacy and harmony with the nature, people and institutions of one's own land towards which for the last twenty years or more I must say I have aspired more than towards anything else. Alice may do as she pleases; *I* will never come abroad again. It is' n't respectable. How is your dear old Frank, or rather *young* Frank,—speaking of the institutions of our native land? I hope he has borne stiffly up, under all the burdens of that terrible New York post of his.

I am writing *this* part of this interminable letter on January 7th. The entire day, yesterday & the day before, consisted of social & business interruptions. There were six people waiting at one time whilst we were at lunch; in the afternoon I had to take Peg to a child's party whilst Alice went for a drive with Mrs. Evans; and in the Evening Alice (for the 1st time in Florence) and I went to the theatre, where by a rare exception, Salvini played. It was a Richardson-Goldoni comedy (on the anniversary of G's death) "Pamela Nubile"—the most charming acting I ever knew.[2] Salvini is even better in comedy than in tragedy although the comedy here was not of the *light* order, so far as his part was concerned. The little self-righteous minx Pamela was deliciously done.—The great evil in Florence is the sociability—it has begun in the last few days to assume really threatening proportions, and I shall have to run away if it gets much worse. So many idle english and americans. I ought to be reading a good many hours a day, with a view to the teaching of the next two or three years.—Good bye, dear Mrs. Child, and a blessing upon you and all your household and kin. Alice sends a happy new year to you with me and we hope pretty soon to hear from your own pen just how things are.

Ever your affectionate, | Wm. James

ALS: MH bMS Am 1922 (347)

[1] Susan Child, daughter of Elizabeth Child.

[2] Alexander Salvini (1861–1896), Italian actor, appeared in Carlo Goldoni (1707–1793), Italian dramatist, *Pamela Nubile,* a play based on the novel *Pamela* by Samuel Richardson (1689–1761), British novelist.

To Hugo Münsterberg

16 P.ª dell' Indipendenza, | Florence, Jan. 7. 93

My dear Münsterberg,

Your welcome letter of Dec. 23rd. arrived yesterday, and all your cordial *glückwünsche* are "reciprocated," with a high rate of interest, by both of us. Long may your satisfaction with Cambridge last. Royce writes me that you are considered on all hands as "an immense success." The President writes "Münsterberg is doing splendidly"; so, since the organism seems so perfectly adapted to its environment, all that is needed is that the environment should continue to please the organism; and *that,* I privately continue to hope, will be the case even after the three years contract has come to an end. In other words, I have been speculating all along on the possibility that your three years term might end by being indefinitely prolonged, and I think that any very anxious canvassing of the question "who shall be M's successor?" is certainly not called for at the present time. The end of next year, or, still better, of the year after next, will be full time enough for that.

Now, as to the special question of Nichols and the work for next year, I got a long letter from Royce the day before yesterday, in which he utters much the same opinions that you do, and I wish that you would communicate what I now say to him, as well as to Palmer as it will save duplication in writing.

I have felt all along that Nichols ought to have independent control of the psychological department of a smaller college where the standard of general cultivation was less high, and the atmosphere less critical than at Harvard University. I tried to make him realize that last year himself, but evidently without success. He is quite too unacademic a character to succeed in the higher teaching with us, and he is too old, too original, and too positive a personality, to be employed permanently as mere laboratory-demonstrator, admirable as his talents and disposition are for that kind of work. He ought to be chief in a smaller place. If such a place offers itself to him for next year, we ought to make him understand that we wish him to take it, and can promise him no advancement at Harvard. At the same time, if no place should offer itself, and we should at the end of this year be seeking a laboratory assistant for the following year, and Nichols desire it, on the full understanding that he must be exerting himself all the while to secure a position elsewhere, it seems to me that it would be for the advantage of the College to keep him, in spite of the moral strain on our sympathies which his presence would involve. The peculiar thing about Nichols is his extraordinary transparency and fundamental generosity of character. He confides all his feelings, hopes, exultations and agonies to you so unreservedly, and when you criticize him tries to prove to you by elaborate reasonings that you don't understand him at all, that it is a real torture to have him near you in the condition of imperfect approval which his sayings and doings must always continue to elicit from you. He is *naif* as a child, with many of the best qualities of a splendid man. On a polar expedition or in a campaign few men would be loved like Nichols, for his energy would be boundless, and his unselfishness and good spirits matchless—but in the arena of modern philosophy his ideas are all too eccentric, and his way of expressing them too queer. No man has made my heart bleed so much; and I am sorry that you are forced to take your turn in the haemorrhage. I think that the sympathetic way in which you write of him does the greatest honour to the essentially humane character of your own disposition. I don't know just what may have happened lately on his part, to bring upon me these rather urgent letters from yourself and Royce, so I dare not write to him immediately a frank letter stating my own opinion as to his future; but I am ready to do so, if you desire it, whenever you let me know.

Now as to the work of next year, I am still of the opinion that I expressed to Royce, Palmer & Nichols last Spring, namely that our present grading and subdivision of the instruction in Psychology is injudicious. What we should aim at is: 1st.) a *large* course of general information as to the chief results and methods; & 2nd.) a course of training for picked men who mean to go more deeply into the study. This latter course, it seems to me, ought not legitimately to contain more than twenty five or at the outside thirty men, including those who wish to become professors. The former course might contain 200, or even more. Our present course 2, if taken by many men who have had already course 1, has to be made too minute and fastidious for the nonprofessional-aspirant, and it is n't quite technical enough for the "picked" man, who should properly be treated more as a strictly professional student. I vote therefore that Phil. 2 be dropped altogether.[1] I propose that Phil. 1 be made a "half-course" (3 lessons a week for ½ the year) with no laboratory work, but experimental demonstrations before the class by the instructor, and that students who have taken Phil 1. be allowed, *after consultation with the instructor,* to enter the more advanced psychology, which should consist of two parts, one (to count as a half course) of laboratory exercises and a thesis, the other of special research and seminary, to "count" according to the time the man may put into it. This seems to me a division founded on two natural groups of men and their legitimate wants. I quite satisfied myself last year that the present Phil 1. & Phil 2 are a clumsy and unnatural arrangement. Some degree of acquaintance with psychology is needed by every liberally educated man, but the saturation point of the ordinary man is soon reached and when subtleties and polemics come in (and they are very quickly reached in Psychology) he groans and fails to assimilate. There is not, (and I think we must frankly confess it) enough positive *Ausbeute* in what we call the science of Psychology, for more than a ½ year of general instruction. In this respect, Physics, Chemistry, Physiology, and Natural History are on an entirely different footing, from Psychol. I trust that these views will recommend themselves to your judgment as practical, and that the philosophical committee will see no objection to the change. If the Psychology of Phil 1. be extended to a ½ year, it would seem natural to have a ½ year of Logic, and one of metaphysics too. I believe in those as well. *All* the subjects are too crowded at present in Phil. 1, whose only advantage is one of external convenience, and simplicity in our list of courses.

As to who shall do the teaching, I have all along supposed that I should myself resume the giving of the larger course next year. I am sorry you speak still so despondingly of your English, but of course to lecture to a large class after one year would be an almost unheard-of feat, and the amount of care and responsibility you have as director of experimental work will be a full man's share. If I also take the *theses* of the second half-course which I propose, and offer a seminary, say on mental-pathology, for either half the year or the whole year, whichever may seem best to go with the seminary-work which you propose, our psychological bill of fare will be provided, without the need of any third instructor beside the laboratory demonstrator.[2] I ought to say frankly, what you of course already know, that nature never made me to be an experimentalist, and that laboratory instruction of any sort assigned to me would certainly be very inferiorly performed. Besides I am too "neurasthenic" (*not* lazy!) to do much of it in addition to teaching, without bad fag at the end of the year.

That is all I have to say about all this troublesome business, and I hope I have both made myself clear, and expressed opinions which will prove to be in accordance with your own.

You speak, at the beginning of your letter, of your last letter, "seit acht Tagen unterwegs." I have never received it, and hope to Heaven it isn't lost. But we haven't lost any letter yet, to my knowledge, since being here, though some letters have been late, and I still trust that yours will come. Please remember us both most cordially to Mrs. Munsterberg—I hear the pleasantest gossip about your household from Margaret Gibbens—and believe me ever yours,

W.J.

ALS: MH bMS Am 1092.9 (3275)

[1] WJ's arguments proved unpersuasive and Philosophy 1: General Introduction to Philosophy, covering logic, psychology, metaphysics, and history of philosophy, and Philosophy 2: Psychology were retained for 1893–94.

[2] In 1893–94 advanced psychology consisted of Philosophy 20a, a psychological laboratory given by Münsterberg, and WJ's Philosophy 20b: Psychological Seminary, which that year was devoted to mental pathology. For WJ's teaching in abnormal psychology see *ML*, lv.

To Josiah Royce

16 P.ª dell Indipendenza | Florence, Jan 7. 93

Dearest Josiah, Having just written 16 pp. to Münsterberg, & asked him to refer them to you, I need not express myself in any detail in

response to your letter of the 22nd ult. with its masterly characteriz-
ing of poor Herbert. J. N. I entirely agree with all you say about his
ought-ing to have an autonomous position in a smaller college. He
is too cranky and crude on the side of his allgemeine Bildung for
the fierce light that beats upon our professorial thrones in Harvard
University. Would that he wouldn't make our hearts bleed so for
him! Not knowing how much *he* knows of your present concern
about him, I have refrained from writing to him direct. The trouble
is that whatever you say to him, he will try to argue to you that it is
false, unmindful of the rule that you must never *reason* with another's
impression of your *character*, but leave him to his blindness & error.
Münsterberg's letter, much to my satisfaction, showed that his views
as to the general policy of the teaching, were quite in accordance
with my own.

I have explicitly proposed to him to drop Phil 2. for next year and
make the Psychology part of Phil. 1 a ½ year's course. I hope that
you and Palmer, when the Committee meets, will agree that this is
best. *I* am absolutely certain of it. Of course I will write to you later
about the courses in detail. I aim, as you know, at the "Cosmology."[1]
Can't you advise me as to a text book? Spencer's 1st Principles, gone
rapidly, lightly and not venemously-over would surely be good; but
it is n't enough, I fear.[2] Lange's Hist. is too long.[3] Possibly Spencer
with lectures and a good deal of thesis, would be good; but I mistrust
too much lecturing without a printed text to follow.—It's very
hard!—How is Santayana getting on this year? And what of Rand,
to whom I hear no allusions? Are you having an easier year of work
than hitherto? I hope so. "Society" is beginning now to threaten
our existence. It is too bad. Berenson & Mrs. Costello have turned
up. Loeser is a dear duck.

Good bye blessings on you all, especially on my dear little Mr. Bradlaugh![4]

Yours ever | W.J.

ALS: MH bMS Am 1092.9 (3611)

[1] For Philosophy 3: Cosmology, see letter of 18 December 1892; for the texts used
see *ML*, liv.

[2] WJ's heavily annotated copy of Spencer's *First Principles of a New System of Philosophy*
is an 1877 reprint of the revised edition (WJ 582.24.4).

[3] Friedrich Albert Lange (1828–1875), German philosopher, *History of Materialism*
(1877).

[4] Nothing was found identifying Mr. Bradlaugh. Possibly, it is an inside joke, perhaps with reference to Charles Bradlaugh (1833–1891), British freethinker and political radical, and Royce as an agitator within Harvard's philosophy department.

To Arthur George Sedgwick

16 Pᵃ dell' Indipendenza | Florence, Jan 21. 92 [1893]
My dear Arthur,

I am very glad to hear directly from you of your well-being and satisfaction with Meran. You say nothing of extreme cold, so I suppose you must have been sheltered from the terrible weather which seems to have afflicted the rest of the Austrian empire. The sufferings of the poor must have been terrible. We have had no discomfort here at all except from the small size of our only warmable sitting room, and the *costplayfulness,* to use the happy German phrase, of the whole expedition. I suppose you can sympathize!—I'm glad your going into the bowels of German. Julian Schmidt's Gesch. d. D. Literatur seit Lessings Tod, I used to think one of the richest messes I ever dipped into.[1] At present my german is all Science & Philosophy. My Italian is—awful! But this nation is resigned to everything.— Vide in last Nation a letter about Padua signed W.J.—I cal'late to go to Germany *solus* about May 1, over the Brenner, and do hope that you will be at Meran. Tell Bs. Schönberg (the title stands for Baroness, not Bess) that nothing will rejoice me (and possibly me & *her**) more than to stop and see them at Brixen.[2]

Best of regards to your wife—Peg sends love to Grace.[3]

Do you find that your great trouble at Meran is that you haven't *time* for anything? It's my great trouble here. I used to think it due to circumstances at home, but now I believe it to be "constitutional."

Yrs ever. | Wm James

I've bought this A.M. seven old Italian paintings of remar[k]able merit for 105 francs, four of 'em with frames

[*]By "her" I don't mean *her,* but my wife. Keep the *text* of this message concealed from her, for Heaven's sake. She's a dear thing.

ALS: MH bMS Am 1092.9 (3717)

[1] Julian Schmidt (1818–1886), German literary historian, *Geschichte der deutschen Litaratur seit Lessing's Tod* (1858).

[2] Elizabeth Ward de Schönberg, sister of Thomas Wren Ward and niece of Mary Dorr.

[3] Probably Grace Ashburner Sedgwick, Arthur Sedgwick's daughter.

To Francis Boott

16 Pᵃ dell' Indipendenza, | Jan 30. 93

Dear Mr. Boott,

Your letter of Dec. 15th was very welcome, with its home gossip and its florentine advice. Our winter has worn away, as you see, with very little discomfort from cold. It is true that I have been irritated at the immoveable condition of my bed-room thermometer which for 5 weeks has been at 40° F. not shifting in all that time more than one degree either way until I longed for a change—but how much better such steadfastness than the acrobatic performances of our American winter-thermometer. You and other sybarites scared us so, in the fall, about the arctic cold we should have, that I used daily to make vows to the creator and the saints that if they would only carry us safely to the first of February I never would ask them for another favor as long as I lived. With the impending winter once *overcome,* I thought, life would be one long vista of relief thenceforth. But practically there has been nothing *to* overcome. I am glad, however, that now that January disappears, we may have some *warm* days, coming more and more frequently. The spring must be really delicious. We are keeping as shy of "Society" as we can, but still we see a good many people, and the interruptions to study (from that, and the domestic causes which abound in our narrow quarters—narrow in winter time, broad enough when fires go out) are very great. Duveneck spent a most delightful evening here a while ago, and left a big portfolio of photogs of Böcklin's pictures and a big bunch of cegars for me two days later. I wish I didn't always feel like a *phrase-monger* with honest artists like him. However there are some fellows who seem phrase mongers to me, Berenson, *e.g.,* so it's "square." We have seen the Huntingtons several times—I like miss Huntington very much.[1] Were you ever struck by the likeness between *Mrs.* H. & Aunt Mary Tweedy—a *family* likeness? She is still more like Lady Rose.[2]—We have a cook, Raffaello, the most modest and faithful of his sex. Our manner of communication with him is *awful,* but he finishes all our sentences for us, and strange to say, just as we would have finished them if we could. Alice swears we must bring him home to America. Should you think it safe? He seems to have no friends or diversions here, and no love except for his sauce pans. But I dread the responsibility of being foster-father to him in our cold and uncongenial land. It would be different if I spoke his lingo.—What do *you* think? And *what* a pretty lingo it is. Italian & German seem to me *the* languages. The mongrels french & english might drop out! *A propos* to English, I return your slip "as *per* request," having been amused at the manifestation of the ruling passion in you. I don't care how incorrect language may be if it only has fitness of epithet, energy, and clearness. But I do pity the poor English department. I see they are talking in England of more study of their own tongue in the schools being required. I wish I knew more details of the Peabody affair.[3] I wrote him a letter of "endorsement" whatever he did. The copy of the Journal which you sent me by Duveneck was enough to make me swear never to return home. I wonder if we can't get up a law making the publication of a man's portrait without his permission a penal offence. The french papers and our papers are a mere —— *stink.*

Mark Twain dined with us last night in Co. with the good Villari and the charming Mrs. V. but there was no chance then to ask him to sing Nora McCarty. He's a dear man, and there'll be a chance yet. He is in a delightful Villa at Settignano, and says he has written more in the past 4 months than he could have done in 2 years at Hartford.—Well! good bye, dear old friend. I hope that this will find both you and Mrs. Greenough well, after the great cold which we hear of. Alice sends you much love, & so do I.

Yours ever,   Wm. James

Duveneck's bronze is still invisible. He is to let me know as soon as it can be seen.

ALS: MH bMS Am 1092.9 (764)

Address: Francis Boott Esq | Cambridge | Mass | Stati Uniti di A.

Postmarks: NEW YORK FEB 12 93   CAMBRIDGE BOSTON MASS. FEB 13 93

[1] Ellen Greenough Huntington (d. 1893), an expatriate American residing mostly in Italy. Miss Huntington is Mary Huntington, her stepdaughter. Ellen Huntington's brother was married to Frances Boott Greenough, sister of Francis Boott.

[2] Lady Charlotte Temple Rose (d. 1883), wife of Sir John Rose (1820–1888), Canadian financier and diplomat, and sister of Mary Temple Tweedy.

[3] The Peabody affair involved Francis Greenwood Peabody, who as a senior at Harvard in 1869, with no thought of the future, was elected "Aligator Crocadilus" of the Hasty Pudding, a Harvard student society, with duties that included the composition of an amusing poem. When years later he become professor of Christian morals, some students discovered the poem and embarrassed him by reciting it in public. Subsequently, the poem disappeared from the safe at the offices of the Hasty Pudding, removed, according to the janitor, by someone who looked very much like Peabody. Peabody's biographical file in the Harvard Archives contains clippings about the affair, including one from the *Journal*, 17 December 1892. The *Journal* is probably the *Boston Journal.*

To Léon Marillier

[February 11, 1893]

The passing thought which I propose that psychologists should adopt as their ultimate datum on the mental side, is expressly intended to make psychology more positivistic and free from subtle disputes than she has been.   Practically all schools agree with common sense that we do have thoughts which pass, altho' they differ as to the genesis & constitution of such tho'ts.   Now I contend that all the facts of our experience are *formulable* in terms of these undecomposed thoughts, on the one hand, and of the 'objects' which they 'know' on the other, quite as simply and more naturally than by the theory of ideas.   Formulating them thus gives us a good honest empirical body of science, which does not of course go to the bottom of all mysteries, but which, as far as it does go, is sound, and as free as possible from containing paradoxes and stumbling blocks in its terms. The farther questions that remain (as to the genesis and constitution of these thoughts etc) seem to me so subtle that they had best be relegated to "metaphysics"; and it is the misfortune of of the age in which I write quite as much as my personal fault, that in trying to show how to make a psychology which shall be 'positivistic' I have to exert myself also to show the metaphysical difficulties that the current theories involve, and of which their supporters seem so profoundly unconscious.   I cannot however well [see] why you should *object* to my formulation; for even if our thoughts *are* compounds of 'ideas', they are at least superficially and practically also all that I say they are, namely integreal pulses of consciousness with respect to the multitude of facts of which they may take cognizance in a single passing moment of time.   All you ought to accuse me of is *insufficiency,* not error.   But I freely admit that in the vehemence of my argumentation in the Chap. on the Stream of Tho't.,[1] I seem to be contending for the unity more as an ultimate and definitive truth than as a peculiarly advantageous methodological assumption.   That Chapter was really written as a bit of popular description, to show (1st) the natural way in which our mental life would appear to a man who has no theories, and (2nd) to show certain omissions and difficulties involved in the account given by the theory of ideas.   I shd. be sorry to have it taken as a 'theory' of my own; and in particular . . . . . I have no definite theory whatever as to just how the consciousness of relations may arise.   I protest heartily against what you say on page 627 that I "superpose upon states of consciousness thoughts which think them."[2] The thoughts are the states of consciousness; and since common sense & natural science think that the things of which we are conscious do exist extra mentem, I prefer to say that the thoughts think *those things*.

Now it is quite true that some of these things are *sensible qualities*, and that in this case there is no distinction between the feeling and its object. At this point, then, to my mind, the whole *problem of cognition* opens. The dualistic views of common sense and science, that the thought is one thing and the object another, breaks down, the object appearing as what you call the *'sensation objectivée.*['] But to trace the consequences of this idea involves one in the most diabolically subtle and insoluble of all the higher metaphysical problems; and a straightforward psychology can never be written in consistent terms in any but dualistic language. Therefore I exclude all this consideration from psychology, and talk of sensation's 'object' just as I do of conceptions or perception's objects. If Erkenntnisstheorie is ever thought out (and I confess that its problems are what for some years past have weighed most heavily on my own mind) there will probably be a reconciliation between the notions of states of Mind compounding themselves and of objects being combined in thoughts. Meanwhile why should you insist on keeping the more paradoxical form of statement? Why protest against the other, in which no one ever has found or ever will find cause of offense?

Copy in WJ's hand:[3] MH bMS Am 1092.9 (3189)

[1] "The Stream of Thought," chap. 9 of *Principles of Psychology*.

[2] Reference is to Marillier's "Psychologie de William James," *Revue Philosophique*, 34:627.

[3] On the front of an envelope found with this letter is the following note in WJ's hand: 'Copy of W.J.'s letter to Marillier | Feb. 11. 1893'. The physical evidence suggests that this copy of the letter was kept in the envelope.

To Hugo Münsterberg

16 P.ª dell Indipendenza, | Feb. 11. 1893

My dear Münsterberg,

Just one word, to say that the letter before the one you wrote about Nichols has never appeared. I am extremely sorry to have missed it, and can form no theory as to how it may have gone astray. I missed a letter from Nichols last summer, but know of no other loss. Possibly yours may turn up yet, as one from Royce did several weeks too late, stamped "Missent—Indian Mail." Your reprint of article about Lab. came this AM. and is very graceful & readable.[1]　Two months in America has made you also one of the *Reclamhelder*! Where will it end?　But such things are really useful to the cause, although I do wish we had some more simply and solidly formulable results to show to the populace than 'exact' investigation has yet ground out!

I wrote to day (I could n't help it) a letter to Ebbinghaus, asking if he thought it did any good to German Science or to his Zeitschrift to print articles so blackguardly in tone as Müller's last, in his largest type.[2]　I expressed myself without reserve as to M's personal indecency.　Don't for God's sake retort in kind—such polemics only degrade Germany in the eyes of the world, and Müller writes himself down as a ruffian and a cad, without any aid from any one else in so defining him.　But what's the use of an editor unless to protect a man from such insults?

As for the matter in dispute Hipp's Chronoscope is getting to be as impossible a thing to discuss with Muller and his kind as Kant's Ding an Sich, so I confess I didn't read what he had to say, barring his insults.　In the business of muscle psychology you know how inhospitable I am to your ideas.　In particular the pp. about 90–91 struck me when I read them as rather an oversubtle way out of a difficulty.[3]　But your whole theory is in process of evolution by way of copious experiments of your own, and the really scientific manner of regarding you, I take it, is not to *jump on you* like this, but to remain a while longer expectant and see what it developes into in your own hands.

Good luck to you all!

Yours | W.J.

ALS: MB

[1] Hugo Münsterberg, "The New Psychology, and Harvard's Equipment for Teaching It," *Harvard Graduates' Magazine* 1 (January 1893): 201–9.

[2] Georg Elias Müller, "Berichtigung zu Prof. Münsterbergs Beiträgen zur experimentellen Psychologie, Heft 4," *Zeitschrift für Psychologie und Physiologie der Sinnesorgane* 4 (1893): 404–14.

[3] Hugo Münsterberg, *Beiträge zur experimentellen Psychologie*, pt. 4 (1892).

From George Frederick Stout

S^T JOHN'S COLLEGE, | CAMBRIDGE. Feb 13th /93

Dear Professor James

I am distinctly in favour of keeping your longer reply.　The issue is very important & cries out for discussion.[1]

Personally I feel strongly opposed to your view & to me Bradley's criticism seemed effective.   Certainly the attempted *reductio ad absurdum* breaks down; for the simple reason that it cuts both ways. The regression in infinitum lies in the very nature of an intensive series, becausive intensive magnitude admits of an infinite number of gradations.   You & Stumpf are left with a series of degrees of resemblance.[2] I cannot see that such a series is in a logically different position to a series of degrees of green or degrees of blue or even degrees of blue & green united such as we have in the transition from pure blue to pure green.

I have criticised your view in a paper published in the Aristotelian Proceedings, No 1. Pt 2 1892.[3] I have there been more modest than Bradley, contenting myself with an attempt to show that the identity-theory has not been *dis*proved, so that if positive reasons can be found for adopting it, there is no reason in the nature of the case why we should not do so.   The positive reasons seem to me forthcoming in connexion with the doctrine of what goes by the name of "Interactions of Presentation."   This doctrine appears to me to have a substantial basis, though the nature of this basis has doubtless been misunderstood.   I agree with you that as mere fleeting contents of consciousness presentations cannot interact & I now agree that an[y] resort to unconscious or even *sub*conscious presentations is quite unsatisfactory   But even this theory seems to me to formulate facts of fundamental importance & the fault lies chiefly in the mode of formulation, which certainly leads to what you call mythology.   But I [do] not agree that the objective conditions, which "Association of ideas" etc. presuppose, can only be thought of from the physiological point of view as given in the sensible phenomena of brain & nervous system.   If we are to give anything like a satisfactory schema of our mental life, we must also approach them from the point of view of introspective reflection as given in the phenomena of mental process. Yet I do not, like you, incline to believe in Free will & a separable soul.   I do not care much about gaining bran-new knowledge about mind.   My absorbing desire is merely for clearness & distinctness. Is this a reprehensible attitude?

Yours very truly | G. F. Stout.

Excuse this rigmarole.   You are under no obligation to answer it.

ALS: MH WJ 583.67

[1] WJ, "Mr. Bradley on Immediate Resemblance," *Mind*, n.s., 2 (April 1893): 208–10 (reprinted in *EPh*), a reply to Francis Herbert Bradley, "On Professor James' Doctrine of Simple Resemblance," *Mind*, n.s., 2 (January 1893): 83–88.

[2] WJ states that in his view he is only following Stumpf (*EPh*, 66).

[3] George Frederick Stout, "A General Analysis of Presentations as a Preparatory to the Theory of Their Interaction," *Proceedings of the Aristotelian Society*, vol. 2, no. 1, pt. 2, pp. 107–20 (pp. 116–20 on WJ).

To Alice Howe Gibbens James

GRAND HOTEL BRUN | BOLOGNA Tuesday [February 21, 1893] P.M.
after dinner | 8 o'clock

Dearest wife & Mother—we got here safely at 10 o'clock and with the exception of lunch have been on our feet 7 hours, seeing 2 museums, several churches, the Old professor pictures, and the streets.[1] Bologna has no charm but there is tremendous strength of character in the building, arcades stairs, courts etc.   The pinacothek is awfully uninteresting, and the poor old professor's collection mostly trash with immense prices attached.   He has 4 *good*, really good figure pieces, at from 5000 dollars to three thousand each, and four capital landscapes, making a set, for which he asks 2000 dollars.   I should gladly own all the eight, but you will be pleased to hear that I have made no offer, not even 10,000 dollars for the lot.   He had two landscapes by the painter of those I destroyed, smaller than those, for which he asks 1500 or 2000 frs. I forget which.   Harry has been serene and though inexpressive has thoroughly enjoyed himself. Our only regret was your absence and Bill's; but as there was a tower like a factory-chimney so high that the eye fell short of the top of it, which he would have forced us to climb had he been here, our grief at his absence was tempered with resignation.—Let him practice in getting both legs round his neck ere I return and meet me walking

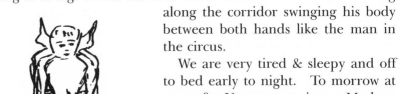 along the corridor swinging his body between both hands like the man in the circus.

We are very tired & sleepy and off to bed early to night.   To morrow at 10.30 for Verona stopping at Modena 3 hours by the way, and arriving at about 8 PM. at the Colomba d'Oro. After Verona, I think we shan't stop till Munich—possibly at Meran, though.[2] Keep back and read letters for a day or too then send to Hôtel Marienbad Munich.   I hope your day has gone well, with a certain amount of simplification.

Yours ever,   W.J.

Kiss all three. I am so proud, darling of the qualities you have developed here in Italy!!

ALS: MH bMS Am 1092.9 (1857)

[1] WJ and son Henry were on their way to Munich to look for suitable schools.
[2] Arthur George Sedgwick was then at Meran; see letter of 21 January 1893.

From Alice Howe Gibbens James

Wednesday, 3 P.M. [February 22, 1893]

Dear William,

Your good letter and Harry's came this morning, to my joy. I hope the keen air does n't mean decided cold for you. I shopped all day with Mrs Brooks and was glad to rest and attend to my own affairs today. I have finished the Life of Miss Dix[1] and read *Baumeister Solneβ,* which I can now take back to Mrs Costelloe.[2] I suppose you gave her her article as I do not see it in her book.[3] I send you the *Nation* and the *Speaker* shall follow.[4] This letter from Mr Peabody disappoints me, it has so hollow a ring.[5] Mrs Child's is more involved than ever—Grace run riot. Shall I send you two numbers of *Lux* which have appeared?[6]

I ought to take Billy and go away from home that you may see what space seems to reign here. You would like it. I like a day of quiet at last, but I miss you and Harry. Billy is at school rehearsing his play this afternoon.—Mrs Brooks has come to say that Mrs Holton has come so I will run over and see her and mail this at the same time. What you write of those pictures makes the old sick feeling come back. Let us never speak of them again. I am guilty of a deed of violence for which I can only atone by future temperateness and gentleness.[7] This proof came yesterday morning, picked up in the Pension by Mrs Brooks![8] Heaven bless you both and keep you warm o'nights.

Your loving | Alice.

ALS: MH bMS Am 1092.9 (295)

[1] Dorothea Lynde Dix (1802–1887), American feminist and reformer. AGJ read Francis Tiffany, *Life of Dorothea Lynde Dix* (1890).
[2] Henrik Ibsen, *Baumeister Solness* (1892).
[3] Mary Berenson published some articles as Mary Whitall Costelloe, but which is the one in question was not established.
[4] *Speaker: The Liberal Review* was published in London from 1890.
[5] Peabody's letter may have had something to do with the Hasty Pudding affair; see letter to Boott of 30 January 1893.

[6] *Lux* (*Nova Lux*) was a psychological periodical published in Rome from 1888.

[7] In his letter to AGJ of 21 February 1893 WJ states that it was he who destroyed certain landscapes.

[8] Writing to AGJ on 4 March 1893 (calendared), WJ referred to "'stout' proofs," suggesting that these are proofs of "Mr. Bradley on Immediate Resemblance."

From Alice Howe Gibbens James

Florence Feb 23ᵈ 1893

My dear William,

This has been a queer day beginning with thunder and such darkness that I backed out from a visit to Santa Croce with Mrs Brooks and stayed at home to read and write a letter to Mary. After the lesson I took Peggy and we wandered forth to the dressmaker, to pay for Harry's suit and to get her hair cut.—There Obrist appeared and has spent the evening so I must make short work of this that Rafaello may mail it tonight. Obrist came to ask the boys to go with him to Vincilliata next Sunday. He has agreed to come for Billy & then return to dinner. I met Mary James at the station. She & Mamie very nice and cheery.[1]

Duveneck came in to say good bye ere he starts for Siscily(!) He has an idea for the tomb stone of which I will write tomorrow. He was amazed that you should be contemplating Munich, of which he tells a sad tale in the way of climate. Miss Loring quite converted me to Stuttgart. Of course with the little children we must pay some heed to climate. They are well, Billy is a good boy and I really am busy all day long. Vasari is delightful, you were so kind to get it![2] And you are always kind to us and I mean to contradict no more when you come back.

Now I must get this into the box so no more, save blessings on you both.

Your loving | Alice

Tell Harry that I shall write to him some day. Stout's letter came this A.M.

ALS: MH bMS Am 1092.9 (293)

[1] Mamie is the nickname of Mary James Vaux.

[2] Giorgio Vasari (1511–1574), Italian artist and biographer of artists.

To Alice Howe Gibbens James

　　　　　　　　　　　Hotel Marienbad | Munich Feb 25. 93
Dearest Alice,
　　I write this at bkfst. just after receiving your letter of the 23rd
enclosing Stout's. Your sociability seems great; and the good Obrist
apparently is smitten by the charms of your white hair. He's a dear
creature! Yesterday mng. we went to the Pinacothek, a superb collection of masterpieces,[1] and then loafed about the city, which is a
noble one. Table d'hote at 1; then nap, and more walk when I left
Harry & spent 1½ with the Stumpf's, who live in a very simple way;
in the evening to the circus—a better one than at Florence. What a
pleasure it is to see a stout well dressed manly looking population—
no beggars—It makes Florence loom like a lazaretto in one's memory.
The air here, too is so strong and good, with that old german smell
of smoke in it to make it feel nourishing!—[Bedroom] I am thoroughly glad, however, that we went to Florence; and when I think of
you, with your sociable and anhänglich disposition, left here next
year, I don't like the idea at all. Mrs. Stumpf praises the climate, &
says that her only remembrances of Munich are of fine days. At
eleven St. is coming to take me to the Realgymnasiumdirector, who
is an old friend of his, and who may put us in the way of finding a
family at least.
　　I must now write *in rê* Stout. Heaven bless you. Kiss Peg, Tweedy,
& even Bill.
　　　　　　　　　　　　　　　　　　　Thine ever! | W.J.
　　Harry has gone off alone to the neue pinacothek, which was
closed yesterday.

ALS: MH bMS Am 1092.9 (1829)

[1] The Alte Pinakothek in Munich was a museum that housed old masters, while the
Neue Pinakothek was devoted to contemporary paintings.

To Alice Howe Gibbens James

　　Marienbad H. Munich | Sunday [February] 26. 1893 | 11.30 AM.
Dearest Alice
　　Your letter of Friday greets us, lying on the table as we enter the
bed-room. I am sorry you are coming the remorse-business (Vide
your last sentence) you had better leave that to me! And when you

dwell upon the quiet time, the rest etc, in spite of company to dinner every night and social duties all day, and say you wish that by changing places with you I could enjoy it, why then it makes me think that *my* absence is what makes the quiet; and I don't wonder that you feel so, so fretful, restless and agaçant was my presence in the last weeks. It can't be helped; I am einmal so gemacht! Munich is delicious; the perfection of weather, mellow tempered sunshine soft full bodied air with just enough smoke-smell in it to give interest, and noble streets and population. Great horizontal effects, and the steep roofs pressing down the great houses so as to make them steadfast and weighty on the ground. The 'pension' question for Harry is no farther advanced. I saw a dreadful place yesterday recommended by the Gymnasiumdirector, a place out of "Jack," filthy with six beds in one small room. I have just called on Schrenk-Notzing—psychical researcher who is very cordial and invites me to 3 social entertainments in one breath—he says I must *advertize*. Meanwhile his wife who is a Stuttgarterin will write to a family there whom she guarantees as good, if they only have room. The[y] also offer good introductions in Stuttgart, and as he is a "freiherr" and a *von*, that probably will suit you better. My own impression is that, school for school, the Munich R!gym is less likely to be good than the Stuttgart one. A poor old building, a dingy director, etc. *But*, I *imagine* we shall all go home together in any case—so the main thing is to lodge Harry favorably at present. I had deep depression of spirits yesterday in this big strange place, with so little living connexion, and what connexion there is too exciting for the nerves. I go now to find no 2. of the gymnasium director's addresses, having called twice and found the man out. It looks little better than the first one.—Then to Stumpf's again to dine—Harry understood everything essential at the theatre last night. A *beautifully* acted play, out at 9.20!

The *beer* here is delicious—I am to go with Schrenk to the Hofbrauhaus at 3.30 this P.M.

Love to you all and remembrances to Mary Holton & family. How I wish we cd find someone who wd. take the two bratlets home!—from Genoa.

Your loving   W.J.

ALS: MH bMS Am 1092.9 (1830)

To Alice Howe Gibbens James

      Hotel Marienbad, München, | Feb. 27. 93 | 12.45. PM.
Dearest Alice—Another letter from you this A.M.—how I could live
without them I know not! But the whirlpool of sociability in which
you are plunged makes me glad I am away.—A musical party at Mrs.
Bigelow Lawrence's is a horror unreckoned on. I have had rather
too much sociability here, since it comes at a bad time of day for my
sleep, but I am luckily free from it to day. Yesterday after Stumpf's
dinner, Schrenk Notzing took me (whilst Harry stayed in hotel) a
delightful drive in his pony phaeton, around & through the town
and we wound up with an hour and a ½ at 3 enormous beer-keller
(the hofbräuhous being the first one,) where I had to drink 3 litres,
and went to the theatre after wards with Harry who was much
pleased by the play—l'Ami Fritz of Eck-Ch.[1] To night we go to see
l'Assommoir.[2] The theatre is really *good* here; and all together I
heartily and thoroughly like the town. It is true that this fine
weather is said to be exceptional at this season. We have made a
little progress to day towards a boarding place. I shall fight it out in
Munich, no matter how long it takes, for it will all be to recommence
if I go elsewhere. You must really not think of Weimar; the Greek
there would be nothing short of a *crime,* in Harry's case; and he could
never get ready to enter by the first week in April. We might however, as a family, find it good for the summer to be near there.

    I have slept badly since being here, and read nothing to speak of,
and all that with the interminableness of our "problems," the expen-
siveness of all this travelling, and the charms of our Irving S.ᵗ home
(if I could only escape over-work there!) make me feel as if it would
be awfully good for us all to be safe back there together again. But
we shall have plenty of time to decide when Harry once is settled.
Just now, I must confess that his utterly unresisting, but also utterly
inert presence rather adds to the weight. But I have got him to
reading Uli der Knecht, which he seems able to follow,[3] and a good
nap which I can get this afternoon will dispel the gloom.

                               Lovingly W.J.
3 o'clock. Nap stattgefunden, so I feel born again, thanks to *you.*
God bless you

ALS: MH bMS Am 1092.9 (1831)

[1] A dramatization of Émile Erckmann (1822–1899) and Alexandre Chatrian (1826–
1890), French authors, *L'Ami Fritz* (1864).

[2] A dramatization of the novel by Émile Zola, *L'Assommoir* (1877).

[3] Albert Bitzius (1797–1854), writing under the pseudonym of Jeremias Gotthelf, *Uli der Knecht* (1841).

To Alice Howe Gibbens James

Marienbad Hotel Tuesday. Feb. 28(?) 1893 | 5 P.M.

Dearest Alice,

No letter from you to day, alas!   But to morrow's will be all the more greedily looked for.   I suppose you couldn't write to *all* of us on Sunday.

I am just in from a dinner at v. Schrenk's, in my honour.   I hate such responsibility; and yet, altho' I was in poor condition as regards sleep, I enjoyed it.   V.S. is a very friendly pleasant fellow with an inferior sort of wife, and they had the 2 Stumpfs a Prof Herz & wife,[1] and two psychological youngsters.   After dinner he showed me his method of hypnotizing, on myself, with only an incipient effect.

Harry stayed by himself away.   We go now probably to decide finally on his place.   I have seen several and 2 or 3 are possible.   One very promising, 2 Frauleins Kern with 4 young gynasiast boarders, sound, delightful women who have (as the mother of a 5th boy told me, who passes his day with them) an extraordinary success with boys.   Separate bedroom probable.   House clean and good &c. Meanwhile Mrs. Stumpf has just told me that rather than see me have more trouble she would take him and put him in her son's bedroom.

Kurz—es wird sich bald heraustellen.   I like Munich überaus, but of course I pine for repose and reading.

The mail hour is near & I go.   Last night we saw the Assommoir at a popular theatre.[2]   Harry catches on splendidly with the plays, and is absolutely contented so far.

Yours ever | W.J.

ALS: MH bMS Am 1092.9 (1832)

[1] Possibly Wilhelm Carl Heinrich Hertz (1835–1902), German poet, literary historian, and professor at Munich, and his wife, Katharina Hertz.

[2] See previous letter.

From Alice Howe Gibbens James

Florence Tuesday, Feb 28 [1893]

My darling William,

I have this moment read your Sunday letter with its dear, queer misunderstanding of my letter. Suddenly the strain of a very wearing decision was removed, Mrs Evans gone, Billy quiet as a mouse and days of rain set in quite isolating us. Then I thought of how you would have enjoyed the long mornings (for being only three we breakfasted earlier) and the silent doorbell. I have had far too much company as you may have gathered but it was good to show Lilla and her cousins some attention, and to treat Mary with the consideration which she likes to receive. And the entertainment was much simpler than you would have offered, still I am tired of it. Don't ever say that it is your absence that makes the quiet—it hurts my feelings as Peggy says. You will never know the way in which I miss you, the want of you all day long and always recurring every time I come in and have no William to interrupt and talk to. Each day I try to spend as you would like, and each day when confusion and hurry invade me I feel glad that it has not destroyed your precious time.— Saturday night Baron Ostensacken called on his way from Rome. He was eager to get back to Heidelberg, and left messages for you whom he was sorry not to see. After lunch yesterday I stayed at home reading *Vanitas*.[1] The woman has done Harry with a free hand and some most malicious touches. Towards 5 o'clock Mrs Le Strange came in and behaved like a human being with talk of the Oliphants, of course.[2] Then Mrs Lawrence appeared and stayed a long time. She has just your mother's accent, & Aunt Kate's which I loved to hear again. She was very entertaining about *Parsifal* and Bayreuth and made me wonder if you and I might not get there a year later when you come over for me.[3] She told me that dear old Mr Brimmer had had a bad fall, and been very ill, in charge of two nurses when she last heard. She urged me very kindly to come next Saturday to her music and told me that a fortnight hence she was going to have a Mass of Palestrina sung by 6 voices a rare treat which you must be sure to hear too.[4] She says Wagner worshipped Palestrina.

Today I shall do an errand for Mrs Brooks, call on Mrs Costelloe, return her *Baumeister*[5] then meet the two Marys at Lilla's for 5 o'clock tea. In Vienna they got very pretty gowns. You know your good theory of music becoming harmful in so far as its appeal to the emotions bears no fruit?[6] I found myself resolving Saturday night, as I listened to Beethoven's *Serenades*—a perfect succession of young raptures—that I would no more offend you with black clothes, even if I do make a mountain of myself.

You must be having a very discouraging time and I hope you understand ere this that I should *prefer* to take my winter at Stuttgart, all things considered.   If you could have heard Obrist's account of Loeser's parents you would have forgiven me for not wishing to be comitted to their hands.   Poor, good Loeser!   Obrist was very *kind*— he did not make fun of them he described how he "worked" to talk to them when Loeser got him in to dinner with them.   I should feel light as a bit of cork this morning, (save for your dear sadness) were I not kept under by the pressure of that letter to Mrs Dorr, not yet sent, alas!   Francis is splendid these days, he races about the house with his horse and his cow and never desists from his pursuit of something to eat.[7]   I forgot to tell you that Miss Loring was here Satur-[d]ay to propose our seeing some sights together, also to visit her Scotch friends the Miss Forbeses.[8]   I am growing very fond of her, she is so really kind.   I am grateful too when people like me a little. It's what Mary Holton will never do!   She distrusts me at bottom.   I think all is plain but the next time we meet the impression has passed off as completely as a dent on a rubber ball.   However I like her, she is so completely the thing she is.   Mrs Holton describes her Granddaughter as the prey of bitter jealously on the part of other English women who resent her marrying their Sir Frederic.[9]   Carrie has had her "feelings hurt" by Mrs Cuyler while both were in Paris.   They did not meet.   Now I shall write to our boy, and you need not show this to him lest he should know how mightily I love his father.   You dear, blessed thing!   As if I would let you be changed, or ever be capable of finding rest in life apart from your side.   God bless you.

Alice

P.S. I dreamed last night that I was going to London alone to hear Harry['s] play in May.   He did n't expect me and I almost died of grief.   *Don't* you wish we could see it together!

ALS: MH bMS Am 1092.9 (298)

Address: William James Esq | Hotel Marienbad | Munich | Bavaria | Germania
Postmarks: FIRENZE 28 2 93   MUENCHEN B.U. 1 MAR 93

[1] Violet Paget, *Vanitas: Polite Stories* (1892).   Jervase Marion, one of the major characters of "Lady Tal," the first story, is supposed to be a caricature of HJ, who complained about the "saucy" satire in his letter to WJ of 20 January 1893 (*Correspondence*, 2:252).

[2] Alice Le Strange Oliphant (d. 1886) was the wife of Laurence Oliphant. She had three brothers, at least two of whom were married. Which Mrs. Le Strange is meant was not discovered.

[3] AGJ did not go to the Wagner festival at Bayreuth but heard *Tannhäuser* in Munich in May 1893.

[4] Giovanni Pierluigi da Palestrina (ca. 1526–1594), Italian composer.

[5] See letter from AGJ of 22 February 1893.

[6] For WJ's account of sentimental character as typifying someone who has many fine emotions which, however, do not lead to action, see *PP*, 129.

[7] Francis Tweedy was the name given originally to Alexander Robertson James.

[8] The Misses Forbes were not identified.

[9] Alice Millard Holton Cuyler, wife of James Wayne Cuyler, was the daughter of Lucinda Holton and the sister of Mary Holton James. Her daughter, May Wayne Cuyler (d. 1959), married Sir Philip Henry Brian Grey-Egerton (1864–1937), a British military officer. For the marriage see *Correspondence*, 2:250–51n.

To Alice Howe Gibbens James

Wednesday March 1. 93 | 4. P.M.

Dearest Wifelein,   Thank Heaven, Harry is disposed of. I have just come from his two future homes, in one of wh. I left him. He is to sleep in a separate bed chamber (for 100 Marks a month with bkfst & supper and all day Sunday) at Frau Oberstlieutenant Wittve Schnitzlein's, Jäger Strasse, 17ᵇ, and to spend his days at the 2 Fraulein Kern's, 10 Trift Strasse, where the young Schnitzlein spends also his days, and where there are 4 young gymnasiasts, three of them just about Harry's age, all of first rate families etc. I don't see how anything more ideal could be hoped for—except that the arrangement is rather dear. I pay 80 Mks. a month to the Kerns for dinner, general oversight in study & regular instruction in german, the latter an hour a day. They seem to be admirable women; and Harry is extremely cheerful at the prospect. The gymnasium rector recommended a professor Friedrich to me as his teacher in Latin, as a man on whose judgment I could rely as to H's ulterior fitness to go there. I wish I had more confidence myself as to that point—I confess I haven't much; and don't feel as if for the one year it was worth while to strain or press much. For 2 years it would have been different. Munich pleases me incessantly. A most sedative-feeling place, and yet alive and grossartig in all respects. When I think from here of Florence, it is as of a place where there was always sand in my eyes. And yet there on the whole I slept; and here I have slept abominably,

and feel quite used up now in consequence.   I will immediately lie
down and see if the settlement of the Harry-business wont make me
go off.

Your monday's letter came last evening.   Nothing to day.   I reenclose your Mother's and Margaret's, and thank you for sending them.
You have earned some repose over Lilla, the Holtons, Mrs. Brooks,
Obrist and all.   Don't send me any thing after receiving this but write
daily, if only a postcard.   I shall probably leave here Sunday, possibly
not till monday however, and stop a night at Innsbruck to prospect
for the summer.   Heaven bless you, and the little ones.

W.J.

I have seen Cossman—a repulsive individual.

ALS: MH bMS Am 1092.9 (1835)

To Alice Howe Gibbens James

Hotel Marienbad, München | March 2. 93
Dearest Alice,

I had a good nap after mailing my letter to you yesterday, and on
returning in the evening after a walk found you[r] two affectionate
sheets to me, and your one to Harry.   I read quietly last evening,
and went to bed late—still bad sleep, but better.   This AM. I went
to talk over things with H's latin teacher,[1] and at 11 waylaid him,
galumphing along to his lesson.   He looked fresh, seemed happy etc.
After his lesson I went to the photographer's with him, but have no
great expectations of the result, they turning the whole thing off so
mechanically.—Glorious weather—no fires needed all this time.   I
ordered some books, went to a dealer's gallery of pictures, and then
to the glorious Old pinakothek—where the Rubens and Vandykes on
the whole strike me most.   I dined off an omelette mit schinken, and
after a nap, am now (4.30) expecting a visit from Harry.   I thought
last night, as I was left alone that if Billy were here also, it would be
a good thing for him, so nicely does Harry seem placed.   But the
expense is great, and Billy is doing so well in his work, that I don't
regret his not being with Harry.   Besides, H. ought to be left alone
for a while.—If *I* feel so disconsolate and homesickish here with you
as near as Florence, how much more so will you feel with me as far
as Cambridge?   Then that house—it seems to me a perfect elysium
with all its beauties and comforts.   I imagine that the mark here will
be about equal to the franc in Italy, and that at the very utmost we

might *hope* to save 1000 dollars. I question whether it will be worth while, even if Harry shd. get in all right, of which I have almost no confidence. When you & I go off to Siena we can take a cool view and talk it over. You've no idea how much simpler it seems to me here than it did in Florence. Meanwhile everyone speaks well of the weather here. Cold, but clear. The photographeress told me this noon that though the cold was much greater than in Dresden, she felt it much less because it was less damp. Nervenleidenden feel well here, they say. I am amused at your *phases* about Stuttgart, when Munich offers so much more. The Vice-consul here, Mr. Corning is a very cultivated man who educated a family abroad, & has lived 12 years in Europe. He spent 5 at Stuttgart, and has been here for 3, and says when his daughter goes back to Stuttgart, she is depressed by the inferiority.[2] He thinks the diff. of climate doesn't make up for the other inferiorities of Stuttgart.—I thank you, my own darling, for your free and affectionate expressions in your letter. We are getting on pretty well with each other, it seems to me, as the years go by. I only wish that my nervous infirmities would not stand so in the way of complete decency on my part.

Kiss old bill, and tell him that his father loves him, in spite of his apparently being so down on him at times. Whom the Lord loveth he chasteneth. Kiss sweet sweet Peg too, and *bat* Tweedy somewhere affectionately for me. I enclose a couple of good things which Billy can copy on pasteboard and make work. Sorry they're so shabby. I will write immediately to Mrs. Dorr.

There comes Harry who says he feels at home already and will write to you as soon as he gets a little more settled.

Ever your | W.

ALS: MH bMS Am 1092.9 (1836)

[1] Professor Friedrich.

[2] James Leonard Corning had one daughter, Mrs. Henry Knote, who lived primarily in Germany.

To Alice Howe Gibbens James

H. Marienbad, Mch 3. 93 | 3.3[o]. P.M

Dearest Alice,

No letter from you yesterday, and none this AM. I live in hopes of what the evening brings.—Harry came in very cheerful yesterday at 4.30 and we went to the riding school & (warmed) swimming bath, to both of which I have decided he shall go. The riding lessons here cost only 33 cents each if one takes the course of 42. That number will doubtless set him up for life, and the chance ought not to be let slip. It is a better *manège* than in Florence, and no doubt the *instruction* (being German) will be positive and thorough. At seven I went to Schrenk's, took tea with another baron, and we spent the evening at a gorgeous café, round a table where were Stumpf and a number of other psychologist's, and where (under Schrenk's direction) I ingurgitated two liters and a half of beer, he saying that *that amount* would make me sleep. Sure enough I did sleep fairly well, and have felt hearty to day. Been to Stumpf's to the Pinacothek, through the streets, and choosing photographs of pictures here to the tune of 53 marks. Forgive! they are a joy for ever, especially the wonderful Rubens things. Nothing else to say! I get no time to read. Am always mulling and grubbing about what to do for next year, and if we go home, *how* to go. I long to see you again, if only we could be a little by ourselves. The social complications here are decidedly infernal infernal in *quantity* I mean, the quality is delightful. I don't get a single day to myself. V. Schrenk made me promise to come to the café again to night after the theatre—no refusal possible, and I must to morrow go to Stumpf's to dine at 1. Stumpf is a dear old fellow a perfect piece, of plain unaffected, earnest, serene, upright, clear thinking. I like his wife too, very much.—I have just written to Mrs. Dorr.

Good bye! Kiss dear Bill. Harry is coming to see me in ½ an hour again.

W.J.

ALS: MH bMS Am 1092.9 (1837)

To Dickinson Sergeant Miller

                    Hotel Marienbad, Munchen, March 3, 1893.
My Dear Miller:

I have been in Germany for a week, putting Harry to school, so to speak; but I can't manage to get farther than Munich, and on Sunday I must return to Florence. I did mean to write to you the first day of my being here, but the fitful fever of my occupation has made any such thing impossible. I thought that by some extraordinary chance some member of your colony might now be here, and that by writing to you I should hear of it and see him—*you,* if you were he. But "I guess" you're all in Berlin still, and that my delay has brought no disaster. Of course I enjoyed your rousing good letter of Jan. 22 amazingly, and was extremely glad to learn that you had been able to travel so much, compare with each other so many universities, etc. It is queer, considering how little positive "truth," that one can teach, accrues from all these visits to people and lecture-rooms, that nevertheless one's subjective personal feeling of being more solidly in the philosophical profession should be so much enhanced thereby. At least I have found it so in past times, and only now begin to be indifferent. I see much of Stumpf here whom I like personally as much as I respect his writings. He is as straightforward and affectionate and faithful as he is clear and subtle intellectually; and although his weak health (sleep, etc.) makes him a poor worker, he has a serene unexcited way of continually forging ahead which comes from a fundamentally phlegmatic temperament. All Münich questions me about Mrs. Piper!! That worthy woman's feminine vanity will be immensely tickled by her fame. v. Schrenk Notzing has been overdoing the entertaining of me, but seems a very amiable fellow, and no fool. For *undiluted* filthy reading, commend me to his suggestions therapie b. kkhaften Erscheinugen, etc.[1] All the other smut I have seen is watered. A queer chapter in human nature!—I was pleased inordinately by your opinion of Harvard as a philosophical school holding itself so *aufrecht* in the face of the enemy. What must it be, now that Münsterberg is there? for verily he is an admirable teacher. I shall go back with all lab. responsibility off my hands, and try, ere Chronos' scythe cut me off, to put some work in on *Erkenntniss*-theorie and metaphysics. I long for clearness in certain places *there*. Florence has been on the whole a good winter-place for us, but since the latter part of January it has become for me a sort of hell owing to the incessant social interruptions and the narrowness of the space (space available in cold weather, that is) in our apartment. A stream of acquaintances pour through Florence, "look one up" at every hour of the day, and expect you to spend hours daily in going round with them. All serious reading has been entirely stopped, not to be resumed I fear till we get away, early in April. I have found a good place to leave Harry in, here, and if he can get into the Realgymnasium class that fits his age, my wife *may* stay over in Münich next winter, whilst I return, a lonely bird, to Cambridge. My decided impression now, however, is that we all shall go back, but by what route I can't now tell. I love this Germany; I love to be again with a strong calm manly-voiced people around me. (The poor Tuscans!

Heaven help them.) The weather here has been simply perfect, and the stronger air with its good taste of old smoke in it, quite regenerating to me. Italy is delicious as a mere tourists' spectacle, but how one can *stay* there I don't understand. Something in air, soil and people intimately disagrees with me. This is the third time it has happened. So you too are a Bocklinite. Strange how that man seems to haunt people. The thing whose photog. I enclose stood out in my memory, killing all else in the Neue Pinakothek. If you've *got* it, give this to Mrs. Hodder. Good bye, my dear boy. Love to the Hodders and Angell, and plenty for yourself.

Ever yours, | Wm. James.

I have read Rickert's book, with highest admiration.[2] It seems tragic that out of such fine work there should come [no] more solid upshot practically. But Rickert is evidently a future force.

W.J.

TC: MH bMS Am 1092.1

[1] Albert von Schrenck-Notzing, *Die Suggestions-Therapie bei krankhaften Erscheinungen des Geschlechtssinnes* (1892).

[2] Heinrich Rickert, *Der Gegenstand der Erkenntnis* (1892).

To Sarah Wyman Whitman

Munich, March 5. 1893

If you have thought, my dear Mrs. Whitman, that my not writing to you through all these long months has come from my not having *thought* of you, or about writing to you, you have greatly erred. The fact is, there are two great obstacles to a letter to you from me, and one of them is *You* and the other is *me*. Until those obstacles are cleared away, you see it must go hard. To common people I can write; but I have to feel awfully conceited to write adequately to you, and as the process of this world's education of me is to take my native conceit more and more out of me, the thing won't go. This is not mere words or fantasticality, but a very sober truth of the kind that shrinks from words about itself—hence the silence etc, etc.—I don't want affectation or fantastic relations, yet the fulness of truth is hard to express, & if revealed to you would seem *flat* in the extreme. Pending the day of judgment, then, I will gravitate to my natural level which is very close to the earth, and there you must get accustomed to bend your eyes when you want to discover W.J.—You will have suffered as much as anyone the loss of Philipps Brooks, but the unalloyed character of the sort of greatness that he possessed swallows up for me the impression of his being cut off. A man who lived himself out so freely could afford to die at any time. I hear in a remote way, now, that Mr. Brimmer has been very ill. I confess that that touches me personally more, and I earnestly hope, for your sake too, that that will come all right. We have been well, and after a divine summer (in many ways) in Switzerland, turned up in Florence as a refuge from the difficulty of choosing which German town. There we have been five months already, keeping house, and I trying to do some study, but largely frustrated by the claims of the sights to see, and the stream of "loved ones from home" and others who have poured through the place, "looked one up" and expected one to be with them for several hours every day. Art-connoisseurs there, too, somewhat instructive, but on the whole more *de*structive, to one's own private "feelinks" about the pictures and things. I have been away for a fortnight with my boy Harry, and have settled him here with two families, teacher etc. In half an hour now I am to pay my bill and leave the hotel. Germany at bottom is better than all the Italies in the world, a race of adult male beings. Modern Art, too, is quite as live a thing as ancient art,—only one must have no formulas. Mine are smashed to comminuted bits. I wish you could come and see it all, *by yourself*—I mean without any one to *talk* it, or about it, to you.—Alice *may* stay over here next winter, but I am by this time pretty well convinced that the balance of wisdom will be for us all to go home together by September. Then I am going to be a sort of Wordsworth, and try to deal worthily with the few things I've got without reaching out for still more raw material which one can never assimilate.—Have you photogs. of Giotto's Arena Chapel things? If not, I wish you would let me bring them to you.

Good bye! Think charitably but not too charitably, of your disciple,

W.J.

I wish you would drop just a line to say how the winter has treated you, to Baring Brothers care. I hope well, and I hope the same as regards Mr. Whitman to whom pray present my best regards.

I enclose one of Bocklin's best things—in the Neue Pinacothek here. You've no idea of the wonderful painting of that great clear blackish wave with the light in the sky coming across it.

ALS: MH bMS Am 1092.9 (3913)

To Henry James III

Friday, Mch. 10. 1893 | 9. P.M.
Darling Boy—Billy and your Mother are just gone to bed—she used
up with a wakeful night last night, Tweedy being sick again much as
he was last time, and poor Peg, though not positively ill, still not yet
out of bed.   Bill seems very quiet, now that you are away, but rather
listless about his school.   He is anxious to give up French now, since
they are about to make him buy a new book, and he says in this whole
winter all that he has learned has been a few tenses of the verb *aimer.*
The weather here is delicious, the light so warm, the shadows so cool,
the windows open etc, so that it is quite a changed place from what
it was when we left.   We hoped for a letter from you this morning,
but none came.   I trust it is because you have had so much to do
that there was no time for it.   If you had been homesick I think you
would have written, so that I regard it as a good sign.   Live energeti-
cally; and whatever you have to do, do it with your might.   These
weeks are a great chance in your life.   Tell me how the latin goes
when you write; and how you like everything.   Go to Stumpfs on
Sunday, I said you would.   And if anything should go wrong anywhere else, or you be in any perplexity, go to him.   He and I made
out together that you should.—I have spent the afternoon designing
for a stone cutter whom I saw about it yesterday, a casket for your
Aunt Alice's ashes.   I think it will be very good-looking, and I have
found in Dante a good inscription for the back: "Ed essa da martiro
e da esiglio venne a questa pace"—["]And she, from martyrdom, and
from exile came unto this peace."   Mrs. Evans writes both despondingly and admiringly of Egypt where she is all alone, the more alone
since she can't speak french.   A letter from Aunt Margaret yesterday,
said the snow was over their fence, and Munsterberg ill with diphtheria.

Your loving | Dad.

ALS: MH fMS Am 1092.4

To Violet Paget

16 Piazza Indipendenza | Florence, March 11. [1893]
Dear Miss Paget,
    I have been four days back from Munich, and a friend here has
shown me *Vanitas.*   The portrait of my brother in the first story is

clever enough, and I cannot call it exactly malicious.[1] But the using of a friend as so much raw material for "copy" implies on your part such a strangely *objective* way of taking human beings, and such a detachment from the sympathetic considerations which usually govern human intercourse, that you will not be surprised to learn that seeing the book has quite quenched my desire to pay you another visit.

As for your brother's case, the idea has come to me, that von Schrenk in Munich, who is personally an agreeable man, who is a hypnotist of great experience, and enormous patience, and who has had most extraordinary results in some very inveterate cases, would be a promising man to consult.[2] His address is

> Freiherr von Schrenk-Notzing
> 2, Max-Josef Strasse
> München

With thanks for your courtesy to us, and regrets, I am truly yours,

Wm James

ALS: MeWC

[1] In her diary for 9 March 1893 Mary Berenson describes her visit to WJ, with Paget's *Vanitas* as the subject of discussion. In her view WJ was quite angry and threatened to break off all social ties with Paget (*Mary Berenson: A Self-Portrait*, ed. Barbara Strachey and Jayne Samuels [New York: W. W. Norton, 1983], 52).

[2] Violet Paget's half brother was British poet and novelist Eugene Lee-Hamilton (1845–1907), who was an invalid for most of his life from an illness that was most likely psychological in origin.

To Hugo Münsterberg

Address hereafter, c/o Baring Bros & Co London | Florence, March 13. 93

My dear Münsterberg,

The bad news has just come, of your diphtheria—fortunately with it the good news that you are already out of danger, though you have been very ill indeed. I telegraphed you last night "accept our house if useful." I hope you understood. I tho't that for a time you might all feel like leaving your own house until it became completely disinfected, or that perhaps Mrs. Münsterberg and the children would like to turn into ours whilst you were convalescing. I am sorry the telegram could not have gone 10 days ago. It will give us real pleasure to think of you in our house, for as long a time as you may find convenient. I sincerely hope that you will have no after-consequences from the infernal disease. At any rate don't go back to work too soon, but give yourself a long time to regain your strength. How on earth can you have caught the thing? Provided the children don't get it!—I was surprised but also pleased to hear that you had Wesselhoeft.[1] The prejudice against homoeopathy is so strong amongst our doctors that I didn't conceive of an MD. like yourself having even social relations with one. I however was brought up in a homoeopathic family, and am as sure as I am of anything in the world that infinitesimal doses of their remedies are *effective*. The trouble is that they are men of one idea; and what with their narrowness, and the gross ignorance on the part of orthodox doctors of things that *they* know, there is no such thing as an all-round *physician* to be had—only sectarians. Wesselhoeft is a noble man, and I am right glad for his sake that you have had him. I turned to him *in extremis* when our child was ill. The child died—general tuberculosis, complicated with whooping-cough; but we shall never forget Wesselhoeft's devotion to the case.[2]

I have been for a fortnight in Munich, leaving my eldest boy in a small school there, and I can assure you that it was pleasant, after 6 months of this debilitated Florence, to breathe the strong smoky transalpine air, and to mingle with the strong German race and hear the deep bass voices again. I have done almost nothing serious in two months. A continual stream of relatives and friends passing through Florence and claiming all one's time. There are more of them here now, and there will probably be no time to oneself till we get into the mountains again, which I trust will happen within a month. In Munich I saw Stumpf a good deal—an honest and kindly man, and a clear headed one, for whom I have a real affection. Schrenk-Notzing was also very hospitable and friendly, and says he may possibly make a trip to America this summer.—I shall send Palmer within a week my proposals for next year's instruction, which I hope you will approve. How has Nichols's instruction turned out in Phil 2. and in the Annex? Can you get at any opinions from the students? When writing to you last, about N., & his possible successor as laboratory instructor, I made no mention of J. R. Angell who was with us last year, & who is really a very strong fellow—more positively efficient than Delabarre. Of all the men I know, I should prefer him. Ask Royce! Well, accept my dear friend our heartiest sympathy, first for you, and next, for Mrs. M., in this terrible trial, from which I trust you will emerge safely, and none the worse.

Yours ever, W.J.

ALS: MB

[1] There were a number of physicians of that name in Boston and Cambridge, including two German-born brothers who were homeopathic physicians: Conrad Wesselhoeft (1834–1904) and Walter Wesselhoeft (1838–1920), both graduates of the Harvard Medical School.

[2] Reference is to Herman James.

To Henry James III

Florence, March 14. 1893

Darling Harry,

Your letter of Sunday came this morning and gave us great joy. I'm glad you say you're contented; glad your riding improves (of course get the spurs for 3 marks); but sorry you find your latin still "mixed" in consequence of the german. Keep your attention alive and don't leave anything only half understood. At the end of the week, Prof. Friedrich will write and then we shall know where we are. Meanwhile do your darnedest in *every* respect. Live *hard*! We are having gloomy weather again, and I "stuffed up" with a cold. Visitors pour along. Last night the Hodders and Angell to dinner. They were very nice, gave a poor account of Berlin, but a very good one of Dickinson S. M., who seems to flourish like a green bay tree there, speaks good german, and stammers no more. We are also having our Royal birthday to day, and there is consequently no school. Billy has been at the skating-rink all the morning, and is inventing new summersaults this afternoon. He has a rope tied now round the bed-knobs, which he uses as a sort of parallel bar. He is an unconquerable little cuss in the way of energy—something like Artemus Ward's "moral kangaroo."[1] I tried to make him write you a letter to day, but he begged off saying he had already written on sunday. Peg is all the sweeter for her illness.—We went to the Villaris the other night, and Gino told me that the rehearsals were going off very well.[2] But Mr. Begg has just left a card, saying that *Sig. Lani* is dead, so the representation is postponed.[3] No special news from home—still mourning over Uncle Joseph's will, which certainly was a curious one for a practical man to make.[4]—I hope that both the Schnitzlein and the Kern household continue to be as pleasant as they seemed when I was there. Say your father "lässt grussen" to both. I enclose one of your photographs which came two days ago.

Your poor mother is out calling.

Your loving | W.J.

ALS: MH fMS Am 1092.4

[1] Artemus Ward, pseudonym of Charles Farrar Browne (1834–1867), American dialect humorist, presented himself as the manager of a traveling show, consisting of "three moral Bares, a Kangaroo (a amoozin little Raskal—t'would make you larf yerself to deth to see the little cuss jump up and squeal . . .)," and wax figures (*Artemus Ward: His Book* [New York: Carleton, 1866], 1).

[2] Gino was not identified.

[3] Neither Mr. Begg nor Sig. Lani was identified.

[4] Probably Joseph M. Gibbens, a businessman, mentioned several times in *Correspondence*, vol. 6.

To Violet Paget

16, Piazza Indipendenza | March 18. 93

My dear Miss Paget,

A woman in tears is something that I can never stand out against! Your note wipes away the affront so far as I am concerned, only you must never, never, NEVER, do such a thing again in any future book! It is too serious a matter.

We are pulling ourselves together to go north in a couple of weeks unless something unforeseen prevents. My wife and I are to make some one or two day excursions first. When the time serves, I will, (if you are willing?) come again and bid you good bye.

Sincerely yours | Wm James

ALS: MeWC

To Josiah Royce

Address Baring's after this | Florence, March 18. 93

My dear Royce,

I wrote to Palmer yesterday, proposing my courses, a letter which you will doubtless see. I didn't expressly ask him to communicate to me *without delay* the result, but I assume that it will be done, for I must govern my reading accordingly. I waited a while hoping to hear from you the recommendation of a text book, but no recommendation coming, I decided on Spencer's 1st. P. & Lotze's Naturphilosophie,[1] which I suppose are safe enough. Theses of course will form an important feature of the course. I am awfully curious to know how *your* work has gone this year, how many extra courses of lectures you have given to crowned heads and leaders of fashion, to teachers and fanatics. Margaret G. writes that your paedagogy lectures have been given to overflowing houses. I forgot to mention them in my letter to Palmer, and God wot I don't want them again unless you all agree to shove them on to me, when of course I cheerfully submit.[2] I have been extremely grieved to hear of Münsterberg's dangerous illness. I hope the convalescence will be good. I have offered him the use of our house, but fear he will have no use for it. I want most fearfully that he should be a big success and blight his miserable detractors. I am very curious to know how matters stand with Nichols. Have you any means of knowing what his success in Phil. 2 and in the Annex has been? I would give anything to hear of him in an independent professorship somewhere. When I wrote to you and M. about him and the question of the assistant next year, I in my haste said nothing of *Angell's* qualifications which were nevertheless livelily present to my mind. *A.* has been here lately, taking a little tour before going probably to Paris for farther work. He is the same definite and satisfactory fellow as ever—not "interesting" personally, on account of his processes being all so sure and definitive, but all the more compulsive of one's admiration. He seems to me a more promising fellow than Delabarre—I don't know Witmer—and I can't imagine a more satisfactory possible assistant for next year than he would be, if Nichols goes. Moreover we cd. of course have him for one year as assistant which would be impossible in the case of the other men (Delab. & Wit) whom M——g mentioned. Please communicate this as my opinion to M——g, together with your own view of Angell. The Hodders also are here now. He is genial and amused as if life agreed with him, she innocent, sweet and devoted to he— her eyes hanging on his features etc. An "enfantillage" is impending in a month, and she naively told my wife that she thought it would be easier to see the sights now than after the baby's birth, so they hurried down now to Italy. Such trust in life is refreshing. I hope they'll pull through—providence ought not to "go back" on such confidence. They appear to have the needful funds.

We are shaking ourselves together preparatory to leaving Florence. I think it now pretty certain that we shall return home in a body. Harry will have to get up his german in the next 3 months in Munich where he is. We shall go pretty straight to England, I think, and try to make out a summer there. The sweet rottenness of Italy disagrees with me, the air is so devitalized that I long to get away. I took a walk & horse-car drive in the outskirts with Mrs. Costelloe yesterday (erst Mary Smith of the Annex) who is more spirited and good natured than ever, but quite infernal when she gets on to the subject of art-history which is now the serious occupation of her life. She has left husband (I imagine a "coldness") and babies and come here to collaborate platonically with Berenson on a catalog of the works of one Lorenzo Lotto.³ B. has a noble gift of the gab, perceptions *dazu,* & learning. Also good visual images without wh. (ah me!) no scholarship in that direction! But he has terrible moral defects I imagine—keeps me off by his constant habit of denunciation of the folly of everyone else and the pretention to the only right and objective knowledge.—I am *so* glad to hear of Gilman's appointment.⁴

Yours ever   W.J.

Love from both of us to both of you, & the babes.

ALS: MH bMS Am 1092.9 (3612)

¹ While the Harvard catalogue lists Lotze's *Outlines of the Philosophy of Nature* among the texts of Philosophy 3 in 1893–94, Lotze's *Grundzüge der Naturphilosophie* (1882) was not translated into English.

² See letter to Harris of 14 November 1891.

³ Lorenzo Lotto (ca. 1480–1556), Italian painter. Berenson published *Lorenzo Lotto: An Essay in Constructive Art Criticism* (1895). Mary Berenson had two children by her first marriage. By the date of WJ's letter, she was formally separated from Frank Costelloe.

⁴ Benjamin Ives Gilman was appointed secretary of the Museum of Fine Arts, Boston.

To Henry James III

Florence, March 26. 1893

My dear old Heinrich,

I wrote yesterday a registered letter to Fraulein Kern, inclosing a 100 Marks, which she will have received before you receive this. I forgot to ask her, in stopping Prof. F.'s lessons,¹ to *pay* him—please tell her so to do. I wish you had told me a little more about the lessons with him. Has it been pure grammar and translation? and do you feel, in spite of the confusion and difficulty that it has given you more control of the latin. I have written to Frl. K., who also agrees that one year at the Gym. would not be advisable for you, to take her younger teacher, and to have him make you read as much latin as possible in the time that remains. He will have to be judge of the book. Perhaps some of their school readers would be better than any regular author like Sallust, only you must not let your self go to your old habit of ending with a vague idea of what is meant, and a part of your daily exercise should be written translation. If

in addition to that you could read a good quantity of easy latin making in writing a list of the words new to you in each days work, I
should think it a good plan. I have written to Browne two letters to
ask what the class is doing, but I dont hear from him yet. It can't
be much longer now.—How do you find the diet? And how do you
like Frl. Kern's German teaching? Do the riding lessons take hold,
so that you feel a better seat & more control? Write a full account
of everything, and read to Fraulein Kern what I say on the previous
page about your new latin lessons, so that she may explain to the
teacher what my idea is, viz. a minimum of grammar, an improvement in reading at sight, a good many pages read, and at the same
time an exercise in exactness and in German by means of the written translation.

Our plans are ripening. To morrow your mother & I go to Lucca,
Wednesday to Siena, and I hope by next monday to start with Billy
for Vevey, whence Mrs. Cérésole writes that you have left so pleasant
an impression that she is eager to have him. A week later, your
mother will start for Lucerne where Mrs. Evans will arrive in due
time, stay with the little ones, and leave us free to go to England and
reconnoitre. At least this is the *last* plan—up to date, and it seems
the most rational one. We are all well. Billy has been having exam⁵
at school, so a stoppage of all work at home. To day I took him to
have his hair cut, & then to the Uffizii. Peg celebrated her birthday
two days ago with the Baldwins and a cake. She is very well, and so
is Tweedy, who is growing bigger all the time. Good bye my dear
old Boy. Profit tremendously by these weeks. Don't get slack.
Throw yourself over BACKWARDS! Wash your hands before meals.
Billy has to be sent away from table nearly every day to do it. If
your Mother were here she would send love, but she is gone with
Frank Loring to an afternoon tea.

Your loving | DAD.

ALS: MH fMS Am 1092.4
¹ Professor Friedrich.

To Henry James III

Florence, Apl. 9. [1893]

Beloved Heinrich,

I scribble this word to you to go in Frau. S.'s letter.¹ Your figure
is fast receding into the dim aisles of memory, you have been so long

away. But, so far from German diet and air not agreeing with you, your freedom from headache seems to show that they agree better than what you got at home. This, I hope, will appease your grandmother's anxious mind.

You write no details about your lessons, either in latin or in German. Do you find the latin teaching particularly good? I hope they are making you learn a lot of German poetry. It will be an invaluable enrichment for all the rest of your life, every verse that you learn now. Also, do mind your reformed walking, and get a new habit ingrained, and practice every day pulling yourself up to your chin. Finally, don't read *a word* of English till you rejoin us again. *Forget your English, if you can.* Write to us in German!

We have been very busy with futilities. The weather is gloriously bright, but rather too peppery hot & dry. Billy has a painting craze upon him, buys coloured powders which he mixes with water so that we have no table glasses left to drink out of, and in company with the Tealdis paints scenes on brown paper which the following day fall off in dust and are trodden in to the floor.[2] But his ardor beats everything, and at Vevay I must try to get someone who goes sketching to take him *mit*.

On Monday I go for two days to Volterra with Hodder & Chas. Atkinson who has just arrived. Mrs. H. comes into my room. On Wednesday or Thursday I take Billy to Vevey, & your Mother follows a week later. Mrs. Evans has just arrived in Venice from Greece, & the Rosses are back. I hope you got through the von Schrenk scrape successfully. One visit is enough. You must call them Herr Baron & Frau Baronin. Love from us all.[3]

Your l. D.

ALS: MH fMS Am 1092.4

[1] Frau Schnitzlein.

[2] The Tealdi family was not identified. They are connected most likely with Aubrey Tealdi, a professor of landscape design at the University of Michigan in the 1930s and son of Mrs. C. A. Tealdi of Florence.

[3] On the otherwise blank fourth page WJ wrote 'For Harry'.

To Frank Duveneck

16 Piazza Indipendenza | April 13. 93

My dear Duveneck,

We saw the monument yesterday, and all I can say is that it is beautiful, *beautiful*, BEAUTIFUL![1] The face with its solemn half-smile, the position of the head, the hands upon the bosom, the somewhat flattened form as if sunk into the couch, the simple delicate drapery, so modest and so real, the serenity and peace of the whole thing! It is a great work, and a great monument; and I wish I could believe that poor dear Lizzie herself took cognizance of it and knew that you had done it. It ought to make you very happy to have expressed by such a completed and permanent piece of work something of the feeling for her which has filled your heart. It will last after you too are gone, as one of the monuments of Florence which people go to see. And it is better that, being a *painter,* you should have been able to do this thing, than if you had done it being a sculptor. It is more particular, more exclusively for her.

Good bye, my dear fellow, I leave on Saturday night. I will write to F.B. my impression of the monument,[2] and I shall hope within the year to see you at our house in Cambridge. God bless you!

Yours ever | Wm James

ALS: MH bMS Am 1092.9 (901)

[1] Duveneck's monument to Elizabeth Boott Duveneck in the Allori Cemetery in Florence.

[2] Francis Boott.

To Hugo Münsterberg

Florence, April 13. 1893

My dear Münsterberg

I have just received your good long letter of the 27th March, on my return from a short trip in the country. It is sad to see the change in your handwriting, and to think of the weeks during which you will still be below par in strength and in feeling of strength. You must have had a hellish time of it; but it will end, and in the next couple of months no one will expect great achievements from you. So "take things easy!" What I should like to know is *where you caught* the d——d thing. Poor Mrs Münsterberg too! I hope that by this time she has rested from her fatigues, but she must have had some pretty distressful weeks.

Your letter is full of the most interesting matters to me, but I write this morning only with reference to the courses for next year. I am sorry that Palmer will not *einwilligen* any more than he would last year. It may be that the matter is already decided, but if not yet, I wish that you would listen to the following remarks, and read them to the committee, before it comes to a final vote on the subject.

You tell me that Palmer wishes to keep the present state of things, but agrees to modify Phil 2, so that I shall give theoretic instruction the first ½ year, and you and the assistant give practical instruction the 2nd half.[1]   If this were actually adopted next year, the Phil 1. Psychology would be *general* (a rapid survey of my smaller book), and the Phil. 2. ought not to go over the same ground again, but should consist of *special subjects* gone over in some detail.   I know of no one book that could then be used for Phil. 2.; and I should think that the theoretic & practical work ought not to be put in different half years, but to go hand in hand.   This of course might also be arranged.   But to the entire plan these objections seem fatal:

1)   The Phil. 1.-psychology given for ⅓ of a year is too short to be sufficient for *the* general course.   Large numbers of fellows will want more, and will crowd into Phil 2. to the great detriment of that course, both on its theoretic and on its practical side; and we shall not have the excuse for refusing them admittance, which we should have if they had already had a good half year of psychology.   I really think that an adequate course of psychology for the purposes of "general education["] can be given in ½ a year, and that much more than that exceeds the power of assimilation of ⅔ of the men who would offer themselves.   I also believe that in a general education Psychology is one of the most important subjects, and that we should aim at a general course which should be both large and sufficiently substantial, more substantial than the Phil 1. Psychology can *possibly* be.

2)   The plan which I propose seems to me exactly to meet the needs.   We have the superficial general student provided for in the 1st half year; the more scientific general student, the medical man, etc, will be satisfied with what he gets added in the 2nd. half year; and the more technical psychologist ought thereupon to go straight into the laboratory & seminaries and occupy himself with special problems.   There is *no waste* whatever of teaching power, on this arrangement.

3)   I protest strongly against having the inner needs of a subject like psychology determined by considerations of outer symmetry in the printed list of courses, considerations which I fear are not absent from the chairman's mind.

4)   I believe the metaphysics also to be much *squeezed* in Phil 1; but of that I say nothing, since I only want to impress my views about Psychology.

If you and Royce agree on the wisdom of the reasons I give (of course at this distance I cannot tell what counter-reasons there may be), I trust that you will vote without hesitation against keeping the present arrangement.* How does Nichols feel about it now? You tell me nothing about his eyes, concerning which we have heard alarming rumors. Poor N.! I feel great sympathy with him in his disappointment about continuing with us, for he has most lovable and admirable qualities. I have no doubt that Wittmer would do admirably if he were willing to take a place *without* definite prospect of advancement. You really *must* not hold out to any one now the hope of succeeding you in 1895. You can't tell how you may feel about staying then, if the Corporation ask you to do so, and you mustn't complicate your decision by any thing which you may be saying now. Leave that decision as free and open to yourself as possible.

In rê Müller, be brief and very dignified! The Stumpf-Wundt controversy ought to be a warning! A couple of my old students who passed through here the other day after a winter at Leipzig told me that Wundt had said to them that there were only two laboratories that he could recommend for the study of Psychology in America, viz. Titchener's and Angell's in California![2] A propos to T., I wish that he might get a clip over the head from you also. The surly grudging tone of his review in the last Mind is ignoble.[3] How can you arouse such malevolence? The true reply, however, is to go on with your work, not to print counter-criticisms. I am glad you are to print this one privately.[4] Ebbinghaus acted unpardonably in allowing Müller's last to appear. He hasn't answered my remarks to him on the subject, but I told him he needn't, and I expected no reply.[5]

I have been extraordinarily pleased with the quality of Rickert's little book. It is really classical in tone,—and so concise.

Well! may good health now attend you all, and serenity follow in its train.

Yours always | Wm James

In a couple of days I leave for Switzerland.

*Of course, whatever you vote, I will do my best to make it a success, even if it be no[t] the plan of my own choice.

ALS: MH bMS Am 1092.9 (3276)

[1] Philosophy 2 was offered in 1893–94 with WJ lecturing during the first half of the year and Münsterberg supervising laboratory work in the second.

[2] Frank Angell at Stanford University.

[3] Titchener reviewed Münsterberg's *Beiträge zur experimentellen Psychologie*, pt. 4, in *Mind*, n.s., 2 (April 1893): 234–41.

[4] Hugo Münsterberg, "Professor G. E. Müller's 'Berichtigung'" (Boston: C. H. Heintzemann, 1893).

[5] See letter to Münsterberg of 11 February 1893.

To Alice Howe Gibbens James

HÔTEL & PENSION MOOSER, | VEVEY, LE 19 Avril 1893
Beloved Weibchen—Billy and I walked up a very dusty road to the Ceresole's yesterday, arriving at ½ past 5, & finding Mme C. & her daughter in the garden. The place seemed to me even more beautiful than last year—one of the most ideally beautiful spots I ever saw. By an odd coincidence a young lady from Berlin was arriving the same evening & for the same purpose. She soon appeared & was welcomed, and for nearly an hour and a half I had to "visit" as Bob's mary would say, waiting for C. to come in and tea to be served. Billy instantly retired with Arnold and was shown all over the place out'doors and in.[1] Arnold has been ill, so will be out of school for 3 weeks more, and then, Madame C. hopes, Billy can go back with him as an externe. I hope he can, but badly fear that he won't be able to do any work. However, if they only let him sit there, 'twill be a great gain for him. Arnold is a wonderfully handsome boy, with a most expressive and interesting face, reminding me of Mlle Chausson, the teacher at Gryon.[2] He is just the size of Billy, and a great reader, his mother said. Billy & he have evidently fallen in love at first sight. B. squirmed when I tried to kiss him for good bye, and there certainly will be no re-enactment of the scenes of last year. Mr. Ceresole at table told him that he expected to see M. Thélin to day and asked B. if he had any message for him, seeming instinctively to understand the joke. He is a strong man, and his wife is a very sweet woman—reversing the rôles in our family. They both spoke fondly of Harry, and she promised to see what might be done to encourage Billy to draw. There is "sketching"-matter wherever one casts one's eye in their neighborhood. In three quarters of an hour, I expect B. & A. to come down to pay me a visit, when I will report again.

I have been leading a quiet day of reading. Last night I grew quite feverish with my cold which has been the heaviest I can remember, and my mind and eyes are equally sore, heavy and pressed upon. Nevertheless I have enjoyed life. The view from the grounds round the house is simply divine. The air probably smells good, but my nose can't now appreciate that fact, though my ears can appreciate the stillness & enjoy the music of the birds. My soul can also appreciate the packing of my trunk by your sweet hands. In the cars I said to myself—there now I've forgotten my portfolio!—but you remembered it. But why did you put in the lanoline soap, that I set out for your sweet hands?

To morrow I go to the hotel de la Paix at Geneva where I hope to get plenty of news from you. I hope every thing goes well at No 16—both in the Hodder's and in your half of the house. I feel as if I ought to be there to help with the packing and getting off, but I know, now that the family is so simplified, that you are enough.

Please get another of those 10 fr. photograph albums, the size I got the last day, at Alinari's. The long big album was a mistake, and it is worth paying two more dollars, to get our photos. into the most manageable shape.

Tell Peg there is a little german boy here in the hotel, 5¾ years old. He is a nice little fellow, but he doesn't know a single letter of the alfabet yet, and when I told him I had a girl of six who could read both french and english he seemed much sprīged.—Love to the whole house, chiefly to you.

W.J.

Billy has come, with Arnold—very dignified & reticent & rather stiff. But everything seems going well.

ALS: MH bMS Am 1092.9 (1839)

[1] Arnold was not identified.
[2] The Jameses were in Gryon in July 1892. Mlle Chausson was not identified.

To Josiah Royce

Geneva, Apl 21. [1893]

Your blessed epistle of the 1st (or 3rd?) rec'd. Next to living in the light of your dear eyes, living far eno' away to get such letters is the greatest boon life can bring me. I giggled so over it at my hotel bkfst. table this A.M. that they nearly put me out of the dining room.— But I am deeply sorry for the sinister intelligence it conveys, and have just written to Palmer to say that since the sacredness of Phil 1 as the only portal has been violated by the erection of your new course he must count me out of it altogether.[1] I have 8 hours without it (with course 2 running through the year) and 8 is my maximum.[2]—An alternative would be that you should treat only Metaphysics & Logic in "Phil 1b," whilst I gave (instead of Phil 2 as heretofore) the two graded half-courses which I have proposed instead of Phil 1.   Phil 1 could then coexist with these new courses, and the present Phil 2 die out.   This pleases me better than the old arrangement favored by P; because there would be then no pretense of *grading* from Phil 1 to the two half courses in Psychology

W.J.

APS: MH bMS Am 1092.9 (3613)

Address: Professor Royce | 105, Irving Street | Cambridge (Mass[)] | Etats Unis d'Am'que

Postmarks: GENEVE 21. IV. 93.   NEW <YORK> MAY 3 93

[1] In 1893–94 Royce taught Philosophy 1b: General Introduction to Philosophy, covering the history of principal problems, logic, psychology, and ethics, while Palmer and Santayana taught Philosophy 1a, covering logic, psychology, metaphysics, and history of philosophy.

[2] In 1893–94 WJ taught Philosophy 3: Cosmology, three hours a week for the year, Philosophy 20b: Psychological Seminary, two hours a week for the year, and the lecture portion of Philosophy 2: Psychology, three hours a week for half the year.

To Carl Stumpf

Meggen, bei Luzern, April 24 [1893]

My dear Stumpf,

I ought to have written to you some time since to tell you of our decisions, which were still inchoate when I was at Munich.   If you could have seen the confusion in which my last six weeks have been spent, however, you would excuse any derelictions on my part.   *Incessant* sociability in florence, pushed to such an extreme that one pair of young American friends came and *had a baby(!!!)* in our appartment, there being no other convenient place for the event to take place in.[1]   Fortunately my wife came away three days ago, and left them in possession—"mother and child well."   I have also done a little travelling in Italy, and for a week past have been in Switzerland putting my second boy in a family at Vevey, seeing some sick cousins at Geneva,[2] and finding this paradise for the rest of the family here. When it became evident that Harry could not be fitted for the Gymnasium in April, we concluded that the whole family had better return together in the summer to America.   It is the *comfortable* decision; and we have been happy in it ever since.   I believe that from the point of view of education, the best possible thing for American boys would be to pass the years from *6 to 10* in German schools.   At Harry's age, however, the advantages of only one single year are doubtful. But three or four months where he is will consolidate his german, so that when he gets home I think there will be little danger of its getting lost as far as the *reading* use of it goes.

We are going to spend most of the summer in England, and have taken the road through Switzerland rather than through Tyrol for economical reasons. This means that my wife, and possibly I will not have the chance of meeting you and Mrs. Stumpf this summer, which we both regret—but of regrets life seems to be made up! We are in this heavenly spot, with the trees all in bloom about us, and shall stay a fortnight at least, before going farther, but my safe address is always 34 De Vere Gardens, London W. I am glad to have said good bye to the sweet rottenness of Italy, of which I shall always preserve the tenderest memories but in which I shall always feel a foreigner. The ugly swiss faces, costume and speech seem to me delicious, primeval, pure, and full of human soundness and moral good. And the air! the air! there can be nothing like it in the world. I was hardly able to read a line in the past 6 weeks in Italy; but in the last few days in Switzerland I have read 250 pp. of Paulsen's Einleitung in die Philosophie. I don't know on what account you spoke so disparagingly of it in Munich—but our tone about a book always depends on what we *expect* of it. To me it seems a wonderful book for the human sympathy that is in it, for the fairness and candor that it breathes, and for its admirable artistic composition. It will probably be a classic translated into all languages, a means of enlarging the narrowness of mind of many scientific materialists, and an adequate expression of the naturalistic pantheism that is in the air to day. It is the work of a thoroughly cultivated man; and although I am not satisfied with the standpoint that satisfies Paulsen, I have learned much both morally and intellectually from the pages wh. I have read, and expect to learn much more from those that remain. It seems to me that if there ever is a *true* philosophy it must be susceptible of an expression as popular and untechnical as this. The man is a *good* man, through and through!

I am sorry that those days those not easily to be forgotten days that I spent in dear old Munich, are likely to be the last ones of our seeing each other for a long time to come. My boy has enjoyed much his visits to your house, and I thank you for inviting him. My love to you both (Mrs James is so sorry not to make the acquaintance of "the Stumpf's,")—

Yours ever | Wm James

ALS: MH bMS Am 1092.9 (3789)
¹ Alfred Hodder and Jessie Hodder, who gave birth to a daughter, Olive Hodder.
² Katharine Rodgers and Henrietta Rodgers.

To Francis Boott

                    Pension Gottlieben, | Meggen, bei Luzern. | April 27. '93
Dear Mr. Boott
    I duly got your letter of the 14th, and should have written to you
ere now save that I was hoping to see the monument and give an
account of my impression.¹   We did see it, on the 12th, a few days
before leaving Florence. It is really a most beautiful thing, very like,
and yet ideal.   The repose, the inclination of the head, the noble
serenity of the face, the somewhat low relief of the body half sunk
into the couch, the tenderness of the drapery, the whole thing in
short give it an extraordinary beauty and distinction which will, I am
sure, make the work hereafter—and for what a long hereafter!—one
of the acknowledged artistic treasures of Florence. Its place is good
too, (relatively speaking, for all the places are huddled in these foreign cemeteries), with a row of cypresses behind its head, the ground
sloping gently towards the feet, and one side free, towards the path.
Poor dear Lizzie! It is pleasant to think of her being associated in a
lasting way with that florence with which she always appeared to us
so identified; and I should think it would be a great gratification to
you that the excellent Duveneck could do such an act for her memory—the better too that he was not a professional sculptor, since it
seems more as if pure love and tenderness had inspired him.—He
looks very well, and no one can know him without affection.
    You wrote of the Peabody trouble. Of course in speaking of the
paper I didn't give you away.   I don't know what clumsiness there
may have been in his way of laying hold of the MS.² But I hold (no
matter what the legal proprietorship may be) that the *moral* owner-
ship of a man's writings resides in the man himself; and that it is an
act of proper spirit to assert it against any adversary, if he sees reason.
The loathesome thing about such incidents is the base view one gets
of the meanness of public opinion—people yelping and catching the
cry from each other, people who have never seen the culprit but who
smack their lips over his crime, like a pack of curs.
    Our last 6 weeks in florence were rather too agitated by social calls.
Amongst other things we had a *baby born* in our apartment(!) by a

pair of innocent friends who came wandering along to florence with that burden and had no other place handy for depositing it. Parents & child, I'm glad to say, doing well![3] *Uberhaupt*, the drouth made florence unpleasant. Such peppery light and air, and such dryness of the skin I never felt. I think the italian air lacks something essential to my organism, which keeps admiring everything, but with a surly kind of inner protest that I can't get over. I am glad to be North of the Alps again with something strong to breathe, and solid things about me. Not that the Italian *houses* are not solid! I wish we could have their solid floors. Here I am, reading & enjoying the air and paradise-like views. Harry is at Munich, & Billy at Vevey, for the next 2 or 3 months. Alice and I hope that we may get to England for the "heft" of the summer, though the expense looks deterrent. My brother Henry speaks of coming on hither from Paris shortly; and I hope he will. What are your plans for the summer? or have you none as yet? I saw in a paper the notice of poor Arthur Blake's death. I hope it was not painful in detail. In a way it must be a relief to his wife.[4] But what a heritage of pathos and sadness such a life leaves behind.

Please take the best love of both of us. Remember us warmly to Mrs. Greenough, and believe me, ever truly yours

Wm James

ALS: MH bMS Am 1092.9 (765)

Address: Francis Boott Esq | Cambridge | Mass | U.S. of A.

Postmarks: MEGGEN 27. IV. 93   NE<W Y>ORK MAY 7 93   CAMBRIDGE BOSTON MASS. MAY 8 93

[1] The monument to Elizabeth Boott Duveneck.

[2] See letter to Boott of 30 January 1893.

[3] See letter to Stumpf of 24 April 1893.

[4] Arthur Welland Blake (1840–1893), a Boston banker, died on 28 February. His widow was Frances Greenough Blake, daughter of Frances Boott Greenough.

To William James, Jr.

Pension Gottlieben, Meggen bei Luzern, April 27. 93

Well, old Bill, how goes it with you by this time? I suppose that you are so domesticated with the Ceresole's that you have forgotten that you ever had any other home. It will make a man of you. Remember your mother, and when tempted by the devil, think how she would like to see you behaving, and thus hold yourself straight. That is the best advice I can give you. Our days here pass by without events.   The Lake is beautiful.   On a couple of German guests at table we practice our German.   We lob round and read and write letters in the morning, and walk a couple of hours in the P.M.   Helène keeps Tweedy out of doors all day, but he doesn't seem over well inside.   Peg is charming now that she has no Bill to quarrel with. Card from Harry this AM.   Of course you have heard from him.

W. James

APS: MH bMS Am 1092.9 (3143)

Address: Monsieur W. James | Chez M. Ceresole   Cure de Blonay | la Chiésaz, sur Vevey | Vaud

Postmarks: MEGGEN 27. IV. 93   FRIBOURG 28 IV 93   VEVEY 28 IV 93   ST LEGIER 28 IV 93

To William James, Jr.

Pension Gottlieben, Meggen, bei Luzern, May 2. [1893] Dearest Bill,   What is the matter with you that you never send us a word?   Are you dead, mad, or simply lazy?—or so happy that you have forgotten that you have any ancestors'?   Pray write immediately and tell us how things go.   They go very well indeed for us in the glorious weather, with the birds singing about us from morning till night.   Tweedy i<sn'>t exactly right, however, and scold & says '*top* a great deal, and shrieks too early in the morning for our comfort.   To day I walked to Luzern and saw the german emperor arrive from Italy in the steamer and walk along the front of some troops that lined the quay bei the Schweitzerhof.[1]   He is quite round and fat, and looked very jolly, smiling and showing his upper teeth, thus— not very successful as a portrait!— —

Your uncle harry comes to morrow or thursday. A long letter from your bro. Harry in Munich showed him to be happy.   Yesterday the Chicago Exhibition opened.

Your loving   Dad.

APS: MH bMS Am 1092.9 (3144)

Address: Monsieur R. James | Chez Monsieur Ceresole, pasteur, | a la Chiésaz, sur Vevey | Vaud

Postmarks: MEGGEN 2.V. 93   VEVEY 3 V 93   ST. LEGIER 3 V 93

[1] William II, emperor of Germany, was in Italy on 1 May 1893, when he began his return journey to Berlin through Switzerland.   He reached Lucerne at 10 A.M. on 2 May and after lunch, according to newspaper reports, went to the railroad station cheered by enthusiastic spectators.

To Crawford Howell Toy[1]

Meggen, bei Luzern, May 3. 1893

My dear old Toy,

What friendship for your person could not prevail on me to do, imaginary duty towards a man whom I hardly know makes me perform. I need hardly say that I refer to the writing of this letter, of all human activities the least congenial to my inert temperament. First then, of the man's business, one Revd Corning, acting consul now at Munich and a very cultivated man, whose syllabus I enclose and who says his stereoptic illustrations are profuse and unequalled. I told him I would be on the look out for a possible call to him to give his lectures, and I send them to you because you are more on the track of enquiries about that sort of thing, from which my ways are rather remote. Lowell Lectures hereafter would be the thing for him.[2] At any rate, pray bear the matter in mind, and keep the syllabus, which I will ask you for again on my return.

I hope that the winter has treated both you and Mrs. Toy kindly,[3] in spite of the cold. We had a mixed, but on the whole a decidedly comfortable and profitable seven months at Florence, and are now slowly making our way with the two younger children, towards England where we shall pass most of the summer. All well; and don't I just *not* envy you all the soul- and body-destroying committees which you must be having to attend! They are what are losing Harvard University. Dadurch wird sie zu Grunde gerichtet. Apart from them I am eager to get home and into Harness and at my own library table again. As mere vacation and recuperation four solid months are always enough.

Pray give the love of both of us to Mrs. Toy, than whom I for one, have seen nothing more inspiring or truly satisfactory since the shores of America sank below the western horizon. Take our love too for yourself, and believe me ever yours faithfully,

Wm James

ALS: MH bMS Am 1092.9 (3818)

[1] Crawford Howell Toy (1836–1919), American Orientalist, professor at Harvard. Correspondence is known from 1885 to 1910.

[2] The lectures were most likely on art history. Corning did not lecture before the Lowell Institute, Boston.

[3] Toy was married to Nancy Saunders Toy.

To Théodore Flournoy

Pension Gottlieben, | Meggen, bei Luzern, | May 5. 1893
My dear Flournoy,

Madame Flournoy's delightful letter to my wife came the day before yesterday, and gave her the greatest pleasure. She will soon write herself, but as I have had an envelope, directed to you, lying on my table for a week past, I "get ahead." She is probably going early next week to Munich to pay a visit of 3 to 5 days to our Harry, to see whom she has a maternal longing. If you are kind enough to invite Billy, I am sure he will be highly pleased. But I advise you to wait for a fortnight longer. He will speak better then; and until he gets into entire equilibrium with his environment at la Chiésaz, he had better not be disturbed. His address there is chez M. A. Ceresole, pasteur, la Chiésaz, sur Vevey.—*This* place is a paradise, and we shall very likely spend the whole month of May here. I find I can read and walk and sleep, and I enjoy it very much. My brother arrived yesterday from London, or rather from Paris.

Can you name me any simple book on the differential calculus which gives an insight into the philosophy of the subject. I was struck by you saying last summer that you tho't Renouvier's view was mistaken. Lasswitz in his Atomistik would seem to hold also what he would call a mystical view. I have just been through a short treatise by one of my colleagues, but it is a thicket of particular formulas & calculations without one general idea, and I want ideas and not formulas.[1] Can you also indicate to me any little manual explaining the political constitution of Switzerland? There must be something for schools. But don't take *any trouble* about either of these things! There is a young German Gelehrter Carl Hauptmann by name here in the house, very modest and simple, author of a book "die Metaphysik in der heutigen Physiologie—Beiträge zu einer Dynamik der Lebewesen."[2] The book is a terribly abstract and unreal affair, insisting that life is pure mechanism but without a single concrete suggestion as to what the mechanism may be. But the man is a charming and human individual with a very pretty and innocent young wife.

Warmest regards! | W.J.

ALS: MH bMS Am 1505 (8)

[1] Possibly William Elwood Byerly, *Elements of the Differential Calculus* (1879).

[2] Carl Hauptmann, *Die Metaphysik in der modernen Psychologie* (1893). The work has an added title page: *Beiträge zu einer dynamischen Theorie der Lebewesen.*

To Eliza Putnam Webb Gibbens

Meggen, bei Luzern, May 9 [8]. 93[1]

Sweet Belle-mère,

Alice, wonderful to relate, has started off all alone to Munich to pay a visit to her first-born. Such is the power of maternal love that she started up suddenly without misgiving or hesitation, and resolved on it three or four days ago, and did it yesterday. She insisted on going third class, in spite of the fact that it would only save her $2.50 on both journeys, that she would have a straight wooden back to her seat and nothing to rest her elbow on for 12 hours, etc. But, from this misguided Ideal, Providence rescued her (*I* could not) by showing her at the station that she would have to spend the night at a hotel in Zurich, there being no third class on through-trains. I mention this only to show the spirit of which she is composed. We always travel third class in Switzerland; but for a woman alone, on an all-day journey it seemed to me uncalled for economy. The swiss trains are as clean and decent as one could desire and open throughout like ours, making an entirely different thing of the journey. Well, A's departure leaves a sort of emptiness which makes me turn to you as the next best substitute, remote as you are. We have been having a terrible three or four days of perplexity about when to return. I *must* be back at least a fortnight before the 26th Sept. (when College begins) to prepare for my work; and I *ought* for the interests of my total character and standing, to return as early as Aug 5 and go to Chicago to the Psychical Congress, and also to see the Exhibition and meet the men of my own sort who are to be there.[2] Alice on her part says that it is her and the children's duty to drink the last possible drop of Europe, and not to sail earlier than Sept. 14th., which would bring the boys home the eve. of their school opening. Accordingly we have engaged passage in the Pavonia for that date. It seems to me a misguided plan; for apart from the aimlessness of hanging round till that date with the children in the narrow quarters to which we shall have been condemned all summer [—you've no idea what it is to live in 2 rooms and never have them off your mind—how we lived through last summer with Billy and Harry to complicate the situation I can hardly now comprehend—it must have been the mere novelty of it that pulled us through] there is the certainty of relatively cold weather and head gales in a slow ship, with awful suffering to Billy, not to speak of what misery the others will catch. I think what weighs most on Alice is a real dread (I am sorry to say) of Cambridge housekeeping, and no feeling of satisfaction in our house, and she hates to face what to her is an evil day. The house is to me such a luxury, and its calm wide spaces and outlook will be to me such a haven of peace after four months more of the fever and fret of our consolidated nursery-existence with Tweedy rousing us every morning any where between 5 and 6, and Peggy "hanging" on all day, that I am quite unable to enter into Alices state of mind, and wish that she were willing to sail about Sept 1st, when the voyage will almost certainly be warm, and very probably smooth, and the two weeks before College begins be weeks of quiet preparation and communion with you and the immediate neighbors. If you should feel as I do about it, I wish you would (without referring to me) hold out in your next letter some alluring picture of the sweetness of Cambridge in the latter ⅔ of September, which may soften her heart. If on the contrary you sympathize with her, as you very likely will, all I beg is that you will not actively write anything to encourage her in her resolution, for I should like it to be a fair fight between us two. It seems to me that her ideal about staying till the last minute is an entirely poetical one. The boys have but one desire and that is to get home; and they will (I fear) be impatient and listless and "on her hands" all the time, when we get them to England with nothing to do.—But halt! I hadn't the remotest intention, when I sat down to address you, of writing all these details, and after they had begun to flow, I stopped and almost destroyed the letter. But on second thoughts, I went on, because I thought it *might* bring something from you that would do good. Don't gather from this that I am "discouraged" about our trip. *Quite* the reverse! It has been very costly; but it has done us all lots of good and I wouldn't have it otherwise. It has had a big *minus* side in the fact that we are primarily and essentially a *nursery*, with adults attached, and I don't think that my truest vocation is to be an appendage to a nursery. The consciousness that I don't perform the duties required is as great a wear and tear as the duties themselves would be if I performed them at all. But the *plus* outweighs the *minus* immensely. Florence is an experience which I would not for a great deal have removed from my life. Alice is rejuvenated mentally. The boys have a greatly enlarged horizon Peggy gabbles french like an ash-shoot, and both she and Tweedy are *entirely* well just now. She has improved on the whole more than any of us, and now that Billy and the continuous opportunity of quarrel which he presented are removed, she has become really a charming little companion. I think you will relish her greatly on her return.

How sorry I am that you had to have another bronchial attack! Pray take the best "care" of yourself until it subsides. Your last letter referred to Mrs. Piper, and to your preparations to receive her into your family. Of *all* the . . . . . . what?—words fail for me to designate this new duty by! But I say nothing more about it, since it has happily blown over. I hope the possibility will never come up again. Is her husband entirely unable to support her?—or are they completely estranged?[3] I am very glad that Mark is building next you. You won't find him "interesting," but I am very glad to have him for a near neighbor, so honest and able a man. I never saw his wife.[4] I hope that Mr. Child's injury proved of no permanent importance. It is a shame for him to get such a shock, anyhow. I rec'd the Philadelphia press with Russian treaty circular & report of Mass meeting. It is good to think of Mack finishing his year with a bit of solid public service like that.[5] They mount up as life proceeds, and make a man important.

The day is cold and cloudy and a fire is lighted in the stove. Tweedy is now asleep in the adjoining room, Peggy comes in from a walk with a couple of the ladies of the house, and when asked for a message says "I send 3 kisses and 100 loves." Take 3 times 3 and 100 times a 100 from me, and give the same to Margy with a smaller and more respectful dose to Aunt Nanny who would be shocked at so much.

Yours ever affectionately, William.

Pray be sure that the clipping of our hedge isn't neglected this Spring.

ALS: MH bMS Am 1092.9 (928)

[1] The contents of the letters to AGJ of 8 May 1893 and from AGJ of 8 May 1893 (both calendared) would indicate that this letter was written on 8 May rather than 9 May.

[2] WJ did not go to Chicago for the World's Columbian Exposition.

[3] Little is known about William R. Piper (d. ca. 1904). The hypothesis that he became estranged from his wife receives some support from the fact that he did not die in Massachusetts; see *EPR*, 400.

[4] Edward Laurens Mark (1847–1946), professor of anatomy at Harvard, built his house at 109 Irving St. His wife was Lucy Thorp King Mark.

[5] In late April 1893 the United States and Russia ratified an extradition treaty that many thought posed a threat to political refugees seeking asylum in the United States. Several groups were formed calling for abrogation of the treaty. While the clippings mentioned by WJ were not seen, it is clear that Salter was agitating against the treaty.

To Alice Howe Gibbens James

                    Thursday, later.—Meggen [May 11, 1893]
Dearest—Here is Margaret's letter which I forgot.   I looked at it
hastily and thought it was Hodder's writing—so I opened it, when I
saw the first line I stopped, so no secrets have been revealed to me.
     Heavy rain this P.M. which I escaped.   Saw Harry and sat with him
during the shower.   He has a tenderer heart than you infer from his
disinclination to live in our immediate contact.   He shed copious
tears, e.g. this P.M. on being reminded of Wilky's last days.
     Do enjoy yourself.   Eat drink, be merry, and have your fling.
                                                        Your | W.
     I am writing to Mary.   My cold is well.
     Write me Mary Salter's address.
ALS: MH bMS Am 1092.9 (1843)

To Mary Sherwin Gibbens Salter

                         Meggen, Lake Lucerne, May 11. 93
My dear Mary
     Alice having abandoned me 4 days ago and gone to munich to see
her first-born—all alone! such is the power of the maternal instinct—
I, left alone and deprived of the wonted ear into which to pour all
my observations, aphorisms, wishes and complaints, turn unto the
cognate channel of your mother and you as the most nearly resem-
bling things to commune with.   I enclose her letter received yesterday morning (nothing has come to day) that you may see in what
good spirits her trip has put her, and in what shape the good Cultur-
mensch has appeared to her fond eyes.   Send it to your mother when
you've done with it—it will please her too.   We are all very well,
Tweedy entirely so at last.   He strikes one as a fundamentally vigorous child, but he has had all sorts of successive maladies of nutrition.
Peg has become a little trump, though in all her mental acts, of questioning, proposing, demanding and enunciating, she is more remarkable for ponderosity and momentum than for the lightness and grace
usually deemed characteristic of her sex.   The depth of her voice
and the blackness of her brow add to the impressiveness, but she is
the most amiable little creature living, in spite of the stern appearance
she so much of the time presents.   We are all in a mess about going
home; but as I unburdened myself of that to your mother, I will spare

your ears. We shall *get* home, somehow! and no doubt have our
money's worth in England before we do so. And glad I shall be of
the roomy quarters in our big house.—[Sunday, 14th] Peg had to
have a "reading" lesson at this point, and what with other duties I
haven't had a chance at this letter again till to day. Alice is still absent, and after hearing Tannhäuser to night at the Munich Hof-
theater, leaves to morrow morning for home, a full seven days in
Munich of which I feel quite proud. I think I shall go as far as
Zurich to morrow to meet her on her way. We are so mixed up with
Mrs. Evans & Miss Gardiner here, not to speak of my bro. Harry at
Lucerne, that it is the only way to get her an hour to myself.—The
weather is glorious to day, after a couple of days with rain. I have
taken the children and Helène across the Lake in a row boat, two
hours, which were rather too much for the youthful Tweedy at the
end. He wanted constantly to get out of the boat, & was only paci-
fied at last by pouring water over his hands. When we were landed
he rolled on the ground and roared to go back again. After a bottle
of milk and a new plaster over his abdomen, we have got him to sleep
at last, and Peggy is supposed to be taken a "writing" lesson sitting
at the table opposite me. I will send you the result—you see she *can*
write, after a fashion, but she throws down her pencil after each letter
and says she's too tired to go any farther—at this moment she is
shedding tears and saying "I'm awfully hungry." How *we* ever got
over these troubles I don't know—to think that my hand which writes
now so easily, had all these impossibilities to overcome.—But there is
the dinner bell which mercifully sets both of us free from the writing
lesson, and interrupts this letter, alas! again. [After dinner]. You
never heard such a forest of song birds as we are in about this house.
The European blackbird (which corresponds in shape and make to
our robin) is the sweetest songster I know. But the whole collection
of them is vastly richer, stronger and sweeter than anything I ever
heard in America. We have got a table girl down stairs with mincing
gait, frizzly bang, puffy eyelinds and conceited doughy complexion,
who, because she does remind one of a type so frequently met with
at home, makes you realize by the contrast how absolutely free, so
far, we have been from *any* human unwholesomeness such as is the
rule in country hotels at home. Heighho! yet I long to be home and
to get into deeper communication with my land, unwholesome as so
many of its people are.—I am so glad that Mack, to whom give my
love, has put thro' the Russian treaty protest.[1] I hope it will be an
effective one. How do the "first steps" sell?[2] And how have they

been noticed. I was highly delighted yesterday to hear of 619 dollars as the last six months profits of my psychologies. Of course this can't be repeated as it is the heaviest sale of the first year of the smaller book. I wish I could be on your hill top at Chocorua for a while *without the babies!*

Affectionately, | W.J.

ALS: MH bMS Am 1092.9 (3649)

[1] See letter to Eliza Gibbens of 9 May 1893.
[2] Salter's *First Steps in Philosophy.*

To Théodore Flournoy

Meggen, bei Luzern, 12 Mai. 1893

Mille fois merci, mon cher Flournoy, de votre envoi plus qu'aimiable, que je vais me mettre tout-de-suite à tâcher de comprendre un peu.[1] L'etat des volumes me donne une terrible idée de votre érudition et de votre profondeur. Pourquoi suis [je] dépourvu du sens mathématique? Toutes les propositions mathématiques me semblent non-seulement inintelligibles, mais *fausses!* Renouvier m'a toujours contenté par son exposition; et voilà qu'il va falloir que je me remette à l'école! Ma femme reste 8 jours à Munich.

W. James

TC: MH bMS Am 1092.1

[1] In his letter of 10 May 1893 (calendared) Flournoy mentioned several books that he was sending to WJ.

From Carl Stumpf

München 17 mai 93

Lieber James!

Es ist mir unendlich leid, dass wir Ihre liebe Frau nun gar nicht mehr gesehen haben, und dass *ich* sie überhaupt nicht kennen gelernt habe! Meine Frau und Schwägerin waren so entzückt von ihr, dass ich es als einen grossen Verlust betrachten muss. Aber sie wird Ihnen bereits erzählt haben, wie wir zu genau gleicher Zeit uns gegenseitig besuchen wollten; wenn dies auf Grund einer telepathischen Anziehung geschah, so verwünsche ich die Telepathie. Die Tage vorher wie nachher war ich gerade so vollständig in Anspruch genom̃en, dass ich meinen Besuch nicht wiederholen konnte, hegte aber doch die leise Hoffnung, dass sie mit Harry unsrer Einladung auf Montag Mittag noch folgen könne. Sie scheint aber bereits vorher zurückgereist zu sein. Und dass ich nun auch Sie selbst, lieber Freund, "auf lange Zeit", wie Sie schreiben, nicht mehr sehen soll, ist mir nicht minder leid: denn ich hatte bei Ihrer hiesigen Anwesenheit infolge Ihrer vielfachen Geschäfte weniger von Ihnen als ich gehofft hatte. Sie sind ein volles Jahr in Europa—ein Jahr, auf das ich mich seit 10 Jahren gefreut hatte—: und von diesem Jahr entfallen auf unser Wiedersehen wenige Stunden, in denen noch dazu Ihr Denken und Fühlen durch dringende Angelegenheiten in Anspruch genoṁen ist! Ich kann Ihnen dies natürlich nicht zum Vorwurf machen, aber ich bin traurig darüber, und um so trauriger, als ich—um es offen zu sagen—das unbestiṁte Gefühl habe, dass Ihre Freundschaft zu mir in den Jahren doch etwas an Lebendigkeit eingebüsst habe, dass Sie vielleicht darin nicht gefunden, was Sie anfangs sich versprachen, oder dass irgend etwas an mir Ihnen direct befremdlich oder unsympathisch erschien. Etwa das Auftreten gegen Wundt? *Ernster*, viel ernster sind wir ja alle beide seit diesen 10 Jahren geworden; das Leben ist auch so kurz u. die Welt so klein, in der wir leben. Aber um so fester möchte ich an denen halten, die ich von Herzen hochschätze und liebe.

Ihr begeistertes Urteil über Paulsens Schrift macht mich begierig, bald mehr darin zu lesen; mein eigenes Urteil rechte ja nur auf ganz flüchtigem Einblick und wird sich sehr wahrscheinlich dem Ihrigen nähern, wenn ich das Buch näher kennen lerne. Den Menschen schätze ich ja ohnedies von jeher sehr hoch, und bewundere den populären Schriftsteller und den Kenner des Lebens.

Die experimentellen Übungen, die ich begonnen, haben unter den Studirenden viel Anklang gefunden, nehmen mir aber, wie Sie richtig voraussagten, unmenschlich viel Zeit und Mühe weg, die eigentlich wissenschaftlichen Arbeiten gehören sollten. Ich bin geradezu angegriffen davon und werde jedenfalls *allein* die Sache künftig nur in ganz kleinem Massstab treiben können; aber vielleicht findet sich ein Assistent.

Wundts Psychologie I Band ist soeben in 4. Aufl. erschienen.

Zu dem, was wir über die Frage der einfachen Ähnlichkeiten besprachen, möchte ich noch Eins bemerken. Wenn Sie finden, dass meinem Argument dadurch zu entgehen wäre, dass man die letzten Elemente weder qualitativ noch quantitativ sondern lediglich *numerisch* abgestuft denkt: so kann ich dies doch nicht für eine wirkliche Lösung der Schwierigkeit anerkennen, da es doch nach allgemeiner Ansicht unmöglich ist, dass mehrere qualitativ völlig gleiche (und auch räumlich nicht verschieden localisirte) Empfindungen im Bewusstsein gleichzeitig existiren. Dieses Prinzip also müsste man aufgeben u. damit aller Erfahrung widersprechen.

Genug für heute—ich muss noch an die Luft, um mir den nächtlichen Schlaf wieder zu erwerben. Leben Sie wol und seien Sie und Ihre liebe Frau Gemahlin aufs Beste von uns gegrüsst.

Ihr getreuer | C. Stumpf

ALS: MH bMS Am 1092.9 (630)

To Henry Rutgers Marshall

Meggen, bei Luzern, May 24. [1893]

I have meant for two months past to write & tell you how good your aesthetic articles seemed to me in Mind.[1] They cover the ground most completely; and I am entirely converted to the relativity-doctrine which you set forth with such effect. I don't believe that "differences of taste" are a provisional infirmity, to be superseded by more evolved insight into "the Beautiful." Any abstract treatment of the "aesthetic Ideal" is inadequate to the innumerable different demands which different men (& the same man at different moments) are entitled to make upon the artist. The clash of opinions, and of mutual disdains lavished on each other by the different dillettantes and experts at Florence had begun to make me doubt of any "objectively true" standard of criticism, and the radicalism of your articles settled my mind entirely.

Wm James

APS: MNS

Address: H. Rutgers Marshall Esq | Century Club | New York | U.S. of A.
Postmarks: MEGGEN 26. VI 93   NEW YORK JUN 6 93

[1] Henry Rutgers Marshall, "The Field of Aesthetics Psychologically Considered," *Mind*, n.s., 1 (July 1892): 358–78; (October 1892): 453–69; "Hedonic Aesthetics," *Mind*, n.s., 2 (January 1893): 15–41.

To Carl Stumpf

Meggen, bei Luzern, Schweiz | May 26. 93

My dear Stumpf;

Your letter of the 17th., just received, touches me very much, and confirms me in my habitual belief that your heart is as strong and active an organ as your head. But how *could* I have conveyed to you the impression that my feeling of personal affection for you, and satisfaction in being able to count you as a friend, had grown less in the past ten years? Older I am indeed, and probably much duller, but I speak sincerely when I say that during my last visit I felt more intimately and closely the charm of your character and our intellectual kinship than when we were together ten years ago in Prag. That was relatively superficial. I only wish it were possible for my wife to repeat to you all the things I said about the impression I had of you, when I got back to Florence. I was, as I now see, a little too afraid, when in Munich, of encroaching on your time and appealing to your hospitality. My own experience of the visits of English people to Cambridge who expect entertainment when I am hard pressed with work, has perhaps made me too sensitive, in that regard, towards others. You were busy & I was relatively idle; I did n't wish to make it possible that you should think me a bore. But with *you*, I see now that the thought of such possibilities ought to have been absent from my mind. Over and above that, however, most men's friendships are too inarticulate. As our Emerson says: "There is more kindness than is ever spoken."[1] And in the beautiful verses of an old friend and neighbor of mine,

> Thought is deeper than all speech,
> Feeling deeper than all thought.
> Heart to heart can never teach
> What unto itself was taught.
> Like the stars that gem the sky,
> Far apart, though *seeming* near
> - - - -
> We are spirits clad in veils,
> Soul with soul can never meet;
> We are columns left alone,
> Of a temple once complete—.[2]
> - - - - - - -

Alas! I find that I have forgotten the words, which sadly express the "dialectic contradictoriness" that is to be found in finite individuality.—Will a "higher synthesis" ever come to give relief? Your letter meanwhile shall be one of my most cherished possessions, and makes me feel freer with you than ever before. I feel free now to express

my amusement at your suggestion that the tone of your polemics
with Wundt should have made my love turn cold. I confess that that
sentence gave me a good long laugh, and makes me laugh again now!
Wundt seems to be "getting himself generally disliked." In this pension we have had a Herr Carl Hauptmann author of a book called
"die Metaphysik in die Physiologie" (which you perhaps know) and
his friend Prof. Avenarius, both with their wives.[3] Hauptmann is a
charming modest man, and his wife an angel, and Avenarius a very
good natured creature (superficially, at any rate), but they both seem
to have Wundt "on the brain," and can hardly talk for five minutes
about any subject without some groaning reference to him. Victor
Hugo says of Bonaparte that he fell because *"il gênait Dieu."*[4] Is that
to be also Wundt's fate? He certainly begins to encroach on God's
omniscience. If only he could show a spark of creative genius *dabei!*
As for Hauptmann, the book does not seem to me as good as the
man. I have not yet read a page of Avenarius's books, but have an
apriori distrust of all attempts at making philosophy systematically
exact just now. The frequency with which a man loves to use the
words "streng wissenschaftlich" is beginning to be for me a measure
of the shallowness of his sense of the truth. Altogether, the less we
have to say about "strenge" the better, I think, in the present condition of our speculations. That is one reason for which I enjoy
Paulsen's book.[5] There is no pretence of "strenge" about it; and yet
the most pedantically written works have no *more* solid *stuff* to give
you than he gives in this absolutely popular and unpretending way.
To me the stuff is theoretically quite unsatisfying; but it is so fundamental and uncomplicated that it admits of addition, possibly without
much alteration; and I cannot but esteem it a great gain for the truth
to have such deep matters treated so absolutely-without technical apparatus. It makes one realize the alternatives in their natural naked-
ness, unveiled by what I must call the humbug which a would-be
"streng wissenschaftlich" treatment generally disguises them in.

On the matter of resemblance, there is a reply from me to Bradley
in the April Mind, I don't know whether you have seen it. I agree
with you that a multitude of qualitatively identical coexistent elements of consciousness is an unintelligible conception; but still, *if* one
chooses to adopt it (as Spencer & Taine, *e.g.* adopt it) it affords a
refuge from the infinite regress of composition, it seems to me.

The dinner bell rings, and I must stop. My wife has been saying
all the morning that we *must* come over to the Munich "Congress" in

1895,[6] we two without the children! *Perhaps* the gods will provide the means! but I have no very strong hopes. Meanwhile I enclose a sheet from her, written yesterday, and am with warmest regards to you all, your faithful friend,

Wm James

ALS: MH bMS Am 1092.9 (3790)

[1] Ralph Waldo Emerson, the opening line of the essay "Friendship," *Essays*, 1st ser. (Boston: Houghton Mifflin, 1884), 183.
[2] Christopher Pearse Cranch, "Enosis" in *Poems* (1844).
[3] Richard Heinrich Ludwig Avenarius (1843–1896), German philosopher. His wife was Maria Semper Avenarius.
[4] Victor-Marie Hugo, *Les Misérables* (1862), vol. 2, bk. 1, chap. 9.
[5] *Einleitung in die Philosophie*.
[6] The Third International Congress of Psychology was held at Munich in April 1896.

To William Wilberforce Baldwin

Vers-chez-les Blanc, | sur Lausanne, 4. VI. 93

My dear Baldwin

Your magisterial handwriting is pleasant to receive—also to feel that you don't forget us. Liquid vaseline was easily got, and our catarrhs which were most obstinate, speedily got well. As for plans, I wish *you* could trace mine. We are trembling on the verge of being able to go to England, my wife and I, without the brats, but I don't feel at all sure that at the last moment the whole thing wont settle the wrong way and we be unable to leave them behind. I am consequently in a state of *Spannung* which probably won't be relieved till Thursday or Friday, the combinations being complex and delicate on which our liberation depends. I can't know till I get to England, whether I go to Chicago early in August or not. Other combinations are to heave in sight there. I will let you know as soon as things are decided. Meanwhile please let *me* know at what time this summer you will be *disponible* for Switzerland, as that will become an ingredient in my various possibilities.—The only solid result of my sabbatical year so far is to urge all human beings hereafter never to take children along if they go travelling for their own good. Please remember that in your patients cases.—Mrs. Glendower Evans leaves to morrow for Schöneck. It surely is not the great Wunderlich? Her case is queer—a little Garibaldi of a woman, who has carried out your prescriptions only too literally if anything, but still loses sleep badly, and (it seems to me) has a more invalid-consciousness than when she arrived. I have suggested the possibility that a little more reading, and less methodical lying down wide-awake in day time might prove better instead of worse, but she spurns the suggestion. I am right glad she will now go to some one who can see her as well as exercise authority over her, for treating by correspondence must surely be unsatisfactory to you. Her letter to you was written under the effect of a very bad sore throat—tonsillitis. She will surely get well!

How does the dutiful Raffaello succeed in your house? I suppose that you are getting rather more leisure time now. Trusting that your sister, and the children are well and that you get good news from America, I am always yours

Wm James

Address Barings

ALS: NNMor

To Margaret Mary James

Hotel S: Romain, Paris, Sunday night. [June 11, 1893]

Sweet Peg,

We rose at ½ past three this morning to get the train for Paris at Geneva, & had a very agreeable 13 hours journey. Your Ma has just gone to bed after promenading the Boulevards with me, and sitting at a little marble table on the sidewalk, sipping coffee & seeing the crowd of idlers go by. I suppose that by this time you feel quite at home at the Ceresoles, and hope that to morrow you will settle down to your regular daily lesson, which every one needs who is six years old to make them right for the rest of the day. Tell Billy to keep for me a book which I ordered sent to him from Zurich. It will come by post. Love to you all 3.

Dad.

APS: MH bMS Am 1092.9 (2977)

Address: Mademoiselle James | Chez Monsieur Ceresole, pasteur | Cure de Blonay | par Vevey | Suisse

Postmarks: PARIS 12 JUIN 93 VEV<EY> 13 VI 93 ST. LEGIER 13 VI 93

To François Pillon

          34 De Vere Gardens, London W. June 17 [1893]
You can hardly imagine how strong my disappointment was in losing you in Paris—when we *might* have found you by going to Alcan's
on Monday, or by writing you before we came.[1] It seems now sheer
folly! But I didn't think of the possibility of your being gone so early
in the summer.—Our 3 young children are *all* in Switzerland, the
older boy in Munich, and my wife and [I] are are like middle aged
omnibus horses let loose in a pasture. The first time we have had a
holiday together for 15 years. I feel like a barrel without hoops!
We shall be here in England for a month at least. After that everything is uncertain. I *may* not even pass through Paris again!
                                              W.J.

APS: MH bMS Am 1092.9 (3497)
Address: Monsieur F. Pillon | 15 Rue Campagne première | Paris
Postmark: KENSINGTON W. JU 17 93
  [1] Félix Alcan, publisher in Paris.

To Charles Ritter

          34 De Vere Gardens, | London W. June 22. [1893]
My dear Ritter,
    Your letter of the 16th only reached me yesterday. I did not an-
swer your charming epistle written from Stuttgart the day after your
arrival, (or from Bern?) because it had no address, and in it you said
you should write again. You are certainly, my dear old Ritter, a master of the manly art of compliment to the feminine sex, and I am on
the whole rather glad that you & my wife don't live near each other,
for seeing you too often would turn her head entirely, and what I
foretold to you in Geneva has come to pass, namely that *you* have
captivated *her* affections also. An occasional visit is all that would be
safe with such inflammable materials—alas! that even an occasional
visit will hereafter be denied to us all, in all probability! I don't know
when we shall come to Europe again, and I am afraid that it will be
impossible to us to go back to Geneva this summer. My wife (who
is after all nearly as lovable as your imagination represents her) has
just consented to abridge her stay in Europe by three weeks, and to
accept my wished for date of return, namely August 24th. She is
enjoying very much her first taste of England, but it is so dark and

strong & tremendous that outsiders like ourselves feel at first annihilated, and I don't feel at all surprised that you should have fled from it after twenty-four hours, to the humanity and simplicity of your own dear little land. The english have less *sentiment* than any other people—all their life goes to activity, not to feeling; and yet the race is so rich in endowments that out of it comes as abundant a supply of geniuses as even Germany seems to produce. Only they are more isolated than in Germany.

We passed a delightful evening with the Flournoys nearly two weeks ago. I hope that you two will soon learn to know each other. It is amusing that I should be the *trait d'union* between two old Genevese! If we return on Aug 24, (I am now about to go out and take passage) I shall probably not see the Chicago exhibition, and I do not feel very sorry. Chicago heat in August is something to be dreaded.

Good bye, my dear old friend, and do not forget us, if we should not meet again this year.

Always affectionately yours | Wm James

ALS: Bibliothèque publique et universitaire, Geneva

To Shadworth Hollway Hodgson

34 De Vere Gardens, W | June 23. 93

My dear Hodgson,

I am more different kinds of an ass, or rather I am (without ceasing to be different kinds) the same kind more often than any other living man! This morning I knocked at your door inwardly exultant with the certainty that I should find you, and learned that you had left for Saltburn just one hour ago! A week ago yesterday the same thing happened to me at Pillon's in Paris, and because of the same reason, my having announced my presence a day too late.

My wife and I have been here six days. As it was her first visit to England and she had a lot of clothes to get, having worn out her american supply in the past year, we thought we had better remain incog. for a week drinking in London irresponsibly, and letting the dressmakers have their will with her time. I early asked at your door whether you were in town and visible, and received a reassuring reply, so I felt quite safe and devoted myself to showing my poor wife the sights, and enjoying her *naif* wonder as she drank in Britain's greatness. Four nights ago at 9.30 P.M. I pointed out to her (as possibly the climax of the greatness) your library windows with one of them open and bright with the inner light. She said, "let's ring and see him." My heart palpitated to do so, but it was late and a hot night, and I was afraid you might be in tropical costume, safe for the night, and my hesitation lost us: We came home. It is too, too bad! I wanted much to see you, for though, my dear Hodgson, our correspondence has languished of late (the effect of encroaching eld) my sentiments to youward (as the apostle would say) are as lively as ever, and I recognize in you always the friend as well as the master. Are you likely to come back to London at all. Our plans did n't exactly lie through Yorkshire, but they are vague and may possibly be changed. But what I wanted my *wife* to see was S.H.H. in his own golden-hued library with the rumor of the cabstand filling the air.

Write and make any suggestion as to how this worst of all bad blunders may be remedied, and we will see what we can do. The worst of it is that, having succeeded in quartering our two youngest in Switzerland (the elder two are also provided for), and being off on a lark *together* for the *first* time since our honeymoon, we are likely to be recalled suddenly to switzerland by any chance stomachache on the baby's part. Moreover when the waterspout of English hospitality at this season begins to break over one, one is led from one invitation to another till one is so tied up that no freedom more remains. But write, you noble old philosopher and dear young man, to yours always

Wm James

ALS: MH bMS Am 1092.9 (986)
Address: S. H. Hodgson Esq | Penrhyn House | Saltburn-by-the Sea | Yorkshire
Postmarks: LO<NDON-W.> JU 24 <93> SALTBURN-BY-THE-SEA JU 24 93
The envelope is endorsed: 'William James | June 23. 1893.'

To Théodore Flournoy

34 De Vere Gardens | June 26. [1893]

My dear Flournoy,

I received your card with the article by Baldwin many days ago, and send back with this your copy of the program of the Etudes modernes. We are staying in my brothers rooms, he being in the country, and enjoying to the utmost the glorious of London at this season, sombre, rich, immense, nothing on the Continent can be compared to it. My wife takes to it as a fish to the water. The great thing is simply to ride through the streets on the tops of omnibuses over the softly rumbling wooden pavement.   I wish you both were here so that I might take your respective "reactions"—not the *time* of them, but the quality.

No decision yet as to how we return.

The amount of literature indicated in the Enseignement moderne is enormous.   It looks as if it must be an indigestion.   It certainly will require skilful teaching, and I shall be extremely curious to know, after 10 years trial of the system, what the results are judged to be. Certainly if the program can be successfully taught to youths under 20, it is safe to say that their education will be more really "humanistic" than on the classic plan.

The evening spent with you is a delicious remembrance.   When we get back to Switzerland we shall immediately communicate with you.   With love from both, to both,

Yours always | Wm James

ALS: MH bMS Am 1505 (10)

To Hugo Münsterberg

c/o Baring Bros & Co | London, July 6th. 1893
My dear Münsterberg

It was a great pleasure to see your handwriting again after so long an interval.   Your letter of June 22nd came yesterday, and gave me some little idea of all that has been going on.   But first of all, *what* a year you have had, of worry, trouble and confusion, not to speak of illness; and now at the end of it, to have to move again and furnish, *per fas aut nefas,* an empty house!   At least it will be a clean one, newly put in order!   You show extraordinary elasticity of spirits, under the circumstances, to write as cheerfully as you do, and not to send up a perfect symphony of groans and wails.   I am sorry you have n't got a better place than Swampscott to pass the summer in; but that too is one of those things that one can only learn gradually after acquaintance with the country; and I hope that your illness and that of your dear wife will prove to have been a sort of prophylactic vaccination against all future American ailments, and that by next summer you will know both the dark and the bright sides of our country so well as to be in equilibrium, and without waste of time or money, know just what to look for and how to find it.   I don't like to hear you after so bad a year, speak of using the vacation for such heavy writing as you propose, and I certainly trust that you will take four weeks *at least* for *complete* repose, so far as psychology is concerned.

I have heard nothing from Royce or from Palmer since the final decision about our next years courses, nor have I yet rec'd the pamphlet of Instruction-courses. (Having written for it to the Secretary, I shall doubtless get it in two weeks now). What you say of Phil 1, makes me suppose, however, that Palmer has had his way, as he usually has it; and that it is to be given, but by someone as yet unknown, so far as the Psychology part of it goes.[1] I am sorry, for I believe in the plan I wrote you about, and feel sure that if you had had the experience in teaching our undergraduates which I have had, you would have been in heartier agreement with me. *Überhaupt,* from what you write, you seem to have been a little over modest in expressing your views. By right of your office, militancy and not neutrality, was your perfectly proper rôle, in any question in which you had an assured opinion.—Poor Nichols! I have just written to Palmer and the President, on my own responsibility, to say that in my opinion he ought to be reappointed now for next year, rather than fall back on a "Durchsc[h]nitts student," which is all you now say we can look to. I am very sorry that Angell couldn't come. He is a wonderfully efficient man, with a head as clear as crystal. We had here some correspondence on the subject, which made me hope he would take what Harvard offered, small as it was. As you know, I never advised Nichols's being dropped unconditionally. I only pronounced him a bad subject for *permanent* place and *promotion* with us, and said he had better go, if an equally good temporary man could take his place next year.

With regard to the Journal of Psychology, what you write is the first I have heard of any negotitiations, and I am in the dark as to whether Hall himself wishes to resign the Journal or whether the others are forcing his hand by threatening to start a rival if he doesn't.[2] It is in many respects badly edited now, and might be better. Only I wish that the Philosophical Review might give up all special Psychology and the two things in some way be consolidated so as to appear once a month, or a philosophical and a psychological part on alternate months.[3] Or any other plan of publication would do, provided we could avoid duplication of matter and dispersion of readers. One solid philosophico-psychological review ought to be enough for the american market, and the jealousies of institutions & rival ambitions of would-be editors ought to be sternly suppressed for the sake of the public interest. The readers ought to be sure of one thoroughly competent notice of whatever of importance appears; and the writers ought to be sure of having all the readers in the country for their articles. *Of course* it ought not to be dominated by men of the Cattell and Scripture stamp—but in my ignorance of the whole matter, I had better say no more!—I wish I could tell you definitively when I shall return. If I consulted my own personal interest I should go in August and have some quiet lonesome weeks of recueillement and meditation of my next year's work in my empty house. But conscience makes cowards of us all;[4] and the "sense of sin" that would come over me on leaving my wife behind to manage single-handed all our impedimenta, children, new servants, etc., will I think make me stay to the end. I have read hardly any thing since the 1st of March on account of external interruptions. I have neither memories nor ideas; and am getting into a rather melancholic state which I hope that the work of next year may rescue me from. You will have ample opportunity of learning what an empty vessel I am after my return. Blessed word "neurasthenia"! Almost as felicitous an invention as "epiphenomenon."—Meanwhile the wife and children are well and happy so far, and if we get safely home with our accretions, I shall be so too.

Love to you both! I am so glad that Mrs. M. is well again,

Wm James

ALS: MB

[1] In his letter of 22 June 1893 (calendared) Münsterberg stated that both Witmer and James Rowland Angell turned down offers, while Nichols, the best man available, was fired. As a result, there was no one to take WJ's place in Philosophy 1 (see letter to Münsterberg of 7 January 1893, note 1).

[2] In his letter of 22 June 1893 (calendared) Münsterberg reported efforts either to take the *American Journal of Psychology* away from Hall or to start a new journal, indicating that his efforts probably had prevented a new journal. In fact, the first issue of the *Psychological Review*, edited by Baldwin and Cattell, two of the persons mentioned by Münsterberg as involved in the negotiations, appeared in January 1894.

[3] The *Philosophical Review* appeared every two months.

[4] From Shakespeare's *Hamlet*, act 3, sc. 1, line 85.

To James Bryce

34 De Vere Gardens, W | July 8. 93

My dear Bryce,

The American Academy, etc. is one of the oldest and most respectable learned bodies in the United States, and contains all the wisdom of our "section of the country" in its sheltering folds.[1] The only trouble about it is that it is rather too respectable and its meetings too slow. It has lost importance as a publishing body now, on account of the rise of so many special Journals. But it is really an honour to be elected by it, and you need not hesitate to accept. Cooke[2] & Jackson[3] are Harvard Professors of Chemistry. The Academy has also a section for historical and philological science.

I echo your wish about London. To lie on one's back under a tree on the mountains, early in vacation time is the only *satisfactory* position for human intercourse, in my opinion. Then what people have in them *comes* out—doesn't have to be pumped out or drawn out etc. May a kind Providence some day provide that mode of coming together for you and me and several of "we-uns," is the wish of

Ever yours | Wm James

ALS: Bodleian Library, University of Oxford

[1] The American Academy of Arts and Sciences had its center in Boston. James Bryce was elected foreign honorary member in the section of moral and political sciences.

[2] Josiah Parsons Cooke was then serving as president of the academy.

[3] Charles Loring Jackson (1847–1935), American chemist.

To Dickinson Sergeant Miller

34 De Vere Gardens, W., July 8, 1893.

Darling Miller,

I must still for a while call you darling in spite of your Toryism, ecclesiasticism, determinism, and general diabolism, which will probably result in your ruthlessly destroying me both as a man and as a philosopher some day, but sufficient unto that day will be its evil, so let me take advantage of the hours before "black manhood comes"[1] and still fondle you for a while upon my knee. And both you and Angell, being colleagues and not students, had better stop Mistering or Professoring me, or I shall retaliate by beginning to "Mr." and "Prof." you. Your letter comes in the nick of time, for I had mislaid the Halle address and wanted to write to you both. First as to Angell, please tell him I am very sorry that he has decided for Minnesota rather than for Harvard, but under the circumstances I cannot complain. Münsterberg has just communicated to me the news in a letter in which he also says that Nichols has not been re-appointed, and that they have no one at all. I trust that under these circumstances Nichols will come back for at least next year. At any rate whatever happens to us, I hope that Angell will have a happy and successful year in Minnesota.   As for yourself, what you say of Erdmann,[2] Uphues, and the atmosphere of German academic life generally, is exceedingly interesting.   If *we* can only keep our own humaner tone in spite of the growing complication of interests!   I think we shall, in great measure, for there is nothing here in English Academic circles that corresponds to the German savagery.   I do hope we may meet in Switzerland shortly, and you can then tell me what Erdmann's greatness consists in.   Our plans for return are not quite settled yet, and the date depends somewhat on whether we find some servants in Switzerland to take back with us.   We have got emancipated from the children for a month, and my wife and I have been enjoying London together, especially she who has never seen it before.   The babes are at the house of M. Ceresole, pasteur, at la Chiésaz above Vevey on Lake Leman, and Harry who has been at Münich since March 1st, will come there in a few days to join them.   We follow later on.   I have done hardly any reading since the beginning of March.   My genius for being frustrated and interrupted, and our unsettled mode of life have played too well into each other's hands. The consequence is that I rather long for settlement, and the resumption of the harness.   If I only had working strength not to require these abominably costly vacations.   Make the most of these days, my dear Miller.   They will never exactly return, and will be looked back to by you hereafter as quite ideal.   I am glad you have assimilated the German opportunities so well.   Both Hodder and Angell have spoken with admiration of the methodical way in which you have forged ahead.   It is a pity you have not had a chance at England with which land you seem to have so many inward affinities.   If you care to come here let me know and I can give you introductions. Hodgson is in Yorkshire and I've missed him.   Myers sails for the Chicago Psychic Congress, Aug. 2nd.   Sidgwick may still be had, perhaps, and Bryce, who will give you an order to the Stranger's gallery.[3] The H. of C., cradle of all free institutions, is really a wonderful and moving sight, and at bottom here the people are more good-natured on the Irish question than one would think to listen to their strong words.   The cheery active english temperament beats the world, I believe, the Deutschers included.   But so cartilaginous and unsentimental as to the *Gemüth*.   The girls like boys and the men like horses! I shall be greatly interested in your article.[4]   As for Uphues I am duly uplifted that such a man should read me, and am ashamed to say that amongst my pile of sins is that of having carried about two of his books with me for 3 or 4 years past always meaning to read, and never actually reading them. I only laid them out again yesterday to take back to Switz. with me. Such things make me despair. Paulsen's Einleitung is the greatest treat I have enjoyed of late. His synthesis is to my mind almost lamentably unsatisfactory, but the book makes a station, an étape, in the expression of things. Good bye— my wife comes in, ready to go out to Lunch, and thereafter to Haslemere for the night. She sends love, and so do I. Address us when you get to Switzerland to M. Ceresole, as above, "la Chiésaz sur Vevey (Vaud)," and believe me ever yours,

Wm. James.

TC: MH bMS Am 1092.1

[1] From the poem "The Gipsy's Malison" by Charles Lamb (1775–1834), British writer.

[2] Benno Erdmann (1851–1921), German philosopher.

[3] Reference is to the House of Commons.

[4] Dickinson Sergeant Miller, "The Meaning of Truth and Error," *Philosophical Review* 2 (July 1893): 408–25.

To Frederic William Henry Myers

Keep addressing me at | 34 De Vere Gardens, W | July 9 1893
My dear Myers,

I have been through the proof with renewed feeling of its eminence as literature and of its value as psychology.[1] Some day it will count as a great document, and in the heat of your appetitive constitution I seem to myself a cynic batrachian. I have absolutely no emendation to suggest, except possibly to ask whether the second "once" in line 10 of sonnet VII is required—the metre being so much better without it. "Lumour" in the following poem I at first had doubts about, but on the whole I now say *stet*.[2] No other word is equivalent.

It was yesterday, and will be to day, impossible for me to get to a sitting with Miss Bailey.[3] Life's fitful fever! To morrow we return from Haslemere and that is our last social engagement. Then to Canterbury, Salisbury, Winchester etc, and to Switz.d again.

Mrs. Tennant told me that you were to go in the Majestic and not in the Lucania after all, she being belated.[4] I am very sorry, for the best part of the fun would have been that ship. Now that *my* decision is made I breathe more calmly—It was but a *wish*, and I see now that I never *could* have left the caravan to its fate.

Of course mum's the word, as to the document. I am touched

by the way, my dear Myers, in which you make me your confidant, contrasted as I am in so many ways with yourself—democratic, misanthropic, cold blooded, hollow-hearted, neurasthenic above all, and abstract where you are concrete. But out of such twinings strong ropes may be made, and if you get *any* such enlargement of *glimpse* through me as I get enlargement of *view* through you, the partnership will be hallowed.

Affectionately yours | W.J.

ALS: MH bMS Am 1092.9 (3311)

[1] Reference is to Myers's autobiography; see letter to AGJ of 18 August 1892.

[2] Myers's published poems include many sonnets, but in their published form they are neither numbered nor called sonnets. 'Lumour' appears in "Saint John the Baptist," published in *The Renewal of Youth and Other Poems* (1882): "The false and fickle lumour of their joy" (Frederic William Henry Myers, *Collected Poems*, ed. Eveleen Myers [London: Macmillan, 1921], 160).

[3] Miss Bailey was not found in the published reports of the Society for Psychical Research. However, several Miss Bs are mentioned at about the right time.

[4] Gertrude Barbara Tennant, mother of Eveleen Tennant Myers and Dorothy Tennant Stanley. Myers was planning to visit the World's Columbian Exposition in Chicago.

To Frederic William Henry Myers

34 D.V.G. July 16 [1893]

Dear Myers,

My children have been in a delightful place, the parsonage of M. Alfred Ceresole, pasteur à la Chiésaz, sur Vevey. I don't know whether they can take another boy till mine leave, a little less than a month hence. My eldest has just gone there from Munich. There are several places at Lausanne, where several boys are taken. I forget the names of most of them now, but can find out in a week. At Aubonne, a little way down the lake, there is a pastor named Laufer whose reputation as a *teacher of classics* stands high, and whose place is pleasant.[1] There is a man named Rosselet in Lausanne who will ere long start with his youths for a walking tour in the mountains. I liked him, but I fear he has several Britishers amongst the boys. There is a charming pastorial couple named Thélin in the town of Lausanne—personally both of them the salt of the earth, though possibly deficient in a sense of humour – – etc. etc. A relative of Flournoy's professor of mathematics—I forget his name—takes boys, is a fine man and has a pleasant wife, and a nice place. etc. etc.[2] If Sir A. wants his boy to have *companions*,[3] I would suggest Rosselet, if a home, Ceresole, Thélin, or Flournoy's man, whose name may presently revive. If teaching, Laufer.

I tho't the dinner delightful. We are far off from the possibility of such a crowd as that in america. *Your* face seemed actually phosphorescent with spiritual light and human geniality.—I have already written to Mrs. Wingfield that I can't go to her to day.[4] I get off on Tuesday to the Continent where my address will be at Vers-chez-les-Blanc, sur Lausanne—I hope that a black cloud that has weighed on my spirits for a month past may there clear off—certainly in London it remains! I enclose introductions to my friends Holmes, Gray, Perry, Bigelow & Fennollosa,[5] *et al.* The two latter have had some training in Buddhism in Japan. Cards will do, as they all know your reputation & writings. Mrs Whitman will very likely ask you to Beverly Farms, and make you acquainted with people there, and through Ho<lmes> you will know everybody.—Farewell and a good voyage to you, & congressional success! We should be installed at 91 Irving S.[t][6] by Sept 4th or 5th.

Yours for the truth! | W.J.

I forget Gray's town address. Wendell professes English and writes on Rhetoric—also novels & biographies. Putnam is one of the best of men, a neurologist. When you come to Cambridge you can see some other colleagues. I give you a card to Gray because he has an ornamental wife.[7]

ALS: MH bMS Am 1092.9 (3312)

[1] Laufer was not identified.

[2] Probably Professor David.

[3] Sir A. was not identified.

[4] Membership lists of the Society for Psychical Research include Mrs. Edward Wingfield, living in Hyde Park, London. But several other Wingfields were involved with the Society in various capacities.

[5] Ernest Francisco Fenollosa (1853–1908), a student at the Harvard Divinity School, from 1878 professor of philosophy and political economy at the Imperial University, Tokyo.

[6] A slip for 95 Irving St.

[7] John Chipman Gray's wife was Anna Sophia Lyman Mason Gray.

To Jacob Gould Schurman

London, July 17. 93

Dear Schurman,

Another book-review—would I could make them shorter, but my pen will run away.[1]

My desciple Miller sent me a letter from you in rê an article of his of whose editorial treatment he had complained. It was very good reading, and the aforesaid Miller seems to have enjoyed it hugely, in spite of the fact that you had chawed him up so. He said it gave him a great appetite for your acquaintance, although he could not agree in your doctrine of editorial duties towards articles that were signed.* He is a delectable young fellow, of whom the world will doubtless hear more. I return home, a somewhat saddened and impoverished man, on August 24th, and on the whole shall be glad to be in harness again—even as a tub may be glad to feel the hoops driven on tight.

I write by lamplight at midday, a classical green London fog having descended on the town!

Best wishes and greetings, from yours ever,

W.J.

[*]It gave me no envy of your editorial tasks!

ALS: NIC

[1] At this time WJ was doing extensive reviewing for the *Philosophical Review* and sometimes it is impossible to identify the book in question. The best possibility is Lucien Arréat, *Psychologie du peintre* in *Philosophical Review* 2 (September 1893): 590–94; reprinted in *ECR*.

From Alice Howe Gibbens James

Vers-Chez-les-Blanc | Monday July 17ᵗʰ [1893]

My darling William,

You will have received my post-card from Vevey and know, that thanks to your prompt telegraphing I did n't go to Berne. Harry found me in the Buffet where I had taken my coffee and was meditating my next move, a ticket to Berne. We returned to Vevey at once, took a carriage to Blonay which waited and carried me back with the children at half past two, for 6 francs! I gave the man an extra one. I settled with Mᵐᵉ Ceresole. She asked if 10 francs a day was too much for Helène & the babies—you know Billy pays six.—I told her that we wished to recompense Mˡˡᵉ Marthe[1] in a satisfactory way and were willing to pay as much for Peggy as for Billy so we reckoned 20 francs a day for the party, added in Billy's unpaid days (ere the others came) also 75 francs for washing and extras, Dr's bill, hat for Billy stockings for him & for the baby. The whole thing came to 852 francs from which we deducted the 100 you advanced. I paid 752 francs to July 17 for everything. It has troubled me since that I did not pay her exactly her demand and leave you to add what you thought fit. But when I saw how much care and attention had been given to the children—Peggy always with Madame or her daughter—I felt as if I must make my gratitude sincere in the only return I could make. But I am not satisfied with myself, at a moment when you are so worried about money. We saved the trip to Berne. Hélène is more fishy and inert than ever so I don't regret her. She has no more heart than an oyster. I shall write to M. Claperède in Geneva & put an advertisement in the paper in Lausanne but I suspect our best chance will be London.[2] I will write to Agnes Clarke to ask her to send you the address of the Intelligence office of which she spoke to me. Perhaps you could there inquire as to the chances of a well recommended person being willing to go to America. Still, wait a little in case I find anyone here.

The Cruchons were really glad to see us. The house is full—the Rodgerses not coming. You cannot think how heavenly and innocent the country looks, green enough now. I feel like Tithonos since you have "returned me to the ground".[3] It taught me a great deal which I hope will benefit you and the household in time—all the experience in London—but the havoc it has made in your vacation, the money it has cost, and the sickening consciousness that you did it all for me alas! the burden of saddens me. To find myself back here in the wide freshness with the little children happy about me seems so normal, so much more like me that I wonder, wonder at myself. I shall always be thankful to have had my glimpse of London, if you only get well again. And I shall always love Harry for his kindness to me and to everybody. And the "Brothers" could hardly have given him a serener face.

As for you William darling, I pray that you may do the one thing necessary to your recovery, without the *least* regard to me.

Peggy is in excellent condition sweet, happy & unexcited. She finds some pleasant young people in the house, and is playing now under my window with a little English child. She keeps coming up to my room to speak to me All the anxiety & questioning which troubled us has gone. I began to give the baby more food today. He had a little beef & potato for his dinner.

He can say anything he wants to in French. At first he would n't come to me saying "peur de Maman" but now he has accepted me again. I shall write my other notes now.

I am sure you will feel better the moment you get into this Swiss country.   Only break the journey by a night on the way.   It would tire you to come through as I did, tho' I didn't mind it myself.

God bless you!

Alice.

ALS: MH bMS Am 1092.9 (302)

[1] Mlle Marthe was not identified. She was most likely a daughter of the Cérésoles.
[2] AGJ was trying to solve the servant problem.
[3] Probably a rough version of Tennyson, "Tithonus," line 72.

To Alice Howe Gibbens James

34 D.V.G. July 19, [1893] | 9 P.M.

Dearest Wife,   your divine letter after settling down arrived this morning and filled me with balm.   Such a good account of the children, and such a pleasant impression of old Switzerland again, as you give.   But why you should start up and incriminate yourself in your relation to me [at this late hour! (subtle joke.)] I know not, nor why you should not be able to see me depressed in spirits without holding yourself responsible.   The logical ground of my depression has been to see that after spending all this money, I am about the same in health, and that the year has gone with very little reading done.   *You* have nothing to do with it at all.   If there is anything in the whole year which does me good to think of, it is this holiday with you.   It is only a pity that it should have outwardly coincided with the above discoveries.   I suppose there is no doubt of my being able to get the room at the Blancs whenever I come again.   I shall go to morrow to see Harry, and on Friday pass on to Paris.   To-day has been a big southerly gale, with warmth and rain.   I've heard from no one but you; and despite the fact that I sent off a notice of Pillon's book,[1] I still feel strangely sad, for me.   I long to break away from London which yet in many ways I love so well.   I paid for the clock £13.10.0 making £18.10 in all, including case, which he warrants strong.   I found at our Japan screen place that a case fit to take the thing over will cost 12 shillings—it becomes questionable whether the screen be worth as much.   He said that if you wished to change it for lighter articles when you come back, you may do so, so I let the matter stand over.   I bo't Harry a first rate Aluminium glass for £10, so in a measure we are quits—but such a purchase also makes me sad.   I am writing a short notice of Myers's little book "Science and a future life with other essays" for the nation—it will please him to see it appear whilst he is there.[2] I am right glad you were generous with Madame Ceresole—I don't understand just how generous you were—and your account of Helen is discouraging.   If the address comes from "Agnes"[3] we can ask our question by writing, as well as I could ask it now.   I am writing to several people, so I will stop, with the old old love,

Your | Wm.

I shall probably leave Paris on Sunday.

ALS: MH bMS Am 1092.9 (1849)

[1] Review of *L'Année Philosophique*, 3d year (1893), ed. by François Pillon, in *Philosophical Review* 2 (September 1893): 629–30; reprinted in *ECR*.

[2] Review of Frederic William Henry Myers, *Science and a Future Life* (1893), in *Nation* 57 (7 September 1893): 176–77; reprinted in *EPR*.

[3] Agnes Clarke.

From Henry Holt

Somewhere in Vermont | July 24/93

Dear James:

Here I am on the same railroad again, & it comes natural to answer your letter.

Your half serious & half burlesque theological exhortations edify me from both stand-points.   I think though that your counsels, if acted upon, would perhaps decrease my habitual range in the directions you propose.   I do not care to accept the view of your friends addicted to the "higher thought," that I am "*soon* to be brought face to face with the "Great Judge":   I prefer my own conviction that I am there all the while.

The "billows of eternity" I know nothing about except the portion of them that I have traversed.   I use the best craft I can find for them, and if I ever get into a different sort of billows, will try to adapt my notions of naval architecture to *them*.

I do not offer any "excuses based on the Spencerian formula of evolution," or on anything else, but try to bear the consequences of my volitions as well as I can.

As for "preparing for the last day," there is very little wisdom in any man who does not do what he can to live as if the present day were his last.   So far as I can see, I should live no differently and think no differently if I believed all the consequences of my acts to be conveniently posponed to some later indefinite settling day. I want to live better and think better than I do, but dont see how I could get any help from such procrastinative doctrines as you preach. In fact, they date, you know as well as I do, from a time when the consequences of conduct were vastly less understood than they are now; and the "higher thought" as far as I can make it out, seems to be mainly an effort to get "higher" than they, or than any real thinking whatever. Whenever you dont attempt it, you're quite a rational and dependable creature: whenever you do, your gyrations make me think of a bird with but half a tail. He cant even fly straight backwards—which you admit a man can at least do, even if he has not "the higher thought."

Dear old Royce! He was in my office the other day professing that the one effort of his life was to "keep free from the business virtues." He has succeeded pretty well, though he hasnt yet quite got rid of the fundamental one—honesty, yet the free range of his "philosophy" is not much hampered by such clogs as consistency, coherency and adaptation to an end. I kind of love the wambling cuss, nevertheless.

Bess Evans would keep well if she would not insist on navigating this puddle on the theory that it's not a puddle at all, and that sails are wings. I declare the attempted aeronautics of you Boston people sometimes almost reconciles me to New York. Yet just you bet your sweet life that I know that as soon as I am reconciled, I am hopelessly damned. The happy mean is not Boston nor yet New York: perhaps it's Burlington, where I hope to enjoy a sunset tonight that will help my faith in Something that cant be vulgarized even by Bostonian pretence of comprehension. I'm afraid though that even at Burlington, I'll find a professor of Philosophy in the University of Vermont who thinks he knows a donkey-path right into the heart of it.

Damn your irreverence, W.J! That's what's the matter with all you fellows.

And Ah! Here's larks! After we've been here (i.e. at Stowe) a week, we're (my Wife, sons & I)[1] going over to N. E. Harbor to sit the rest of the season under the shadow of a bishop![2] "William of Albany" he signs himself, and his shadow is very large and round, and he's a very dear old man, and very sensible for a bishop. I am a bit afraid though of finding a certain not unfragrant feminine oppressiveness in the atmosphere. Glancing at your letter I just read your acknowledgement of my last "written on the train" & I read you as going on to say: "Evidently that is the way to write letters—when one is *en traine*" But the last five words were not there, but were only in my anticipatory imagination

My son Roland shares your enthusiasm for railroads.[3] He is just well of an attack of typhoid—pneumonia and all, and we feared the journey would tire him, but he seems rather to revel in it.

What odd coincidences do turn up! We are just stopping at Middlebury where, I just told Roland, he had typhoid when a child.

Guess I've said all I had to say, and a good deal more, as people usually do. What wd. life be if they didn't?

My Wife whom you accuse of being a poet, joins me in love to you & your Wife whom I accuse of being a poem.

Yours ever | H. Holt.

I've forgotten your bankers, & have to send this *via* the shop.

ALS: MH bMS Am 1092 (423)

[1] Henry Holt had seven children by his first wife.

[2] The Holts were traveling to North East Harbor, Mount Desert, Maine. The bishop was not identified.

[3] Roland Holt (1867–1931), publisher and author.

To Henry James III

[July 26, 1893][1]

Dear old Heinrich—Keep a stiff upper lip. Your mother and I were quite down hearted after leaving you behind, and reflected that we often think we want a thing, and when we have got it we find it wasn't exactly what we wanted. [In *my* case it was the absence of you and Bill that I sighed for for a while!] In the village we met that poor lame man who had been all that time coming up—and it stabbed me to the heart that I had prevented your tender hearted mother from taking him into the carriage.—We both resolved hereafter to obey *immediately* any such humane impulse. I hope that you are by this time getting to feel less strange with the Cérésoles, and that on the whole life looks promising. I am sorry that the young one is not yet there. I didn't understand that he was to be away. God bless you, my dear boy.

Your "loving Dad"

ALS: MH fMS Am 1092.4

[1] WJ's letter is on the same sheet of paper as AGJ's letter to son Henry, which is dated 26 July 1893.

From George Herbert Palmer

Boxford, | July 26, 1893.

Dear James:

I do not wonder you are annoyed, sitting silent in Europe while entangling operations go on here unreported. But I assure you I have pressed your interests as heartily as one can who is not entirely in sympathy with them. Fearing, too, that I might not say all you would wish to have said, I have shown to the President as soon as they were received the several letters of instruction you have sent.

Phil. 1, established at your earnest request, has been singularly successful. While it has had the reputation of being a stiff course, it has been taken by a large number of students, and by students of a high grade. Since it was so useful in supplying all the higher courses with excellent material, I was unwilling to sacrifice it to the supposed needs of one of its parts, psychology; especially when Münsterberg, after hearing the whole matter discussed, declared that psychology would be helped by the continuance of the course. The vote finally stood Münsterberg, Peabody and myself in favor of the old Phil. 1 with Royce and Santayana against it. It was accordingly allowed to remain; but, as you know, Royce offers a paralell one in addition.[1] Both the President and Dunbar warned me that to abandon Phil. 1 would put the Department to a serious disadvantage in comparison with other Departments.

I have steadily urged on the President the appointment of such an Assistant in the Laboratory as could give the psychological instruction in Phil. 1. I have told him I thought it unjust to force you into teaching which you did not approve. I have shown him that you will have a full year exclusive of this elementary work. I have asked Royce to make similar representations to him, and I have shown him your written protests. But thus far he has refused to do anything. He says he wants to talk with you before making any change. The Corporation, he says, are unwilling to pay the Assistant next year more than $250, or at the most $300. The large amount this year was possible because Nichols was your substitute and paid out of your salary; but no such payment can continue after your return. I tried to get Delabarre and Angell, thinking that with them the honor and experience would count for more than pay; but they could not be had. I agree with you that Nichols is far better than any one we are likely to obtain at that sum. I have told Eliot so, and I shall send him your letter. But he has a strong aversion to Nichols, and has said to me that he would never appoint him again to any place in the University. He calls him "unwholesome", and one can see that the term is founded in fact. I am sorry for Nichols, and have recommended him unsuccessfully to three other places.

Though I sent in the proof of our pamphlet on June 1, I have not yet seen a copy of it.[2] The printing-office has been unusually crowded with work, partly I suppose on account of the World's Fair. But I hope it will not be long now before you receive a copy.

Half a dozen of us from Harvard agreed to go to West Chop this summer;[3] but finding the attendance was likely to be very small, we persuaded the managers to give up the school. We have therefore had the more time in beautiful Boxford, and we are both feeling the invigorating effect of the happy life. I wish I could be sure you are having half so good a time.

I have missed you all the year. Frequently as my judgment differs from yours, you are never long out of my life without making it poorer. Nobody will welcome you home more warmly than
Your admiring friend and fellow, | G. H. Palmer

TLS: MH bMS Am 1092.9 (429)

[1] See letter of 21 April 1893.

[2] Reference is to the printed announcement of courses offered by the Philosophy Department.

[3] West Chop is a village on Martha's Vineyard. No information about the school was found.

To Hugo Münsterberg,

Vers-chez-les-Blanc, | sur Lausanne, Switz? | July 29. 93
My dear Münsterberg

Your letters are always delectable—that of July 14th. received yesterday P.M., no less than all the rest. You will ere this have received one from me in which I make a statement of the general principles which I believe ought to guide those concerned in the question of deciding upon the psychological periodical for America. Your present letter does n't make me change them in the least, but gives me some more insight into the matter-of-fact situation. I suppose the discussion arose in the bosom of the American psychological Society, and that some personal ambitions (personal in a large sense as including universities) had a little to do with starting it. But as I believe that America has hitherto been most happily free from bad personal rivalries in scientific matters, and is remarkable for the humanity and fairness that prevails in such affairs as this, I have earnest hopes that the decision will be made on purely objective grounds, & that individuals will sacrifice their own desires to the good of the greatest number. To me a few points seem clear, at least until I shall have heard objections which I cannot myself frame.

1) One journal is infinitely better than two, even if both were equally good.

2) It is "objectively" quite immaterial at what university it shall be produced. That question can be solved passively, so to speak, by getting the other questions solved first.

3) I can personally see no objection to a "board" of Editors, with proper division of labor. There will have to be one laboring and drudging chief-editor in that case, and he should be the most wide-awake and practical and sympathetic and unoriginal man.

4) Since Hall has borne the brunt of the fight single-handed all these years, it is certainly fairest that the new journal should be continuous with his journal, & if need be, bear its name. I can hardly think him unwilling, on principle, to enlarge its scope.

5) I should personally prefer to see a monthly journal, as catholic as the Revue philosophique, though with more psychology and better bibliography. A fusion of Hall's & Schurmann's would do this—but I fear others will not feel as I do in this matter.

6) The worst *possible* thing is several one-sided journals repeating partially each other's matter, with their *raison d'être* based on University rivalries. It will be literally *shameful* to the U.S. of A., if we descend to that. We must resist it by every possible means. Therefore I am in principle totally opposed to a "Harvard" Journal, and refuse to consider the idea of such a thing until joint harmonious action is proved impossible.[1]

7) Can't the American psychological Association meet, and vote 1st the ideal form of journal which is needed, leaving out no feature which, after discussion, is strongly insisted on by any one man? Can't they, 2nd., elect a chief-editor from the number who are willing to be candidates, on this programme, and elect him for 5 years, with such assistant-editors as are then willing to serve, amongst whom the work can be portioned out along the lines of least resistance, these to be discovered by the editors themselves. In all case of disagreement, then & thereafter, the chief editor should have power to decide.

8) My own wretched insufficiency of working strength absolutely precludes my serving, under any circumstances, as any kind of editor.

Of course I should hope to be engaged as some sort of contributor; and I will heartily support any editor who will make the thing broad, and distinguish good work from bad, so as in the bibliography *e.g.* only to print the former. The shorter bibliography of the Revue Philosophique, *e.g.,* is disgraceful.

9) You may communicate these remarks of mine to any one you see fit. As I pen them in this sylvan solitude, they will doubtless seem delightful *naïfs* and abstract, to yourself and others who realize all the difficulties of the concrete situation. It is easy to understand that men like Hall and Schurman who are now autonomous, should not like to bring in a body like the Psychol. Ass.ⁿ to sit above them, nor complicate their decisions by the opinions of associate editors. Therefore it is not to be expected that they should cordially cooperate. But on the other hand, they should recognize that *clearly formulated* demands for improvement of their journals, if such be agreed on by the psychological association, are binding upon them morally. The association on its side ought to help, and be faithful to, *any* editor who should with sincerity and intelligence, once in his position, produce the sort of journal which it defined as ideal, and it should relentlessly frown down any attempt to start rival publications, of which the motive then could only be personal restlessness or the jealousy of some university.—It is hard for me to believe that one journal (monthly if need be) will not suffice for many years to come, for all the *matter* required.

Don't think of a Harvard publication, my dear Münsterberg, until all hope of something general is extinct! You speak of the *Kleeblatt,* Jastrow Baldwin, & Cattell. B. seems to me a broad man, and a strong one, though not a clear writer. Cattell is absurdly narrow, and Jastrow too newspapery. Still abstractly, & obeying a program generally agreed on, they might make very good editors. Baldwin's mansuetude of disposition seems well shown by his willingness to serve with Jastrow. J. wrote a very insulting and abominable short notice of his Psychology, and Hall printed it, as he never should have done.[2] The great trouble, I suppose, is with Hall. He is absolutely without judgment, can't tell good from bad, and has n't a definite or clear idea in his head. Yet his enthusiasm, initiative, and vast & vague bibliographic knowledge, together with what he has done, give him certain *rights* which can hardly be ignored. If he could only be nominal chief-editor, whilst some one else exerted the real power,— that might be the solution.

I hope swampscott will agree with you all round, and that you'll get a good rest, to launch you with the greater momentum on next year.   Love to you both from yours ever

Wm James

We return in Cephalonia to Boston, Aug 24

ALS: MB

[1] In his letter of 14 July 1893 (calendared) Münsterberg suggested that if the negotiations between Hall, Baldwin, and Cattell lead nowhere, Harvard should establish its own journal, which would cover not only experimental psychology but also the broader field of philosophy.

[2] See letter of 11 January 1891.

To Alice Howe Gibbens James

Zermatt, Aug 7. 1893 | 9. P.M.

We had a glorious 10 hours on the Riffelberg & Gorner Grat to day—the very perfection of weather and sublimity, and with no great exertion—some five hours walk in all.[1]   Billy is delightful.   On returning just in time for the table d'hôte, I found your big envelope of enclosures for all of which thanks.   The Cunard thing on my part was to give you a chance to change if you tho't fit at the last hour.[2] You may possibly do it yet if after having Mrs Evans, Mack and Mary, you think it best to stay over.   Decide yourself!—I rejoice in the new cook—the promised one.   Poor Helène![3]—To morrow we go from here to the Hotel Jungfrau on the Æggischorn via Brig & Viesch. On Wednesday up that horn and down to Brig over Rieder Alp & Belalp thence home

W.J.

APS: MH bMS Am 1092.9 (1852)

Address: Mrs. James | Vers-Chez-les-Blanc | sur Lausanne

Postmark: ZERMATT 8 VIII 93

[1] WJ and his two older sons were on a walking tour of about eight days, which began on 3 August 1893.

[2] In his card of 6 August 1893 (calendared) WJ suggested that should AGJ want to delay their return she should telegraph the Cunard Line and change their reservations from 24 August to 24 September.

[3] In her letter of 5 August 1893 (calendared) AGJ stated that the servant Helène had departed and had been replaced by Marie Garin, whose friend was a good cook and wanted to come to the Jameses.

To Hugo Münsterberg

V. ch. l. B. Aug. 11. 93

Dear Münsterberg—I have already written to Baldwin and Cattell about the Journal, asking Baldwin to send the letter to you, so, to avoid repetition, I will be very brief on that matter now. I am not altogether surprised that you have all come to grief in your negotiations with Hall; his personal psychology is a very queer and tortuous one, containing, however, elements of sincere devotion to truth. He hates clearness—clear formulas, clear statements clear understandings; and mystification of some kind seems never far distant from everything he does. Yet I think he does not mean to deceive, nor is he a liar in any vulgar meaning of the term. He shrinks with an instinctive terror from any explanation that is definitive, and irrevocable, and hence comes to say & do things that leave an avenue open to retreat—at bottom it is all connected with timidity in him—as a *dreamer* he is bold, when it comes to acting, he wills-and-wills-not. But what I least like in his journal and other writings of his as president, is the religious cant he finds it neccessary to throw in. Yet in a certain sense even that is not insincerely meant! He has too complicated a mind!—As I said to Baldwin and already to you, I can't be any kind of editor and I can't contribute money. This year has been a perfectly ruinous one to me financially, making a far worse hole in my capital that I ever thought possible, or than I ever should have consented to in advance, and I must "lie low" and live within my income for many years to come. I am heartily sorry that you have had so similar an experience.[1] But the first year is always the worst, and I trust that there will be no deficit whatever hereafter. What *is* abominable is that your things should have been so badly packed in Freiburg.[2] Have you no redress? I cannot imagine anything more exasperating, especially for your poor wife, who has no laboratory-successes to console her for so many domestic disasters. I am glad you have liked Swampscott; and both myself and wife are eager to see you again and hear all the gossip of your year from your own mouths. She starts tomorrow for London, I follow in 9 days, on the 24th we sail.

Yours ever | W.J.

ALS: MB

[1] In his letter of 26 July 1893 (calendared) Münsterberg reported that he lived less well on $7,000 a year in Cambridge than he had on $2,500 in Freiburg.

[2] In his letter of 26 July 1893 (calendared) Münsterberg stated that twenty-two cases of household goods had arrived, with most things broken.

To William Wilberforce Baldwin

Vers-chez-les-Blanc | sur Lausanne, Aug 12. [1893]

My dear Baldwin,

After long wondering where you might be, I only received yesterday on returning from 8 days in the M^{ts} with my boys, your letter of July 31st, in which you tantalizingly describe the charms and salubrities of a certain "here" but convey no hint as to [where] the province of the earth or vulgar denomination of the so delectable abode may be. I suspect, from a certain vague and wild aroma that impregnates your description that it is probably somewhere in the Mountains in Italy. Your amateur polyclinic is delightful—I wish I were there to keep the records for you. But what an idea it gives of an "over-instigated" nature, not to be able to keep his hands off of his fellow creatures even when driven to the Mountains for a rest! *Therapism*, or *therapo-mania* as another morbid craving like *cocainism* or *morphino-mania*—I'll mention it in my course on mental pathology next year. I daresay those italian peasants are sweet creatures to deal with, though, and offer a great temptation. The two chief things that will remain over to me from this year, will be the impression of swiss air, and of italian graciousness of disposition. For our museless race, the mere glimpse of an entire people with whom the muses are familiar, is a revelation; and I thank God that *real* worths are known to him alone, and that there are such diverse voices in the human concert.

My wife leaves here to day with our eldest boy for England, and I follow, a week from to morrow, with the rest of the caravan, including three domestics whom we have with much trouble found. We sail for Boston, Aug. 24th; I am not likely soon to visit Europe again, must repair the financial breach etc; but I wish I could hear some day soon that you were likely to come home and settle in Boston. There is not a medical man of your artistic fibre in the place, and you would be sure of quick success. Of course the climate means more wear and tear. Anyhow, my dear Baldwin, good success and happiness to you and all of yours, wherever you decide to abide. I shall always count it one of the great gains of the year to have learned to know you. Cordialest regards from both of us to Mrs. Baldwin,

Yours ever | Wm James

ALS: NNMor
Address: Sig. Dott. Baldwin | 1 via Palestro | Firenze | Italie
Postmarks: LAUSANNE 12 VIII 93   FIRENZE 14 8 –93

To Josiah Royce

near Lausanne, Aug. 14. 93

My dear Royce,

I have languished from hearing no word from you since that great letter you wrote me about the beginning of the proceedings concerning the electives for next year. I at last wrote to Bolles for the pamphlet, by which I see that the worser plan was followed;[1] and since then I have heard from Palmer about it. No one can play the rôle which that inimitable Being has created, after he has gone. The letter describes at great length all the things he did to further my desires and interests so far as he was in sympathy with them. I am "never long away without making his life the poorer" etc. etc. Dear, dear, old G.H.P.—one must love him in spite of everything. But the upshot of it is that Eliot, unable to pay any one for teaching Psychol. in Phil 1 is to "talk with me" about it immediately after I return. Now it seems to me that the plainly god-appointed instructor for that 3rd of Phil 1. is G.H.P. himself and that he must be made to do the work. If that were so, in spite of the title of your course, I should think that you and I, between us, could make something like what I have regarded as the ideal arrangement, you giving logic for ½ a year or less, metaphysics for ½ or more, & I Psychology for ½ a year, all to beginners, and the 2nd half year of psychol. being only to the picked men who were worth spending laboratory-time upon. Phil 1. would then be a superfetation. I wish you would seriously think of playing into my hands in this way—into the hands of EDUCATION as well!

Do you remember whether my refusal to teach in Phil. 1 came *before* the final vote by the committee? That is an important tactical point.

Munsterberg, Baldwin and Cattell are all bombarding me with letters about a new psychological Journal. I only partly know the circumstances which have led up to their decision, but am urging that it be a "Psychological Review" to appear on the alternate months with Schurmans, same publisher, type etc. and he to give up Psychology. Then we should have a full all round philosophical periodical appearing monthly. I wish you would do anything you can to convert

Schurman.   What I most fear is another little inadequate back-shop sectarian affair like Hall's.   Cattell hardly seems broad enough in his ideas to be a good editor.—I hope you have been having a salubrious time at Davidson's.   I wish I could look in on you.   Am uberhaupt very eager to get home.

Yours ever | W.J.

I see no lectures to teachers on paedogogy advertized.   Does that mean that nary one of [us] is to give them?[2]

Of course you have no time to answer this letter—it is only meant to prepare your mine[3] for what I expect you to talk about after my arrival.

ALS: MH bMS Am 1092.9 (3614)

[1] Frank Bolles (1856–1894), American nature writer, secretary of Harvard University.   WJ had asked for the printed announcement of courses.

[2] The question refers to the summer of 1894 since the 1893 session began in early July.   No lectures to teachers were found in 1893 and 1894.

[3] A slip for 'mind'.

To Lionel Dauriac

Vers-chez-les-Blanc | sur Lausanne, Aug 15. 1893

Dear Mr. Dauriac,

I am thoroughly ashamed of myself for having been so long the receiver of attentions from you in the way of books, and of articles about my book, and yet of never having written to express my acknowledgments, thanks, protestations or anything at all.   You however, have lived long enough to understand the state of mind of a man who has once got badly behindhand with an office of this kind. He abandons himself to his negligence; and that he has sinned so long becomes a reason why he should continue to sin longer.   I fully meant to write to you after your first article in M. Pillon's Année about my book, but I reacted on that by simply giving a little abstract of it in the Philosophical Review, and somehow let the letter go.[1]   Of this second article I have also given a little abstract which I will cause to be sent to you;[2] but hearing all the pleasant and affectionate talk about you at the good Pillon's the other day has at last brought a letter to birth.   The letter will, however hardly be worthy of such a long preface, for all I wish to say in it is that I am your constant reader, and admirer of your philosophic talent and originality, which never fail to instruct me; and that in particular I feel deeply flattered at the serious manner in which you have found it worth while to write about my book. The criticisms in your first article were I think entirely just—I only excuse myself by saying that the see saw between the mechanical and the spiritual point of view of which you complain is characteristic of the present incoherence of our knowledge, and that until the genius comes whom we wait for, who shall bring unity into our formulations, every sincere writer must alternately turn his face now to one, and now to the other set of facts, and so be more or less inconsistent with himself. Of your criticism on my emotion-theory, I will only say that although I well understand it, it hasn't convinced me, for it only affirms but does not prove. It is also a little too Herbartian for my taste. I confess that my theory of the emotions has for my own mind no *systematic* importance whatever. They probably have some cerebral process to which they are correlated, and I see no *consequences* involved in the process being of the sort which I assign rather than of any other sort. I still hold to the theory as regards all the coarse emotions because it seems verified by my own introspection in ever concrete emotional experience upon which I am able to turn my attention promptly.

I am eager to read your psychologie du musicien, which through accidental circumstances I have missed.[3] When I get back to Cambridge (Mass)—we sail from Liverpool on August 24th—it will be one of the first things that I shall attack.

Believe me, dear Monsieur Dauriac, with most cordial regards, yours most gratefully and fraternally

Wm James

ALS: Sorbonne

[1] Lionel Alexandre Dauriac, "Du positivisme en psychologie (à propos des *Principes de Psychologie* de M. William James)," *L'Année Philosophique* 2 (1892): 209–52. WJ reviewed the volume in *Philosophical Review* 1 (November 1892): 649–52; reprinted in *ECR*.

[2] Lionel Alexandre Dauriac, "Nature de l'émotion," *L'Année Philosophique* 3 (1893): 63–76. WJ reviewed the volume in *Philosophical Review* 2 (September 1893): 629–30.

[3] Lionel Alexandre Dauriac, "Psychologie du musicien," *Revue Philosophique* 35 (June 1893): 449–70; (July 1893): 595–617.

To Alice Howe Gibbens James

Vers chez les Blanc—|Tuesday, 4. P.M. Aug. 15. 1893

Sweet Alice,

This is the most exquisitely *agreeing* place I ever was in. After writing a card to you yesterday, I had a delightful hour walking up the Berne road, and off into a forest to the left, read till 9.15 in the dining room, & slept like a top at night.   This morning, lying in woods and despatching 120 pp. of Physics, and now another nap.   It will probably never exactly return as long as we live.   The children are well, especially Peggy, who seems very happy, *jouant son petit rôle* in the society of the place.   She is evidently destined for a social career.   She spent the morning in the woods with the Greniers,[1] who are certainly extraordinarily nice children, esp? Robert.   Tweedy is still deficient in colour, and serious.   He doesn't cry but he is prone to whimper.   He is very happy with the big wagon of the Wilsons which he drags about, and is dragged in.   This A.M. I tho't it my duty to give him a taste of the woods, but he evidently didn't appreciate their beauty, refused to do anything when there, and finally was led back by the "tall" Marie.   The latter looks cheerful and vigorous. She is probably not endowed with a very rich sense of humor, but I love to see her healthy strength.   I think that Tweedy misses you. He hates to have me go away, and acts as if he lacked something in life.   He sleeps well however and his looks improve daily.   Mrs. Wilson's husband came yesterday—a good looking, wiry active man with a small head, who hates Lausanne.   I imagine they chafe a good deal upon each other, and he sacrifices his life to hers.   He told me that they took her away from Cooperstown in the midst of puerperal fever, and their child died in the cars before she reached New York.   They also lost their eldest child.   She turns out a decidedly intelligent woman.   She gives me her Galignani every day,[2] and Miss Blumer her J'l de Genève,[3] so I am well off.—I pity you in this heat, which must be bad in London, and long to get news of your first 24 hours there.   I hope the clothing problems of both of you don't depress your spirits.   I wrote a note to J. B. Greenough this A.M.   Madame Weber is very "nice," with me, and expresses great sympathy with you, wishing you could have been more in her life.[4]   The book-box ought to have painted on it "W James c/o Cunard SS. Co. Liverpool for *Cephalonia* Aug 24"   Smith can get it done.[5]   I do hope, darling that all goes smoothly where you are.   Give love to the Clarke's, as well as to Hen- & Har-ry.

Your loving husband,   W.J.

How is Harry struck by England?

On re-reading, I fear I give a false impression of Tweedy.   He has never been as poor looking as just before you left.   All I mean is that he hasn't got up to his maximum before his indigestion.

ALS: MH bMS Am 1092.9 (1855)
¹The Grenier family was not identified.
²*Galignani's Messenger* was a newspaper published in Paris.
³*Journal de Genève* was a newspaper started in 1867 in Geneva. Miss Blumer was not identified.
⁴Madame Weber was not identified.
⁵Smith was one of HJ's servants; see *Correspondence*, 2:440.

To Charles Ritter

Vers-chez-les-Blanc | sur Lausanne, 18. VIII. 93

My dear Ritter,

Your charming letter of the first reached me duly, and the inexorable hours have at last brought us to the pass which you invoke, in which I am to write you "un petit mot avant de partir de la Suisse." In 4½ hours I shall be in the train for Paris, and next Thursday shall be at sea for Boston. It is with a tragic sort of regret that I say good bye to this place and to Switzerland, on the whole the most faultless country that I know, and the most beauteous, for some thing tells me rather solemnly that I shall most likely never return again. I *ought* to *hineinleben* myself in to my own land a little more, and this voyage has been my pecuniary ruin! So if I ever come back, it will not be for many many years. I shall have to commune with Switzerland in memory as you say you have to do with so many things. We take two excellent Vaudoises women with us who will to some degree keep us *en rapport*. And my children will come back some day, whether I do or not! My wife and eldest boy have been broiling and frying in England for a week past, and I take on to night the rest of the caravan,—five tickets.

Among the charms of my holiday has been that of seeing you again, even for so short a time. I only wish I saw you less burdened as to the eye and ear. But your patience and philosophy under such afflictions are an object-lesson in morals, my dear Ritter, and I shall try not to forget them. It is so much easier to lament than to endure silently as you do. Good bye, keep well, and improve, if possible, and don't forget your "old friend of 1860," whose affection for you is always warm.

Wm James | "Cambridge (Mass) | U.S. of A."

ALS: Bibliothèque publique et universitaire, Geneva

To Grace Norton

[September 1893]
My dear Grace,
    I am home! May I breakfast with you?[1]
Water, bread, and an egg is all that I habitually take. If the nutritive equivalent of the egg be supplied in any other way, I shall be more than satisfied, so don't fear me.

With hope, yours | W.J.

ALS: MH bMS Am 1092.9 (3346)

[1] The *Cephalonia* with the Jameses and their servants on board reached Boston in the early afternoon of 2 September 1893.

To Parke Godwin

95 Irving St, Cambridge Mass | Sept. 4, 1893
Dear Mr. Godwin,
    I have just got back from Europe to find a mass of "reading matter" on my table waiting for me, and amongst it your address on poor Geo. Curtis, which has caught my eye and compelled perusal to the end.[1] It is extraordinary that at your age you should have written a thing so full of fire & literary vitality. Of course the subject was one that appealed to your heart, but the result is of the happiest, and worthy of the admirable man and citizen who is gone.
    I stayed a couple of days in Paris with the good Pillons—the best of human beings both of them, but with that curious french timidity about the outer world which made me think of two mice living in a hollow cheese. It would never enter their conceptions of possibility to take, *e.g.* a journey to England, seven hours away. Pillon told me that you had ordered his photograph, and seemed to wonder greatly at this inscrutable unknown American who followed his career with such sympathy. Have you, by the way, read Renouvier's paper on Schopenhauer in the last Année Philosophique.[2] R. is 80 and almost deaf, but he never wrote anything more vigorous or deep-cutting, and the *form* of this paper make it one of his best works.
    And now comes something which I tremble to write, and which I might best have begun by. I am about to *beg;* and I never should have tho't of begging of *you* if you hadn't sent me the oration, and if the matter of Pillon's photograph had n't reminded me of your paying for the index to the Critique philosophique many years ago. This

made me think that you might wish to waste money on philosophy or Psychology, and might help me out of my present scrape, which is briefly this.

We are starting, that is Baldwin of Princeton, Cattell of Columbia, and practically all the good psychologists of the country with two exceptions,[3] are starting a new psychological Journal. We have vainly tried to get Hall of Clark University whose American Journal of Psychology is considered by all to be carried on in too narrow a way, to consent to enlarge it and better it, and are determined now to have a thoroughly broad and worthy thing which will cover the whole field. There are enough trained men in the country now to make the journal a success as regards quality, but we need to guarantee the finances to the publisher for the first couple of years. The publisher will be Macmillan,[4] probably, and the first number appear Jany 1st. I have undertaken to raise a few hundred dollars—Are you willing to contribute one hundred (or more if you wish) to such a cause?[5] It may all come back to you in a couple of years.

An early answer will oblige and put me out of my misery. If negative *just write "No" on a postcard* and I will understand.

Remember that you have brought this on yourself! and believe me your once young and now senescent friend

Wm James

ALS: NN

Address: Parke Godwin Esq | Century Club | New York | N.Y

Postmark: CAMBRIDGE SEP 5

[1] Parke Godwin spoke on George William Curtis on 17 December 1892 before the Century Association in New York City. First published as a pamphlet, the address is included in Godwin's *Commemorative Addresses* (1895).

[2] Charles Renouvier, "Schopenhauer et la métaphysique du pessimisme," *L'Année Philosophique* 3 (1893): 1–61.

[3] The exceptions were Hall and Joseph Jastrow, but the latter contributed to the first volume (1894) and became a cooperating editor during the first year.

[4] The publisher of the *Psychological Review* was Macmillan & Co., in New York and London.

[5] Godwin contributed $100; see letter to Cattell of 30 December 1893.

To Sarah Wyman Whitman

95, IRVING STREET, | CAMBRIDGE. Sept 5. [1893]

Dear Mrs. Whitman

I meant to write to inform you of our arrival to day, but your note forestalls me. Your letter on the steamer was a most agreeable surprise, and had we sunk I should have gone down clasping it in my hand.   But since Friday beckons, no more need be said now.   Alice can't detach her self so soon from all the nameless duties which are involved in our settlement, with 28 trunks and boxes to unpack, 13 of them arrive only to morrow, no parlor maid and two other "girls," (imported) who don't speak a word of english if anyone rings at the door, so I must come alone.   Our voyage was incredibly smooth.

It will indeed be good to look upon your face and hear your voice again!

Yours always | Wm James

ALS: MH bMS Am 1092.9 (3915)

To Carl Stumpf

Cambridge (Mass) Sept. 12. 93

My dear Stumpf

Let me announce to you that we have arrived safely at home after an admirably smooth voyage, and that after 15 months of pensions & hotels the comforts of our own house are most enjoyable.   It has been a costly, but on the whole a profitable year to all, especially to the children who have been made much more perceptive and intelligent than they would have been without all the travel they have had.

I also have a business matter to propound to you.   The American Journal of Psychology edited by G. Stanley Hall has always left much to be desired.   Its field is very narrow and much of its work ill done. During the past year Profs. Baldwin, Cattell and Munsterberg have been negotiating with Hall to see if some arrangement might not be made for improving the Journal, but everything has failed, and the result is that a new Journal is to be started, under the title (probably) of "the Psychological Review," with Baldwin and Cattell as chief editors, and all the Professors of Psychology in the american universities (except Jastrow and Hall) as co-operating editors.   Such names as Ladd, Münsterberg, Donaldson, James, Scripture etc etc.[1]   I cannot but hope that the new Review will prove good.   It will be published by the great house of Macmillan in both countries.

The Editorial Committee now request you (through my hand) to permit your name to be placed on the title-page as co-operating editor.   Binet has already allowed his name to be so used for France.   I feel quite sure that the *character* of the Review will be such that you need have no mistrust about your name being connected with it.   On the other hand what the editors particularly desire is that your name figuring on the title should be a guarantee to other Germans of your own confidence in the capacity of the other editors. We do not expect that you should take your *duties* very seriously, but should be exceedingly grateful for any thing you may be able to send in the way of

1.) Articles;

2.) Reviews or bibliographic abstracts;

3.) Suggestions as to articles, information about books of which we ought to give a prompt account, etc.

4.) Items of "news" from the German psychological world which might interest our readers.

I will undertake either myself to translate or to guarantee a good translation of any MS., long or short, which you may send for publication.

Pray think favorably of this. We all, including Münsterberg, think that there is no German psychologist whose name would so honour and adorn the new Journal, as yours. And I earnestly hope that you may yield to our desire.

I hope that you are having a good vacation in the Tyrol. Nothing agrees with *me* as well as the mountains. With affectionate regards to all your family, I am as ever yours faithfully

Wm James

ALS: MH bMS Am 1092.9 (3791)

[1] Ten cooperating editors are listed in the first volume of the *Psychological Review:* WJ, Stumpf, Alfred Binet, John Dewey, George Stuart Fullerton, Moses Allen Starr of the College of Physicians and Surgeons in New York City, and those mentioned by WJ except for Scripture.

From Frederic William Henry Myers

Oct. 10, '93, Leckhampton House.

My dear James:

I have been asked by the Council of the S.P.R. to approach you informally on a matter which they did not wish to lay officially before you until your wishes are known—Will you allow us to elect you President of the S.P.R. for the year beginning Feb. 1894?

We do not ask for your presence on *this* side of the water;—we shall be content to know that you are present on the *other. That,* indeed, is one of the two main reasons which have led to the very strong expression of opinion on which I am now acting.

The *first* reason is, of course, your position as a psychologist—Since you *do* sympathise with us,—since you *have* given your name as a Vice-President,—we feel that it will be only a natural extention of your kindness, if you will allow us to draw from that name the full advantage which its presence among our own—at the head of our own—can bestow.

The second reason is also a weighty one—We are unfeignedly in accord with one at least of Berkeley's views;—that the Anglo-Saxon headship in each several matter should gladly and unreservedly be located on that side of the Atlantic where its location may best subserve the common good.   Let our Society,—"Domiciled" as it is in London,—enjoy the opportunity of showing that it aspires to be international in something more than in name! We honestly think that at this juncture it is *best* to have an American President;—that the stimulus to our cause on your continent far outweighs your absence from our London meetings;—at which, I need hardly say, a humble Secretary will always be ready to read any number of *Presidential addresses* with all the respectful seriousness at his command!

We trust that you will grant our prayer! We cannot see that it will hurt you;—and we see very clearly that it will *help* us.

Kindest remembrances to your group! Sept. 10, '93 was a red-letter day for me, in more ways than one.

Yours always,| F. W. H. Myers.

TC: MH bMS Am 1092.9 (414)

From Benjamin Paul Blood[1]

Amsterdam Oct 13. 1893

Prof James
My dear Doctor—

(since "Sir" does not suit) I have hesitated about accepting your generous offer to locate 20 of my pamphlets—on the title page of which I was tempted to inscribe *A Treatise of No Earthly Use*—but have concluded that by sharing the labor of addressing them the scheme might serve.   The devil trust you to fold, lick stamp and direct 20 packages! I have therefore mailed you 20 p's in 20 stamped envelopes. I also send you a clipping print of your too kind letter, which if it violates any privacy you will excuse when I tell you about it. I was reading your note near by a reporter friend of mine, and I groaned, with ancient Pistol:

"Old do I wax, and from my weary bones
Honor is cudgelled—"[2]

My boy asked what was the matter, looking over my shoulder, and I asked "Am I a fool and a babe and a suckling?" and he said "He's got you right, whoever it is"—and seeing the signature, he said "Gi' me that!" and snatched it. There was more followed, for I was set upon by an exclusive set to give them an evening of reading and remark upon philosophy, and there amongst other things arose your notion of a Spatial Quale,[3] and more print about you followed, until you would think, to read it, you were Goddlemighty,—which being a palpable mistake I show you no more.—You are right in your remark on the Anaesthetic literature: all critical glory fades before him who agonises in the coil and twist of the aboriginal anaesthetic mystery. I often mumble to myself a sentence of your's like this: "There is no identity save that of the difference between identity & difference";[4] then I correct it and say: There is also the identity of the *sameness between* identity and difference; then I try to eliminate the *between* and substitute *of* for *between,* & so on. But enough of that. Believe that I shall be glad to have you bother your colleagues with The Flaw etc,[5] and that I grieve only that I can but poorly repay your kindness.

Ever with highest regard, | Benj. Paul Blood

ALS: MH bMS Am 1092.9 (53)

[1] Benjamin Paul Blood (1832–1919), American writer and mystic. Correspondence is known from 1882 to 1910. For WJ's view of Blood see "A Pluralistic Mystic" (1910), reprinted in *EPh.*

[2] From Shakespeare's *Henry V,* act 5, sc. 1, line 90.

[3] WJ, "The Spatial Quale," *Journal of Speculative Philosophy* 13 (January 1879): 64–87; reprinted in *EPs.*

[4] Probably a reference to the appendix of WJ's "On Some Hegelisms," a collection of notes made while under the influence of nitrous oxide (*WB,* 220).

[5] Benjamin Paul Blood, *The Flaw in Supremacy* (1893). For the complete title see *EPh,* 230.

To James McKeen Cattell

CAMBRIDGE Oct 16. [1893]

<My dear Cat>tell

I have no special criticism to make on the table you send me, which seems a complete carving-out of the field. Of course the number of pages is conjectural, and may very likely be departed from.

As for myself, I should like to keep up with the literature of "hallu-cinations," "hypnotism<">> & "sleep,<">> [*manuscript excised*] taken wide [*manuscript excised*] of my competent [*manuscript excised*] in that latter if [*manuscript excised*] to have an expert there.[1]

I confess that I don't hanker after space, having probably reached my saturation point with that matter, but you can try me if you will. Hyslop's paper for example, I should rather not opine upon, because it seems to me that he is a prominent enough man to print whatever he writes;[2] and edito [*end of letter missing*]

AL incomplete: DLC

[1] WJ was a regular reviewer for the *Psychological Review* until 1897.

[2] James Hervey Hyslop, "Experiments in Space Perception," *Psychological Review* 1 (May 1894): 257–73; (November 1894): 581–601.

To Harald Höffding

95 Irving St. Cambridge, Mass | Oct. 23. 1893

My dear Sir,

I thank you for sending me the reprint of your article in Phil. Stud. VIII. 1. zur Theorie des Wiedererkennens.[1] As your statement now stands, p. 90, I can have little objection to it; and it may be that the suggestion of my friend Prof Baldwin (Philosophical Rev. July 1893, p. 402)[2] that the sense of familiarity is due to the easier reinstatement of *motor adjustments of attention* that have already been once performed is calculated to reconcile the associationists with you. *We* (the associ-ationists[)] have had exclusively in mind *sensory* associations, and that was possibly too narrow a view.

One word about the last sentence of your article. I cannot admit that I am inconsistent.[3] I believe that the only associations by simi-larity that exist are those where the resemblance *is* compound. Be-tween simple qualities I see no ground for supposing that association by similarity takes place. One degree of heat as such doesn't remind us of another degree of heat as such, though it may recall the total situation where we experienced the other heat, and then, secondarily, *that.* (Cf. Principles of Psychol. I. 578–9; also Ehrenfels Vierteljsch. f. wiss. P. XIV, 282).[4] I think there is no inconsistency.

I rejoice to have your authority for believe that there must be pos-tulated as an ultimate fact the relation of resemblance, and in general

I must express my gratitude and admiration for the suggestive and vital character of your psychological work.

Believe me with high respect

Yours truly | Wm James

Professor Höffding

ALS: MH bMS Am 1092.9 (999)

[1] Harald Höffding, "Zur Theorie des Wiedererkennens," *Philosophische Studien* 8 (1892): 86–96.

[2] James Mark Baldwin, "Internal Speech and Song," *Philosophical Review* 2 (July 1893): 385–407.

[3] Höffding quotes *PP* 544 on the one hand, and *PP* 466 and 651–52 on the other, and claims that these remarks by WJ on association by similarity are inconsistent.

[4] Christian von Ehrenfels (1859–1932), Austrian philosophical writer, "Über Gestaltqualitäten," *Vierteljahrsschrift für wissenschaftliche Philosophie* 14 (1890): 249–92.

To George Holmes Howison

CAMBRIDGE Oct 28. [1893]

My dear Howison,

Your kind letter just arrives in the twilight, and though I am laid up with tonsillitis and feverishness, my emotions of affection are so called out that I can't help scribbling you an immediate line. How well you seem to keep it up, off there, with your "Union," your Plato and all![1] I think of you as lonely, remote, and heroic. But I dare say that where you are, there is the centre for your own consciousness, and it is we who are "off there." Well, of course there is no absolute "here" or "there" in pure space, <b>ut *to this* relative here you ought erelong to make a visit. I have longed for years to visit California and see you and your University, but the chance never comes. I break down every two or three years and have to ruin myself by going to Europe, which each time seems a safer place for a long holiday than California.—As for your Laboratory, I don't think that the *results* ground out of all the labs. have so far been important, so you can easily console yourself on that score. But of course it is a healthy and cheerful thing for the young to be in touch with the concrete facts of the human organism as well as with the abstract product<s> of its intellectual functioning, so you had better get a Lab. when you can, and stock it well with apparatus illustrating the Senses, if with nothing else.—I am unutterably amused, or rather amused and saddened, by your extraordinary reference to my book on Metaphysic.

I have never even attained to the dream of the possibility of such a thing, much less to the execution, and I now foresee that I never shall. A curious sense of incapacity, a sere-and-yellow-leafiness has come over me in the past year which makes all psychologizing and philosophizing seem a nullity, and the cultivation of the soil to be a man's only honest pursuit. At any rate my intellectual higgledy-piggledyism can never lead to a system of metaphysics. That sort of thing is for a higher order of mind than W.J.'s—yours for instance. Why don't *you*, who write so well, and who have such systematic ideas, put them down in due form?—I take note of all you say of Hegel. *I* am a hegelian so far as the transcendency of the immediate and the principle of totality go, but I can't follow H. in any of his applications of detail, and his *manner* is pure literary deformity. Don't you admire Royce's chapter on Hegel in his Spirit of Modern Philosophy?[2] Has Hegel really said much more than those few pages express, in all his tedious writings? But hold! All I wanted, my dear H., was to grasp you by the hand once more. Your faithful pupil Bakewell is developing finely here—a noble fellow. Best respects to Mrs. Howison,[3]

Your faithful friend, | Wm James

ALS: MH bMS Am 1092.9 (1032)

Address: Professor Howison | Berkeley | California

Postmarks: BOSTON. MASS. OCT 29 1893   BERK‹ELEY› CAL NOV 3

[1] Howison established the Philosophical Union of the University of California, which presented discussions of philosophical problems to both student and general audiences.

[2] Josiah Royce, *The Spirit of Modern Philosophy* (1892), chap. 7, "Hegel."

[3] Howison was married to Lois Caswell Howison.

To Katharine Outram Rodgers

95 Irving St. Cambridge | Oct. 30. 93

My dear Katharine,

Nearly two months is too long a time to have let pass without giving you any news of our fortunes. *But*—you know how the days bring the press and how letters get postponed. But for the providential visitation of a mild tonsillitis with fever etc. which makes me keep my bedroom and stop work, I doubt whether even now I should be writing, although for the last three Sundays I have resolved that I shouldn't go to bed without having got off something to you, so that a letter would not have been postponed many days later than this. Our voyage was almost supernaturally smooth, and our home looked delightful, altho' Alice's first impulse was to try to let it to a couple of "parties" whom she heard wanted a house at any price. This hero-ically meant but really silly piece of would be economy was frustrated by the tenants dropping off after keeping us hanging for a fortnight, so we are not "scattered," and are just comfortably settling into fires for the winter—an ambiguous sounding phrase—all that it means is the autumn has been so wonderfully warm that no need of fire has arisen till within two or three days. Our sky and air are delicious— but after 15 months in Europe the whole human background here seems rather grim, with its over-strained seriousness over narrow practical and spiritual horizons, and its jerky angular unsmiling ways and manners. You have to go below the surface to appreciate America—Europe you can appreciate without an effort, for the work that with us is in the doing, over there has been done. One must n't mix one's continents—it give[s] one nothing but the heartache. *You* stay over there, and *I* will stay over here, and we will write! I verily believe that for a man (I don't say for you, for you Italy would be better, but for a man) *Switzerland* is on the whole the best country in the world. Work goes very hard, I seem to have forgotten every-thing, but I'm told it is a common case & will expect it to pass. This is a somewhat gloomy sounding epistle, but I can't write long, aching as I am, and it will do to waft my love to you both by. I do hope you can send me some good news of yourselves in return. I trust that your winter will be mild and your quarters comfortable whether they be in Geneva or elsewhere.

Love from us both to you both. | Wm James
I have delayed this to get your address from your brother Rob.[1] I'm glad you're at Vevey, where I hope the skies will smile. Switzer-land seems a paradise to me—so GOOD! Alice sends you much love & means to write. Your last letter to her she describes as "de-lightful."

W.J.

ALS: MH bMS Am 1092.9 (3186)
[1] Robertson Rodgers (1845–1915).

To James Mark Baldwin

Camb. Oct. 31, '93.
I don't know a monkey or a monkey's keeper on this terrene globe. There may be some dime museum monkeys in Boston but there's

no menagerie, and one can't get a dime museum attendant to make observations. In spite of every inducement, *I* didn't make any on my baby!

W.J.

From Frederic William Henry Myers

Nov. 16, '93, Leckhampton House.

My dear James:

I am very sorry that you are feeling ill; but a touch of something is mixed with my sympathy that I may as well have out—It seems to me that your mental and physical disorganisation and decay is never by any chance perceptible to anyone but *yourself;* and moreover, that when you are actually in the presence of friends you are able to make an effort (if such it be) which presents you to them as a source of wisdom and delight,—"as light and life communicable"; which makes them rather wish that they were even as you than grieve over any hidden malaise within you, and yet it seems to me that you lack one touch more of *doggedness* which would render you of even more helpfulness in the world than you are—why on earth should you not in *public* matters act upon other people's view of you and not on your own? We all wanted you to place your name at our head;—we should have been satisfied, however little you had actually *done;* why not have let us have our way? To *underrate* one's own importance in the eyes of others may be (though rarer) as great a nuisance to them as it is to *overrate* it. We must not push you further now; but I warn you that we shall ask you again another year,—and that unless we have evidence to your decrepitude from someone besides yourself, we shall then take it somewhat unkind if you won't oblige us!

Mrs. Piper is all right—and the universe is all right—and people will soon pay up more money to S.P.R.—and an eternity of happiness and glory awaits you—and I am sure Mrs. James would agree to much in this letter—and the dear spirits are hovering around us in the Summer Land.

Yours always, | F. W. H. Myers.

To Dickinson Sergeant Miller

95 Irving St., Cambr., November 19, '93.

My dear Miller:

Your jolly good letter has waited so long for an answer because I wanted to find a moment that was unhurried. I rejoice that the lecturing goes so well.[1] With so much work, and the whole business new, you must expect a good deal of wear and tear to your nerves before the year is out, but it will pass away like a tale that is told, and in after years be unremembered. From all accounts you are the pilgrim to Germany who profited most by his time last year and who most steadily forged ahead accumulating and making no wasteful mistakes. Herein is seen the advantage of a pertinacious and methodical disposition—would that I had been like you at your age. I should not now be sitting so disconsolate! I have found the work of recommencing teaching unexpectedly formidable after our year of gentlemanly irresponsibility. I seem to have forgotten everything, especially psychology, and the subjects themselves have become so paltry and insignificant seeming that each lecture has appeared a ghastly farce. Of late things are getting more real; but the experience brings startlingly near to one the wild desert of old-age which lies ahead, and makes me feel like impressing on all chicken-professors like you the paramount urgency of providing for the time when you'll be old fogies, by laying by from your very first year of service a fund on which you may be enabled to "retire" before you're sixty and incapable of any cognitive operation that wasn't ground into you twenty years before, or of any emotion save bewilderment and jealousy of the thinkers of the rising generation. I am glad to hear that you have more writings on the stocks. I read your paper on Truth and Error with bewilderment and jealousy. Either it is Dr. Johnson *redivivus* striking the earth with his stick and saying, "Matter exists and there's an end on't,"[2] or it is a new David R. Hume, reincarnated in your form, and so subtle in his simplicity, that a decaying mind like mine fails to seize any of the deeper import of his words. The trouble is, I can't tell which it is. But with the help of God, I will go at it again this winter, when I settle down to my final bout with Royce's theory, which must result in my either *actively* becoming a propagator thereof, or actively its enemy and destroyer. It is high time that this more decisive attitude were generated in me, and it ought to take place this winter. I hardly see more of my colleagues this winter than I did last year. Each of us lies in his burrow, and we meet on the street.　Münsterberg is going really *splendidly,* and the Lab. is a bower of delight.　But I do not work there.　Royce is in powerful condition, but his unit of discourse is getting more inexorably than ever to be the full hour lecture with some slopping over into the next hour at the end, so that minds of a less commensurate receptivity sometimes dread his deliverances, solid and instructive as they invariably are.　Bakewell and Pierce are hearty.　Nichols I have hardly seen.　He keeps much to himself, seems in good condition, and is piling up a mass of experimental and theoretic material, difficult to cast into shape (as always with him), but probably involving facts of novelty and ideas of real importance.　Hodder lives at Winthrop, Mass., and *lies low*—his wife reports him very busy and I am sorry to hear, *not* very well.　*She* is a sweet thing.　Uphues sent me his new book the other day, with its preface in which we both lie embalmed like flies in amber, and a request that I review it, which, if I get any time to read it, I propose to do in the new Psychological Review.[3]　It is scandalous that I should still remain so ignorant of his writings.

Good bye, dear Miller.　My wife sends her love.　Don't let your heart get too much entangled with your "fair charges".　Cast away illusion and delusion—perhaps you're in the best circumstances for so doing—with regard to the eternal feminine.

Yours ever, | Wm. James.

TC: MH bMS Am 1092.1

[1] Miller taught at Bryn Mawr College in 1893–99, when he became an instructor at Harvard.

[2] Samuel Johnson (1709–1784), British author and lexicographer.　According to James Boswell, in the course of a discussion of the views of George Berkeley on 6 August 1763, Johnson kicked a stone and thought Berkeley refuted.

[3] Goswin K. Uphues, *Psychologie des Erkennens vom empirischen Standpunkte,* vol. 1 (1893).　In his preface Uphues describes *Principles of Psychology* as the most important work in systematic philosophy in recent years and mentions Miller's "Meaning of Truth and Error."

To James Ward

95, IRVING STREET, | CAMBRIDGE. Nov. 19. 93

My dear Ward,

Your note, enclosing the purest, most white souled and least regrettable or revokable post card I ever wrote, came back to me yesterday and made me wonder at your telepathic insight into its source, for as I don't well recognize your handwriting, I dont expect you to recognize mine. The queer part of the business is that I don't remember myself what was the message destined for the post-card's surface. Evidently it was unimportant, or I should.—Hark! even now the act of writing brings up to me the fact that I sent you the laboratory catalogue which Münsterberg prepared for our "Exhibit" at Chicago,[1] (—at least I think I did) and this card was probably intended to call your attention to it as something handy for reference concerning apparatus, makers, and prices—in fact a useful publication as well as an advertisement of our own resources. I must say that M. is proving a splendid laboratory teacher. Perfect order and clock work regularity so that everything goes without waste of thought or time. My own decay of memory will be apparent to you, without more explicit reference. I don't know whether my other faculties are going to follow suit or not!

Best regards to you and respects to your wife all the same.

Yours always | Wm James

ALS: MH bMS Am 1092.9 (3836)

[1] Hugo Münsterberg, *Psychological Laboratory of Harvard University* (1893).

From George Herbert Palmer

3 Mason St. | Dec. 3. [1893]

Dear James:

In view of what you told me today I decide to take the Psychology of Phil. 1 myself, without reference to Eliot.[1] You need not therefore write him. This decision I have reported to Münsterberg & I have expressed to him hearty regret at not having before made clear my wish not to override his judgment in the matter of Phil. 13.[2]

How all this misunderstanding has come about I cannot guess, for even now I cannot see what I could have kindly done differently. It certainly surprised & pained me that you & Royce could imagine in what I did anything so plot like & overbearing. But since confusion has arisen—through my wrong doing or not—it is better that I should stand whatever hardship follows than allow the agitation to go farther. I hope I shall not be turned out of house & home, & that I shall get through the course in some sort of fashion. But at any rate so far as I can settle it the matter is now settled.

Always faithfully yours, | G. H. Palmer

ALS: MH bMS Am 1092.9 (430)

[1] See letter of 21 April 1893.

[2] Philosophy 13: Comparative Religion, taught by Charles Carroll Everett, was not given in 1893–94 but was offered the next year.

To Smith Baker

Cambridge, Dec 8. 93

Dear D.r Baker,

I'm delighted—can I do anything towards inquiring about rooms? We have gone over general psycho-pathy, cranks and geniuses, morbid impulses etc. and systematized delusions.[1] We begin hysteria next week. I wish that you might be here for that. We next take up double personality and other trance states, slipping into the history of witchcraft etc if possible. The more classic types of insanity follow, and if there is time we shall touch upon criminological literature.

Once more, welcome. Is the Rev. Smith Baker just installed at East Boston a relative of yours?[2]

Very truly yours | Wm James

ALS: OO

[1] Reference is to Philosophy 20b: Psychological Seminary, dealing with questions of mental pathology.

[2] Smith Baker (1836–1917), American clergyman, then pastor of Maverick Church, East Boston.

To Richard Hodgson

Cambr. Dec 8. 93[1]

Dear Hodgson,

The Piper-sitting with the Bourgets yesterday was a fairly successful one, though there was much confusion owing to the number of clues that were started and could not develope in the 2 hours and 20 minutes that the trance lasted.[2] Mrs. P. makes on me, I confess, an impression of greater weakness of mind & character than before. I put the light on the table after she got entranced and there it remained for most of the time, her head sunk down on her left arm and averted. My wife entering towards the end, thought that the strained attitude was in consequence of the light, and was probably injurious, prolonged as it was. I think such things should be considered. Poor Mrs. P. ought to have every "chance."

I have urged B. to send me a written account. Meanwhile something interesting occurred to my servant Marie.

In Weir Mitchell's very bad sitting,[3] 6 weeks or so since, the name "Marie" kept coming, & he failed to connect it with anyone whom he knew. I tho't of our *bonne,* but said nothing, as I didn't wish to confuse M.'s hour. Yesterday the sitting opened with Mme. Bourget holding Mrs. P's hand, and this same name "Marie" and "I want you to tell my sister Marie, in the body," kept coming through the hand, mixed with much other matter. At last a name "Carrie", or "Garie" came, which was so like Marie *Garin's* surname that I got her to come up to see if she were the Marie in question. Immediately she took Mrs. P.s hand the other hand wrote "sunstroke". "I passed away with sunstroke, I am glad to see my dear sister Marie. Tell mother I am happy. The children are well with her. There has been great confusion but the two children will be well with her etc." I don't give the exact words, some of which came through mouth. There were other names and references which Marie could n't understand. One of these was "James." Mme. Bourget said to Marie "thats Jacques in french, have you any Jacques?" The hand then wrote Jack Alexandre, Jacques Alexandres being the name of an uncle of Maries who many years ago came to America and had never been heard from. Louise, Daniel, Julie, Eugenie, Charles were mentioned, all being members of Maries immediate circle, Louise her mother's name. The whole thing very brief.

Now Maries brother had had a grave sunstroke shortly before we left Switzerland in August. In Sept. Marie got a letter from her mother saying he was dead. The mother Louise, has Marie's two children with her. No member of this family ever mentioned this to Mrs. P. I mentioned it to you and Myers, as a good possible test for Mrs P. before the news had come of the death, but Myers's sitting was otherwise so full that Marie was crowded out. Marie herself hardly speaks two words of english, and only knows two persons in Cambridge, servants who know nothing of Mrs. Piper. She is very reticent and says she does not *think* she has mentioned her brothers death to these persons, one of whom is a recently arrived italian servant and the other a french canadian servant of the Münsterberg's.

My impression is that both Marie and the Bourgets should have a second sitting But the price prevents M. & is likely to prevent the B's. Can any of the Society money be used? You ought to preside at the B's next sitting, I at Maries.

Yours always | Wm James

ALS: Cambridge University Library

¹ WJ's letter is quoted in part in Richard Hodgson, "A Further Record of Observations of Certain Phenomena of Trance," *Proceedings of the Society for Psychical Research* 13 (February 1898): 494–95. The manuscript letter has marks of editing, probably made by Hodgson.
² For references to Bourget's account of the sittings see *EPR,* 396, 397.
³ For Mitchell's comments on his sitting see *EPR,* 420.

To Frederic William Henry Myers

95, IRVING STREET, | CAMBRIDGE. Dec 17. 93.

My dear Myers,¹

I telegraphed you this morning "James accepts"—the Presidency of the S.P.R. being understood.² This is in consequence of a letter from Pearsall Smith informing me that the council still desire it and regard it as a matter of importance.³ They are bent on having a king-log, so they shall be humored. I had no idea, when I got your first invitation, that it was a matter of the slightest real *importance,* or so regarded, by any of you; and I much regretted to perceive, from your reply to my own letter of declination, that the latter, so far as you were concerned, had been a genuine disappointment. Since however in that reply, you treated the refusal as definitive and implied that its consequences were then evolving, I have let the matter drop from my own attention, and was all the more surprised yesterday AM. by P.S.'s letter treating the presidency as still undecided, and asking me to reconsider. To tell the truth I supposed the true inwardness of the offer to lie in your friendly wish, yours and the Sidgwick's, to pay me a compliment, which friendly wish I thought almost as well acknowledged by "declined with thanks" as by "accepted."

My state of mind is also revolutionized since that time. I had a pretty bad spell, and know now a new kind, of melancholy. It is barely possible that the recovery may be due to a mind-curer with whom I tried 18 sittings.⁴ What makes me think so is that I am enjoying an altogether new kind of *sleep,* or rather an old kind which I have been bereft of for so many years that I had forgotten its existence, and considered myself sleeping as well as I ought to, and told her so, when I went to her, saying my only trouble was my mind. She's the one who revolutionized my sister-in-law. Two other cases of brain-trouble, intimate friends of mine, treated simultaneously with me, have entirely recovered. It is a good deal of a puzzle. I should like to get this woman into a lunatic asylum for two months, and have every case of chronic delusional insanity in the house tried by her. That would be a real test, and if successful would *have* to produce some effect. I may possibly bring it about yet!

My college work is all-engrossing, as ever. For a presidential address, even, I should be at a loss for matter. When, by the way, is such a thing due? Here nothing goes on but Mrs. Piper—toujours Piper! I wish we could unearth a little variety. I appreciate your strictures[5] as to the absence of doggedness in me—but you must remember that tenacity like *yours* is what puts you in the IMMORTAL GALAXY which I have already previously enumerated, and that if it were a common possession, you would lose your distinction! We are all well and I hope that you are the same. With warm regards to both of you from both of us,

Yours ever | Wm James

ALS: MH bMS Am 1092.9 (3313)

[1] In the top margin of the page Myers wrote: '[return when we meet]'.
[2] WJ was elected president of the Society for Psychical Research for 1894.
[3] Robert Pearsall Smith was a member of the council and wrote WJ on its request.
[4] Reference is to Miss Clarke.
[5] Above the word 'strictures' Myers wrote '[very mild ones!]'.

To Alice Howe Gibbens James

Newport. Sunday 24. 12. 93

Dearest Alice,

You will have been overcome by post-cards from me, so I now write a letter. I had a good day in Providence yesterday—the weather was so beautiful & warm (no snow being left hereabouts) and the two boat trips so lovely. I was well-received at the Asylum, but the lunatic whom I went to see did not turn out particularly interesting. Mrs. Tiffany is very sweet, but Tweedy has deteriorated somewhat—I mean he is more indifferent, and lets himself go more—not unnatural at over 80! But don't let *us* die of old age. The walking here is soft as pap which rather spoils things, but I've done some reading and a great deal of browsing in Magazines and Lowell's letters.[1] There's no place like home—if it were only a little more in the country. I imagine you having a rather jolly couple of days with the children all well and together. I don't think I am probably very much missed.—I broached the change of name to Tweedy.[2] He cares nothing about the matter anyhow, so you need trouble yourself no more. Poor little Tweedy—give him my love! Send letters here up to Monday night.   I will telegraph of my New York address as soon as I know what it is to be.

Yours eternally—with a Merry Christmas to all the babes, Harry, Billy, Peggy & Tweedy,

W.J.

ALS: MH bMS Am 1092.9 (1856)

Address: Mrs. William James | 95 Irving Street | Cambridge | Mass

Postmark: NEWPORT R.I. DEC 24

[1] *Letters of James Russell Lowell,* ed. by Charles Eliot Norton, 2 vols. (1894).

[2] The Jameses were changing the name of their youngest son.

From Alice Howe Gibbens James

95, IRVING STREET, | CAMBRIDGE. Christmas Eve
[December 24, 1893]

Darling William,

How I hope that you are enjoying yourself! We miss you so much that some compensating joy ought to be won for you.   At five o'clock we marched upstairs to your room where in the centre of the table stood a tree decorated and lighted by the boys and at its base were really some sweet little gifts.   Harry & Billy are *delighted* with their books and they are both reading them now (8 o'clock) that Mother, Aunt Nannie and Margie have gone home.   Peggy is joyous over her sled, tea set and books and the baby! He eat steadily his paper of popped corn while he walked round & round the tree, and once or twice he lifted up his voice to say "Bébé a trois ans" evidently considering the whole illumination as *his* fête.   Harry has a bottle of cologne for you, and Bourget sends you the Cliff Dwellers[1] together with the Révue you lent him.

Chandler Gibbens was here last evening & I paid for the tea.[2] He says the #108 is too good tea for ordinary people to like! He says it is as good as the famous Caravan tea which sells for $3.00 a pound. I asked him what it (108) would cost at retail; he said "$1.50 more or less." I think we had better take a box of it, don't you? The box holds less than 20 lb.

Well! we are all tired and going early to bed, but it pays to take pains and give as much pleasure as our little tree has.   The women are really pleased and excited by their gifts, and the both beg me to thank you.   Altogether we have had a thoroughly successful Xmas, and had you been here I should have been satisfied.   The lack of you is like missing the air I breathe; and just how keen a want it is I think you will never imagine because you are a man and not a woman.   Heaven bless you and give us all a good new Year.

Your loving | Alice.

ALS: MH bMS Am 1092.9 (306)

[1] Henry Blake Fuller (1857–1929), American novelist, *The Cliff-Dwellers* (1893).

[2] Chandler Gibbens (ca. 1858–1911), a tea merchant in Boston.   His relationship to AGJ, if any, is unknown.

To Alice Howe Gibbens James

THE WINDSOR | NEW YORK. Thursday [December 28, 1893]
Hom[e] to morrow by bed-time—beloved wife.   Very crowded hours here.   Miller read a fine paper.[1]   To night to dine with Alexander—to morrow to Lunatic Asylum on Ward's Island,[2] and home by P.M. train.

I don't see how I can go to Masons as per your letter just rec'd,[3] since I've made an appointment with a Canadian whom I fear I can't reach by telegraph for that evening.[4]   But I will find out to morrow and telegraph him if I can.—

No time for mor[e]

No need to change *your* plan or take tho't about Masons   I will arrange all

W.J.

ALS: MH bMS Am 1092.9 (1798)

Address: Mrs James | 95 Irving St | Cambridge | Mass

Postmarks: NEW YORK N.Y. DEC 28 93   CAMBRIDGE. BOSTON MASS DEC 29

[1] WJ was in New York City for the second annual meeting of the American Psychological Association, held at Columbia College on 27–28 December 1893.   He was elected president.   Miller read a paper that was published as "The Confusion of Function and Content in Mental Analysis," *Psychological Review* 2 (November 1895): 535–50.

[2] The Manhattan State Hospital on Ward's Island, New York City.

[3] WJ knew several Masons.   Perhaps, Ellen Frances Mason (d. 1930), resident of Boston and Newport, philosophical writer and philanthropist, and her sister Ida M. Mason.   Correspondence with Ellen Mason is known from 1895.

[4] The Canadian probably was John Clark Murray (1836–1917), a psychologist teaching at McGill University, Montreal.   One letter is known (1885).   Murray was in New York City attending meetings of the American Psychological Association.

To James Mark Baldwin

Cambridge Dec 30. 93

Dear Baldwin,

Life was such a fitful fever on Thursday and Friday A.M. (I having made an appointment to visit the Ward's Island Asylum) that I had no chance to look you up and see how you were. I hope your ailment was a brief one. You were missed at the various meetings and at poor Alexander's dinner, which went off very pleasantly, and I dare say that you yourself lost a little of that curious solidification of one's sense of what the concrete psychological Treiben and Industry is in our country, which I gained from hearing the other man talk on the second day. I think Cattell appeared to great advantage all through, and I received from Ladd a curious impression of a consciousness in him of his own commanding position.[1] With best wishes for your health and happiness next year, yours and all of yours', I am ever cordially

Wm James

ALS: Bodleian Library, University of Oxford

[1] George Trumbull Ladd gave the presidential address at the meeting of the American Psychological Association.

To James McKeen Cattell

Cambridge, Dec 30. 93

Dear Cattell

I hope that after life's fitful fever you sleep well. I think that the whole thing was a success, and that *you* distinguished yourself by your tact, good humor and flexibility of intellect! I am only sorry that poor Baldwin had to absent himself the second day.

I enclose a check for 100 dollars towards the expenses of the review, being ⅖ of the 250 which M——g & I promised to raise. You may perceive that it is from that veteran man of letters Parke Godwin and not from Harvard University, which had a big deficit last year and is lying low at present. Knowing Godwins weakness for philosophy, I successfully applied a stimulus calculated to elicit this generous reaction—I imagine that even Scripture would not despise the operation because the time was not accurately measured. The remaining $150.00 will be supplied whenever you notify us that they are needed. If you endorse this check to Macmillan's order it will be a voucher to the good Godwin that the money has found its destination. *He ought also to be added to the free subscription list.* I have lost his N.Y. address which will be in the Directory.

Happy new year | W.J.

I suggest that copies of no 1. be sent also to Henry Holt, Thos. W. Ward, and Gouverneur M. Carnochan in N.Y.[1] [Addresses in Directory] and to George B. Dorr, of 18 Commonwealth Avenue, Boston. They may be tempted to subscribe. Also to Dr. W. S. Bigelow, 70 Beacon S:, Boston.

Happy New Year, | W.J.

ALS: DLC

[1] Gouverneur Morris Carnochan (1865–1915), American publisher, a Harvard graduate, associated with WJ in psychical research.

To Théodore Flournoy

Cambridge, Dec. 31, 1893.

My dear Flournoys,

We must address you in the plural as we are ourselves plural. She is holding the pen and I am dictating the words because a sharp attack of tonsillitis keeps me from writing myself and I don't want 1893 to pass by without your receiving a word of greeting from us. We had a most magnificent voyage home and found everything in our house charmingly clean and cheerful. But I found it terribly hard to get at any teaching again. One loses so quickly an artificial discipline like that of a professor's life that in my 15 months I had quite reverted to the "Feral" state. I seemed to have forgotten all my psychology and the subject of psychology *Ueberhaupt* had shrunk to nothing in my consciousness. I had two months of profoundest melancholy from which I gradually emerged and am now all right again. But I now know that 15 months is too long a vacation for a man whose work, at all times, is done with effort. In another way too, we are both melancholy after our vacation. So much Italy and so much Switzerland make one's native land seem *strange* to one. A non-conducting film has grown up between us. We both look back to Switzerland as the terrestrial paradise and I must say, my dear Flournoy, that your position in the world as a citizen of that fortunate republic, with your pleasant house in Geneva, and your not-too-burdensome professorship, with those salubrious mountains open to you for your summer vacation, with your central position for travelling etc. etc. make you a most enviable man. The impression Switzerland leaves on us is that of extraordinarily healthy civilization. The neurotic *fin-de siècle* element which is killing the larger countries, including our own, has got but comparatively little hold on you as yet. All human lives have their dissatisfactions but the algebraic sum of these and the healthy satisfactions seems to me on the whole to be a maximum just where you are placed.

We had last week a meeting of most of the psychologists of the country in New York. On the whole a very profitable two days. When you see all the little homunculi from whom the work comes its majesty of the latter shrinks, but at the same time it *solidifies* in one's imagination. Münsterberg is a great success here. In so far as I can see he hasn't a personal fault. He is very enthusiastic about America too and considers that ideality is a distinguishing trait of the American character—rather a pleasant contrast to the usual German accusation that we have no soul for anything but dollars.

We are starting a new Psychological Journal of which you will receive a specimen and possibly become a subscriber. Everyone seems to be publishing a Psychology in these days. Ebbinghaus, Külpe, Müller, Ladd, Stout, and who knows who besides. It seems as if some precipitation of truth ought to result from all this industry and I hope it will. Those who wait before emitting their own thunder till all this irrigating shower has passed by, and fertilized the ground will be in the best position to write something good. Madame Flournoy will be pleased to hear that our two Swiss women are perfect treasures,—the best women we have ever had in the house. And they, like Münsterberg, take an optimistic view of America. How we should like to look in on you by some sort of theosophy this morning. I think the sight of *les demoiselles* would instantly cure my tonsillitis.

Let Madame Flournoy take this letter from both of us, and believe in the sincere affection with which we wish you each and all (not forgetting the Good Fraulein) a happy New Year.

Yours ever faithfully, | Wm James

TC: MH bMS Am 1092.1

To Ferdinand Canning Scott Schiller

Dictated

95, IRVING STREET, | CAMBRIDGE. [January 1, 1894]
Dear Mr Schiller,

I was much mortified to fail to appear at Hodgson's dinner last night; but in the afternoon tonsillitis with a high fever began, and I had no choice. It seems to have been an unlucky Christmas time in many social ways, and I especially regret not meeting you.

We had a good Psychological Association meeting in New York, and wondered why some of you Cornell people didn't come.[1]

Hoping to see you somewhere before 1894 is over, I am, with a happy New Year to you

Very truly yours | Wm James

MLS (AGJ): CSt

[1] Schiller left Oxford in 1893 and for a time served as an instructor at Cornell, at the same time working for his doctorate.

From Charles Sanders Peirce

C. S. PEIRCE. "ARISBE" | P.O. MILFORD, PA. 1894 Jan 1. 1 A.M.
My dear James:

A happy New Year to you, and unless your situation has been exceptional, may it be as unlike the dead year now in hell as possible!

I wrote to you enclosing a copy of a prospectus of my treatise on philosophy. I directed it to Columbia College, where I assumed you would be, and asked you to write me a letter expressive of your interest with leave to print the same.[1] No answer has yet come. Perhaps you were not there. I now enclose *another* prospectus. A third and fourth are to come. I do not feel at all sure of getting subscribers enough to begin. If I do begin, I feel pretty sure there will be interest enough in the thing before I get through.

There is nothing in your psychology which serves my purposes better than your distinction between *substantive* and *transitive* parts of the train of thought. I had been forced to emphacize a precisely corresponding distinction in logic, where one of the most important & difficult operations is to catch the transitive on the wing & nail it down in substantive form. But the word "transitive" has been used for other purposes. For one thing in the logic of relatives (by De Morgan & me)[2] by another in the closely related theory of Substitutions & now you propose to add to the confusion & render your own thought hard to get at by using this same word. Why is this word better than "transient" for your purpose? If I were you, having called the other "substantive," a word well chosen & derived from the terminology of grammar, I would call these others *adjective*, & would either go to grammar for both terms or for neither. You might term them *volatile* and *sessile* or, after Homer's ἔπεα πτερόεντα and ἀπτερό-εντα, *winged* and *unwinged*, or, if you want Greek, *planetic* and *aplanetic*. Perhaps you mean "transitive" to be taken from grammar. If so, the analogy is not clear. Besides, that would spoil your *substantive* which surely has nothing to do with the substantive verb. I wish to make use of the distinction, & hence would like to know what improved terminology you would accept.

very faithfully | C S Peirce

I think it would be better to leave grammar-words for *logic*, and take *psychological* terms from othe[r] quarters. Now, would not "volatile" and "sessile" make a pretty and expressive pair of epithets?

ALS: MH bMS Am 1092 (668)

[1] Peirce expected WJ to be at the meeting of the American Psychological Association in New York City. Associated with Peirce's letter of 26 December 1893 (calendared) are two prospectuses of his book. For Peirce's project see Brent, *CSP,* 233–36.

[2] Augustus De Morgan (1806–1871), British mathematician and logician.

To Charles Sanders Peirce

Dictated

95, IRVING STREET, | CAMBRIDGE. Jan 3. 1894

My dear Charles,

I am five days in with the Grippe and didn't know there was so much length and breadth and thickness of me to be made miserable. Let this explain my tardiness. I enclose a line which you can print, for I suppose you would like that quickly, being too weak to add a word more.

Yours with best wishes | Wm. James | by A.H.J.
Harvard University

My dear Peirce,

I am heartily glad to learn that you are preparing to publish the results of your philosophizing in a complete and connected form.[1] Pray consider me a subscriber to the whole series. There is no more original thinker than yourself in our generation. You have personally suggested more important things to me than, perhaps, anyone whom I have known; and I have never given you sufficient public credit for all that you have taught me. I am sure that this systematic work will increase my debt.

Always faithfully yours | William James.

ML (AGJ): MH bMS Am 1092.9 (3374)

[1] Peirce printed and circulated WJ's remarks (see letter of 27 February 1894).

To Grace Norton

[January 14, 1894]

My dear Grace,

Many thanks for your giftlet, a truly "cultured" one, inside and out—how do you Nortons' ever find such things? You always do.

I *need* to meditate on poverty, for I find as I grow older and more luxurious, that a terrible lust for money possesses me. Ambition and avarice are apparently the moral infirmities of age. Don't fall a prey yourself!

I am still on this blessed 16th. day of it, quite prostrate with my influenza catarrh. Strength, appetite, everything, departed. The gout is nothing in comparison.

Once more, dont fall a prey.

Excuse the awkwardness of my paper. I didn't perceive that I was writing the first page on only a half sheet, and then I was too "sick" to rewrite.

With much love, and Christmas wishes, believe me, dear Grace, ever yours,

Wm James

ALS: MH bMS Am 1092.9 (3345)

To Charles Sanders Peirce

Cambridge Jan 24. 94

My dear Charles,

My interminable "grip" has thrown me into such arrears that I am lucky to write to you at all. You have very likely forgotten by this time your question about "substantive" and "transitive" states. To my mind it is well not to strain language already in use any more than one can help in creating technical terms. "Volatile" and "sessile" seem decidedly too metaphorical; and in thinking over the matter I don't see why plain "relational" is not after all the most practical epithet to adopt.

I hope that subscribers to your magnum opus come in. It may be that if the more distant thunder had been held in reserve and the first 3 volumes alone announced at present, the circular would have met with a better response, but it ought to be responded to as it is. In case of a renewed circular with such letters as mine printed, might it not be well to draw a line between the earlier and later volumes, expressing the later as something hoped for and conditional upon the success of the former? People are afraid of schemes too vast and ambitious—and also threatening to be too expensive. *I* hope for the whole set, but all men are not as I!

Yours heartily | Wm James

P.S. Do you, by the way, know of any other author than Delboeuf and in a manner yourself, who has treated the inorganic as a sort of product of the living? I know I have come across such a speculation but I can no longer think where.

ALS: MH bMS Am 1092.9 (3375)

To Carl Stumpf

95 Irving St. Cambridge, Mass. | Jan. 24. 94

My dear Stumpf,

I had been promising myself the pleasure of writing you a letter of New Year's greeting on January 1st, but Jan. 1st found me in bed with influenza and I have regained my strength so slowly that with all the arrears of duty I had to attend to as soon as I began to get well, this letter has been postponed to this day.—First of all, let me congratulate you on the Berlin Professorship, for which you were of course the most suitable candidate, and your appointment to which made Baldwin, Cattell Münsterberg and myself all very glad. I only feared that Berlin might prove a rasping, fatiguing, and *ungemüthlich* place to live in, and that you might be buying honour, if you accepted the appointment, at the price of peace of soul. But Münsterberg tells me that they have exempted you from responsibility about a laboratory; and that is a great point gained. I may say that I myself enjoy inward peace and a good professorial conscience for the first time, now that Münsterberg has taken charge of the entire experimental field. Needless to say that if I had lived 1000 years I should not have done what he has been doing in the past two years here. He is a wonderful organizer, methodical to the last degree, our laboratory being a picture to look upon since he has taken hold; and he is moreover a most high minded and lovable human being, so that I can only be thankful for the inspiration that led me to tempt him away from Freiburg. My only fear now is that his stay with us may be short, for although he likes America so far, and perhaps sees it in too ideal a light, his ambition of course would be better fulfilled by a German Professorship. But the future will decide. We have a three weeks' holiday from lecturing at present, and with characteristic energy he has gone to California in order to visit the educational institutions there, and the principal colleges on the way. Some 13,000 kilometers of railroad in 3 weeks seems to me a bit too much!—We had a rare passage home, the Ocean like a lake, and we found our own clean house just as we had left it, and very comfortable after our fifteen months of pension-life. But I found it very hard to begin teaching again. I had been rather melancholy all summer, but it grew acute with my lectures. *I* shrank to nothing, *psychology* shrank to nothing—etc. It passed away, however, and now not a trace of it is left. But it has taught me the lesson that 15 months is too long a vacation for a man like me to take. Teaching is such an artificial discipline, that one loses the habit of it almost immediately, and seems to forget all that one ever knew. At present I have "Cosmology" and "Mental Pathology" (taken in a wide sense), 3 + 2 hours a week throughout the year, and "psychology" (3 hours a week) until the middle of march.[1]—Our new Psychological review, of which your name adorns the cover, promises well. I think that B. & C. will be good editors, and if you will only occasionally write a few pages, or give them timely advice about German books or news, the thing will succeed. It is a bad time to start such an enterprise, for the country is groaning under the worst financial depression it has ever known. With the passage of the bill reducing the tariff, & with the beginning of the Spring, business will probably revive.[2] Meanwhile every one is trying to save money, and the poor are in a sad condition of distress. Fortunately the winter so far has been a mild one.—Our university has even had to dismiss instructors; but our *own* income is, so far, not reduced, altho' we are trying to spend as little as possible in order to repair the frightful ravages left by our European year.—Ladd is just out with a new and heavy-looking "psychology."[3] From all the new psychologies either published or about to appear, there *ought* to be *some* sedimentary deposit of truth—I devoutly hope that it may be

clearly discernible by all!   To me the sort of thing that Pierre Janet
has just done in his "Etat Mental des hystériques" seems to outweigh
in importance all the "exact" laboratory measurements put together.[4]
For of what laboratory experiments made with brass instruments can
one say that they have opened an entirely new chapter in human
nature, and led to a new method of relieving human suffering?   Not
even of the ophthalmoscope can *all* that be said.—We had Helmholtz
here, by the bye, in the autumn.   A fine looking old fellow, but with
formidable powers of holding his tongue, and answering you by a
friendly inclination of the head.   His wife was a *femme du monde*, however, and fully made up for his lack of conversation.[5]   Another coun-
tryman of yours, Hagen from Konigsberg, for many years Professor
of Entomology at Harvard, died here this winter after a sad illness of
nearly three years.   Also a *herrlicher Mensch.*—I think of the strong
good air, the horizontal spaces, the noble architecture both German
and Greek, of Munich, the beer, the pictures the whole civilization
there, as an *el Dorado* to which I wish I could return.   I should think
that you and Mrs. Stumpf would hate to leave so good a dwelling
place.   I fear I never may return.   One should not be a cosmopolitan, one's soul becomes "disaggregated" as Janet would say.   Parts of
it remain in different places, and the whole of it is nowhere.   One's
native land seems foreign.   It is not a wholly good thing, and I think
I suffer from it.   But it is a danger that menaces not *you*.   Please take
the heartiest wishes from both of us for your continued prosperity in
1874.[6]   Harry too sends Gluckwünsche and regards to Rudi and the
younger boy.   I am as ever,

                    Your most affectionate   Wm James

ALS: MH bMS Am 1092.9 (3792)

  [1] See letter of 21 April 1893, note 2.

  [2] For economic conditions see *Correspondence*, 2:288n, 2:325n.

  [3] George Trumbull Ladd, *Psychology: Descriptive and Explanatory* (1894).   WJ reviewed the book in *Psychological Review* 1 (May 1894): 286–93; reprinted in *ECR*.

  [4] Pierre Janet, *État mental des hystériques* (1894).   WJ reviewed the work in *Psychological Review* 1 (March 1894): 195–99; reprinted in *ECR*.

  [5] Hermann Helmholtz toured the United States while visiting the World's Columbian Exposition.   His wife was Olga von Velten Helmholtz.   For more comments
about the visit see *Correspondence*, 2:279–80.

  [6] A slip for 1894.

From Charles Sanders Peirce

Milford Pa 1894 Jan 28

Dear William

In writing you yesterday I had not your note before me & so over looked some things.

You ask whether I know of anybody but Delboeuf & myself "who has treated the inorganic as a sort of product of the living?" This is good. An instance, no doubt, of that wonderful originality for which I am so justly admired. Your papa for one believed in creation, & so did the authors of all the religions. But my views were probably influenced by Schelling,—by all stages of Schelling, but especially by the *Philosophie der Natur.*[1] I consider Schelling as enormous; and one thing I admire about him is his freedom from the trammels of system and his holding himself uncommitted to any previous utterance. In that, he is like a scientific man.

If you were to call my philosophy Schellingism transformed in the light of modern physics, I should not take it hard.

But my philosophy is simply the *synechistic philosophy.*

I consider *relational* as the most perversely bad designation it would be easy to give for your "transitive" states. If you find *volatile* and *sessile* too metaphorical, it probably indicates that you conceive the states a little differently from what I do. All naming has to be metaphorical, and as you seem unable to describe these states in plain language, with only quite familiar metaphors, you will have to choose between a positively incorrect designation and a highly metaphorical one.

My reasons for not liking relational are two

1ˢᵗ that word should be preserved to mean "dealing with relations," and cant be spared.

2ⁿᵈ When you shoot one of your "transitive" thoughts on the wing, transfix it and make it "substantive," *then* you have the idea of a relation; and until the thought ceases to be transitive it has no consciousness of the relation. While it is transitive, it is in a certain sense what you might call *relative* but it is not *relational.*

Homer speaks of winged and unwinged words to denote two different kinds or grades of attention. That is, that is what seems to be meant, if anything is meant. Words are always winged in the Iliad, I believe, and unwinged in the Oddyssey. Shall we say *pteroent* and *apteroent*?

I am quite of your opinion that "it is well not to strain language already in use any more than one can help in creating technical terms." This is one reason for liking *volatile* and *sessile* states of mind, those terms not being already in use. But "substantive" "transitive" and "relational" are all in use in senses widely different from those you would give them & just *so* different as to create false suggestions.

Yours faithfully | C. S. Peirce

I have heard that within a few years some have urged views like mine but have not seen the papers.

ALS: MH bMS Am 1092 (670)

[1] Friedrich Wilhelm Joseph von Schelling (1775–1854), German philosopher.

To Alfred Church Lane

95 Irving Street, Cambridge. | Feb. 13, 1894

My dear Lane:

I am delighted to hear authentic news of you again—only the other day I was wondering to what spheres you had flitted. Now you appear in the character of a geologist, whereas when I knew you you were a mathematician. I am pegging away in the same old manner, in a larger house, with more children, a balder head, and a poorer memory, but otherwise much the same.

As for your expts., the way you suggest with cards is a good one, probably the best to begin with. It is fearfully dull work, and might be exchanged for words or diagrams if the statistics were favorable. Of course in any case the thing to be guessed must be, not *chosen* then and there by the agent, but taken at random in some way.

I beg you to send me your results, positive or negative. I also wish you would ask Professor McNair to put down for me on paper his two dreams, and any thought transference phenomena of which he may have knowledge—unpublished phenomena, I mean.[1]

He will confer on me a deep obligation, if he will be so very kind as to take this trouble.

Believe me, with cordiallest greetings,

Yours always truly, | Wm. James

TC: MH bMS Am 1092.1

[1] Probably Fred Walter McNair (1862–1924), American educator and mathematician, for a time Lane's colleague at the Michigan College of Mines.

To Charles Sanders Peirce

Cambr. Feb. 27. 94

Dear Chas.,

I wish that you had printed my note intact—the last sentence would have been a tardy reparation for real omissions on my part which I have regretted.[1]

Your brother tells me that you have some lectures and would like to give them.[2] I am writing to the director of the Brooklyn Institute to suggest etc. But I dare say this is officious, as you most probably know each other. He is Franklin W. Hooper, of 502 Fulton St Brooklyn.[3] My friend Thos. Davidson, who is in the lecturing line, says that the B.I. is a very good place to *have* lectured in, for its lists are consulted by other parties. I hope the subscriptions come in satisfactorily.

Yours always | Wm James

ALS: MH bMS Am 1092.9 (3376)

[1] See letter to Peirce of 3 January 1894.
[2] Charles Peirce's brother was James Mills Peirce.
[3] Franklin William Hooper (1851–1914), director of the Brooklyn Institute of Arts and Sciences.

To James McKeen Cattell

95 Irving St March 1. [1894]

My dear Cattell,

1) I will see to Bradley[1]

2) I return note to Creighton, which I think good.

3) I return the Nichols correspondence. Of course he made no *complaint* of you; but felt cast down, being so poor, at the probable size of the bill. I will try to induce him to abridge the paper.

4) Thank you! I don't care to see MS. of Association report. Enough reading on hand now with exams students theses, Ladd and Paulhan,[2] and the entire subject of "Cosmology["] now being lectured on by me for the first time!

Yours as ever | W.J.

ALS: DLC

[1] Unwilling to review Bradley's *Appearance and Reality*, WJ undertook to find a reviewer for it. The review in *Psychological Review* 1 (May 1894): 307–11 is by Alfred Hodder.

[2] The report of the American Psychological Association meeting appeared in *Psychological Review* 1 (March 1894): 214–15. WJ was writing a review of Ladd (see letter to Stumpf of 24 January 1894) and reading Frédéric Paulhan's *Les Caractères* (1894).

To George Holmes Howison

95 Irving S! Cambridge | March 3. 94

My dear Howison,

I want to write you a word *in rê* Herbert Nichols who is candidate for any good opening in Psychology, and who has a hope that possibly your contemplated place at Berkeley may be thrown open to him. He was thrown out of employment here by Munsterberg's arrival as head of the laboratory and my return to teach psychology, and has been working by himself through the winter in Cambridge. We have no place for him, since he ought to be autonomous in his department, and we only require now from year to year an assistant at 300 dollars.

He is a mature man with his character formed and great merits and defects of both of which I will give you a candid account. The chief defect, and the only serious one, is a certain complication and obscurity of statement in theoretical matters, which I think every one feels. He is sometimes tactless, too, from an excess of frankness and confidingness—he alienated Eliots friendship in this way. He is also a little imaginative about people and their relations to him—but what man eager and disappointed in a career, is not liable to this, when thrown amongst those who can make or mar his destiny?

Per contra, his good spirits, helpfulness, devotion and generosity are endless. He is a terrible worker, with very tough nerves, an excellent mechanician, full of inventiveness, having a broad acquaintance with all psychophysical instruments and methods, and great patience with students, as well as lots of original ideas, as his papers on pleasure and pain in Schurmann's review, as well as his forthcoming papers, on the skin will testify. As head of a psychological department, laboratory and class instruction, I should think he would be sure to be a success. His teaching, with my book as a text, last year, was successful, both in College and in the Annex. Of his metaphysics I take little account, for I find them obscure. What would be *plain* in him as an intellectual influence is the usual biologico-evolutionary standpoint, which however little ultimate, has at any rate to be swallowed digested and superseded (with incorporation) by the *Truth*—whate'er that be—and which would be the almost inevitable influence in any of the younger psychologists. I write to you now to ask you if you can, *without in any way making your self responsible,* forecast what is most likely to happen next year. If N. feels that he has anything like a favorable chance with you, he will do certain things now otherwise than he might if there were no prospects on the Pacific Coast. So pray write to me freely: no harm will come, in any event, and some good may come to both N. & yourselves. To sum up, there is no end of *go* and capacity in him, but he is a less *academic* type of character than most such candidates are. I wish you could be here to see him—Can't you take a trip East this Spring?

Münsterberg is colossal in jeder Beziehung!

We are all well—I suffering much from the sense of my inadequacy, both intellectual and corporeal, to my tasks, but the years elapse notwithstanding with no public exposure—. I wish I could pay you a flying trip somewhat longer than that which Munsterberg paid.[1]

Yours ever | Wm James

ALS: MH bMS Am 1092.9 (1033)

Address: Professor Howison | Berkeley | California
Postmark: CAMBRIDGE STA MAR 5 94

[1] See letter to Stumpf of 24 January 1894.

To George Stuart Fullerton

Cambr. March 13 or 14 [1894]

My dear Fullerton:

I need not say that Hodgson and I have been much disappointed at the reply of the Seybert Commission.[1] Having irretrievably lost our tails ourselves we should naturally have been pleased at the reduction of such very foxy vulpines as you 'uns to the same status.

You give no motive for the refusal, so that I am in doubt whether it be the expense, or your feeling that the facts known to you about Mrs. P. do not establish a presumption strong enough to make it your duty to spend valuable time etc., etc. Of course the latter ground would seem to show that our judgment, after all the time we have spent, still cuts a tolerably pitiable figure in your eyes. We however are philosophical enough not to care for that, for we know the darkness in which men grope and we understand the tremendous odds which such opinions as ours have to overcome, especially in the minds of men who have had so untoward a run of luck as you had in your investigations. We are therefore not so much chagrined or discouraged as disappointed. But in return for this benignant disposition on our part we should like to ask you a favor which we think you will not refuse, and that is that (entirely regardless of what might be the effect on our feelings if we were "sensitive") you candidly set down in writing the veritable grounds of your refusal.   In case Mrs. P. and the likes of her ever did hereafter *prevail,* it might be an interesting document in the history of opinion concerning her case, and the difficulties that lay in our path.   In fact I think you will all easily understand and sympathize with our desire to possess such a document.

Pray send it, then, long or short, and greatly oblige,

Yours sincerely, | Wm. James.

TC: MH bMS Am 1092.1

[1] WJ cited the refusal by the Seybert Commission to provide funds for the investigation of Mrs. Piper as an example of the prejudice of orthodox science against psychical research (see *EPR,* 194).   Members of the commission claimed that there was no money; see letters of 19 October 1890 and 19 March 1894.

To William Dean Howells

95, IRVING STREET, | CAMBRIDGE. March 19. 94

My dear Howells,

Your note from Barnegat Park, N.J. arrived duly, and the "pressure" on things upon me is best shown by the length of time it has taken to get it to Bob and back, and to return it "as per" your request. You must be lapped in a sea of such affectionate responses from people from whom the humanity of your muse has melted out the native hardness.   And both Bob and I are much pleased to learn of one more reader of poor old H. J. whose readers in these latter days seem so few.   This Ilsley I never heard of, but he seems a quite ideal personage in his tranquil California.[1]   Only as for "one real American not being afraid of any other," I fear Father would have snorted at the lack of reality in the dictum.   If there is any one *I* am really afraid of it is the dry-hearted American whom you meet in travelling, and to whom the sort of trivial conversation you engage in with every one you meet in Europe, is an object of nothing but disdain.   I dined yesterday at New Bedford, whither I had rushed for a snatch of Sabbatical rest, at a table with 4 others.   Each of us gulped his food in silence, each fearing the others' contemptuous or painful reception of a sudden remark.   I was immensely struck in the South two years ago by the uncomfortable state I threw every one into to whom I spoke at table.   They looked away, became uneasy, and hastened to leave. Speech must have an *object,* for the 'real' American to tolerate it.

But more than enough! Can't we go together in June for a couple
of weeks to the North Carolina M^{ts} I wish you would say yes!   I
hope you are all well, and good news from the Architect. Commend
us both to Mrs. Howells.

Yours ever | Wm James

ALS: Menninger Foundation

[1] In 1888, with reference to a reader of his father, WJ wrote a letter to an Ilsley
who was identified as Samuel Marshall Ilsley (1863–1946), an engineer then living in
Milwaukee (see *Correspondence,* 6:304–5). It was not established whether WJ simply
forgot about the 1888 letter or two different Ilsleys are involved.

From George Stuart Fullerton

March 19th '94.

My dear James:

I enclose an answer from Dr. Furness, our chairman. The Seybert
Commission will not act if he will not.

You know him well enough to know that when he appears to be
bursting with merriment he is most serious. He sends me his letter
to you with a request to tear it up if its tone of levity can be regarded
as in any sense a violation of the unities. I send it to you as it is, for
it expresses his real thought.

I am really sorry.

Sincerely yours, | Geo. S. Fullerton.

TC: MH bMS Am 1092 (276)

From Horace Howard Furness

222 West Washington Square. [March 19, 1894][1]

My dear James

Your letter of the 14th inst. to Fullerton, that dear lad has just sent
me as Acting Chairman of the late Seybert Com. with an implied
urbane request that, in answering it, I should with alacrity mount a
pillory where you and Hodgson to your hearts content can pelt me
with dead Phinuits and, between the showers of pickled peppers,
make the Summerland shake with the Homeric laughter of Piperian gods.

I'm willing. What do I care for the disgrace, any more than the darkey who ran away from the battle in the late Rebellion, when I am dead and "the power ob perception am gone."

First: in declining to investigate Mrs. Piper, there is no need of a Chairman's dictum, the Treasurer's is all sufficient. We have not now and we never had any money for such investigations—but, bless me! it just occurs to me that there is no need to enter into any explanations with you in regard to this fact—all you have to do is to ask Mrs. Piper! Just let Phinuit scratch round and hunt up Henry Seybert, and then you'll find out how nicely the latter played his little game.

Secondly, and to be serious, the sessions of two members of the Seybert Com. (Weir Mitchell and myself) with Mrs. Piper were such unalleviated, not to say, ridiculous, failures, that we cannot from our own personal experiences ask our fellow-members to interrupt their busy professional vocations with an avocation of so barren a promise—as far as Spiritualism is concerned. We have no ground to build on. We are like the little cherubims in Barham's Ingoldsby Legends who could not sit down because they had not *de quoi*.[2]

Thus far the Seybert Commissioner, now let me speak in my own person. I can believe that through the agency of Mrs. Piper and of kindred temperaments imagined revelations may be made of the illimitable human mind, which may force a re-creation of all our conceptions of it, and in the revolving years the chasm may be bridged between the dieseits and the jenseits, and a jenseits may be proved. Thus far, however, no shred of irrefragable proof has been adduced by Spiritualism that a hereafter exists.

'J'y suis et j'y reste,' and resting thus I cannot see what immediate good can be gained by spending shekels on Mrs. Piper for that which is not genuine Spiritualistic presentiment.

Heyho, dear boy,

Yours faithfully, | Horace Howard Furness.

TC: MH bMS Am 1092 (284)

[1] Dated with reference to Fullerton's letter.

[2] Richard Harris Barham (1788–1845), British author, *Ingoldsby Legends* (1840).

To Katharine Peabody Loring

Cambridge, March 20th. [1894][1]

Dear Katherine,

It is pleasant to greet you as a professional psychologist-sister. I never expected you would come to that. Just as I feel like stepping out too having disgorged all that I am as a P——ist into those volumes, and having nothing left over to teach with.

No nothing of mine has ever been translated into German. But your pupil can easily order either the Briefer Course or the Principles from Macmillan in London who vend them there.

On the whole for your pupils purposes I should think that Höffding's Outlines of Psychology, a danish book translated both into German and English would be the best attainable thing. How queer for a German to seek the springs of higher truth in America!

We are having a splendid winter in point of health, and the children are coming on most satisfactorily. I am glad Camden agrees so well with you all.[2] Please give my respects to your father and regards to your sister, and with Alice's love and mine believe me always truly yours

Wm James

ALS: Beverly Historical Society and Charles W. Galloupe Memorial Society

[1] Dating uncertain, with 1896 the latest possible year.

[2] Caleb William Loring died in Camden, S.C., in January 1897, indicating that this is the Camden in question.

To Henry Holt

95 Irving St. Camb. March 27 1894

Dear Holt

The Introduction to filosofy is what I ment—I dont no the other book.

I will try Nordau's Entartung this summer—as a rule however it duznt profit me to read Jeremiads against evil—the example of a little good has more effect.[1]

A propo of kitchen ranges, I wish you wood remoov your recommendation from that Boynton Furnace Company's affair.[2] We have struggld with it for five years—lost 2 cooks in consequens—burnt countless tons of extra coal, never had anything decently baikt, and now, having good rid of it for 15 dollars, are having a happy kitchen for the 1st time in our experience—all through your unprinsipld recommendation! You ought to hear my wife sware when she hears your name!

I will try about a translator for Nordau—though the only man I can think of needs munny more than fame, and coodn't do the job for pure love of the publisher or author or on an unsertainty.

Yours affectionately | Wm. James

TC: MH bMS Am 1092.1

[1] Max Simon Nordau, *Entartung*, 2 vols. (1892–93). Holt did not publish a translation. WJ's review of the English translation, *Degeneration* (1895), is reprinted in *ECR*.

[2] In 1889 WJ had corresponded with Holt concerning the stove at 95 Irving St.
(see *Correspondence*, 6:612–13).

To Henry Pickering Walcott

95 Irving St. April 1. 94

My dear Walcott,

Senator Harvey[1] has just sent me Doc 155, being a bill to punish
persons advertizing or announcing them selves as doctors etc without
qualifying by examination.   This seems to be the bill you had in
mind, whilst you were ignorant of the existence of the one which
was sent me with the petition which I signed, and against which my
thunderbolts were hurled in the *Transcript*.[2]   I have forgotten the
number and verbiage of that bill, but it made the treatment of patients penal by persons without a license gained by examination.   I
regard therapeutics as in too undeveloped a state for us to be able
to afford to stamp out the contributions of all fanatics & one-sided
geniuses.   Twenty years ago massage, then practiced exclusively by
fanatics and irregulars, wd. have been gladly stamped out by conservative M.D.'s under the provisions of such a bill.

Of the existence of this document 155 I in my turn was ignorant.
Of course I accept its principle, and would gladly vote for it were I
a legislator.   I shall write to the *Transcript* to that effect, I think.

Yours always truly | Wm James

ALS: MB

[1] Edwin Bayard Harvey (1834–1913), American physician, in 1894 elected to the
senate of Massachusetts.

[2] In his letter to the *Boston Evening Transcript*, 24 March 1894, WJ objected to a
proposed law requiring everyone practicing medicine in Massachusetts to be licensed.
In a second letter to the *Transcript*, 4 April 1894, he expressed his support for a
different bill.   This bill, Document 155, which simply made it a crime for anyone
without a state license to present himself as a physician or call himself a doctor, passed.
Walcott was then a member of the State Board of Health.   Both of WJ's letters to
the *Transcript* are reprinted in *ECR*.

To George Holmes Howison

Cambridge April 2 94

My dear Howison,

Your characteristically free, good, and eloquent letter, arrived duly the day before yesterday. I have to be more stingy in my reply being rather overloaded just now.

I thank you heartily for your complete confidence *in rê* Nichols. I will inform him without any details that he must practically indulge no hopes in your quarter.[1] That certainly will be for him a great point gained.

As for Mr. Stratton, I can answer an abstract question, but how can I know whether he is the concrete man who realizes the concept. My impression is that a man of 27, already caught with metaphysical fever would hardly be likely to grow into a successful laboratory-psychologist *in the long run* unless he happened to be also an individual of a lively mechanical and experimental turn of mind originally. I should fear other wise that he would drift away from the laboratory and find it quiddling and irksome, and that book work would absorb his attention more and more as he grew older. The first enthusiasm, however, might carry him well over the first few years, and after that there might be changes. Perhaps I am influenced too much by my own career; but unless he loves to tinker *anyhow,* I shouldn't hope a great deal. There are, to be sure, tinkers & metaphysicians in one, but the combination is rarer than is either separate element. Munsterberg and Wundt are such, and so may be Stratton for aught I know.

But if you love Stratton otherwise, and you can work well together and he is willing to make himself a psychologist, let me confidentially whisper in your ear what I think you can perfectly well do. Make him a *demonstrator* so far as the laboratory goes, and give up the notion of having a laboratory of *original research.* My private impression is that that business is being overstocked in America, and that the results are not proportionate to the money expended. I refer especially to "exact" work like that of Wundt's Laboratory. I fear that in a few years, if nothing more significant in the way of ideas emerges from it all, there may be a reaction which will make trustees repent of their enterprise in founding laboratories and places. At any rate we have now as many labs. as America *needs.* And with the natural experimenter Angell at Palo Alto, the Pacific Slope ought to be satisfied, I should think with a man at Berkeley who should be a competent psychologist and exhibiter of classic experiments without having to torture his brain to devise new varieties of insipidity for publication, as he would have to do if appointed on the basis lately fashionable. If Stratton has any psychology at all in him, two years would be ample to teach him what has been acquired and to enable him to teach, and show his pupils the physiology of brain, senses, and psycho physic methods in general. *I* always enjoyed that much of psychology, but I was bowed down with weight of woe that I couldn't invent original investigations or find the patience to carry them out.

If this strikes you as promising, and Stratton wants to study in a lab. two years, I am absolutely sure that the best one in the world is Münsterberg's. I don't believe there is any comparison between him and other men as teachers, and all his operations are models of methodical arrangement. (I don't mean by that to say that his results are infallible). Moreover he always keeps going a great variety of things, so that his students get a wide acquaintance with facts and methods. I say then, either two years here, or one year in Germany for the language, and the other here. I found the men in M's private little lab. at Freiburg last year all admitting that he was the only *teacher* in Germany.

As for Charles Peirce, it's the most curious instance of talents not making a career. He dished himself at Harvard by inspiring dislike in Eliot. I always supposed that he dished himself at the Johns Hopkins by his matrimonial irregularity which took place whilst he was there and made some little scandal.[2] He is now so mature in character, with rather fixed ½ bohemian habits and no habit of teaching, that it would be risky to appoint him. I yield to no one in admiration of his genius, but he is paradoxical and unsociable of intellect, and hates to *make connexion* with any one he is with. With all this curious misanthropy, he has a genuine vein of sentiment and softness running through him, but so narrow a vein that it always surprises me when I meet it. Anyhow he's a genius, and I look forward with avidity to his work.

When shall we have your work, into which you cast the quintessential extract of all your untiring labors?

Good bye! Affectionate regards from

Wm James

Thos. Davidson has been staying with us for a week. Matured and improved by the good years.

As a visiting lecturer Peirce might be really inspiring.

ALS: MH bMS Am 1092.9 (1034)
Address: Professor Howison | Berkeley | California
Postmark: CAMBRIDGE STA BOSTON MASS. APR 2 94

¹ In his letter of 25 March 1894 (calendared) Howison indicated that he would not hire Nichols because he and Nichols would not get along.

² In his letter of 25 March 1894 (calendared) Howison asked confidentially why Peirce was not given a professorship at Harvard or elsewhere. Peirce was divorced in 1883 and remarried the same year. He taught at Johns Hopkins in 1879–84.

To Josiah Royce

April 3. '94

My dear Royce,

Palmer came straight to M——berg the next morning, & said that my claims were all right, and that either M——g must give up his proposed psychological seminary and take the Phil 1 Psychol., or you give up your Schop. etc or ½ of it and take the Kant. That *he* himself should do anything he did not mention as a possibility, nor did M——g suggest it. On the contrary, he gave a ½ consent to do the Phil 1. plan.¹

I think this ought to be carefully considered by the department. I dislike to have any of our announced work given up, and my *impression* is that I am more likely to succeed than M——g in Phil 1, though I confess that may be a mistake. I should far rather on selfish grounds give the Kant and let M——g give the Phil I, only that does not give any sweet chance of either worrying our seraphic chairman or getting work out of him.

I find that in both the Economic and the mathematical dep^{ts} men lecture from 8 to 11 or 12 hours a week. Ashley is an exception lecturing only 5 hours.²

How a man can support the inward sense of sneaking that Palmer must carry I don't see. Bah!

W.J.

ALS: MH bMS Am 1092.9 (3615)

¹ In 1894–95 Philosophy 1: General Introduction to Philosophy was given by Palmer, WJ, and Santayana, with WJ responsible for the psychology segment. Royce gave, among other courses, Philosophy 12: Kant and Schopenhauer, and Münsterberg gave Philosophy 20a: Psychological Laboratory. WJ also gave Philosophy 3: Cosmology and Philosophy 20b: Psychological Seminary, on questions in mental pathology.

² Sir William James Ashley (1860–1927), British economic historian, then professor at Harvard.

To Frederic William Henry Myers

95, IRVING STREET, | CAMBRIDGE. May 4. 94

Dear Myers

Here is a test for telepathy! Note the date!

I woke this morning early with a vivid imagination that even now a letter might be on its way inviting me to accept a Professorship at the university of Cambridge. I am already discussing with my wife the quarter of the town in which we will take up our residence.

Don't you think that as believers in telepathy such a "psychosis["] on my part imposes some duties on Sidgwick and yourself? In a former occasion I had a similar lively early morning imagination that a person whom I didn't even know to be ill had remembered me in her will. No natural reason whatever to think she would. But 24 hours later I read of her death in the papers, and six weeks later heard from her executor that she had left me $5000.[1] Shall such things be suffered to remain exceptions? Shall they not rather be the rule? Shall a man have them happen to him only once in a lifetime?

To pass from ebriety to sobriety, I have been on my back for a month with a big subcutaneous abscess. But I am now breeched and walking and in a few days expect to be out and about my business. The Cosmos meanwhile has had a happy rest from my inquisitions and expositions.

Hodgson writes good accounts of the Piper sittings in N.Y. I am curious to see him on his return, and will then communicate to you my impressions of the past and my propositions for the future, especially with reference to your poor brother's bequest.[2]

Trusting that we are soon to be neighbors, yours being the part of the town which I favor, I am with warm regards to you all,

yours | W.J.

ALS: MH bMS Am 1092.9 (3314)

[1] For WJ's legacy from Alice Sturgis Hooper see *Correspondence*, 5:67.

[2] In his letter to Henry Lee Higginson of 15 March 1894 (calendared) WJ listed securities amounting to about $20,000 from the estate of Arthur Thomas Myers for the Society for Psychical Research. WJ wanted Higginson's advice, whether to keep the securities or sell and reinvest.

To Alice Howe Gibbens James

Wednesday 16th May 94 | 10.40 P.M

I returned home *via* Miss Clark, who said little, but went at me like a little bull-dog. I am to go for another treatment to morrow at 8.30 A.M. Rather fussily busy day, and very dull seminary this evening on the Character of Swedenborg.—It was a touching thing of you to have provided liver for me this evening—I had been thinking of presently ordering it for myself.—I went in this P.M. to see about Tweedy's shoes. They will try to rectify the distorted pair—as for the other pair I didn't know what to do but to bring them back, since the man in the shop who was bro't me as most of an expert could throw no light on the cause of the wearing over. Harry went to Spy pond again, and with Margaret to the Hindoo this evening.[1] Tweedy has had a fine day, perfectly happy and good.

W.J.

ALS: MH bMS Am 1092.9 (1858)
Address: Mrs William James | Chocorua | N.H.
Postmark: CAMBRIDGE STA BOSTON MASS. MAY 17 94

[1] Swami Vivekânanda (1863–1902), a Hindu monk, lectured at Sever Hall at 8 P.M. on 16 May 1894.

To Alice Howe Gibbens James

Cambr. Thursday May 17 1894 | 2.30 P.M

Sweet Alice;

I write a word now, so as not to be caught with too much to say to night at bed time.

1) Tweedy's shoes (the new ones which I took out & bro't back again) seem to fit him very well. He has worn them to day.

2) He is perfectly happy, asks for no one, and seems better than when there are so many people with him.

3) I took your mother back the $20 you gave me. She says she lent you 30. I told her I supposed you had kep the other 10.

4) We had 31 dollars in the bank, the which I extracted.

5) I went to Miss Clarke again this A.M. Slept very well last night, and have felt unusually well to day.

6) D.r Driver called to ask how I was. Said most important thing for Billy is not to cool off suddenly when hot. That throws blood on to kidneys.

7) Marie has nicely cleaned up the house against the party to night.

10.30 P.M. Mrs Dorr and Mrs Shaw appeared at 4 o'clock and stayed till 5.30. Mrs. S. was really beautiful, so earnest an[d] veracious, and told so nicely all her own experience.[1] It is nothing but the old story of religious conversion in a new form. I am very glad she came. Then I went to say good bye to Theodora & Helen,[2] taking tweedy with me, and returned for the dinner. We had a very nice young Langdon Mitchell, son of Weir M., husband of an actress, and himself a poet & playwright and a good deal of a man of the world.[3] It was very lively from the word go, Mary T. charming in manner and talk,[4] Mitchell a great addition, and Margaret extremely nice—I'm very glad she was there.

I am impatient to know how you got there, and what are your impressions. No doubt there'll be a letter to morrow. Give my love to Bill and tell truthful Peg that the house is a different place, and a sad & lonely one, with[out] the sound of her soft low voice. Without thine too, Alice!

Thy | W.J.

Jae Walsh writes (I've mislaid his letter) that the dividend will be $3000 net per share. Lilla & her bro. Dick[5] are going to Europe, and he & his wife, both out of health are going later, with the children.[6] I have written to him, to dissuade from *that*.

ALS: MH bMS Am 1092.9 (1859)

[1] Mrs. Shaw's narrative is one of several anonymous accounts in *The Varieties of Religious Experience* (1902); for a list of possibilities see *Varieties* (Cambridge: Harvard Univ. Press, 1985), 442. There are at least three possible Mrs. Shaws. The likeliest one appears to be Pauline Agassiz Shaw (1841–1917), philanthropist, daughter of Louis Agassiz. The narrative in *Varieties*, 91–92, describes certain events in 1881 when the narrator was forty, exactly the age of Pauline Shaw.

[2] Perhaps Helen Maria Child Sargent (d. 1903), daughter of Francis James Child and wife of Frederick Le Roy Sargent.

[3] Langdon Elwyn Mitchell (1862–1935), American lawyer and author, son of Silas Weir Mitchell. His wife was Marion Lea Mitchell.

[4] Perhaps Mary Tappan.

[5] Richard Montgomery Lawrence Walsh (1848–1908), a stockbroker and amateur painter, brother of James William Walsh.

[6] James William Walsh and his wife, Susan Newbold Lawrence Walsh.

To Thomas Davidson

Cambr. May 19. 94

Dear Davidson,

Your friendly letter came yesterday. Bakewell gave you a wrong account. I am feeling very hearty, working well, and no relapse of the peccant spots into bad ways. Wife, Bill & Peg at Chocorua, where, the former says, the drought is sickening.

As for my "Talks on the recent state of Psychology["] or whatever it be (for I have sent your letter to my wife), I must beg you to desist.[1] I am unwilling to be pledged to *anything,* least of all to Psychology, which, for some inscrutable reason, has completely vanished from my ken, so far as power to talk about it goes. I may not get to Keene Valley, I may not stay more than two days at your end of it, I may not open my head when there if I do, and I positively decline to be "announced."

Yours, in haste, W.J.

ALS: MH bMS Am 1092.9 (868)

[1] Apparently in Davidson's letter, now lost, he had asked WJ to lecture at the Glenmore Summer School of the Culture Sciences in Keene Valley.

From Charles William Eliot

17 QUINCY S! | CAMBRIDGE. 20 May '94

Dear Dr. James:

You carry me back farther than anybody else—to 1861.[1] I can see that I there had some of the same qualities & powers that I have now; but I had little range of observation, no breadth of experience, and small capacity for sympathetic imagination.

You and I have, I think, the same fundamental reason for being moderately content with the years that are past:—We have a sense of growth and of increased capacity for useful service. We find our lives enriched and amplified from year to year. So long as that enlarging process goes on, we shall be content. If it stops suddenly we shall be content to that date.

I thank you for including in the list of my serviceable qualities "devotion to ideals". I have privately supposed myself to have been pursuing certain educational ideals; but so many excellent persons have described the fruits of the past twenty five years as lands, buildings, collections, money and thousands of students, that I have sometimes feared that to the next generation I should appear as nothing but a successful Philistine.

As to the next President it seems to me that you might be more hopeful of a good succession. He will not have to do all the things that I have done; for the organization has been greatly improved within fifteen years. At this moment it happens that not a single one of our ten Deans is able-bodied; but that condition can hardly be chronic. With ten robust, energetic Deans, the President might lapse into a figure-head, or a public speaker.

Your coming to the University and your career as a teacher and writer have been among my most solid grounds of satisfaction. So your words of cheer are of especial value to me.

Sincerely yours | Charles W. Eliot

ALS: MH Archives

[1] In 1861 WJ had entered the Lawrence Scientific School of Harvard University, where Eliot was an instructor in chemistry (see *Correspondence*, 1:2).

To Alice Howe Gibbens James

Monday night [May 21, 1894] | 11. P.M.

Dearest Alice,

Your letter of Saturday and yesterday breathed a more tranquil spirit, and glad I was that it was so. I had a headache this AM. & couldn't study, so, after writing a lot of Mrs. Piper invitations to University men, I went to town, got back babys shoes etc etc. saw "Gorilla" again etc.[1] Charles Norton has sat here an hour, and I have had to write an important business letter about Nichols, to Dick!! Miller, who has been getting an offer of a place for him at Bryn Mawr. M. is a little trump. I enclose a letter from C.W.E. in reply to a love letter which I wrote him on the 25th anniversary of his election. It is characteristic—and good!—Who is mabel page?[2] I never heard her name. I am ashamed to send you such a shabby line in return for your good ample letter, but I must to bed. To morrow AM. to Miss Clarke again.—Tweedy is splendidly well. Fatter than when you left.

W.J.

ALS: MH bMS Am 1092.9 (1861a)

[1] The show was not identified. There was an animal show in town, but it did not feature gorillas.

[2] Mabel Page was not identified. Perhaps she is the one mentioned in an 1887 letter; see *Correspondence*, 6:589.

To Alice Howe Gibbens James

May 23. 94 | 10.45 P.M.

Dearest Alice,

Your letter came this P.M., saying that you would stay up rather than bring the children down, but I prefer to wait a while to see what your farther reflexion may bring. I am glad that Billy is better, and that the place is already improving. It takes the Garden to make the place look well. I hope we can get some manure from the Sherwin's.[1] I regret you[2] hear you write as if Chocorua were something to escape from, because, apart from the money question, the thought of going up there has seemed very sweet to me, and the prospect of a tenant makes me in one sense feel quite sad. Guess who turns up now? I haven't heard yet from Walker or his "party," but the *Taussigs* say they may take it, and will go up to look at it next week! I told them 400 dollars. Mrs. T's father-in-law is ill, so they cant go together, and prefer all to pass the summer in America. All goes well here. The cook is a sweet depressed careful and conscientious creature—Marie rather a spoiled beauty, and acting as if she had too much to do. She has indeed been doing a good deal, but the darning of stockings is what she likes to do.* She has had very little time *out* with tweedy who keeps rather dirty, but is better than I have ever known him in tone and look. He sleept this morning till after seven AM., and s'ts till ½ past 3 PM. The effect of removing the poison of the maternal presence? or that of the fraternal? or of the sorellar?

Harry is judicious—much occupied with his insects and Ed Cogswell.[3] I saw Mr Turner to day having a big hole dug in his lot, for no other reason, apparently but to taste its possession the more completely. They haven't touched our money yet.[4] I saw Ames last night—quite well and lecturing. I have been aimlessly busy to day, part of the time over the Piper sittings. Jackson refuses,[5] regarding her, from the Perry's account, to be an ingenious fraud. Shaler has a sitting Friday P.M., & Norton Saturday morn. Dont mention it! I am ashamed to be sending you such shabby letters, but it is 11 o'clock. I have had an old pupil, D! Taylor, to tea, who bro't our laboratory a splendid set of brain preparations.[6] I took him to the Seminary, which went off all right. My headache has remitted to day but is back again this evening—It is distinctly neuralgic in character. I got too late to Miss Clarke's this AM. but I go again to morrow. I am developing such sympathy with you on the housekeeping basis. To be suddenly called to Boyson leaves nothing possible but to order beefsteak or chops,[7] and I wonder how you (with the prices too staring you in the face!) can have been so varied profuse, and thoughtful as you have always proved.   How glad I am that it is not *after your death* that I make that discovery.   That would indeed be a "victory" for the grave over your loving husband

Wm.

Kiss sweet old Peg, and even Billy.   I wish I were with you, but things are reeling off finely here.

*Has taken up carpets to day.

ALS: MH bMS Am 1092.9 (1863)

[1] Thomas Sherwin (1839–1914), a businessman, was related to AGJ and Isabel Fiske Edwards Sherwin.   The Sherwins, who had a home in Chocorua, had at least four children.

[2] A slip for 'to'.

[3] Edward Russell Cogswell (b. 1874), in later years a landscape architect.

[4] If Turner is Samuel Epes Turner, whose lot adjoined WJ's, it is possible that WJ bought a parcel from him to complete his holdings.

[5] Unidentified, but perhaps Charles Loring Jackson; see letter to Bryce of 8 July 1893.

[6] Dr. Taylor was not identified.

[7] George Boyson was a grocer in Mount Auburn Street.

To Richard Hodgson

May 24 [1894]

Dear H.,

I return Langley's letter.   His prudence makes me feel as if you and I must be great moral heroes, especially you.   How he (—and many others—) will wish on the day of judgment that they had put themselves on record with our quintet (Lodge, Myers, Mrs. S.[1] you and I) in order to be then sharing our prominent position of honour and profit.   Let the tho't of that nerve us to our great task!

Did you ever take a copy of my record of Bourget's sitting at this house?

Yours etc. | W.J.

ALS: Cambridge University Library

[1] Eleanor Sidgwick.

To Alice Howe Gibbens James

95 Irving S! May 24. 94 | 11.15 P.M

Dearest Alice,

A day of pouring rain. Marie has got up both carpets, Tweedy is divine, we had a delicious stewed breast of veal, and Louise is a dear old personality with her pained face, and delicate sense of what is good. I believe she thinks we can't tell any differences. I slept better last night and got a nap this P.M., and have had but little headache, intermittently. On the whole I am hopeful. I came in at 10.30 from examining Bigham for PhD. at Palmer's (we passed him with difficulty)[1] and found Hodgson waiting to see me because Mrs. P. had struck, and said to day she wouldn't come for the sittings I had arranged for to morrow. I have been writing her a letter which H. thinks will fetch her. The Shalers come to morrow.[2] I got your letter this P.M. With all this rain you must need your patience, and I wish I had lent Andrew my rubber coat. Between Mrs. Gignoux,[3] the Taussigs and Mr. Walkers friend we *ought* to get a tenant. The latter gives no sign of life yet, however. How I wish you were coming back to morrow. I dread to break the negative news to Marie.

Thy own   W.J.

ALS: MH bMS Am 1092.9 (1864)

[1] John Bigham received his doctorate from Harvard in 1894 and after teaching for a short time became a businessman.

[2] In his letter to AGJ of 25 May 1894 (calendared) WJ reported that the Shalers' sitting with Mrs. Piper was a "very decent success."

[3] Mrs. Gignoux was not identified.

To Granville Stanley Hall

95 Irving S! Cambr. May 27. [1894]

My dear Hall,

I have been too busy to answer your letter till now, and meanwhile Mrs. P. who has been sitting almost every day since last Sept. has intimated that she is tired out, and must take a long vacation, so that in any case nothing can be done till next fall, when possibly you will be invited again.[1]

But the particular tests that you propose would almost certainly fail. She has little or no "clairvoyant" power, and so far as her achievements can be explained by mind reading, it is the subliminal reser[v]oir that she gets at, and not the momentary consciousness of the sitter. The only way to take her is on her own ground. Sit and see what names and facts the "aura of your person" suggests to her; or bring an object closely associated with some other person (recently dead if possible), give it to her to handle and see what it brings out. Out of 27 sittings which she has just given in N.Y. to total strangers (strangers in great part to Hodgson too, who was present) she failed completely I believe in only two.—I forgot when I wrote to you that you had already had a sitting with her in the early days, & had failed to get anything. This might invalidate any positive results with you, of the kind that she gives, on the ground of of recognition and exploration [*end of letter missing*]

AL incomplete: MH bMS Am 1092.9 (962)

[1] In his letter to AGJ of 25 May 1894 (calendared) WJ wrote that he suspected that Hall's letter "is meant to be refused so that he can say we wouldn't sit under certain simple conditions that he proposed."

To Alice Howe Gibbens James

Sunday | Cambr. May 27. 94 | 10.15 P.M.

Dearest Alice,

I had hoped to write you a long, rambling gossipping, loving letter to day, *before* bed time. But I naturally keep it till the end, and I have been at the desk from morning till now over other things. This gives a false idea of my assiduity, however, for I have been away from the desk *some,* and wasted much time when there. However, all the morning and ½ the afternoon went to an examination paper in Phil 3. and the rest of the time to letters. I bicycled a little after bkfst. and went in to Royce's. Harry Fox was out in the sun on their door step, surrounded by the admiring neighborhood. The Royce children improve very much, and Ned is becoming a real beauty for expression. We lunched at the Childs in Co. with Bessie Moore, a well finished thing, whom I like to meet.[1] After tea here, to Miss Clark's. My headache comes and goes, even now whilst I write. There is a good deal of news, the most important item of which is that Cowie writes that it is impossible to save the wall, every one including our own architect calling it unsafe.[2] I wired him to go on and cooperate in the rebuilding. We are now not legally liable to the tenants at all; but to tear down their wall and leave them to shelter themselves at their own expense from the weather doesn't seem exactly honorable, so we shall have to be at some expense on their account. I have written to ask Cowie his candid opinion of the extent of our duty, and I will consult Danforth here who will take the landlord's point of view. At any rate it will swallow the whole Wyckoff fund and more.

I gave a rousing good lecture yesterday in spite of a bad head, & went in to the Saturday Club dinner, where I sat between John Gray and Wolcott Gibbs.[3]   Chas. Norton was there, after a sitting with Mrs. Piper and Hodgson here in the forenoon, and was convinced of the genuineness of the performance, and of the inexplicability of certain things, though it was a distinctly poor sitting. The Shalers was much better. Still, N. is *morally* a convert, which is a great point gained. At ½ pas 4 I went to Mrs Whitman's but found her on the sidewalk stepping into a cab to go to Brookline where Chas. Sargent was receiving the British admiral in the open air amongst his azaleas etc.[4] She scooped me up, and I enjoyed it greatly, going in to find all my old friends, Edith (Emerson) Forbes,[5] Mary (Forbes) Russell, Jennie (Watson) Perkins,[6] Lizzie Head,[7] Mrs. Roger Wolcott,[8] and in the hostess, my long lost Minnie Robeson of Newport, whom I used to dandle on my knee, and call "sister" whilst she called me "brother."[9] She also remembered well the time. After all, human intercourse is good, and it seems mean to cultivate so little of it. With me, however, it is all a matter of health and eyes. Mrs. W. was in great spirits about going to Europe. She sails with the Brimmers, has a week in London, after that to Paris, and then no plans. I spoke to her of the diary, and think I will send it to her.[10] —Bowditch, Hodg[s]on & Co, have given up N. Carolina, and go to Keene Valley; but if we let the place, I shall still be much tempted by N.C. I gave your note to Mrs. Taussig to night. She says they can't go before Wednesday, and that the Gorhams will want the place by the 15th. *What I should like* would be to be *there with you* till the 15th., and then, you coming back here, go to N.C. Tweedy is better than ever—I think the cutting of his hair must have restored him! Marie appeared to day in an iridescent gown & hat, looking like a rainbow or the queen of Switzerland. An army in full flight would have stopped to look at her. She washed the floor of my bedroom yesterday, and I must say on the whole has done very well, and her sulks have quite passed over. The cook is a dear old thing, washing and cleaning all the time. Yesterday the hall, to day the dining-room, etc., etc. Well!

Good night, dearest.   Kiss old bill; and oh! how I long for truthful Peg, with the low soft voice, and the arms going up regularly like clockwork three times a day twelve times in succession, the chin up and the shoulders back all the time, and never a frown or a tear or a peevish word!   What a daughter to possess.—Only two more lectures now!

Thine forever | W.J.

ALS: MH bMS Am 1092.9 (1866)

[1] Probably Elizabeth Fisk Hewins Moore, second wife of Charles Herbert Moore (1840–1930), professor of fine arts at Harvard.

[2] Reference is to the stores in Syracuse.

[3] Oliver Wolcott Gibbs (1822–1908), a chemist, professor at Harvard, a member of the Saturday Club.

[4] Two British warships were in port visiting Boston.

[5] Edith Emerson Forbes (1841–1929), daughter of Ralph Waldo Emerson, wife of William Hathaway Forbes, who was a son of John Murray Forbes.

[6] Jane Sedgwick Watson Perkins (1838–1912); for her family see *Correspondence*, 1:5n.

[7] Boston directories list three women named Head at 61 Westville, including an Elizabeth Head.   No information about her was found.

[8] Edith Prescott Wolcott, wife of Roger Wolcott (1847–1900), American politician.

[9] Mary Allen Robeson Sargent.

[10] Reference is to AJ's diary; see letter to Whitman of 28 May 1894.

To Sarah Wyman Whitman

95, IRVING STREET, | CAMBRIDGE. May 28. [1894]

Dear Mrs. Whitman,

I think it best to leave poor sister Alice's diary with you to day.[1] Some parts of it will say nothing to you for lack of a key to the persons etc.; some will bore you; but there are some beautiful things well said, and beside the dramatic pathos as it nears the end—she with her cancer—it seems to me a very vivid expression of one of the most vivid and able characters I ever knew—This little note of personal expressiveness in literature being literally *all* that remains behind objectively of her life.   My real reason for sending it to you is that it brings you more into the intimacy of the James family.   But please mention it to no one.   Not to Katherine Loring, should you meet her.   My brother Bob is still ignorant of its existence, and my wife hasn't yet communicated the fact to her mother and sister.   So you see how you are singled out!

I feel very happy now that I know you are going away!
"Exsudation" and "sylvan" are permanent acquisitions!

Yours (also a permanent acquisition) | W.J.

Don't be in haste to read the diary—that's why I send it now.

ALS: MH bMS Am 1092.9 (3923)

[1] AJ's diary was published as *The Diary of Alice James,* ed. Leon Edel (1964). For another publication and the history of the diary see *Correspondence,* 2:302n.

To Alice Howe Gibbens James

Cambr. May 28 [1894] | 11. P.M.

Dearest Wifelet,

It seems doomed that I shall never get at you before 10 o'clock. To night I am just in from the performing lions etc.,[1] and finding Harry's window alight, went up to see him.   He says that Mary arrived in good spirits and condition.   I had offered to Margy in the morning to do anything towards receiving her, but Margaret was going in, and I knew I should spoil the company, so this afternoon, feeling the absolute need of a little change, I took a car to city point, and on the way back stopped at the beast show, which was very fine indeed.   I shall see Mary to morrow morning.   Your letter came this PM. enclosing Hall's etc.   I am sorry you are so eager to get back, but I think it extremely natural under the circumstances.   I am apparently never to have any decent times with you, for when you get back I must get off, for the reason that that is the only way to get the refreshment I need.   We can go for a couple of days to Newport together, however.   All this is on the supposition that my letter of yesterday, speaking of my wish to go to you, hasn't altered your desire. I can take Tweedy up there and leave Marie here if you say so.—The good Julie, what a treasure she is.   But Marie is also a treasure, so pure in heart apparently, and really friendly in disposition.

Mrs. Piper turned up this P.M. very much disgruntled that we had taken her manifesto seriously and wishing to go on sitting indefinitely again.   So we have Chas. N. again to morrow.   The poor innocent little woman—she has to stamp her foot and shake her head occasionally, to make believe she has any individuality left.   It does seem to me to be all smoothing out into a sheet of tissue paper.   But she too is pure in heart—after all a good thing.   I tied up Alice's diary and left it at Mrs. W.'s door.   I have been reading it the past few nights— it *is* hard; but there are wonderful bits in it.   I went to Chapel this

A.M. had an honour exam[n], a student to dinner.   Mrs P. & another visitor this PM., so not much got done.   The City point Marine Park Anlage looks promising, but much of the way thither through so. Boston is mean.   I took supper in Eliot Street off 4 slices of rye bread, a lot of Limburg cheese, and six slices of Bologna Sausage, (but not the hard black kind) and 2 glasses of beer.   Poor M——g. is quite disconsolate and wife-sick in his empty house.   It will end by his going to Keene Valley.

The lamp is going out—so good night, and heaven bless you, and all of you.

Your | Wm.

A letter went up for Julie this AM.

ALS: MH bMS Am 1092.9 (1867)

[1] WJ saw Hacenbeck's Trained Animals.   The show was nearing the end of its Boston engagement of about a month at the Columbia Theatre.   He passed up the Woman Suffrage Association Festival, where Julia Ward Howe was among the main speakers.

To Alice Howe Gibbens James

Cambr. May 29. 94 | 9.15 P.M.

Dearest Alice,

Your post-card came this P.M., and at 6 I saw Taussig, who said they couldn't go up till next week, so all you have to do is to post back here as quick as possible after getting this—Thursday morning if you can, so that I may clasp you in my arms again.   After all, it is just as well that the Taussigs should have it all to themselves.   Mrs. Fassitt declines, but says she may go up next week to see Mary's house;[1] and the Walker's friend (who was not Mrs. F.) also declines, so that the T's are our last chance.—A beautiful day to-day.   I gave my last lecture in Phil. 3., and it would have done your proud wifely heart good to hear the solid applause.   I have been conscious of a most excellent *rapport* with the men all the year, and next year I think I can make of it a good course.   The relief of finishing is great.   To morrow night the end of my seminary, Friday the exam[n], and then the end of everything, when I must *instantly* get away.—Mary looks finely.— Andrew[2] got home to find that the man whom he had left in charge of his affairs had stolen 56 dollars and cleared out.   The police have tracked him to Newport.—Poor Grace Thayer has had to have her leg amputated—they feared a malignant growth.[3]   I have just been there to inquire and the accounts are good.   Chas. N. & Sally had their second sitting this P.M.   No result, mrs. P. could hardly get entranced.   It is a pity—but N. is already a *moral* convert, and that is all I care for.

Bring a list of all the desiderata of the place with you!   The Fitchburg R. R. has a train for Somerville at 1.30, 1.45, 2.25 P.M.[4]   I can meet you neither Thursday nor Friday at the morning train, but I can in the evening, so let me know when to expect you.   I exult in the speedy prospect.

W.J.

ALS: MH bMS Am 1092.9 (1868)

[1] Mrs. Fassitt (perhaps Fassett) was not identified.

[2] AGJ put an asterisk before 'Andrew' and wrote '*Our coloured servant.' in the left margin.

[3] Grace Thayer was not identified.

[4] The Fitchburg Railroad operated trains to Vermont and Canada through Somerville, near Cambridge.

From Alice Howe Gibbens James

Tuesday noon. [May 29, 1894]

Darling William,

Yesterday Moore brought the mail and as the flies were biting his horse I wrote you a miserable post-card only.[1]   Today he is coming again with an order.   It is well that the Taussigs are not coming till Thursday for another day of rain has come.   Yesterday I discovered another woodbine still alive and Billy and I dug about and manured it then tidied up around the woodshed and planted a few more nasturtiums all in time for this beautiful rain.   The country needs it all. Indoors we are having a cheerful day.   I have been covering a sofa with Billy's help and we have a great log burning in the fire place so with plenty to do we keep very cheerful.   Twice a day I play a game of authors with the children,—the same game we played with in Weymouth so long ago.

How nice it was that you went with Mrs Whitman to the Sargents. And how curious that the heroine of Mrs Dorr's tale should be an old friend of yours.[2]   You remember what I told you of the Saratoga hotel episode.   Somehow the news from Syracuse does not afflict me because it [is] *not* bad news.   The wall once done we shall be so much to the fore for the future.   Moreover it will absolve you from refunding to Bob part of the purchase money!   (This is amiable on my part—a joke!) What do you suppose is the cause of your headache? I don't see how you lecture with it aching. You seem so high and far from me, as if days and weeks were to go on without my being with you. Heaven soften the heart of Mrs Gorham and incline it towards Chocorua. Please send me a check for 25 dollars after June 1. Moore will cash it.

AL: MH bMS Am 1092.9 (341)

[1] Moore was not identified, but he may be Fred Moore; see letter to AGJ of 10 June 1891.

[2] See letter to AGJ of 17 May 1894.

To Margaret Mary James

June 5th. 1894

Sweet Peg

I take my pen in hand to write good night to my darling little daughter. We have had a supper party for students and your ma has gone to bed, dead tired, and I must follow. Either I or your grandma will come to you on Thursday night. Much love to Billy.— Miller was here at the party.—I hope you can read this yourself.[1] I also hope you keep yourself straigt, and throw your arms up quite regular.

With love to you all and "bien des choses à Julie," I am

Your loving   Dad.

ALS: MH bMS Am 1092.9 (2979)

Address: Miss M. M. James | c/o Mrs. William James | Chocorua | N.H

The postmark is illegible.

[1] WJ is referring to the fact that he was printing, using capital letters. At the end of the letter, however, he wrote 'I am . . . Dad' in cursive.

To George Holmes Howison,

Newport, R.I., June 11. '94

My dear Howison,

I got duly your letter of the 25th., but tho't that I would see Stratton before replying. Everything will go on now as if nothing had happened. M——g took Stratton's visit too seriously and you took M.'s letter too seriously—hence your fears. M. is sensitive by nature and has smarted under the ferocious enmity which he has aroused in some of his colleagues in Germany, one of the ugliest incidents in the academic life of that country that I know. You have no conception of the hideous virulence of some of it. Well, knowing that they will disdain to discriminate between a vacation course at Harvard and a regular academic course, he felt that if S. should go to Leipzig with only his summer course to brag about, they would rejoice in hearing that that was all that the great M——g could do, and speread wide the news of his superficiality. Moreover, he thought that after the correspondence, etc., Mr Stratton might expect more, whilst he, M., couldn't physically give more than the one hour a day to the whole class. Thus between his reputation abroad, his desire to do much for S., and his inability thereto, he felt "bad" and wrote you the letter of which you send me a copy.

Stratton seems perfectly to see into the situation, and if he only insists on making it clear in Leipzig that what he took with M. was a vacation demonstration course for ordinary teachers, and not one for professionals, all will go smoothly, and you need not fret any more.

My work, Gottlob! is over, and I am on my way for a fortnight in the N. Carolina M$^{\underline{ts}}$ to "recuperate" withal. Warm regards to you both, from

Yours always | Wm James

ALS: CU-B

To Alice Howe Gibbens James

Newport June 11. '94

Dearest Alice,

I am having two and a half sleepy days here, with *no* headache yesterday, and no *regrets*. The postponement of a day is no harm, I take it. I received your letter with its enclosures from Logan etc.,[1] but can't tell whether it was written Saturday or Sunday, so I still hope for another to day by the later mail, with something possibly from Cowies in it. Went yesterday to see the Warings and the Coleman's,[2] also to Miss W.'s studio[3] and to a sewage purifying apparatus which W. has invented, in the port. Am going again now to the Coleman's to see his mexican sketches and photogs. All are sorry you are not along. Tweedy is very nice—no such impression as I gave you. I hope things, especially cesspools, carpets and clothes, will go well at the house. I have finished Tess which I found here.[4] What a descent into the melodramatic and improbable in the last 3rd of the book. It shows how hard perfection is to carry through. The first

⅔ merited to belong to a perfect whole. Tess is much like you, except that she was a bit more patient. I am really anxious to hear how it was with Peggy after her fright. Address me *once* at Blowing Rock, Mitchell Co, N.C. but don't enclose anything very valuable. Then up till Friday (say) at Linville ditto.

Love to you all.

Your | W.J

ALS: MH bMS Am 1092.9 (1870)

[1] Logan was not identified.

[2] Samuel Colman (or Coleman) (1832–1920), American landscape painter, at the time living in Newport.

[3] Daisy Waring.

[4] Thomas Hardy (1840–1928), British author, *Tess of the D'Urbervilles* (1891).

To Alice Howe Gibbens James

Blowing Rock, N.C. | Wednesday June 13. [1894] | 9.30 P.M. Beloved Wife, The journey hither proved much simpler this time than the last. The train from Jersey City at 4.30 was a Pullman car one with but few people and we reached Hickory at ½ past 12, and took immediately the narrow gauge road to Lenoir where we had a poor dinner, but got a good light wagon and horse to bring us up here for $4.00. The journey as far as Lenoir was very hot, but a tremendous thunder shower cleared the air whilst we were dining and laid the dust, and we were soon winding our way up amongst the sweet smelling woods to this lofty ridge which we reached in 5 hours, walking the last hour of the way. The hotel is just open and clean, and the air deliciously pure and neither warm nor cold. I did wish for you by my side as we were driving into the lower valleys. C.F.A. is a good companion however in your absence. You can telegraph me here, and I am trusting that if anything goes wrong you will not fail to do so. It seemed queer to have to go off without news from your mother of how she found the young ones at Chocorua. I have no doubt we shall enjoy the summer better there than ever before, the more for the lack of horse cow & man complication; and it will be good for us all to develope our pedestrian powers.—I wrote you very briefly concerning my visit to Elly. Her eldest, Minny, is much changed and looked morbidly interesting and delicate(!) Her mother told me in secret that she was engaged to a very nice fellow named Peabody, now studying law, who would inherit wealth and comes from good people.[1] Rosina has outgrown her blowsiness, but is not as handsome as she promised to be. Her mother says she cares nothing for the male sex, but gets excited about "Causes," such as woman's suffrage. "Bay" was a broad faced, smiling, plain thing with the look of health and happiness about her that is so much better than ordinary beauty. (*You* have both!)—I long for news, but so far I'm glad we came here, and if the weather keeps good we shall no doubt make it a real success. The country is suffering much from drouth so far. Good night! my own darling from your loving

W.J.

ALS: MH bMS Am 1092.9 (1871)

[1] Mary Temple Emmet (Minny) Peabody (b. 1872), daughter of Ellen Hunter, married Archibald Russell Peabody (1873–1908) on 23 August 1894.

To Alice Howe Gibbens James

Blowing Rock, Friday June 15. 94 | 9 P.M.

Dearest Alice,

I slept two hours yesterday afternoon, 10 last night, 1½ this morning, and 1½ this afternoon, and shall drop asleep now the minute I go to bed. That shows that the change of air takes a holt. But it is not conducive to eloquent letter writing, the state of brain that goes with it. This afternoon I got your letter of Tuesday, with your mother's enclosed. Poor Billy I was more afraid about Peggy than about him, and I am sorry that he received such a shock. I hope hers was slight—your mother says nothing about her. Nor do you say whether Bowditch writes that he will send away the man. I am going to write immediately to Harry about the legacy and Bob.

C.F.A. and I spent the morning on one high hill top with our books, and the afternoon after our naps in doors on another to which we were led by the only other guest in the house, a certain Col. Atkinson, a northerner settled in this state who has been all over creation and is an exceptionally intelligent man and good talker.[1] But the country is in a deplorable condition, a months drouth, covering everything with powdery dust, the foliage half killed by an untimely hard frost two weeks ago, so that all the foreground trees are stripped of leaves and the rhododendrons killed, the air full of whitey mist, so that there are no distant views, and the heat oppressive the moment one begins to go up hill. No tonic in the air; but a most delicious cool softness when one sits still and gets the breeze. Such weather can't last forever, but it can only be relieved by copious rain, which on the

whole will be even worse *for us*. But I'm glad we came all the same—
it is a complete change, and you see by my sleep how it does take
hold.   I enclose you an article from the Richmond paper which is
evidently scientific—on cake-making. I think we shall stay here over
tomorrow and then advance to Linville. I hope that Harry gets on
right well, and does a right smart sight of study, now that my disturbing presence is gone.—As for you, your presence seems like one
of those elusive things, too good to have ever been quite true.

Your   Wm.

ALS: MH bMS Am 1092.9 (1873)

[1] Colonel Atkinson was not identified. Hoffman Atkinson (d. 1901), a colonel from
the Civil War, a businessman and diplomat, had lived in several countries and traveled
extensively, but his obituary does not place him in North Carolina.

To Alice Howe Gibbens James

                    Linville, Mitchell Co. N.C. | June 18. 94 | 11. A.M.
Dearest Wifelet—*What* a rich fat envelope that was which the hotel
clerk handed me an hour ago, with your letter of the 13th and all
the enclosures. I am glad that the two walls are to be separate after
all, even tho' we lose 4 inches of space thereby. It saves all possible
complications in the future. As for Harry, his agonies are most characteristic—but under the circumstances we will of course keep the
thing an absolute secret from every one, including Bob.[1] I wrote to
K.P.L. by this mail to that effect, also to Mrs. Whitman, already on
her way. If Chadwick's english friend really should want our place,
would it not be sinful for us to refuse the Newcastle offer—a queer
one anyhow, and from whom. The advantage of Newcastle would
be nearness, and the learning of boating by the boys. I fear the air
would not agree with me, though, as well as that of our own dear
little place.—I will accept the offer of the Brooklyn institute, condi-
tionally on the Presidents giving me leave to absence myself from six
lectures on Saturday AM.'s.[2]

We had a most exquisite drive from B.R. yestreen.[3] The road is
unsurpassably lovely in its way, and strange to say it had been rained
over the previous day for a good part of its extent. Linville is to
B. R. as hyperion to a satyr. The hotel is *perfect,* all but the baggy
wire mattresses, which however are easily got over by dragging the
mattress off on to the floor. The blight of the trees is here invisible
and we shall stay until it is time to go home, say Saturday of this

week, without extending our tour. *Don't write again after receiving this!*
I am feeling very hearty—walked 6 or 8 miles of the road yesterday—
and am going off into the woods with C.F.A. for a couple of hours
now.—I suppose that this will reach you at Chocorua, but I send it
to Cambridge. Darling wife—the thought of your recognition of me
does me unspeakable good all these days. Love to noble old Harry!

Your | Wm.

ALS: MH bMS Am 1092.9 (1874)

[1] For HJ's distress about the possibility of AJ's diary becoming public knowledge,
see *Correspondence*, 2:309–12. HJ wanted RJ to have a copy because he feared an
outburst from RJ should he discover that the diary was being kept secret from him.

[2] Eliot allowed the absences. WJ gave six lectures at the Brooklyn Institute of Arts
and Sciences in January and February 1896 on "Recent Researches into Exceptional
Mental Phenomena" (see *ML*, 458), but the fact that arrangements were being made
more than a year in advance casts some doubt as to whether these are the lectures
in question and raises the possibility that other lectures were being discussed.

[3] Blowing Rock, N.C.

To Alice Howe Gibbens James

Sunday, June 24. 94 | 10.30 P.M.

Dearest Wifelet,

Home an hour ago, to find harry with Gurdon[1] & Roger W.[2] in his
bed room. He looks well, and I do hope he'll pass. No handwriting
of yours since your letter of last Monday A.M.—Can it be that Mr.
Stratton has been sending *your* letters back to you with others that
he says he's sent?

We started from Cranbery yesterday at seven A.M. & have consequently travelled more than 36 hours. The way was intensely dusty
and hot until this P.M., but the Shenandoah Valley was beautiful &
interesting. The good part of the trip was Linville—and that was
really good. How I long for that forest-perfumed air again! How I
should have relished having you here—you and I all alone in the
house—on my arrival. But such is not our destiny. I will get
through what I have to do as quickly as I can, but I am pretty sure
I can't get off before Thursday afternoon. Wednesday is commencement, and I ought, being here so near it, to stay for that. Moreover
I must write a review of Marshall's book on Pleasure, pain, and aesthetics, which I have read on my journey, and see to a lot of final
things.[3] Harry exam⁵ last till Saturday. I hope that you are in equilibrium there, and not too lonely. You have a servant apiece, if you

count the dog as one!   I have bro't back $15.50, and am in prime
elastic condition, both of body and mind.   C.A. & I went on Friday
up grandfather mountain which did me a lot of good, and on Saturday at 6 A.M.   I went on an entrancing walk of 5 miles on one of the
forest roads—I never breathed such sweet air.   Good night my own
dearest, I am so glad I am near unto you again, safely and soundly.
This house of ours looks sweet in tone, and I am ready for a bath
and bed.

Your   Wm.

Kiss Peggy and Billy tenderly for me—also Tweedy and Tommy.[4]
How I hope the Cochrans will come to the scratch.[5]

ALS: MH bMS Am 1092.9 (1878)

[1] Gurdon Saltanstall Parker.

[2] Roger Wolcott (b. 1877), graduated from Harvard in 1899, a lawyer.   For his parents see letter to AGJ of 27 May 1894, note 8.

[3] WJ, review of Henry Rutgers Marshall, *Pain, Pleasure, and Aesthetics* (1894), in
Nation 59 (19 July 1894): 49–51; reprinted in *ECR*.

[4] Tommy was not identified.

[5] Perhaps Emily Belden Walsh Cochran, a relative (see *Correspondence*, 2:301).

To Alice Howe Gibbens James

Cambr. June 24. [25] 94[1]

Dearest Alice,

Your letter came this afternoon with all its inclosures, encluding
the check from Geo. Kennedy who seems a very generous person.[2]
I feel badly about Ladd, whose tone is one of deep personal irritation,
and the discussion is on ground for which there is no objective solution, and is a most unprofitable matter.   It makes one feel like writing
no more reviews!*   For black ants, try borax and suger powdered
together.   I have bo't some insect-powder to bring up.

Poor Bob Davis   Or rather poor B.D.'s mother & wife.   How the
latter will idealize him now![3]

I bkfstd. at your ma's & lunched & supped at the Club.   M——berg
has had a very painful (not dangerous, he says) time with his heart
during the past week.   I spent the morning writing letters.   In the
late P.M. went to the marble cutter's, who has done nothing so far, and
to the cemetery, where the poor little pine is dead again, and the rose
bushes *so* sickly.[4]   Harry was with me.   I saw Warner who is in great
heart.   I called at Brooks's to see about the lot-sale, but the house

was closed.[5] The day is muggy warm. I lack sleep and must close. I have been to your mother's again this evening. Thank you for your dear expressions of affection in your letters!

> Your own—W.J.

If a dog acts queerly, you should always keep him tied or enclosed, and under observation until you notice him distinctly delirious, when it will probably be hydrophobia. But such a thing seems to me incredible in so young a pup. I came very near bringing home a young bear-cub from Linville. I could have bo't him for $5.00.—Middleton missed the train to day.—

> Good night! | W.J.

How bad this french news is![6]

*I have just re-read it—its tone is not what I thought when I hastily ran over it this P.M., so I don't care.

ALS: MH bMS Am 1092.9 (1877)

[1] This letter was written probably on 25 June, not 24 June, as evidenced from its contents and from those of the preceding letter.

[2] Perhaps George Golding Kennedy.

[3] Robert Howe Davis (1868–1894), an 1891 graduate of Harvard, died in California on 19 June. On 13 June he had married Katherine Lewis. His parents were William Whitney Davis and Julia Wilder Robinson Davis.

[4] WJ is referring to AJ's tombstone and to the grave of Herman James.

[5] Perhaps J. Mason Brooks, a real estate agent in Cambridge.

[6] Marie-François-Sadi Carnot (1837–1894), president of France, was stabbed to death at about 9 P.M. on 24 June 1894.

To James Mark Baldwin

> Cambridge, June 25. [26] 94[1]

My poor Baldwin,

I am *very* sorry; but the hopelessness and springlessness of early convalescence is well known, and in the twinkling of an eye all will be changed a little later on.[2]

My wife and I may possibly pay a visit at Bar Harbor in August. If we do I shall go over to SW.H to see you.[3]

Cattell has sent me proof of Ladd's retort, which I have enjoyed for its literary cleverness—Ladd is certainly a growing man in this respect,—but I have felt rather badly because I seem to discern an undertone of personal irritation which perhaps is justified by what I wrote of the youths & maidens etc.[4] It makes me wish never to write a review again! I respect and admire Ladd's capacity very much, and this particular "Galileo" and "Lavoisier" discussion we have stumbled into, is about as profitless a thing as one can conceive.[5]

Sursum *cor*—my dear Baldwin. The sun will shine on you yet.

Yours always | Wm James

ALS: Bodleian Library, University of Oxford

[1] Possibly misdated. On 26 June WJ wrote AGJ that he had been misdating his letters for three days, which would make 26 June the correct date of this letter.

[2] Baldwin was recovering from measles.

[3] Bar Harbor and Southwest Harbor are villages on Mt. Desert Island, Maine.

[4] Ladd responded to WJ's review of *Psychology: Descriptive and Explanatory* in "Is Psychology a Science?" *Psychological Review* 1 (July 1894): 392–95.

[5] For the reference to Galileo and Lavoisier see *ECR*, 485.

To James McKeen Cattell

Cambr. June 26. 94

Dear Cattell,

Hyatt says he cannot review Bateson.[1] As it is a book I have been desirous of reading carefully, and as only the more psychological parts of it (if there be any) are desirable for the Review, I should be glad to try my hand at it briefly myself, *if you can't get a really competent biologist.* Mail it to me at *Chocorua N.H.* if you so decide.

Ladd's article rather fills me with sadness for I fear he is personally hurt. The literary cleverness of the reply must however be some consolation to him! It is great. Of course I can make no retort, for I am on the barren heath of mere subjective peevishness and dissatisfaction, so long as no real theory of body and mind exists. I refuse however to believe that there *is* no matter for theory hidden away in the facts, or that the human mind will forever be without one. I am sorry (or half-sorry) that I let out my feelings as I did, in my review.

Yours truly | Wm James

ALS: DLC

[1] WJ reviewed William Bateson, *Materials for the Study of Variation* (1894) in *Psychological Review* 1 (November 1894): 627–30; reprinted in *ECR*.

To Alice Howe Gibbens James

Tuesday, June 26th. [1894] | 6 P.M.

Dearest Wife,

A bad day! no letter from you, and even worse than that, both Harry & I forgot the dentists engagement. It has been daily on my mind, only yesterday I looked at the calendar for it, but some judicial blindness has fallen upon me, I have misdated my letters for three days past, and I tho't that to day was the 25th and to morrow the bespoken 26th. It fills me with disgust for myself. Harry went there at noon, and I at half past two o'clock, but we both found the Office closed. To set off against this, I have received $267.77 from Holt, and Eliot permits me to accept the Brooklyn Institute proposal.[1] Your mother is much pleased at finding that she has about 900 dollars to her credit in the sinking fund. *We* have about $250; and the Wyckoff lawyer, so Warner judges, is ready to pay up as soon as Henry's document goes in, so we may be put to no embarrassment at all. A book has come from Henry containing two of his comedies, written to act, with the announcement of a volume to contain two more. Poor boy! it is pathetic to see him failing even before he starts. I will bring up the volume, and you shall read it aloud.[2]

It has been an intensely hot day. I have looked all over for my linen coat but cannot find it. Have you put it away, or taken it along? I have been grappling with a review of Marshall's aesthetics, an excessively irksome task, which does not "go" at all. Perhaps I had better not let that detain me here but bring it to be finished by your side. I have just been over at Hyatts, the whole family on the lawn, playing tennis with Nichols, looking so cool and good, and secluded.[3] Mrs. H. sent you her love. She must be an able woman in her sphere of wife and house-angel. They had a delicious iced drink.—*10 P.M.* I stopped to go to dinner at the Club, whither I had invited Nichols. M——berg was there, sick of his bargain about the summer school, and troubled to day with his heart. After which, adjournment to our top piazza, where, with Miller the Strattons, Nichols & Harry, the rest of the evening was passed.—The day has been intensely sultry. To-night is cooler, with some threat of rain to morrow. I have engaged Farlow's gown for Commencement, & M——berg Palmer's. P. has gone to Ann Arbor to deliver an oration, & Royce to Minneapolis for exam.ˢ Harry who has just gone to bed, has given me your sweet letter to him. I see that it is now quite impossible for me to get off before Friday, so don't expect me on Thursday. In any case you

won't come to the Depôt. At most you might be at Nickerson's Hotel
without the children, and we walk home together. But don't do this
unless its convenient in every way. I am sorry to hear that Louise is
so un-Walt Whitman like in her powers of enjoying whatever comes
along.—It is a warning to one's self!

Good night, my dear One.

Yours, | Wm.

Tell sweet Peg that I came mighty near bring[ing] home a new pet
for her, a sweet young bear 4 months old who sucked my fingers like
a child, and whom I might have bo't for 5 dollars at Linville.

I deeply regret not having bo't you a Transcript to night.[4] I have
just been to your mothers, finding them cooling off on the porch,
but they had not read their copy.

ALS: MH bMS Am 1092.9 (1879)

[1] See letter to AGJ of 18 June 1894.
[2] HJ, *Theatricals* (1894), containing *Tenants* and *Disengaged*.
[3] Alpheus Hyatt and Andella Beebe Hyatt had four children.
[4] The *Boston Evening Transcript*.

To Alice Howe Gibbens James

Cambr. June 27. 1894 | 10. P.M.

Dearest Alice,

Dentist yesterday filled the hour, so no expense. Harry had 5 fill-
ings put in the P.M., & goes next Monday for 5 more(!). I run till
the fall.

Your letter this P.M. with thanks! I will aim at the Friday noon-
train or die, though it is very hard to get "through."

I breakfasted at the Child's he very well looking—Helen reported
to be "wild" with joy, ever since the first 3 days of the ship. Went to
Sanders in Farlow's red faced gown.[1] "Parts" very good indeed.
John Fiske, James Thayer, Lane,[2] and others, got degrees of LLD.
Great plaudits over Fiske. Too late for dinner ticket but after dinner
got standing admission to Memorial. Choate's address to Eliot very
common and poor. Eliot's reply too cold.[3] Chas. Norton presided,
with no great success—I left before the other speakers got at it.
Went then on a round of visits, Burnett (poor plucky thing),[4] Hooper
(he very talkative about trip, and very well, Nelly sending love to
you)[5] Ross, Cary,[6] Stoughton,[7] Shaler,[8] Agassiz,[9] Grace Norton, & your
Ma. Ready now for bed, with a morrow busy with affairs. Good

night! Harry gone safely to bed, in preparation for his exam.ⁿ to morrow.

Good night! good night! It has been intensely hot all day till about 6 P.M.

I lied about our share of the Estate interest in Higginson's hands. We already drew it out, and paid it either to Bob or to Turner. We own but 141 dollars of the Savings Bank fund.

Your loving (and sweating) | W.J.

ALS: MH bMS Am 1092.9 (1880)

[1] WJ attended Harvard's commencement exercises in a borrowed gown.

[2] George Martin Lane (1823–1897), American classicist, professor at Harvard, re-tired in 1894.

[3] Joseph Hodges Choate (1832–1917), American diplomat. The dinner at Memo-rial Hall was to mark Eliot's twenty-five years as president of Harvard.

[4] Mabel Lowell Burnett or her husband, Edward Burnett (1849–1925), American politician, at the Lowell home on Elmwood Avenue.

[5] Ellen Sturgis Hooper (b. 1872), daughter of Edward William Hooper.

[6] WJ could have used Brattle Street for his stroll home, stopping at 92 Brattle St., the home of Sarah Gray Cary (1830–1898) and Emma Cary (1833–1918), sisters of Elizabeth Cary Agassiz.

[7] At 90 Brattle St., next door to the Cary sisters, lived Mary Fiske Stoughton, widow of American diplomat Edwin Wallace Stoughton (1818–1882) and step-mother of John Fiske.

[8] Shaler lived at 25 Quincy St., along a possible route from Brattle Street to Irving.

[9] Alexander Agassiz lived at 36 Quincy St., toward Irving Street from the Shaler home.

To Henry Rutgers Marshall

Chocorua, N.H. | July 5. '94

My dear Marshall,

I have at last read your book and sent off a review to the Nation. I feel as if I owed you contrite apologies for the delay. You may remember that I gave you warning; but I didn't think myself that the procrastination would extend so far. I was sick in bed for five weeks in the spring, and my miserable head made it impossible to do any reading beyond what was neccessary for my College tasks. The book is a robust one, easier to feel vaguely dissatisfied with than to correct. But my candid opinion is that it will remain as one of the landmarks in the history of the subject. I wish it might have been a little less drily written!

It seems to me more and more as if pain proper were a specific sensation, and that you are wrong in lumping it with all the other displeasures. One verbal point: Why, when in common speech *pleasant* is a sufficiently good word, should writers on ethics and aesthetics think it neccessary always to employ the barbarous form *pleasurable*?

I hope that you are well, and having, or being-about-to-have, a good wholesome vacation. After such a book, you'll have to turn to writing another one to make you feel happy. Why not take up special effects in aesthetics? Not much hope?—I was gloating lately over some specimens of the new blown glass vessels etc which Mr. Tiffany has been making, and which surpass anything venetian. Many of them very dull and dingy in tone, with such effects as any candy window or heap of rotting vegetables will present. Yet they seemed so unspeakably *precious*? Why so? It may be that your formula, of mutual reinforcement of elements by contrast etc will cover the case. But this ought to be shown in detail. Why not take up these glasses as a specific problem?—The best thing about your aesthetics is its empiricism, and subjectivism.

Yours always faithfully | Wm James

ALS: MNS

To James Mark Baldwin

Chocorua, N.H. | July 8-94.

Dear Baldwin:

I am glad that you are so much better and that you are in such a nice place as you describe. We both thank you for the cordiality of your invitation. Did I say August. As matters have turned out, our visit to Mt. Desert, *if it comes off at all* is more likely to come off in September than in August. But, for certain good reasons, it may not be possible for it to come off at all. Nothing would please me so much as a few days with you, if they could be vouchsafed by envious Time. I haven't yet read your article on imitation!,[1] and have but just glanced on your report on Psychology in the July Number.[2] I shall soon catch up, however, now that I am here. I am glad you are working on the question of emotional expression. I am just writing a discussion on Wundt's, Lehman's, Iron's Sollier's comments on Lange's and my theory.[3] When must the Cyclopedia article on personality be finished? I have asked the question of Mr. —— who wrote me on behalf of the publishers, but I get no reply.[4]

Always truly yours, | Wm. James.

TC: MH bMS Am 1092.1

[1] James Mark Baldwin, "Imitation: A Chapter in the Natural History of Consciousness," *Mind,* n.s., 3 (January 1894): 26–55.

[2] James Mark Baldwin, "Psychology Past and Present," *Psychological Review* 1 (July 1894): 363–91.

[3] WJ, "The Physical Basis of Emotion," *Psychological Review* 1 (September 1894): 516–29. For references to the writings of Wundt, Lehmann, David Irons (1870–1907), Scottish psychologist, Paul Auguste Sollier (1861–1933), French psychologist, and Carl Georg Lange (1834–1900), Danish physiologist, see *EPs,* 362, 375, 376.

[4] WJ, "Person and Personality," *Johnson's Universal Cyclopaedia* (1895); reprinted in *EPs.* The publisher was A. J. Johnson in New York City.

To Alice Howe Gibbens James

Ridgefield,[1] Friday | July 20th [1894]

Dearest wife,

The C's met me at the station at 6 oclock yesterday and we drove 3 miles to their hill top, a wide viewed rolling country, with a good many rich settlers—a fine new stone house very handsomely furnished with the strippings of the old world, splendid plumbing and bathtub off my room, and a noble bed in which I slept well. The country is somewhat parched (though nothing like what it was at Boston), the thermometer 86° here in the coolest place. The Craftses have been hanging pictures and putting up ceramic treasures all the morning in expectation of a party of people to lunch. I am resigned, but far from eager. The two hosts, their two youngest daughters and the governess are the only inmates at present, and I am glad you didn't come, as you would have felt the slightly negative and benumbing influence of C.—as indeed I do. In the presence of such heavy *things,* the lightness of our little wayside life seems quite ideal. Half the good of being in the country disappears when instead of a cottage, you have a ponderous mansion to keep up—and dress for.—I have been sitting on the piazza reading Bradley's Appearance and Reality—not very happy, for my bad spirits about myself keep up. *What* a dose I gave you! and *why*—that is what I ask, and get no answer save out of an evil tree there comes for[th] evil fruit etc.—I hope that you keep up the family prayers in my absence.

Kiss dear old Harry & Billy and give my love & reverence to your Mother.

Your Wm

ALS: MH bMS Am 1092.9 (1882)

[1] James Mason Crafts lived in Ridgefield, Conn.

To Alice Howe Gibbens James

Cambr. July 23. 94 | 6. P.M.

Dearest Alice

I am just back from Ridgefield, after a cool ride, and am to stay here, writing my Encyclopedia article, until Friday when I go to Shaler's.   I got one letter from you at the Craftses and am naturally rather anxious for news.   Your account of Bill's drowning adventure was rather provokingly vague, since "after a raft" didn't explain why he had to swim ashore, or what became of the boat, nor did you say how much "overtired" he got.   I hope it has all passed off, whatever it was, and that he now, having had the experience of a boat accident, will be able to boss every future situation of the sort he may fall into. There is nothing like familiarity with danger to give a cool head. Please give the dear boy my love, and say how glad I am it was no worse.   I find Mrs. Stratton ill with cholera morbus since last night, and D.ʳ Mackintire in attendance.[1]   Royce having gone to get Mrs. Child to come and show her some feminine sympathy, he, she, & Henrietta[2] have just arrived, and are conferring with Stratton—9.30. St. told Mrs. C. that his wife was asleep so Royce, & I and a man named Aikins Prof.ᵗ at Cleveland, whom I first knew at Yale,[3] have been to the Club to dine, and after a short visit to M——berg's house, I returned there to look at the Magazines, and then came home, through the cool good smelling night.   Cambridge air is good too, and the rain of Saturday night has freshened up things very much. I should say that Simon has kept your mother's place as green as Stratton has ours and Fox his.[4]

Now, as for the Craftses, they were busy as beavers the whole time getting their house in order—it is a heavy contract.   I consequently didn't see a great deal of them in the forenoon, which was O. K. as it enabled me to get on with Bradley's book.   We drove in the P.M. of Friday & Saturday but the air was so sultry, and the roads so dust laden and the sky so filled with sullen heat haze that it reminded me of London in the hot days last summer, and I could only try to compute what it *should* be in good weather.   It certainly is not preferable to Chocorua, and I confess I don't well see why the Craftses chose it for such a heavy investment.   But he says it grows on one very much. There is something niggardly about him, but nothing of the sort about her.   I *relish* her, straight; and she seemed unfeignedly sorry not to have you there.

All is quiet overhead; and for the next few days I expect to be busy over the tedious article "personality." I am quite rested and in good spirits and slept perfectly all 4 nights at the Craftses, and expect to do so tonight. I have got the nation's check and your other enclosures, and long to get news from you. I dare say one letter has gone to Ridgefield and will be returned. I have ordered all letters to be sent from the P.O. here until farther orders, & will send everything to you. I hope that the drain has started, & isn't giving you too much perplexity. Perhaps, though, it hasn't started yet.

Best of love to your Mother, & no end to yourself from your own
Wm.

ALS: MH bMS Am 1092.9 (1883)

[1] The only physician of that name in Cambridge was H. B. McIntire, at 4 Garden St.

[2] Henrietta Child.

[3] Herbert Austin Aikins (1867–1946), Canadian-born professor of philosophy at Western Reserve University in Cleveland, received his doctorate from Yale in 1891.

[4] Simon is Simon Hassett.

To James Mark Baldwin

Cambridge, July 24. [1894]

I have begun "personality" taking for granted the existence of a short "person" article. Or shall I write both "person" and "personality"?—or run them into one article with two titles? This last would seem best.

Of course, I assume that another hand is to treat of person legally and theologically.

W.J.

TC: MH bMS Am 1092.1

To Alice Howe Gibbens James

Irving S!, July 25. 94 | 10.15 P.M.

Dearest Alice

Your letter of Sunday arrived here this A.M. forwarded from Ridgefield, and this afternoon came yours of yesterday. Little Bill seems delicate, according to your account, but your general mood is serene, so I feel happy. I am just in from the Club, where I had Jim Putnam to dinner, and a very pleasant circle after the thunderstorm on the piazza, farlow, royce, Munsterberg, Warner, etc etc. Lemonade to wind up. The personality article goes bravely on, and will be finished to morrow. It is the only genuine *rubbish* that I ever wrote. I bkfstd. with Grace N. at 10 o'clock and went out at 1 and bought some ice cream with which I regaled the Strattons. At 4 I went into town to find your Aunt Maria, but again failed to find the house.[1] Can't you send me the number? Last night I enjoyed myself very much at the theatre, the company being poor, and the Grande Duchesse having all the life taken out of it by omissions and flat english jokes. But the prima donna was a ladylike and interesting french woman, and I experience[d] a good amount of cosmic emotion, with a revelation of truth at the end of it consisting in the sudden perception that my own real circumstances were richer and fuller of cosmic elements than any play I knew.[2] The lucid scene spread roundabout our house at Chocorua, the living you in your rarity and love within, Switzerland and France tamed and made domestic properties, with the singing whistling Marie visible all over the place at once, with 10 times the beauty of any prima donna, the incomparable Tweedy and his brethren, the unique mother-in law—the precious tutor[3]—all of it came shining in upon me at once to show how much richer the reality at our doors is than any possible fiction. It was a great illumination for which I remain most grateful. It is queer how you *feel* things sometimes all at once, which you fail to grasp by thinking. I doubt whether you can feel this as I did, certainly the mere enumeration will not make you. I have got to take Grace Norton there tomorrow night. She said she had never been to a comic opera in her life. It is a little of a nuisance to have the Strattons in the house with one, but they are as neat as wax, and thanks to him the place is luxuriantly green. Cogswell has paid 3000 to Jae Walsh's representative on our account and we ought to have the money this week.[4] I go on Friday to the Shaler's at North Tisbury Duke's County Mass. to stay till monday and then to visit Cotuit and So. Yarmouth. Don't address me there unless in case of need, but have a good letter mailed for me on Monday next, so that I may get the news on my return. The Cummings's were here to day, Mrs. C. evidently *guter Hoffnung.*—I don't seem to find time for anything, but am determined not to worry, and will now go to bed, altho' I feel as if there was some important thing still left unsaid.

Love to you all, and chiefly to you, my wife,

W.J.

ALS: MH bMS Am 1092.9 (1884)

[1] An unidentified relative of AGJ.

[2] Camille D'Arville (1863–1932), Dutch-born actress and singer who in advertisements for the show was said to be as "cool as a ton of ice," was performing in *The Grand Duchess*, probably an English version of the comic opera *La Grande Duchesse de Gérolstein* (1867) by Jacques Offenbach (1819–1880), French composer.

[3] Lamar Middleton.

[4] Probably part of the settlement of the Wyckoff estate. Cogswell was not identified but was possibly a lawyer handling the Wyckoff matter; see letter to AGJ of 26 June 1894.

To Alice Howe Gibbens James

Cambr. July 26. '94 | 9.30. P.M.

Dearest Alice,

I am just back from Grace N's where I have been dining and spending the evening on the window-porch listening to the first cricket of the year. She decided not to go to the theatre, much to my relief, because Phil. Davis and the young widow were to return to night, and it seemed to her incongruous—which testifies to her moral delicacy, I think.[1] I finished my article at one o'clock (the only *deliberate* rubbish I ever wrote)[2] and after dining at the Club, went to see about Alice's tombstone, which will be up when we come back. The wreath is awful, but it can't be helped. The day was cooler, and after the rain of yestreen, Cambridge looked charming as I walked back. I went through Browne & Nichols's new building in order to tell of it to the boys. They are lathing and shingling it. It is an immense structure with two very large fine rooms on the western end, and a third one in the attic. Lots of smaller rooms, and what promises to be a good system of warming and ventilating. The air is to come over hot water pipes in the cellar, and be discharged near the ceilings, & the big ventilating openings start near the floor. I hope it will work. At any rate the boys must feel more comfortable in such fine spacious rooms. Returning I coincided with the postman who gave me your letter. The Savings bank book is absolutely unfindable. Ask your mother if it be possible that I may have left it in her house. The last I remember of it, I *think,* is showing her the account, when I was explaining to her how much she had. But I may not have shown it on the book itself. Look in my red portfolio, either in the smaller sitting room or in my bed room, as a last desperate hope. We shall each owe for the rebuilding about 1100 dollars. Of this your mother has already 680 in Cowies hands, 120 in mine, and something like 180 in the Savings Bank, leaving 120 to make up. If the Wyckoff money comes in in time I can pay instanter and settle later. In any case I can do that. But if she has any floating cash, she had better send it, to diminish the possible borrowing. If I could get at the Savings bank fund, together with my College salary due Aug 1. we could pay without borrowing, even if the Wyckoff money were postponed.—I labelled and docketed all the old receipted bills this afternoon, wishing to do something 'considerate' of you after finishing my article. I hope you are recognizant. Don't you wish me to send up to Chocorua the bed from Beverly, and order Grant's mahogany thing to take its place? Write me any "wants" that I may fulfill them on my way back next week.—Jordan & Marsh have never sent out the bathing suits,[3] so, if you say so I will demand the money back. But a house where the women can have no bathing suits seems to me a queer thing.—Good night! good night!

W.J.

ALS: MH bMS Am 1092.9 (1885)

[1] Philip Whitney Davis was a brother of the deceased Robert Howe Davis. For the young widow see letter to AGJ of 24 June 1894.

[2] WJ, "Person and Personality."

[3] In his letter of 18 July 1894 (calendared) WJ wrote AGJ that he had ordered two "female bathing suits 6.25" from Jordan & Marsh, a Boston department store.

From Paul Bourget

27 Juillet 94

Merci de votre petit mot, mon cher William James, auquel je réponds tard et hâtivement. Le ashy side dont $\overline{vs}$ parlez a déjà laissé son goût dans mon pauvre esprit par suite de la nécessité d'une trop lourde correspondance, et pas souvent helas! avec des correspondants tels que vous!

Si $\overline{vs}$ ne m'avez pas oublié, croyez que je pense souvent à vous et au paisible Cambridge. J'y ai remué, grâce à vous, quelques idées et la lecture que j'ai faite de toute la fin de votre livre de psychologie me reste comme un grand enseignement des *possibilités* de la science moderne de l'esprit. Et puis il y a des mots que l'on garde, ce que $\overline{vs}$ m'avez dit, et que $\overline{vs}$ avez certes oublié sur le bienfait de la *drudgery*, un autre sur la bonne coutume de fixer quelquefois sa pensée sur quelque idée première et presque sans forme, et cette formule: "nous vivons sur la surface de notre être." Si apaisante pour le coeur, je ne saurais dire pourquoi.

Tandis que v̄s *psychisaitez* dans le voisinage de l'aimable professeur Norton, je peine sur mon Outre Mer, vaste résumé de mes sensations d'Amérique.__ J'oserai v̄s demander de ne pas lire ce livre en traduction.[1] V̄s ne soupconnez pas ce que devient une prose d'analyste Français transportée dans l'Anglais de quelque *reporter,* ce qui est mon cas. Je ne suis pas trop mécontent du livre, en égard à la difficulté qu'il représentait, et j'espère n'avoir jamais violé la loi sacrée de la *privacy.*

Votre frère me laisse sans nouvelles, ce dont je ne lui en veux pas. Nous autres, pauvres diables d'hommes de lettres, nous avons quelquefois de trop légitimes lassitudes de cet outil que vos compatriotes ont sagement remplacé par le type-writer. Je pense qu'il est toujours en Italie, ce dont j'espère ne pas l'envier trop longtemps.

Quand reviendrez vous en Europe? Si, à defaut de vous-même, vous envoyez, on the other side, un de vos charmants fils, rappelez vous et rappelez lui que vous avez un ami très vrai 20. rue Barbet de Jouy, ce qui est entre parenthèses, ma nouvelle adresse à Paris. Je v̄s [*illeg.*] de la campagne, à la veille de rentrer vaquer aux devoirs de cette installation. Vous savez ce que c'est que de transporter une bibliothèque!

Voulez-vous dire les souvenirs de Madame Bourget à Madame James et respects. J'y joins pour vous toutes les affectueuses pensées de votre dévoué

Paul Bourget

ALS: MH bMS Am 1092 (41)

[1] Paul Bourget, *Outre-Mer: Impressions of America* (1895).

To Sarah Wyman Whitman

Cambridge, July 31. 1894

Dear Madam,

How goes it? Hot, no doubt, but not as hot as here, I'm sure, and England and France and the rich old world of it, all pouring into your mind. I hope it makes your soul happy, and that youth, health and vigor are already coursing through your veins. It was a touching and beautiful sight to see for a moment You, the unvanquished, laid low. A little shade over the lamp, etc.—it adds to the total effect of richness! I got your letter from the steamer, and appreciate the kindness, and am so glad the treacherous sea was good. A week ago,

I left the Crafteses after a pleasant visit of three days, and had the anguish of seeing him, as he was driving me to the Station, take one of your lapidary envelopes from the P.O., and put it into his mail bag, so that I knew not, nor ever shall know, what it contained. Otherwise it gave a pleasant sense of the continuity of your existence. She, the fair "Clem" is a trump to the core. He is a good and knowing man, but why always hang back so niggardly-like? Their house is charming, the window beautiful (but what means *ciel-à-ciel*?) and as for Ridgfield, it is a good place, but I don't understand why it was the only proper place. But places grow on one, I know, and drouth and heat were raging full sore when I was there.—By way of contrast I have been for two days at Martha's Vineyard with the Shalers. How he exists with that romantic magnanimous circus going on in his head all the time, I don't know. It would mean acute mania in the rest of us, but *his* clock never runs down. But he is a dear and inestimable being, the sketch of what all men should be, and when he dies a great light will go out and darkness cover our College world.—I get awful accounts from poor H. J. of the hell which Italy proved to be for him with social duties taking all his time.[1] Not a day to himself. Be kind to the poor boy, if you meet! He says Italy is closed to him forever!— Likewise don't mention (except to him) even the existence of my sister's diary. Beside him K.P.L., my wife, and myself, you are the only person who has heard of it. You had a right to.—I have been here three days writing cyclopedia articles etc. a sorry trade, and to-morrow I go back to my simple cot in N.H. Cambridge in summer time has a delicious freedom, partly due to contrast with the conditions of term-time, partly because of the positive emptiness and shirt-sleeve life. The Quincy S! Club helps greatly.[2]

This you see is not a philosophic or witty letter. Neither is it a "human cry." Only a friendly word; a nod or smile, as it were. Don't write back unless you *must*(?!). The best thing for you now to indulge in is a system of elaborate selfishness. Forget everything!—I am sorry, now, that I write to remind you of my own trumpery existence. *Be* selfish, and animal, if you can, for three months; and in the final awful Book, I am sure, those days will be credited more highly to your account than all the rest.

Good night!

Your | W.J.

I have just been trying to write something that would do to inscribe on silver for Du Maurier. But so classic a task doesn't suit my gothic pen. Possibly it will come!

ALS: MH bMS Am 1092.9 (3917)

[1] For HJ's complaint see his letter of 29 June 1894, *Correspondence*, 2:314–16.
[2] The Colonial Club was located at 20 Quincy St., the former home of the Jameses.

To Théodore Flournoy

Chocorua (New Hampshire) | Aug 1894

My dear Flournoy,

I have thought of you often in this summer season, as the contrast between the last two summers and this one has brought you up in memory as an "associate" of the bygone periods. I wonder whether you are again at Salvan, or have passed to some new mountain height unknown to us. Wherever it be I hope it is as good a place as the Vers-chez les Blanc & Pension Cruchon which you introduced to us, and which now stand apart in my imagination as places of almost unique tranquility, salubrity and happiness. Here in this warmer and lower region, expressive as it is artistically, I find myself thirsting for that incomparable strong and sweet air, and recollecting how it felt when one began to get it, above the Croisettes, after walking or driving in the Postwagon at the end of a hot day at Lausanne or on the lake. Everything disappears in the maelstrom of time, and I much doubt whether I ever see the Pension Cruchon again!—But I must not get into the Obermann vein, which I find of late is rather growing upon me, but tell you of our destinies, which are much what they always were. I got through the University year somewhat halt-ingly, having the influenza at Christmas time, and being so fatigued at the end of March that in desperation, and at the advice of a medi-cal friend who had had good success with it in his practice, I tried Brown-Sequard's famous injections.[1] The result after eight of them was an abscess which kept me in bed 5 weeks. But between Royce and Münsterberg my instruction got given and the year closed hap-pily. I got off to the North Carolina Mountains early in June, and since then have been for the most part here with the family, who are all well, save little Tweedy who today has a rather severe bronchial attack. Our little lakeside and Mountain slope look pretty, even after Switzerland, only the air has not that magnificent quality. Having spent so much money abroad, we are living on an economical basis, without horse, man, cow, or pig. But *es geht*, and although I lose freedom, by having to do a good deal of work which naturally would be taken by the man, and by the neccissity of going on foot when otherwise I should drive, it is probably good for my constitution. My intellect is somewhat stagnant. I enjoyed last year reading a good deal of stuff which might connect itself with lectures on "Cosmology,"[2] but no reactions of my own have yet set in, and as for psychology, it has passed away from me altogether since the publication of my book. Münsterberg now lectures very fluently & on the whole very effectively in English and creates enthusiasm amongst the students. He is still in Cambridge conducting a "summer school" in psychology. The University gets such professors as are willing, to give these summer schools for the benefit of teachers who come from all parts of the country to work up particular subjects. Each subject is lectured on every day for six weeks. There are 500 students in all, this year, of whom munsterberg has 40, half men, half women. It is very useful work, and it shows his energy that he should be able to take it. On the whole he is one of the most *faultless* men whom I have ever known, in point of character.—By the way, if a young *Wadsworth*, formerly of Harvard, has made your acquaintance in geneva, be a little cautious with him. He is very intelligent, acute and witty, but with a distinct tendency to mental aberration. He left Cambridge with a delusion about Munsterberg having insulted him, and was going to Geneva to study with Schiff,[3] so that it is very likely you may have met him.—I have just read a book "Appearance and Reality" by F. H. Bradley, pub.[d] a year ago, which is destined to bring the whole of english philosophical discussion up to a higher plane, dialectically, than it has ever known before. I mistrust it, both premises and conclusion; but it is one of those vigorous and original things that have to be assimilated slowly. Your colleague Gourd would probably enjoy it, although it is so different from his own book in the theses it defends, because it is pure metaphysics from beginning to end.[4] It undoubtedly will be epoch-making in our literature.—But enough! This is only to let you all know that we love you. Those dear demoiselles! How I should like to see and hear them. Our Harry is now bigger than I am, and the brief period of about six months in which I could get rid of clothes that I didn't like, by transferring them to him, is now gone by forever, alas. Pray send a line, before the summer is over to let us know how it has fared with you all. Accept the affectionate regards of both of us for both yourself and Madame Flournoy, and believe always faithfully yours,

Wm James.

Our regards also to Frl. Hühnersdorf, who, I hope, is with you still.

ALS: MH bMS Am 1505 (12)

[1] Brown-Séquard described his extract in several pamphlets, including *Effets physi-ologiques d'un liquide extrait des glandes sexuelles et surtout des testicules* (1892).

[2] WJ's Philosophy 3: Cosmology.

[3] Moritz Schiff (1823–1896), Swiss physiologist.

[4] Jean-Jacques Gourd, *Le Phénomème* (1888).

To Hugo Münsterberg

Chocorua, N.H. | Aug 1. 94

My dear Munsterberg

I left you in such a hurry that I hardly said good bye, and as I think of myself in this rural freshness and stillness, and of you "toiling and moiling" in the heat of Cambridge and staleness of the labora-tory, merely to save the souls of a handful of barbarians whom you never saw before,[1] the contrast between our outward lots afflicts me with a sense of injustice, and I feel like wafting you a word of sympa-thy and affection to express my sense of that fact. If I could, I would do my share in some way, but I simply *can't,* and there's an end of it. Perhaps there is a region of Being where the power goes with the willingness. If there is, you may form a different opinion of me from the one you have now, where I have no reserves of strength whatever, and where the whole problem for me reduces itself to keeping such a hygiene as will enable me to get through the teaching year without having to resign because I break down.

But enough of this!

I am glad that Lough is turning out so well—I did him injustice. I wish that you could stop here on your way to Keene—just to see for 24 hours how we live—plainly enough. But I can easily see how in your present condition of body you wish to minimize the number of miles between you and your wife. Nevertheless, if you feel like 48 hours more on the way and a trip through the White Mountains, you could take us in passing, by buying a ticket for Burlington (Ver-mont) via the White Mountains and stopping over at West Ossipee, 4 hours from Boston, which is our station. Burlington is on Lake Champlain, which you cross by steamer to get to Westport, and thence drive to Keene. I pray for your speedy recovery and am al-ways yours affectionately

Wm James

ALS: MB

[1] The barbarians were teachers; see previous letter.

To James Mark Baldwin

                                        Chocorua N.H. | Aug. 25. 94
My dear Baldwin,

Your hospitality and friendliness are worthy of the golden age. We have had so many friends with us this summer—four of them at this moment—that other things have languished and what can be done in September will depend on what is done between now and then, the ups and downs of my constitution being always a Hauptmoment which can't be exactly foreseen, since the tide of well being, when it comes, has to be taken at the flood to do a little work in, and when it ebbs is a good time to get away for a change, and the ebb and flow are rather capricious. At any rate my *wife* can't get away from housekeeping, so with heartiest thanks to Mrs. Baldwin and yourself she begs you, with much regret, to count her out.

I will let you know at the earliest possible moment just what the possibilities are. I should like extremely to be with you. Please say to Jastrow how sorry I am that his letter reached me so late, and that he couldn't stop here. Possibly he may do so on the way down, or may meet me in Cambridge on Tuesday or Wednesday of the 1st week in September. I have to go there for two days then. I suppose the letter I sent him at Phila. was forwarded to S.-W.H.[1]

I am at present trying to dig some rational truth out of myself for a future number of the Psych. Rev., but it comes hard and has to be blasted, and I fear will result in shapeless débris.[2]—By the way, how Titchener seems to have taken upon himself the office of sole protector, defender and guardian of Wundt.[3] Yesterday came his Brain-review of W. & Külpe. His loyalty is commendable, but he rather overdoes the business in my opinion, and his luminousness is less than his zeal. But he's an amazing fellow for getting up details. Warm regards to both yourself & Mrs. B. Also to Cattell & Jastrow.

                                                              W.J.

ALS: Bodleian Library, University of Oxford

[1] Southwest Harbor, Maine.

[2] WJ, "The Knowing of Things Together," *Psychological Review* 2 (March 1895): 105–24; reprinted in *EPh*.

[3] Review by Edward Bradford Titchener of Wilhelm Wundt, *Grundzüge der physiologischen Psychologie*, 4th ed. (1893), and Oswald Külpe, *Grundriss der Psychologie* (1893) (WJ 747.51), in *Brain* 17 (1894): 90–102.

To Francis Boott

                                                    Chocorua, N.H. Sept 5. 94

Dear Mr. Boott,

Your letter, your charming booklet, and your vial of quinine have all arrived. The two latter objects were uncalled for and unexpected, but in spite of that the book has been most welcome, and Alice, reading it aloud to me at bed time every night, is not yet "through"—so you see it wears well. It is a much more artistic performance than Stevenson's and Lloyd Osbourne's last book, the Wrecker, in which it seemed to me that the matter had decidedly overflowed and slopped round the form.[1] Too much inchoate frontierism of event, character and language. Literature has to assimilate her stuff slowly to get it plastic.— —Kneisel just interrupts by coming to say good bye.[2] He doesn't look so imposing in his town dress. The drought here is very bad still, and we have had some awful days with smoke. But they, I suppose, are the same everywhere, during this terrible summer. I feel as if your visit hadn't been just what it should be. I caught a cold on Saturday and for Sunday and Monday was *sicker* than a cold ever made me before; and then my sympathy went out to you retrospectively more than it had done at the time. When a man as *stricken in years* as you makes a visit, nothing ought to go wrong, and I now feel as if I went wrong in escorting Mrs. Evans over the mountain. But the great thing is to have given you an insight into what Mary Tappan calls our "interesting" mode of life in the country. Our visitors are now all gone except Gurdon Parker, a friend of Harry's. Mrs Gibbens and Margaret went to Cambridge through yesterday's heat. I am settling to my summer's task which I hoped to have finished by Sept. 1st. but which, alas!, promises to drag through the month, an article namely on what it is the fashion nowadays to call "epistemology."[3] I fear I shan't get away either to Adirondacks or Mount Desert—but so runs the world away! In a week I shall probably run down to Cambridge for a visit. I hope you may be there. Alice sends you her love and remorse for your taking cold. It seems to have been an epidemic. Peggy I and the baby & all the Kneisels have had it.

Best regards to Mrs. Greenough.

                                             Affectionately yours | Wm James

ALS: MH bMS Am 1092.9 (766)

Address: Francis Boott Esq | Cambridge | Mass; forwarded to ['Waltham' *del.*] Hawthorne Inn | East Gloucester

Postmarks: CHOCORUA N.H. SEP 7 1894　CAMBRIDGE STA. BOSTON MASS. SEP 7 94
GLOUCESTER MASS SEP 8

[1] *The Wrecker* (1892) by Robert Louis Stevenson (1850–1894), British novelist, in collaboration with his brother-in-law, Lloyd Osbourne (1868–1947).

[2] Franz Kneisel (1865–1926), Romanian-born violinist, in 1885 became conductor of the Boston Symphony Orchestra.

[3] WJ, "The Knowing of Things Together."

To Thomas Davidson

Cambr. Sept 13. 94

My dear Davidson,

Margaret read me yesterday your letter announcing that you are to sail on the 25th. May the trip rejuvenate (—not that you need *that!*—) you, and in all ways do you good. It turns out impracticable again for me to go to Keene Valley—it was what I feared! To morrow I go to S. W. Harbor & Bar H. for a couple of visits, and in ten days buckle down again to work feeling more stale than I ought to at this time of year

You ask for introductions to frenchmen. I have no personal acquaintance with anyone except poor Pillon who lives on such a invalid economical scheme with his wife that he would be terrified at the sight of a red-hot scotch cowboy like you. But if you insist I'll give you a letter—you will gain absolutely nothing from him. Pierre Janet I have corresponded with, and he showed me his ward at the hospital. He is now in medical practice (I believe) whilst still retaining his professorship at the Lycée Rollin. I am so much cursed with english men who come to see me here with cards and letters that I have resolved to be ultra-scrupulous about giving introductions to my foreign acquaintances to anyone who has n't pretty definite business with them. Janet must be one of the busiest men in Paris, and I have no claims on him, nor you any definite business, I imagine. How is that I would give you letters to any intimate friends ad libitum, but I have none, absolutely none except Pillon, and after a fashion Stumpf, on the Continent. Hardly any in England either except Myers. Write what you want, and believe me yours always

Wm James

ALS: MH bMS Am 1092.9 (869)

Address: Professor Thos. Davidson | Keene | Essex Co. N.Y.

Postmarks: CAMBRIDGE STA BOSTON MASS. SEP 14 94　KEENE N.Y. SEP 17 1894

To Alice Howe Gibbens James

Boston P.O. | Thursday [September 13, 1894] | 5.15
Dearest wife—I send the mileage book back.—7 fares in it just eno'
for the rest of you, including Middleton.—Nothing from Cowie yet.
I slept well and bkfst with your Mother & lunched at the Club. Pottered round house most of time. It is *sweet,* that house in its emptiness, and the weather is so fine and all that I am tempted not to go
away at all. My trouble is not fatigue—I've done no work this summer to fatigue me in the least. It comes from a stratum deeper than
mere hygiene can touch, the weakness in my head, and I believe that
if I stayed at home now and began immediately to electrify myself it
would be a good use to put the time to. Nevertheless I imagine that
I shall go to M! Desert to morrow. I have given up Keene V. anyhow—what I need is not the violent exercise incidental to those
mountains, all beautiful as they are. I have been to get the Cabot
stain—a sample in a little tin can which will come with the other
things.[1] Try a part of the shingles where it won't make too ugly a
blotch if it fails. I have drawn the check for Aunt Nanny, drawn the
$439.81 from the Savings Bank etc.
Keep well, dearest   Health is the one thing. Kiss Harry, Billy,
Peggy, Tweedy,—and Middleton.

Your   W.J.

ALS: MH bMS Am 1092.9 (1888)

[1] Perhaps paint from Charles Cabot, a painter in Boston.

To Alice Howe Gibbens James

Cambr. Sept 14. 94
Dearest Alice,
I have decided to stay over for Snow's funeral on Sunday, so here
I still am.[1]   Pottered about house all the A.M. arranging galvanic battery & writing letters. Lunched at Club. Went to town to get grass
seed, return shoes etc. Took tea at your mother's, called at the Cummings's and have just come in from Royce's. The crickets sound
sadly, taking one back to things that are past, past, past—and altogether the world seems in the sere and yellow leaf with the wan dull
day and the dusty and dessicated vegetation. My thought has been
of you all day—I have cramponné'd myself to your existence as a sort
of protection, not very manly, but occasionally a good thing to do.

A letter from Cowie came—dividend of $575 this month but the final bills not yet sent in.   He says there is no trouble anywhere in view. Last night I went to Royces and found Mrs. R. just arrived.   She says she could kiss every square foot of the house.   It certainly was in a beautiful state of cleanness, thanks to Josiah having had in what she described as a "drove of negresses" to clean it.   One of them said to him "I suppose that you are the *janitor* of the building."   *Your* letter came this P.M.—I thank Harry for working so nobly—he is a fine boy. See, please, if you can't make both him and Bill learn some poetry by heart ere they come down.   I suggest Helvellyn which they'll find in John Forbes's Collection.[2]   I wish I could tell you more, but everything is shrunken inside and out.   Miller was here this A.M.—fine creature.—I think I must have left Mrs. Shaler's type written letter about her crystal gazing in the lower table drawer.   Please take good care of it if you find it.   "Proceedings" have come with Mrs. Sidgwick's report on halls.—splendidly done—400 pp.[3]   I enclose poor Garrison's letter.—The reviewer is a born idiot.[4]

Good night, O my own darling.   My depression will lift!   How many I've been through before.   Kiss the bairnies.

W.J.

ALS: MH bMS Am 1092.9 (1889)

   [1] Freeman Snow died on 12 September 1894.

   [2] "Hellvellyn," a poem by Sir Walter Scott.   John Forbes's collection was not identified.

   [3] "Report of the Census of Hallucinations," *Proceedings of the Society for Psychical Research* 10 (August 1894): 25–422.   The author is said to be "Prof. Sidgwick's Committee."   WJ is using personal information in attributing the report to Eleanor Sidgwick.

   [4] The only review noted that was likely to have offended WJ is the somewhat flippant review by William Healey Dall (1845–1927), American naturalist, of Andrew Lang's *Cock Lane and Common Sense* (1894) in the *Nation* 59 (30 August 1894): 161. For WJ's own review of the book see *ECR*.

To Alice Howe Gibbens James

Sunday night, 9.30. | Sept. 16. 94

Darling, darling Alice,

   Two days have passed—no letter from you yesterday—naturally enough—but last night Salter gave me good news.   I find it very hard not to go back, but believe that I am the better for not doing so, and probably go on Tuesday to M! Desert.   My battery has developed all sorts of obstacles in the rigging and is n't yet in working order.[1]   Last night I dined with dear old Nichols at the Club, and wrangled with him for 2 hours about a very foolish criticism he was going to publish concerning M'berg's "Contributions" in the last Phil. Rev.   I hope I have kept him from publishing it in that shape.[2]   I then called on Grace Norton, and then read Mrs. Sidgwick's report till bedtime.[3]   This A.M. I got reading solidly for the first time. Snow's funeral was attended by all of us hereabouts except Child.   It was at his bro' in law Lewando's in Boston.[4]   Minot J. Savage offici- ated, not having known Snow, & did well *for that sort of thing.*[5]   But when you bury me do it in a cathedral with a ritual.   Dignity befits the business better than sincerity.   Savage was very sincere, with his doubts and timidly expressed hopes.   But to have a private individ- ual shoved in, without authority, or official majesty, without associa- tions or context, in his bare personal nudity, expressing individual opinions—it does n't meet the case.   Savage was queer!   Poor dear old Snow.   Returned for a nap, the[n] walked to the Cemetery to see Alice's monument which looks very well indeed, much better than I tho't it would in the way of composition & keeping with the rest. The little pine is dead again.   I had meant to bring down another from Chocorua.   But I suppose that it would go the same way, and that an oak will be better worth trying.   I wonder if harry can bring down a very small oak to plant there when he comes.   If it compli- cates things too much, no matter.   Dined with Miller at the Club, after making a call on the Childs, and have been ever since at your mothers and the Davis's.[6]   I met Carroll Everett looking like a *bon- vivant,* and seeming very well.   Lyon was at the funeral with his beard shaved, hardly recognizable.   He says his wife is better.[7]   I have felt better to day, but need a solid night of sleep to get as I should be. It is a queer condition but nothing for you to be anxious about.   God bless you, dearest.   How I cling to you.   I send you a letter from H. arrived yesterday[8]—also 4 others, dating from an innocent time— 1859–60.   Wilkys earlier one seems to me quite delicious—17 years old.   Keep them carefully.   I am sending up the things by Mack. Two corks for stopping the hillside spring must be *carefully kept.*   The smaller one probably just fits the pipe, which must be plugged *tight* before the key under the house is turned so as to let the water out of the pipe.   The faucets over both sinks should also be left open. Harry can see to this if Ross does n't.   Most mysterious disappear- ance of my last wash here from mrs Malone, including pale blue

canvass shirt & army & navy store pajamas.   Can they be still at Chocorua.   Oceans of love to you all.

W.J.

ALS: MH bMS Am 1092.9 (1890)

¹WJ was doctoring himself with electrical currents.

²"Studies from the Harvard Psychological Laboratory," *Psychological Review* 1 (September 1894): 441–95, communicated by Hugo Münsterberg, consisting of reports by
students of work done in the Harvard Psychological Laboratory.   No published criticisms by Nichols were found.

³See previous letter.

⁴Freeman Snow married Mathilde Lewando, who died in childbirth.   The funeral
was at 80 St. Stephen St., and according to Boston directories neither of the two
Lewandos lived at that address.   One Lewando operated a chain of cleaning estab-
lishments, the other was a cigar maker.

⁵Minot Judson Savage (1841–1918), American Unitarian clergyman and author.
Correspondence is known from 1881 to 1910.

⁶Probably Julia Davis.

⁷David Gordon Lyon was married to Tosca Woehler Lyon.

⁸For HJ's letter of 7 September 1894 see *Correspondence*, 2:322–24.

From Alice Howe Gibbens James

Chocorua Sept 16ᵗʰ [1894]

My darling William,

I was so sorry when your letter came yesterday, with its decision
to stay over Sunday, that I had not mailed mine on Friday night.
There was nothing in it, only when you are sad-hearted I like to have
you know that I am thinking of you and loving you.

I wish that you might always "cramponner to my existence" in
these times of withering.   It would draw some serviceableness out of
me—or out of something better—and oh! you will never know how
I long to be near to you and to help you when these lonesome days
befall.   There seems to me but one cure—to "lay hold on immortal
Life."   Not in the old sense of looking to the future, you know I don't
mean that.   I mean the consciousness of the Divine in which our
incompleteness is forgotten.   This seems to me sometimes the only
vital thing in life, the only real living.   If I could so live you would
not be sad any more.   So dear, the more you ask the more shall I be
led to seek, and if you only will not turn away from me in your depression we shall see it fade away.   I hope that it has gone already,
but you won't mind my saying this, and telling you will help me to
keep the faith.

The boys began their poetry at once after breakfast   Harry took Helvellyn and Billy *Abou Ben Adhem*—a short one, because *East, West,* his long effort, is at the Hill Top.[1]   I shall not forget about Mrs Shaler's letter.[2]   It is not in the drawers of the desk but I shall probably find it in clearing up.   The magazines have been much read and enjoyed, but nothing is as good as Cowper's letters.[3]   I think I shall read his poems and then go through the book again.   *He* lived by faith through many a dreary year.

Middleton has gone to dine with the Mangasarians and now the 3 boys are starting to walk to the Hill Top, and return to tea.[4]   Everything here goes on successfully.   Tomorrow the much-belaboured tennis court will be ready to plant.   Yesterday I had a lot of wood sawed and our cellar cleared up.   So I think the closing up will be done very easily.   Do take a *good* holiday and stay away till Wednesday night that you may find us settled when you get home.

How I love you, and bless you, and believe in you, my dear one.

Alice.

ALS: MH bMS Am 1092.9 (308)

Address: William James Esq | Bar Harbour | Mt Desert | Maine | Care of George Dorr Esq

Postmarks: CHOCORUA N.H. SEP 17 1894   BAR HARBOR. ME. SEP 17

[1] For "Hellvellyn" see letter to AGJ of 14 September 1894.   "Abou ben Adhem" is a poem by Leigh Hunt (1784–1859), British writer.   "East, West" was not identified. The Salters owned a summer home near Chocorua and called it the Hill Top.

[2] See letter to AGJ of 14 September 1894.

[3] William Cowper (1731–1800), British author, *The Letters of the Late William Cowper, Esq., to His Friends,* available in numerous editions.

[4] Mangasar Mugurditch Mangasarian (1859–1943), born in Turkey, at the time a leader in the Society for Ethical Culture and Salter's replacement as leader of the Chicago congregation.   His wife was Akabie Mangasarian.

To Sarah Wyman Whitman

95, IRVING STREET, | CAMBRIDGE. Sept. 18. 94

Just a line, beloved Madam, to thank you for your letter from Nancy which, though it contained no phrases fit to feed a love sick fancy on—supposing such a thing to exist—showed you to be my genuine friend—otherwise you wouldn't have done such a kind thing at all!   No lovesick fancies in this quarter now, but much sadness and a general tenebrific condition, owing to my head being in bad "shape" and dark pictures of the future obtruding.   I have lived through plenty such periods, and know how little they mean, but meanwhile it stops the impulse to write freely and abundantly—I can't describe it better than in Jonathan Edwards immortal words—did you ever read them?—to the trustees of Princeton College who had asked him to be president of that institution.　I take down the book and copy them:—"I have a constitution, in many respects peculiarly unhappy, attended with flaccid solids, vapid, sizy, and scarce fluids, and a low tide of spirits; often occasioning a kind of childish weakness and contemptibleness of speech, presence and demeanor, with a disagreeable dulness and stiffness, much unfitting me for conversation, but more especially for the government of a College."[1]—Imagine C.W.E. writing an official letter like that!—Well, I *sursum corda* myself by the thought of your pluck, that unique "blend" of heroism and graciousness, height attained without precipices, etc.　And how glad is the poor thing that is W. J. that for a while your fancy is getting *food* instead of the crumbs and scraps that have had to serve its turn so long.

Dont waste a minute in writing again, but go in for a chockfullness of enjoyment and experience.　Bless you for the last letter!

Your faithful　W.J.

ALS: MH bMS Am 1092.9 (3918)

[1] Jonathan Edwards (1703–1758), American clergyman and theologian, in his letter of 19 October 1757 to the trustees of the College of New Jersey at Princeton upon his election as president of the college.　Edwards was inducted in February 1758 and died shortly thereafter.　The letter is quoted in Sereno Edwards Dwight, *The Life of President Edwards* (1830), 568–71.

To Alice Howe Gibbens James

Cambr. Wednesday [September 19, 1894] | 9 P.M.

Darling Alice,

Here I am still, as immovable as I accuse you of being.　But things go better with me, and in spite of interruptions, I manage to get through a mite of work.　The floor men won't be out till to morrow,[1] so I could n't go to M! Desert if I would, and unless my head gets bad again I think I won't.　I feel strongly like going to *you,* but I confess that a certain dread of being unwelcome to you in the midst of your "improvements," of being a burden, a "cross" to bear, etc. makes me shrink!?!?!?

The news of the day is that Brooks met me in the club, saying he had got a letter from Mogen, asking him to give an account of Louise to a Mrs. Iselin at New Rochelle.　[She must be one of the rich swiss

Iselins, friends of the Craftses, yacht people etc]. I told him of her jealousy etc. and he agreed with me that he had better refer Mrs. I. to you. Of course we can't stand in the way of her bettering her wages, but I fear if the I's have a large establishment that she won't be adequate.—It will be too bad to lose her, to lose the state once enjoyed, of being sure of something that tastes good when you bring a friend in to dinner! She has arrived with a headache and gone straight to bed. Mary ditto at your mother's. Tom Ward & his wife called this P.M.—a most unsatisfactory visit.[2] The M——bergs are back, neither of them in good condition, she very thin, he too fat and pasty, and she anxious about him.—I found young Witmer a friend of Miller's, and psychologist of Penn[a] University who had come up with his colleague Newbold to see Mrs. P.[3] She had ivy poisoning and wouldn't see them, although she had telegraphed them yesterday to come! I took him to the Club to dine, and we talked Piper—to my loathing. He is a conceited little ignoramus on the subject, and I think I must make a resolution and keep it, not to be inveigled into any Piper conversations again, but refer people to what is printed or to Arlington Heights.[4]—I am very sorry to hear from Louise of your having another bad headache. I hope twill prove short.

Heaven bless you

Good night. | W.J.

Love to Harry, Billy Peggy, Tweedy, Marie and Julie.

ALS: MH bMS Am 1092.9 (1893)

[1] In his letter to Baldwin of 19 September 1894 (calendared) WJ states that he has engaged "floor scrapers & other carpenters" and must wait until they finish "to-morrow night."

[2] The wife of Thomas Wren Ward was Sophia Read Howard Ward.

[3] William Romaine Newbold (1865–1926), American educator. One letter is known (1900). He described his sittings with Leonora Piper in "A Further Record of Observations of Certain Phenomena of Trance," *Transactions of the Society for Psychical Research* 14 (December 1898): 6–49.

[4] Leonora Piper lived in Arlington Heights.

To Frank Thilly

95, IRVING STREET, | CAMBRIDGE. Sept 20. '94

Dear Professor Thilly,

I have the highest opinion of the execution of Paulsen's book, but a low opinion of the simple naturalism there propounded as a philosophy. If you care for a page and a half of preface in which I should

say that, I will gladly write you one.[1] I really think that as a statement of simple naturalism it should be held to supersede all other
books.

I congratulate you on so speedy a conclusion of your task. Such
things are so apt to drag. I wish that I could hear you speak of the
work yourself now that you are so intimate with it. I hope to be able
to use it in my class in "Cosmology" but am not quite sure yet.

Truly yours | Wm James

ALS: NIC

[1] For Thilly's translation of Paulsen and WJ's preface see letter of 5 January 1890,
note 2.

To Alice Howe Gibbens James

Cambr. Wednesday Sept 26 1894 | 9.15 P.M.

Dearest darling Alice,

How many days you have been without a letter from me. I left
here Friday P.M. and had no chance to write on Sunday. Monday I
didn't because I thought I should find you all here at home when I
should arrive this AM. But I arrived to an empty house! How the
work seems to drag out—it reminds one of old times. I had no idea
it would take so many days, but I hope that it *interests* you all the
time. My M! Desert visit was a success, especially yesterday with its
fine weather, which we spent on a big walk over the Mountains. I
had no idea of the strength of that little Island. I stayed 2 days with
Baldwin, who is a really beautiful fellow, and "growing" like a bay
tree, and one and a half with the dorrs—just long enough with both,
and Im very glad I didn't leave home sooner and drag it out there.
Mrs. D. excessively friendly to me and all but insulting to poor Holt.
Mrs. Holt sweet. Mrs. Delafield[1] & daughter there. Mrs. Fred
Jones & daughter[2] & Geo. Vanderbilt at dinner.[3] I got one letter
from you there, and on reaching home this morning the earlier one
which Mrs. Dorr had sent back here for me. Darling Alice that one
letter is enough to make me good. Qui vivra verra—I shall try, and
with you and the Almighty to boost me may get over the bar.—I
have found my clothes of which I wrote—I had given them to Mrs.
Windmark,[4] not Mrs. Malone, to wash, and she has them returned.
But Mrs. Shaler's letter (type written)?!?[5]—and that little tortoise shell
penholder. Please bring back the dull lamp scissors. Let Billy not
lose my knife. The Old english valise trunk in the ice house room

might be bro't back. Also the india rubber piazza scraper, either in end room or your ma's room closet.—I had a bad conflict between M! Desert and going to you, the which I will explain when we meet. I am glad on the whole I chose what I did, though I am missing Heaven and home. I went to the 1 o'clock train to meet you, but Margaret had told me you would probably overstay the school opening, so I did what I have had on my mind for 6 months, and for which this was the only chance, namely without going to the 3-something train for you I went at 2.20 to Westboro to see the Cranches and am only back since ½ past eight when your letter of yesterday enclosing Miller's greets me. The Hospital is the most cheerful one I have ever seen. Mrs. C. poor soul has entirely lost her memory—didn't know who I was and asked my name several times. Carrie is very stout, looks well and talks well, seems in fact quite natural and rational, and ought to be out of such a place.[6] I am *very* glad I went. Poor souls, poor souls! I enclose 3 letters which will interest you. I answered Mrs. Iselins as you would have done. You are right about not taking L. back,[7] merely to remain unsettled. I wrote to Loisette that he had duped me sweetly, and that I bore him no malice, but that I really could[n't] let him consume M'berg's time at the lab.—I came from Bar Harbor with Miss Devens who has taken to bicyling.[8] Margaret will go next! Kitty Temple (Emmet) was here this A.M. having been to see about Grenville's installation.[9] Gives a good report of everybody. I left Margaret just now with Mr. White, who is growing fat already on the prospect of pensioned idleness.[10]—Good night, blessed wife, how glad I shall be to "fold" you once more to my arms. Kiss the boys, & Peg. I went over B. & N's school in their company on Friday last—it is really fine, the building, and I hope it will pay them.[11] Good night! good night! Till Friday—I suppose the 11 o'clock train will run all this week.

Your loving Wm.

Tell Billy I haven't so much as peeped at the enclosure for him which was thrown through the slot of the door this P.M. whilst I was away.

Love to Aunt Nannie.

ALS: MH bMS Am 1092.9 (1892)

[1] Mrs. Delafield was not identified. For another reference to her see *Correspondence*, 6:318.

[2] Mary Cadwalader Rawle Jones (1850–1935), American socialite, wife of Frederic Rhinelander Jones, a gentleman of leisure and the brother of Edith Wharton. One letter is known (1909). Their daughter was Beatrix Cadwalader Jones Farrand (1872–1959), a landscape architect.

[3]George Washington Vanderbilt (1862–1914), American businessman, builder of the Biltmore mansion in Asheville, N.C.

[4]Mrs. Windmark was not identified.

[5]Apparently, Mrs. Shaler's letter was not in the lower table drawer; see letter to AGJ of 14 September 1894.

[6]Caroline Cranch, daughter of Christopher Pearse Cranch and Elizabeth de Windt Cranch. For Caroline's obsession with HJ see *Correspondence*, 1:382n.

[7]The servant, Louise.

[8]Miss Devens was not identified. For another reference to her see *Correspondence*, 6:373.

[9]Grenville Temple Emmet (1877–1937), in later years a lawyer and diplomat, was entering Harvard College.

[10]Charles Joyce White (1839–1917), professor of mathematics at Harvard, resigned effective 1 September 1894.

[11]Browne and Nichols.

To Frederic William Henry Myers

Cambr. Sept. 29. 94

Dear Myers

Yours of the 20th. is just in, along with my family from the country and the beginning of the College year. As it's a "broken day", I answer immediately.

I tingle for exact details about Eusapia.[1] You don't even say whether Lodge is absolutely convinced, but I suppose he must be from the general context. I shall have to think over the question of sending his report to Science or elsewhere, after seeing it in proof.[2] I don't see what is to be gained in this matter by haste, and I hope that Piper may come first in Proc. and be once for all got out of the way,[3] and the tables cleared for the more startling material and discussion that is sure to follow.

As for my Presidency another year, leave that question awhile open.[4] I have no ideas whatever to communicate in an address, and have been cursing my good nature in accepting the post for the past month. My cerebral symptoms have been so bad (at end of vacation!!) that I have resolved to do no odd literary "chores" whatever, am withdrawing my name as editor from Psychological Review etc,[5] and shall concentrate wholly on teaching and what traces of "original" work there may be left in my carcase. Nevertheless, I recognize that 1 year is a short term and makes the Society seem restless, and having accepted I may be in honour bound to go on if elected again. The only *trouble* is the addresses, which have to spread out Nothing into literary form, and literary form being one of my bugbears. If this one should *go*, I shall be ready to face the next.

But what a stomach for the fray *you* have! The whole society organization is *widerlich* to me. Perhaps it wouldn't be so were it not the American branch.

As for Principia, Macmillan's edition (you say "Macmillan") is Latin and costs $12.00. What I had in mind was copies of some earlier english edition of the P., & of the Optics, which wd. be relatively cheap.[6]

Lombroso swings fairly round the circle of illogicality and credulity. The vastest donkey of the age.[7] But I love his treuherzigkeit.

I am right glad you have enmeshed Langley and like him. He seems to me a rather massive personage, though I can hardly say that I know him.

Crookes admirable for President![8] Of course no objection. I will look up paper on levitation—I fancy the article Langley means is a very old one.[9]

Mrs. Sidgwick's report is simply stupendous for care and definiteness![10]

One think[11] I should like to command you as president, and that is to publish titles & Indices, both of Proceedings and Journal, *with* the last number of each vol. The present arrangement is infernal. How came you to fall into it?

Love to you all, from yours fondly

W.J.

I expect to see Hodgson the day after to morrow, after his month in the wilderness his animal spirits must be quite untameable.

Balfour's address excellent.[12] His contempt for the poor devils who get out the truth before the bell has rung, shows the effect of political life on his imagination.

ALS: MH bMS Am 1092.9 (3315)

[1] Eusapia Palladino (1854–1918), Italian physical medium. For a note on her career, including her exposure in 1895, see *EPR*, 417.

[2] Oliver Joseph Lodge, "Experience of Unusual Physical Phenomena Occurring in the Presence of an Entranced Person (Eusapia Paladino)," *Journal of the Society for Psychical Research* 6 (November 1894): 306–36. The *Journal* was for circulation only among members. The report was not published elsewhere.

[3] The next major report concerning Leonora Piper appeared in 1898; see *EPR*, 485.

[4] WJ was still president in 1895.

[5] WJ is still listed as a cooperating editor in the 1895 volume of the *Psychological Review*.

[6] Macmillan had numerous printings of *Newton's Principia,* starting in 1863. There were numerous English editions of Newton's *Opticks.*

[7] Lombroso was among the first to study Eusapia Paladino and believed that she possessed an unknown psychic force that she could transmit through the ether.

[8] Crookes succeeded WJ as president in 1896.

[9] Perhaps William Crookes, "Notes of Séances with D. D. Home," *Proceedings of the Society for Psychical Research* 6 (December 1889): 98–127, describing many marvels, including things rising in the air on their own account.

[10] See letter to AGJ of 14 September 1894.

[11] A slip for 'thing'.

[12] Arthur Balfour gave the presidential address, published in *Proceedings of the Society for Psychical Research* 10 (August 1894): 2–13.

To Oliver Joseph Lodge

Cambridge, Oct. 4, 1894.

Dear Professor Lodge,—

Your kind letter of the 22nd came duly the other day, and yesterday I received from Hodgson your report.[1] I need not say that I have read it with "*Spannung.*" This seems to be a rather grave moment for all of us. We are changing places with a set of beings, the "regular" spiritualists, whom we have hitherto treated with a species of contempt that must have been not only galling but asinine and conceited in their eyes, and we are since using—you at least in your admirable methodological reflexions are using—language towards our hard-hearted colleagues almost identical with that which we have so often heard the aforesaid spiritualists use to us. Say what we will about the occasion of our supercilious demeanor being fraudulent occasions, and those (as now) of our converted demeanour being genuine, the fact remains of a queer mixture of roles, and I confess nothing seemed to me more humorous than to hear you in this report claiming and contending for rules and principles of evidence that I had practically pooh-poohed so often in the mouth of my good though soft headed friend Brackett, *e.g.* whose book on "materialized apparitions" is based on the performance of 3 female mediums who have hoodwinked the very eyes out of his head.[2] The fact seems to be that the abstract talk is reasonable enough on both sides; but the only thing that counts much for a man is what he sees himself. I very much fear that your testimony will make but little impression on your professional colleagues, and that you will be but another Crookes case to be deplored.[3] If this thing is true, however, the chasm will have to be filled with many Curtius-like dead bodies of good men before the world passes over[4]—*then* indeed their fame will have a resurrection. You ask what I think of popular publication. I must confess myself extremely averse, the more averse the longer I think of it, to go out of our regular course. Nothing really important will be gained by it, and the Society will thereby give itself an appearance of excitability and eagerness, the absence of which is now among its chief decorations. The more startling the secrets we have to disclose, the more, in my opinion, should we calmly pursue the tenor of our way and publish proceedings at their due date. The world won't be converted for many years. When it is converted we shall seem all the more dignified and sublime to have been so imperturbable. Send the report as a pamphlet to members, if you like, in advance of the proceedings, though I confess I doubt even the necessity of that. But don't *sell it publicly* apart from the total context of the other witnesses evidence; and by no means send it to Nature, Science, or the XIXth Century. This bluntly is my both personal and presidential opinion, though I don't know what penalty could follow if the advice were disobeyed![5]

I think that the very breadth & philosophic character of your report which will make it so admirable a concomitant of other testimony, going more into the details of the phenomena, decidedly unfit it for effectiveness amongst circles ignorant of the general subject, as scientific circles are. They will make pious exclamations of pity, deplore your "vagueness" etc., etc. This is one reason why even an immediate circulation among members seems to me of doubtful utility. The stuff will keep; and the bigger the bomb to be exploded at once in the proceedings, the greater the shock. Pardon my brevity and frankness. I find it hard to express how much I admire yours—and your clearness too. Your paper is that of *a man* dealing with *facts*, and is refreshing after the pedantry and pretentious timidity of orthodox deliverances. May the days of your eclipse be short, and may you live to be the leader of a new orthodoxy at no remote date. Most cordially and faithfully

Yours | Wm. James.

TC: MH bMS Am 1092.1

[1] See previous letter.

[2] WJ and Edward Augustus Brackett (1818–1908), American sculptor and poet and an investigator into spiritualism, were involved in the case of Hannah Ross; see *Correspondence*, vol. 6. In his book *Materialized Apparitions: If Not Beings from Another Life, What Are They?* (Boston: Colby & Rich, 1886) (Phil 7068.86.40), Brackett discusses several mediums; see *Correspondence*, vol. 6.

[3] Crookes was one of a few important scientists to publish his belief in the authenticity of certain mediums. This did not serve to convert others but merely hurt his own reputation.

[4] Possibly Ernst Curtius (1814–1896), German archaeologist.

[5] In his letter of 13 October 1894 (calendared) Lodge stated that the decision not to publicize the report had been made before the arrival of WJ's letter.

To Oliver Wendell Holmes, Jr.

95, IRVING STREET, | CAMBRIDGE. Oct. 9. 94

Dear Wendell

I have but just learned (owing to my paper not having been left at the door yesterday) that your poor Father has at last said good bye to the life he loved so well and with which he was so well matched.[1]

Peace be to him; and to you in the great loneliness which this will make for you in many respects. One of the great big and important memories of my younger days passes with him, and like so much else now becomes a part of history. How much and how little!

My most affectionate regards, to both you and your wife, to whom the world will now seem for a while so different.

Yours ever | Wm James

ALS: MH-L

[1] Oliver Wendell Holmes, Sr., died on 7 October 1894.

To Francis Greenwood Peabody

[October 18, 1894]

Dear Peabody:

I hate to say no to anything, especially to anything proposed by you, but pray don't propose me for this committee of fifty, council of ten, or Garibaldi thousand, whatever it may be.[1] Do you fellows think you can scare alcohol by the portentousness of your names? Never! It seems to me we *know* quite enough for all practical purposes already, and that this is a kind of swell front to a house about 3 feet deep. I confess that the sight of the report of the physiological Committee with its proposal to have more dogs sacrificed, and an expert in the library to look up the literature of the subject for several weeks made me quite sick inside.

What is *effective,* it seems to me, is the example of abstinence, and the gradually progressive weaning of the people from the habit of expecting to drink on all occasions. Your aqueous dinners to the Club e.g. do more than your name on this circular will ever do. As in all things, the real cure is the substitution of the better ideal—one needn't then be at pains to drive out the worser one. For our students, e.g. the admiration of, and belief in that pure early-morning health, that is better than all drunkenness, and no man that has drunk anything the day before can ever feel, will do more for temperance than anything. I admit it is something to *live up to*!

Excuse the appearance of churlishness that this letter wears. I am no man for committees anyhow.

Yours fondly, | W.J.

TC: MH bMS Am 1092.1

[1] Peabody served as secretary to a committee of fifty prominent citizens, which undertook the task of investigating the problem of alcohol. Known as the Committee of Fifty, it published *The Liquor Problem* (1905).

To Sarah Wyman Whitman

95 Irving St Oct 29. 94

Dear Madam

'Twas I, not she, who called under the fortuitous cover of her card.

My ankle is quite well for moderate distances, and I expect to call again in spite of "not-at-home"s. Don't take my poor little cousinesses *au sérieux*. They will be too happy with the student-society which can be only too amply provided here. I should like to show the glories of you to the little artist one, who is the most satisfactory and simple child, inarticulate as every real artist ought to be,* and making her living now by a pretty bad vein of work, *en somme,* drawing modern society jokes for the papers.[1] But she really has, or had once, a lot of real fancy in her. I have only seen her once in the past seven years.

I can't get over your having been to Europe! It is such a jolly bit of fitness in this disjointed world.

Adieu!

Yours as always | W.J.

*P.S. This is not meant for a "dig" at *you*! Cf. Du Maurier, Hunt,[2] etc etc.

ALS: MH bMS Am 1092.9 (3919)

[1] Reference is to Ellen Rand.

[2] William Morris Hunt (1824–1879), American painter.

To William Wilberforce Baldwin

Cambridge Nov 5. 94

My dear Baldwin,

Your letter *in rê* Raffaello came duly more than a week ago, and I have vainly tried to snatch a moment in which to answer it, ever since. Your account of the harmony in which you were living, thanks to him, gave me a creepy feeling as if I had made an *attentat* on your lives.* I am glad it has turned out as it has, and that you may forget in due course of time my nefarious designs upon you. Please recollect that when I wrote I didn't know that R. was still with you at all, and that he had taken the initiative (as I understood his rather diplomatic letter) in the proceedings. So pray forgive us yourself and beg Mrs. Baldwin to forgive us too. The plan was more my wife's than mine, for I dreaded being responsible for the happiness of so unhilarious a being as R., with my miserable supply of Italian; and überhaupt I was not sure it would work. We have set one of our Swiss women to cooking, and she will do well enough. I often think with a tender regret of our pleasant winter in the Piazza dell' I., and wish I might take a dip into florence again. But you, when are you coming here? Morton Prince said to me not long ago, that in a year, if you came, you would have the biggest practice in Boston, which, take it as a whole, is a decent place to live in, though deficient in people like yourself, of artistic temperament, especially deficient perhaps in the medical profession.

We are all doing well, I neurasthenically groaning along, but *doing* it still. Like the woman who said she had always observed the curious fact that if she lived through the month of January she lived through the rest of the year, I have observed that if I life through October, I struggle on till the summer vacation, and so it will doubtless be this year.

Give Fritz and his brother Peggy's best remembrances, please; and take, for yourself and Mrs. Baldwin (and your sister if she is still with you) those of both of us.[1] Pray greet Raffaello also, and believe me ever truly yours

Wm James

I only discovered after turning the page that the sheet was torn— pray excuse the shabby appearance of the letter.

*Much as I once felt when after vainly trying to shoot a hoary battle-scarred tom cat that used to infest our garden I made a call

on some neighbors and found him coiled up on the parlor table in
the midst of the ladies of the family—a very queer feeling, I remember.

ALS: NNMor

¹ No information about Baldwin's family was found.

To Ellen James Temple Emmet Hunter

Sunday Nov 18. 94

Dear Elly

Here is my final dying message about Rosina.

Alice and I have had a full and explicit talk about the matter such
as we have had no opportunity of having until this A.M. We have
ventilated every point involved, have sounded the matter to the bottom, and have ended with hearty laughter. I am now filled with
wonder at the nightmarish scruples that have been possessing me for
twenty four hours, beginning at 3 A.M. Saturday, and lasting till my
talk with Alice this Sunday A.M. I can, however, explain how they
arose. Alice has fits of morbid low spirits and depression about herself, which sometimes get very acute. On Thursday she had one of
her bad sick headaches which lasted till Friday A.M. Then I perceived that she had a tendency to shun the childish merriment and
din that we were making together. Rosina also showed jealousy of
Bay sitting next to me at the table. My own brain, always ready to
fly off on the wings of fancy, put all sorts of things together in the
night, [for a fortnight now I have been in one of my bad wakeful
times] and the result was my talk yesterday and letter written in bed
before dawn this A.M.—You will be amused at the hysterical picture
this suggests of the James family—it is certainly not a fair average,
as you know. The upshot of it all is this honest opinion which I am
ready to be hanged for that Rosina *ought* to come, that you *ought* to
make an effort to send her, that both my incomparable Alice and I
will be as parents to her, that there is *no* cause for anxiety of any sort
whatever, no matter what I may have given you to understand to
the contrary hitherto. You can depend on the sober and deliberate
character of this judgment, so I hope that we shall soon see the girl
arrive and instal herself. Please recollect that, commencing at this
late day for college work, it is important that she be not detained
with you one day more than is absolutely required. Remember also

Cam. F.!¹ Alice is earnest in her desire to have her come. You don't perhaps sufficiently realize what an important thing it may be in her future to have even this one year here, if it should end there.

Always yours affectionately | Wm J.

Poor little R. must never be allowed to suspect the lurid conceptions of possibility to which her innocent presence has given rise.

Monday A.M. Just one more word to corroborate all that I have said. There is n't a single doubt about the matter. I make myself absolutely responsible and guarantee success.

W.J.

ALS: MH bMS Am 1092.9 (1074)

¹ Probably a reference to William Cameron Forbes.

To James Mark Baldwin

Cambr. | Dec. 1. 94

My dear Baldwin

"Broadly you burgeon and grandly you grow"—long may you keep a doing of it! I have read the proof with the greatest interest and admiration. If much of the book has the same originality and vigor, it will be epoch-making. It is all new to me. I had never tho't of *synergy* as the condition of synthesis, and the whole thing is as yet so unassimilated by me that I can't tell whether I can make use of it or not.¹ It is very magnanimous of you to let me have it in advance, instead of keeping it all back to kill me with when I have had my say at the meeting. I fear that I can't use it much yet, for my own speculations (so far as I have made any) run on somewhat incongruent lines. I haven't written a line yet, and imagine that nothing may come at all. Of course there *need* be no presidential address—it isn't part of the to be constitution, I hope, but a free gift if it comes, any year, and I am disposed to think, if my paper does materialize, that since it will be wholly technical in form, it will be better to give it as one of the common communications and not as a presidential address.² The latter should be some rather broadly *zusammenfassend* review of the situation, I should say.

I make no comment on your text *now*. What jolly good type you have got.

Yrs ever | W.J.

P.S. Is anyone noticing Hirsch's Genie u. Entartung for the review? If not I will do so briefly.³

ALS: Bodleian Library, University of Oxford

[1] In the preface, dated December 1894, to his *Mental Development in the Child and the Race: Methods and Processes* (New York: Macmillan, 1895), xi, Baldwin thanks WJ for reading parts of the manuscript. But "synergy" is not Baldwin's term. In the article on synergy by Baldwin in the *Dictionary of Philosophy and Psychology*, ed. by James Mark Baldwin (1901–5), the only reference is to WJ's "Knowing of Things Together."

[2] WJ gave "The Knowing of Things Together" as his presidential address to the American Psychological Association at Princeton on 27 December 1894.

[3] WJ's review of William Hirsch, a physician, *Genie und Entartung* (1894) (Phil 5425.5.6*), appeared in *Psychological Review* 2 (May 1895): 290–94; reprinted in *ECR*.

To Charles William Eliot

95 Irving S! Dec. 7. '94

Dear Mr. Eliot

Mr. B. F. Randall is a harmless and optimistic lunatic who bored me to death last year.[1] I got him however to come to my course in Mental Pathology and discourse about himself, so that he served as clinical material. I don't know just what his present condition may be. His letters should be simply ignored.

Sincerely yours | Wm James

ALS: MH Archives

[1] No information about B. F. Randall was found.

From Charles Montague Bakewell

Jerusalemer Str 44^{IV} | Berlin, Dec. 23, '94.

Dear Professor James:

I had expected to get a letter written to you some time before this, but the days are as bad here as at home in their rapidity. I had supposed that wonderful restfulness in the people and in the air that one hears about so much would make it otherwise. But said "restfulness" is all a fiction—at least in Berlin. I am having a pleasant and profitable stay here, though it is not exactly what I had anticipated. Philosophy in the proper sense of the term seems dead or dying. The young men here who do not devote themselves to the microscopic analysis of some petty dust heap in the universe, nor yet like Simmel carry on a simultaneous fanciful construction,[1] treat of broader fields to be sure, but in a painful, encyclopædic fashion— like Dessoir and Schmekel (Schmekel.)[2] One imagines himself listening to a sort of philosophical century dictionary,[3] sounding through a phonograph. In spite of this tediousness I am getting something from Schmekel. (After all I have heard of people who have learned to use their native tongue by poring over Webster's dictionary. But I have always suspected that the result of such procedure would be a withered style.) Paulsen is much better. He seems to have landed on the shoals of Hume and Schopenhaur, but at least he is no mere machine. He is the connecting link between the good old philosophers and the modern philosophasts.—I have not however any occasion to make the complaint which students often make of Berlin, I have found the Professors and other *Gelehrten* quite as available as one could wish. It is very plain that the older philosophers and theologians here are quite apprehensive of the present German situation. I have got the same story entirely independently from all the men whom I have met. And the sum of it all is: the young men of the present day are for the most part adventurers, or else mere *Brodgelehrten,* to use Schillers term. Philosophy is driven as a trade. The young philosophers don't take the trouble to make the acquaintance of any of the *great* German philosophers. Kant is still much read, but from the outside, to find arguments to bolster up crudely formed notions.—And Kant is better than the Bible to use as a prop for every conceivable theory, shallow or profound. The philosophical devils have learned to quote the Kantian scriptures for their own purposes.

I spend a good part of my time in the library. Ueberweg's history has been brought down to date by Heinze in its bibliography,[4] and, thanks to Zeller's influence perhaps,[5] the library contains everything on Greek philosophy down to the minutest monographs. I am having a good time with the literature, though the air in the reading-room is painfully thick and reeks with all sorts of odors in which a general unwashedness is predominant. The arrangement of the library is clumsy in the extreme, especially after one has been enjoying the smoothness and simplicity of the British Museum. But I have been here long enough to be accustomed to clumsiness, and to endure all things from German officials from cab-drivers up.

The trick of writing "scholarly" books is a very simple one, so simple that it is laughable so many should be fooled thereby. Perhaps this is especially obvious in the case of the monographs which have been appearing of recent years in such quantities on questions concerning Greek philosophy. You remember Ruskin's remark on Grote's history—undoubtedly harsh there[6]—But I feel much the same about many of these books of learning. Any Junior in Harvard

College could write books like these if he had the time and impudence to try. I am now decidedly of the opinion that it requires more ability to refrain from publishing a "scholarly" work these days than to publish one.

Well, perhaps I have written heresies enough for one letter. I should hardly have dared to express myself so freely in some of these criticisms if I had not such good authority behind me.—Besides the larger lights, I have seen quite a little of two very clever German students; the one, a self-satisfied North-German, embodies in himself many of the results of these evils; the other, a pleasant open and fair-minded Frankfurter, of his own accord told me a tale of woe worse in some ways than the one I have told above.—I could tell you some entertaining stories, too, in evidence, but they are too long for letters.

Do not think from all this that I am unhappy, or disappointed at having come here. I am managing to make as good a use of my time as I could wish, and am getting that view of Greek phil. as a whole this term which I wished.—But I should not be satisfied to remain in a similar situation next semester. I am trying to find out where some man of note is to be heard in minute work upon some special field, preferably, the period immediately after Aristotle, or the Neo-platonic period. If I find any such I shall seek him out whether in France, Italy, or Germany.—I am "short" on Cambridge news, I hope you have been enjoying good health this year, and that you will have a spare moment to write me a line. When you do will you tell me whether you know of any available work in which *Ch. Pierce* has published his views on *egoism, idism* & *tuism* of wh. you once spoke to me[7]—

With best holiday greetings to Mrs James and Miss Gibbens, and regards to your colleagues,

Yours sincerely, | Chas. M. Bakewell.—

Mr Davidson has gone to Italy, stopping in Rome on his way to Egypt. I hear from him that he is quite unwell, and is undecided as to what his plans will have to be. We enjoyed much his flying visit, which goes without saying. Pierce sends his cordial regards & says he will write you in a day or two.

C.B.

ALS: MH bMS Am 1092.9 (9)

[1] Georg Simmel (1858–1918), German philosopher and sociologist.

[2] August Schmekel (1857–1934), German historian of philosophy.

[3] *Century Dictionary* (1889–91).

[4] Friedrich Überweg (1826–1871), German historian of philosophy, *Grundriss der*

Geschichte der Philosophie (1880–86), as revised by Max Heinze (1835–1909), German historian of philosophy.

[5] Eduard Zeller (1814–1908), German historian of philosophy.

[6] In a letter to the *Pall Mall Gazette*, 15 February 1886, with reference to George Grote (1794–1871), British historian, *History of Greece* (1846–56), Ruskin wrote: "there is probably no commercial establishment . . . whose head clerk could not write a better one, if he had the vanity to waste his time on it." Ruskin's list of bad authors includes, among others, St. Augustine, John Stuart Mill, and Charles Darwin.

[7] Charles Sanders Peirce, in an 1863 oration at a high school reunion; see *Writings of Charles S. Peirce: A Chronological Edition*, (Bloomington: Indiana Univ. Press, 1982), 1:113.

From Alice Howe Gibbens James

Dec 31. 1894 | Midnight

My own dear William,

The New Year is here and Heaven send it be a happy one for you and all my dear ones! I think I might do more to make it so than I ever have done if I can only keep true to the course I choose in hours of insight.

I hope you did all you wished to in New York and are now safe in Newport. This afternoon we made a pleasant visit to Mrs Miller.[1] What a lovely face she has. After supper we went to hear John Burns and truly my eyes have beheld a hero and my ears were not deaf to his great accents.[2] If he comes to Boston do be sure that you hear him. His appeal to the working men to take their part in Municipal reform and his account of what the London County Council has accomplished in this direction was one of the most stirring bits of human history which I have ever heard. He wasted neither time nor temper in denunciations. He simply stood up and talked to workingmen of their duties and responsibilities toward each other and to the city in which they dwelt. And the trumpet blast of scorn for "charity" was good to hear. I could work for such a workingman.

Mack has gone to a dinner given in his honour and Mary. I must now go to bed. I can finish this in the morning. How dear you are and how I love you!

Tuesday a.m. It was so late—after 2 o'clock—when Mack came home last night that we all slept this morning. John Burns is to speak to morrow night in Boston and you will only just have reached home, so you will not hear him. I am sorry for this. Miller was in the audience last evening. He asked me if I ever had got such an impression of *strength*—"even to the man's hair on his head."

Yesterday I wrote to Mrs Baldwin, so that civility is accomplished.[3] I also wrote to Harry. I did not tell him that he *must* come back on Wednesday but I hope that he will return before Saturday

It is great fun to hear the talk and feel the real life going on in Mack's world. So you see I am not only enjoying my visit but gaining from it in many ways. I hope that you slept at Newport, and that everything has gone well with you. I long to see the children. How they will welcome you!

Dearest love to them and to you.

Your loving | Alice

ALS: MH bMS Am 1092.9 (309)

Address: William James Esq | 95 Irving St. | Cambridge | Mass

Postmarks: CHESTNUT STA. PHILA. PA JAN 1 1895   CAMBRIDGE STA. BOSTON. MASS. JAN 2 1895

[1] Anna Emlen Hare Miller, mother of Dickinson Sergeant Miller.

[2] John Elliot Burns (1858–1943), British labor leader and politician, then touring the United States and speaking before various labor groups.

[3] Probably Helen Green Baldwin. The letter was most likely a letter of thanks. While attending meetings of the American Psychological Association, WJ planned to visit the Baldwins, who were then living at Princeton.

Calendar

1890

From Charles-Robert Richet. [1890, with reference to publication of *Principles of Psychology*]. Thanks WJ for his letter. Is reading WJ's psychology. Thinks Binet will review it for *Revue Scientifique* [a favorable unsigned notice appeared in *Revue Scientifique* 47 (7 February 1891): 181–82]. Is WJ interested in occult psychology and what does he think of Myers's inquiries in this area? Experience will decide (ALS: MH bMS Am 1092 [798]).

To Henry Holt. Cambridge, 11 January 1890. Is now satisfied with first chapter of *Principles*, which he has rewritten after rereading the "entire physiology of the brain." Discusses cuts that are to go in the first 100 pages of the book. Will be in New York City with a "good installment of Ms. by the end of the month" (TC: MH bMS AM 1092.1; published in part in *PP*, 1557).

From Henry Holt. 13 January 1890. Will be pleased to see WJ on the 30th. WJ is not to worry about cuts until the book is finished. Discusses bills he has received from psychical research societies. Asks whether Preble would be a good man to write a Latin book [see letter of 15 January 1890] (Letterbook: NjP).

To William Mackintire Salter. Cambridge, 22 January 1890. Invites Salter on behalf of the Harvard Philosophical Club to lecture in the spring, in the same manner as Adler did two years ago. Sends love to "poor Mary and our dear Mother in Law" (ALS: MH bMS Am 1092.9 [3667]).

To Henry Holt. Cambridge, 28 January [1890]. Will be staying with his cousin, Mrs. Post [Mary Ann King Post (1819–1892), living at 30 W. 25th St., New York City, daughter of Ellen James King, WJ's father's sister, and widow of Minturn Post, a physician]. Discusses plans to meet with Holt. AGJ will not be accompanying him because their son is convalescing (TC: MH bMS Am 1092.1).

To William Mackintire Salter. Cambridge, 13 February 1890. Discusses arrangements for Salter's lecture at the Sanders Theatre in March. Eliza Gibbens was enthusiastic about Salter's "last Sunday's discourse." WJ glad that Salter liked Royce's review [of Salter, *Ethical Religion* (1889) in *Nation* 50 (30 January 1890): 95–96]. Has read Davidson's review [of *Ethical Religion* in *Ethical Record* 2 (January 1890): 230–34] and Salter's reply [*Ethical Record*, 234–38] (ALS: MH bMS Am 1092.9 [3669]).

To William Mackintire Salter. Cambridge, 20 February [1890]. WJ agrees to the time set for the lecture. Glad of the prospectus of Salter's book [unidentified] and advertisement in *Nation* [an ad for the *Ethical Record* appeared in *Nation*

50 (13 February 1890): 142]. WJ must end his letter because a "hypnotized student" is waiting to have "all his ills" cured by "suggestion." Asks what Salter meant by Eliza Gibbens and Mary Salter being "on the mend" (ALS: MH bMS Am 1092.9 [3671]).

From Alfred Binet. Paris, 20 February 1890. Has received WJ's article [unidentified], of which he had learned in *Open Court*. Asks if WJ has published personal researches on double consciousness as he would like to use them. With reference to the question of the cerebral center of consecutive images and his publication of Parinaud's experience [Henri Parinaud (1844–1905), French oculist; for references and WJ's comments on Binet's letter see *PP*, 717n], Binet concedes that WJ's student [Delabarre (see *PP*, 717n)] is right. Wrote WJ several months ago but letter was returned because address was poorly written. Thanks WJ for sending him an article [WJ, "The Psychology of Belief," *Mind* 14 (July 1889): 321–52], which he used in his own article on the psychology of denial ["L'Inhibition dans les phénomènes de conscience," *Revue Philosophique* 30 (August 1890): 136–56] (ALS: MH bMS Am 1092 [38]).

To Charles William Eliot. 7 March 1890. Asks permission for Hodgson to use a room at Harvard. He would sometimes sleep there (ALS: MH Archives).

From Robertson James. Concord, 11 March [1890, with reference to WJ's comment about RJ's spirit rappings (*Correspondence*, 2:134)]. He and Mary have had nine mediumistic sittings since Sarah Moore [unidentified] was there, four of those times with George Augustus King [1834–1919, a lawyer in Boston and Concord] and Ellen Frances Whitney [1843–1933, librarian in Concord]. No raps were heard, except tonight when he sat alone. He doesn't expect to achieve mediumship but will continue to sit, this time alone (ALS: MH bMS Am 1095 [46]).

From Edward Appleton Bangs [b. 1860, graduated from Harvard in 1884, a lawyer, dealt in real estate in Florida]. Boston, 12 March 1890. Proposes the theory that in sexual intercourse one person can make a moral impression upon the other beyond what is produced by normal social association. Men who associate with bad women often deteriorate and there have been women elevated by sexual association with refined persons (ALS: MH bMS Am 1092 [32]).

To Katharine Hillard [d. 1915, translator and writer on Italian culture and theosophy; only this letter is known]. Cambridge, 26 March 1890. Surprised that she is a theosophist. WJ is finishing book [*Principles*] (ALS: known only from description in dealer's catalogue).

From Phillips Brooks. Boston, 26 March 1890. Apologizes for missent letter. The note that WJ did not receive explained that Brooks would be unable to hear Salter's lecture and to accept WJ's invitation to his home to meet Salter (ALS: MH bMS Am 1092 [57]).

From Henry Holt. 29 March 1890. Will be glad to see WJ, but will not start printing the book until WJ has finished. Invites WJ to dine (Letterbook: NjP).

From Henry Holt. 7 April 1890. For the contents of this letter see the notes to letter of 8 April 1890 (Letterbook: NjP; published in part in *TCWJ*, 2:46–47).

From Henry Holt. 14 April 1890. Received copy of contract for *Principles*. If manuscript is not ready by 1 May, "let that day be a day of fasting over your sins" (Letterbook: NjP).

To J. Raymond Derby [unidentified]. Cambridge, 18 April 1890. Allows Derby to use WJ for testimony about the charms of Derby's "place." WJ himself has decided to buy a cheaper place at Chocorua (ALS: OU).

From Henry Holt and Co. New York, 25 April 1890. Reports sale of three copies of Maude's book (Letterbook: NjP).

To Christine Ladd Franklin. Cambridge, 29 April [1890]. For contents of this letter see letter of 19 May 1890, note 1 (ALS: NNC; published in *SUC*).

From Henry Holt. 5 May 1890. Has given WJ grace of four days. "Who's the Demon now?" [see letter of 21 March 1890] (Letterbook: NjP).

From Henry Holt. New York, 8 May 1890. Responding to WJ's letter of 7 May 1890, Holt thinks book will fit in one volume and will look no worse than Ira Remsen's [1846–1927, American chemist, *Inorganic Chemistry* (1889)]. When giving WJ a month's extension, he did not think WJ would use it as an excuse for not meeting the deadline proposed by WJ himself (Letterbook: NjP; published in *PP*, 1560).

From Henry Holt. 10 May 1890. Reiterates that he will not set any of the book until he has the complete manuscript. Asks WJ for his definition of "Science," because Holt believes there are enough truths in psychology to make it a science (Letterbook: NjP; published in part in *PP*, 1561).

To Alice Howe Gibbens James. Cambridge, 17 [16] May 1890. Lectured on Ansel Bourne. Relates day's activities and mentions Edmund Tweedy, Chubb, Margaret Gregor, Gifford, Mrs. Gourlay, the servant Ellen, Ellen Dixey, & Gurdon Parker. Bishop Keane [John Joseph Keane was delivering the Dudleian lecture; see letter of 1 November 1891, note 3] came to get advice about psycho-physic laboratory at Catholic University. Psychology will be finished by Sunday. Mr. Rand's [Edward Lothrop Rand (1859–1924), a lawyer and gardener, lived nearby at 49 Kirkland St.] bees "swarmed" in the Jameses' back yard. Stanley Hall received "stunning blow" [see letter of 16 May 1890] (ALS: MH bMS Am 1092.9 [1713]).

To Alice Howe Gibbens James. Cambridge, 19 May 1890. Worked on manuscript, revising and sorting figures for woodcuts. Frances S. Meeker died. Forgot to go to funeral but will visit Anna Meeker and apologize. Margaret Gregor is very sweet (ALS: MH bMS Am 1092.9 [1715]).

To Alice Howe Gibbens James. Cambridge, 21 May 1890. Busy with illustrations. Expects to send manuscript tomorrow in the "leather colored trunk" that Elizabeth Walsh sent with Katharine Walsh's things. Harder to send letters late at night as P. O. box opposite Lovering's [Joseph Lovering (1813–1892), professor of natural philosophy at Harvard] has discontinued midnight pickup. AGJ should tell her mother that she will have Syracuse money by Friday. Briggs came and promises to do everything. WJ dined with Taussig and afterwards visited Anna Meeker, inviting her for a visit in view of her "ancient relation to father." Mailed AGJ Chubb's copy of Tolstoi's last [see letter to AGJ of 27 May 1890], "a tremendous thing but hardly fit for Margaret" (ALS: MH bMS Am 1092.9 [1716]).

From Joseph Vogelius. 23 May 1890. Manuscript received. WJ sent only twelve books rather than the thirteen he said he was sending (Letterbook: NjP).

To Louisa Loring. Cambridge, 25 May [1890]. Thanks her for the filled-out [census of hallucinations] blanks. Sends respects to her father and love to Katharine Loring (TC: MH bMS Am 1092.1).

To James Ward. Cambridge, 26 May 1890. Read with "keen pleasure" Ward's article ["The Progress of Philosophy," *Mind* 15 (April 1890): 213–33]. Encloses next year's philosophic program (ALS: MH bMS Am 1092.9 [3832]).

To Sarah Wyman Whitman. Cambridge, 27 May 1890. Expresses sympathy on the death of Gemma Timmins. Will be great loss for the Brimmers (ALS: MH bMS Am 1092.9 [3898]).

To Alice Howe Gibbens James. Cambridge, 28 May 1890. Notified that manuscript had arrived at Holt's. Encloses letter from Elizabeth Walsh and asks that it be returned as he wants to send it to AJ. Breakfasted at Child's. Briggs is working at the house. [Timothy W.] Haley, the plumber, is coming. Has to read Hume's thesis, give last lecture, see Ansel Bourne, and visit Mrs. Dorr. Wants AGJ to come on Saturday and hopes that children's colds will be better. AGJ should have Snell's [a workman in Chocorua] money soon (ALS: MH bMS Am 1092.9 [1721]).

From Joseph Vogelius. 29 May 1890. Returning eleven books from which they have taken photographs for illustrations. Asks for English text to replace the German in the illustration from Ludwig Edinger [1855–1918, German neurologist; see *PP*, 48] (Letterbook: NjP).

To Alice Howe Gibbens James. 30 May [1890]. Spent four hours with Ansel Bourne, who, examined in and out of trance by specialists, "doesn't develope." WJ has changed his mind about AGJ coming to Cambridge and instead will go to Chocorua. Will not pay Mrs. Möller until he sees AGJ. Will warn Holt to send proofs by 1 September [see letter to Holt of 3 June 1890] (ALS: MH bMS Am 1092.9 [1724]).

To Alice Howe Gibbens James. Cambridge, Sunday [1 June 1890]. Will not be able to leave tomorrow. Expecting letter from Mitchell about Bourne. Plans for AGJ to come to Cambridge should he not be able to go to Chocorua (ALS: MH bMS Am 1092.9 [1725]).

From Joseph Vogelius. 4 June 1890. Returning *Philosophical Transactions* and Exner book [Siegmund Exner (1846–1926), Austrian physiologist; see *PP*, 1307–8] from which illustrations were made. Discusses questions concerning the illustrations (Letterbook: NjP).

To Minna Timmins Chapman. Cambridge, 9 June 1890. Expresses sympathy on death of Gemma Timmins. AGJ was in Chocorua and WJ was delivering the last lecture of a course and neither could come to the funeral (ALS: known only from description in dealer's catalogue).

From Joseph Vogelius. 12 June 1890. Sends proofs of the illustrations. Discusses some problems connected with them. Will begin printing as soon as proofs are returned (Letterbook: NjP).

To William Noyes. Tamworth Iron Works, N.H., 17 June [1890]. Asks Noyes to send Ansel Bourne's photograph to Hodgson. Has written to Mitchell to find someone to continue studying Bourne (APS: MH bMS Am 1092.9 [3364]).

From Joseph Vogelius. 19 June 1890. Sends first lot of proofs in duplicate. Expects to start sending thirty pages of proof per day (Letterbook: NjP).

To Granville Stanley Hall. Tamworth Iron Works, N.H., 20 June 1890. Happy to hear from Hall, who will recover [see letter of 16 May 1890]. Cannot go to Ashfield because he expects to be working on proofs all summer. Invites Hall to visit Chocorua for talk about psychology and to bring his son (ALS: MWC; published in *SUC*).

To Henry Lee Higginson. Tamworth Iron Works, N.H., 20 June [1890]. Did not expect a reply [see letter of 11 June 1890]. The speech was impressive in its simplicity and originality (ALS: MH bMS Am 1821 [57]; published in Bliss Perry, *Life and Letters of Henry Lee Higginson* [Boston: Atlantic Monthly, 1921], 334).

To Granville Stanley Hall. Tamworth Iron Works, N.H., 21 June [1890]. Invitation to Hall was intended to include Hall's young son (ALS: MWC).

To Henry Holt. Tamworth Iron Works, N.H., 21 June [1890]. Regrets that he and AGJ cannot accept Holt's invitation. He will be working on proofs during the summer. Perhaps they can visit Holt in September. Regards to Mrs. Holt (TC: MH bMS Am 1092.1).

From Joseph Vogelius. 23 June 1890. Received WJ's telegram and sends duplicates of galleys 1–28. Galleys 29–57 were sent on 20 June, and 58–102 are being sent now (Letterbook: NjP).

From Joseph Vogelius. 26 June 1890. Has received galleys 1–57 from WJ. Sending additional proofs. Discusses illustration from Luigi Luciani [1842–1919, Italian physiologist]. Glad that WJ likes type. Estimates book will come to some 1500 pages (Letterbook: NjP).

From James Sully. London, 27 June 1890. Heard from Dr. [illegible] that WJ is bringing out a psychology in which WJ's articles on the emotions, sense of effort, perception of time, belief, and space appear. Sully is rewriting his "Outlines of Psychology" and wants to refer readers to WJ's book rather than the articles. Should WJ's book not be out in time, could WJ send a list of chapters in which the articles will appear? (ALS: MH bMS Am 1092 [1120]).

To Alice Howe Gibbens James. Cambridge, Saturday [5 July 1890]. Returned rested. Apologizes for having spoken impatiently. Is sending licorice powder (ALS: MH bMS Am 1092.9 [1726]).

From Joseph Vogelius. 8 July 1890. Sending many page proofs and galleys. Having calculated that at the present pace the book will not be on time, they have induced the printer to acquire additional type to speed typesetting. The book should be in type by 15 August (Letterbook: NjP).

To Alice Howe Gibbens James. Cambridge, 10 July 1890. With Coggeshall's help worked on proofs all day, except for dinner at Royce's. Last night visited Mary Tappan, whose father is a "gentlemanly old man" (ALS: MH bMS Am 1092.9 [1730]).

To Alice Howe Gibbens James. Cambridge, 11 July 1890. Proof is coming "thick and fast." Dined tonight with the Childs and the Reverend Edward Hull [probably Hall]. Will send AGJ $20. Plumb sent $400. Forgot their anniversary yesterday (ALS: MH bMS Am 1092.9 [1731]).

To Frances Rollins Morse. Cambridge, 13 July [1890]. Will stay in Cambridge until proofs are finished. They give him a sense of his "voluminous garrulity" and he needs a day at the shore. If she will invite him for an evening after "Wednesday next," he will accept and "reknit the thread of old times" (ALS: MH bMS Am 1092.9 [3203]).

To Alice Howe Gibbens James. Cambridge, 17 July [1890]. Meant to send letter by Salter but he left too early. WJ gave him money for AGJ without counting it. Is expecting information from Hodgson, which he will add to proof. Upon hearing of WJ's visit to the Morses at Beverly tomorrow, Sarah Whitman invited him for lunch with [Georgina] Schuyler. Was with Chamberlin last night, a "köstlich being." Asks if AGJ can come to Cambridge on the 26th or the 28th? Although he had dreaded AGJ's visit the former time "for very good reasons!" it had turned out a success (ALS: MH bMS Am 1092.9 [1735]).

To Frances Rollins Morse. Cambridge, 17 July [1890]. Will explain when he arrives why he can only spend one night (ALS: MH bMS Am 1092.9 [3205]).

From Joseph Vogelius. 17 July 1990. Discusses sending proof. They have decided to begin second volume with chapter 17 (Letterbook: NjP).

To the Editor of the *Boston Post*. Cambridge, 19 July 1890. Read the admirable notice of HJ's *Tragic Muse* in paper of 19 July and wishes to know the reviewer's name (ALS: DLC).

To Alice Howe Gibbens James. Cambridge, 19 July 1890. Sarah Whitman's lunch for [Georgina] Schuyler included the Grays [Horace Gray (1828–1902), American jurist, and Jane Matthews Gray], the Rockwells, "Mrs Prof. Sumner" [Jeannie Whittemore Elliott Sumner, wife of William Graham Sumner (1840–1910), American economist], Mrs. Templeman Coolidge [Katharine Scollay Parkman Coolidge (1858–1900), wife of John Templeman Coolidge (1856–1945), American artist], and Arthur Dexter [1830–1897, writer on art]. WJ corrected proofs for two hours in Mrs. Whitman's studio. The letter mentions Fanny Morse, the Eliots [probably Mary Lee Morse and John Wheelock Elliot], the Childs, Eliza Gibbens, and the Henry Higginsons. Ida Higginson discussed her plans to form a lunch club for "refined females," which AGJ must join. AGJ must not miss the *Post*'s review of *The Tragic Muse* (ALS: MH bMS Am 1092.9 [1737]).

To Alice Howe Gibbens James. Wednesday [23 July, 1890], 10 A.M. AGJ's mother goes to see Margaret Gregor off at noon. Corrected proofs, then breakfasted at the Club with [James Jefferson] Myers, Danforth, and Wilson [unidentified]. Longs for AGJ's "gentle presence," but her mother will stay till Monday [28 July] to see Aunt Nanny off and AGJ should not come till after, since "there is a *kind* of romance" in being alone together. Wishes Coggeshall were away, but as he is "almost invisible" it does not matter much (ALS: MH bMS Am 1092.9 [1749]).

To Alice Howe Gibbens James. Cambridge, 23 July 1890, 8:45 [P.M.]. Going to Boston to mail proofs. Dined with Grace Norton. Discusses AGJ's coming to Cambridge to help with proofs. Is writing about tombstone. Wrote AJ this morning (APS: MH bMS Am 1092.9 [1741]).

From Joseph Vogelius. 23 July 1890. Between 300 and 400 pages are in type, using up all the type the printer has. WJ should give preference to page proofs. Anything WJ can do to release the matter now in pages will speed up the process. WJ should not mention to the printer the expected completion date, because they are pushing him as hard as they can (Letterbook: NjP).

To Alice Howe Gibbens James. Mary Tappan's, Thursday [24 July 1890]. Had dinner at the Adams House [a Boston hotel]. Went to the Putnams, saw Lizzie

[Elizabeth Cabot Putnam (1836–1918), author and social worker, sister of James Jackson Putnam], who was "rather less daft than usual." Mentions Mr. Tappan, Mary, and Miss Gaudelet. AGJ's mother will go to Chocorua Saturday and AGJ can come to WJ on Monday. Wonders why Billy catches so many colds (ALS: MH bMS Am 1092.9 [1773]).

To Henry Holt. Cambridge, 27 July 1890. Proof going well; first volume is in pages. Asks if 100 copies can be printed not in the usual gray ink but in black, as is done for elementary school books like Trowbridge's *New Physics* [1884] and Joseph Henry Allen [1820–1898, American clergyman and author] and Greenough's *Caesar's Gallic War* [1883]. Likes the quiet life with only proof to worry about. Didn't respond to Holt's invitation to go to Burlington; perhaps will go in September (TC: MH bMS Am 1092.1; published in *TCWJ*, 2:49).

To Alice Howe Gibbens James. Cambridge, 27 July 1890. Margaret Norton brought AGJ's reassuring note about Billy. Continue giving Harry iron for his headaches. James Jackson Putnam may have to examine him again. Went to Hodgson's, but he is away, perhaps at Bar Harbor. Dined at Parker House and drank half a bottle of sauterne, went to Mary Tappan's, slept well, breakfasted at Child's. Will go to Medford to see a blind man named Perry for psychological reasons. Is enjoying the quiet time with nothing to do but read proof but misses AGJ. They should speak to Andrew about his sulks. Ask Salter who the William Clarke [1852–1901, English writer] is who writes in the *Ethical Record* (ALS: MH bMS Am 1092.9 [1744]).

To Alice Howe Gibbens James. Cambridge, Monday evening [28 July 1890]. Has been dictating psychic research letter to Mary Tappan. Had dinner with Mary, Miss Gaudelet, and Mr. Tappan. Well into proofs for volume 2. Will send her $100 (ALS: MH bMS Am 1092.9 [1750]).

To Alice Howe Gibbens James. Cambridge, 29 July 1890. Glad that Billy is well again, but he should not "bully his dam." Proofreading is "forging ahead magnificently." Had breakfast of "real chops & potatoes" at Parker House. Has not been feeling well, probably because he works late and has supper when he is in "starving condition." Mentions Mary Tappan, Francis Boott and Mr. Tappan, who probably will not live long. Royce is back but will return in ten days to the Dorrs (ALS: MH bMS Am 1092.9 [1745]).

From Joseph Vogelius. 29 July 1890. Discusses errors in the numbering of figures, which always occur when the author deals directly with the printer. Drummond has agreed to make corrections at no charge. Sends remaining plate proofs of first volume (Letterbook: NjP).

To Alice Howe Gibbens James. Cambridge, 1 August 1890, 1 P.M. Received seventeen dollars from Houghton Mifflin Co., not for sales, but for melted plates. Slept well thanks to sulfonal. Correcting proof. Will pay Grant and Mann. Discusses finances. Lifted chest weights. Happy about Margaret Mary (ALS: MH bMS Am 1092.9 [1751]).

To Alice Howe Gibbens James. Cambridge, 1 August 1890, 7 P.M. Feels happy and plans to go to the theater and dine at Parker House, while correcting proofs. Clement Lawrence Smith [1844–1909, professor of Latin and administrator at Harvard] said that William Slater gave John Fiske $3,000 for WJ's laboratory, bringing total to more than $4,000. Happiest of all that the Jacksons going to Chocorua means that AGJ can come to him and "we'll have high jinks together, celebrating the final completion of the old book by a grand carouse which Boston will not soon forget" (ALS: MH bMS Am 1092.9 [1752]).

From Oliver Wendell Holmes, Jr. Beverly Farms, 1 August 1890. Invites WJ to come to Beverly. [Probably WJ sent the letter on to AGJ because on it there is a note in his hand explaining that the invitation is the result of a hint to Fanny Holmes] (ALS: MH bMS Am 1092 [391]).

From Joseph Vogelius. New York, 1 August 1890. Drummond will now send one set of proofs by letter postage, so that WJ receives them earlier. They marvel at WJ's ability to keep up. The chief proofreader, Theodore Neu, is very interested in the book and will not allow anyone else to touch it. Has enclosed part of plate proofs. Diagrams will be all right. Is WJ working on index? (ALS: MH bMS Am 1092.9 [235]; published in part in *PP*, 1566).

From Joseph Vogelius. 2 August 1890. Discusses ways of fitting in the note [unidentified] for p. 133 which WJ sent Drummond. Pages 134–282 have already been cast and making changes in them would cost about thirty dollars (Letterbook: NjP).

To Henry Holt. Cambridge, 7 August 1890. Asks if he may send John Bundy the proofs of WJ's chapter on Hypnotism to print in his *Journal*. Final galleys of book in hand (TC: MH bMS Am 1092.1; published in part in *PP*, 1566).

From Hugo Münsterberg. Freiburg, 11 August 1890. Delabarre brought WJ's letter. At first, Münsterberg did not think that color contrast was a good subject for Delabarre's dissertation and suggested other topics. He will talk about it to Riehl, who will be Delabarre's examiner. Münsterberg could not attend the Paris conference, but hopes to be in London in two years and renew WJ's acquaintance. Will send WJ portions of his *Beiträge* [see letter of 13 May 1890, note 7]. He feels at times that he is doing what WJ has already done in *Principles* (ALS: MH bMS Am 1092.9 [357]).

To Henry Holt. Cambridge, 12 August 1890. Is pleased at the chance that the Holts will visit Chocorua and gives directions for reaching the house. All did nobly in proofreading. Now only the index remains. What will they ask for the book? Wants to see Holt's place in Burlington (TC: MH bMS Am 1092.1; published in part in *TCWJ*, 2:49).

To Henry James III and William James, Jr. Cambridge, 13 August 1890. Has worked like a slave and will be glad to get to Chocorua. Has got them spoon hooks and line. Discusses repairs to Billy's gun. Sends regards to Grandma, Aunts Mary and Margy, Margaret Mary, Fräulein, Hubbard, Bridget, Ellen, and Andrew and "all the rest of the livestock" (ALS: MH fMS Am 1092.4).

To Katharine Peabody Loring. Cambridge, 13 August 1890. Wishes her "Godspeed" on her journey. Could think of nothing to send to AJ, but he and AGJ have written notes to her (ALS: CSt; published in *SUC*).

From Joseph Vogelius. 15 August 1890. The preface will help to make the two volumes equal in length. Book should be published in late September. Changes cost $0.50 per hour. The first volume required 312 hours, the second, 263½. The cost is $287.75. The allowance is $130.00, 10% of the cost of composition, leaving $157.75 chargeable to WJ (Letterbook: NjP).

From Robertson James. Milwaukee, 16 August [1890, with reference to AJ's condition]. Returned from two days at Nashotah with Frank Bigelow [perhaps Frank Gordon Bigelow (b. 1847), a banker in Milwaukee]. Caroline James and the children were there. Received check and is glad Syracuse matters are going well but pained for AJ's sake and hopes Katharine Loring can go to her. He and Mary are leaving for New Hampshire. Is disgusted at hearing nothing discussed in Milwaukee except "Western smartness" and "the mammoth fortunes it brings." Many of RJ's friends have lost everything in trying to make fortunes. RJ's daughter will probably spend the winter in Florida with the Holtons (ALS: MH bMS Am 1095.2 [22–24]).

From James Sully. 18 August [1890]. Thanks WJ for table of contents. Expects WJ's book will be out first as he is only halfway in revising his own. Asks WJ to send him an early copy as he would like to see it before issuing his own. He and family are by the sea and will return to Hampstead in September (ALS: MH bMS Am 1092 [1121]).

From Sarah Orne Jewett. South Berwick, Maine, 21 August 1890. She and Mrs. Fields are sorry not to be able to contribute [see letter to Dorr of 12 August 1890]. Slater's interest in WJ's work not greater than theirs. Great pleasure to see WJ and AGJ (ALS: MH bMS Am 1092 [453]).

To Sarah Orne Jewett. Tamworth Iron Works, N.H., 27 August 1890. Thanks her for letter. He will call on her should a need for contributions arise again. He just returned a contribution from Larrowe. Wishes that she could have stayed over Sunday. Helen Merriman is "one of the finest women living" (ALS: MH bMS Am 1743 [112]).

To Alice Howe Gibbens James. Jefferson, N.H., 5 September 1890, 10 A.M. Grand views. Met the George Kennedy family who were returning from Mt. Washington. Their two oldest children are in Berlin with Miss Ingell [unidentified, but see *Correspondence*, 6:264n]. WJ tried to persuade them to go by Tamworth, hoping to convince Kennedy to subscribe to the Society for Psychical Research, but "he seemed to smell the trap, and would not." Ride from Glen House was fine although Brown was lazy and the luggage did not arrive as promised. The "handsomest spot" for a home is E. A. Crawford's [perhaps Ethan Allen Crawford who built a hotel at Fabyan, N.H.] at Jefferson Heights. WJ's trip has impressed him with the "desirability" of the Chocorua area for summer homes and he feels confident as to its future. Bought the September *Atlantic Monthly,* which is full of "crisp and breezy literature." House full of "decent-seeming" people but the flies are worse here than at Tamworth (ALS: MH bMS Am 1092.9 [1756]).

From Miss Q. Wisconsin, 22 September 1890. Following the death of their mother, she and her sister in Wisconsin heard their brother singing although he was in North Dakota. He later confirmed that he sang the very song they heard (Frederic William Henry Myers, "The Indications of Continued Terrene Knowledge on the Part of Phantasms of the Dead," *Proceedings of the SPR* 8 [1892]: 220).

From Joseph Vogelius. 22 September 1890. WJ's *Principles* to be ready on the 24th. Price probably will be $7. They have several orders and have promised the book on the 25th. Asks if they should hold it back for a few days to give WJ time to get circulars ready (Letterbook: NjP).

To Alice Howe Gibbens James. Cambridge, 25 September 1890. A day of "much agitation and little progress." Met his Philosophy 10, which has only six students. Harry is happy. Royce has been talking with WJ for an hour and he did not do the reading that he intended. Bought an *Atlantic Monthly* and will send it (ALS: MH bMS Am 1092.9 [1760]).

From Joseph Vogelius. New York, 25 September 1890. Price fixed for *Principles* at $6, but retailers usually sell at 20% discount, bringing price to under $5. They regret that some printer's points show on the top margin but printing new set would take four to five weeks. WJ's twenty copies will be expressed to him today; complimentary and individual copies will go out later (ALS: MH bMS Am 1092 [419]).

To Ellen James Temple Emmet Hunter. Cambridge, 28 September 1890. Her letter gave him great pleasure. Glad that she is going to Europe with daughter Mary and hopes that the rest of the family will follow and stay abroad for some years. WJ was too busy to visit her. Invites her to visit them in November before she leaves. Harry is with WJ, beginning school at Browne and Nichols. AGJ and the rest are in Chocorua for several weeks longer. AGJ to give birth in December. AJ not well and telegraphed HJ to come from Italy and Katharine Loring to come from Beverly. Katharine moved her to London, where they are looking for lodgings near HJ. For AJ, death "would be the greatest release," but she will have no such luck soon. Sends regards to everyone, including Henrietta and Leslie Pell-Clarke, to whom he will send copy of *Principles* (ALS: MH bMS Am 1092.9 [1068]).

To Sarah Wyman Whitman. Cambridge, 30 September 1890. Learned from [Howard] Cushing that she was still in the country, so is sending her his "two fat tomes," which are a "dismal piece of work on the whole" (ALS: MH bMS Am 1092.9 [3902]).

From Joseph Vogelius. 30 September 1890. Encloses list of persons and journals to whom free copies of *Principles* will be sent. Of those on WJ's list, WJ will not be charged for copies to Ladd, Hall, Howison, Jastrow, and Schurman, since Holt planned to send them copies on his own. Has WJ given Royce a copy? If not, Holt will include him. They are arranging for an English edition and will not send free copies to England. It is better that they come from the English publisher (Letterbook: NjP).

From George Angier Gordon [1853–1929, Scottish-born clergyman, on 3 June 1890 married Susan Huntington Manning]. Boston, 1 October 1890. Thanks WJ for the two volumes of *Principles,* which will be for him "a memorial of friendship," and for the congratulations on his wedding (ALS: MH bMS Am 1092 [300]).

From Silas Weir Mitchell. 1 October [1890]. Thanks WJ for *Principles.* He will read them when he can "feed on them slowly—absorbingly" (ALS: MH bMS Am 1092 [554]).

To Alice Howe Gibbens James. Cambridge, 2 October 1890. Philosophy 20a students to come after tea; Miss Calkins is admitted. Mary Salter "got off." Scully [unidentified craftsman] revarnished hall and stairs. Discusses selling of Brown, perhaps by Isburgh [see letter of 6 October 1890]. Has written to James Walsh to hurry him, saying that WJ needs the money. Mr. Tweedy came this A.M., looking older and feebler. WJ retrieved Billy's gun from the store. Harry works hard. WJ could not go to Temple's today. AGJ's mother should not carry the pear trees—everything can be sent together by express. AGJ should bring the bureau (ALS: MH bMS Am 1092.9 [1765]).

From Charles Augustus Strong. Worcester, 2 October [1890]. Thanks for *Principles*. Read the chapter on conscious-automaton theory with great interest. Has difficulty accepting WJ's theory and would like to discuss it with him (ALS: MH bMS Am 1092 [1053]).

From Joseph Vogelius. 2 October 1890. In reply to WJ's letter of 30 September, they have sent *Principles* to Salter (Letterbook: NjP).

From Francis Ellingwood Abbot. 3 October 1890. Thanks for the *"opus magnum."* Sent WJ his *Way Out of Agnosticism,* but as he has not heard from him, presumes it was lost in the mail (Letterbook: MH Archives).

To Alice Howe Gibbens James. Cambridge [5 October 1890]. Picked apples, lunched with Ashburners, gave *Principles* to Everett. WJ does not think SPR will survive the year. Send Brown to Isburgh. AGJ's mother arrived. Paul Ross will prepare for spring after AGJ leaves. Harry in good shape. Hodgson talks incessantly about Tom [unidentified], who is paying for his medical education. Return the *Puck* that he sent as Harry wants to see it. Frontispiece best caricature he has seen (ALS: MH bMS Am 1092.9 [1767]).

To Samuel Burns Weston. Cambridge, 6 October 1890. Agrees to be advertised among contributors to the *International Journal of Ethics* and has at least "one ethical thunderbolt" to contribute ["The Moral Philosopher and the Moral Life"]. Will write notice of *Journal* for *Nation,* but Weston himself should suggest WJ to Garrison [unsigned note in *Nation* 51 (30 October 1890): 345, does not appear to be by WJ] (ALS: Archives of the Society for Ethical Culture, New York City).

To Alice Howe Gibbens James. Cambridge, 7 October 1890. Margaret Gregor arrived and is helping Ellen prepare tea for Elliot—the Scottish visitor—and James Putnam. Discusses selling of horses. Borrowed $600.00 from the bank and paid taxes. Child endorsed. Briggs's bill is $107.00, not $10.70 as WJ thought. Has begun Stanley's *In Darkest Africa* (ALS: MH bMS Am 1092.9 [1769]).

From Joseph Vogelius. 7 October 1890. They expect an order from England and will print a new edition of *Principles*. Does WJ have more corrections, besides the ones he has sent? They did not print an errata slip but corrected the plates. Returning Dr. Harris's letter [see letter to Harris of 9 October 1890] (Letterbook: NjP).

To Alice Howe Gibbens James. Cambridge, 8 October [1890]. Will get Wesley P. Balch [dealer in livestock] to sell the horses, rather than Isburgh (APS: MH bMS Am 1092.9 [1770]).

From Thomas Davidson. Keene, 8 October 1890. Thanks for *Principles* (ALS: MH bMS Am 1092.9 [122]).

To Alice Howe Gibbens James. Cambridge, 9 October 1890. Is coming on Friday [10 October] but she should not meet him at West Ossipee station in the darkness and in her "interesting condition." Robertson [unidentified] will take him to Nickerson's and he will walk from there. Margaret Gregor is "sweetness incarnate" (ALS: MH bMS Am 1092.9 [1771]).

From Ida Agassiz Higginson. 9 October [1890]. Thanks for *Principles* (ALS: MH bMS Am 1092 [362]).

From Joseph-Remi-Léopold Delbœuf. Liège, 12 October 1890. Has received WJ's letter of the first [letter unknown] and does not understand Sidgwick's phrase "Delbœuf's man for my money." Is publishing a long article on his travels, which he did not want to write. Also "Pourquoi mourons-nous?" [*Revue Philosophique* 31 (March 1891): 225–57; (April 1891): 408–27], a sequel to his *Matiére brute* [1887]. Is writing on determinism and has asked for his letters from WJ and Fouillée. His article will appear in the *Revue Philosophique*. Has stumbled upon a mathematical way of representing the development of species. Has published an article on the psychology of lizards and has studied Émile-François Maupas [d. 1916]. As professor of Latin and Greek has published on Aristophanes and a revised edition of *Chrestomathie* [see *Correspondence*, 6:227n]. Would like to publish on hypnotism in the *Forum* rather than in Berillon's journal [Edgar Bérillon (1859–1948), editor of *Revue de psychologie appliquée*], because the *Forum* pays better. Since the death of his wife [see *Correspondence*, 6:613], does not know why he keeps on writing. Is morose only when alone; in public, continues to be a good companion. Thinks that those who have chosen pleasure have made the right choice. Congratulates WJ on expected child. (ALS: MH bMS Am 1092 [163]).

From Sarah Wyman Whitman. 12 October 1890. Apologizes for not writing. Mentions Sargent [see letter to Whitman of 15 October 1890, note 1]. She and Bryce are sorry that WJ cannot dine with them. Thanks him for the "two fat tomes." The "prick and pungency" of his way of writing makes it exciting to her. Mentions Chamberlain [see letter to Whitman of 15 October 1890]. Some day she will tell him about her conflict with Elizabeth Phillips [unidentified; name uncertain] (ALS: MH bMS Am 1092.9 [685]).

To Alice Howe Gibbens James. Cambridge, 13 October [1890]. Journey went well and Margaret Mary was amiable the entire time. Discusses plans to meet AGJ when she returns. Asks her to bring Tennyson's poems and Goethe's *Faust* and to give Andrew the enclosed (ALS: MH bMS Am 1092.9 [1772]).

To Caroline Wells Healey Dall [1822–1912, American author and reformer; only the present letter is known]. Cambridge, 14 October 1890. Harry Norman Gardiner told WJ that Mrs. Dall has had telepathic experiences, including an apparition of Theodore Parker [1810–1860, American transcendentalist theologian]. Asks her for written statements. WJ is collecting many such documents in the hope of discovering "laws" (ALS: MHi).

From Hugo Münsterberg. Freiburg, 14 October 1890. Thanks WJ for *Principles*, which express the present state of psychology. Münsterberg has compiled a list of important psychological literature, examining 200 journals. Siebert has arrived and has begun work on reaction time (ALS: MH bMS Am 1092.9 [358]).

From Théodule Ribot. Paris, 14 October 1890. Thanks for *Principles*, which he will use immediately in his course. Thinks that in attention the motor side is more important. Will read with interest WJ's treatment of abstract ideas that the new psychology, except for Taine, neglects. Ribot has prepared a questionnaire on the subject. Will arrange to review WJ in *Revue Philosophique* [see letter to AJ of 23 August 1891, note 6] (ALS: MH bMS Am 1092 [793]).

From Théodore Flournoy. Geneva, 15 October 1890. Thanks for *Principles*. Will read all of it because WJ expresses ideas that were drifting vaguely through

Flournoy's mind. Mentioned WJ in his introduction to *Métaphysique et psychologie*, which he sent to WJ. In Flournoy's psychology classes, students will hear WJ's name often (ALS: MH bMS Am 1092 [201]; published in English translation in *WJTF*).

From Ernst Mach. Prague, 17 October 1890. Thanks for *Principles* (ALS: MH bMS Am 1092 [539]).

To Ellen James Temple Emmet Hunter. Cambridge [23 October 1890 (postmark)]. Gives her HJ's address. HJ writes [*Correspondence*, 2:151–52] that AJ is "surprisingly well" and that he will "rejoice to see Elly T." Family returned from the country. Wishes he could go to the Tweedys in November when she will be there. AGJ sends love (ALS: MH bMS Am 1092.9 [1069]).

From Joseph Vogelius. 1 November 1890. Macmillan Co. in England took 250 copies of *Principles*. The interleaved copy [*AC85.J2376.890p] is being bound (Letterbook: NjP).

From Silas Weir Mitchell. 3 November [1890]. Thanks for *Principles* (ALS: MH bMS Am 1092 [555]).

From Joseph Vogelius. 3 November 1890. Complimentary copies for England will be sent along with Macmillan's copies. Copies for Germany and France were sent when book was issued. Giving Macmillan twenty-five additional free copies (Letterbook: NjP).

From Joseph Vogelius. 5 November 1890. They charged WJ $276.47 for 63 copies sent at WJ's request (Letterbook: NjP).

To Harriet Jackson Lee Morse. Cambridge, 7 November 1890. Condolences on death of Samuel Morse. Prays that she and her children will find "unknown resources for weathering this trial" (ALS: MCR).

To Oliver Wendell Holmes, Jr. Cambridge, 10 November [1890]. Holmes's praise of *Principles* did his heart good. Believes that only "two other living persons" have "performed the feat" of finishing the book. Wishes that it had "some construction" instead of "criticism" (ALS: MH-L).

From Carl Stumpf. Munich, 17 November 1890. Has only leafed through *Principles*, but will write WJ as soon as he reads it. Psychology is making progress in America, but there is little of it in Munich. Only in the area of hypnotism are contributions being made, by Carl Ludwig Du Prel [1839–1899, German oculist and philosophical writer], Schrenck-Notzing, and Schmidkunz. Is interested in Janet's book [see letter of 23 March 1890] for the theory of personality. WJ's "Hidden Self" pleased him, but he remains unsure about telepathy and spiritualism. Glad that WJ speaks strongly about Wundt's lack of clarity. In December WJ will receive an article in which Stumpf criticizes the experimental work being done in Wundt's school (ALS: MH bMS Am 1092.9 [626]).

From Joseph Vogelius. 17 November 1890. As WJ requested, a complimentary copy was sent to Fullerton (Letterbook: NjP).

From Joseph-Remi-Léopold Delbœuf. Liège, 18 November 1890. Has not written to WJ because he has been disgusted with life since the death of his wife. Has plans for many articles but cannot work on them. Liégeois and [Armand] Sabatier [1834–1910, French scientist and philosopher, teaching at Montpellier] have visited him. Finds his country dominated by a fanatical clergy and perhaps only a political revolution will put him back in touch with life. He has become a grandfather, his daughter Henriette having a boy. Has had little time to read WJ's *Principles*. Asks what WJ thinks of the work of Binet, which Delbœuf finds easy to read but not profound. Discusses free will. The central problem is to reconcile causality with freedom (ALS: MH bMS Am 1092 [162]).

From François Pillon. Paris, 21 November 1890. Thanks WJ for *Principles*. This has been a terrible year. His wife has been seriously ill, although now is nearly well, and his nephew Bourdillet [unidentified], a young man about to become a professor of philosophy, died in July. Pillon had placed all his hopes in this nephew, whom WJ once met (ALS: MH bMS Am 1092.9 [476]).

To Thomas Davidson. [December 1890]. London SPR has but two officers in America: Langley and Hodgson. Advised Hodgson not to approve circular because it appears to involve separate organization, but if it is only for a meeting to increase membership they will sign it [see letter to Davidson of 13 December 1890, note 1] (ALS: MH bMS Am 1092.9 [867]).

From William Mackintire Salter. Chicago, 9 December 1890. Discusses statements about Eliza Salter made by Leonora Piper while entranced (Published in *EPR*, 439–40).

From John Murray Forbes. Boston, 10 December 1890. WJ's letter led him to read SPR publications, which he did not find of sufficient interest to subscribe to. Is returning Langley's note (ALS: MH bMS Am 1092 [260]).

From Shadworth Hollway Hodgson. London, 13 December 1890. Thanks WJ for *Principles*. Very pleased that WJ mentioned him in the preface and cites his writings. Although they sometimes differ, they both belong to the "*experiential* as distinguished from the *empiricist* school of thought." Has made progress on his own book but WJ's has put "a spoke into its chariot wheels." George Croom Robertson looks well. Hopes that WJ, as a corresponding member of the Aristotelian Society, receives their *Proceedings* regularly. Met Justin Winsor [1831–1897, librarian at Harvard and historian], at home of Godfrey Lushington [1832–1907, British lawyer] (ALS: MH bMS Am 1092.9 [207]).

From William Dean Howells. Jefferson, Ohio, 13 December 1890. Looks forward to WJ's *Principles*, which he will see when he returns home. Was reading Henry James's *Society the Redeemed Form of Man* [1879] to his father. Thinks it wonderful thinking, but now understands what WJ meant "by his having his God perpetually set up over against him" (ALS: MH bMS Am 1092.9 [237]).

To Elinor Gertrude Mead Howells. Cambridge, 14 December 1890. Lest she think WJ's son Henry is a gifted artist, the drawing was something he copied and was left in the volume as a mark. Harry not gifted but copies well. Her husband will find the second volume [of *Principles*] more interesting for browsing (ALS: MH bMS Am 1784.5 [15]).

From James Sully. 15 December 1890. Thanks WJ for *Principles*. Has read the first thirty pages. Wants to review it for *Mind*, if he can find the time. Will send a copy of his own book due out next summer (ALS: MH bMS Am 1092 [1119]).

From Mary Sherwin Gibbens Salter. Chicago, 17 December 1890. Thanks for stenographic report of the Piper sitting. Thinks she did not tell Leonora Piper that Eliza Salter handled the knife before her death. Perhaps her sister

Margaret did so. [Note added by WJ: thinks he could have mentioned the knife incident but does not remember] (Published in *EPR*, 440).

From William Mackintire Salter. Chicago, 17 December 1890. Concerns names of Salter's relatives given by Leonora Piper at a sitting in Chocorua a year ago (Published in *EPR*, 440).

To Parke Godwin. Cambridge, 20 December 1890. Thanks Godwin for the favorable notice he gave *Principles* "on the 12th" [unidentified] but chides him for not sending WJ copies of it (TC: MH bMS Am 1092.1).

From Andrew Seth Pringle-Pattison. St. Andrews, 23 December 1890. Thanks WJ for *Principles*. Promises to read it and then discuss it with WJ. Finds WJ's writing helpful. Is working on lectures for Edinburgh (ALS: MH bMS Am 1092 [986]).

From Henry Sidgwick. Cambridge [England], 24 December 1890. WJ's postcard with the correction arrived too late as *Proceedings* had been printed [see letter to Myers of 15 July 1890], but the correction will be attended to at the first opportunity. Thanks WJ for *Principles*. Will read it after he finishes writing *The Elements of Politics* [1891]. Hodgson wrote Myers in cheerful tone about prospects for psychical research. Sidgwick hopes his hopefulness justified. He and Mrs. Sidgwick witnessed table-rising. Difficult to communicate it to others because dependent on faith in the participants and not on scientific basis (ALS: MH bMS Am 1092.9 [615]).

From Frederic William Henry Myers. Cambridge [England], 28 December 1890. Thanks WJ for *Principles*. Struck by the great increase of subject matter, as compared to Ward, Bain, and Sully, which WJ's psychical researches supplied. WJ's book better than Spencer's or Sully's. Does not think the SPR in America is moribund. Wants to hear what [name illegible, perhaps Carey] does (APS: MH bMS Am 1092.9 [412]).

From Henry Holt and Co. 31 December 1890. Statement [in part illegible] listing various amounts and leaving a balance of $115.77 (Letterbook: NjP).

1891

To Paul Carus. Cambridge [1891]. Sends Delbœuf's final article, which can be shortened [perhaps Joseph-Remi-Léopold Delbœuf, "On Criminal Suggestion," *Monist* 2 (April 1892): 363–85]. It is very sensible, but the anecdotes are too numerous (AL: ICarbS).

From Edward Allen Fay [1843–1923, American educator, then teaching at Gallaudet College, Washington, D.C.]. [1891]. Assures WJ that Melville Ballard, WJ's deaf-mute witness, is trustworthy (Published in *EPS*, 278–79n).

From Joseph Claybaugh Gordon [1842–1903, professor at Gallaudet College, Washington, D.C.]. [1891]. Assures WJ of Ballard's competence (Published in *EPS*, 279n).

From Warring Wilkinson [1834–1918, principal of the California Institution for the Education of the Deaf and Dumb, and the Blind]. [1891]. Theophilus d'Estrella [see *EPs*, 374] can be trusted to report his experiences accurately (Published in *EPs*, 279n).

From Granville Stanley Hall. [January 1891]. Could not respond to WJ's note immediately and has since mislaid it. Has seen but one copy of the *Christian*

Union, probably later than WJ himself [Hall's unsigned notice of WJ's *Psychology* appeared in *Christian Union* 43 (1 January 1891): 22]. WJ's book "stimulates reaction" in him and he differs with WJ more than he thought, as WJ will see from Hall's signed review [see letter of 30 January 1891, note 3] (ALS: MH bMS Am 1092.9 [177]).

To Mary Whiton Calkins. Cambridge, 1 January 1891. Wishes her a happy new year. Hopes that she will consult him soon (ALS: MWelC).

From William M. Reily. 2 January 1891. Describes a woman who has been starving [see *EPR,* 384] (ALS: SPR, New York City).

To Samuel Pierpont Langley. Cambridge, 3 January 1891. He knows of no article on hypnotism as described by Langley. Hodgson mentioned one by [Christian Archibald] Herter [1865–1910, American pathologist, "Hypnotism: What It Is and What It Is Not," *Popular Science Monthly* 33 (October 1888): 755–71]. Forbes did not subscribe in spite of Langley's letter [see letter of 10 December 1890 (calendared)] (ALS: Smithsonian; published in *SUC*).

From Andrew Preston Peabody. Cambridge, 3 January 1890 [1891, with reference to the death of Peabody's daughter, Maria L. Peabody, on 30 December 1890]. Thanks WJ for his sympathy (ALS: MH bMS Am 1092 [655]).

To Mary Gray Ward Dorr. Cambridge, 9 January 1891. Declines invitation as he had accepted another engagement (ALS: MH bMS Am 1092.9 [891]).

From Sarah Wyman Whitman. [19 January 1891]. Invites WJ to tea for [Richard Harding] Davis [1864–1916, American author], son of Rebecca Harding Davis [1831–1910, American author]. Banter about WJ's statement regarding a shortened term at Harvard [see *ECR,* 32–41]. Some day will tell him what she thinks of *Principles* (ALS: MH bMS Am 1092.9 [686]).

To Sarah Wyman Whitman. 19 January 1891. Must decline her invitation again. Perhaps he will see her at the Dorrs. Saw Daniel Merriman's church in Worcester [with stained glass by Sarah Whitman]—better than anything he has seen since St. Mark's in Venice (ALS: MH bMS Am 1092.9 [3907]).

To James Ward. 24 January 1891. Letter is listed in Houghton catalogues, but is lost and was not seen (MH bMS Am 1092.9 [3833]).

From Joseph Vogelius. 27 January 1891. In reply to WJ's card of 24 January states that a copy of *Principles* was sent to the *Vierteljahrsschrift für wissenschaftliche Philosophie.* They are preparing a new edition and WJ should inform them of any changes (Letterbook: NjP).

To Henry Holt. 1 February 1891. For content see letter of 3 February 1891 (TC: MH bMS Am 1092.1; published in part in *PP,* 1576).

From Henry Holt. 12 February 1891. Advertisements will appear in volume 2 of *Principles.* Asks about condensed version. Notes that Ladd is out with one [*Outlines of Physiological Psychology* (1891)]. Thanks WJ for his frank opinion of the *Educational Review* [see letter of 3 February 1891] and asks if he will do the same for the next number (Letterbook: NjP).

From William Leonard Worcester. Little Rock, 23 February 1891. Asks if WJ can send him an article on belief by Marty ["Über subjectlose Sätze," *Vierteljahrsschrift für wissenschaftliche Philosophie* 8 (1884): 161–92]. Relates anecdote about a squirrel's reasoning, which cannot be reconciled with WJ's views concerning the intelligence of brutes [see *PP,* 1470] (ALS: MH bMS Am 1092 [1184]).

From Jacques Loeb. Naples, 2 March 1891. Thanks WJ for *Principles*, which is marked by originality and naturalness, and hopes that it will stimulate psychology in Germany. Loeb called on WJ recently while visiting the United States, but WJ was out. Wanted to talk about psychical phenomena in the lower animals, about which Loeb's views resemble those of Mach and Carl Sachs [1853–1878, German physician]. Would like to return to America to teach (ALS: MH bMS Am 1092 [510]).

From Andrew Seth Pringle-Pattison. St. Andrews, 11 March 1891. Is applying for the Chair of Logic and Metaphysics at Edinburgh University, recently vacated by Alexander Campbell Fraser [1819–1914, Scottish philosopher; two letters to WJ are known, from 1898 and 1901] and seeks testimonial from WJ. Has read parts of *Principles* (ALS: MH bMS Am 1092 [987]).

From George C. Bartlett. New York, 18 March 1891. At Frank B. Carpenter's [unidentified] request is sending WJ a copy of *The Salem Seer* [1891; reminiscences of Charles H. Foster] (TL [signature typed]: MH Phil 7054.43.3B).

From George C. Bartlett. New York, 25 March 1891. Reply to WJ's letter of 21 March. Defends his belief that Foster is genuine. WJ is mistaken in accusing Foster of trickery. WJ speaks of Foster's failure at a séance at Mr. Mountford's [unidentified] and says that Bartlett knows about Truesdell's [unidentified] accusations that Foster reads the messages while relighting his cigar (TL [signature typed]: MH Phil 7054.43.3B).

From Annie Payson Call. 28 March 1891. Thanks WJ for his notice [Call, *Power through Repose* (1891), *Nation* 52 (19 March 1891): 246–47; reprinted in *ECR*] (ALS: MH bMS Am 1092 [63]).

From Joseph Vogelius. 2 April 1891. Sending WJ two complimentary copies of volume 1 of *Principles* (Letterbook: NjP).

To Alpheus Hyatt. 7 April 1891. Declines invitation. Went to [Francis Greenwood] Peabody's, who is going to Europe (ALS: NjP).

From Elisha Benjamin Andrews [1844–1917, American historian and administrator, president of Brown University]. Providence, 14 April 1891. Is interested in Delabarre and thanks WJ for his testimony. Wants to build up psychology department (ALS: RPB).

To Samuel Porter. Cambridge, 19 April 1891. Giżicki finds Ballard's statements [see *PP*, 256–59] "incredible." Since WJ takes them from Porter's article [*PP*, 1343], asks for his opinion of Ballard's credibility (ALS: Miss Porter's School).

From Samuel Porter [April 1891, placed here with reference to preceding letter from WJ]. Assures WJ of Ballard's competence (Published in *EPs*, 278n).

From Henry Holt. 22 April 1891. Thanks WJ for his note of 20 April. Information about Windelband will be useful. Will keep WJ informed concerning sales of *Principles* (Letterbook: NjP).

From Henry Holt. 25 April 1891. WJ's royalties on sheets of *Principles* sent to England will be $0.33⅓ per set (Letterbook: NjP).

From Henry Holt. 25 April 1891. They [prospective publishers of translations of *Principles*] probably will act as they have written. The book is not protected by international copyright, but any modifications and abridgements will be protected since they will appear after the law goes into effect (Letterbook: NjP).

From Joseph Vogelius. 25 April 1891. As of 31 December 1890, 544 copies and

250 sheets were sold, yielding royalties of $409.73. Charges were $235.06. Sending $87.34 [the other half was sent later] (Letterbook: NjP).

From Carl Stumpf. Munich, 14 May 1891. Discusses difficulties with translation of *Principles*. Stumpf cannot assist Cossmann because their personal relations are poor. Cossmann now is negotiating with Giżycki. WJ should not be angered by Schmidkunz [see letter to AGJ of 14 August 1891, 9:15 A.M.], because Schmidkunz identifies psychology with hypnotism. Sully's review of volume 2 of the *Tonpsychologie* [see letter of 24 October 1891] is peevish and discourages Stumpf from working on volume 3 (ALS: MH bMS Am 1092.9 (627)].

To Alice Howe Gibbens James. Chocorua, Tuesday, 10 [9] June [1891]. All is well. Waiting for Sumner Gilman [unidentified] who has key to barn (APS: MH bMS Am 1092.9 [1776]).

From Joseph-Remi-Léopold Delbœuf. Liège, 11 June 1891. Has returned from a tour of Swiss and German laboratories and is disappointed by their experiments. Explains at great length that because of the death of his wife he is unable to finish articles on hypnotism, including the one WJ is interested in. Explains how one lizard would not eat while its companion lizard could not be found after it escaped. Will now have to combat the anti-psychological thesis of Liégeois. A law is being passed in Belgium that would have prevented Delbœuf from making his experiments. Asks whether WJ is responsible for Delbœuf's nomination as corresponding member of a medico-legal society in New York. Tarde is quite ill. Delbœuf's article about Montpellier was a success. Wants to have the *Monist* manuscript back, even if it is published [see letter to Carus of 1891] (ALS: MH bMS Am 1092 [164]).

To Alice Howe Gibbens James. Cambridge, Thursday night [25 June 1891]. Busy but not much progress. Lunched with John Murray Forbes. Margaret Gregor arrived and is pleased with Briggs's plan of the house. Will go to see Edmund Tweedy tomorrow. Going to Club for lunch and will see Pierce and Benjamin Ives Gilman (ALS: MH bMS Am 1092.9 [1780]).

From Henry Holt and Co. 25 June 1891. Sends royalty check for $87.33 (Letterbook: NjP).

To Charles William Eliot. Cambridge, 26 June 1891. Discusses housing for the psychological laboratory in Dane Hall. Spoke with Garfield about the outside staircase, and they propose something more expensive than what the Corporation approved. Eliot must notify Garfield if he is to go forward (ALS: MH Archives).

To Alice Howe Gibbens James. Cambridge, 26 June 1891. Gives AJ's address. Margaret acts "splendidly, altho I gave her an exhibition of my temper." Pierces are to come on Saturday and discussion follows about finding clean sheets. Mentions Annie and Mrs. Malone. Check arrived from Holt. Many unforeseen expenses. Going now to Mrs. Gourlay's and McNamee's, then to catch the Newport train (ALS: MH bMS Am 1092.9 [1781]).

To Alice Howe Gibbens James. Newport, 28 June 1891. Missed the Friday trains, so took train yesterday. Tweedy wept when speaking of his wife and looks poorly. His niece Mrs. Tiffany and her stepson are here. WJ still feeling effects of the "grip." Will go to Boston tonight. Never felt as solidly "welded (or wedded)" to her as now. Tell Margaret Mary that unless she improves Harry Fox will take Toby away (ALS: MH bMS Am 1092.9 [1782]).

To Frederick Law Olmsted. Chocorua, July 1891. Thanks for letter of 28 June. Would like more details about Olmsted's "open-eyed sleep-visions." The more facts are accumulated, the better the chances that they will fall into "natural groups" (APS: DLC).

From Frederick Law Olmsted. 8 July 1891. In response to WJ note, describes in detail [10 pp.] incidents of sleeping with open eyes and the haunting of their house (TC: DLC; published in part in *The Papers of Frederick Law Olmsted*, ed. Charles Capen McLaughlin [Baltimore: Johns Hopkins Univ. Press, 1977], 1:168).

From François Pillon. Paris, 9 July 1891. Thanks WJ for his letter of 23 May. WJ best understands what the death of Bourdillet means to Pillon [see letter of 21 November 1890 (calendared)]. If WJ has read Pillon's "La Première preuve cartésienne de l'existence de Dieu, et la critique de l'infini" [*Année Philosophique* 1 (1891): 43–190], he understands how important for Pillon is the clarification of the ideas of infinity and perfection and how Pillon tries to connect phenomenalist criticism with modern philosophy. A phenomenalist is not only a disciple of Kant, but also of Hume, Descartes, Berkeley, and others. The review of literature in *Année Philosophique* is limited to writings in French, and thus Pillon could not include WJ's *Principles* or Sidgwick's *Methods of Ethics*. But Dauriac is now preparing a critical notice of *Principles* for the *Année*. Like WJ, Pillon admires Tarde but cannot understand why Tarde does not realize that belief in determinism does not rest upon science but upon metaphysics (ALS: MH bMS Am 1092.9 [477]).

To Frederick Law Olmsted. Chocorua, 11 July 1891. Thanks for narrative (ALS: DLC).

From Alice James. Kensington, 30 July [1891]. Thanks WJ for his fraternal letter. She would have felt wounded had he "walked round & not up to my demise." His philosophy of the "transition" is hers also. She congratulates him upon arriving at fifty at the point she reached at fifteen. He exaggerates the tragedy of her death and should remember that women need less "to feed upon" than men. Despite the poverty of her experience, she has always had a significance for herself. This year has been one of the happiest because she was "surrounded by such affection & devotion." Annie Ashburner Richards [wife of Francis Gardner Richards, related to Anne and Grace Ashburner; three letters are known from 1873 to 1878] has been perfect in her friendship. William Baldwin has had an "inspiring effect." Sends love to AGJ, to Henrietta Child, and to Mrs. Child (MLS [Katharine Peabody Loring]: MH bMS Am 1094 [1491]; published in *DLAJ*).

From Joseph Vogelius. 31 July 1891. Received WJ's letter of the 21st to Holt, who is on vacation. WJ should read the proofs himself. Upon receiving manuscript [*Briefer Course*] they will send some proofs by 1 September. Sales of *Principles* will be good in the fall (Letterbook incomplete: NjP).

To Frederick Law Olmsted. 2 August 1891. Returns Olmsted's account [see letter of 8 July 1891 (calendared)] (ALS: DLC).

To Alice Howe Gibbens James. 10 August [1891]. Delightful day on Gerrishe's

Island [Maine]. Dined with Hodgson. Mrs. Wm. P's [unidentified] address is Union, N. H. Neither Warner nor Hodgson can go with him and it may be too hot to go to Virginia (APS: MH bMS Am 1092.9 [1784]).

To Alice Howe Gibbens James. Cambridge, 13 August 1891. Tea at Ashburners with Charles, Sara, the Richard Nortons, and George Curtis. Breakfast at Child's. Finished manuscript [*Briefer Course*]. Sent check for $175, twice the amount of Plumb's first installment for month, half for her, half for her mother. When Clary's note is cashed, $100 more apiece will follow. Tell Eliza Gibbens that Bradley and Storer will send deed to be recorded, then send it to her. Will leave the check with Charles Norton. Will leave tomorrow. Received letters from her and Harry (ALS: MH bMS Am 1092.9 [1786]).

To Alice Howe Gibbens James. Washington, D.C., 15 August 1891. Slept well on train. Will spend night in Danville and arrive at Asheville, N. C., tomorrow (ALS: MH bMS Am 1092.9 [1788]).

To Grace Ashburner. Linville, N. C., 25 August 1891. Has been thinking of her but has had many letters to write to family: AGJ, HJ, Katharine Loring, and Ellen Emmet, who is soon to marry a Scot [George Hunter]. There follows a long description of the area, an "Eden" in which the "serpent has not yet made his appearance." If WJ had Child's "pen," he might do justice to it. The development is managed by a "charming" North Carolinian [Hugh MacRae; for WJ's published description of the area see *ECR*, 133–35] (ALS: MH bMS Am 1092.9 [724]).

To Daniel Merriman. Chocorua, Thursday [late August 1891, dating uncertain and assumes that 'Thursday' is an error]. Returned from the South two days ago. Telegram from Merriman arrived too late for WJ to go. Hopes to bring AGJ before the middle of the month to bid the Merrimans good bye (TC: MH bMS Am 1092.1).

To Alice Howe Gibbens James. Cambridge, 11 September 1891. Will sail tomorrow at noon on the *Eider*. Said good-bye to everyone. Mentions Theodora and "Aunt" Annie. Is in mood for going and won't allow thoughts of other duties to "mar the harmony" (ALS: MH bMS Am 1092.9 [1793]).

From William Noyes. Somerville, Mass. 18 September [1891]. Describes his experiments while riding on a train of trying to "get an apparent motion directly opposite the motion of the train." Hopes to have the results of the measurement of Mrs. Prince's brain as compared with that of an insane person when he returns next week (ALS: MBCo).

To Grace Norton. London [ca. 25 September 1891]. Declines invitation for that evening. Apologizes for not informing her sooner but HJ had destroyed her note with her address. Found berth on the *City of Paris*. Happy to hear from HJ that her trip has been successful (ALS: MH bMS Am 1092.1).

To Smith Baker. Cambridge [9 October 1891]. Has just returned from England. The best book is Theodore Ziehen's [1862–1950, German psychiatrist] *Leitfaden der physiologischen Psychologie* [1891, Phil 5265.1*]. Regrets that Baker will not come here (APS: OO).

From L. J. Bertrand [a Huguenot minister then living in Neuilly, France]. 10 October 1891. In response to several letters from WJ, is sending a description of his experience of clairvoyance (Published in Myers, "Indications of Continued Terrene Knowlege," 194–95).

From Joseph Vogelius. 12 October 1891. Enclosed are sample pages of *Briefer Course*. Should they send proofs to A. Zimmer, German publishers from Stuttgart, who have applied for price of sets? (Letterbook: NjP; published in *BC*, 468).

From George Croom Robertson. London, 13 October 1891. Disappointed to have missed WJ. Saw Sidgwick, who supplemented Robertson's impressions of WJ received from letters. Hopes for a visit from WJ next year. Doubtful that he will be at International Congress of Experimental Psychology in 1892. Has begun college year and is relieved not to have any manuscripts to read. [Robertson retired as editor of *Mind*.] Wife sends her regards (ALS: MH bMS Am 1092.9 [526]).

From Joseph Vogelius. 14 October 1891. Sent first lot of proof [of *Briefer Course*]. Will be glad to send proof to Germany and France [to prospective translators]. Asks for Boirac's address. Cossmann is in Frankfurt (Letterbook: NjP; published in *BC*, 468).

To Sarah Wyman Whitman. 20 October [1891]. Declines invitation as AGJ has headache and he is too busy. Went to London to visit his dying sister, whom he found "positively hilarious over the prospect of speedy release." Hopes to see her when she returns from Beverly (ALS: MH bMS Am 1092.9 [3911]).

From Henry Holt and Co. 24 October 1891. As of 30 June, 310 sets of *Principles* at $0.60. Sending $93.00 (Letterbook: NjP).

From Joseph Vogelius. 24 October 1891. Sending books by express. Title will be *Psychology*, but title page and advertisements will carry the words *Briefer Course* (Letterbook: NjP; published in part in *BC*, 470).

From Joseph Vogelius. 2 November 1891. Sending proofs to Cossman and Boirac. Discusses layout of pages in chapter 7 (Letterbook: NjP; published in part in *BC*, 480).

From Joseph Vogelius. 4 November 1891. Preparing to print a new edition of *Principles*. Will WJ send his list of corrections? Discusses prices of pamphlet [see *BC*, 480] (Letterbook: NjP; published in part in *BC*, 481).

From Francis Albert Christie [1858–1938, American theologian]. Cambridge, 6 November 1891. Attended WJ's lecture of Thursday [5 November] and wants to know why in listing human instincts WJ omitted the "combative instinct." As a teacher, he has noticed it and appealed to it to get boys to learn. Often, those who had no desire to imitate, who did not want prizes, or to whom ideas of excellence were meaningless, were moved by desire to battle with a problem (ALS: MH bMS Am 1092.9 [4536]).

From Joseph Vogelius. 16 November 1891. WJ's letter of 12 November ordering 100 copies of the pamphlet only reached him this morning. As can be seen from the enclosed envelope, the letter was not posted until [illegible] and thus came too late because the printer on Saturday [illegible] (Letterbook: NjP).

From Joseph Vogelius. 24 November 1891. WJ's letter of the 18th was first indication that he expected *Briefer Course* on a certain day for his classes. Will try to accommodate him and will gain time if he will do the cuttings and insertions in galley proofs rather than in pages. Does WJ want to see plate proofs? (Letterbook: NjP; published in *BC*, 481).

To William Torrey Harris. Cambridge, 27 November 1891. Declines to write text-book, having promised himself after *Principles* that he would "never, never, never, write a text book again" (ALS: CLSU; published in Wallace Nethery, "Pragmatist to Publisher: Letters of W. James to W. T. Harris," *Personalist* 49 [1968]: 489–508).

To William Noyes. Cambridge, 30 November 1891. Thanks Noyes for the chronoscopic apparatus. Hopes to be able to work it but if Sanford failed, he doesn't think there is much hope for him (ALS: MH bMS Am 1092.9 [3358]).

From John Murray Forbes. Milton, Mass., 2 December 1891. Discussion of contributions of money and portraits for a club. Lists names of men whose portraits might hang in a gallery. 27 December 1891. Meant to write WJ but was too busy. Is Professor Royce an original member? Remembers something about that. Met Raphael Pumpelly [1837–1923, American geologist and traveler] and converted him. Toughest opposition is Charles Norton (ALS: MH bMS Am 1092 [261]).

From Alice James. Kensington, 2 December [1891]. Describes her physical condition. Katharine Loring's remedy [morphia], which calms her nerves and lets her sleep, more helpful than Tuckey, her hypnotizer [from note in WJ's hand it is clear that he sent the letter on to RJ] (ALS: MH bMS Am 1094 [1493]; published in *DLAJ*).

From Joseph Vogelius. 2 December 1891. Printer cannot deliver the extra type for *Briefer Course* in time for book to be ready for WJ's classes. Gives WJ three alternatives that would allow him to have text for his classes (Letterbook: NjP; published in part in *BC*, 481).

From Joseph Vogelius. 4 December 1891. Asks if WJ has any more corrections before *Briefer Course* goes to press. Will print the book at same time as the pamphlet for WJ's class. Asks if 200 copies are enough for WJ's class. Discussion follows about printing schedule. Thanks WJ for his offer to pay half the cost of the pamphlets but they will supply them free (Letterbook: NjP; published in part in *BC*, 481).

From Joseph Vogelius. 6 December 1891. WJ shall have 206 copies of the first 96 pages of *Briefer Course* for his classes. Asked about WJ's index question, Holt responded: "Tell Prof. James that his reputation can stand letting the book go out without an index, but ours can't" (Letterbook: NjP).

From Henry Holt. 7 December 1891. Is Windelband the one about whom WJ expressed a very good opinion last spring? Someone from the University of Michigan wants to translate him (Letterbook: NjP).

From Joseph Vogelius. 11 December 1891. Sending the entire lot tomorrow, including the sixteen additional copies of the pamphlet that WJ requested (Letterbook: NjP).

To Alice Howe Gibbens James. Newport, Monday [21 December 1891]. Note from Hodgson arrived. Called on Mrs. Calvert's medium [Elizabeth Steuart Calvert (1803–1897), wife of George Henry Calvert (1803–1889), author, mayor of Newport] but did not get a sitting. Called on Theodora Woolsey [unidentified]. Enjoyed Daisy Waring's table at dinner but should have enjoyed it more had AGJ been there. Will go to Katharine and Richard Emmet's at New Rochelle tomorrow and to New York City Wednesday morning. Send mail in care of Cattell at Columbia College. Wish her mother and Margaret Gregor a merry Christmas (ALS: MH bMS Am 1092.9 [1799]).

From Joseph Vogelius. 21 December 1891. Discussion of missing page proofs. Duplicate proofs will be mailed to WJ, who should not let this accident prevent him from going away. They will print new leaves for pages 86 and 89 as they dislike putting in an errata slip (Letterbook: NjP).

From Joseph Vogelius. 22 December 1891. Received missing page proofs of pp. 342–61 but are still lacking pp. 338–41 (Letterbook: NjP).

From Henry Holt and Co. 23 December 1891. Encloses royalty check for $82.49, balance due as of 30 June (Letterbook: NjP).

To Jacob Gould Schurman. Cambridge, 28 December 1891. Discusses setting of "Thought Before Language" [reprinted in *EPs*]. Missed Creighton who brought card from Schurman. Met Caldwell, a "nice fellow." Schurman has probably received WJ's reply to Ladd ["A Plea for Psychology as a 'Natural Science'" (reprinted in *EPs*)]. Hopes the *Philosophical Review* will be a success (ALS: MH bMS Am 1092.9 [3708]).

From Joseph Vogelius. 29 December 1891. Sending the last page proofs of text and also the front matter. Would like index by 31 December, otherwise they cannot have bound copies ready by 12 January 1892. Jastrow wants to examine book for use in his class. They have promised it by 15 January (Letterbook: NjP; published in *BC*, 472).

From Joseph Vogelius. 31 December 1891. Received WJ's letter of the 30th. If the index is ready WJ should express it to Drummond. They still hope to have book in WJ's hands on the 12th. WJ should see that booksellers send their orders (Letterbook: NjP; published in part in *BC*, 472).

1892

From Henry Holt and Co. 5 January [1892]. Returning Arey's [possibly Melvin Franklin Arey (1844–1931), an educator in Iowa] letter. Have done everything they can to present WJ's books to the audience Arey mentions, as can be seen from the number of copies sold in normal schools (Letterbook: NjP).

From Joseph Vogelius. 6 January 1892. Received his letter of the 5th. Still hopes to be able to ship books on the 11th. Price for teachers should be about $2. *Principles* has sold about 516 copies as well as 100 sheets to England since 1 July 1891 (Letterbook: NjP; published in part in *BC*, 472).

From Jane Lee Waring [sister of George Edwin Waring, and a longtime follower of Harris, whom she is reported to have married in March 1892 when she was sixty-two]. Santa Rosa, Cal., 8 January 1892. Thomas Lake Harris [1823–1906, English-born spiritualist, founder of utopian communities, active in the United States, at this time the subject of reports of sexual and financial irregularities] asked her to answer WJ's letter. Describes in great detail how her contact with Harris and his teaching helped her to overcome sorrow. Encloses letter from Dr. Pulsford [unidentified] (ALS: MH Autograph File).

From Joseph Vogelius. 11 January 1892. *Briefer Course* is ready. Teachers' price is $1.60 (Letterbook: NjP; published in part in *BC*, 473).

From Joseph Vogelius. 12 January 1892. Asks WJ to supply reference page on enclosed proof as printer left it blank (Letterbook: NjP; published in part in *BC*, 473).

To Jacob Gould Schurman. Cambridge, 14 January 1892. Wishes he could have been at meetings of the American Psychological Association. Hopes to visit

Cornell. Found "Thought Before Language" [reprinted in *EPs*] in his drawer and will send it at once. Has seen a copy of the *Philosophical Review* and thinks it good (ALS: MH bMS Am 1092.9 [3709]).

From Joseph Vogelius. 14 January 1892. Glad that WJ is pleased with the appearance of *Briefer Course*. Will print cancel sheet for pp. 51 and 52. Sent Cossmann and Boirac plate proofs of the pages. Sold Macmillan & Co. 500 copies of *Briefer Course* for England (Letterbook: NjP; published in *BC*, 473).

From Joseph Vogelius. 14 January 1892. Need to print new edition of *Briefer Course* at once. WJ should send any corrections (Letterbook: NjP; published in part in *BC*, 473).

To Jacob Gould Schurman. Cambridge, 15 January 1892. Wants to review Schmidkunz, *Psychologie der Suggestion* [1892 (reprinted in *ECR*)], and Frédéric Courmont [French physician], *Le Cervelet* [reprinted in *ECR*] (APS: MH bMS Am 1092.9 [3710]).

From Henry Holt and Co. 19 January 1892. Have distributed thirty-one free copies of *Briefer Course*. WJ will be charged for ten (Letterbook: NjP).

To Francis Ellingwood Abbot. Cambridge, 21 January 1892. Prodding Abbot about his subscription for the Robertson testimonial [upon the retirement of Robertson as editor of *Mind*] (APS: MH Archives).

To Lester Frank Ward. Cambridge, 22 January 1892. Prodding Ward about subscribing for the Robertson testimonial (APS: RPB).

To Frances Rollins Morse. 2 February 1892. Thanks her for her gift of a book (ALS: MH bMS Am 1092.9 [3207]).

To Charles Renouvier. Cambridge, 4 February 1892. Thanks Renouvier for sending the second edition of *Les Principes de la nature* [1892; for WJ's review see *ECR*]. Has not had time to read it. Sent Renouvier a copy of *Briefer Course*. WJ has eighty laboratory students, leaving him little time for reading (ALS: MH bMS Am 1092.9 [3533]; published in *TCWJ*, 1:708).

To Charles William Eliot. 7 February 1892. Approves proposed scheme of retirement allowances, at 60 years of age after 20 years service (ALS: MH Archives).

From John Dewey. Ann Arbor, 8 February 1892. Sends $5 for Robertson testimonial. *Briefer Course* is a lively book and helps destroy the superstition that every "scientific book ought to be a corpse." Thinks highly of Harvard graduates. George Herbert Mead "grows on us everyday" (ALS: MH bMS Am 1092.9 [132]).

To Harry Norman Gardiner. Cambridge, 14 February 1892. Discussion of the census of hallucinations, mentioning the Gilfillan, Kent, and Blodgett cases. Asks if Miss Stoffel [unidentified] can show Gardiner the letter that refers to a particular incident. Anyone who pays can attend the International Congress of Experimental Psychology. Myers asks if American participants will object to a date change. Neither WJ nor anyone he knows plans to go (ALS: MH bMS Am 1092.9 [911]).

To James Ford Rhodes [1848–1927, American author; correspondence is known from 1892 to 1907]. Cambridge, 14 February [1892 (assigned by archivist)]. Returning Dr. Lowman's [unidentified] letter. Found the case of the soldier interesting (ALS: MHi).

From Granville Stanley Hall. Worcester, Mass., 16 February 1892. Hears inspiring accounts of WJ's experimental department at Harvard. WJ should publish in the *American Journal of Psychology* (MLS: MH bMS Am 1092.9 [178]).

To Mary Whiton Calkins. 17 February 1892. Thanks her for the optical papers. Delabarre will arrive in March (APS: MWelC).

From Hans Schmidkunz. 18 February 1892. Thanks WJ for his letter of 26 November 1891 and book. Briefly comments on "our" antimaterialistic pamphlet (ALS: MH Phil 7140.8.5).

To Sarah Wyman Whitman. 1 March [1892]. Returning Chapman's manuscript [John Jay Chapman, *The Two Philosophers: A Quaint, and Sad Comedy* (1892), published anonymously, about the controversy between Royce and Abbot], which should be published. Abbot seems to be going mad (ALS: MH bMS Am 1092.9 [3937]).

To William Noyes. Cambridge, 2 March 1892. His chronoscope arrived so he will return Noyes's. WJ wants to take his graduate students in mental pathology to visit an asylum. He is considering South Boston. Asks for the superintendent's name (ALS: MH bMS Am 1092.9 [3360]).

From Sarah Wyman Whitman. 22 March 1892. Condolence letter on AJ's death. Is going to join the Brimmers in Bermuda (ALS: MH bMS Am 1092.9 [688]).

From Joseph Vogelius. 26 March 1892. Encloses *Briefer Course* corrections. Pages 94 and 100 need condensing (Letterbook: NjP; published in *BC*, 486).

To Hugo Münsterberg. Cambridge, 5 April 1892. Leaving on a trip. A prospective donor to support Münsterberg's hiring has "grown cold." There will be nothing final about the position until the first week in May (ALS: MB).

From Charles William Eliot. California, 6 April 1892. Approves inviting Münsterberg at $3,000 salary plus $600 expenses. Consult Hooper and Walcott. Keep Santayana only through next year (Telegram: MH bMS Am 1092.9 [148]).

From Hugo Münsterberg. Freiburg, 8 April 1892. Now thinks he will not need $12,000 for three years. The $9,000 WJ suggested at first will be enough to live on. Two years would be enough to organize the laboratory. Four years are out of the question. Is seeking the advice of friends. WJ knows that Münsterberg would like to accept (ALS: MH bMS Am 1092.9 [361]).

From Hugo Münsterberg. Freiburg, 12 April 1892. Has received WJ's telegram and will go to Berlin to consult colleagues and to Danzig to consult his family. He is concerned that an American stay will harm his prospects in Germany and that he will become too specialized, moving too much toward experimentation and physiology and away from broader philosophical questions. However, he is much attracted by the new experiences that America offers. Asks for permission to dedicate a book [unidentified] to WJ (ALS: MH bMS Am 1092.9 [362]).

From Hugo Münsterberg. Freiburg, 12 April 1892. Thanks WJ. Decision by end of April (Cablegram: MH bMS Am 1092.9 [362]).

From William Leonard Worcester. Little Rock, 19 April 1892. Extensive reply to WJ's lost letter concerning criticism of *Principles* published by Worcester in the *Monist* [see *EPs*, 375, for the articles and WJ's annotations]. Worcester still holds that all beliefs can be expressed by judgments and does not understand to what WJ has reference "as beliefs not capable of being formulated as judgments." He supposed WJ to hold that fundamental in every belief and volition was a "free choice, between alternatives." He did not suppose WJ to maintain seriously the "infallibility of the method" that WJ says is infallible. Worcester's own loss of belief in God contradicts WJ's claim, because Worcester continued to pray after he had come to think that there was no one to pray to. Is sorry now that he did not send his second article, on emotion, to WJ before sending it to the publisher (ALS: MH bMS Am 1092.9 [712a]).

From Henry Holt and Co. 25 April 1892. As of 31 December 1891, 513 copies of *Principles* at $0.60 and 100 sheets at $0.33⅓, for a total of $341.14. Charges were $97.03. Sending [amount illegible] (Letterbook: NjP).

From Hugo Münsterberg. Freiburg, 29 April 1892. Grateful to WJ for his efforts. Is afraid of not being able to learn English well enough and of separation from his mother tongue and fatherland. The latter is especially important because he is inclined not only toward science but also toward poetry and politics. Otherwise, he and his wife are much drawn to America (ALS: MH bMS Am 1092.9 [364]).

From Hugo Münsterberg. Freiburg, 30 April 1892. Accepts three-year position but has not received an official offer. Wants to be certain that WJ has not changed his mind after learning that Münsterberg lacks talent in languages and wants the freedom to end his service for any reason. Discussion follows concerning the move to America. Hopes to see WJ there but understands that WJ may be in Europe, in which case he will turn to Royce and Nichols (ALS: MH bMS Am 1092.9 [365]).

From Hugo Münsterberg. Freiburg, 3 May 1892. Awaits WJ's telegram. Has almost decided to accept (Cablegram: MH bMS Am 1092.9 [367]).

From Hugo Münsterberg. Freiburg, 3 May 1892. After acceptance, some details remain. As the second laboratory assistant he suggests Wadsworth [see letter to Münsterberg of 15 May 1892, note 6]. German newspapers are writing about their negotiations, learning about them from American sources and not from Münsterberg (ALS: MH bMS Am 1092.9 [366]).

From Henry Holt and Co. 4 May 1892. Sending copy of *Principles* to Christian Ufer [b. 1856], Altenburg, Germany (Letterbook: NjP).

From Michael Anagnos. 5 May 1892. In answer to WJ's letter, they will be pleased to have him and his students visit Helen Keller on 7 May (Letterbook: Perkins School for the Blind).

From Andrew Seth Pringle-Pattison. Edinburgh, 6 May 1892. Flattered by Harvard's interest, but nothing could induce him to leave Edinburgh. Hears that Chicago has taken people from Cornell. James Seth [1860–1924, Scottish philosopher] has been offered a position at Brown and will probably go. George Croom Robertson, whose wife is ill, is resigning his chair. Hopes that WJ will visit Edinburgh when he is in London for the International Congress of Experimental Psychology (ALS: MH bMS Am 1092 [988]).

To Jacob Gould Schurman. Cambridge, 12 May 1892. Asks if Schurman would like a notice of Pillon's *Année Philosophique* [see *ECR*] and a report of a paper by Augustus Désiré Waller [1856–1922, British physiologist; see *ECR*] (APS: MH bMS Am 1092.9 [3711]).

To Jacob Gould Schurman. Cambridge, 18 May 1892. Received his card. D'Estrella better see the proof as his is the important part [see *EPs*, 281–89], but WJ is afraid that d'Estrella could remove all the "naivete" from his narrative.

Will send the Pillon and Waller reports and hopes next year to send an article on Renouvier's philosophy (ALS: MH bMS Am 1092.9 [3712]).

From Joseph Vogelius. 20 May 1892. [Letter mostly illegible.] Discusses remittances and 500 copies at a greatly reduced price (Letterbook: NjP).

From George Croom Robertson. London, 21 May 1892. Poignant letter about his wife, who will not live to welcome WJ when he comes. Her illness is "of that dire nature which to you also is but too well known" (ALS: MH bMS Am 1092.9 [527]).

From Henry Lee Higginson. Boston, 22 May 1892. Told clerk to send credit to WJ for £2,000. There is much to be said in favor of "spending & enjoying." Will administer finances so that WJ can live in "earthly comfort & peace." Has been asked to speak on Memorial Day [Higginson spoke at Harvard on 30 May] (ALS: MH bMS Am 1092 [340]).

From Sarah Wyman Whitman. 23 May 1892. Sends list of addresses and a "little box" for his postage stamps. Bids WJ farewell (ALS: MH bMS Am 1092.9 [688]).

To Hugo Münsterberg. Antwerp, 7 June 1892. Received letter. Good voyage. Proceeding to Freiburg and will arrive Friday or Saturday (ALS: MB).

From Mrs. George Hackett. 7 June 1892. Describes Maggie O'Neill, who has spoken seven or eight languages identified by a linguist (ALS: SPR, New York City).

To Théodore Flournoy. Freiburg, 13 June 1892. Has come to Europe with entire family to spend at least fifteen months and asks for advice about finding a quiet spot in Switzerland where they can stay. Is also writing Charles Ritter. Münsterberg has given him Flournoy's good news about the professorship and laboratory. May write later to inquire about a summer tutor for his sons. Will Flournoy be at the International Congress of Experimental Psychology? WJ does not plan to go (ALS: MH bMS Am 1505 [2]; published in *WJTF*).

From Théodore Flournoy. Monday [13 June 1892]. Recommends the home of Professor David, near Lausanne, as a pension for WJ's sons. Also possible are the homes of Theodore Biéler, Lausanne; Paul-Jean Oltramare [b. 1854], "master of the College of Geneva"; and Louis-J. Thévenaz, also of the College of Geneva (ALS: MH bMS Am 1092 [202]; published in English translation in *WJTF*).

From Henry Holt and Co. 25 June 1892. Sends $160.38, royalties to 1 January 1892 (Letterbook: NjP).

To Alice Howe Gibbens James. Tuesday [28 June 1892]. At Gourd's, had long talk with [Daniel Auguste] Chantre [1836–1912, a theologian at the University of Geneva] and Flournoy. At meal was seated next to Miss Lucy Woods [possibly Lucy R. Woods, a teacher, living at 415 Boylston St., Boston, near Joseph M. Gibbens, AGJ's uncle] who is on her way to France with Miss Allen [unidentified]. Will now go to see Ritter (APS: MH bMS Am 1092.9 [1803]).

To Alice Howe Gibbens James. Ouchy, 30 June [1892]. Still looking for a pension for their sons. Will be in Aigle tonight (APS: MH bMS Am 1092.9 [1804]).

From Carl Stumpf. Munich, 30 June 1892. Heard from Münsterberg that WJ is in Europe. Very happy at prospect of seeing WJ. Outlines advantages and disadvantages of a Munich stay. Advised Münsterberg, who is talented but sometimes too hasty, to take the position at Harvard. Marty's review was not really an evaluation of the power and advances of WJ's work [see letter of 24 June 1892] (ALS: MH bMS Am 1092.9 [629]).

To Théodore Flournoy. Lucerne, 4 July 1892. Was charmed by David and his wife but both of the Jameses' sons will stay with pastors: one at Ormonts, the other at Gryon. WJ's address will be Gryon. Regards to Mme Flournoy (ALS: Bibliothèque publique et universitaire, Geneva; published in *WJTF*).

To Henry Pickering Bowditch. Gryon, 13 July 1892. Asks for Clements's address [George Henry Clements (1854–1935), an artist, and his wife, Caroline Curtis Dixwell Clements (1856–1931), Bowditch's cousin]. Banter about the trials of traveling with young children. Will probably be in Paris for the winter. At Freiburg visited the Münsterbergs, he "a civilized & liberal minded human being, with a genius for experiment" (APS: MH bMS Am 1092.9 [796]).

To Alice Howe Gibbens James. Lausanne, 15 July 1892. Relates day's events. Met the Flournoys, who had heard of nothing available but said that David might still take in one boy. WJ considering the hotel for the family quarters, but the problem of finding families for the boys is difficult (ALS: MH bMS Am 1092.9 [1810]).

To Alice Howe Gibbens James. Lausanne, 17 [July 1892]. Received her "cheerful letter." Asks where the boys went on their long walk. If she goes to Villars, she should ask about rooms in the hotel (APS: MH bMS Am 1092.9 [1811]).

To Alice Howe Gibbens James. Lausanne, 17 [July] 1892. Visited several places, two of which are possible for the boys. Supposes real reason why they can't find suitable place is that they "dread alienating the interesting William" and look for excuses. Visited the Flournoys at the pension where there are rooms for August and where Peg would have playmates. But it is a "regular barracks," which he could not stand (ALS: MH bMS Am 1092.9 [1812]).

To François Pillon. Lausanne, 21 July 1892. May decide to stay in Lausanne for winter. If they decide for Paris, he will be there in September. Greatly perplexed about what to do with "these *infernal* children." Will write notice of the *Année Philosophique* [see *ECR*]. In what year did the *Critique Philosophique* begin? Asks why Pillon did not accept Hodgson's invitation (APS: MH bMS Am 1092.9 [3494]).

To Jacob Gould Schurman. Lausanne, 27 July 1892. Sends one report [of the *Année Philosophique*]. Report on Waller will follow. Hopes to send an article on Renouvier's *Principes de la nature* [see *ECR*] by Christmas. Fees should be sent to Lee, Higginson, & Co. Hopes that d'Estrella did not sophisticate "Thought Before Language." Switzerland is "*good*" (ALS: MH bMS Am 1092.9 [3713]).

To Alice Howe Gibbens James. Disentis, 3 August 1892. Arrived last night. Very good walk and stage ride. Weather clearing. Hopes son William is feeling better. Asks her to tell HJ that WJ has been "saying lots of forgotten things to him" since he came away (APS: MH bMS Am 1092.9 [1816]).

To Alice Howe Gibbens James. Chur, 4 July [3 August 1892]. Walked through streets of "this ancient town." Will take stage to Samaden, which is said to be full of snow (APS: MH bMS Am 1092.9 [1817]).

To Charles Ritter. Lausanne, 10 August 1892. Is going to Stuttgart to look for winter quarters. One son is with pastor's family in Lausanne, the other in

Vevey. Requests card of introduction to some one of Ritter's friends in Stuttgart (APS: Bibliothèque publique et universitaire, Geneva).

From Charles Ritter. Geneva, 11 August 1892. Sends WJ cards of introduction to three friends in Stuttgart: Ed. Märklin, Ad. Rapp, and the widow of Félix Martin [all three unidentified] (ALS: Bibliothèque publique et universitaire, Geneva).

To Alice Howe Gibbens James. Chamonix, 19 [August 1892]. Spent "most delicious day yesterday," reading and resting. Met Harvard man who told him that Alice Palmer was going to Chicago as dean (APS: MH bMS Am 1092.9 [1820]).

To Charles Ritter. [22 August 1892]. Sorry to have missed Ritter during WJ's unannounced visit to Geneva. He wanted Ritter to meet AGJ. WJ did not go to Stuttgart in the end. Will probably go to Florence for winter. Left Ritter's Lemaître [see letter to Ritter of 4 July 1892]. Found Flournoy an "admirably solid man" (ALS: Bibliothèque publique et universitaire, Geneva).

To William Wilberforce Baldwin. Pallanza, 14 September 1892. Stopped here on their way to Florence. Son Alexander Robertson became sick. Asks whether there is milk safe for babies in Florence, where they will go to Signora Grotti's pension and then look for an apartment (ALS: NNMor).

From Hugo Münsterberg. Cambridge, 17 September 1892. Describes voyage, their settling in Cambridge, which was very difficult at first, and first impressions of America. Royce and Nichols received them hospitably as did Margaret Gregor. Palmer has also visited. Laboratory was delightful surprise. Nichols unavailable as an assistant, so Münsterberg is making do. Royce has made a great impression and they speak German together. Decided against renting the James house because it is too big and requires too many servants (ALS: MH bMS Am 1092.9 [368]).

From Ewald Hering. Prague, 1 October 1892. Thanks WJ for letter. Hering suffers much because he makes little progress in learning English. Is making a collection of his work on light and color and will send it to WJ when complete. Thinks he is better understood in England and America than in Germany, where he is opposed by the deserved authority of Helmholtz and Emil Heinrich Du Bois–Reymond [1818–1896, German physiologist], and the undeserved authority of Wundt. WJ's German is quite good (ALS: MH bMS Am 1092 [333]).

To James Jackson Putnam. Florence, 7 October 1892. They are settled for the winter. Likes to think of the Putnams enjoying "our good little Lake [Chocorua]" and asks if he or Charles Pickering Putnam [1844–1914, American physician, brother of James Putnam] have bought land there. Coming abroad "with a pack of children is not the same thing in reality as it is on paper" and advises Putnam to come with only his wife. Description follows of their domestic life. Their cook Raffaello Maltini speaks only Italian and they converse by means of "raw latin roots." Their governess [Hichbrunner], who looks like "Luther in his more corpulent days," speaks some Italian. Liked Germany but Switzerland was better. Hopes his sons' school will be good. AGJ much refreshed in spite of her maternal cares. His winter reading will include "*Naturphilosophie* and *Kunstgeschichte*." Asks if Putnam has seen the

Münsterbergs. Love to the family, including Annie Cabot Putnam [d. 1924] and Madeline Yale Wynne [1847–1918, an artist] (ALS: MBCo).

From Charles Howard Hinton [1853–1907, British philosophical writer; correspondence is known from 1892 to 1904]. Boston, 8 October 1892. When he landed in America, learned that WJ was abroad. Discusses the 4th dimension. No one prints what he writes. He is looking for a position (ALS: MH bMS Am 1092 [368]).

From Francis Marion Crawford. 9 October 1892. Asks WJ to read Marchesa Lily Conrad Theodoli's *Under Pressure* [1892]. She is Crawford's friend (ALS: MH bMS Am 1092 [147]).

From Hugo Münsterberg. Cambridge, 9 October 1892. Is conducting the laboratory in English, with eleven students. Nichols suggested Fletcher Bascom Dressler as an assistant. The best students are Edgar Pierce, Arthur Pierce, Bigham, Gulick [possibly Edward Leeds Gulick (1862–1931), teacher and clergyman, a graduate student at Harvard in 1892–93], and Wendell T. Bush [1866–1941, American philosopher, a graduate student at Harvard in 1891–93]. It helps with his English to have Royce, Santayana, and Nichols present. Is attending Royce's Hegel seminar. This evening he and his wife will be guests of Eliza Gibbens and will meet Mary Salter. Is making notes for a book on America. There will be a meeting in December of the society [American Psychological Association] founded by Hall, with Fullerton as chairman. They should send photographs of laboratory apparatus to the World's Columbian Exposition in Chicago. Jastrow is planning for the Exposition to do extensive statistical studies. Münsterberg finds such striving for publicity strange. The Boston papers noted that Yale has acquired an Ewald chronoscope, but Münsterberg does not think well of it. Found distasteful Krohn's article ["Facilities in Experimental Psychology, at the Various German Universities," *American Journal of Psychology* 4 (August 1892): 585–94]. Encloses an eight-page address in English setting out his own proposed laboratory work for students (ALS: MH bMS Am 1092.9 [369]).

To John Graham Brooks. Florence, 16 October 1892. Letter of introduction for WJ's nephew, Edward Holton James, a Harvard freshman and a "good boy," who is going to Freiburg (ALS: MCR).

To Jacob Gould Schurman. Florence, 16 October 1892. Apology for sending his report so late. Wishes Schurman well in his presidential career (ALS: MH bMS Am 1092.9 [3714]).

From Josiah Royce. 17 October 1892. Banter about how much he misses WJ. Lectured at Davidson's school and grew fond of Davidson. Visited the Dorrs. The Münsterbergs are settled in the Mulford house. He is great success with the students. General discussion of the start of term at Harvard and particularly the habit of a new student from Russia to talk with Royce endlessly. [The new student was Boris Sidis (1867–1923), Ukrainian-born psychiatrist. Correspondence is known from 1896 to 1907.] Mentions Palmer. The Harvard overseers have Royce's nomination [for a professorship] and some are worrying about his great crime against Abbot (ALS: MH bMS Am 1092.9 [545]; published in *LJR*).

To Théodore Flournoy. Florence, 19 October 1892. Sends an article by his former assistant [Herbert Nichols, see letter of 6 November 1892], whose theories have some merit. WJ and family are settled and boys have begun school. Florence is "delicious" (APS: MH bMS Am 1505 [5]; published in *WJTF*).

From Francis Marion Crawford. Sorrento, 24 October 1892. Thanks WJ for promising to read the book [see letter from Crawford of 9 October 1892 (calendared)]. He is sailing to America to do some readings. His wife [Elizabeth Berdan Crawford] is delighted with WJ's photograph (ALS: MH bMS Am 1092 [148]).

From Henry Holt and Co. 25 October 1892. As of 30 June, due $382.70 for 907 copies of *Briefer Course*, 500 sheets of the same, and 240 copies of *Principles*. Charges were $128.00. Sending part ($190.07) now, the rest in 60 days (Letterbook: NjP).

From Hugo Münsterberg. Cambridge [11 November 1892]. Has no need of comforting concerning Nichols, with whom he is becoming friends. Neither Bolton [possibly Thaddeus Lincoln Bolton (1865–1948), then a student at Clark] nor Dressler could come as assistants and he gave the job to Edgar Pierce, the smartest of his students. Has eleven men in the laboratory, more than are at Clark or Yale. The seminar has some fifteen men and is going well. Not sure where to publish the research of his laboratory. Eliot said there was money for separate publication. Royce and Nichols are on Münsterberg's side. Scripture asked him about supporting a new journal in psychology that would publish all the work of the Harvard laboratory. Cattell would be publisher, Yale would provide the funds. But he is not interested in advancing Scripture's ambition (ALS: MH bMS Am 1092.9 [370]).

To Frederic William Henry Myers. Florence, 19 November 1892. Returns proofs, which are so well done that he can add nothing. This should affect the opinion of "soi-disant scientists." Glad that Myers will use Bakewell's observation [see letter of 14 November 1892] (ALS: Trinity College, Cambridge).

To Editor of the Philosophical Magazine [Jacob Gould Schurman]. Florence, 21 November 1892. Reminds Schurman that fee for "Thought Before Language" should be sent to d'Estrella. WJ's fees should be made payable to order of Eliza Gibbens. WJ will review Fouillée [see *ECR*] (APS: NIC; published in *SUC*).

From Joseph Vogelius. 29 November 1892. There is repetition in the chapter on "Association" [*Briefer Course*]. Asks for corrections since new edition will be printed soon (Letterbook: NjP; published in *BC*, 473).

From James Bryce. 30 November [1892]. Got WJ's address from HJ. Disappointed that he did not see WJ in Italy. Invites him to the Riviera where he is going soon. Otherwise, hopes to see WJ in London (ALS: MH bMS Am 1092 [60]).

To Alice Howe Gibbens James. Padua, 7 [December 1892]. Describes ceremony [the Galileo festival] at Padua. George Howard Darwin and Fayrer spoke and WJ received honorary Doctor of Letters and Philosophy degree (APS: MH bMS Am 1092.9 [1826]).

To Carlo Francesco Ferraris. Florence, 12 December 1892. Expresses appreciation for ceremonies at Padua (ALS: unknown; published in *SUC*).

From Ellis F. Moyse. 22 December 1892. Describes an apparition seen by a girl who on Halloween ate an apple and combed her hair (ALS: SPR, New York City).

From Josiah Royce. Cambridge, 22 December 1892. They are all writing to WJ about Nichols. Gives his own long evaluation of Nichols, who in Royce's opinion is "impossible, as a colleague, and as a contributor to thought" and should not be kept after this year, particularly "with men like Delabarre within easy reach." Nichols is brilliant and ambitious but lacks judgment. Royce was made professor (ALS: MH bMS Am 1092.9 [546]; published in *JRL*).

From Henry Holt and Co. 24 December 1892. Encloses royalties of $191.35 (Letterbook: NjP).

From Théodore Flournoy. Geneva, 30 December 1892. Read Marillier [see letter to AJ of 23 August 1891, note 6]. Not satisfied, but is pleased that WJ's book is presented to the French public by more than a report and hopes that the plan to translate the book will be accomplished. Read WJ's "Thought Before Language" and found it thought-provoking. Won't speak to WJ about his laboratory, which bores him. He is to speak on Kant's philosophy to a group of Eastern European students who barely understand French. His children have been skating with Mlle Hühnersdorf (ALS: MH bMS Am 1092 [203]; published in English translation in *WJTF*).

1893

To Henry Lee Higginson. [1893]. If Higginson is ever "pushed," he may use "that amount" to make things go easier (Fragment in *The Life and Letters of Henry Lee Higginson*, 414).

To Katharine Peabody Loring. Florence, 4 January 1893. Florence is comfortable but expensive. AGJ is undecided whether to stay here next year. Their social circle is expanding and beginning to threaten his peace. HJ writes that he may reach Florence in about six weeks. "Boston and Cambridge seem to me as highly vitalized as Florence in the XVth century" (ALS: Beverly Historical Society & Charles W. Galloupe Memorial Society).

To William Wilberforce Baldwin. Florence, 9 January 1893. Asks Baldwin to send bill (ALS: NNMor).

To William Wilberforce Baldwin. Florence, Thursday [12 January 1893]. Will come on Saturday (ALS: NNMor).

To William Wilberforce Baldwin. Florence, 13 January 1893. Sends eighty francs. Baldwin should have asked for more. WJ is sleeping better (ALS: NNMor).

From James Rowland Angell. Berlin, 13 January 1893. Plans to visit the hospitals of Hippolyte Bernheim [1840–1919, French hypnotist] and Jean-Martin Charcot [1825–1893, French neurologist] and asks for WJ's advice as to best way of gaining access. Has enjoyed the company of the Hodders. Work at Berlin has "fizzled out" and he is going to Leipzig to work on several experiments. Hopes that letters from his cousin [Frank Angell] to Wundt and Külpe will make it possible for him to work on his own. Has become engaged to Marion Isabel Watrous. Given WJ's maxim that "a man married is a man marred" he has to apologize to WJ who is his "spiritual father." Letters from Pierce and Nichols describe Cambridge as prosperous and speak of Münsterberg warmly. Expects to spend six weeks in Italy and hopes that Hodders will come (ALS: MH bMS Am 1092 [16]).

To Théodore Flournoy. Florence, 30 January 1893. Sends "The Moral Philosopher and the Moral Life" which while "'chock-full' of truth" is too condensed. Everything is well (APS: MH bMS Am 1505 [7]; published in *WJTF*).

To Charles Ritter. Florence, 15 February 1893. Is going to Stuttgart to look for a place for his sons and asks for letter of introduction to some friend of Ritter's who can give WJ information. Plans to go to Weimar and elsewhere. Hopes that it has been a good year in spite of Panama scandals (ALS: Bibliothèque publique et universitaire, Geneva).

From William Dean Howells. New York, 19 February 1893. WJ is fortunate to be in Florence with Clemens, who is "one of the first minds in the world." Howells is writing about the various books that he has loved at different periods in his life. The first was *Don Quixote*. He also plans to write about the literary life of Cambridge. He is taking great delight in HJ's work, which is "simply perfection." Finds New York City interrupting and hopes for the quiet of Cambridge (TLS: MH bMS Am 1092.9 [239]).

From George Frederick Stout. 19 February 1893. Manuscript [see letter of 13 February 1893] had already been sent to the printer when WJ's second letter arrived as well as his postcard asking for the substitution of 'immediate' for 'simple' in the title. Stout wants a full discussion as does Ward. The matter rests on the question of intensive magnitude. Asks for WJ's support in getting his fellowship renewed (ALS: MH WJ 583.67).

To Alice Howe Gibbens James. Munich, Friday [24 February 1893]. Enjoyed Verona and reached Munich early this morning. Son Henry is a good traveler. Hopes that AGJ is not "slaving" too much over Helen Brooks and that Mary Holton James arrives today. Asks AGJ to give his love to Elizabeth Walsh. AGJ's, Francis Greenwood Peabody's, and Elizabeth Child's letters came, along with proofs and the *Nation*. AGJ should keep the *Nation* and the *Speaker,* sending only important letters, such as those from Münsterberg or Royce (ALS: MH bMS Am 1092.9 [1833]).

From Alice Howe Gibbens James. Florence, 24 February [1893]. Lucinda Holton, Mary Holton James, and Mary's daughter are coming to dinner tonight. Discusses their travel plans. Helen Brooks is in "Galleries." Will call on the Baldwins, Elizabeth Walsh, and Mary Costelloe. Duveneck proposes a monument like the "others in the lot," with a bronze vase, the proposal of Shaw [unidentified]. AGJ prefers the Etruscan box. Obrist was very nice last evening (ALS: MH bMS Am 1092.9 [294]).

From Alice Howe Gibbens James. Florence, 25 February 1893. Letters from WJ and son Henry have reassured her. She has been thinking about going to Weimar and he should not get angry with her because she is again considering Weimar. Mary Holton James says that Edward is very pleased there. Lucinda Holton, Mary Holton James, and her daughter dined last night. Helen Brooks came. AGJ showed them his pictures and Mary Walsh James thought that the one with a white horse could be by Philips Wouwerman [1619–1668, Dutch painter, known for depicting horses]. Yesterday she returned the box to Dr. Baldwin and called on the Kirkes [unidentified], saw Elizabeth Walsh and her cousins. She can do little for Elizabeth Walsh and the Lawrences [the Walshes had a number of Lawrence cousins]. Coolidge [for a possible Coolidge see letter of 19 July 1890 (calendared)] called with a note from Mrs. Bigelow Lawrence inviting AGJ for an evening of music. Has received an entertaining letter from Myers. Margaret Mary sticks at her side (ALS: MH bMS Am 1092.9 [296]).

From Alice Howe Gibbens James. Florence, 27 February [1893]. AGJ is sick with headache. Mrs. B[rooks] came for lunch. Mary Walsh James came to dine with Obrist. Elizabeth Walsh and the Holton party will leave in a few days. The music was fine [see preceding abstract] but too "exclusive" since only several listeners were present. Mrs. Peruzzi [unidentified], a "disagreeable woman," invited her and WJ. Linda Villari has sent *Vanitas* [see letter from AGJ of 28 February 1893]. AGJ thinks the portrait of HJ inexcusable. Asks WJ to destroy letter from Eliza Gibbens after reading it (ALS: MH bMS Am 1092.9 [297]).

From Alice Howe Gibbens James. Florence, 1 March [1893]. Likes Elizabeth Walsh and hopes they see more of her. Met Loeser and called on Mary Costelloe. Has put off her excursion with Mary Loring and said goodbye to Mary Holton James and her daughter. Does not understand why WJ clings to Munich when WJ always preferred the Stuttgart school (ALS: MH bMS Am 1092.9 [299]).

From Alice Howe Gibbens James. Florence, 2 March [1893]. Glad that the Stumpfs offer to take son Henry, but WJ should make sure that Henry learns German. Called on Elizabeth Walsh. Sorry to have refolded Stout's "Communication" (ALS: MH bMS Am 1092.9 [300]).

To Alice Howe Gibbens James. Munich, Saturday [4 March 1893]. His friends have left and he can remain incognito correcting the "'stout' proofs." Plans to see the pinakotheks. Is now inclined toward return to America. Letter from Stout came (ALS: MH bMS Am 1092.9 [1834]).

From Alice Howe Gibbens James. Florence, 4 March 1893. AGJ returned from the dentist and cried over WJ's sad letter. Is it lack of sleep or some fresh trouble he is hiding from her? Sometimes she opposes him, but really wants only "that which will give you the most satisfaction." Asks WJ to come home soon. Son William does not want to go with Obrist. Paid dental bills. Elizabeth Walsh and her cousins will leave on Monday (ALS: MH bMS Am 1092.9 [301]).

From Josiah Royce. Cambridge, 4 March 1893. It has been a good year. Describes in detail disagreements between himself, Palmer, and Münsterberg over the fate of Philosophy 1. Palmer favored keeping the course, certain of the support of Eliot and Dunbar. Münsterberg seems to be taking notes of American department meetings for "future generations." Peabody and Santayana were also present, the latter seeming indispensable. Nichols was not invited and was told that he will not return next year. Royce describes in detail the teaching plan (ALS: MH bMS Am 1092.9 [547]; published in *JRL*).

To William Wilberforce Baldwin. Florence, Friday [10 March 1893]. Alexander Robertson has a swollen gland and WJ asks Baldwin to come tomorrow (ALS: NNMor).

To Charles Ritter. Florence, 17 March 1893. Apologizes for having troubled him about Stuttgart and letters of introduction. WJ now prefers Munich (ALS: Bibliothèque publique et universitaire, Geneva).

From Hugo Münsterberg. 27 March 1893. He and his wife have been seeing the beauties of America. His father died and Münsterberg himself has been sick.

Wesselhoeft [see letter of 13 March 1893] became their physician because he speaks German. Münsterberg did not know that Wesselhoeft was a homeopath. Some of his medicines help, but the worst is that he consults other homeopaths, one of whom did "butchery" on Münsterberg's neck. Plans for a separate publication for the laboratory are dormant until WJ returns. Arthur Pierce, Edgar Pierce, Bigham, McLeod [unidentified], and perhaps Kozaki want to work for the doctorate. Eliot wants them to take part in the World's Columbian Exhibition. Many schools are sending their entire laboratories to demonstrate reaction time experiments. Harvard is taking part in the experiments of Jastrow and Donaldson. They need to send at least a catalogue of apparatus [Hugo Münsterberg, *Psychological Laboratory of Harvard University* (1893), an illustrated pamphlet prepared for the Harvard exhibit]. His article was not for publicity but to interest Harvard people [see letter to Münsterberg of 11 February 1893]. They need more rooms in laboratory, having fewer rooms than Scripture or Titchener. Münsterberg wanted Nichols to remain as assistant, but Eliot, Palmer, and Royce decided to let him go. Nichols needs a position and Münsterberg has written to Baldwin, who is leaving Toronto for Princeton. As assistant, Palmer prefers Delabarre, James prefers Angell, and he himself, Witmer. Witmer is the most original and hardworking of the young psychologists. Palmer is opposed to WJ's plan of giving psychology in Philosophy 1. Everyone agrees that Philosophy 2 should be shared between WJ and Münsterberg. He has decided to print privately an answer to G. E. Müller, because without an answer he will appear to have lost (ALS: MH bMS Am 1092.9 [371]).

To Elizabeth Glendower Evans. Florence, 6 April 1893. Welcomes her to Italy, sure that she will have much to tell about Egypt and Greece. Their plans are uncertain and AGJ needs to confer with her. WJ would like for them to spend the summer near each other. He is tired of Florence where he has not an hour for serious reading (ALS: MCR).

To George Frederick Stout. Florence, 9 April [1893]. Sends reply to E. Ford [see *EPs*]. Liked Bradley ["Consciousness and Experience," *Mind*, n. s., 2 (April 1893): 211–16] who this time was clear (ALS: unknown; published in *SUC*).

To Alice Howe Gibbens James. Luzerne, Sunday [16 April 1893]. Son William has gone to bed. They had a most beautiful railway journey. Many things in Italy are sweet but WJ is glad to have left it and be heading homeward. Wants to know the outcome of AGJ's discussions with Elizabeth Evans about travel plans. Gives instructions about the handling of his things. Hopes that Jessie Hodder and the baby are well (ALS: MH bMS Am 1092.9 [1846]).

To Alice Howe Gibbens James. Vevey, 18 April 1893. Have just arrived and will shortly proceed to the Cérésoles. Son William seems to be enjoying the journey. Found Bern very picturesque. Advises AGJ as to where to stay with Elizabeth Evans on their journey north. Hopes Jessie Hodder and the baby are well. Loeser may send an Italian pamphlet for which AGJ should pay. Asks her to get photographs of the Masaccio [15th-century Italian painter] paintings and "that roman inscription" from Steele [unidentified]. Insist on a talk with Baldwin about Margaret Mary's nose (ALS: MH bMS Am 1092.9 [1838]).

To Alice Howe Gibbens James. Geneva, 20 April 1893. Has been talking with

Henrietta and Katharine Rodgers, who are old women and must stay in Europe because of the latter's "uterine tumor." Gives AGJ instructions about her journey. AGJ says nothing about Jessie Hodder. Glad that Elizabeth Lawrence has invested in "Carnelio" [unidentified] (ALS: MH bMS Am 1092.9 [1840]).

To William Wilberforce Baldwin. Meggen, 24 April 1893. Thanks Baldwin for his help during the winter. Hopes that Mrs. Baldwin will have a good journey. Encloses testimonial for Maltini (ALS: NNMor).

To François Pillon. Meggen, 24 April [1893]. Will stay here for at least two weeks before going to London. May turn up in Paris with AGJ (APS: MH bMS Am 1092.9 [3495]).

From Henry Holt and Co. 25 April 1893. As of 31 December 1892, $437.40 for 2,167 copies of *Briefer Course* at $0.20; $181.80 for 303 copies of *Principles* at $0.60. Total $619.20. Charges $26.06. Sending $283.54 (Letterbook: NjP).

To James John Garth Wilkinson. Meggen, 28 April [1893]. The Siljeström book [Petr Adam Siljeström (1815–1892), Swedish writer, *Tretton aftnar hos en Spiritist* (1886); the copy in Harvard's Widener Library (Phil 299.3), given through WJ on 16 September 1893, has the author's name added by hand on the title page and a note in what appears to be WJ's hand that the book was given by Wilkinson]; and "John Lone's paradox" [unidentified] will go to the Harvard library, which is well run, with free access and no resulting harm. Will visit him when they reach London (APS: MH bMS Am 1237 [18]).

To Henry James III. Meggen, 2 May [1893]. Sending payment to Fräulein Kern, who says that Henry is not diligent enough. He must establish the habit of performing each task "accurately and exactly." Have heard nothing from son William. HJ has his fourth attack of gout. The World's Columbian Exposition opened yesterday (ALS: MH fMS Am 1092.4).

From Friedrich Paulsen. Steiglitz, 3 May 1893. The reception of *Principles* in Germany has not been favorable and he has seen articles making fun of the book. Is happy that Paulsen's book is well received in America. Hopes that WJ will come to Berlin. Has heard about WJ from Ebbinghaus and Kuno Francke (ALS: MH bMS Am 1092 [651]).

To William Wilberforce Baldwin. Meggen, 4 May [1893]. Druggists in Luzern could not decipher Baldwin's prescription. HJ arrived tired from Paris, sick with gout, an attack made mild by a "new remedy." Hopes Mrs. Baldwin's voyage went well. Thinks he may go home on 5 August 1893 and attend the "Psychical Congress" at the World's Columbian Exposition (ALS: NNMor).

To Charles Ritter. Meggen, 5 May 1893. They will stay here perhaps a month. AGJ goes to Munich to visit their son. Hopes Ritter will visit them (APS: Bibliothèque publique et universitaire, Geneva).

To William James, Jr. Meggen, 6 May 1893. William seems happy at the Cérésoles. AGJ has written about schooling, but Mme Cérésole will know what is best. He should answer his brother Henry whether he received the old German stamps (APS: MH bMS Am 1092.9 [3145]).

From Robertson James. Concord, 6 May 1893. Sends check for $105.17, WJ's share of the Syracuse rents for April. Visited Eliza Gibbens and Margaret Gregor. The country is approaching depression, for which the "silver shysters" are to blame. Has found a mental healer who puts him to sleep merely by sitting with him in a room. A "hard year with terrors," but his family will return soon [WJ probably sent this letter on to HJ] (ALS: MH bMS Am 1095.2 [22–24]).

To Alice Howe Gibbens James. Luzerne, Monday [8 May 1893]. Has been walking with HJ. Children well. Sends greetings to son Henry (ALS: MH bMS Am 1092.9 [1847]).

From Alice Howe Gibbens James. Munich, 8 May 1893. AGJ enjoyed the play *Sappho* but is sorry to have missed Wagner's *Tannhäuser*. Son Henry understands the letter from Browne. He is more alive than he was in Florence, having learned almost nothing in "Marke's school." Report from Fräulein Kern is good. Placing Henry in Munich is among the best things WJ has done. Describes some of her activities (ALS: MH bMS Am 1092.9 [301a]).

To Alice Howe Gibbens James. Lucerne, Tuesday [9 May 1893]. Children well. HJ came for a visit. Sorry that the Hauptmanns left. Hopes AGJ likes the Stumpfs (APS: MH bMS Am 1092.9 [1842]).

From Théodore Flournoy. Geneva, 10 May 1893. Discusses Freyer [perhaps Paul Freyer, *Studien zur Metaphysik der Differentialrechnung* (1883)] and Hermann Cohen [1842–1918, German philosopher, *Das Princip der infinitesimal-Methode* (1883)] on infinitesimals. Forgot to look for a manual of Swiss government. Sorry about WJ's difficulties with the servant Hélène. Has been interested in a certain Kreps [unidentified] who uses mental suggestion on his daughter. Is writing on colored vision. WJ's visit of three weeks ago was a pleasant surprise (ALS: MH bMS Am 1092 [204]; published in English translation in *WJTF*).

From Sarah Wyman Whitman. Boston, 10 May 1893. "Of all recent years this one since you went away has been the most strenuous for me, in those things which affect one's inner and outer activities." The death of Phillips Brooks brought tenderness but not grief. Minna Choate Pratt [see *Correspondence*, 6:238] and Helen Choate Bell [see *Correspondence*, 6:622] have returned from abroad (ALS: MH bMS Am 1092.9 [689]).

To Alice Howe Gibbens James. Luzerne, Thursday [11 May 1893]. Congratulates her on decision to extend stay in Munich. Hopes she enjoyed *Tannhäuser*. Letter from Caroline James suggests that she "might mean business," but she seems not too eager to "defend the family honour" (ALS: MH bMS Am 1092.9 [1841]).

To Alice Howe Gibbens James. Lucerne, Friday [12 May 1893]. Glad that she is staying over in Munich. Has finished reading Johannes Immanuel Volkelt's [1843–1930, German philosopher] *Erfahrung und Denken* [1886] (APS: MH bMS Am 1092.9 [1844]).

To Alice Howe Gibbens James. Lucerne, Saturday [13 May 1893]. Had letters from Eliza Gibbens and Henry Holt, the latter indicating royalties of $619 (APS: MH bMS Am 1092.9 [1845]).

To Oliver Joseph Lodge. Meggen, 13 May [1893]. Myers was premature in saying that WJ will go. WJ prefers the *Lucania* but is unsure when he will leave and Lodge should make his plans independently (APS: Cambridge University Library).

From Henry Holt and Co. 13 May 1893. At WJ's request, sending him Baldwin's *Elements of Psychology* [1893]. Sent copy of *Principles* to Loeser (Letterbook: NjP).

From Henry Holt. On Central Vermont Railroad, 15 May 1893. The business side of WJ's letter of 14 March was attended to. Has built a new barn at Burlington. Since WJ left, has none with whom to discuss philosophy. Butler came occasionally and Royce has written. Envies Elizabeth Evans, who sees WJ. Has read Du Maurier's *Peter Ibbetson* [1891]. Has been thinking about the French criminologists WJ recommended through the book by Havelock Ellis [1859–1939, English author; correspondence is known from 1899 and 1900]. Tried to imagine a criminal and found their ideas contradictory. Describes prison escape. Cannot decide about Arthur Sherburne Hardy [1847–1930, American diplomat and writer], whose *The Wind of Destiny* [1886] he has with him (ALS: MH bMS Am 1092 [422]).

To Théodore Flournoy. Meggen, 18 May 1893. Is returning from Zurich with AGJ. Finds Flournoy's note inviting son William for a week. Thinks week too much (APS: MH bMS Am 1505 [9]; published in *WJTF*).

To William James, Jr. Meggen, 18 May [1893]. His note came in Mme Cérésole's letter. Discusses William's and Henry's school work and William's visit to the Flournoys (APS: MH bMS Am 1092.9 [3146]).

To Charles Ritter. Meggen, 18 May [1893]. Will remain in Meggen for a week and then leave for England. Can Ritter visit them? HJ is returning to England after three weeks (APS: Bibliothèque publique et universitaire, Geneva).

To Charles Ritter. Meggen, 18 May 1893. Sent a card addressed to Geneva and sending this one to Zurich. Urges Ritter to pay them a short visit (APS: Bibliothèque publique et universitaire, Geneva).

To Katharine Outram Rodgers. Meggen, 24 May [1893]. AGJ is going to visit her and her sister. They have two sisters [Elizabeth Evans and her sister] from Boston visiting them, one an invalid. HJ visited for ten days (ALS: MH bMS Am 1092.9 [3554]; published in *SUC*).

To François Pillon. Meggen, 25 May [1893]. They plan to leave for London shortly. Do not know if they will stop in Paris but will return in July and visit Pillon. He should keep the *Année Philosophique* until WJ asks (APS: MH bMS Am 1092.9 [3496]).

To Sarah Wyman Whitman. Meggen, 25 May [1893]. Sending her a newspaper clipping with a "manly" speech by Zola. They plan to leave in about ten days and spend the summer in England. In August he may leave the family behind and go to Chicago for the World's Columbian Exhibition and psychical congress (ALS: MH bMS Am 1092.9 [3914]).

To Henry James III. Vers-chez-les-Blanc, Sunday, 4 June [1893]. Sends 100 marks to Fräulein Kern. AGJ does not want the photographs, which are poor, but he should order them anyway. Wants him to learn jumping at the riding school. Son William likes Mme Cérésole (APS: MH fMS Am 1092.4).

To George Frederick Stout. Vers-chez-les-Blanc, 5 June [1893]. Agrees to recommend Stout [see letter to Owens College of 16 June 1893 (calendared)]. Asks for reprints of Stout's articles which should be sent to HJ's address. Can wait for Bradley's reply [see *EPh*, 208] (ALS: unknown; published in *SUC*).

To Mme Alfred Cérésole. [7 June 1893]. Has sent the toys the use of which AGJ has explained. She should pay the postage, since he could not know at the store what the postage would be (APS: MH bMS Am 1092.9 [824]).

To William James, Jr. Paris, Thursday [15 June 1893]. Leaving for London, having stayed in Paris one additional day. Mme Cérésole sends good reports of him (APS: MH bMS Am 1092.9 [3147]).

To Owens College, Manchester. London, 16 June [1893]. Recommends Stout for a professorship, to succeed Adamson (ALS: unknown; published in *SUC*).

To George Frederick Stout. London, 16 June [1893]. Reached London last night and is now reading Stout's articles. In 1891–92 fell behind in his reading. Asks what is the matter with Adamson (ALS: unknown; published in *SUC*).

To William James, Jr. London, 17 June [1893]. Describes journey. HJ gave them "luxurious quarters." AGJ is getting dresses. Richard Hodgson has had a major operation on his abdomen (APS: MH bMS Am 1092.9 [3148]).

From Robertson James. Concord, 21 June 1893. The McCarthys [see *Correspondence*, 2:271n] ask the Jameses to surrender their first mortgage on the store in exchange for a second mortgage on the whole McCarthy property. Cowie thinks it a poor idea. RJ and Eliza Gibbens have refused (ALS: MH bMS Am 1095.2 [22-24]).

To Henry James III. London, 22 June 1893. Describes procedure for passing through customs. Edward James is here with three "pups" that occupy his whole time and money. What Henry wrote about Alexander Sch[nitzlein] is sad (ALS: MH fMS Am 1092.4).

From Hugo Münsterberg. Cambridge, 22 June 1893. Thinks Nichols was the best man and is distressed that Eliot and Palmer fired him. Witmer and James Angell have turned down offers. Also disturbing are efforts to take the *American Journal of Psychology* away from Hall. Glad that at meetings in New York he prevented the founding of a new journal. Fears that Baldwin, Jastrow, Scripture, and Cattell will decide everything and Münsterberg will remain in the minority. Thinks decisions should await WJ's return. His first year at Harvard has been good. Enjoyed a week at the World's Columbian Exposition. His colleague, Hermann Eduard von Holst [1841–1904, professor of history at Freiburg and Chicago], is unhappy at Chicago. Describes summer plans and their house for next year (ALS: MH bMS Am 1092.9 [372]).

From Henry Holt and Co. 25 June [1893]. Charges of $12.98 for copies of *Principles* sent to Ritter, Carl Hauptmann, and to professor [name illegible] in Zurich (Letterbook: NjP).

To Shadworth Hollway Hodgson. London, 27 June [1893]. Will not be able to visit Hodgson at Saltburn since they have to return to Switzerland. Tomorrow they will visit Louis Dyer [1851–1908, American scholar] at Oxford. Glad that Hodgson is working on the "Metaphysician" [*The Metaphysic of Experience* (1898)] (ALS: MH bMS Am 1092.9 [987]).

From François Pillon. Paris, 27 June 1893. WJ's letter of 23 June gave much pleasure. Urges WJ to spend more than a day in Paris when he passes through. There are sights in Paris WJ could show AGJ. Invites WJ to stay at any time convenient for WJ (ALS: MH bMS Am 1092.9 [478]).

To Katharine Outram Rodgers. London, 6 July 1893. They have returned from Harrow [visiting Joseph Clarke]. Describes various hotels in Switzerland.

Plans are unsettled. AGJ has enjoyed London, but WJ finds the people tiresome and wants to return to Switzerland (ALS: MH bMS Am 1092.9 [3555]).

From Hugo Münsterberg. Swampscott, Mass., 14 July 1893. Thanks WJ for card about Müller. Negotiations between Hall, Baldwin, and Cattell will not lead to agreement. There is mistrust of Hall, while Hall does not want a board. Has suggested that Eliot provide $250 for support of one of the plans. The result may be two journals, something which Münsterberg does not want. Thinks Hall competent, while Baldwin, Cattell, and Jastrow lack an authoritative voice. Persuaded them to ask WJ and not Münsterberg to represent Harvard. He and WJ should act together. Münsterberg wants to avoid the impression that he is WJ's subordinate, as Scripture is to Ladd, Titchener to Schurman, Witmer to Fullerton. If there is a split, it might be best for Harvard to establish its own journal, with WJ, Royce, Hanus, Santayana, and Münsterberg as publishers and possibly involve Palmer and Everett (ALS: MH bMS Am 1092.9 [373]).

To Alice Howe Gibbens James. Tuesday [18 July 1893]. HJ is better. WJ paid HJ for life of Isaac Newton and for freight and had a "fierce talk" about payment for their food. HJ will be hurt if WJ presses the matter further, and WJ will buy HJ a field glass instead. Visited the National Gallery and the offices of the SPR. Read Pillon's book and will write about it [see *ECR*]. M. B. [unidentified] wrote a nice note and WJ is sorry to have lost her. Met Miss Head [unidentified] of Meggen. Describes his shopping. Feels lonely (ALS: MH bMS Am 1092.9 [1848]).

From Hugo Münsterberg. Swampscott, Mass., 26 July 1893. Will respond to WJ's letter in detail later. Baldwin and his family have been here. Nicholas is in better spirits. The assistantship has been given to Arthur Pierce. Münsterberg's financial position is difficult. He now thinks that Hall lied to him about the journal and that Baldwin and Cattell will establish their own. WJ and Münsterberg will be named among the publishers. He now thinks two journals are good, with shorter items going to the new one and the longer student dissertations going to Hall. Schurman is not involved. Harvard will help with the cost of the new journal (ALS: MH bMS Am 1092.9 [374]).

To Henry James III. Vers-chez-les-Blanc, 28 July [1893]. Have been here since Monday [24 July]. Asks Henry to come to Vevey, because WJ wants to see him and son William. WJ was sick in London. He and AGJ are looking for servants (APS: MH fMS Am 1092.4).

From Charles Ritter. Geneva, 1 August 1893. Recalls with great pleasure his day with the Jameses at Meggen. Has not seen Flournoy in the three weeks since Flournoy's return (ALS: MH bMS Am 1092 [808]).

To Alice Howe Gibbens James. Aigle, Saturday [5 August 1893]. They have come in the stage and are shopping. Can have rooms in Zermatt, which they plan to reach tomorrow afternoon (APS: MH bMS Am 1092.9 [1850]).

From Alice Howe Gibbens James. Vers-chez-les-Blanc, 5 August 1893. Dreamed that she was helping Boott die. Hélène has left and Marie [Garin], a real treasure, has arrived. Discusses arrangements for return to America. Spent a day with Eugenia [unidentified] and Elizabeth Evans. Little Eugenia [unidentified] is ill and nervous. They are coming tomorrow. Asks WJ to telegraph her since she feels lost not knowing where WJ is. Will write to Harry and Clarke. Margaret Mary has gone to church with Mlle Cruchon. Alexander Robertson has taken wonderfully to Marie Garin. Marie likes Hortense. Instructs WJ to buy some "*unset* stones" at Interlaken (ALS: MH bMS Am 1092.9 [303]).

To Alice Howe Gibbens James. Zermatt, Sunday [6 August 1893]. Asks AGJ to inform the Cunard line of a change from the *Cephalonia* of 24 August to the *Pavonia* of 24 September. She should answer letter from Charles Follen Atkinson. Sons Henry and William are well (APS: MH bMS Am 1092.9 [1851]).

From Sarah Wyman Whitman. Boston, 10 August 1893. Has met and liked Frederic Myers, who said little during dinner given by Annie Fields. Glad that WJ is returning (ALS: MH bMS Am 1092.9 [690]).

To Alice Howe Gibbens James. Lausanne [13 August 1893]. Thinks she must be already in London. Margaret Mary went to church with Louise Cruchon. Alexander Robertson is well. WJ gave him a book (APS: MH bMS Am 1092.9 [1853]).

To Alice Howe Gibbens James. Chailly, Monday [14 August 1893]. Sorry that AGJ missed her train. Children well. Miller writes about the death of a brother. A "common" French couple here. Mrs. Wilson is very cultivated (APS: MH bMS Am 1092.9 [1854]).

From Alice Howe Gibbens James. Harrow, 16 August 1893. Has had a headache, but is enjoying herself today. Discusses arrangements for return trip. Told the Cunard Line that WJ would pay on Tuesday. Son Henry's bicycle has come. Discusses the making of clothes for herself and children. HJ very much wants William, Henry, and WJ to come for the last two days. Sam Emerson [unidentified] says her "blue stone from Interlaken" is cut better than most diamonds (ALS: MH bMS Am 1092.9 [304]).

To Théodore Flournoy. Queenstown, Ireland, 25 August [1893]. He and AGJ send their last farewells (APS: MH bMS Am 1505 [11]; published in *WJTF*).

To Smith Baker. [September 1893]. On typed appeal for funds for the American Branch of the Society for Psychical Research. Asks whether Baker is interested (Note: OO).

From James McKeen Cattell. Garrison-on-Hudson, 16 September 1893. Hall has not accepted any of the proposals about a psychology journal made by Cattell and Baldwin. Cattell is willing to go along with what was agreed upon in Cambridge, a bimonthly *Psychological Review*, owned and edited by Cattell and Baldwin, with the support of WJ, Münsterberg, Ladd, Fullerton, Dewey, and Donaldson. If WJ thinks it best, Cattell is willing to consider union with the *Philosophical Review*. Cattell thinks it best to have a journal publishing reviews and shorter articles of general interest, and an annals, published when materials become available, for monographs and longer research. Cattell's and Fullerton's papers fit better in an annals. Hyslop and Nichols have offered long papers not of general interest. An issue of the annals could contain the work of a single laboratory, edited by the instructor in charge if he so wishes, as Scripture does. Cattell would prefer to edit the annals, and Baldwin, the journal. Discusses financial arrangements. Sending postcard from Schurman together with Cattell's reply and copies of this letter to Baldwin and Münsterberg (TC: MB).

From James Mark Baldwin. Toronto, 18 September 1893. Cattell has written to WJ and others without consulting Baldwin (see above abstract). Baldwin wrote Cattell favoring what was agreed upon in Cambridge. Cattell asked Münsterberg for his views and Münsterberg should see this letter. Donaldson joins the *Review*. Jastrow takes a department of literature (ALS: MB).

To Wincenty Lutoslawski. Cambridge, 27 September 1893. He and Münsterberg will be happy to show the Harvard laboratory (ALS: CtY).

To Henry Lee Higginson. 13 October 1893. Is waiting for the dinner of the Club on Friday (*The Life and Letters of Henry Lee Higginson*, 403).

To Wincenty Lutoslawski. Cambridge, 16 October 1893. Invites Lutoslawski to his seminar on mental pathology [Philosophy 20b] on 18 October, when they can make arrangements for other visits. Also invites him for lunch on 19 October. Gives directions for reaching the laboratory. Münsterberg has already made arrangements to see Lutoslawski (ALS: CtY).

From Henry Holt and Co. 25 October 1893. As of 30 June, for 259 copies of *Briefer Course* at $0.20 and 157 copies of *Principles* at $0.60, royalties due of $166. Changes cost $4.20 (Letterbook: NjP).

From Joseph Vogelius. 27 October 1893. Has WJ's request to send *Principles* to Byerly. Sorry that remittance was delayed (Letterbook: NjP).

To Homer Horatio Seerley [1848–1932, president of Iowa State Teachers College]. Cambridge, 11 November 1893. D. W. Hugh [unidentified] writes that Seerley has an interesting case of hallucination in the family. Asks for written account (ALS: University of Northern Iowa, Cedar Falls).

From William Dean Howells. New York, 27 November 1893. Is in New York City and cannot come to meet Bourget (ALS: MH bMS Am 1092.9 [240]).

From Paul Bourget. Brookline, Mass., Friday [1 December 1893]. Will be glad to spend two evenings with WJ. WJ should not forget his promise to arrange a sitting with Leonora Piper [see *EPR*, 396, 397] (ALS: MH bMS Am 1092 [42]).

From Paul Bourget. Boston, 3 December 1893. There is a curious theory derived from Gnostic sources by Jacques Matter [1791–1864, French historian, *Histoire critique du gnosticisme* (1828)]. Certain spirits, including those of animals, become associated with human souls. These make an irrational soul, opposed to our rational one. Such associations would account for the fact that men sometimes acquire the characteristics and even the appearance of certain animals (ALS: MH bMS Am 1092 [40]).

From Frédéric Paulhan. Nîmes, 10 December 1893. Thanks WJ for presenting Paulhan's *Caractères* to readers of the *Psychological Review* [see letter of 27 May 1894; Paulhan may have thought, erroneously, that WJ would write the review] (ALS: MH bMS Am 1092 [650]).

From Théodore Flournoy. Geneva, 18 December 1893. Since WJ left Europe has become dangerous, due to dynamite explosions set off by anarchists. Hopes that WJ's "twenty-eight large pieces of luggage" and the "army" of packages arrived safely. Thanks WJ for receiving Louis Wuarin [b. 1846, Swiss writer], who attended one of WJ's classes. Wuarin brought back a brochure about the Harvard laboratory. Flournoy does not envy Harvard its equipment; what he has is sufficient for him. He has three students in the laboratory, two of them women, using experiments borrowed from Sanford and Nichols. His theoretical course has about thirty-five students. There are few good mediums in Geneva. He is reading Myers's articles. Fräulein Hühnersdorf is a great help and he hopes that the servants WJ picked up in Switzerland are good helpers. Flournoy's son Henri is having difficulties in school. Hopes that it is Henri's rapid physical growth that is keeping back his intellectual one, as is suggested by Willliam Townsend Porter [1862–1949, American physiologist] (ALS: MH bMS Am 1092 [205]; published in English translation in *WJTF*).

From Frederic William Henry Myers. Leckhampton House, 18 December 1893. Thanks WJ for accepting presidency of SPR. The SPR council had asked Robert Pearsall Smith to write WJ. Banter about an American becoming president of a British society (TLS: MH bMS Am 1092.9 [416]).

From Alice Howe Gibbens James. Cambridge, 25 December [1893]. Alexander invites WJ and Münsterberg, who can answer for himself, to dine. Hughes carelessly let both furnaces go out. Julie is relighting one (ALS: MH bMS Am 1092.9 [305]).

From Henry Holt and Co. 26 December 1893. Charges of $7.68 for copies of *Principles* to Byerly and Edward Lincoln Atkinson (Letterbook: NjP).

From Charles Sanders Peirce. Milford, Pa., 26 December 1893. Will not go to meetings of the American Psychological Association. Sending prospectus of his great book [preserved with letter]. Asks WJ to write a supporting note, which Peirce can print. The first two volumes are nearly ready. Has recently suffered severe blows that make life a "horrid bore" (ALS: MH bMS Am 1092 [667]).

From Henry Holt and Co. 27 December 1893. Noticed error in yesterday's remittance. Sending $3.88. WJ is due $75.32 (Letterbook: NjP).

To Parke Godwin. Cambridge, 30 December [1893]. Thanks for check, which Godwin sent without waiting for a reminder [see letter to Cattell of 30 December 1893]. WJ was in New York City for meetings of the American Psychological Association but had no time to see Godwin. Tweedy is little changed and happy enough. WJ will send photograph of his father (TC: MH bMS Am 1092.1).

1894

From Frederic William Henry Myers. Leckhampton House, 3 January 1894. Thanks WJ for accepting presidency of SPR. Arthur Balfour will give an address on 26 January and resign his post to WJ. A Mr. Casey [unidentified] has been telling him about Leonora Piper. "Let us preach Piper and the Resurrection, none making us afraid!" Moses [probably William Stainton Moses (1839–1892), British clergyman and spiritualist] offers strong evidence (TC: MH bMS Am 1092.9 [417]).

To James Mark Baldwin. Cambridge [4 January 1894]. Sixth day of being sick with the "grip." *Psychological Review* has come. The printing is quite stunning (TC: MH bMS Am 1092.1).

To Smith Baker. Cambridge, 8 January 1894. Is sick with "grippe." Baker should not come before 12 February, when the second term begins (APS: OO).

To Josiah Royce. 8 January [1894]. Invites Royce to drop by to discuss Philosophy 3 (ALS: MH bMS Am 1092.9 [3635]).

To Henry Lee Higginson. Cambridge, 15 January 1894. Had not verified contents of envelope given him by Warner, which contained bank savings book and a receipt. Short discussion of finances follows (ALS: MH-BA).

To Parke Godwin. Cambridge, 16 January 1894. Encloses four photographs of Henry James. Godwin should keep the one with his initials on the back but return the others (ALS: NN).

To James McKeen Cattell. Cambridge, 22 January 1894. Sends review of Janet and of similar works [including work by Sigmund Freud; see *ECR*, 470–76]. Asks that they be printed consecutively and requests two sets of proofs, one for a medical friend. Thanks Cattell for sending him copy of Ladd [*Psychology: Descriptive and Explanatory* (1894) (see *ECR*)] (ALS: DLC; published in *SUC*).

To James McKeen Cattell. Cambridge, 26 January 1894. Bradley's [*Appearance and Reality* (1893) (WJ 510.2)] is important. Unable to review it, WJ will find someone else. Royce is reviewing it for another journal (APS: DLC).

From Charles Sanders Peirce. Milford, Pa., 27 January 1894. His philosophy "leads to positive predictions comparable with observation" and it has taken much selection to compress it into twelve volumes. Each volume is really separate. They should sell well. Has issued only a hundred circulars and is astonished by the many subscriptions. Needs money for advertising. Is on the brink of starvation. Plans to sell his place since no bank will lend anything on it (ALS: MH bMS Am 1092 [669]).

To James McKeen Cattell. Cambridge, 28 January 1894. Nichols is quite concerned about the cost of printing his work [unidentified]. WJ thinks that a specimen table would suffice, but Nichols and Münsterberg think all the tables are needed. WJ is unfamiliar with the investigation but some results seem startling (APS: DLC).

To Smith Baker. Cambridge, 30 January 1894. Discusses arrangements for housing Baker while at Harvard (ALS: OO).

From Alfred Church Lane. 4 February 1894. Asks for advice on conducting telepathy experiments (ALS: SPR, New York City).

To Paul Henry Hanus. Cambridge, 12 February [1894]. Asks for full name of the McClellan who wrote a "padagogic psychology" [James Alexander McLellan (1832–1907), *Applied Psychology* (1889)] (AP: MH Archives).

To Frederic William Henry Myers. Cambridge, 14 February 1894. Arthur Myers was "gentle, modest, true, and brave," a view also held by HJ [see *Correspondence*, 2:273] (AL incomplete: Trinity College, Cambridge).

To James McKeen Cattell. Cambridge, 18 February [1894]. Sends some "stuff" for *Psychological Review*. Asks for two copies of the March issue, which includes the Janet review [see letter to Stumpf of 24 January 1894]. Thinks page numbers in the table of contents would improve the journal. Asks that Marshall's new book be sent to Santayana [see letter to AGJ of 24 June 1894] and thanks Cattell for proofs of Fullerton ["The Psychological Standpoint," *Psychological Review* 1 (March 1894): 113–33], whom he will answer in a "general theoretic" article he hopes to write next summer [probably "The Knowing of Things Together"] (ALS: DLC; published in *SUC*).

From Henry Pickering Bowditch. [28 February 1894]. Asks if WJ has read Joseph Weatherhead Warren's [1849–1916, American physician] "Alcohol Again" [see *ML*, 457]; recommends Warren's "Notes on Progress in Physiology" [*Bos-*

ton Medical and Surgical Journal 126 (18 February 1892): 167–70; (10 March 1892): 238–41] and Russell Henry Chittenden's [1856–1943, professor of physiological chemistry at Yale] "The Influence of Alcohol on Proteid Metabolism" [*Journal of Physiology* 12 (1891): 220–32]. On the front of the postcard WJ notes that Chittenden finds "little or no change of N. metabolism in dogs" (APS: MH bMS Am 1092.9 [4527]).

From George Stuart Fullerton. Philadelphia, 1 March 1894. Furness and Mitchell will have nothing to do with Leonora Piper as they were not impressed by her (TC: MH bMS Am 1092 [275]).

To John Knowles Paine. Cambridge, 9 March 1894. Refuses invitation (ALS: MHi).

From Henry Holt and Co. 13 March 1894. [Letter is illegible.] (Letterbook: NjP).

To James Mark Baldwin. Cambridge, 14 March [1894]. Wishes he could go with Baldwin to Columbia [S.C., Baldwin's birthplace]. May start for the North Carolina mountains in early June. Received the Nordau [see letter of 27 March 1894], which is "hideous" (TC: MH bMS Am 1092.1).

To Henry Lee Higginson. Cambridge, 15 March 1894. For contents see letter of 4 May 1894 (ALS: MH-BA).

From Théodore Flournoy. Geneva, 18 March 1894. Thanks WJ for photograph, letter, copy of *Psychological Review*, and the review of Flournoy's *Des phénomènes de synopsie* [1894; see *ECR*]. Hopes WJ has recovered from angina attack. Gave number of public lectures, including two on "occult psychology." Had large audience but "displeased almost everyone": the medical people for not rejecting telepathy and spiritism and the spiritualists for not boosting their cause. His own view not settled: mediums he contacted did not furnish decisive phenomena. Instead he relied on WJ's *Principles* and *Proceedings of the SPR*, especially the article by Myers on subliminal consciousness. Recently met Harriet Clisby [1830–1931, a physician, studied in New York City in about 1865, lived in Boston for many years and died in England], who had been entertained in home of WJ's parents and had met WJ and HJ when they were young. Grieved by Arthur Myers's death (ALS: MH bMS Am 1092 [206]; published in English translation in *WJTF*).

From George Holmes Howison. Berkeley, 25 March 1894. Thanks WJ for letter about Nichols, but his own defects and those of Nichols are much alike and they would not get along. Psychology at Berkeley is a branch of the philosophy department and Howison wants someone without contempt for metaphysics and neither a materialist nor an agnostic. Should Stratton, Howison's young assistant, be sent to study experimental psychology to a place suggested by WJ, Hall, and Münsterberg? Stratton is not primarily interested in laboratory psychology but in idealist ethics. Can he learn enough in two years to establish a good laboratory? These questions would not arise if Howison could get an experienced man, who is not "an empiristic bigot & fool," and a young man of a broad culture and philosophic good sense, called for laboratory work. Thinks he can get Scripture or Krohn or James Angell. Titchener could be induced and perhaps Sanford. Asks why Peirce has no academic career. Peirce wrote that he hoped for a place in California and that Howison prevented the appointment. Howison has a very high opinion of Peirce, but supposes that "in certain vital respects of life" he is not qualified for an academic career, based on information received from Peirce's college associates. If Howison is mistaken, he would like to know so as to write Peirce and make amends (ALS: MH bMS Am 1092.9 [255]).

From Henry Holt. 26 March 1894. Sent a copy of the book to "the particularly pure Anthony" [unidentified] as WJ requested. Invites WJ to visit (Letterbook: NjP).

From Henry Holt. 28 March 1894 [date uncertain; the letter, also sent to Butler, Royce, and others, is mostly illegible]. Asks what WJ thinks of Paulsen's *Introduction to Philosophy*. Mentions Windelband and Richard Falckenberg [1851–1920, German philosopher] (Letterbook: NjP).

From Henry Holt. 29 March 1894. "Delited" by improvement in WJ's "spontaneous spelling." Discusses translation of Nordau's *Entartung* [most of letter illegible] (Letterbook: NjP).

From Silas Weir Mitchell. [April 1894]. Question concerning his impressions of Leonora Piper in her hysterical condition. Asks if WJ wants him to have another sitting with her. Learned about a case of levitation and has received interesting letters from Coleman Sellers [1827–1907, an engineer in Philadelphia, or his son, Coleman Sellers, Jr. (1852–1923), also an engineer], which he may be allowed to show WJ (ALS: MH bMS Am 1092 [557]).

To Carl Stumpf. Cambridge, 1 April 1894. Letter of introduction for his former pupil, Arthur Henry Pierce (ALS: MH bMS Am 1092.9 [3793]).

To James Mark Baldwin. Cambridge, 8 April [1894]. Will write on telepathy or personality for Johnson's *Cyclopaedia* (see *EPR, EPs*) (TC: MH bMS Am 1092.1).

To Julius Hawley Seelye. 12 April 1894. Letter lost and not seen, listed among manuscripts at Amherst College. Likely, a letter of sympathy on the death of Seelye's daughter, Elizabeth James Seelye Bixler (b. 1862), who died 10 April 1894.

To George Holmes Howison. Cambridge, 16 April [1894]. Is in bed with "painful abscess." Münsterberg will give a summer school course in experimental psychology. Davidson is staying with WJ (APS: MH bMS Am 1092.9 [1035]).

From Henry Holt and Co. 25 April 1894. Due $535.53 for 1,791 copies of *Briefer Course*, 290 copies of *Principles*, and 100 sheets. WJ charged for *Briefer Course* sent to Thomas Cochran [see *Correspondence*, 2:301] and Levi Reuben [unidentified], and for *Principles*, to Dr. Howard James [see *Correspondence*, 2:432] (Letterbook: NjP).

To Sarah Wyman Whitman. Cambridge, 2 May 1894. Charming letter commiserating with her for losing a drawing competition. Her "conceptions were certainly beautiful things" that would have "worthily adorned any hall of Justice in the world." He is still on his "couch of agony." Mary Dorr paid him long visit (ALS: MH bMS Am 1092.9 [3916]).

To George Holmes Howison. Cambridge, 9 May 1894. Pleased to hear that the Strattons are coming to Cambridge. They should come to WJ's house. Bakewell, "a fine fellow," is to take the oral examination for his Ph.D. in WJ's house tonight, having had his thesis, a protest against Hegelian monism, accepted (ALS: MH bMS Am 1092.9 [1036]).

To Ellen James Temple Emmet Hunter. Cambridge, 16 May 1894. Regrets that he cannot invite her daughters and Katharine Emmet's for a visit but he is only now up from five weeks on his back with an abscess. Invites her for October and asks about the visit to Tweedy. AGJ will return from New Hampshire in ten days. Sends "powerful love" to everyone (ALS: MH bMS Am 1092.9 [1073]).

From Alice Howe Gibbens James. [17 May 1894]. Thankful that he found Miss Clark. Son William has not slept well for two nights. "Andrew is perfection" and Julie is pleased with the place and him. Maggie [a horse] in excellent condition. WJ must not forget Mrs. Whitman's crystal. AGJ will return next week. Does not know Margaret Gregor's plans. Eliza Gibbens has taken good care of this place (ALS: MH bMS Am 1092.9 [340]).

To Alice Howe Gibbens James. Cambridge, 18 May 1894. Her letter and postcard show her to be in the "heart-sunk state," but he is sure that once they are together she will be happy. He lunched at Grace Norton's with Theodora Sedgwick. Took his class to the McLean Asylum. Hodgson came to tea, weary with the Leonora Piper "agency." Margaret Gregor will take his place and go on Tuesday with Philip Davis. Alexander Robertson sleeps "magnificently," son Henry "serene" and racing on his bicycle with Christopher R[oyce]. Will not forget about Sarah Whitman's crystal. Sends love to son William and Margaret Mary (ALS: MH bMS Am 1092.9 [1860]).

To Alice Howe Gibbens James. Cambridge, 19 May 1894. Tries to reassure her that her "low heartedness" will pass but fears that if the rain continues she will "really be depressed." Miss Farrell will come on Saturday and he wants to know what AGJ wants done. Arrived at the Childs too late to bid Helen [Helen Maria Child Sargent (d. 1903), their daughter] farewell. Went to Miss Clark's, lunched at Münsterberg's with Johannes Gad [1842–1926, German physiologist] and Bowditch, saw a performance of "Athalie" at the Annex, which was very poor. Selma Münsterberg impressed him very much. Examined Kishimoto for the doctorate. Sorry that son William does not sleep. Alexander Robertson in "perfect shape." Sunday. Tea at the Norton's with the Cummingses and [Grace W.] Minns [see *Correspondence*, 6:636]. Lost his temper at Royce for refusing to see Leonora Piper. But WJ does not feel that Royce thinks he, Hodgson, and Myers are "dupes," as Münsterberg does (ALS: MH bMS Am 1092.9 [1861]).

From George Holmes Howison. Berkeley, 19 May 1894. The Strattons will not need WJ's hospitality, as they can stay with the father of Oliver Bridges Henshaw [1870–1898, graduated from Harvard in 1893, an instructor in philosophy at the University of California]. Henshaw has done well both as student and as assistant. Howison hopes that Henshaw will find a place in English at California. He and Ernest Norton Henderson [1869–1938, American educator, then a fellow in philosophy at the University of California] will remain as assistants. Glad to hear about Bakewell's success. His view of Hegel is like Howison's, who believes that Hegel intended to "rout pantheism" but failed. Royce follows Hegel's pantheism (ALS: MH bMS Am 1092.9 [256]).

To Alice Howe Gibbens James. 22 May 1894. Still has a headache but no "brain-fag" and hopes it is due to Miss Clarke's "'chemicalization,'" by whose ways he is irritated. Had dinner at club with John Edward Russell [1848–1917, American philosopher; correspondence is known from 1900 to 1910], who is taking over Everett's work. Margaret Gregor reported that Philip Davis had "bully sitting" with Leonora Piper. Mentions Ikeda [see letter of 24 October 1891]. Has heard of a family interested in renting Chocorua. Called on Mrs. Fiske whose nephew was one of the five drowned students [Mary G. Fisk, widow of James C. Fisk, lived at 32 Quincy St., Cambridge, and was a neighbor when the Jameses lived at 20 Quincy; four students drowned off City Point, Boston, on 15 May] (ALS: MH bMS Am 1092.9 [1862]).

To Henry Holt. Cambridge, 25 May [1894]. Asks if translation of Paulsen's *Einleitung*, "a wonderful book," will be published by 1 January as he wants to use it in class (Letterbook: NjP).

To Alice Howe Gibbens James. Cambridge, 25 May [1894]. Mentions Hughes, Miss Farrell, and Eliza Gibbens in connection with household routine. The Shalers had successful sitting with Leonora Piper, who will sit for Charles Norton tomorrow and then not sit until the fall. Taussig told WJ to rent [the Chocorua place] to someone else since he is uncertain about Mrs. Gorham. Will send Alexander Robertson to Eliza Gibbens while he goes to Sarah Whitman's, who is going abroad. Tell Margaret Mary that Tommy [unidentified] is his "only consolation now that *she* is gone." Mentions chatting with Mrs. Peabody [unidentified]. Asks AGJ to return Hall's letter, which WJ suspects "is meant to be refused so that he can say that we wouldn't sit under certain simple conditions that he proposed" (ALS: MH bMS Am 1092.9 [1865]).

From George Holmes Howison. Berkeley, 25 May 1894. Sends WJ copy of Münsterberg's letter, which upsets Stratton's plans. Howison had not realized that he was "crossing M.'s grain by the plans laid out for S." Assured of only one year's leave, Stratton feels the need for the European experience. Howison had not heard of any German laboratory more valuable than Wundt's and does not agree with Münsterberg that Wundt is "antiquated" or with Wundt's people that Münsterberg is "an ass and a charlatan." Did not realize that Wundt was such a "sore point." Asks WJ to advise Stratton (ALS: MH bMS Am 1092.9 [257]).

To James Mark Baldwin. Cambridge, 27 May [1894]. Sends photograph. Pleased that Binet will review Paulhan's *Caractères*. Does not understand what Baldwin meant when he wrote that he sent WJ letter through the Johnson Cyclopaedia people, but WJ has not received it (ALS: Bodleian Library, University of Oxford; published in *SUC*).

To James Mark Baldwin. Cambridge, 30 May 1894. Agrees to write about personality and telepathy but not spiritualism [see letter of 8 April 1894 (calendared)], for which he recommends Hodgson. Invites Baldwin to join him for a trip to the North Carolina mountains (ALS: Bodleian Library, University of Oxford; published in *SUC*).

From Alice Howe Gibbens James. Wednesday [30 May 1894]. Torrents of rain all day. Drake [unidentified] and she worked "like beavers." Expecting the Taussigs tomorrow. Would like to be at Chocorua with WJ, but she cannot miss her dressmaker. Ask Miss Lemke [unidentified] while she is at Eliza Gibbens's if she can work for the Jameses (ALS: MH bMS Am 1092.9 [342]).

From Alice Howe Gibbens James. [June 1894; beginning of letter missing]. Should the Taussigs offer, AGJ would like them to bring the sofa cover. AGJ is preparing for their visit. Son William wants to stay in Chocorua. Misses the baby. Discusses problems in the garden. Wants to see WJ before he leaves for the S. C. [a slip for North Carolina] mountains (AL incomplete: MH bMS Am 1092.9 [344]).

To James Mark Baldwin. Cambridge, 1 June [1894]. Probably won't leave until 7 June. Only companion certain of going is Charles Atkinson (ALS: Bodleian Library, University of Oxford).

To Alice Howe Gibbens James. 1 June [1894]. Felt so sure she was coming that he met three trains, then received her letter asking him to go to Chocorua. Just returned from Eliza Gibbens, where he saw the Byerlys and Taussigs, who probably won't rent Chocorua. They should not expect to be able to "dump" their children upon Mary Salter, who could take one or two, but will have "old Mr. Salter" [William Salter (1821–1910), a clergyman, father of William Mackintire Salter] and other guests. WJ thinks they'd better keep their own place for the summer. Tempted to go to Chocorua but instead asks AGJ to come to Cambridge. Disgusted that the Taussigs and Mrs. Gorham have kept them dangling about Chocorua. Margaret Gregor and Mary Salter told the Taussigs that they would not need a horse there. No sign of benefit from Miss Clarke's treatment. Charles Atkinson and Baldwin are waiting for WJ to lead them to the North Carolina mountains. Will go see Sarah Whitman tomorrow. Discusses finances. Trowbridge had "miserable sitting" with Leonora Piper (ALS: MH bMS Am 1092.9 [1869]).

To George Thomas Smart [1863–1928, English-born clergyman and author; only the present letter is known]. 3 June 1894. Invitation to tea at 95 Irving St. (TC: MH bMS Am 1092.1).

To James Mark Baldwin. 6 June [1894]. Asks for old examination paper on Baldwin's book to give as a makeup exam. Will notify about North Carolina (ALS: Bodleian Library, University of Oxford; published in *SUC*).

From John Trowbridge. Cambridge, 7 June 1894. Describes sitting with Leonora Piper. Was struck by "insane cunning in the groping." Does not think she was pretending to be entranced (Published in Hodgson, "A Further Record of Observations of Certain Phenomena of Trance," *Proceedings of the SPR* 13 [February 1898]: 526).

To James Mark Baldwin. Cambridge, 8 June [1894]. Sorry that Baldwin can't go [to North Carolina]. Thanks for the examination paper (ALS: Bodleian Library, University of Oxford; published in *SUC*).

To Alice Howe Gibbens James. Blowing Rock, N.C., 14 June [1894]. No news. Almost alone in the settlement. Vegetation killed by recent frost. Had two hours' nap and a walk to a hilltop. Air is delicious (APS: MH bMS Am 1092.9 [1872]).

To James Mark Baldwin. Linville, N.C., 18 June 1894. Hopes Baldwin recovered from measles but he should have no regrets about missing the trip. Frost killed rhododendron blossoms and now there is terrible drought and intense heat. Linville beautiful, laurels and azaleas everywhere. Will go back end of week. Has "slept & 'rested' famously" (ALS: Bodleian Library, University of Oxford; published in James Mark Baldwin, *Between Two Wars* [Boston: Stratford, 1926], 2:207).

To Alice Howe Gibbens James. Linville, N.C., 19 June [1894]. Wishes she could be "wafted here" to enjoy the forest air. He and Charles Atkinson walked five miles. Would gladly summer here except for the expense of coming.

Telegraphed Cowie to ask about first payment. Read [William Henry Hudson (1841–1922), English-born author] *A Naturalist in La Plata* [1892] now reading [Sir James Matthew Barrie (1860–1937), British author] *The Little Minister* [1891], which he got from Tweedy. Leaving Thursday (ALS: MH bMS Am 1092.9 [1875]).

To Alice Howe Gibbens James. Thursday, 23 [21] June 1894. Enjoying the place so much that have given up a day in Cranberry. Comments on her dream about going downstairs to see why the dog was howling. Going up Grandfather Mountain and back by the Linville River. Charles Atkinson "rather languid." Will be in Cambridge Monday [25 June] (ALS: MH bMS Am 1092.9 [1876]).

From Henry Holt and Co. 25 June 1894. Sends $257.77 (Letterbook: NjP).

To Henry Lee Higginson. Cambridge, 26 June 1894. Is withdrawing all money from the sinking fund to rebuild a wall on the Syracuse property. Asks for advice about railway bonds in the same account that belong to HJ and Eliza Gibbens (ALS: MH-BA).

To Mary Gray Ward Dorr. Chocorua, 3 July 1894. AGJ showed him invitation but impossible to make any promises because of work schedule. AGJ must be with family in August. Sorry to miss the Crafts, but perhaps he and AGJ can come in September (ALS: MH bMS Am 1092.9 [892]).

To George Malcolm Stratton. Chocorua, 5 July 1894. Asks Stratton to send him reference from Worcester's articles in the *Open Court* [likely an error for the *Monist*] concerning anesthetic patients and comments upon Worcester by a physician [Henry Johns Berkley (see *PP*, 1473)], which WJ has in the interleaved copy of *Principles* [*AC85.J2376.890p]. Also send shoestrings that are in library table. Supposes Münsterberg's lectures begin today and is curious about number of students (ALS: CU-B; published in *SUC*).

To George Malcolm Stratton. Chocorua, 6 July 1894. Needs Lehmann's *Die Hauptgesetze des menschlichen Gefühlslebens* [1892; WJ 749.39], which contains notes [WJ was working on "The Physical Basis of Emotion"], and Charles River Bank deposit slips (ALS: CU-B; published in *SUC*).

To Henry Holt. Chocorua, 8 July 1894. Letter of introduction for Ellery Sedgwick, who wants employment in publishing house (Letterbook: NjP).

To James Mark Baldwin. Chocorua, 14 July 1894. Since Cattell is to visit Baldwin, WJ is sending his contribution ["The Physical Basis of Emotion"] to Baldwin's address. Nichols, who is staying with WJ, has "all manly moral qualities" although fate seems against him. Regards to Helen Baldwin and Cattell (ALS: Bodleian Library, University of Oxford; published in *SUC*).

To Alice Howe Gibbens James. Cambridge, 18 July 1894. Journey went well. He and Nichols did not talk much. AGJ should not be too hard on Nichols, who is "ravaged by some inward trouble." Lists seventeen errands he ran while in Boston, mentioning shops and people including Hodgson, who is going to the Dorrs; Jordan, Marsh where he bought two "female" bathing suits; Jacob Shamos, a tailor, where he spent $10 on a coat, vest, and shirt; his home, well looked after by the Strattons. At Grace Norton's he learned that Richard Norton is engaged to a daughter [Edith] of John Williams White. At the Club saw Münsterberg, who is still suffering with pain but pleased with summer school which has forty students and who read two poems to WJ and Royce. Selma Münsterberg returns from Keene. Mrs. Hermann Hagen left America unwillingly and with only $300 a year. Saw Brooks and Lawrence [Lawrence Graham Brooks (b. 1881), son of John Graham Brooks] at the Club. Royce delighted with the Strattons. WJ does not want to go to the Crafts but must. Asks AGJ to forget his "unmanliness" for there will be better days (ALS: MH bMS Am 1092.9 [1881]).

To Alice Howe Gibbens James. Cambridge, 30 July [1894]. Anxious about the "money affair" so came straight home from Buzzard's Bay instead of taking train to Cape Cod. Found Warner's check for $3,000 [see *Correspondence*, 2:320–21] and on the strength of it ordered Norfolk jacket, *Mind*, and French and German philosophical journals, "which I stopped last December." Thanks for suggestions "à la Myers." Strattons not at the house. WJ dining at Colonial Club. Santayana also there with Lord Russell [Francis Stanley Russell, 2d Earl Russell (1865–1931), brother of Bertrand Russell]. Caroline Little Böcher [wife of Ferdinand Böcher] is dead. "Shaler is immense! not a man but a continent" [WJ was visiting Shaler on Martha's Vineyard]. WJ cannot understand how Shaler lives "with that circus going on in his head." Has not received letter from Kishimoto (ALS: MH bMS Am 1092.9 [1886]).

From Henry Holt and Co. August 1894. [Letter is illegible.] (Letterbook: NjP).

To James McKeen Cattell. Chocorua, 6 August [1894]. Could Cattell add Münsterberg's name to the note in "The Physical Basis of Emotion" where Miller and Nichols are mentioned [see *EPs*, 307n] (APS: DLC; published in *SUC*).

From Sarah Wyman Whitman. Nancy, 7 August 1894. Enjoying her trip. In London saw Thomas Francis Bayard [1828–1898, American statesman, then serving as ambassador to Great Britain], who is having a political holiday, and Bryce. Sargent's work for the Boston Public Library seems an assemblage rather than a composition, "a museum of idols rather than a picture of the world's religions." In Paris, James Abbott McNeill Whistler [1834–1903, American painter] and his pictures gave her great joy. Will not write about cathedrals she is seeing. Is going with Elizabeth Lawrence to Beyreuth for the music (ALS: MH bMS Am 1092.9 [691]; published in *Letters of Sarah Wyman Whitman* [Cambridge: privately printed, 1907]).

To James McKeen Cattell. Chocorua, 11 August 1894. Sends review of William Bateson [see *ECR*] and will send notice of Sir Francis Galton [1822–1911, British scientist, "Discontinuity in Evolution," *Mind*, n. s., 3 (July 1894): 362–72; notice not known] in September. Hopes that he and Baldwin do not quarrel (ALS: DLC; published in *SUC*).

To George Malcolm Stratton. Chocorua, 14 August [1894]. Hopes this note arrives before he leaves for Europe and that he has gained much from summer school. Will send note to Stumpf when Stratton goes to Berlin. Leave key to house with Grace Norton (ALS: CU-B; published in *SUC*).

To James Edwin Creighton. Chocorua, 23 August 1894. Wants to write short notice of Uphues's *Psychologie des Erkennens* [review not known] (APS: NIC).

To William Wilberforce Baldwin. Chocorua, 28 August 1894. Discusses Raffaello Maltini, who had written to say he would be glad to come to America. They could pay him $20 per month. HJ wrote that Baldwin was to come home for visit this summer. WJ would have liked to have seen him. Regards to his sister and Mrs. Baldwin. 20 September. Kept letter back until now because their French cook decided to stay (ALS: NNMor).

To Mary Gray Ward Dorr. Chocorua, 28 August 1894. AGJ regrets that she must refuse invitation to visit. They have had company since 1 July and their cook is leaving next week. WJ would like to postpone his reply to invitation until he sees how his work goes. Perhaps he can come on the 15th (ALS: MH bMS Am 1092.9 [893]).

From Henry Holt and Co. September 1894. [Letter is illegible.] (Letterbook: NjP).

To Alice Howe Gibbens James. Cambridge, 12 September [1894]. Comfortable trip and "*bad* pie at Portsmouth." Discusses lock, which he forgot. Wrote to Bowditch [see letter of 11 May 1891] about the hay and Andrew and to Bazzell [unidentified, reading uncertain]. Strattons left everything "neat as a pin," unlike the Pierces. Had tea with Eliza Gibbens and Margaret Gregor. Davidson leaves for Europe on the 25th, "so that complication is removed." Snow died suddenly. Rebecca Cummings "grossartig." Cooke had stomach cancer [Josiah Cooke died on 3 September 1894] (ALS: MH bMS Am 1092.9 [1887]).

To Mary Gray Ward Dorr. Cambridge, 13 September [1894]. Will be with Baldwin at Southwest Harbor on Saturday [15 September] and can call on her at Bar Harbor several days later (ALS: MH bMS Am 1092.9 [896]).

To Ada Goodrich Freer. Cambridge, 14 September 1894. Myers wrote that she has a paper about her messages. Invites her to read it at SPR meeting, probably in December. "Mrs. Sidgwick's" report on the Census of Hallucinations is "simply magnificent," while in the United States psychical research languishes (ALS: CLSU).

From Hugo Münsterberg. Swampscott, Mass., 14 September 1894. His health has much improved at Swampscott. Sends the essential part of his letter to Eliot, written without consulting WJ because Münsterberg did not want to place WJ in an "uncomfortable dilemma." Asks that WJ show the Eliot letter to Royce. Münsterberg himself will explain everything to Palmer. In the letter to Eliot, Münsterberg explains that his leave of absence from Germany cannot be extended beyond the two years. If he stays longer at Harvard, he will lose his place in Germany. He likes Harvard, but does not want to make a permanent decision as yet. Asks Eliot for leave for two or three years. No one in America is qualified to replace Münsterberg as permanent director because no one is interested in the research Münsterberg has begun. But if he is granted leave, either Pierce, or Lough, or MacDougall [probably Robert MacDougall (1866–1939), Canadian-born educator and missionary, receiving his doctorate from Harvard in 1895] could oversee the technical side of the laboratory, and Münsterberg would communicate his "experimental thinking" by mail (ALS: MH bMS Am 1092.9 [375]).

To James Mark Baldwin. Cambridge, 15 September 1894. May not be able to make trip because he has to stay for Snow's funeral (TC: MH bMS Am 1092.1).

To Alice Howe Gibbens James. Cambridge, 17 September 1894. Visited Eliza Gibbens and Margaret Gregor. Salter took WJ's supplies with him. May not go to Mt. Desert because too much talk there will do him "no good at all." Discusses floor polishes and mentions Oliver J. Briggs [one of the builders of WJ's house], Charles Butcher [dealer in floor polish], Mrs. Alphonse Naus Van Daell [a neighbor, see Biographical Register of *Correspondence*, vol. 8], Mrs. Riley [unidentified], Grant, and Mann. Likes the Shaler family. WJ has had "frightful spell" of melancholy. Tell Harry and Billy to read German and French and some poetry after Middleton leaves (ALS: MH bMS Am 1092.9 [1891]).

To Dear Madam [unidentified]. Cambridge, 18 September 1896. Thanks for the second part of her "Notes" (ALS: CSmH).

To Charles [?] Robertson. Cambridge, 18 September 1894. Thanks Robertson for his brother's *Philosophical Remains of George Croom Robertson* [1894]. WJ's "love and admiration" for his brother were "intense." Did Robertson see WJ's memorial note [see *ECR*]? Would have sent him copy but did not know where to send it and now has none left (ALS: MH bMS Am 1092.9 [3535]).

To James Mark Baldwin. Cambridge, 19 September 1894. Has had many delays, and WJ may not go at all [to Southwest Harbor]. But if he does, he will start Friday night [21 September]. Hoped late telegram did not inconvenience Baldwin (ALS: Bodleian Library, University of Oxford).

To Hermann Obrist. Cambridge, 20 September 1894. Letter of introduction for Thomas Davidson (ALS: MH bMS Am 1092.9 [3365]).

From Oliver Joseph Lodge. Liverpool, 22 September 1894. Discusses his report on Eusapia Palladino [see letter of 29 September 1894] and proposed number of the *Proceedings of the SPR* about her [not published]. Hopes for contributions from Richet, Henry Sidgwick, Myers, Finzi [Dr. George Finzi, an honorary associate member of the SPR, living in Milan], Julian Ochorowicz [1850–1917, Polish psychologist], and perhaps Lombroso. Asks WJ as president of the SPR whether the case should be published in more scientific journals. Important to publish before William Thomas Stead [1849–1912, British journalist, then editor of *Borderland*, a periodical devoted to spiritualism] prints "garbled reports." Her case shows that objects can be "moved without ordinary kinds of contact." It is philosophers who must find a theory, it is not a matter for physics (ALS: MH bMS Am 1092 [496]).

To James Mark Baldwin. 26 September [1894]. Just back after "glorious day yesterday." Realized he had forgotten to pay telephone bill and that Baldwin probably had paid it, so sends dollar as "fractional reimbursement" (ALS: Bodleian Library, University of Oxford; published in *SUC*).

To Clara Kathleen Barnett Rogers [1844–1931, English-born singer and writer, known as Clara Doria; correspondence is known from 1894 and 1901; see also *Correspondence*, 2:439]. Cambridge, 1 October 1894. Has not forgotten that he has HJ's copy of her book [probably *The Philosophy of Singing* (1893)] and will bring it soon (TC: MH bMS Am 1092.1).

From Théodore Flournoy. Geneva, 2 October 1894. Has not answered WJ's letter because of graphophobia, a real illness. Considered having Brown-Séquard injections but the treatment did not help his friend and WJ's letter was not encouraging. Discusses at length the remodeling of their house. Has ignored the philosophical journals but liked Royce's "The Case of John Bunyan" [*Psychological Review* 1 (1894): 22–33, 134–51, 230–40] and was pleased by WJ's disposing of Wundt ["Professor Wundt and Feelings of Innervation" (see *EPs*)]. Returned from the mountains ahead of his family in order to work on an article for Binet but is having difficulty writing. Mentions his children, Alice, Blanche, Marguerite, and Henri. His wife had begun letter to AGJ but has not finished it. Sends regards to Münsterberg. Thanks WJ for warning him about Wadsworth (ALS: MH bMS Am 1092 [207]; published in English translation in *WJTF*).

From Oliver Joseph Lodge. Liverpool, 13 October 1894. Received WJ's letter today and WJ's advice agrees with their position, as they had already decided to avoid publicity [see letter of 29 September 1894]. Only question now is whether to issue the pamphlet to members. Had not intended that WJ should see his first draft, which WJ probably got from Hodgson. Asks WJ to make further suggestions (ALS: MH bMS Am 1092 [497]).

To Frank Thilly. Cambridge, 14 October 1894. Asks when preface is needed [to Paulsen's *Introduction to Philosophy*] and if he can have proofs of the book to read (ALS: NIC).

To James Mark Baldwin. Cambridge, 24 October [1894]. Sends review of writings on hallucination and hopes it might get into the January *Psychological Review* [see *EPR*, 64–73]. Glad of the favorable prospects for Baldwin's health. "Dilation of the stomach and *lavage*" have now become a reality (ALS: Bodleian Library, University of Oxford; published in part in *SUC*).

From Mary M. Clarkson Manning [unidentified, from Portland, Maine]. Portland, 28 October [1894]. Describes a psychic experience. Many years ago at night she called out the name of her sister, who was several hundred miles away. The sister reported hearing being called (Published in *Journal of the SPR* 7 [June 1895]: 100–101).

From Edward Charles Pickering [1846–1919, astronomer, professor at Harvard; correspondence is known from 1894 and 1895]. 6 November [1894]. In response to WJ's inquiry, discusses the spectrum of a newly found star (Letterbook: MH Archives).

To James Mark Baldwin. 13 November 1894. Mislaid Robert Lilley's [b. 1839, Scottish-born lexicographer, managing editor of *Johnson's Universal Cyclopaedia*] address. Can Baldwin send it? "Telepathy" finished. Banter about WJ having written "Princeton Mass" (TC: MH bMS Am 1092.1).

To James Mark Baldwin. 19 November 1894. Accepts invitation for AGJ and himself to be guests of the Baldwins during the American Psychological Association meeting (ALS: Bodleian Library, University of Oxford; published in *SUC*).

From Mary McNeill Scott [unidentified]. Boston, 21 November 1894. Has met WJ at Sarah Whitman's and corresponded with him. Sends long manuscript about a haunting in New Orleans (ALS: SPR, New York City).

From Sarah Jane Farmer [1847–1916, organizer of summer encampments devoted to comparative religion]. 26 November 1894. Concerns the case of Henry Guy Walters [see Biographical Register of *Correspondence*, vol. 8] (Published in *EPR*, 144).

To James Mark Baldwin. 28 November [1894]. Sends paper by Leon Solomons, which should appear as contribution from the Harvard laboratory [no contributions from the Harvard laboratory were published in 1895]. WJ would like to see proof. Asks Baldwin to also send him proof of the translation of Stumpf ["Hermann von Helmholtz and the New Psychology," *Psychological Review* 2 (January 1895): 1–12] as Stumpf wants him to see it (TC: MH bMS Am 1092.1).

To Frank Thilly. Cambridge, 1 December 1894. Has not received proofs of Paulsen's book, which he needs for preface (ALS: NIC).

To Alice Howe Gibbens James. Cambridge, 3 December 1894. Mary Salter wrote Margaret Gregor that AGJ is ill with a cold. Urges her not to hurry home. Took care of business in morning, committees all afternoon, and Philosophy 20b in evening. Rosina Emmet, son Henry, and Margaret Gregor went to concert and now are chatting with Middleton. Alexander Robertson looks splendid. Son William spent night at Warners having been on a sleigh party. Has bills to pay but McCarthy check and Radcliffe salary have come. Love to the Salters (ALS: MH bMS Am 1092.9 [1894]).

To William Temple Emmet [1869–1918, a lawyer, son of Katharine Emmet; only present letter is known]. Cambridge, 11 December [1894]. Wrote to Henry Higginson, who said that picture was Frank's [perhaps Francis Lee Higginson; see letter of 14 February 1892]. Frank has happy memories of Emmet's aunts, Mary Temple [see *Correspondence*, 4:618–19] and Ellen Hunter, and will give Emmet the picture. WJ thinks it has "*tone*" very like Emmet's mother but not a close likeness. Told Frank that Mr. Keogh [unidentified] would pay what Frank had paid, but Frank does not remember its cost. Emmet should communicate through WJ or Grenville Emmet [see letter to AGJ of 26 September 1894] as Higginson has had "domestic calamity" (ALS: known only through dealer's catalogue).

To William Cameron Forbes. Cambridge, 11 December [1894]. Invites Forbes to dinner on the 20th and to spend the night. Regards to his parents and brother Ralph Emerson Forbes [d. 1937, graduated from Harvard in 1888] (ALS: MH bMS Am 1364 [154]).

From Joseph Estlin Carpenter [1844–1927, British clergyman; correspondence is known from 1894 to 1909]. 14 December 1894. Describes sitting with Leonora Piper. Is convinced that she has extraordinary powers but does not know what they are (Published in Hodgson, "A Further Record of Observations of Certain Phenomena of Trance," *Proceedings of the SPR* 13 [February 1898]: 529).

To James Mark Baldwin. Cambridge, 15 December [1894]. Cannot commit to lunch on either Thursday [27 December] or Friday. Has had trouble sleeping and excitement at Princeton will make it worse. WJ and AGJ are due at Philadelphia on Sunday [30 December]. Hopes to dine with the Sloanes [William Milligan Sloane (1850–1928), then professor of history at Princeton, and his wife, Mary Espy Johnston Sloane]. Feels "astonishingly well" but the "address hangs between wind and water" (ALS: Bodleian Library, University of Oxford).

From Henry Holt and Co. 21 December 1894. Sending royalty check for $141.02 (Letterbook: NjP).

To Sarah Wyman Whitman. 25 December 1894. A letter of thanks for the "splendid medallion" she gave them. Wishes her a merry Christmas (ALS: MH bMS Am 1092.9 [3920]).

Biographical Register

Abbot, Francis Ellingwood (1836–1903), American philosopher, a participant with WJ in several philosophy clubs in Cambridge. Correspondence is known from 1876 to 1903.

Adams, Henry (1838–1918), American historian. In 1872 he married Marian (Clover) Hooper. Correspondence is known from 1882 to 1910.

Adamson, Robert (1852–1902), Scottish philosopher.

Adler, Felix (1851–1933), American philosopher, founder of the Society for Ethical Culture, husband of Helen Goldmark Adler. Correspondence is known from 1888 and 1901.

Agassiz, Alexander (1835–1910), American naturalist, son of Louis Agassiz by his first wife. Correspondence is known from 1905 and 1907.

Agassiz, Louis (1807–1873), Swiss-born naturalist, appointed to teach zoology and geology at Harvard in 1847. One letter to WJ is known (1865).

A.K. *See* Walsh, Catharine

Alexander, Samuel (1859–1938), Australian-born philosopher, active in England.

Ames, James Barr (1846–1910), American lawyer and writer.

Anagnos (Anagnostopoulus), Michael (1837–1906), Greek-born journalist and educator, then associated with the Perkins Institution for the Blind. Correspondence is known from 1892.

Andrew, a black servant brought from Aiken, S. C., by AGJ in 1888 and employed by the Jameses into the 1890s.

Angell, Frank (1857–1939), American psychologist, a cousin of James Rowland Angell, received his doctorate at Leipzig in 1891. After teaching at Cornell he went to Stanford in 1892, where he spent most of his teaching career. One letter is known (1906).

Angell, James Rowland (1869–1949), American psychologist, received his doctorate from Harvard in 1892. After a year of teaching at the University of Minnesota, he went to Chicago in 1894, where he spent most of his teaching career. Correspondence is known from 1892 to 1908.

Anne, Miss. *See* Ashburner, Anne

Arthur. *See* Sedgwick, Arthur George

Ashburner, Anne (1807–1894), sister of Grace Ashburner.

Ashburner, Grace (1814–1893), sister of Sarah Ashburner Sedgwick, who was the mother of Arthur George Sedgwick, Sara Ashburner Sedgwick Darwin, Susan Ridley Sedgwick Norton, and Theodora Sedgwick. Correspondence is known from 1891 to 1893.

Atkinson, Charles Follen (d. 1915), in 1861–65 attended the Lawrence Scientific School, later a businessman in Boston.

Atkinson, Edward Lincoln (1865–1902), a clergyman, as a student served as tutor in the James family. One letter is known (1899).

B., Ansel. *See* Bourne, Ansel

Bain, Alexander (1818–1903), Scottish philosopher and psychologist.

Baker, Smith (1850–1922), American educator and neurologist. Correspondence is known from 1891 to 1897.

Bakewell, Charles Montague (1867–1957), American philosopher. Correspondence survives from 1894 to 1909.

Baldwin, Helen Green, wife of James Mark Baldwin.

Baldwin, James Mark (1861–1934), American psychologist, one of the editors of the *Psychological Review,* husband of Helen Green Baldwin. Correspondence is known from 1890 to 1910.

Baldwin, William Wilberforce (1850–1910), American physician and author, residing mostly in Florence, Italy. Correspondence survives from 1892 to 1905.

Balfour, Arthur James Balfour, 1st earl of (1848–1930), British statesman and philosopher. One letter to WJ is known (1902).

Ballard, Melville, instructor at the Columbia Institution for the Instruction of the Deaf and Dumb and Blind (now Gallaudet College).

Barnum, Phineas Taylor (1810–1891), American showman.

Bartlett, George Alonzo (1844–1908), professor of German at Harvard.

Bartlett, George C., writer on spiritualism, living in New York City. Correspondence is known from 1891.

Bateson, William (1861–1926), British biologist.

Bay. *See* Rand, Ellen Gertrude (Bay) Emmet

Berenson, Bernhard, (1865–1959), Lithuanian-born art critic, married Mary Smith Costelloe in 1900, her second marriage.

Berenson, Mary Smith Costelloe (1864–1945), daughter of Hannah Whitall Smith and Robert Pearsall Smith and sister of Logan Pearsall Smith. In 1884–85 she studied philosophy at the Harvard Annex (later Radcliffe). On 3 September 1885 she married Frank Costelloe. After they separated in 1892, she lived with Bernhard Berenson, whom she married in 1900.

Bierwirth, Heinrich Conrad (1853–1940), German-born professor of German at Harvard.

Bigelow, William Sturgis (1850–1926), Boston physician, trustee of the Museum of Fine Arts in Boston. Correspondence is known from 1887 to 1908.

Bigham, John (1864–1940), received his doctorate from Harvard in 1894, in later years a businessman.

Billy. *See* James, William (son)

Binet, Alfred (1857–1911), French psychologist. Two letters from 1890 and 1895 are known.

Blodgett, Elizabeth Wild, wife of Charles Blodgett (d. 1903), a physician in Holyoke, Mass. Elizabeth Blodgett was attempting to communicate with her dead sister, Hannah Wild. One letter is known (1888). For the case see *Correspondence,* 6:419–20n.

Blood, Benjamin Paul (1832–1919), American writer and mystic. Correspondence is known from 1882 to 1910. Blood sent WJ numerous clippings and pamphlets, many of them preserved in the James Collection of Harvard's Houghton Library. For references see the notes in *EPh* to WJ's essay on Blood, "A Pluralistic Mystic" (1910).

Bob. *See* James, Robertson

Bôcher, Ferdinand (1832–1902), professor of modern languages at Harvard.

Böcklin, Arnold (1827–1901), Swiss painter.

Boirac, Émile (1851–1917), French philosopher, undertook to translate WJ's *Psychology: Briefer Course* but did not complete his work.

Boott, Francis (1813–1904), American composer, father of Elizabeth Boott Duveneck, lived mostly in Italy after the death of his wife in 1847. Correspondence survives from 1892 to 1900.

Bourget, Minnie David, married Paul Bourget in 1890.

Bourget, Paul-Charles-Joseph (1852–1935), French writer, journalist, husband of Minnie David Bourget. Correspondence survives from 1893 and 1894.

Bourne, Ansel (b. 1826), a workman afflicted with multiple personalities, hypnotized and investigated by WJ. For WJ's note on the case see *EPs*, 269.

Bowditch, Henry Pickering (1840–1911), American physiologist, professor at the Harvard Medical School. Correspondence is known from 1867 to 1910.

Bradley, Francis Herbert (1846–1924), English philosopher. Correspondence is known from 1895 to 1910.

Bridget, a servant of the Jameses in the early 1890s.

Briggs, Oliver J., and Briggs, William A., carpenters and builders in Cambridge, builders of WJ's house at 95 Irving St.

Brimmer, Martin (1829–1896), for many years president of the Museum of Fine Arts in Boston.

Brimmer, Mary Ann Timmins, wife of Martin Brimmer and aunt of Gemma Timmins.

Brooks, Helen Lawrence Appleton Washburn (1846–1938), widow of Francis Tucker Washburn, wife of John Graham Brooks.

Brooks, John Graham (1846–1938), an 1875 graduate of the Harvard Divinity School, a writer on social problems. Correspondence is known from 1892 to 1907.

Brooks, Phillips (1835–1893), American Episcopalian clergyman. One letter is known (1890).

Brown, a horse owned by WJ in 1890.

Browne, George Henry (1857–1931), one of the founders of the Browne and Nichols School for Boys in Cambridge.

Brown-Séquard, Charles Édouard (1817–1894), Mauritian-born physiologist of mixed American and French parentage.

Bryce, James, Viscount Bryce (1838–1922), British historian and politician, husband of Marion Ashton Bryce. Correspondence is known from 1882 to 1902.

Bundy, John Curtis (1841–1892), editor of the spiritualist *Religio-Philosophical Journal* in Chicago.

Butler, Nicholas Murray (1862–1947), American educator, president of Columbia University. Correspondence is known from 1909.

Byerly, William Elwood (1849–1935), American mathematician, professor at Harvard.

Caird, Edward (1835–1908), Scottish philosopher. Correspondence is known from 1899 and 1907.

Caldwell, William (1863–1942), Scottish-born educator, taught at Cornell University in 1891–92, spent most of his career at McGill University in Canada.

Calkins, Mary Whiton (1863–1930), American philosopher, teaching at Wellesley College, then taking graduate courses at Harvard. Correspondence is known from 1890 to 1909.

Call, Annie Payson (1853–1940), American mental health writer. One letter is known (1891).

Captain, a horse owned by WJ in 1890.

Carlyle, Thomas (1795–1881), Scottish historian and essayist.

Carrie. *See* James, Caroline Eames Cary

Carus, Paul (1852–1919), German-born editor and philosophical writer. Correspondence is known from 1891 to 1910.

Cattell, James McKeen (1860–1944), American psychologist. Correspondence is known from 1893 to 1910.

Cérésole, Alfred, a pastor near Vevey, Switzerland, who with his wife took in pupils, including some of WJ's children in 1892 and 1893.

Cérésole, Mme Alfred, wife of Alfred Cérésole. According to WJ, she was a niece of Louis Agassiz. One letter is known (1893).

C.F.A. *See* Atkinson, Charles Follen

Chadwick, James Read (1844–1905), American physician and medical librarian. Two letters from 1874 are known.

Chamberlin, Eleazer Davis, a relative of AGJ.

Chaplin, Winfield Scott (1847–1918), professor of engineering.

Chapman, John Jay (1862–1933), American critic and essayist, husband of Minna Timmins Chapman. Correspondence is known from 1891 to 1910.

Chapman, Minna Timmins, wife of John Jay Chapman. One letter is known (1890).

Child, Elizabeth Ellery Sedgwick (b. 1825), wife of Francis James Child. Correspondence is known from 1885 to 1903.

Child, Francis James (1825–1896), professor of English at Harvard, married Elizabeth Ellery Sedgwick in 1860. The Childs had three daughters, Helen, Susan, and Henrietta, and a son, Francis Sedgwick. Correspondence is known from 1878 to 1896.

Child, Francis (Frank) Sedgwick (1869–1935), a clergyman, son of Francis James Child and Elizabeth Ellery Sedgwick Child.

Child, Helen. *See* Sargent, Helen Maria Child

Child, Henrietta Ellery (b. 1867), daughter of Francis James Child.

Chubb, Percival (1860–1960), English-born educator, associated with the Society for Ethical Culture.

Claparède, Édouard (1873–1940), Swiss psychologist, related to Théodore Flournoy. Correspondence is known from 1902 and 1907.

Clark, Sir Andrew (1847–1893), British physician, known for treatment of cancer.

Clarke (or Clark), Miss, a healer in Boston. For a suggestion as to her identity see *Correspondence*, 2:293n.

Clarke, Agnes, wife of Joseph Thacher Clarke.

Clarke, Joseph Thacher (d. 1920), American writer on archaeology, living in Harrow, England. AGJ met Clarke in 1868 in Dresden when she lived there with her mother and sisters. Sometimes WJ writes Clarke's name without the 'e'. Correspondence survives from 1898 to 1908.

Clary, O. Ware, dealer in rubber goods at 211 S. Salina St., Syracuse, a tenant of the Jameses.

Clemens, Samuel Langhorne (Mark Twain) (1835–1910), American novelist. Correspondence is known from 1900.

Coggeshall, Frederic (1861–1911), Boston physician, an 1886 graduate of Harvard. According to his Harvard class biography, he took twice as many courses as were required and was a member of the Philosophical Club.

Cooke, Josiah Parsons (1827–1894), American chemist, professor at Harvard.

Corning, James Leonard (1828–1903), American clergyman, diplomat, and art historian.

Cossmann, Paul Nikolaus (b. 1869), undertook to translate *The Principles of Psychology* into German but did not complete the task.

Costelloe, Frank (Benjamin François Conn) (1855–1899), an Irish lawyer, studied philosophy at Oxford, first husband of Mary Smith Costelloe Berenson.

Costelloe, Mary Smith. *See* Berenson, Mary Smith Costelloe

Cowie, William (1846–1913), Syracuse real estate agent, elected mayor of Syracuse in 1890. In 1892 he became business agent for the Jameses.

Crafts, Clémence Haggerty, wife of James Mason Crafts.

Crafts, James Mason (1839–1917), American chemist, president of the Massachusetts Institute of Technology from 1898 to 1900, husband of Clémence Haggerty Crafts.

Cranch, Christopher Pearse (1813–1892), American artist and poet.

Crawford, Francis Marion (1854–1909), American novelist. Correspondence is known from 1892.

Creighton, James Edwin (1861–1924), American philosopher, later editor of the *Philosophical Review*. Correspondence is known from 1894 to 1897.

Crookes, Sir William (1832–1919), British physicist, chemist, and psychical researcher.

Cruchon, Mme, keeper of a pension at Vers-chez-les-Blanc, near Lausanne, Switzerland. She likely had a daughter named Louise.

Cummings, Edward (1861–1926), sociologist and clergyman, teaching at Harvard, husband of Rebecca Haswell Cummings. They were the parents of Edward Estlin Cummings (1894–1962), American poet. One letter is known (1887).

Cummings, Rebecca Haswell (d. 1947), wife of Edward Cummings.

Curtis, George William (1824–1892), American editor and author.

Cushing, Howard Gardiner (1869–1916), an 1891 graduate of Harvard, later an artist in Boston.

Danforth, Allen (1846–1909), Harvard administrator.

Darwin, George Howard (1845–1912), English mathematician and astronomer.

Dauriac, Lionel-Alexandre (1847–1923), French philosopher. Correspondence is known from 1893 and 1904.

David, Professor, an otherwise unidentified friend and relative by marriage of Théodore Flournoy, a prospective teacher of WJ's sons.

Davidson, Thomas (1840–1900), Scottish-born writer. For WJ's appreciation of

Davidson see "Thomas Davidson: Individualist" in *ECR*. Correspondence survives from 1880 to 1900.

Davis, Julia Wilder Robinson, widow of William Whitney Davis.

Davis, Philip Whitney (b. 1871), a businessman, brother of Robert Howe Davis.

Davis, William Whitney (d. 1878), a singer and music teacher, husband of Julia Davis and father of Philip Davis and Robert Davis.

Delabarre, Edmund Burke (1863–1945), American psychologist, received his doctorate in Freiburg in 1891, professor at Brown University. WJ incorporated Delabarre's essay on the law of contrast into *The Principles of Psychology*; see *PP*, 662–74.

Delbœuf, Joseph-Remi-Léopold (1831–1896), Belgian philosopher and psychologist. Correspondence survives from 1882 to 1891.

Dessoir, Max (1867–1947), German psychologist and aesthetician.

D'Estrella, Theophilus (1851–1929), instructor in art at the California Institution for the Education of the Deaf and Dumb, and the Blind.

Dewey, John (1859–1952), American philosopher. Correspondence is known from 1891 to 1909.

Dibblee, Annie Meacham, California friend of Ellen James Temple Emmet Hunter. Annie Dibblee had at least four children. Her husband was Albert Dibblee about whom no information was found.

Dixey, Ellen Sturgis Tappan (b. 1849), sister of Mary Aspinwall Tappan, wife of Richard Cowell Dixey. Two letters to her are known.

Dolmateff, Mme, unidentified person in Switzerland, who offered rooms or board.

Donaldson, Henry Herbert (1857–1938), American neurologist.

Dorr, Charles Hazen (d. 1893), husband of Mary Gray Ward Dorr and father of George Bucknam Dorr.

Dorr, George Bucknam (1853–1944), a student at Harvard with an interest in philosophy, son of Mary Gray Ward Dorr. Dorr was associated with WJ in psychical research. Correspondence survives from 1886 to 1909.

Dorr, Mary Gray Ward (ca. 1820–1901), Boston hostess, had a summer home at Bar Harbor, Maine. She was the mother of George Bucknam Dorr and an aunt of Thomas Wren Ward, WJ's friend from their early years in Newport. Correspondence survives from 1886 to 1901.

Dressler, Fletcher Bascom (1858–1930), a psychologist.

Driver, Stephen William (b. 1834), a physician in Cambridge.

Drummond, Robert, printer at 3 Hague St., New York City.

Du Maurier, George Louis Palmella Busson (1834–1896), British novelist and illustrator.

Dunbar, Charles Franklin (1830–1900), professor of political economy at Harvard.

Duveneck, Elizabeth Boott (1846–1888), daughter of Francis Boott, studied painting and in 1886 married Frank Duveneck, one of her teachers. One letter to WJ is known (1877).

Duveneck, Frank (1848–1919), American painter, husband of Elizabeth Boott Duveneck. One letter from WJ is known (1893).

Ebbinghaus, Hermann (1850–1909), German psychologist.

Eliot, Charles William (1834–1926), in charge of the chemistry laboratory at the Lawrence Scientific School in 1861–63, president of Harvard from 1869. Correspondence is known from 1875 to 1910. For Eliot's early impression of WJ see *LWJ*, 1:31–32.

Eliot, Grace Hopkinson (d. 1924), second wife of Charles William Eliot.

Ellen, a servant in the James household in about 1890.

Elliot, a Scottish visitor in 1890.

Elliot, John Wheelock (d. 1925), Boston physician, husband of Mary Lee Morse Elliot.

Elliot, Mary Lee Morse, sister of Frances Rollins Morse and wife of John Wheelock Elliot.

Ellis, William Rogers (1846–1903), dealt in real estate and insurance in Cambridge.

Emmet, Katharine (Kitty) Temple (1843–1895), one of WJ's six Temple cousins, daughter of Robert Emmet Temple and Catharine Margaret James Temple and wife of Richard Stockton Emmet. The Emmets had six children. Correspondence is known from 1861 to 1868.

Emmet, Richard Stockton Emmet (1821–1902), husband of Katharine Emmet.

Emmet, Rosina Hubley (b. 1873), daughter of Ellen James Emmet Temple Hunter. Correspondence survives from 1895 to 1910.

Ermacora, Giovanni Battista (1869–1898), Italian physicist and psychical researcher.

Evans, Elizabeth Glendower (1856–1937), American social reformer, widow of Glendower Evans (1859–1886), a Harvard student befriended by WJ. Correspondence is known from 1886 to 1906.

Everett, Charles Carroll (1829–1900), professor of theology at Harvard. Four letters from Everett to WJ are known from 1881 to 1898.

Ewald, Julius Richard (1855–1921), German physiologist.

Fairchild, Sally (b. 1869), daughter of Elizabeth Nelson Fairchild and Charles Fairchild (b. 1838), a lawyer and banker associated with Henry Lee Higginson. One letter is known (1906). For a note about her see *Correspondence*, 3:274n; for her sister, Lucia Fairchild Fuller, see *Correspondence*, 6:343n.

Fanny. *See* Morse, Frances Rollins

Farlow, William Gilson (1844–1919), American botanist. Correspondence is known from 1899 and 1900.

Farrell, Miss, unidentified person, perhaps Margaret A. Farrell, a carpetmaker.

Fayrer, Sir Joseph (1824–1907), British physician.

Ferraris, Carlo Francesco (1850–1924), Italian economist and politician. One letter is known (1892).

Ferrier, David (1843–1928), British physician and neurologist. One letter is known (1891).

Fields, Annie Adams (1834–1915), American author. One letter is known (1888).

Fiske, John (1842–1901), American philosopher of evolution and historian. Correspondence is known from 1880 and 1898.

Flournoy, Marie-Hélène Burnier (d. 1909), wife of Théodore Flournoy.

Flournoy, Théodore (1854–1920), Swiss psychologist, husband of Marie-Hélène Burnier Flournoy. Extensive correspondence survives from 1890 to 1910.

Föhrenbach, a hotelkeeper in Freiburg.

Forbes, John Murray (1813–1898), a businessman in Milton, Mass. Two letters to WJ are known from 1890 and 1891.

Forbes, William Cameron (1870–1959), a businessman and diplomat, grandson of John Murray Forbes and Ralph Waldo Emerson. Correspondence is known from 1894 to 1907.

Foster, Charles H. (1838–1888), spiritualist medium from Salem, Mass., known as the Salem Seer.

Fouillée, Alfred (1838–1912), French philosopher.

Fox, Henry Heywood (1880–1935), a businessman, son of Jabez Fox.

Fox, Jabez (b. 1850), a lawyer living at 99 Irving St.

Francke, Kuno (1855–1930), professor of Germanic languages at Harvard.

Franklin, Christine Ladd (1847–1930), American writer on mathematics, logic, and psychology. Correspondence is known from 1888 to 1892.

Franklin, Fabian (1853–1939), American mathematician, husband of Christine Ladd Franklin.

Fräulein, refers to any one of several governesses working for the James family, including Fräulein Hühnersdorf.

Freer, Ada Goodrich (1857–1931), British psychical researcher and folklore collector, who sometimes wrote under the pseudonym of Miss X. For a note on her see *EPR,* 412. One letter is known (1894).

Friedrich, Professor, an unidentified German who taught Latin to WJ's son Henry in Munich in 1893. Possibly he was Johann Friedrich (1836–1917), an Old Catholic clergyman and church historian and member of the theological faculty in Munich.

Fullerton, George Stuart (1859–1925), American philosopher. Correspondence is known from 1894 to 1909.

Furness, Horace Howard (1833–1912), American lawyer and Shakespearian scholar. Furness made several trips to Boston to investigate psychical phenomena. Correspondence is known from 1886 to 1910.

Gardiner, Miss, sister of Elizabeth Glendower Evans.

Gardiner, Harry Norman (1855–1927), professor of philosophy at Smith College. Correspondence is known from 1890 to 1909.

Garfield, Leonard D., superintendent of buildings at Harvard.

Garin, Marie, a Swiss servant of the Jameses in the 1890s.

Garrison, Wendell Phillips (1840–1907), associated with the *Nation* from its founding in 1865. Correspondence is known from 1875 to 1906.

Gaudelet, Miss. The obituary of Harriet Hooper Chase Gaudelet (d. 1901), widow of Alfred Gaudelet, mentions two daughters, Mrs. William Amory and Mrs. John Peters. Miss Gaudelet is either one of the two, or still another daughter.

Gibbens, Eliza Putnam Webb (1827–1917), AGJ's mother. Correspondence survives from 1883 to 1910.

Gibbens, Margaret. *See* Gregor, Margaret Merrill Gibbens

Gifford, Ralph Waldo (1867–1925), tutor in the James family in 1890, later a lawyer.

Gilman, Benjamin Ives (1852–1933), American author and museum official. Correspondence is known from 1888 and 1889, with one undated letter.

Giotto (ca. 1266–1337), Italian artist.

Giżycki, Georg von (1851–1895), German philosopher. One letter to WJ is known (1884).

G.N. *See* Norton, Grace

Godkin, Edwin Lawrence (1831–1902), American journalist, co-founded the *Nation* in 1865. Correspondence is known from 1885 to 1902.

Godwin, Parke (1816–1904), American editor and author. Correspondence is known from 1883 to 1897.

Gorham, an unidentified family interested in renting WJ's house in Chocorua.

Gourd, Jean-Jacques (1850–1909), professor of philosophy and rector of the University of Geneva.

Gourlay, Mrs., an unidentified woman who did household chores for WJ in Cambridge. Cambridge directories for the period list an Adelaide H. Gourlay, a widow.

Grace. *See* Norton, Grace

Grant, unidentified tradesman in Cambridge.

Gray, John Chipman (1839–1915), American lawyer and educator. Correspondence is known from 1872 to 1899.

Greenough, Frances Boott, sister of Francis Boott and wife of American architect Henry Greenough (1807–1883).

Greenough, James Bradstreet (1833–1901), American philologist, professor at Harvard. One letter to WJ is known (1899).

Gregor, Margaret Merrill Gibbens (1857–1927), sister of Alice Howe Gibbens James, married Leigh Gregor in 1899. One letter is known (1893).

Gurney, Edmund (1847–1888), British aesthetician and psychical researcher. Correspondence is known from 1882 to 1888.

Gurney, Ellen Sturgis Hooper (1838–1887), sister of Edward William Hooper and Marian Hooper Adams and wife of Ephraim Whitman Gurney. Ellen Gurney suffered periods of mental breakdown.

Gurney, Ephraim Whitman (1829–1886), professor of history at Harvard, husband of Ellen Sturgis Hooper Gurney. One letter to WJ from 1877 is known.

Hagen, Hermann August (1817–1893), German entomologist, professor at Harvard from 1870. While the Jameses named one of their children after him, there was friction between the two families (see *Correspondence*, 5:571).

Hall, Cornelia Fisher (d. 1890), first wife of Granville Stanley Hall.

Hall, Edward Henry (1831–1912), Unitarian clergyman, serving as a pastor in Cambridge at the time.

Hall, Granville Stanley (1844–1924), American psychologist, a graduate student at Harvard in 1876–78, receiving his doctorate in 1878. In 1888 he became president of Clark University, Worcester, Mass. Correspondence survives from 1878 to 1909.

Hall, Robert Granville (b. 1881), son of Granville Stanley Hall.

Hammond, a resident of Chocorua who helped WJ with repairs.

Hanus, Paul Henry (1855–1942), German-born educator, appointed assistant professor of History and Art of Teaching at Harvard in 1891. Correspondence is known from 1891 to 1907.

Harper, William Rainey (1856–1906), American educator, president of the University of Chicago.

Harris, William Torrey (1835–1909), American philosopher and educator, founder of the *Journal of Speculative Philosophy* in 1867. Correspondence is known from 1877 to 1903.

Harry, refers usually to WJ's son, but sometimes to HJ.

Hassett, Simon, a gardener in Cambridge.

Hauptmann, Carl Ferdinand Maximillian (1858–1921), German poet and scientist.

Hauptmann, Martha Thienemann (1862–1939), first wife of Carl Hauptmann.

Hazer, Warren H., a photographer at 213 S. Salina St., Syracuse, a tenant of the Jameses. His business failed in 1898.

Hélène, a servant in the James household in 1893.

Helmholtz, Hermann Ludwig Ferdinand von (1821–1894), German physiologist, physicist, and psychologist.

Henrietta. *See* Pell-Clarke, Henrietta Temple

Herbart, Johann Friedrich (1776–1841), German philosopher.

Hering, Ewald (1834–1918), German physiologist. One letter is known (1892).

Hichbrunner, Fräulein, a Bernese governess employed by the Jameses in late 1892.

Higginson, Henry Lee (1834–1919), American banker, a partner in the firm Lee, Higginson and Co., WJ's financial adviser. Correspondence is known from 1880 to 1910.

Higginson, Ida Agassiz, wife of Henry Lee Higginson. Two letters to WJ are known, one from 1890 and one from 1896.

Hipp, Matthäus (1813–1893), German-born inventor, developer of the chronoscope, an instrument for measuring very short intervals of time.

Hodder, Alfred LeRoy (1866–1907), a graduate student in philosophy at Harvard, in later years a writer. His common-law wife was Jessie Donaldson Hodder. Correspondence is known from 1906, with one undated letter.

Hodder, Jessie Donaldson (1867–1931), American social worker, common-law wife of Alfred Hodder. In 1906, after Hodder married someone else, the Jameses did a great deal to help Jessie Hodder survive the crisis.

Hodgson, Richard (1855–1905), Australian-born psychical researcher. Correspondence is known from 1888 to 1904.

Hodgson, Shadworth Hollway (1832–1912), British philosopher. Correspondence is known from 1879 to 1910.

Höffding, Harald (1843–1931), Danish philosopher. Correspondence is known from 1893 to 1910.

Holmes, Fanny Bowditch Dixwell, wife of Oliver Wendell Holmes, Jr. There is evidence that at one time WJ had a romantic interest in her.

Holmes, Oliver Wendell, Sr. (1809–1894), American author and physician, one of WJ's examiners in the Harvard Medical School. One letter is known (1888).

Holmes, Oliver Wendell, Jr. (1841–1935), American jurist. Correspondence is known from 1866 to 1907. There are also a number of undated letters.

Holt, Florence Taber (d. 1947), second wife of Henry Holt.

Holt, Henry (1840–1926), American publisher, married Florence Taber in December 1886. Correspondence is known from 1878 to 1906.

Holton, Lucinda Caroline Millard, a relative of President Millard Fillmore, wife of Edward Dwight Holton and mother of Mary Holton James.

Hooper, Edward William (1839–1901), a lawyer in Boston, brother of Marian

Hooper Adams and Ellen Sturgis Hooper Gurney and husband of Fanny Chapin Hooper. Hooper served as treasurer of Harvard University. One letter is known (1888).

Hortense, a servant of the Jameses in Switzerland.

Howe, Alice Greenwood (1835–1924), sister of Mary Greenwood Lodge and wife of George D. Howe.

Howells, Elinor Gertrude Mead (1837–1910), wife of William Dean Howells. One letter is known (1890).

Howells, William Dean (1837–1920), American novelist. Correspondence is known from 1874 to 1910.

Howison, George Holmes (1834–1916), American philosopher. Correspondence is known from 1879 to 1909.

Hubbard, an unidentified tutor or friend of the James boys, possibly Gardiner Hubbard Scudder, son of Samuel Hubbard Scudder (1837–1911), American naturalist. The younger Scudder graduated from Harvard in 1892.

Hughes, an unidentified workman in Cambridge.

Hühnersdorf, Fräulein, a governess working in the James household in the late 1880s and early 1890s. She later worked for the Flournoys.

Hume, James Gibson (1860–1949), Canadian philosopher, a graduate student at Harvard. One letter is known (1889).

Hunter, Ellen (Elly) James Temple Emmet (1850–1920), one of WJ's six Temple cousins, daughter of Robert Emmet Temple and Catharine Margaret James Temple. After the death of their parents, the young Temples were brought up by their aunt Mary Tweedy and her husband, Edmund Tweedy, in Newport and Pelham, N.Y. In 1869 Ellen Temple married Christopher Temple Emmet (1822–1884), a physician and lawyer, and moved to San Francisco. The Emmets had four children: Mary Temple Emmet Peabody, Rosina Hubley Emmet, Ellen Gertrude (Bay) Emmet Rand, and Edith Leslie Emmet. On 1 September 1891 Ellen Temple Emmet married George Hunter. The Hunters had one child, George Grenville Hunter (b. 1892). Correspondence survives from 1888 to 1909.

Hunter, George (1847–1914), Scottish-born second husband of Ellen James Temple Emmet Hunter.

Huntington, Mary Elizabeth (b. 1840), stepdaughter of Ellen Greenough Huntington.

Hyatt, Alpheus (1838–1902), American naturalist, husband of Andella Beebe Hyatt. One letter is known (1891).

Hyslop, James Hervey (1854–1920), American philosopher and psychical researcher. Correspondence is known from 1903 to 1910.

Ibsen, Henrik (1828–1906), Norwegian dramatist.

Iselin, Hope Goddard, second wife of banker and noted yachtsman Charles Oliver Iselin (1854–1932). Born in the United States, Charles Iselin, who had a summer home near New Rochelle, N. Y., had studied in Switzerland.

Jackson family, an unidentified family associated with S. Weymouth, Mass.

James, Alexander Robertson (22 December 1890–1946), WJ's son, a painter, initially named Francis Tweedy, later renamed Alexander Robertson because he disliked his original name. Correspondence survives from 1895 to 1909.

James, Alice (1848–1892), WJ's sister, moved to Europe permanently in November 1884. For her life see Jean Strouse, *Alice James: A Biography* (Boston: Houghton Mifflin, 1980). Correspondence survives from 1861 to 1892.

James, Alice Howe Gibbens (1849–1922), WJ's wife. Correspondence survives from 1876 to 1910.

James, Caroline (Carrie) Eames Cary (b. 1851), wife of GWJ.

James, Edward (Ned) Holton (1873–1954), a journalist, son of RJ. For additional information see *Correspondence*, 3:438–39.

James, Garth Wilkinson (1845–1883), WJ's brother, husband of Caroline Eames Cary. Their first child, Joseph Cary James, was born in 1874; their second, Alice James (later Alice James Edgar), in 1875. Correspondence survives from 1866 to 1883.

James, Henry (1811–1882), WJ's father. Correspondence survives from 1860 to 1882.

James, Henry (1843–1916), author, WJ's brother. For correspondence see *Correspondence*, vols. 1–3.

James, Henry (Harry) (1879–1947), WJ's son, a lawyer and biographer. Correspondence survives from 1882 to 1910.

James, Herman (Humster) (31 January 1884–9 July 1885), WJ's son.

James, Margaret Mary. *See* Porter, Margaret Mary James

James, Mary Lucinda Holton (1849–1922), wife of RJ. Correspondence survives from 1878 to 1907.

James, Mary Robertson Walsh (1810–1882), WJ's mother. Correspondence is known from 1861 to 1874.

James, Mary Walsh. *See* Vaux, Mary Walsh James

James, Robertson (1846–1910), WJ's youngest brother, husband of Mary Holton James. Their first child, Edward Holton James, was born on 18 November 1873; their second, Mary Walsh James (later Mary Walsh James Vaux), on 18 August 1875. For details see *BBF.* Correspondence survives from 1868 to 1910. There are also undated letters.

James, William (Billy) (1882–1961), WJ's son, an artist. Correspondence survives from 1888 to 1910.

Janet, Pierre (1859–1947), French psychologist. Correspondence is known from 1887 to 1895.

Jastrow, Joseph (1863–1944), Polish-born psychologist. One letter is known (1906).

Jewett, Sarah Orne (1849–1909), American writer. Correspondence is known from 1890 to 1902.

Jordan, Mary Augusta (1855–1941), American educator and editor, on the faculty of Smith College. Correspondence is known from 1891.

Julie, a servant of the Jameses in the 1890s.

Kate, Aunt. *See* Walsh, Catharine

Katharine (Katherine). *See* Loring, Katharine Peabody

Keller, Helen Adams (1880–1968), American deaf and blind author and lecturer, then a student at the Perkins Institution for the Blind. Correspondence is known from 1908.

Kennedy, George Golding (b. 1841), a physician, member of the visiting committee on the herbarium at Harvard, husband of Harriet White Kennedy. The identification is uncertain because in his letter to AGJ of 5 September 1890 (calendared) WJ says that Kennedy's two older children were in Berlin with Miss Ingell, but at the time both were about twenty, perhaps too old to need supervision. The youngest child, a daughter, was Mildred Kennedy (b. 1877).

Kern, the last name of two unidentified women with whom WJ's son Henry boarded in Munich in early 1893.

Kipling, Rudyard (1865–1936), English author. One letter to WJ is known (1896).

Kishimoto, Nabuta, a Japanese graduate student at Harvard in 1893–94. One letter is known (1898).

Kozaki, Nariaki, a divinity student at Harvard, later a theology instructor in Japan.

K.P.L. *See* Loring, Katharine Peabody

Krohn, William Otterbein (1868–1922), writer on psychology.

Külpe, Oswald (1862–1915), Latvian-born psychologist.

Ladd, George Trumbull (1842–1921), American philosopher and psychologist, professor at Yale. Correspondence is known from 1887 to 1909.

Lane, Alfred Church (1863–1948), American geologist, received his doctorate from Harvard in 1888. Correspondence is known from 1894 and 1907.

Langley, Samuel Pierpont (1834–1906), American astronomer, a vice-president of the SPR from 1890. Correspondence is known from 1891.

Larrowe, Marcus Dwight, writer on mnemonics under the pen name of Alphonse Loisette.

Lasswitz, Kurd (1848–1910), German philosopher.

Lawrence, Elizabeth Chapman, widow of Timothy Bigelow Lawrence (1826–1869), the United States consul in Italy.

Leaf, Walter (1852–1927), British scholar.

Lehmann, Alfred Georg Ludwig (1858–1921), Danish psychologist. Correspondence is known from 1899.

Leslie. *See* Pell-Clarke, Leslie

Liégeois, Jules (1833–1908), French jurist and psychological writer.

Lilla. *See* Walsh, Elizabeth Robertson

Lloyd, Alfred Henry (1864–1927), American philosopher and university administrator, graduated from Harvard in 1886 and remained there as a graduate student.

Lodge, Sir Oliver Joseph (1851–1940), British physicist and psychical researcher. Correspondence is known from 1893 to 1910.

Loeb, Jacques (1859–1924), German-born physiologist, active in the United States. Correspondence is known from 1888 to 1897.

Loeser, Charles Alexander (1864–1928), graduated from Harvard in 1886, later an art collector. One letter is known (1905).

Loftie, Henry (1839–1917), maker of wigs and fishing gear, one of the James tenants at 213 S. Salina St., Syracuse.

Loisette, Alphonse. *See* Larrowe, Marcus Dwight

Lombroso, Cesare (1835–1909), Italian sociologist and physician.

Longfellow, Henry Wadsworth (1807–1882), American poet.

Loring, Caleb William (1819–1897), a lawyer and businessman, father of Katharine Peabody Loring and Louisa Putnam Loring.

Loring, Francis William (1838–1905), American painter who lived in Europe for extended periods of time.

Loring, Katharine Peabody (1849–1943), AJ's companion. Correspondence is known from 1887 to 1894.

Loring, Louisa Putnam (1854–1923), sister of Katharine Loring, active in charity work. One letter is known (1890).

Loring, Mary Greely (1831–1913), sister of Francis William Loring, lived mostly in Italy after 1875.

Lotze, Rudolph Hermann (1817–1881), German philosopher.

Lough, James Edwin (1871–1952), American psychologist, received his doctorate from Harvard in 1898.

Louise, a servant of the Jameses in the 1890s.

Lowell, James Russell (1819–1891), American poet, editor, diplomat, married Frances Dunlap in 1857, his second marriage. Two letters from WJ are known: one undated, one from 1883.

Lutoslawski, Wincenty (1863–1954), Polish philosopher. Correspondence is known from 1893 to 1910.

Lyon, David Gordon (1852–1935), American educator and Orientalist, husband of Tosca Woehler Lyon.

Mach, Ernst (1838–1916), Austrian physicist and philosopher. Correspondence is known from 1884 to 1909.

Mack. *See* Salter, William Mackintire

MacKay, Donald (d. 1894), a graduate of the University of Toronto, a graduate student at Harvard in 1889–90. Although no information was found placing him in Germany in the summer of 1891, he is the most likely candidate.

McNamee. John McNamee was the proprietor and Benjamin F. McNamee the business manager of the Union Marble and Granite Works, near Mount Auburn Cemetery, Cambridge.

MacRae, Hugh (1865–1951), an 1885 graduate of the Massachusetts Institute of Technology, a businessman active in North Carolina.

Macvane, Silas Marcus (1842–1914), Canadian-born professor of history at Harvard.

Malone, Mrs., a woman in Cambridge who sometimes did WJ's laundry.

Maltini, Raffaello, the Jameses' cook in Florence.

Manly, John Matthews (1865–1940), American scholar, received his doctorate from Harvard in 1890, a professor of English at the University of Chicago from 1898.

Mann, unidentified tradesman in Cambridge.

Margaret. *See* Gregor, Margaret Merrill Gibbens

Marie. *See* Garin, Marie

Marillier, Léon (1842–1901), French psychologist. Correspondence is known from 1893.

Marquand, Allan (1853–1924), American educator and author. Correspondence is known from 1902 to 1906.

Marshall, Henry Rutgers (1852–1927), American architect and writer on aesthetics. Correspondence is known from 1887 to 1909.

Marty, Anton (1847–1914), Swiss philosopher of language.

Mary, Aunt. *See* Tweedy, Mary Temple

Mary. Numerous Marys are mentioned in the text. Which one is meant is usually clear from the context. Mary Holton James is found in connection with RJ or in Europe; Mary Salter, in connection with her husband or AGJ. Others appear in their own contexts. However, at times, the Jameses employed servants named Mary, and while there are no clear references to servants of this name in the present volume, there is some risk of error.

Mascagni, Pietro (1863–1945), Italian composer.

Maude, John Edward (1855–1885), English-born clergyman, graduated from Harvard College in 1881, received a Master of Arts degree from the Harvard Divinity School in 1883.

Mead, George Herbert (1863–1931), American philosopher, tutor to WJ's children in 1888.

Meeker family. Frances S. Meeker (d. 1890), daughter of David and Frances Meeker, was born in Elizabeth, N.J. She lived in Somerville, Mass., and was sixty-six years old at the time of her death. WJ also mentions Anna Meeker, perhaps her sister.

Merriman, Daniel (1838–1912), American clergyman, husband of Helen Bigelow Merriman. The Merrimans spent their summers at Intervale, N.H., near Chocorua. Correspondence survives from 1891 to 1905.

Merriman, Helen Bigelow (1844–1933), American author and artist, wife of Daniel Merriman. Correspondence survives from 1891 to 1901.

Middleton, Lamar (1872–1909), American journalist, tutor to WJ's children in 1894.

Miller, Dickinson Sergeant (1868–1963), American philosopher, instructor at Bryn Mawr College from 1893 to 1899, taught at Harvard from 1899 to 1904, when he received a permanent appointment at Columbia University in New York City. For several summers he served as tutor to WJ's children. Correspondence survives from 1893 to 1910.

Mitchell, Silas Weir (1829–1914), American neurologist and author. Correspondence is known from 1885 to 1894.

Möller, Mrs., unidentified, perhaps Mrs. Helga Möller, a dressmaker in Cambridge, or Mrs. Benedikta Möller, a physician in Cambridge.

Moring, Anna L. (d. 1890), a neighbor of the Jameses, lived at 12 Quincy St.

Moring, Charles (d. 1890), described as an idiot, son of Anna L. Moring.

Morse, Frances (Fanny) Rollins (1850–1928), a social worker, a close friend of AJ and WJ. Correspondence between her and WJ is known from 1875 to 1910.

Morse, Harriet Jackson Lee, mother of Frances Rollins Morse and wife of Samuel Torrey Morse. Correspondence is known from 1890 to 1900.

Morse, Samuel Torrey (d. 1890), father of Frances Rollins Morse and husband of Harriet Jackson Lee Morse.

Mulford, Elisha (1833–1885), American clergyman and author, lecturer at the Episcopal Theological School in Cambridge.

Mulford, Rachel Price, widow of Elisha Mulford.

Müller, Georg Elias (1850–1934), German psychologist.

Münsterberg, Hugo (1863–1916), German-born psychologist, from 1892 WJ's colleague at Harvard. His wife was Selma Oppler Münsterberg. Correspondence survives from 1890 to 1910.

Münsterberg, Otto (1854–1915), a Danzig businessman, brother of Hugo Münsterberg.

Münsterberg, Selma Oppler, wife of Hugo Münsterberg.

Myers, Arthur Thomas (d. 1894), British physician, brother of Frederic William Henry Myers.

Myers, Eveleen Tennant, wife of Frederic Myers. Correspondence is known from 1901 to 1906.

Myers, Frederic William Henry (1843–1901), British essayist and psychical researcher, husband of Eveleen Myers. Correspondence is known from 1885 to 1901.

Myers, James Jefferson (1842–1915), a lawyer, graduated from Harvard College in 1869.

N., Charles. *See* Norton, Charles Eliot

N., Grace. *See* Norton, Grace

Nanny (Nannie), Aunt, an unidentified relative of AGJ.

Ned. *See* James, Edward Holton

Neu, Theodore F., proofreader for printer Robert Drummond.

Nichols, Edgar Hamilton (1856–1910), author of mathematics textbooks, one of the founders of the Browne and Nichols School for Boys in Cambridge. Correspondence is known from 1910.

Nichols, Herbert (1852–1936), American psychologist, received his doctorate from Clark University in 1891, for a time instructor at Harvard.

Nickerson, John Henry, innkeeper in Chocorua.

Nordau, Max Simon (1849–1923), German physician and writer.

Norton, Charles Eliot (1827–1908), American art historian, professor at Harvard, married to Susan Ridley Sedgwick Norton. Correspondence survives from 1864 to 1908.

Norton, Eliot (1863–1932), a lawyer, son of Charles Eliot Norton. One letter from WJ is known (1899).

Norton, Grace (1834–1929), sister of Charles Eliot Norton. Extensive correspondence survives from 1884 to 1908.

Norton, Margaret Palmer Meyer, wife of Eliot Norton.

Norton, Richard (1872–1918), son of Charles Eliot Norton.

Norton, Rupert (1867–1914), American physician, son of Charles Eliot Norton. Correspondence is known from 1905.

Norton, Sara (Sally) (b. 1864), daughter of Charles Eliot Norton. Correspondence is known from 1888 to 1907.

Noyes, William (1857–1915), American physician, then serving as pathologist at McLean Asylum. Correspondence is known from 1889 to 1896.

Obrist, Hermann (1862–1927), Swiss artist and teacher, whom WJ met in Florence in 1893. One letter is known (1894).

Oliphant, Laurence (1829–1888), British novelist, journalist, and mystic.

Olmsted (Olmstead), Frederick Law, Sr. (1822–1903), American landscape architect. Correspondence is known from 1891.

Osten-Sacken, Carl Robert, Freiherr von der (1828–1906), Russian diplomat and entomologist. One letter from 1900 is known.

P., Mrs. *See* Piper, Leonora Evelina

Paget, Violet (1856–1935), British author living in Florence, writing under the pseudonym Vernon Lee. Correspondence survives from 1893 to 1909.

Paine, John Knowles (1839–1906), American composer, professor of music at Harvard.

Palmer, Alice Elvira Freeman (1855–1902), American educator, wife of George Herbert Palmer.

Palmer, George Herbert (1842–1933), American philosopher, WJ's colleague at Harvard, husband of Alice Elvira Freeman Palmer. Correspondence survives from 1887 to 1909.

Parker, Gurdon Saltanstall (1878–1941), son of Henry Ainsworth Parker, graduated from the Lawrence Scientific School in 1900, an architect in New York City.

Paulhan, Frédéric (1856–1931), French psychologist. One letter is known (1893).

Paulsen, Friedrich (1846–1908), German philosopher. Correspondence is known from 1893 to 1902.

Peabody, Andrew Preston (1811–1893), American clergyman, Plummer Professor of Christian Morals at Harvard to 1881. One letter to WJ survives (1891).

Peabody, Francis Greenwood (1847–1936), professor of Christian morals at Harvard. Correspondence is known from 1894 to 1909.

Peg (Peggy). *See* Porter, Margaret Mary James

Peirce, Charles Sanders (1839–1914), American philosopher. His second wife was Juliette Froissy Peirce. From 1861 he was an aide in the United States Coast and Geodesic Survey. Correspondence is known from 1875 to 1910.

Peirce, James Mills (1834–1906), mathematician, dean of the graduate faculty at Harvard, brother of Charles Sanders Peirce. Correspondence is known from 1895 to 1899.

Pell-Clarke, Henrietta Temple (b. 1853), one of WJ's six Temple cousins, daughter of Robert Emmet Temple and Catharine Margaret James Temple and wife of Leslie Pell-Clarke.

Pell-Clarke, Leslie (1853–1904), husband of Henrietta Temple Pell-Clarke. Two letters from 1887 are known.

Perez, Bernard (1836–1903), French educator, whose work on the development of children is cited in *The Principles of Psychology.*

Perry, a blind man living in Medford, Mass., whose psychic experiences were studied by WJ.

Perry, Thomas Sergeant (1845–1928), American literary scholar. Perry met the Jameses in Newport in the summer of 1858 and was especially friendly with HJ. He married Lilla Cabot in April 1874. Correspondence is known from 1860 to 1910.

Phinuit, Dr., a supposed French physician who for a time acted as Leonora Piper's spirit control. For his origin see *EPR,* 398.

Pierce. Several different Pierces are mentioned in the text, and sometimes it is not clear which one is meant. A Pierce, or Pierces, looked after WJ's house in 1891, but it is unlikely that he was either Arthur Henry Pierce, who was unmarried in 1891 when he began his graduate studies, or Edgar Pierce, who was still an undergraduate. The graduate-student years of Arthur Henry and Edgar overlap, and which one is meant was not always established.

Pierce, Arthur Henry (1867–1914), American psychologist, a graduate student at Harvard in 1891–94, received his doctorate in 1899. Correspondence is known from 1895.

Pierce, Edgar (1870–1929), a graduate student at Harvard in 1892–95, receiving his doctorate in 1895, in later years a businessman in Cambridge.

Pillon, François (1830–1914), French philosopher. Correspondence is known from 1882 to 1910.

Pillon, Mme François, French translator, wife of François Pillon.

Piper, Leonora Evelina (1859–1950), American trance medium. WJ's extensive studies of Mrs. Piper are reprinted in *EPR*. There is evidence of correspondence from 1889 and 1908, but no evidence has been found to indicate that any letters survive.

Plumb, George Mallney (1863–1931), real estate agent, WJ's business agent in Syracuse in 1890–92.

Porter, Margaret Mary (Peg, Peggy) James (1887–1952), WJ's daughter. Correspondence is known from 1892 to 1910.

Porter, Samuel (1810–1901), American educator, instructor at the National Deaf-Mute College, Washington, D.C. Correspondence is known from 1882 to 1891.

Preble, Henry (1853–1929), instructor in Latin and Greek at Harvard to December 1888, later worked in real estate and as a translator. See letter of 15 January 1890.

Prince, Katharine (Kitty) Barber James (1834–1890), WJ's cousin, daughter of WJ's father's brother, William James. Katharine Prince was frequently in mental institutions; in 1861 she married her psychiatrist, William Henry Prince. Correspondence survives from 1863 to 1887.

Prince, Morton (1854–1929), American physician and psychiatrist. One letter is known (1905).

Putnam, Elizabeth (Lizzie) Cabot (1836–1922), author and social worker, sister of James Jackson Putnam, Charles Pickering Putnam, and Annie Cabot Putnam.

Putnam, James Jackson (1846–1918), American neurologist. Correspondence survives from 1877 to 1910.

Raffaello. *See* Maltini, Raffaello

Rand, Benjamin (1856–1934), philosophical librarian and bibliographer, a graduate student at Harvard. Correspondence is known from 1900 to 1905.

Rand, Ellen Gertrude (Bay) Emmet (1876–1941), an artist, daughter of Christopher Temple Emmet and Ellen James Temple Emmet Hunter.

Renan, Joseph-Ernest (1823–1892), French historian and critic.

Renouvier, Charles (1815–1903), French philosopher. Correspondence is known from 1872 to 1896.

Ribot, Théodule-Armand (1839–1916), French psychologist. Correspondence is known from 1882 to 1907.

Richet, Charles-Robert (1850–1935), French psychologist, editor of the *Revue Scientifique*. Letters to WJ are known from 1885 to 1907.

Rickert, Heinrich (1863–1936), German philosopher.

Riehl, Alois (1844–1924), Austrian philosopher.

Ritter, Charles (1838–1908), Swiss scholar whose friendship with WJ dates to the 1850s. Correspondence is known from 1859 to 1902.

Robertson, Caroline Anna Crompton (d. 1892), wife of George Croom Robertson.

Robertson, George Croom (1842–1892), British philosopher. Correspondence is known from 1878 to 1892.

Rockwell family, an unidentified family several of whose members WJ encountered socially.

Rodgers, Henrietta Dorrington (b. 1843), sister of Katharine Outram Rodgers.

Rodgers, Katharine (Katie) Outram (1841–1922), granddaughter of Helen Robertson Rodgers, WJ's maternal grandmother's sister. She lived in Europe for extended periods. WJ's letters to her are preserved from 1893 to 1909.

Rogers, Clara Kathleen Barnett (Clara Doria) (1844–1931), English-born singer and writer on singing. For her comments about WJ see *Correspondence*, 2:439. Correspondence is known from 1894 to 1901.

Rosina. *See* Emmet, Rosina Hubley

Ross, Denman Waldo (1853–1935), American educator and art collector.

Ross, Frances Waldo (d. 1904), mother of Denman Waldo Ross.

Ross, Paul, a workman in Chocorua.

Rosselet, an unidentified teacher in Lausanne, Switzerland.

Royce, Christopher (1882–1910), oldest son of Josiah Royce.

Royce, Edward (b. 1886), second son of Josiah Royce.

Royce, Josiah (1855–1916), American philosopher, one of WJ's closer personal friends. Correspondence survives from 1878 to 1910.

Royce, Katharine Head (b. 1858), translator, wife of Josiah Royce.

Royce, Stephen (b. 1889), youngest son of Josiah Royce, in later years an engineer.

Rupert. *See* Norton, Rupert

Ruskin, John (1819–1900), British author and critic.

Russell, Mary Hathaway Forbes, wife of Henry Sturgis Russell (1838–1905), a public official.

Sally. *See* Norton, Sara

Salter, Eliza (1888–1889), daughter of William Mackintire Salter and Mary Sherwin Gibbens Salter.

Salter, Mary Sherwin Gibbens (1851–1933), sister of AGJ and wife of William Mackintire Salter. Correspondence survives from 1890 and 1893.

Salter, William Mackintire (1853–1931), husband of Mary Sherwin Gibbens Salter, a lecturer in the Society for Ethical Culture, author of numerous works in philosophy. Correspondence survives from 1880 to 1910.

Sanford, Edmund Clark (1859–1924), American psychologist.

Santayana, George (1863–1952), Spanish-born philosopher, WJ's colleague at Harvard. Correspondence is known from 1886 to 1908.

Sargent, Charles Sprague (1841–1927), professor of arboriculture at Harvard, director of the Arnold Arboretum. His wife was Mary Allen Robeson Sargent.

Sargent, Helen Maria Child (d. 1903), daughter of Francis James Child and wife of Frederick Le Roy Sargent.

Sargent, John Singer (1856–1925), American painter.

Sargent, Mary Allen Robeson, wife of Charles Sprague Sargent.

Saussaz family, keepers of a pension in Switzerland.

Sawin, Moses M., an expressman with offices in Harvard Square.

Schiller, Ferdinand Canning Scott (1864–1937), British philosopher. Extensive correspondence is preserved from 1893 to 1910.

Schmidkunz, Hans (1863–1934), German psychologist. One letter is known (1892).

Schnitzlein, Frau Wittve, wife of a military officer, boarded WJ's son Henry at Munich in 1893.

Schrenck-Notzing, Albert von (1862–1929), German physician and psychical researcher.

Schurman, Jacob Gould (1854–1942), Canadian-born educator, editor of the *Philosophical Review,* president of Cornell. Correspondence is known from 1887 to 1893.

Schuyler, Georgina (ca. 1840–1923), member of a prominent New York family, a friend of Sarah Wyman Whitman.

Scripture, Edward Wheeler (1864–1945), American psychologist.

Sedgwick, Arthur George (1844–1915), American lawyer and journalist, from time to time associated with the *Nation,* acquiring a part interest in it in 1872. He was a nephew of Grace and Ann Ashburner and the brother of Theodora Sedgwick and Sara Ashburner Sedgwick Darwin. He was married to Lucy Tuckerman Sedgwick. Correspondence is known from 1868 to 1893.

Sedgwick, Ellery (1872–1960), American editor, graduated from Harvard in 1894. His mother was a sister of Elizabeth Ellery Sedgwick Child. Correspondence is known from 1904 to 1910.

Sedgwick, Lucy Tuckerman (d. 1904), wife of Arthur George Sedgwick.

Sedgwick, Theodora (also Marian Theodora) (1851–1916), sister of Arthur George Sedgwick, Susan Ridley Sedgwick Norton, and Sara Ashburner Sedgwick Darwin. Many letters from WJ to Theodora Sedgwick are known from 1874 to 1910.

Seelye, Julius Hawley (1824–1895), American clergyman, professor of philosophy at and president of Amherst College, husband of Elizabeth Tillman James Seelye. One letter is known (1894).

Seth Pringle-Pattison, Andrew (1856–1931), Scottish philosopher. Correspondence is known from 1888 to 1909.

Seybert, Henry (1801–1883), a businessman and spiritualist from Philadelphia. In his will Seybert established the so-called Seybert Commission for the investigation of spiritualism.

Shaler, Nathaniel Southgate (1841–1906), professor of geology at Harvard. Correspondence survives from 1868 to 1901.

Shaler, Sophia Penn Page, wife of Nathaniel Southgate Shaler. Correspondence is known from 1906 to 1909.

Sidgwick, Eleanor Mildred Balfour (1845–1936), British educator and psychical researcher, wife of Henry Sidgwick. Correspondence survives from 1892 to 1909.

Sidgwick, Henry (1838–1900), British philosopher, president of the English Society for Psychical Research in 1882–84 and 1888–92. He was married to Eleanor Sidgwick. Correspondence survives from 1887 to 1900.

Siebert, Wilbur Henry (1866–1961), American educator and historian. A Harvard graduate student in 1888–90, he was studying history and philosophy in several European universities.

Slater, William Albert (1857–1919), graduated from Harvard in 1881, a businessman and philanthropist, living in Norwich, Conn.

Smith, Robert Pearsall (1827–1898), a Quaker preacher, supporter of psychical research, husband of Hannah Whitall Smith and father of Mary Berenson.

Snider, an unidentified tradesman, perhaps Lazarus Snider, a tailor in Boston.

Snow, Freeman (1841–1894), American legal scholar and historian.

Spencer, Herbert (1820–1903), English philosopher. Correspondence is known from 1879.

Stanley, Dorothy Tennant, wife of Sir Henry Morton Stanley and sister of Eveleen Myers.

Stanley, Sir Henry Morton (1841–1904), British explorer in Africa.

Stone, Edward James (1831–1897), British astronomer.

Stout, George Frederick (1860–1944), British philosopher, served as editor of *Mind* from 1892. Correspondence is known from 1893 to 1905. According to Frederick J. Down Scott, most of WJ's letters to Stout were in the possession of his son, Alan K. Stout (*SUC*, 566n). These letters were not found and seem to have been lost upon the death of Alan Stout.

Stratton, Alice Elenore Miller, wife of George Malcolm Stratton.

Stratton, George Malcolm (1865–1957), American psychologist, graduated from the University of California in 1888, in 1894–96 was a student at Leipzig, receiving his doctorate in 1896. In May 1894 he married Alice Elenore Miller. Correspondence is known from 1894 and 1895.

Strong, Charles Augustus (1862–1940), American philosopher and psychologist, graduated from Harvard in 1885, instructor in logic and psychology at Cornell University in 1887–89, husband of Elizabeth Rockefeller Strong. Correspondence survives from 1886 to 1910.

Strong, Elizabeth Rockefeller (1866–1906), wife of Charles Augustus Strong and daughter of John Davison Rockefeller.

Stumpf, Carl (1848–1936), German psychologist. Extensive correspondence is known from 1882 to 1910.

Stumpf, Hermine Biedermann, wife of Carl Stumpf.

Stumpf, Rudi, son of Carl Stumpf.

Sully, James (1842–1923), British psychologist and philosopher. Correspondence is known from 1880 to 1909.

Taine, Hippolyte-Adolphe (1828–1893), French philosopher, psychologist, and critic.

Tappan, Mary Aspinwall (1852?–1941), daughter of Caroline Sturgis Tappan, sister of Ellen Tappan Dixey. Correspondence is known from 1874 to 1910.

Tappan, William Aspinwall, a friend of Ralph Waldo Emerson, father of Mary Aspinwall Tappan. William Tappan lived in Lenox, Mass.

Tarde, Jean-Gabriel (1843–1904), French sociologist.

Taussig, Edith Thomas Guild (d. 1910), wife of Frank William Taussig.

Taussig, Frank William (1859–1940), American economist, teaching at Harvard.

Temple, a nursery man from whom WJ bought plants and seeds.

Temple, Elly. *See* Hunter, Ellen James Temple Emmet

Thayer, James Bradley (1831–1902), American lawyer, professor of law at Harvard. One letter is known (1895).

Thélin, a pastor in Switzerland with whom WJ's son William boarded in 1892 for a brief time. The stay was not a happy one; see *Correspondence*, 2:228.

Theodora. *See* Sedgwick, Theodora

Thilly, Frank (1865–1934), American philosopher and psychologist. Correspondence is known from 1894 to 1908.

Tiffany, Mrs., an unidentified person connected with Newport and Edmund Tweedy.

Tiffany, Louis Comfort (1848–1933), American decorator, known for work with stained glass.

Timmins, Gemma (d. 1890), sister of Minna Timmins Chapman and niece of Mary Ann Timmins Brimmer.

Titchener, Edward Bradford (1867–1927), English-born psychologist, active in the United States. Correspondence is known from 1892 to 1910.

Toby, a pet animal at Chocorua in the early 1890s.

Trowbridge, John (1843–1923), American physicist, teaching at Harvard. One letter is known (1894).

Tuckey, Charles Lloyd (1855–1925), British physician.

Turner, Samuel Epes (d. 1896), a neighbor of the Jameses living on Francis Avenue, who was killed by a van (see *Correspondence*, 2:399). Although the possibility of confusion exists since a Henry H. Turner of the Chamber of Commerce lived at 40 Irving St., the references are more likely to Samuel Turner since in 1896 he had just completed building his house.

Tweedy. In this volume the reference is either to WJ's son, later known as Alexander Robertson, or to Edmund Tweedy of Newport.

Tweedy, Edmund (d. 1901), with his wife, Mary Temple Tweedy, a guardian of WJ's Temple cousins. According to his obituary, Edmund Tweedy, an intimate friend of Nathaniel Hawthorne, was eighty-nine years old when he died. The Tweedys lived in Pelham, N.Y., and owned a villa at Bellevue Court, Newport. Edmund Tweedy contributed to the *Harbinger* and in the 1840s served as treasurer of a Fourierist association. Two letters are known from 1867 and 1898.

Tweedy, Mary Temple (Aunt Mary) (d. 1891), wife of Edmund Tweedy. She was a sister of Robert Emmet Temple and an aunt of WJ's Temple cousins. Correspondence is known from 1878 to 1889.

Tyndall, John (1820–1893), British physicist.

Uphues, Goswin K. (1841–1916), German philosopher, professor at Halle.

Vaux, Mary Walsh James (b. 1875), daughter of RJ and wife of George Vaux, Jr. Correspondence is known from 1906 and 1907.

Vercelli, J., operated a restaurant at 88 Boylston St., Boston.

Villari, Linda White Mazini (1836–1915), translator and author, wife of Pasquale Villari.

Villari, Pasquale (1827–1917), Italian historian and politician, husband of Linda Villari. Correspondence is known from 1903.

Vogelius, Joseph (b. 1848), an assistant to Henry Holt.

Wadsworth, William Scott (1868–1955), a student at Harvard's Lawrence Scientific School in 1887–91, later a physician in Philadelphia and a writer on medical subjects.

Walcott, Henry Pickering (1838–1932), American physician, acting president of Harvard in 1900–1901. Correspondence is known from 1894 to 1910.

Walker, unidentified friend of Edward Cummings.

Walsh, Catharine (Aunt Kate) (1812–1889), WJ's mother's sister. She was briefly married to Capt. Charles H. Marshall but left him before 1855 and lived mostly with the Jameses. Correspondence survives from 1868 to 1886.

Walsh, Elizabeth Robertson (Lila, Lilla) (1850–1901), daughter of James William Walsh, WJ's mother's brother. Correspondence is known from 1889.

Walsh, James William, Jr. (1852–1908), a New York stockbroker, son of James William Walsh, WJ's mother's brother. One letter to WJ from 1889 is known.

Ward, James (1843–1925), British philosopher and psychologist. Correspondence is known from 1880 to 1910.

Ward, Thomas Wren (1844–1940), a banker, an 1866 graduate of Harvard, son of American banker Samuel Gray Ward and Anna Hazard Barker Ward. His mother was the sister of William H. Barker, husband of Jeanette James, WJ's aunt. Correspondence is known from 1866 to 1902.

Waring, Daisy, an artist living in Newport, daughter of George Edwin Waring.

Waring, Euphemia Johnston Blunt (d. 1932), wife of George Edwin Waring.

Waring, George Edwin (1833–1898), an engineer living in Newport.

Warner, Joseph Bangs (1848–1923), WJ's attorney. Correspondence is known from 1896 to 1903.

Wendell, Barrett (1855–1921), professor of English at Harvard. Correspondence is preserved from 1886 to 1908.

Weston, Samuel Burns (1855–1936), American clergyman, publisher, and editor, a lecturer of the Society for Ethical Culture. Correspondence is known from 1890 to 1899.

White, John Williams (1849–1917), American classicist, professor of Greek at Harvard.

Whitman, Henry, Boston businessman, husband of Sarah Wyman Whitman.

Whitman, Sarah Wyman (Mrs. Henry Whitman) (1842–1904), Boston hostess and artist. Correspondence is known from 1888 to 1904.

Whitman, Walt (1819–1892), American poet.

Whitwell, Maria A. (May) (d. 1908), an artist in Boston.

Wild, Hannah (d. 1886), sister of Elizabeth Wild Blodgett.

Wilkinson, James John Garth (1812–1899), British homeopathic physician, a writer, a Swedenborgian friend of Henry James, and the husband of Emma Anne Marsh Wilkinson. Correspondence is known from 1882 to 1893.

Wilky. *See* James, Garth Wilkinson

Wilson, an unidentified family staying near Lausanne, Switzerland, in 1893.

Windelband, Wilhelm (1848–1915), German philosopher.

Witmer, Lightner (1867–1956), American psychologist, from 1892 director of the psychological laboratory at the University of Pennsylvania. In 1909 he savagely attacked WJ's psychology, claiming that the popularity of *The Principles of Psychology* was evidence of the low state of the science.

Worcester, William Leonard (1845–1901), American physician, author of several critical articles on WJ's psychology. Correspondence is known from 1890 to 1892.

Wundt, Wilhelm (1832–1920), German psychologist and philosopher.

Wyckoff, Henry Albert (1815–1890), son of Mary Robertson Wyckoff and Albert Wyckoff, and brother of Helen Rodgers Wyckoff Perkins. Mary Wyckoff and WJ's maternal grandmother were sisters.

Zola, Émile (1840–1902), French novelist.

Textual Apparatus

All alterations are recorded here except for strengthened letters to clarify a reading and mendings over half-formed letters or over illegible letters and words. Each entry is keyed by page and line number to the individual letter. The line numbers begin anew with each letter and include all elements in the letter but do not include the editorial heading that precedes each letter or the notes that follow. Alterations in letters dictated by James are in the hand of the amanuensis unless the alteration is noted as '(WJ)'.

In recording alterations, the reading to the left of the bracket, the lemma, represents the reading of the present edition and is the final version in the manuscript. (A prefixed superior ^{1} or ^{2} indicates which of any two identical words in the same line is intended.) The processes of revision are described in formulaic terms to the right of the bracket. The use of three dots to the right of the bracket almost invariably indicates ellipsis rather than the existence of dots in the manuscript. This is the only violation of the bibliographical rule that material within single quotes is cited exactly as it appears in the original document. The abbreviation *intrl.* is used when an addition is a simple interlineation (with or without a caret); when a deletion positions the interlineation, the *intrl.* is dropped and the formula reads *above deleted* (i.e., *ab. del.* 'xyz'). The word *inserted* ordinarily refers to marginal additions or squeezed-in letters, words, or punctuation on the line of writing that cannot properly be called interlines but are of the same nature; *over* means inscribed over the letters of the original without interlining. The words *altered from* are used to indicate that the letters in a word have been changed and letters added or deleted to form a new word (i.e., 'she' *alt. fr.* 'they'). When a description within square brackets applies to the preceding words, an asterisk is placed before the first word to which the description in brackets applies; thus it is to be taken that all words between the asterisk and the bracketed description are a part of the described material. The full details of this system may be found in Fredson Bowers, "Transcription of Manuscripts: The Record of Variants," *Studies in Bibliography* 29 (1976): 212–64.

The following abbreviations as here defined are used in recording alterations:

ab.	above
aft.	after
alt.	altered
bef.	before
bel.	below
bkt.	bracket
cap.	capital
db. qt.	double quotation mark
del.	deleted
exclm. mk.	exclamation mark
foll.	following

fr.	from
illeg.	illegible
init.	initial
insrtd.	inserted
intrl.	interlined
l.c.	lower case
mrgn.	margin or marginal
orig.	originally
ov.	over
paren	parenthesis
poss.	possible or possibly
qst. mk.	question mark
sg. qt.	single quotation mark
tr.	transposed
underl.	underline
vert.	vertical or vertically
w.	with

To William Mackintire Salter 28 January [1890]

5.4 lecture] *bef. del.* 'ann'

To Samuel Burns Weston 14 February 1890

6.7 on] *insrtd.*
6.13 copies] *ab. del.* 'numbers'

To William Mackintire Salter 16 February [1890]

7.9 suggests] *bef. del.* 'm'
7.9 reasoned] *bef. del.* 'th'
7.10 reasoning] *aft. del.* 'the'

To William Mackintire Salter 27 February [1890]

7.4 have] *bef. del.* 'ever'
7.6 composing] *aft. del.* 'ca'
7.7 (of] *paren ov. comma*
7.8 only] *intrl.*
7.10 none] *aft. del.* 'not'

To Charles Sanders Peirce 16 March [1890]

8.1 16] '6' *ov.* '8'
8.12 captivate] *aft. del.* 'be'
8.17 is] *ov.* 'was'
8.18 his] *ab. del.* 'th'

From Alice James 16 March 1890

8.4 for] *aft. del.* 'but'
9.7 by] *ab. del.* 'and'
9.7 showing] 'ing' *insrtd.*
9.8 agents] *bef. del. comma*
9.8 complacently] *intrl.*
9.15 20] *ab. del.* 'thou'
9.24 here,] *intrl.*
9.26 in this house] *ab. del.* 'here'
9.31 allowed] *bef. del.* 'me any other'
9.35 face] *bef. del. comma*
9.38 that] *intrl.*
10.4 soul] *bef. del. comma*
10.7 there] *aft. del.* 'surr'
10.19 announces,] *bef. del.* 'that'
10.21 who] *bef. del.* 'in'
10.26 all] *ab. del.* 'one's'
10.27 your] *ab. del.* 'one's'
10.27 flat?] *qst. mk. ov. semicolon*
10.29 against] *ab. del.* 'for'
10.38 insisted that] *ab. del.* 'thought'
10.39 the] *intrl.*
11.4 naïvely] *aft. del.* 'plaintively'
11.10 monosyllabic] *intrl.*

From Pierre Janet 23 March 1890

14.13 nerveuse?—] *qst. mk. and dash ov. ellipsis dots*

To Harry Norman Gardiner 26 March 1890

15.9 not] *intrl.*
15.10 question of the] *intrl.*
15.12 (relatively)] *intrl.*

From Granville Stanley Hall 1 April 1890

16.7 now] *intrl.* (Hall)
16.12 goes] *intrl.* (Hall)

To Alice James 2 April 1890

17.27 tagging] *aft. del.* 'keeping me company.'
18.7 asked] *bef. del.* 'me'
18.12–13 —as . . . else.] *insrtd.*
18.14 see] *ab. del.* 'say'
18.21 ¹the] *ov.* 'M'
18.22 Tragic] 'T' *ov.* 't'
18.25 daughters] 'u' *ov.* 'g'
18.25 years] *apostrophe del. bef.* 's'
18.26 Dibblee,] *bef. del.* 'her'
18.29 next] *intrl.*

To Henry Holt 8 April 1890

21.3 me.] *period insrtd. bef. del.* 'but not sealed. I found the copy you sent me last spring after writing to you, and meant to destroy it when the others came. I imagine I destoyed one of those which you sent, by mistake, as the one which I found is blank, and I fancy you sent 'em both signed. I have copied in this writing which I find on the other one of the pair, signed both, and you can sign them.'

To Henry Holt 7 May [1890]

22.9 a page] *alt. fr.* 'are'
22.12 having] *aft. del.* 'being'
23.1 now, that] *intrl.*
23.3 (460)] *intrl.*

From Charles Augustus Strong 13 May 1890

25.12 *motorischen*] '*ischen*' *intrl.*
26.34 purely] *intrl.*
28.37 present] *intrl.*

To Granville Stanley Hall 16 May [1890]

31.8 knew] *aft. del.* 'were'

To Alice Howe Gibbens James [16] May [1890]

32.5 circular] *intrl.*
32.10 He] *alt. fr.* 'The'

To Alice Howe Gibbens James [18] May 1890

33.1 9.50] '9' *ov.* '10'
33.3 but] *alt. fr.* 'by'
33.7 AM.] 'A' *ov.* 'a'
34.3 with] *aft. del.* 'wh'
34.4 Edwin] *intrl.*
34.6 wife's] *intrl.*

To Christine Ladd Franklin 19 May [1890]

34.16 your] *aft. del.* 'the'
34.16 I] *bef. del.* 'f'

To Alice Howe Gibbens James 22 May 1890

35.2 Dearest] 'est' *intrl.*
35.4 shape,] *bef. del.* 'I'
35.8 intending] *aft. del.* 'wh'

To Charles William Eliot 23 May 1890

36.9 her] *bef. del.* 'th'
36.12 this] 't' *alt. fr.* 'T'
36.20 appear] *aft. del.* 'f'

To Mary Whiton Calkins 24 May [1890]

37.4 you] *bef. del. closing db. qt.*
37.8 women] *aft. del.* 'me'
37.10 say] *bef. del.* 'that'

To Alice Howe Gibbens James 24 May 1890

37.9 and loving] *intrl.*
38.2 threw] 'ew' *ab. del.* 'ough'
38.7–8 —and . . . be!] *intrl. w. caret ov. period*

38.17 any] *ab. del.* 'the'
38.17 and] *ov. dash*
38.24 one] *aft. del.* 'only'
38.35 or] *ab. del.* 'on'
39.4 going] *aft. del.* 'bein'
39.6 ¹etc] 'tc' *ov.* 'ct'
39.8 always] *intrl.*

To Alice Howe Gibbens James [25 May 1890]

40.10 get] *ab. del.* 'have'
40.21 are] *ov.* 'I a'
40.22 Miss] 'M' *ov.* 'm'
40.23 So] 'S' *ov.* 'I'

To Alice Howe Gibbens James 26 May [1890]

41.20 Heaven] *final* 's' *del.*

To Alice Howe Gibbens James 27 May [1890]

41.5 roomy] *ab. del.* 'roomy ['r' *ov.* 'w']'
41.6 worse] *aft. del.* 'wh'
42.5 could] 'c' *ov.* 'w'
42.17 dear] *bef. del.* 'Billy &'
42.17 Billy] 'ill' *ov.* 'ab'
42.19 *Harry*] *aft. del.* 'Billy ['Bi' *ov.* 'Ha']'

To Alice Howe Gibbens James [28 May 1890]

43.3 mad] *final* 'e' *del.*
43.7 was] *ab. del.* 'is'

To Alice Howe Gibbens James 29 May [1890]

44.11 ought] *bef. del.* 'to'

To William Noyes 3 June [1890]

45.7 to . . . possible] *tr. fr.* 'if possible to send you'
45.15 afraid] *bef. del.* 'you'
45.20 influence] *intrl.*
46.1 their] 'ir' *insrtd.*

To Henry Lee Higginson 11 June [1890]

47.10 hit] *aft. del.* 'made'

To Grace Norton 26 June [1890]

48.16 at] *bef. del.* 'his'
48.23 Miss] *aft. del.* 'the'

To Charles William Eliot 2 July 1890

49.19 whether] 'whe' *ab. del.* 'ei'

To Hugo Münsterberg 2 July 1890

49.6 I] *ab. del.* 'and'
50.2 American] *intrl.*

To Alice Howe Gibbens James 7 July 1890

50.7 threatened] 'ed' *insrtd.*; *bef. del.* 'to'
50.24 she] *aft. del.* 'th'
51.1 is] *intrl.*
51.4 We] *aft. del.* 'called'
51.7 those] *aft. del.* 'I got one'
51.9 sunset,] *bef. del.* 'which'
51.9–10 tangled] *bef. del.* 'ry'
51.20 for . . . treatment;] *insrtd. for del.* 'your letter'; *bef. del.* 'a letter from'
51.22 funeral] *aft. del.* 'clipping c'
51.28 ²was] *ab. del.* 'looked so good and'
51.35 3] *intrl.*
51.38 letters] *aft. del.* 'blanks'

To Alice Howe Gibbens James 8 July [1890]

53.1 8] *alt. fr.* '9'
54.15 ¹as] *intrl.*

To Alice Howe Gibbens James 9 July 1890

54.7 till] *aft. del.* 'th'
55.2 returned] *bef. del.* 'wh'
55.2 enclosed] *aft. del.* 'fol'
55.7 bkfst] *final* 's' *del.*
55.7 lunch] *final* 'e' *del.*
55.10 ¹and] *intrl.*
55.13 it] *aft. del.* 'It'
55.16 sallowness] *bef. del.* 'h'
55.17–18 with me] *intrl.*
55.22 Great] *aft. del.* '(!)'

To Ellen James Temple Emmet Hunter 13 July 1890

56.13 pure] *ab. del.* 'more'
57.4–5 I . . . proofs.] *written on the back of the envelope*

To Alice Howe Gibbens James 13 July 1890

57.3 but] *aft. del.* 'f'
57.4 hour] *aft. del.* 'one-'
57.4 -long] *intrl.*
58.9 left] *aft. del.* 'after'
58.25 2] *intrl.*
58.29 loneliness] *aft. del.* 'pensive'
58.30 human] *intrl.*

To Alice Howe Gibbens James 14 July 1890

59.7 contentless] *bef. del.* 'loves'
59.9 manifold] *aft. del.* 'aspe'
59.21 day] *bef. del. comma*

To Alice Howe Gibbens James 15 July 1890

60.10 breeze] *aft. del.* 'f'
60.24 Brocks] 'B' *ov.* 'b'
61.13 &] *intrl.*

To Frances Rollins Morse 15 July [1890]

62.3 prefer] *bef. del.* 'me'

To Frederic William Henry Myers 15 July 1890

62.4 have] *bef. del.* 'told you that I'
62.11 here] *intrl.*
62.11 correcting] 'ing' *ov.* 'ed'
62.11 ²the] *intrl.*
62.12 I] *intrl.*
62.17 Myers] *intrl.*
62.18 to read] *intrl.*

To Alice Howe Gibbens James 16 July 1890

63.11 are] *ab. del.* 'is'
63.14–15 nauseated] *aft. del. opening paren*

To Alice Howe Gibbens James 20 July 1890

64.7 book] *final* 's' *del.*
64.10 of] *bef. del.* 'of'
64.12 He] *alt. fr.* 'she'
64.15 you by] *intrl.*

To Alice Howe Gibbens James 21 July 1890

65.6 adjourned] 'd' *ov.* 'j'
65.11 A.M. on] *alt. fr.* 'noon I'
65.12 Coggeshall] *ab. del.* 'Duveneck'
65.13 lot] *bef. del.* 'oppo'
65.32 Billy] *bef. del.* 'is co'

To Alice Howe Gibbens James 22 July [1890]

66.7 green stamp] *tr. fr.* 'stamp green'
66.8 Billy's] *aft. del.* 'Mrs'
66.11 reading] *bef. del.* 'proofs'
66.19 11.10] *ab. del.* 'night'

To Alice James 23 July 1890

67.14 coolness] *bef. del.* 'and'
67.14 clouds] *aft. del.* 'col'
67.20 bring] *aft. del.* 'f'
67.25 away] *bef. del.* 'the'
68.4 close] *ab. del.* 'flat'
68.14 3] *ov.* '4'
68.15 ²and] *ab. del.* 'but'
68.29 Rockwells'] *bef. del.* 'and'
68.33 ²the] *intrl.*
68.35 His] 'is' *ov.* 'e'
69.1 in] *ab. del.* 'of'
69.3 Anyhow] *aft. del.* 'Ay'

To Sarah Wyman Whitman 24 July 1890

70.4 them] *intrl.*
70.5 which] *aft. del.* 'of'
70.16 can] *intrl.*
70.17 it offends me] *ab. del.* 'I can do'
70.20 May] *aft. del.* '*Si vieillesse pouvait,* they might be an inspiration even now.'

To Alice Howe Gibbens James 25 July [1890]

71.8 is] 's' *ov.* 't'
71.15 is] *ov.* 'be'

71.22 laws] 's' *added*; *aft. del.* 'a'
71.23 testing] *aft. del.* 'ex'

To Alice Howe Gibbens James 25 July [1890]

72.1 25] '5' *ov.* '6'
72.12 it)] *paren ov. period*
72.25 on] *insrtd. for del.* 'with'

From Frederic William Henry Myers 26 July 1890

73.8–9 Blodgett's] ''s' *insrtd.*
73.9 sister] *aft. del.* 'sister [*intrl.*] deserves'
73.12 but] *bef. del.* 'the h'
73.13 containing] *aft. del.* 'send it if'
73.34 over] *bef. del.* 'ag'

To Mary Whiton Calkins 30 July 1890

75.6 make] *bef. del.* 'you and'

To Alice Howe Gibbens James 30 July 1890

75.11 when . . . asleep] ('his' *alt. fr.* 'he'); *intrl.*
75.12 vain] *aft. del.* 'f'
75.13 "rubbing] *bef. del. db. qt.*
75.15–16 viz. . . . it,] (*in MS* 'it. [*period in error*]'); *intrl.*
75.16 you.] *period ov. dash*
75.17 A] *ov.* 'a'
76.3 (until . . . today!)] *parens ov. commas*
76.6–7 apparently] 'ly' *insrtd.*
76.7 supreme] ¹'e' *ov. hyphen*; 'me' *aft. del.* | 'macy of the'
76.10 &] *intrl.*
76.10 floors] *bef. del.* 'and the'
76.11 you] *intrl.*
76.16 My] 'M' *ov.* 'I'
76.21 of] *intrl.*
76.38 my] *bef. del.* 'onl'

To Alice Howe Gibbens James 31 July 1890

77.10 Grace] 'G' *ov.* 'g'
77.15 caught] *aft. del.* 'g'
77.19 poached] 'p' *ov.* 'b'
77.20 cake] *intrl.*
78.9 ¹it] *ab. del.* 's'

78.12 We] *aft. del.* 'Wh'
78.14 (after] *aft. del.* 'whe'

From Charles Augustus Strong 1 August 1890

81.21 demands] 'mands' *insrtd.*

To Alice Howe Gibbens James 3 August 1890

82.1 Aug] *bel. del.* 'July'
82.8 in the middle.] *ab. del.* 'at the beginning.'
82.11 yet] *intrl.*
82.12 day] *aft. del.* 'morrow'
82.28 hours] *bef. del.* 'ou'
82.29 operetta] *aft. del.* 'country'
82.35 after] *intrl.*
82.38 vague in expression] *ab. del.* 'relaxed'
83.1 ask] *aft. del.* 'g'
83.7 material] *bef. del.* 'exce'

To Alice Howe Gibbens James 4 August 1890

85.1 Aug] *bel. del.* 'July'
85.5 10.15] '10' *ov.* 'te'
85.8 at 2.] (*period repeated in error in MS*); *intrl.*

To George Bucknam Dorr 12 August 1890

85.5 refer] *bef. del.* 'f'
85.6 not—] *dash ov. period*

To Alice James 13 August 1890

86.3 on] *bef. del.* 'a'
87.6 letter] *final* 's' *del.*

To William Dean Howells 27 August 1890

87.9 it] *final* 's' *del*
87.12 of] *bef. del.* 'hu'
87.12–13 entire] *bef. del. illeg. letter*
88.4 wife] *aft. del.* 'f'
88.6 naturally] *intrl.*
88.6 couldn't] *bef. del.* 'natur'
88.9 the] *ab. del.* 'your'

To Hugo Münsterberg 27 August 1890

88.11 have] *ab. del.* 'did'
88.12 ¹done] *ab. del.* 'do'
88.14 important years] *ab. del.* 'critical period'
89.4 be] *intrl.*
89.12 are] *ov.* 'o'
89.14 them] 'th' *ov.* 'at'
89.14 such] *intrl.*
89.17 have] 've' *ab. del.* 'd'
89.18 importance] 'c' *alt. fr.* 't'
89.25 criticised] *aft. del.* 'be'
89.25 others] *apostrophe del. aft.* 's'
89.25 besides] *ab. del.* 'than'
89.27 be the stimulus] *ab. del.* 'give rise'
89.27 psychological] *aft. del.* 'work'
89.29 in my book] *intrl.*
89.38 Physics] *bef. del.* 'and m'
89.39 laws] *aft. del.* 'elementary'
89.40 or . . . is] *ab. del.* 'or of'
89.40 *fact*] *final* 's' *del.*
90.2 think] *aft. del.* 'find'

To Alice Howe Gibbens James 3 September 1890

90.4 mountaineous and] *ab. del.* 'and'
90.5 Brown] 'B' *ov.* 'b'
90.7 each] *aft. del.* 'the'
90.9 You and] *ov.* 'It is'
90.11 though] *aft. del.* '&'
90.12 their] 'ir' *insrtd.*
90.12 own] *intrl.*
90.22 hither] *final* 'to' *del.*
91.2 Some] *aft. del.* 'I had the'
91.6 verse,] *bef. del.* 'and'
91.8 phrases] *intrl.*
91.8 etc.] *bef. del.* 'rap'
91.11 level] *ab. del.* 'smiting'
91.12 tender] *aft. del.* 'level'
91.19 cease] 'c' *ov.* 's'
91.21 my] *alt. fr.* 'I a'

To Sarah Wyman Whitman 9 September 1890

92.4 now] *insrtd.*
92.8–9 their looks.] *intrl.*
92.10 believing] *ab. del.* 'knowing'
92.16 An] 'A' *ov.* 'a'; *aft. del.* 'It is'

To Alice Howe Gibbens James 22 September 1890

93.9 just] *aft. del.* 'the'

To Alexander McKenzie 22 September 1890

93.9 document] *intrl.*

To Alice Howe Gibbens James 23 September [1890]

94.10 ¹her] *final* 'e' *del.*

To Alice Howe Gibbens James 24 September [1890]

95.11 Graduate] *aft. del.* 'Phi'
95.11 Psychology] *ab. del.* 'Philosophy'
95.12 4] *ov.* '3'

To Alice Howe Gibbens James 26 September 1890

95.2 writing] *aft. del.* 'lo'
95.3 see] *bef. del.* 'if'
95.3 who] *aft. del.* 'br'
96.4 work] *intrl.*
96.7 Ellen] *aft. del.* 'Ali'
96.8 by your letter] *intrl.*
96.12 told] *aft. del.* 'd'
96.17 having] *intrl.*

To Alice Howe Gibbens James 28 September 1890

97.1 4.30] *intrl.*
97.6 were] *ab. del.* 'well'
97.8 yesterday] *bef. del. opening paren*
97.15 hereafter] *alt. fr.* 'herefater'
97.18 struggle] *aft. del.* 'is the'
97.24 They] *ab. del.* 'He'
97.28 shall] *bef. del.* 'giv'
97.31 alone] *final* 's' *del.*
97.35 with] *bef. del.* 'one'

To Alice Howe Gibbens James 30 September [1890]

98.3 in] *ab. del.* 'to'
98.10 voice] *aft. del.* 'is now'
98.15 graduates] *aft. del.* 'Phil'
98.18 undergraduates] *ab. del.* 'men'
98.19 thus] *bef. del.* 'beg'
98.23 evidently] *aft. del. start of* 'h'

99.4 day,] *comma ov. period; bef.* 'Am [*cap. in MS retained in error*]'

To Alice Howe Gibbens James 1 October [1890]

99.1 Oct] *bel. del.* 'Sept'
100.3 too] *insrtd.*
100.6 Dec] *aft. del.* 'I re'
100.6 me] *bef. del. comma*

To Alice Howe Gibbens James 3 October 1890

101.2 pair of] *insrtd.*
101.4 means] *ab. del.* 'is'
101.4 merit] *intrl. w. caret ov. comma*
101.15 me] *bef. del.* 'unles'
101.32 other aspect] (*in MS period in error aft.* 'aspect'); *ab. del.* 'thing else'

To Alice Howe Gibbens James 6 October 1890

102.6 have] *aft. del.* 'do you'
102.9 favorite] *aft. del.* 'best'
102.17 But] *intrl. bef.* 'We [*cap. in MS retained in error*]'
102.21 both] *intrl.*
103.5 which] *bef. del.* 'had'
103.13 William] *bel. del.* '*Wm J [*bel. del.* 'Alice *[!] [*undel.*]']'
103.14 freight] *intrl.*

From Granville Stanley Hall 14 October [1890]

104.5 at one birth] *intrl.*
104.6 noble] *bef. del.* 'alu'
104.14 weekly] *intrl.*

To Sarah Wyman Whitman 15 October 1890

104.6 make] *aft. del.* 'to rouse me and'
105.9 under] *ab. del.* 'in'
105.11 battering] *aft. del.* 'practical'
105.13 insides,] *ab. del.* 'feelings,'
105.19 cat] *ab. del.* 'card'
105.25 week,] *comma ov. period bef.*
'Though [*cap. in MS retained in error*]'

To Christine Ladd Franklin [16 October 1890]

106.4 last] *aft. del.* 'Chap'
106.8 over] *aft. del.* 'of'
106.8 existence of] *intrl.*
106.8 propositions] *aft. del.* 'truth'
106.10 Nation] *aft. del.* 'unknow'

From Horace Howard Furness 19 October 1890

106.4 then] *intrl.*
107.6 likewise] *aft. del.* 'us'
107.15 shown] 'n' *ov.* 'ed'
107.21 reigns] *aft. del.* 'regn'
108.8 apparition] *aft. del.* 'appoait'

To Simon Newcomb 22 October 1890

109.7 very] *aft. del.* 'a'
109.8 (said] *ab. del.* 'saied'
109.8 to] *bef. del.* 'y'
109.12 speak] *aft. del.* 'define'
109.19 that is] *intrl.*

To Silas Weir Mitchell 12 November [1890]

111.4 inflict] *bef. del.* 'those'
111.6–7 the hope of] *intrl.*

From George Croom Robertson 12 November 1890

111.15 off,] *bef. del.* 'whic'

From Thomas Davidson 19 November 1890

113.10 Martineau] *bef.* 'of' *undel. in error*

To Alice James 26 November 1890

114.12 money] 'ey' *aft. del.* 'th'
114.29 *hypnotism*] 'n' *insrtd.*
114.30 D! Lloyd Tuckey] '!' *ov. opening db. qt.; in MS closing db. qt. aft.* 'Tuckey' *undel. in error*

To Carl Stumpf 1 December 1890

115.1 Dec] 'D' *ov.* 'N'
115.4 in] *ab. del.* 'about'
115.7 you] *aft. del.* 'it'
115.13 have] *aft. del.* 'move'
115.15 ²that] *aft. del.* 'my'
115.17 neither of] *intrl.*
115.17 ever] *init.* 'n' *del.*
115.19 volumes] *aft. del.* 'f'
115.21 sometimes] *aft. del.* 'to con'

To James Mark Baldwin 7 December 1890

116.8 Are] 'A' *ov.* 'a'
116.10 paths] *alt. fr.* 'pathos'
116.10 hand?] *qst. mk. aft. del. comma*
116.11 right] *aft. del.* 're'
116.11–12 response to] *intrl.*
116.14 another] *aft. del.* 'the'
116.15 those] *intrl.*
116.19 will] *intrl.*
116.20 have] *intrl.*
117.20 it] *aft. del.* 'the'
117.21 and] *intrl.*
117.24–25 sympathetic . . . etc] *intrl.*
117.25 whether] *bef. del.* 'the'
117.25 no).] *period insrtd. bef. del.* ', and'
117.25 It] 'I' *ov.* 'i'
117.27 *possible*] *intrl.*
118.9 had] *bef. del.* 'did'
118.24 natively] *intrl.*
118.27 experiences] *ab. del.* 'facts'
118.27 however] *aft. del.* 'of'
119.1 stimulus] *aft. del.* 'eye m'
119.2 for] 'f' *ov.* 'to'
119.2 indeed,] *insrtd.*
119.5,7 native] *intrl.*
119.5–6 ²of . . . sensation—] ('visual' *intrl.*); *intrl.*
119.8 a] *ab. del. illeg.*
119.8 range of] *intrl.*
120.11 way] *aft. del.* 'weigh'
120.13 excitements] *bef. del.* 'Stimulus by Reaction | Near objects Both'
120.25 lingers] *aft. del.* 'does'
120.27 have] 've' *ab. del.* 'd'
120.30 significance] *aft. del.* 'ultimate theoretic'
120.31 uselessly] *intrl.*

120.32 they] *bef. del.* 'do'
120.32 our] *ab. del.* 'the'

To Sarah Wyman Whitman 7 December 1890

121.4 5.30] '.30' *intrl.*
121.5 business] *intrl.*
121.6 tell] *aft. del.* 'to'
121.14 you] *aft. del.* 'f'
121.19 (!)] *intrl.*
121.21 pigment] *aft. del.* 'and'
121.25 acquaintance.] *bef. del. start of qst. mk.*
121.28 ability] *aft. del.* 'more'
121.29 amount] *bef. del.* 'of'

To Thomas Davidson 13 December 1890

122.5 circular] *intrl.*
122.10 rather] *bef. del.* 'rather'
122.13 *facts*] *bef. del.* 'at first'
122.26 thereby] *aft. del.* 'and'
123.1 would thus] *ab. del.* 'will carry'
123.2 would] *ab. del.* 'will'
123.3 &] *intrl.*
123.3 in other ways] *intrl. in MS aft. the comma foll.* 'interfering'
123.4 ²name] *intrl.*
123.8 view] *aft. del.* 'few'
123.18 proved] *bef. del.* 'an'
123.19 keep] *aft. del.* 'stay here at'
123.19 in Boston,] *intrl.*
123.30 stands,] *bef. del.* 'is [*undel. in error*] moribund'
123.30 its] *ab. del.* 'the'
123.33 I] *final* 't' *del.*
123.35 stands,] *comma ov. period; bef. del.* 'You can'
123.41 of] *insrtd.*
123.41 clerk-hire] *intrl.*

From William Leonard Worcester 24 December 1890

125.25 is] *intrl.*
125.32 the sensations] *ab. del.* 'them'
126.3 your view,] *ab. del.* 'it,'
126.5 motor processes] *ab. del.* 'senstion'
126.11 distressful] *ab. del.* 'disagreeable'

126.24 something in your] *ab. del.* 'a'
126.28 of sensation] *intrl.*
126.38 indirect] *ab. del. illeg.*

To Sarah Wyman Whitman 25 December 1890

128.8 yet] *ov.* 'and'
128.14 again] *bel. del.* 'for'
129.1 repeated] *aft. del.* 'renewed'

From Charles Carroll Everett [January 1891]

129.10 often minor] *intrl.*

To Sarah Wyman Whitman 2 January [1891]

130.5 strong] *bef. del.* 'and a s'
130.11 I've] *aft. del.* 'But'

To Jacob Gould Schurman 4 January 1891

131.3 on] *bef. del.* 'your'

To James Mark Baldwin 11 January 1891

132.14 Stanley Hall] *ab. del.* 'Clark University'

From George Holmes Howison 12 January 1891

133.5 read,] *bef. del.* 'o'

From James Ward 12 January 1891

136.9 psychology] *alt. fr.* 'psychologist'

To George Holmes Howison 20 January 1891

138.7 writes] 'w' *ov.* 's'
138.11 D] *ov.* 'd'

To Mary Whiton Calkins 27 January 1891

138.7 hither] *aft. del.* 'hithert'

To Frederic William Henry Myers 30 January 1891

139.15 narratives] *bef. del.* 'which with'
139.23 publicity and] *intrl.*
139.23 bring in] *insrtd.*
140.7 over] *aft. del.* 'of'
140.22 were] *bef. del.* 'both'

To Jacob Gould Schurman 7 February 1891

142.9 rather] *aft. del.* 'raf'

To Sarah Wyman Whitman 10 February 1891

143.5 the] *ab. del.* 'sorts of'

To Jacob Gould Schurman 11 February 1891

143.9 I] *final* 'f' *del.*

To James Mark Baldwin 7 March 1891

144.9 for] *alt. fr.* 'to'
144.13 quality] *ab. del.* 'nature'
144.19 by] *aft. del.* 'with'
144.20 suddenly] *aft. del.* 'suddlen'

To David Ferrier 7 March 1891

145.11 even] *intrl.*

To Samuel Burns Weston 12 March 1891

145.5 year:] *colon aft. del. dash*
145.10 pages] *aft. del.* 'pap'
145.14 it] *aft. del.* 'Uberhaupt I s'
145.16 can't] 'c' *ov.* 's'
145.17 dread] *bef. del.* 'of'
145.17 our american] *intrl.*
145.17 be] *insrtd.*
146.2 Cliffords] *aft. del.* 'and'

To Helen Bigelow Merriman 21 March [1891]

146.6 part] *ab. del.* 'mind'
146.18 significance,] *comma alt. fr. semicolon*
146.22 but] *aft. del.* 'to'

To Thomas Sergeant Perry 23
March 1891

147.5 Plato] *bef. del.* 'excep'
147.14 of] *bef. del.* 'so large po'

To George Santayana 29 March
1891

147.1 '91] '9' *ov.* '8'
147.5–6 (in . . . lavish)] *parens ov.
commas*

To Samuel Burns Weston 2 April
1891

148.14 a skeleton] *aft. del.* 'something'

To Charles William Eliot 7 April
1891

149.6 we] *ab. del.* 'you'
149.6 practical] *aft. del.* 'inst'

From James Mark Baldwin 13
April 1891

150.7 readings.] *bef. del.* '(in'
150.8 use] *intrl.*
151.5 I] *intrl.*
151.7 with] *intrl.*
151.16 *from . . . similarity.*] *intrl. w. period repeated in error*
151.26 *all;*] *bef. del.* '& it is not *of* anything till'
151.27 successive] *intrl.*
151.27 until] *final* 'l' *del.*
152.7 attention plus] *intrl.*
152.11 The] *aft. del. opening db. qt.*

To William Mackintire Salter 24
April [1891]

154.11 to have done] *ab. del.* 'me to do'
154.16 they] *bef. del.* 'as a matter of
fact'
154.16 naturally] *intrl.*
154.17 and *urgent*] *intrl.*
154.18 from . . . demander] *ab. del.
insrtd.* '*the demander [*insrtd. for del.*]
'in *abstracto* the impe')'
154.19 demands.] *period ab. del. comma*
154.19 From . . . *demandee*] *insrtd. for
del.* 'if one places himself in the ab-

stract & impartial situation of the philosopher whom['e' *del.*] I have depicted. *In concreto*'
154.20 he] *ab. del.* 'the individual
thinker'
154.21 by any thinker] *intrl.*
154.21 much] *ab. del.* 'well'
154.22 of] *ov.* 'no'
154.23 too,] *ab. del.* 'also,'
154.25 then] *intrl.*
154.25–26 sort of] *intrl.*
154.26 God] 'G' *ov.* 'g'
154.30 our] *aft. del.* 'our'
154.32 every] *ab. del.* 'a'
154.32 obligation,] *bef. del.* 'imposes an
obligation'
154.33 even] *intrl.*
154.33 it,] *comma alt. fr. period*
154.33–34 so . . . there.] ('actually'
intrl.); *insrtd.*
154.38 so] *ab. del.* 'and'
154.38 I] *ab. del.* 'it has'
154.38 grieve] *final* 'd' *del.*; *bef. del.* 'me'

To Carl Stumpf 25 April 1891

155.3 translations] *alt. fr.* 'translating'
155.7 Jena] 'e' *ov.* 'a'
155.10 abridged] *aft. del.* 'smal'
155.14 looked] *aft. del.* 'over'
155.14 over] *intrl.*
155.26 come] *aft. del.* 'advise'

From James Sully 25 April 1891

156.19 in] *bef. del.* 'an'

To Frederic William Henry
Myers 5 May 1891

157.4 arrived] *aft. del.* 'published'
157.10 crown] *bef. del.* 'of'
157.16 to you] *intrl.*
157.19 ordinary] *alt. fr.* 'ordinarily'
157.23 dependent] *aft. del.* 'entirely'
158.4 Yours] *alt. fr.* 'Yrs'

To Samuel Porter 6 May [1891]

158.13 while] *bef. del.* 'to s'
158.15 Were] *insrtd. for del.* 'Have'

From John Dewey 6 May 1891

159.5 coming] *ov.* 'they'
159.6 know] *bef. del.* 'that'
159.21 suppress] *ab. del.* 'propose'
159.28 [*not*] *bkt. ov. paren*
160.7 (content)] *intrl.*
160.8 Self] *alt. fr.* 'see'
160.8 while] *intrl.*
160.9 him)] *paren ov. comma*
160.9 Hegel's] *aft. del.* 'But'
160.9–10 (or Self)] *intrl.*
160.12 him] *intrl.*
160.30 well] *aft. del.* 'fo'

To William Dean Howells 8 May [1891]

161.5 that] *bef. del.* 'I might'
161.5 by] *aft. del.* 'from'
161.8 book's] *intrl.*
161.9 symptoms] *ab. del.* 'intoxication'

From John Dewey 10 May 1891

162.7 preceptual] *bel. del.* 'preceptual'
162.15 —at] *dash insrtd.*
162.17 any] *alt. fr.* 'the'
162.20 arouses] *ab. del.* 'awakens'
162.22 himself] *alt. fr.* 'my self'
162.23 by] *ab. del.* 'from'
162.29 limit] *aft. del.* 'give'
162.30 psychology] *aft. del.* 'phys'
162.31 even] *ab. del.* 'from'
162.33 towards] 'wards' *intrl.*

To Alice Howe Gibbens James 11 May 1891

163.10 seemed] 'ed' *insrtd.*
163.12 all] *bef. del. illeg.*
163.15 for quiet] *intrl.*
163.17 which] *aft. del.* 'and'
163.19 again] *bef. del. false start*

To Théodore Flournoy 31 May 1891

164.3 received] *bef. del.* 'your'
164.9 book] *bef. del.* 'f'
164.19 summer] *intrl.*
164.20 but] *intrl.*
164.21 for] *insrtd. for del.* 'of'
164.21 finished] *aft. del.* 'read'

165.1 more] *bef. del.* 'for'
165.1 so] *intrl.*
165.4 of] *bef. del.* 'V'

From John Dewey 3 June 1891

165.4 ethical] 'e' *ab. del.* 'a'
165.8 obligation,] *comma ov. period*
165.8 and] *ov.* 'I was'
165.18 was] *ov.* 'is'
165.19 philosophical] *ab. del.* 'news-paper'
166.10 is] *insrtd. for del.* 'wit'
166.16 ¹the] 'e' *ov.* 'is'
166.21–22 in . . . press] *intrl. w. caret ov. comma*
166.25 very] *ov.* 'thesis'
166.27 have] *intrl.*
166.32 his] *insrtd.*
167.1 psy.] *bef. del.* '& to Ll'

To Alice Howe Gibbens James 10 June [1891]

167.12 He . . . night.] *intrl.*
167.13 The] *aft. del.* 'In look'
167.20 Clancy] 'C' *ov.* 'c'
167.22 having] *bef. del.* 'since'

To William Dean Howells 12 June 1891

168.8 which] *aft. del.* 'y'
168.9 fidelity with] *ab. del.* 'way in which'
168.10 stick] *aft. del.* 'keep to the'
168.10 ways] *bef. del.* 'in which'
168.11–12 —all] *insrtd.*

To Mary Augusta Jordan [13 June 1891]

169.7 You] *aft. del.* 'Yo [*ov.* 'I']'

To Alice James 14 June 1891

170.4 and] 'a' *ov.* 'I'
170.4 ¹you] *bef. del.* 'w'
170.26 dome] *final* 'd' *del.*
171.1 everlasting] *aft. del. opening db. qt.*
171.3 degree of insignificance] *intrl.*
171.3 better] *bef. del.* 'stop'

To Sarah Wyman Whitman 20 June 1891

172.3 at 6 o'clock] *intrl.*
172.16 dear] *intrl.*
172.17 baltimoreans and] *intrl.*
172.19 gave] 'a' *ov.* 'i'
172.24 (including your own)] *parens ov. commas*

To Alice Howe Gibbens James 22 June 1891

173.6 would] *bef. del.* 'try'
173.6–7 Doctor] 'D' *ov.* 'd'
173.13–14 until . . . later.] *intrl.*

To Alice Howe Gibbens James 24 June 1891

174.5 little.] *intrl. w. period repeated in error*

To Mary Augusta Jordan 29 June 1891

175.4 fact] *bef. del.* 'the'
175.13 English] 'E' *alt. fr.* 'e'
175.16 I] *aft. del.* 'you'

To Charles William Eliot 3 July 1891

176.9 to recuperate,] *intrl.*
176.13 now] *init.* 'k' *del.*
176.22 power,] *bef. del.* 'more'
176.30 be] *intrl.*

To Alice James 6 July 1891

177.3 telling] *bef. del.* 'about the'
177.19 now] *intrl.*
177.22 respectively] *intrl.*
177.29 just] *bef. del.* 'those'
177.30 inscrutable] 'in' *ov.* 'un'
177.32 than] *aft. del.* 'that'
178.8 when] *aft. del.* 'to'
178.8 (as . . . cases)] *parens ov. commas*
178.11 from] *bef. del.* 'the world's'
178.14 life,] *comma ov. period*
178.14 till . . . down.] *intrl.*
178.15 your] *ab. del.* 'that'
178.16 Everyone] *aft. del.* 'You'
178.22 thought,] *comma insrtd. bef. del.* 'of you'

178.23 activities] *alt. fr.* 'activity,'
178.23 long] *bef. del.* 'and non'
178.25 bore] *ab. del.* 'stood'
178.26 you. But] *period ov. comma;* 'B' *ov.* 'b'
178.33 extinguished)] *paren ov. comma*
178.40 ²—] *insrtd.*
179.8 everything?] *bef. del.* 'They must have the most rights.*" [*db. qt. del. in error*]'

To Hugo Münsterberg 8 July 1891

179.4 find it] *ab. del.* 'feel that it is'
179.5 such] *aft. del.* 'th'
179.7 an] 'n' *added bef. del.* 'man of'
179.16–17 psychic] *final* 's' *del.; intrl.*
180.1 this] *bef. del.* 'cl'
180.6 farther] *intrl.*
180.8 experimental] *aft. del.* 'theoreti'
180.9 of] *bef. del.* 'science'
180.10 only] *bef. del.* '['flex' *del.*] as'
180.12 army . . . critics] *ab. del.* 'of them'
180.25 ²a . . . life?"] *ab. del.* 'longevity?"'
180.27 one] *ab. del.* 'he'
180.32 of you] *intrl.*

From Hugo Münsterberg 28 July 1891

183.1 Und] *aft. del.* 'W'

From Katharine Peabody Loring 30 July [1891]

183.16 mitigated] *aft. del.* 'entirely'
183.18 to tell you] *intrl.*
183.18 suffer] *bef. del.* 'much'

To Mary Whiton Calkins 12 August 1891

184.8 think] 'k' *ov.* 'g'
184.10 rules for] *intrl.*
184.19 here] *intrl.*

To Alice Howe Gibbens James 12 August [1891]

184.4 ¹South] 'S' *ov.* 's'
185.12 ¹her] *aft. del.* 'y'

185.16 old] *intrl.*
185.20 been] *aft. del.* 'ever'

To Alice Howe Gibbens James 14 August 1891

186.10 being] *aft. del.* 'f'
186.15 Pall] *aft. del.* 'Coffin follow'
186.21 thou] 't' *ov.* 's'; *final* 'gh' *del.*
186.37 amuse] *bef. del. period and* 'Yo'
187.3 wrote] *ab. del.* 'drew'
187.3 .95] *intrl.*

To Alice Howe Gibbens James 16 August 1891

187.3 though] *aft. del.* 'ride'
187.5 Asheville] 'A' *ov.* 'a'
188.8 Miller] *aft. del.* 'Mr M. as'

To Alice Howe Gibbens James 17 August 1891

188.4 reconciled] *aft. del.* 'co'
188.7 Howe'er] *aft. del.* '['I am getting' *del.*] My ol''
188.13 good;] *semicolon insrtd. for del. comma bef. del.* 'col'
188.15 An] *aft. del.* 'At'
188.16 before] *bef. del.* 'my'
188.18 &] *intrl.*
189.1 over] *aft. del.* 'of'
189.23 carried] *bef. del.* 'there'

From Shadworth Hollway Hodgson 19 August 1891

190.9 moot] *ab. del.* 'moot ['m' *ov.* 'p']'
190.12 seat] *bef. del.* 'of'
190.13 sensations] *bef. del. comma*
190.16 sympathetic] *ab. del.* 'systemig'
190.17 for . . . system.] *intrl. w. caret ov. period*
191.4 citation] *aft. del.* 'q'
191.8–9 and . . . book,] *intrl.*
191.25 personally to miss] *ab. del.* 'to lose'
191.26 as] *ab. del.* 'from'
191.28 in] *intrl.*

To Alice James 23 August 1891

192.7 (in . . . vitality)] *parens ov. commas*
192.15 received] *bef. del. comma*

192.25 man] *bef. del.* 'has'
192.29 Vie] 'V' *ov.* 'v'
192.29 aux] *ab. del.* 'dans'
192.31 He] *aft. del.* 'And'
192.34 patiently] *bef. del.* 'and'
193.3 review] 'r' *ov.* 'R'
193.4 in November] *intrl.*
193.4 pp.] *bef. del.* 'ag'
193.8 Our] 'O' *ov.* 'My'
193.10 broad] *intrl.*
193.12 year,] *bef. del.* 'and the intimacy of our'

To Ellen James Temple Emmet Hunter 24 August 1891

194.10 "feverishly"] *intrl.*
194.18 On] *final* 'e' *del.*
195.3 beautiful,] *bef. del.* 'and'
195.7 of] *ab. del.* 'for'
195.8 know,] *comma insrtd. for del. exclm. mk.*
195.24 Remind] *ab. del.* 'Tell'
195.25 knows] *aft. del.* 'need'
195.28 best)] *paren insrtd.*
195.28 news] *bef. del. closing paren*

To Alice Howe Gibbens James 25 August 189[1]

196.3 hotel] *bef. del. comma*

To Ellen James Temple Emmet Hunter 30 August 1891

196.9 that] *bef. del. false start*

To John Jay Chapman 4 September 1891

197.6 hand] *aft. del.* 'arm'
197.7 from] *bef. del.* 'the'
197.14 in] *intrl.*
197.14 intoxications] *bef. del.* 'revolve'
197.17–18 discussable] *aft. del.* 'recogn'
197.28 beef,] *bef. del. dash*

To Charles William Eliot 11 September 1891

198.7 My] *aft. del.* 'Phil'
198.8 took] *aft. del.* 'to[start of 'k']'
198.8–9 Phil. 2.] *ab. del.* 'the course'
198.9 in that course] *intrl.*
198.12 be] *intrl.*

To Alice Howe Gibbens James 12
September 1891

199.27 Office] 'O' *ov.* 'o'
200.1 last] *alt. fr.* 'on'

To Carl Stumpf 21 September
1891

200.5 on] *insrtd.*
201.7 still] *bef. del.* 'a barbarian'
201.8 &] *insrtd.*
201.11 volumes] *aft. del.* 'f'
201.15 strong] *aft. del.* 'forte is'
201.16 purely] *bef. del.* 'logic'
201.28 many] *aft. del.* 'my'
201.33 the . . . all] *intrl.*
201.36 to] *bef. del.* 'your'
201.36 that] *bef. del.* 'the'
201.37 that,] *bef. del.* 'the'
202.5 here] *aft. del.* 'f'
202.6 treated] *bef. del.* 'lik'
202.7 existent] *intrl.*
202.7 not] *bef. del.* 'ps[*start of* 'y']'
202.11 matter] *bef. del.* 'until'

To Alice Howe Gibbens James 21
September 1891

203.28 Gardens] *aft. del.* 'Park,'
203.36 &] *ab. del. closing paren*
203.37 Saturday] *aft. del.* 'Sund'
203.38 After] *aft. del.* 'Now that'
203.38 ships] *aft. del.* 'other lines'
204.5 as] *bef. del.* 'dead'
204.7 such] *intrl.*
204.7 me] *aft. del.* 'to'
204.15 some] *bef. del.* 'chu'

To Alice Howe Gibbens James 25
September 1891

205.12 becomes] 'be' *intrl.*
205.12 it] *aft. del.* 'It'
205.21 ²the] *intrl.*
205.21 Thursday] 'T' *ov.* 't'

To Alice James [1 October 1891]

206.6 ship] *aft. del.* 'wh'
206.17 opportunity] 'rtunity' *aft. del.*
'nity'
206.25 amongst] *aft. del.* 'amogn'

207.1 relieve] *bef. del.* 'any sp'
207.6 Bell's] *bef. del.* 'Dinner'

To Frances Rollins Morse 19 October [1891]

209.1 19] *ab. del.* '29'

From Carl Stumpf 24 October
1891

210.31 einfachen] *ab. del.* 'Definition
der'
210.41 davon] *bef. del. comma*
211.9 Schwester] *aft. del.* 'Ür'

To Oliver Wendell Holmes, Jr. 26
October 1891

213.7 Even] *bef. del. illeg.*
213.8 your] *aft. del.* 'te'

To Charles William Eliot 29 October [1891]

213.5 for . . . years] *intrl.*
214.2 will] *aft. del.* 'w'

To Alice James 1 November 1891

214.11 his] *aft. del.* 'its'
214.15 on.] *intrl.*
215.10 boy] *aft. del.* 'eld'
215.15 Carrie] *aft. del.* 'Carry'
215.18 ²Mary] 'M' *ov.* 'm'
215.23 (when] *ab. del.* 'who was'
215.27 this year] *intrl. aft. comma in
error*
215.29 blind] *aft. del.* 'and pour'
215.30 maternal] *intrl.*
216.6 pompous] *aft. del.* 'good'

To Mary Whiton Calkins 6 November 1891

216.3 but] *intrl.*
216.8 hitch] *bef. del.* 'up'
217.6 Newton] *ab. del.* 'Bableone'

To Sarah Wyman Whitman 8 November 1891

217.6 just now] *intrl.*
217.8 know] *aft. del.* 'have'

To Charles Sanders Peirce 12 November 1891

218.6 there] *bel. del.* 'his'
218.7 element of] ('element' *ab. del.* 'sense'); *intrl.*
218.8 mass] *aft. del.* 'volume'
218.9 thick] *bef. del. comma*
218.10 justify] *ab. del.* 'warrant'
218.10 animus] *intrl.*
218.11 however] *intrl.*
218.12 that] *intrl.*
218.18 &] *bef. del.* '2'
218.20–21 Such . . . nostrils.] ('ies' *of* 'controversies' *ab. del.* 'y'); *intrl.*
218.24 passages] *aft. del.* 'a [*undel. in error in MS*] parallel'
218.25 rejoinder] *intrl.*
218.29 bring . . . odour,] *ab. del.* 'mix the Review in a controversy of unseemly tone,'
218.30–31 address . . . Corporation.] *ab. del.* 'pamphlet.'
218.31 a] *ab. del.* 'as a'
218.32 risk] *ab. del.* 'take'
218.34 bring] *aft. del.* 'pr'
218.35 threatening,] *comma ov. period*
218.35–36 since not treating] *alt. fr.* '*The not-treating [*alt. fr.* 'Treating']'
218.36 threatened] *aft. del.* 'p'
218.36 might] *aft. del.* 'implied that this'
218.37 admitted] *bef. del.* 'that'
218.37 original] *intrl.*
218.37 to be] *ab. del.* 'was'
219.2 of] *intrl.*
219.7 scholastic] *aft. del.* 'talentless'
219.15 Abbot] 'A' *ov.* 'a'
219.15 in his own favor] *intrl.*
219.15 introductory] *intrl.*
219.18 which] *aft. del.* 'whom'
219.18 entire] *final* 'ly' *del.*
219.19 special] *intrl.*
219.19 about himself] *intrl.*
219.24 what] *aft. del.* 'and'
219.29 in] *aft. del.* 'wh'

To William Torrey Harris 14 November 1891

220.1 14] '4' *ov.* '2'
220.8 here] *bef. del.* 'to teachers'
220.10 Paul] *intrl.*

From Charles Sanders Peirce [14 November 1891]

220.12 abstain] *aft. del.* 'am'

To Charles Sanders Peirce 16 November 1891

222.5 deal] *aft. del.* 'g'
222.6 novelists] *aft. del.* 'literary'
222.8 reasoned] *aft. del.* 'proof'
222.10 book,] *bef. del.* 'unless'
222.11 go] *ab. del.* 'make'
222.13 understand] *ab. del.* 'imagine'
222.19 a] *ab. del.* 'crit'
222.19 usually] *intrl.*
222.24 was] *ab. del.* 'can be'
222.28 ¹that] *intrl.*
222.30 sure.] *bef. del.* 'Vo'

From Charles Sanders Peirce 17 November 1891

224.30 Even] *intrl.*
224.30 in] 'i' *ov.* 'I'
224.31 Magnus] *ab. del.* 'Tait'
225.4 makes much of] *ab. del.* 'says a great deal about'
225.8 at] *aft. del.* 'finally'

To Henry Rutgers Marshall 18 November 1891

225.15 however,] *intrl.*
226.1 "energy"] *aft. del.* 'eng'
226.2 mean] *bef. del.* 'ar'
226.3 vastly] *ab. del.* 'infinitesimally'
226.3 &] *ov. dash*
226.3–4 probably . . . pain.] *intrl.*
226.9 expresses] *ab. del.* 'is'
226.9 real,] *comma insrtd. bef. del.* 'one, as'
226.9–10 distinguished] 'ed' *insrtd.*
226.16 our] *aft. del.* 'the'
226.21 at least] *intrl.*
226.26 one] *bef. del. qst. mk.*
226.26 round out] *ab. del.* 'fill'
226.29 ²& pains] *intrl.*
226.30 &] *intrl.*
226.35 to] *ab. del.* '['to give us the' *del.*] ['first steps' *del.*] the'
226.38 I] *aft. del.* 'I [*ov.* 'Al']'

To Alice James 22 November 1891

227.5 the] *aft. del.* 'with'
227.7 likely] *aft. del.* 'natu'
227.12 been] *bef. del.* 'ha *not be [undel. in error]*'
227.13 heart-] *bef. del.* 'contract-'
228.6 going] *bef. del.* 'th'

From John Dewey 22 November 1891

229.19–20 (when . . . same)] *parens ov. dashes*
229.22 different] *bef. del.* 'from'
229.23 should] *bef. del.* 'wind [ov. 'aft.']* up in'

From Sarah Wyman Whitman 22 November [1891]

230.6 you] 'y' *alt. fr.* 's'
230.30 silence] *aft. del.* 'sile'

From Charles Sanders Peirce 30 November 1891

231.4 partly] *ab. del.* 'wholly'

To Mary Whiton Calkins [15 December 1891]

232.8 does] *aft. del.* 'did'
232.12–13 explain] *bef. del.* 'simil'
232.14–15 from . . . adhering] ('are found' *intrl.*); *intrl. w. caret ov. semicolon*
232.16 by] *intrl.*
232.16 giving] *alt. fr.* 'give'

To Mary Whiton Calkins 20 December 1891

233.15 with] *bef. del.* 'th'

To Edward Bradford Titchener 3 January 1892

233.3 very] *intrl.*
233.11 ¹I] *aft. stroke indicating new paragraph*
233.12 have] *aft. del.* 'and'
234.5 of wh.] *intrl.*
234.6 think] *bef. del.* 'of'

234.10 me,] *bef. del.* 'that'
234.11 M.] *bef. del.* 'starts up,'
234.12 starts] *aft. del.* 'that his'

From Robertson James 12 January [1892]

235.1 I] *aft. del. false start*
235.11 use] *aft. del.* 'l'

To Henry Rutgers Marshall 31 January 1892

237.8 even] *insrtd. aft. del.* 'satisfaction of the'
237.9 seems] *aft. del.* 'ca'
237.9 effectively] *bef. del.* 'the'
237.11 instantly] *intrl.*
237.11 to the mind] *intrl.*
237.12 volition] *aft. del.* 'volitt'
237.12 we] *aft. del.* 'wh'
237.14 direction] *insrtd. for del.* 'way'
237.14 prompt] *intrl.*
237.15 consciousness] *bef. del. comma*
237.15 potential] *intrl.*

To Edward Bradford Titchener 1 February 1892

238.5 as] *aft. del.* 'I am sorry'
238.10 it] *aft. del.* 'it [ov. 'I']'
238.11 your] *aft. del.* 'him'
238.13 that] *ab. del.* 'myself'
238.13 I was] *insrtd.*
238.19 gratitude] *bef. del.* 'f'
238.19 with] *ab. del.* 'to'
238.22 any] *ab. del.* 'his'
238.24 then] *intrl.*
238.24 it,] *bef. del.* 'that'
238.27 When] 'e' *ov.* 'a'; *aft. del.* 'No'
238.30 assuming] *aft. del.* 'ignori'
238.30 that] *bef. del.* 'the'
239.1 in others] *intrl.*
239.1 acknowledge] *ab. del.* 'submit to'
239.3 think] 'k' *alt. fr.* 'g'
239.5(*twice*) his] *ab. del.* 'the'
239.19 from] *bef. del.* 'b'
239.24 I] *aft. del.* 'only'

From Henry Rutgers Marshall 2 February 1892

240.15 exists] *alt. fr.* 'existed'
240.15 follow] *final* 'ed' *del.*

To William Noyes [6 February 1892]

241.4 Thursday] *bel. del.* 'Tuesday'
241.5 Tuesday] 'ue' *ov.* 'hur'
241.5 8] *ab. del.* '7.45'

To Mary Whiton Calkins 14 February 1892

241.4 just] 'j' *ov.* 's'
241.7 know] *bef. del.* 'better'
241.14 go] *bef. del.* 'until next'

To Hugo Münsterberg 21 February 1892

243.5 University] *bef. del.* '?'
243.5 years] *bef. del.* '?'
243.14 50,] *bef. del.* 'and'
243.16 make] *ab. del.* 'run'
243.22 for 3 years] *intrl.*
243.23–24 (if . . . succeed)] *intrl.*
243.27 back] *bef. del.* 'af'
243.27–28 Of . . . permanence.] *intrl.*
243.32 hours] *aft. del.* 'ye'
243.35 it] *intrl.*
244.2 *pledge*] *aft. del.* 'engage you'
244.2 in case] *alt. fr.* 'since'
244.3 should] *ov.* 'might'
244.3 might] *aft. del.* 'would'

To Christine Ladd Franklin 3 March 1892

245.6 sabbatical] *alt. fr.* 'sabbatatical'
245.14 that] *ab. del.* 'it'
245.23 much] *intrl.*
245.23 has] *bef. del.* 'ma'

From Hugo Münsterberg 7 March 1892

246.6 sehr] *aft. del.* 'w'
247.34–35 für . . . drei] *ab. del.* 'pro'
247.39 wissenschaftliche] *intrl.*

To Charles William Eliot 21 March 1892

249.10–11 are . . . take] *intrl.*
249.11 15th] *bef. del.* 'are unfit to go on'
249.15 besides] *intrl.*
249.18 event] *bef. del.* 'allow Nichols'

249.19 might] *aft. del.* 'ought'
249.22 telegraph] *aft. del.* 'tell'
249.25 own] *intrl.*
249.27 oblige] *aft. del.* 'make'
250.4 it] *bef. del.* 'was before'

To Hugo Münsterberg 23 March 1892

250.7 have] *bef. del.* 'the'
250.15 certainly] *ab. del.* 'probably'
250.17 University] *ab. del.* 'College'
251.5 believe] *ab. del.* 'remember'
251.12 we] *aft. del.* 'I'

To Charles William Eliot 24 March 1892

251.14 M.] *ab. del.* 'him'
251.18 living.] *intrl.*
252.2 am] *aft. del.* 'are'
252.2 the] *ov.* 'his'
252.2 his] *aft. del.* 'th'

To Shadworth Hollway Hodgson 28 March 1892

254.13 shall] *intrl.*
254.15 s/Bex,] *intrl.*
254.35 the neighborhood of] *intrl.*
255.4 imagined] *aft. del.* 'always'
255.8 braver] *aft. del.* 'more'
255.9 more] *intrl.*
255.19 10 days] *ab. del.* 'a fortnight'

To Henry Pickering Bowditch 2 April 1892

256.12 10,000] *aft. del.* '3000.'
256.15 him] *bef. del. closing paren*
256.28 in] *aft. del.* 'f'
256.29 There] *aft. del.* 'I don't'
256.35 any] *insrtd.*
256.36 acquiring] *aft. del.* 'having a man as'
256.40 5500] *bef. del.* 'f'

To Josiah Royce [6 April 1892]

257.6 altogether.] *intrl. w. caret ov. period*

To Clarence John Blake 11 April 1892

258.8 when] *bef. del.* 'I m'

To Charles William Eliot 11 April 1892

258.6 you] *bef. del.* 'again'
258.8 N.H.)] *bef. del.* 'whether'
258.9 answer] *bef. del.* 'it'
259.3 had] *intrl.*
259.3 written] *alt. fr.* 'wrote'
259.14 such] *ab. del.* 'more'
259.19 were] *ab. del.* 'are'
259.19 see] *final* 'n' *del.; aft. del.* 'have'

To Hugo Münsterberg 13 April 1892

260.5 Washington)] *bef. del.* 'in'
260.11 this] *ab. del.* 'next'

To Hugo Münsterberg 19 April 1892

260.3–4 to write] *aft. del.* 'th'; *bef. del.* 'y'
260.11 hesitation] *bef. del. comma*
261.4 now] *bef. del.* 'publishing our pam'
261.8 to you,] *intrl.*
261.18 before the] *aft. del.* 'f'; *bef. del.* 'rea'
261.28 a] *aft. del.* 'more'
261.30 about] *ab. del.* 'for'
261.33 saw] *ab. del.* 'say'
262.5 Irish] 'I' *ov.* 'i'

To Mary Aspinwall Tappan 29 April 1892

262.6 it is] *intrl.*
263.8 into] 'to' *intrl.*
263.11 barring . . . vehemence] *intrl.*
263.13 air] *ab. del.* 'atmosphere'
263.19 talk] *aft. del.* 'talks'

To Michael Anagnos 30 April 1892

263.9 could] *aft. del.* 'go'

To Hugo Münsterberg 3 May 1892

264.1 May] *ab. del.* 'April'
264.3 accepting] *bef. del.* 'yo'
264.12 publication] *bef. del.* 'will'

To Hugo Münsterberg 15 May 1892

265.7 last] *aft. del.* 'days'
265.16 Even] 'E' *ov.* 'I'
265.16 should] *intrl.*
265.17 think] *bef. del.* ', that you will'
265.18 which] *bef. del.* 'y'
266.3 German] *intrl.*
266.6 I] *aft. del.* 'it'
266.10 entirely public] *ab. del.* 'let'
266.16 be] *bef. del.* 'an'
266.24 to] *bef. del.* 'the'
267.4 ²a] *intrl.*
267.5 complete] *intrl.*
267.16–17 Psychological] 'sychologi' *ab. del.* 'hilosophi'
267.22 sure] *bef. del.* 'your'
267.23 the] *ab. del.* 'next'
267.36 neccessity of] *intrl.*
267.36 starting] *bef. del.* 'of'
267.37 the] *insrtd. for del.* 'with the'
267.37 has been that] *ab. del.* 'of'
267.37–38 has been] *ab. del.* 'being'
267.38 —] *ab. del. comma*
267.38 an] *final* 'd' *del.*
267.39 logical,] *aft. del.* 'and'; *bef. del.* 'mind'
268.2 responsibility] *aft. del.* 're'
268.3 find] *aft. del.* '['then establish more harmonious relations with' *del.*] find that'
268.3 (in] *paren ov. comma*
268.6 My] *aft. del.* 'My ['M' *ov.* 'W'] fr'
268.15 at home] *intrl.*

To Hugo Münsterberg 15 May [1892]

269.9–10 decidedly] *intrl.*

To Eleanor Mildred Sidgwick 15 May 1892

269.6 you] *alt. fr.* 'to'
269.12 with] *bef. del.* 'all'
269.14 was] *aft. del.* 'let'
269.14 go,] *bef. del.* 'until'
269.17 as] *alt. fr.* 'I'
270.3 with] *aft. del.* 'to see'
270.6 aiding] *tr. fr. aft.* 'importunity'
270.7 make] *aft. del.* 'be'
270.9 perhaps] *ab. del.* 'somewhat'
270.9 It] *bef. del.* 'will'

270.14 twelve month] *ab. del.* 'year'
270.17 scientific effect] *ab. del.* 'result'
270.20 here] *intrl.*

To Richard Hodgson 25 May 1892

271.4 hither] *final* 'to' *del.*
271.10 of] *bef. del.* 'unalas'
271.12 with] *bef. del.* 'and'
271.15 my] *aft. del.* 'My'
271.16 J. W] *intrl.*
271.16 by me] *intrl.*
271.16 few] *bef. del.* 'f'
271.17 In] *aft. del.* 'The A. Schedules are so little'
271.22 analysis] *bef. del. paren*
271.25 over] *aft. del.* 'of'
271.29 by] *insrtd. bef. del.* 'from'
271.38 as yet] *intrl.*
272.3 meanwhile] *intrl.*

To Charles William Eliot 25 May 1892

272.8 for] *intrl.*
272.11 next year.] (*period insrtd.*); *tr. fr. aft.* 'course' *w. guideline ov. period foll.* 'appropriation'
272.11 The] 'T' *ov.* 't'

To Charles Sanders Peirce [25 May 1892]

273.5 Monist.] *period ov. comma; bef. del.* 'Tha'

To Charles Ritter 13 June 1892

274.1 13] '3' *ov.* '2'
274.3 a] *intrl.*
274.7 advice] *bef. del.* 'wh'
274.8 week] *bef. del.* 'f'
274.10 spot the knowledge] *ab. del.* 'place'
274.24 said] *aft. del.* 'I'

To George Croom Robertson 15 June 1892

275.6 that] *intrl.*
275.10 this] *ab. del.* 'a'
275.10 has] *bef. del.* 'many'
275.14 me] *aft. del.* 'my'

275.18 own] *intrl.*
275.20 you] *bef. del.* 'otherwise'
275.22 ulterior] *intrl.*
275.25 be] *ab. del.* 'bad'
275.32 take] *final* 's' *del.*
275.32 us] *intrl.*

From George Croom Robertson 17 June 1892

276.11 2 or 3] *intrl.*
276.16 continue] *intrl.*
277.3 for] *intrl.*

To Alice Howe Gibbens James [19 June 1892]

277.3 ²to] *bef. del.* 'come to'
277.4 thorn] *aft. del.* 'pilaster and'
277.10 are] *bef. del.* 'dedgeihing'
277.11 Abfahrt] 'A' *ov.* 'a'
277.18 even] *intrl.*
277.21 Even] *aft. del.* 'If'
278.7 Montreaux] 'M' *ov.* 'm'

To Alice Howe Gibbens James 20 June 1892

278.7 come.] *bef. del.* 'Unfortunately'
278.8 balconies] *alt. fr.* 'balcony'
278.12 3] *ov.* '2'
278.17 letter] *bef. del.* 'from'
278.22 doing] *aft. del.* 'go'
278.27 at my leisure] *intrl.*

To Alice Howe Gibbens James 21 June 1892

279.5 when . . . that] *intrl.*
279.12–13 the least] *intrl.*
279.14 If] *aft. del.* 'There'
279.15 you must know] *ab. del.* 'you let me say'
279.15 There] *aft. del.* 'You'
279.16 Badische] 'B' *ov.* 'D'
279.16 1st] *intrl.*
279.16 2nd] *intrl.*
279.17 2nd or] *intrl.*
279.19 whether] *intrl. bef. del.* 'that [ab. del.* 'of']'
280.3 together] *intrl.*
280.14–15 Your . . . off—] *written on the back of the envelope*

To Alice Howe Gibbens James [21 June 1892]

281.1 my] *intrl.*
281.7 exactly] *aft. del.* 'w'

To Charles William Eliot 22 June 1892

281.5 I] *intrl.*
281.17 the whole] *alt. fr.* 'they are'
281.17 family] *ab. del.* 'all'
281.17 has] *insrtd.*
281.19 feelings] *ab. del.* 'ways'
281.20 shall] *aft. del.* 'have'
281.23 the sight of] *ab. del.* 'to see'
281.24 ¹with] *intrl.*
281.24 of] *intrl.*
281.25 revelation] *bef. del.* 'to me'
282.2 man] *bef. del.* 'to be with'
282.4 lumber-merchant's] *intrl.*
282.15 on] *intrl.*
282.15 condition] *final* 'ally' *del.*
282.22 fees] *bef. del.* 'of the'
282.30 pay] *bef. del.* ', at'

To Josiah Royce 22 June 1892

283.6 (days] *paren ov. comma*
283.7 to] *aft. del.* 'f'
283.10 finally] *intrl.*
283.12 future] *ab. del.* 'the'
283.13 travel] *aft. del.* 'hope'
283.17 we] *intrl.*
283.23 painfully] *intrl.*
283.29 humor] *aft. del. false start written at some earlier time* 'I am afraid that when M. is once there people will deem the need less urgent'
283.32 to] *intrl.*
283.35 him] *intrl.*
283.37 out,] *bef. del.* 'h'
284.7 in talking about] *ab. del.* 'over'
284.10 most] *bef. del.* 'cospopo'
284.13 ours.] 's.' *insrtd.; aft. del.* 'to'; *bef. del.* 'tongue.'
284.16 before] *aft. del.* 'when'
284.16 wife,] *bef. del.* '['tr' del.] ['
284.20–21 of contraction] *intrl.*
284.24 talks] *aft. del.* 'and'
284.25 and we] *aft. del.* 'though'; *bef. del.* 'go on'
284.30 contemptuous] *intrl.*

284.31 at] *ab. del.* 'and contempt of'
284.35 who] *ab. del.* 'and'
284.36 calm] *aft. del.* 'free.'
284.39 is] *ab. del.* 'his'
284.40 make] *aft. del.* 'plan, and'
284.41 be] *bef. del.* 'enor'
285.2 way,] *bef. del.* 'who will probably be called back'
285.7 have] *ab. del.* 'send me'
285.8 Programs] *bef. del.* 'sent me fo'
285.10 ²for] *ab. del.* 'by'
285.11 to deal with] *tr. fr. aft.* 'people' *w. guideline placed in error aft. period foll.* 'lady'
285.15 as . . . place.] *intrl.; period foll.* 'House' *undel. in error*

To Carl Stumpf 24 June 1892

285.6 wife] *aft. del.* 'f'
285.13 us,] *comma ov. period*
285.13–286.1 while at school.] *intrl.*
286.4 with] *intrl.*
286.7 wish] *aft. del.* 'wh'
286.7 My] 'M' *ov.* 'B'
286.8 any] *aft. del.* 'ang'
286.10 in Germany] *intrl.*
286.12 in other things,] *tr. fr. aft.* 'tertia,'
286.13 merely] *intrl.*
286.14 account] *aft. del.* 'the'
286.14 a] *ab. del.* 'the'
286.23 the] *intrl.*
286.24 inquiries,] *comma ov. period bef. del.* 'I do hope that'
286.27 July] *aft. del.* 'August'
286.28 enough,] *bef. del.* 'the'
286.28–29 after . . . year] *intrl.*
286.32 all the same] *intrl.*
286.32 succeed;] *semicolon insrtd. bef. del.* 'all the same;'
286.34 psycho] *final* 'logical' *del.*
287.1 thinker] *aft. del.* 'exper'
287.3 with] *bef. del.* 'hea'
287.12 suggests] *bef. del.* 'inward'
287.12 inner] *intrl.*
287.15 far] *intrl.*

To Alice Howe Gibbens James [30 June 1892]

287.4 most] *ab. del.* 'every'
287.4 things] 's' *insrtd.*
288.7 all] *intrl.*

To Alice Howe Gibbens James 2 July [1892]

288.3 to be] *intrl.*
289.1 good] *bef. del.* 'face'
289.2 now] *aft. del.* 'goe'

To Alice Howe Gibbens James 2 July 1892

289.6 a] *intrl.*
289.7 a] *ab. del.* 'a ver'
289.8 house or] *insrtd.*
289.11 about] *ab. del.* 'for'
289.12 I] *bef. del.* 'f'
289.13 ¹&] *ab. del.* 'the'
289.13 probably] *aft. del.* 'p'
289.14 The] *aft. del.* 'In any'
289.31 with . . . time] *intrl.*
289.31 only] *ab. del.* 'possible'
290.5 season] *bef. del.* '['fu' *del.*] ca'
290.5 make] *bef. del.* 'time Se'

To Charles Ritter 4 July 1892

290.12 material] *aft. del.* 'physical'
290.18 breadth of] *intrl.*

To Hugo Münsterberg 6 July 1892

291.3 rather] *intrl.*
291.6 (sur Bex)] *ab. del.* 's/Ollon'
291.7 my] *intrl.*
291.7 family,] *bef. del.* '&'
291.11 I see that] *intrl.*
291.15 were] *aft. del.* 'well'
291.21–22 Münsterbergs] *apostrophe del. bef. final* 's'
291.26 etc.] *aft. del.* 'the'
291.28 but] *aft. del.* 'by'
292.9 St,] *bef. del.* 'any'
292.9 good] *bef. del.* 'one'
292.9–10 if . . . and] *intrl.*
292.13 the . . . be] *ab. del.* 'it is'
292.18 It] *aft. del.* 'My'
292.25 advance] *aft. del.* 'aad'

To Robertson James 10 July 1892

293.10 ²he] *intrl.*
293.13 His] *aft. del.* 'As for Clary'
293.14 lest] *ab. del.* 'should'
293.14 should] *ab. del.* 'have'

293.14 fail] *final* 'ed' *del.*
293.17 William] 'W' *ov.* 'C'
293.19 all] *intrl.*
293.30 reasons] *aft. del. intrl.* 'tempor'
293.31 seemed] *bef. del.* 'of the'
293.31 & Plumb's counsellors] *intrl.*
293.32 empty] *intrl.*
293.32 would] *bef. del.* 'sh'
293.33 then.] *bef. del.* 'You'
293.34 a] *ab. del.* 'the'
293.37 just] *bef. del.* 'what a'
294.2 come] *final* 's' *del.*
294.5 fits] *alt. fr.* 'of its'
294.9 village] *aft. del.* 'f'
294.15 ²with] *intrl.*

To George Croom Robertson 11 July 1892

294.5 because] *bef. del.* 'because'
294.11 have] *intrl.*
295.8 for] *aft. del.* 'for'
295.9 strength.] *period insrtd. for del. comma*
295.9 The] 'T' *ov.* 't'
295.10 ²to] *intrl.*
295.21 pivot of] *ab. del.* 'key to'
295.21 a] *intrl.*
295.21 puzzle] *intrl.*
295.25 from] *aft. del.* 'we'
295.28 Robertson,] *bef. del.* '"to'
295.30 relic.] *bef. del.* 'I f'
295.30 am] *bef. del.* 'sorry'

To Grace Ashburner 13 July 1892

296.3 in Europe] *ab. del.* 'here'
296.3 weeks] *intrl.*
296.7 duty] *aft. del.* 'and'
296.7 have] *bef. del.* 'to'
296.9 To] *aft. del.* 'The'
296.10 novel] *aft. del.* 'a *holiday* with'
296.10 anxieties] *alt. fr.* 'anxiety'
296.10–11 education,] *bef. del.* 'and with'
296.12 their questions,] *intrl.*
296.17 to] *bef. del.* 'the wear and tear of'
296.24 (!!)] *intrl.*
296.27 Up] *aft. del.* 'Upon'
296.29 dropped] 'ed' *ov.* 'ing'
296.36 after] *alt. fr.* 'from'; *intrl.*
297.4 otherwise,] *comma ov. period*

297.4 only] *ab. del.* 'But'
297.6 started on] *intrl.*
297.13 arrangements,] *bef. del.* 'and'
297.19 We] *aft. del.* 'Alice'
297.20 and ideal] *intrl.*
297.22 the] *intrl.*
297.37 to] *final* 'o' *del.*
297.40 Being] 'B' *ov.* 'b'

To Robertson James 13 July 1892

298.3 have] *intrl.*
298.6 unless] *bef. del.* 'he'
298.10 only] *intrl.*
298.14 one] *aft. del.* 'Bagg.'
298.17 hope] *bef. del.* 'to'
298.19 to . . . fee,] *intrl.*
299.3–4 the money] *ab. del.* 'it'
299.6 alpine] *aft. del.* 'swiss'
299.6 will] *ab. del.* 'enclose'
299.13 wear] *final* 's' *del.*
299.18 later:] *intrl.*

To Elizabeth Glendower Evans 15 July 1892

299.3 our] *aft. del.* 'y'
300.3 have] *bef. del.* 'som'
300.12 someone] *aft. del.* 'more'
300.12 *July 17th—Lausanne*] *intrl.*
300.14 I] *aft. del.* 'It'
300.18 lake] *intrl.*

To Eliza Putnam Webb Gibbens 18 July 1892

300.4 to] *intrl.*
301.6 some day] *intrl.*
301.10 boys] *aft. del.* 'family'
301.20 see] *bef. del.* 'Alic'
301.20 it] *aft. del.* 'the'
301.21 there] *intrl.*
301.22 so] *bef. del.* 'th'
301.26 mere] *intrl.*
301.30 ¹the] *intrl.*
302.10 splenetic] 'netic' *aft. del.* 'ntic'

To Alice Howe Gibbens James [18 July 1892]

302.7 (*without* the boys)] *intrl.*
303.5 family] *intrl.*
303.7 that] *bef. del.* 'his'

303.7 ²the] *ab. del.* 'a'
303.8–9 children . . . older.] *orig.* 'children, 2 girls older, and a boy of seven.'
303.14 Back] *bef. del. comma*
303.14 Vevey,] *bef. del.* 'and'

To Théodore Flournoy [19] July 1892

304.2 our] *aft. del.* 'my'
304.11 now] *intrl.*
304.22 all of] *intrl.*
304.30 a] *ab. del.* 'next'

To Alice Howe Gibbens James 19 July 1892

305.5 and a] *ab. del.* 'a'
305.5 ²a] *intrl.*
305.19 year] *bef. del.* 'of'
305.20 recommends] *bef. del.* 'B'
305.28 Dolmateff.] *ab. del.* 'Cérésole'
305.30 by] *bef. del.* 'your'

To Shadworth Hollway Hodgson 22 July 1892

306.6 but good] *intrl.*

To Henry James III 27 July 1892

306.1 Hotel] 'H' *ov.* 'R'
306.12 victuals] *bef. del.* '& sl'
307.1 Harry] 'H' *alt. fr.* 'h'

To Alice Howe Gibbens James [1 August 1892]

307.12 Evil] 'E' *alt. fr.* 'e'
307.18 so] *bef. del.* 'inan'
307.22 more] *intrl.*
307.22 during] *intrl.*
308.1 Allemands,] *comma alt. fr. exclm. mk.*
308.2–3 orders] *aft. del.* 'org'
308.4–6 It . . . of] *insrtd.*

To James Mark Baldwin 9 August 1892

308.1 Cruchon] 'on' *ab. del.* 'an'
308.12 next summer,] *intrl. w. caret ov. comma*
308.17 vastly] *aft. del.* 'decidedly'

309.3 by] *bef. del. false start*
309.5 may] *bef. del.* 'be'
309.12 Americans] *intrl.*
309.13 are] *ab. del.* 'I'
309.17 striking] *aft. del.* 'straki'
309.19 will be] *ab. del.* 'is'
309.22 at] *aft. del. illeg.*
309.22 ²a] *ab. del.* 'an American'
309.22–23 in America] *intrl.*
309.23 is] *intrl.*
309.25 that] *intrl.*
309.27 more] *bef. del.* 'actve'
309.30 my] *ab. del.* 'boy'

To Hugo Münsterberg 9 August 1892

310.13 soon] *ab. del. illeg.*
310.26 already] *bef. del.* 'done the same thing'
310.29 President] *aft. del.* 'the'
311.1 may] *aft. del.* 'may in'
311.16 her] *aft. del.* 'the'
311.19 You] 'Y' *ov.* 'y'; *aft. del.* '—In the continued uncertainty,'
311.19 better] *bef. del.* 'still'
311.19 me] *intrl.*

To Josiah Royce 10 August 1892

311.5 can] *final* ''t' *del.*

To William Wilberforce Baldwin 18 August 1892

313.3 sending] *aft. del.* 'ask'
313.14 apply] *bef. del.* 'early ('

To Alice Howe Gibbens James 18 August 1892

314.15 till] *aft. del.* 'th'
314.31 younger] 'er' *ab. del.* 'est'
314.33 ¹&] *intrl.*
315.5 more] *bef. del.* 'hm'

To Hugo Münsterberg 24 August 1892

316.10 that] *intrl.*
316.14 Sumner] *ab. del.* 'Irving'
316.19 there] 're' *ov.* 'y'
316.22 us,] *bef. del.* 'I a'

To Théodore Flournoy 19 September 1892

317.6 our] *aft. del.* 'the'
317.15 with] *bef. del.* 'so'
317.20 Switzerland] 'S' *ov.* 's'
317.23 me] *intrl.*
317.26 vast] *final* 'e' *del.*
317.26 stretched] *aft. del.* 'on top of Monte Motterone'
317.28 before] *aft. del.* 'f'
318.1 logically] *aft. del.* 'a'
318.4–5 Criticism] 'C' *ov.* 'c'
318.6 inadmissible] *ab. del.* '*bar*'
318.13 flânerie] *aft. del.* 'Fla'
318.13 the] 'e' *ov.* 'is'
318.17 she nor I] *ab. del.* 'us'
318.18 contrasted] *ab. del.* 'situated'
318.23 than] 'n' *ov.* 't'
318.25 take] *aft. del.* 'th'
318.30 work] *aft. del.* 'do'
318.32 with] *aft. del.* 'me'
318.36 reflections.] *period ov. comma*
318.37 Until] 'U' *ov.* 'u'
318.37 take] *aft. del.* 'keep'
318.37 destiny] *ab. del.* 'vocation'

To Charles William Eliot 1 October 1892

319.11 authority,] *bef. del. intrl.* '&'
319.14 as . . . of] *ab. del.* 'of'
319.17 its] *ab. del.* 'the'
319.18 answering] *aft. del.* 'the'
319.18 ²the . . . philosophy] *ab. del.* 'I'
319.19 laboratory] *intrl.*
319.21 himself] *intrl.*
320.2 M.] *bef. del.* '(outside of Phil 2)'
320.4 But] *intrl. bef.* 'As [*cap. in MS retained in error*]'
320.5 in . . . instruction] ('higher *intrl.*); *intrl.*
320.9 ¹that] *ab. del.* 'as'
320.16 stand and] *intrl.*
320.18 want] *ab. del.* 'lack'
320.27 been] *bef. del.* 'g[*illeg.*]'

To Hugo Münsterberg 5 October 1892

320.1 Oct] *ab. del.* 'Sept'
321.1 must] *intrl.*
321.6 our] *intrl.*

321.11 few] *alt. fr.* 'of'
321.11 by] *alt. fr.* 'but'
321.13 about] *bef. del.* 'wishing'
321.15 convenient] 't' *ov.* 'ce'; *aft. del.*
'great'
321.15 arrangement] *intrl. w. guideline*
aft. semicolon in error
321.19 class- . . . work] *intrl.*
321.20 other] *intrl.*
321.24 manual] *intrl.*
321.29 young] *intrl.*
321.36 proper] *intrl.*
321.39 naked] *intrl.*

To Charles Ritter 5 October 1892

322.12 sunny] *aft. del.* 'warm'
322.12 boy's] *ab. del.* 'children's'
322.14 of it,] *intrl.*
322.16 taken] *ab. del.* 'our ap'
322.17 read] *final* 'y' *del.*
322.22 ihrem] *ab. del.* '*ihriem*'
322.22 zu] *intrl.*
322.24 form] *aft. del.* 'final'; *bef. del.*
'into'
322.25 finally] *intrl.*
322.26 freely] *alt. fr.* 'freed'
322.27 those] *aft. del.* 'them'
322.29 Renan's] 'Re' *ov.* 'ren'
322.29 So] *bef. del.* 'But what a'
322.31 couldn't] *aft. del.* 'can't'

To Ellen James Temple Emmet Hunter 9 October 1892

325.6 into] *bef. del.* 'an english'
325.6 ¹a] *ov.* 'or'
325.7 Switzerland] 'S' *ov.* 's'
325.15 leave] *bef. del.* 'them'
325.15 yours] *ab. del.* 'away'
325.16 your] *aft. del.* 'the'
325.19 a] *ab. del.* 'an exclus'
325.20 we] *ab. del.* 'I'
325.21 relatives] *alt. fr.* 'realatives'
325.28 (and] *paren ov. comma*
326.12 marriage] *bef. del.* 'has been'

To Grace Ashburner 19 October 1892

326.5 to you] *intrl.*
326.6 ¹to] *intrl.*

326.8 that] *intrl.*
326.8 you] *ab. del.* 'that you'
327.2 answer.] *bef. del.* 'Useless'
327.5 rest] *aft. del.* 'm'
327.8 almost] *intrl.*
327.10 most] *aft. del.* 'wh'
327.14 rooms] *aft. del.* 'bed'
327.22 Rindge] *bef. del.* 'over the door'
327.27 element.] *ab. del.* 'chief need'
327.32 a] *intrl.*
327.34 to them hereafter] *intrl.*
327.35 would . . . in] *ab. del.* 'lost for'
327.36 do] *final* 'es' *del.; intrl.*
327.36 amount] *final* 's' *del.*
327.37 shan't] *bef. del.* 'stay'
328.3 eye,] *bef. del.* 'the'
328.5 turning] *ab. del.* 'making'
328.5 into] *intrl.*
328.8 other] *intrl.*
328.9 difference] 'ce' *ov.* 't'
328.13 strange to say] *intrl.*
328.24 When] 'W' *ov.* 'I'
328.25 patience] 'ce' *ov.* 't'

To James Ward 1 November 1892

329.5 ¹to] *intrl.*
329.6 giving out] *ab. del.* 'imparting'
329.8 Your] *aft. del.* 'The heartily'
329.11 enough] *aft. del.* 'to me'
329.16 of terms] *intrl.*
329.16 of states] *intrl.*
329.21 analysis followed] *ab. del.* 'synthesis preceded'
329.21 synthesis] *ab. del.* 'analysis'
329.21 ²analysis] *aft. del.* 'alna [ab. del.*
'synthesis seems to me on']'
329.27 even] *intrl.*
329.28 description] *bef. del.* 'even'
329.29 would] *intrl.*
329.29 appear] *aft. del.* 'makes us understand anything'
329.30 must] *bef. del.* 'th'
329.35 admit] *bef. del.* 'that'
329.35 one] *ab. del.* 'you'
329.35 call] *bef. del.* 'an'
330.1–2 the doctrine that] *ab. del.* 'that'
330.2 feeling] *ab. del.* 'pleasure'
330.2 are] *aft. del. intrl.* 'ex'; *bef. del.*
'springs of action'
330.12 really] *aft. del.* 'd'

330.21 brain] *bef. del.* 'the'
330.21 states] *intrl.*
330.26–27 have just written] *ab. del.*
'wrote'

To Alice Howe Gibbens James 2 November 1892

331.5 your] *intrl.*
331.9 surrender] *aft. del.* 'am'
331.19 feel] *aft. del.* 'fel'
331.22 in] *bef. del.* 'introducing their'
331.32 separation] *bef. del.* 'fr'

To Alice Howe Gibbens James 4 November 1892

332.2 35] *aft. del.* '3 [*ov.* '4']'
332.16 Times] 'T' *ov.* 't'
332.16 ²&] *intrl.*

To Alice Howe Gibbens James 5 November 1892

332.4 less] *bef. del.* 'great'
332.9 Back] *ab. del.* 'Home'
333.1 prosaic] *aft. del.* 'and'
333.3 ruins] *bef. del.* 'the'
333.7 off] *bef. del.* 'all'
333.9 salt] *bef. del.* 'c'
333.9 They] 'T' *ov.* 't'
333.14 general] *intrl.*
333.15 the chief] *ab. del.* 'one of the'
333.15 actress] *final* 'es' *del.*
333.15 think] 'k' *ov.* 'g'
333.20 ²more] *bef. del.* 'th'

From James Rowland Angell 6 November 1892

333.7 so] *intrl.*
334.35 to you] *intrl.*
334.35 finished.] *period insrtd. bef. del.*
'to you'
335.7 out] *bef. del.* 'too'

To Alice Howe Gibbens James 7 November [1892]

336.1 ?] *intrl.*
336.1 6] *ov.* '9'

From James Ward 10 November 1892

337.14 analysis] *bef. del.* 'before'
337.40 psychological] *intrl.*
338.17 transgressors] *ab. del.* 'it'

To Eliza Putnam Webb Gibbens 12 November 1892

339.8 &] *intrl.*
339.11 will] *bef. del.* 'soon'
339.24 will] *intrl.*
339.24 do] *bef. del.* 'for'
339.33 so] *ov.* 'as'

To Frederic William Henry Myers 14 November [1892]

340.5 fell] *bef. del.* 'ore'
340.12 there] *bef. del.* 'I'
340.18 carte] *bef. del. false start*
340.19–20 And quite] *ab. del.* 'Anyhow'
340.22 black] *aft. del.* 'pl'
340.28–341.1 psychological] *ab. del.* 'intellectual'
341.2 has] *intrl.*
341.2 that of] *intrl.*

To James Ward 15 November 1892

342.4 heart] 'eart' *ab. del.* 'ead'
342.12 common] *bef. del.* 'pa'
342.15 calls] *ab. del.* 'judges'
342.15 them] *bef. del.* '['as' *del.*] them'
342.18 ²to] *ab. del.* 'you'
342.19–20 the fact of] *intrl.*
342.20 determinate] *intrl.*
342.20 need] *aft. del.* 'need'

To Francis Boott 18 November 1892

343.10 into] *ab. del.* 'up'
343.11 temporarily] *alt. fr.* 'temporary'
343.16 thermometer,] *bef. del.* 'etc'
343.16 general meteorological] *intrl.*
343.19 boys] *aft. del.* 'children'
343.19–20 English] 'E' *alt. fr.* 'e'
343.21 their] *intrl.*
343.25 all] *bef. del.* 'of'
343.31 days] *aft. del.* 'hou'

To Hugo Münsterberg 24 November 1892

345.3 seem] *bef. del. comma*
345.6 continues] *ab. del.* 'lasts'
345.11 much] *intrl.*
345.14 Keep] *aft. del.* 'Ch'
345.18 writes] *aft. del.* 'tells'
345.20 now] *intrl.*
345.20 a] *intrl.*
345.21 as] *bef. del.* 'you'
345.29 work] *bef. del.* 'is any'
345.35 towards] *ab. del.* 'dur'
345.36 they] 'y' *ov.* 'ir'
345.38 Their] *bef. del.* 'first'
345.40 period] *ab. del.* 'phase'
345.41 also] *intrl.*
346.7 & fundamental] *intrl.*
346.8 opportunities] 'ortu' *ab. del.* 'o'
346.15 attack] *bef. del.* 'Wr'
346.20 hardly] *aft. del.* 'ka'

To Alice Howe Gibbens James [7 December 1892]

347.8 on] *final* 'e' *del.*
347.21 slept] *aft. del.* 'sp'

To Alice Howe Gibbens James 8 [December 1892]

348.7 wide] *bef. del.* 'wh'

To Charles William Eliot 10 December 1892

348.1 Dec] *ov.* 'Nov'
349.1 laurel] *bef. del.* 'leaf'
349.3 on it] *intrl.*
349.13 the neccessity of] *intrl.*

To Josiah Royce 18 December 1892

350.4 am] *ab. del.* 'will'
350.5 ask] *bef. del.* 'you'
350.9 $3000,] *bef. del. dash*
350.19 holy] *aft. del.* 'la'
350.27 Italianism] *bef. del.* 'of various degrees of'
350.31 that] *ab. del.* 'we w'
350.32 ¹as] *intrl.*
350.32 modernized] *bef. del.* 'as B'
350.38 hitherto] *ab. del.* 'ever'

350.40 all] *aft. del.* 'della' *and false start of letter*
351.4 and acquaintance but] *intrl.*
351.6 winter] *bef. del.* 'I have'
351.9 think] 'k' *ov.* 'g'
351.10 live] *aft. del.* 'lif'
351.17 is] *ab. del.* 'are'
351.17 nourishing] 'nou' *intrl.*
351.17–18 proposals] *aft. del.* 'bids'
351.18 "Cosmology"] *aft. del.* 'Naturph'
351.27 Principes] *aft. del.* 'Nat'
352.7 last night] *intrl.*
352.8 here] *intrl.*

To Carl Stumpf 20 December 1892

352.4 Luzern,] *bef. del.* 'or'
353.5 by] *aft. del.* 'about'
353.13 We] *ab. del.* 'I'
353.24 production] *ab. del.* 'work'
353.30 there.] *intrl.*
353.32 seems] *bef. del.* 'not in'
353.34 up] *intrl.*
353.35 mathematical] *final* 'ly' *del.*
353.37 however that] *intrl.*
353.39 work] *aft. del.* 'exact school upshot of'
354.2 activity] *aft. del.* 'he'
354.10 may] *intrl.*

To Mary Sherwin Gibbens Salter 26 December 1892

354.10 Mack] *ab. del.* 'make'
355.2 need] *aft. del.* 'neet'
355.2 short] *aft. del.* 'spo'
355.3 unsociably] *aft. del.* 'unsob'
355.5–6 till midnight] *intrl.*
355.6 one's] *ab. del.* 'the'
355.9 Peggy] 'P' *ov.* 'B'; *bef. del.* 'and'
355.13 thrust)] *paren ov. comma*
355.14 Harry] *bef. del.* 'and'
355.18 once more.] *ab. del.* 'again.'
355.23 brevity,] *bef. del.* 'and'
355.26 Borgia,] *bef. del.* 'dully written but'
355.28 old] *aft. del.* 'of'
355.28 pope] *bef. del.* 'is'
355.30–31 Beware . . . Borgias!] *intrl.*
355.32 however] *intrl.*
355.39 whole] *intrl.*

356.3 wolves] *bef. del.* 'ready to'
356.4 very] *insrtd.*

To Grace Norton 28 December 1892

356.3 you] *bef. del.* 'th'
356.12 poor] *bef. del.* 'wr'
356.21 imitated] *ab. del.* 'caught'
356.21 manner] *bef. del. closing paren*
356.25 little] *bef. del.* 'l'
356.26 dispel] *aft. del.* 'make'
356.26 let] *aft. del.* 'lett'
357.11 looking through] *ab. del.* 'in'
357.14 good,] *bef. del.* 'as'
357.24 geography] *aft. del.* 'dem'
357.31 runs] *ab. del.* 'goes'
357.37 being] *intrl.*
358.14 hope] *bef. del.* 'it'
358.18 dears] *bef. del.* 'in the'

To Théodore Flournoy 3 January 1893

361.1 "innervating"] *ab. del.* 'nerving'
361.4–5 soleil] *ab. del.* 'ciel'
361.9 ²the] *ab. del.* 'our'
361.13 at] *intrl.*
361.25 blessed] *aft. del.* 'and'
361.26 up] *aft. del.* 'K'
361.29 ²of] *intrl.*
361.30 things] *insrtd.*
361.30 knew] *bef. del.* 'anything'
361.32 during] *intrl.*
361.32 I] *intrl.*
361.32 never] *bef. del.* 'wipe out the reparation'
361.33 volumes] *aft. del.* 'f'
361.34–35 ²and . . . me,] *intrl.*
362.6 escapes] *aft. del.* 'avoids'
362.9 from] *intrl.*
362.9 whom] 'm' *insrtd.; bef. del.* 'otherwise the world would'
362.12 be] *aft. del. false start*

To Grace Ashburner 5 January 1893

364.12 Curtis's] *aft. del.* 'G'
364.13 continued] *orig.* 'conditio' *alt. in error to* 'condinued'
364.17 come] *bef. del.* 'before'

364.25 little] *init.* 'l' *ov.* 's'; *aft. del.* 'dis'
365.1 these] *aft. del.* 'all'

To Elizabeth Ellery Sedgwick Child 5 January 1893

366.4 Mrs] 'rs' *ov.* 'iss'
366.4 Annex,] *bef. del.* 'whom'
366.17 tough] *aft. del.* 'strong ambition and'
366.20 contempt] *aft. del.* 'scorn and'
366.25 spirit] *bef. del.* 'is'
366.27 peace] *aft. del.* 'ease,'
366.33 as] *ab. del.* 'with'
367.15 ²from] *ab. del.* 'on [*ov.* 'in']'
367.16 girls] *aft. del.* 'boys'
367.18 make] *bef. del.* 'a'
367.19 months] *bef. del.* '. ['in' *del.*] You have to make yourself'
367.22 I'm] *bef. del.* 'g'
367.23 rather] *aft. del. false start*
367.24 And] *bef. del.* 'it'
367.30 or . . . Frank,—] *intrl.*
367.34–35 & business] *intrl.*
368.2 little] *bef. del.* 'mi'

To Hugo Münsterberg 7 January 1893

369.1 what] *aft. del.* 'the'
369.1 ¹as . . . Palmer] *intrl.*
369.3 to have] *aft. del.* 'ha'; *bef. del.* 'a'
369.9 employed] *bef. del.* 'in'
369.17 it,] *intrl.*
369.22 feelings,] *bef. del.* 'to and'
369.23 exultations] *bef. del.* 'ang'
369.28 best] *intrl.*
369.32 and] *bef. del.* 'que'
369.32 queer.] *ab. del.* 'crude.'
369.39 immediately] *intrl.*
370.3 Royce,] *bef. del.* 'and'
370.4 and] *bel. del.* 'of the'
370.6 2nd.)] *paren ov. comma*
370.11 if] *ab. del.* 'which is'
370.12 too] *ab. del.* 'two'
370.15 strictly] *bef. del.* 'technical'
370.21 (to] *paren ov. comma*
370.23 man may] *ab. del.* 'pupil'
370.23 put] *final* 's' *del.*
370.33 Physiology,] *intrl.*
370.34–35 from Psychol.] *intrl. bef. del.* 'Some day we must have Physiology taught in the University apart from

the course given in the medical school.'

370.35 views] *aft. del.* 'As to who'
370.38 ¹a ½ year] *ab. del.* 'six months'
370.38 have] *bef. del.* 'six months'
370.39 one] *intrl.*
370.39 those] *alt. fr.* 'that'
371.2 myself] *intrl.*
371.9 whichever may] *ab. del.* 'as'
371.9 seem] *final* 's' *del.*
371.9 go with] *ab. del.* 'suit'
371.11 beside] *final* 's' *del.*
371.16 without] 'out' *insrtd.*
371.20 last] *aft. del. opening db. qt.*
371.26 ever] *final* 'y' *del.*

To Josiah Royce 7 January 1893

371.3 express myself] *ab. del.* 'answer'
372.1 22nd] *aft. del.* '22n'
372.10 never] *intrl.*
372.11 *character,*] *comma ov. period*
372.11 but . . . error.] *intrl.*
372.16 1] *aft. del.* 'one'

To Arthur George Sedgwick 21 January [1893]

373.17 Bs] *alt. fr.* 'Mrs'
373.18 (and] *paren ov. comma*
373.28 message] *insrtd.*

To Francis Boott 30 January 1893

374.9 the] *ab. del.* 'our'
374.20–22 (from . . . out)] *parens ov. commas*
374.22 great] *bef. del. closing paren*
374.24 photogs of] *intrl.*
374.24 bunch] *final* 'e' *del.*
374.38 —What . . . think?] ('W' *alt. fr.* 'T'); *insrtd.*
375.2 as] *underl. del.*
375.4 fitness] *aft. del.* 'any'
375.4 energy] *aft. del.* 'and'
375.7 Peabody] *aft. del.* 'peopl'

To Hugo Münsterberg 11 February 1893

377.4,6 missed] *ab. del.* 'lost'
377.7 yours] *ab. del.* 'it'
378.3 cause,] *comma aft. del. qst. mk.*

378.7 (I] *paren ov. dash*
378.7 ²to] *ab. del.* 'from'
378.8 or] *insrtd.*
378.8 his] *aft. del.* 'to'
378.10 reserve] *bef. del.* 'ast'
378.14 But] *bef. del.* 'Ebbinghaus'
378.17 thing] *final* 's' *del.*
378.17 Kant's] *ab. del.* 'the'
378.19 how] *bef. del.* 'I'
378.21 an] *intrl.*
378.23 manner] *ab. del.* 'way'

From George Frederick Stout 13 February 1893

379.7 in] *aft. del.* 'in point'
379.8 even] *intrl.*
379.12 2] *ov.* 'II'
379.16 do so.] *added aft. period undel. in error*
379.26 which] *bef. del.* 'Interaction of'
379.31 introspective] *intrl.*
379.31 mental] *bef. del.* 'life.'

To Alice Howe Gibbens James [21 February 1893]

380.10 at] *intrl.*
380.12 the] *intrl.*
380.20 at his absence] *intrl.*
380.27 Verona] *aft. del.* 'Bologna,'

To Alice Howe Gibbens James 25 February 1893

383.9 simple] *aft. del.* 'hum'
383.15 went] *aft. del.* 'stayed'
383.16–17 next year] *intrl. w. caret in error aft. comma*
383.18 her] *final* 'e' *del.*
383.20 way] *aft. del.* 'f'

To Alice Howe Gibbens James 26 [February] 1893

384.11 The] *aft. del.* 'I a'
384.13 filthy] 'fitty' *alt. to* 'filty' *in MS in error*

To Alice Howe Gibbens James 27 February 1893

385.7 I] *intrl.*
385.11 hofbräuhous] *bef. del. closing paren*

385.12 went] *ab. del.* 'when'
385.15 this] 'is' *ov.* 'e'
385.24 all] *intrl.*
385.26 there!] *intrl.*
385.26 as] *bef. del.* 'if I longed'
385.28 shall] *intrl.*
385.28 settled] *aft. del.* 'here'

To Alice Howe Gibbens James 28 February 1893

386.11 an] *intrl.*
386.16 them)] *paren ov. comma*
386.16 an] *final* 'd' *del.*
386.18 Meanwhile] *bef. del.* 'the'

From Alice Howe Gibbens James 28 February [1893]

387.38 music] *aft. del.* 'of'

To Alice Howe Gibbens James 1 March 1893

389.1 March 1. 93] *ab. del.* 'Feb 29. *9 [undel. in error]*'
389.3 in . . . him.] *intrl.*
389.12 regular] *intrl.*
389.12 the latter] *intrl.*
389.13 women; and] *semicolon ov. colon bef.* 'And [*cap. in MS retained in error*]'
389.21 yet] *aft. del.* 'g'
390.2 wont] *aft. del.* 'wnt'

To Alice Howe Gibbens James 2 March 1893

390.13 Old] *aft. del.* 'pin'
390.13 pinakothek—] *dash ov. comma*
390.14 dined] *aft. del.* 'am'
390.19 H.] *bef. del.* 'to'
391.7 Dresden] 'D' *ov.* 'd'
391.11 educated] *aft. del.* 'brought'
391.14 thinks] *aft. del.* 'things'
391.22 Kiss] 'K' *ov.* 'S'
391.24 they're] *alt. fr.* 'there'

To Alice Howe Gibbens James 3 March 1893

392.7 at] *bef. del.* 'another Ca'

To Sarah Wyman Whitman 5 March 1893

394.6 one] *ab. del.* 'of'
394.8 feel] *aft. del.* 'be an'
394.9 take] *bef. del.* 'the possibi'
394.11 mere] *ab. del.* 'me'
394.11 fantasticality] 'ity' *aft. del.* 'ly'
394.15 gravitate] *aft. del.* 'aspire to'
395.5 more] *aft. del.* 'even'
395.5 hope,] *comma insrtd. bef. del.* 'that'
395.8 which] *ab. del.* 'a'
395.10 but] *aft. del.* 'f'
395.12 one] *intrl.*
395.13 there,] *intrl.*
395.14 one's] *bef. del.* 'naif'
395.20 —] *intrl.*
395.22 , or] *aft. del.* 'to you'
395.37 idea] *aft. del.* 'I[start of 'd']'
395.38 blackish] *intrl.*
395.38 with] *ab. del.* 'and'

To Henry James III 10 March 1893

396.7 about to make] *ab. del.* 'making'
396.12 trust] *aft. del.* 'thi'

To Violet Paget 11 March [1893]

397.11 inveterate] *aft. del.* 'invetat'

To Hugo Münsterberg 13 March 1893

398.3 strength] *aft. del.* 'health'
398.10 what] *aft. del.* 'the'
398.21 strong] *aft. del.* 'gro'
398.21 hear] *aft. del.* 'it'
398.32 turned] *aft. del.* 'proved'

To Henry James III 14 March 1893

399.14 there,] *intrl.*
399.24 left] *ab. del.* 'written'
399.29 Say] *aft. del.* 'Reme'

To Violet Paget 18 March 1893

400.4 you] *final* 'r' *del.*

To Josiah Royce 18 March 1893

401.2 Palmer] *aft. del.* 'Royce'
401.2 all] *intrl.*

401.3 cheerfully] *intrl.*
401.8 know] *bef. del.* 'of the'
401.24 as] *intrl.*
401.24 together] *intrl.*
401.30 to Italy.] *intrl. w. caret ov. period*
401.32 funds.] *bef. del.* 'Angell'
402.3 on] *intrl.*
402.5 without wh.] *aft. del.* 'wh'; *bef. del.*
  'alas'

To Henry James III 26 March 1893

403.2 words] *aft. del.* 'new'
403.4 him] *aft. del.* 'it'
403.5 —] *intrl.*
403.5 how] *bef. del.* 'to'
403.8 read] *bef. del.* 'to your teacher
  and'
403.9 new] *intrl.*
403.12 by] *bef. del.* 'the'

To Henry James III 9 April [1893]

404.13 gloriously] *bef. del.* 'warm and'
404.19 get] *aft. del.* 'put'

To Frank Duveneck 13 April 1893

405.1 somewhat] *aft. del.* 'flat'
405.6 ought] *aft. del.* 'must'
405.10 better] *aft. del.* 'p'
405.10 that,] *comma insrtd. bef. del.* 'you
  should h'
405.10 been] *aft. del.* 'done the thing,
  tha'

To Hugo Münsterberg 13 April 1893

405.18 the committee,] *ab. del.* 'Royce,'
405.18 it] *insrtd. for del.* 'the committee'
406.4 ²the] *intrl.*
406.7 special] *bef. del.* 'cha'
406.8 then] *insrtd.*
406.8 Phil. 2.] *ab. del.* 'the class'
406.11 plan] *final* 'e' *del.*
406.17 already] *intrl.*
406.17 good] *intrl.*
406.19 more] *bef. del.* 'that'
406.24 more] *bef. del.* 'subje'
406.28 gets] *bef. del.* 'in the'

406.29 and] *bef. del.* 'for'
406.30 & seminaries] *intrl.*
406.33 having] *ab. del.* 'making'
407.13 ¹as] *intrl.*
407.21 Mind] 'M' *ov.* 'm'
407.35 even] *aft. del.* 'if'

To Alice Howe Gibbens James 19 April 1893

408.6 arriving] *bef. del.* 'at'
408.31 sore,] *bef. del.* 'and'
408.33 divine. The] *period insrtd. for del.
  comma;* 'T' *ov.* 't'
408.33 smells] *aft. del.* 'seems'
408.34 though] *ab. del.* 'but'
409.14 is] *ab. del.* 'was'
409.14 boy] *bef. del.* 'of'
409.14 hotel,] *aft. del.* 'in'
409.16 alfabet] *aft. del.* 'la'
409.16 six] *insrtd.*

To Josiah Royce 21 April [1893]

409.10 8] *ab. del.* 'that'
409.11 only] *aft. del.* 'P'
410.3 would be then] *ab. del.* 'is'

To Carl Stumpf 24 April [1893]

410.6 excuse] *aft. del.* 'have'
410.8 (!!!)] *intrl.*
410.18 ever] *aft. del.* 'every'
410.21 year] *bef. del. comma*
411.1 he] *bef. del.* 'h'
411.4 England] *aft. del.* 'Italy'
411.5 Tyrol] *aft. del.* 'the'
411.20 but] *intrl.*
411.20 about] *bef. del.* 'abo'
411.23 its] *ab. del.* 'the'
411.26 expression] *ab. del.* 'resumé'
411.28 Paulsen,] *bef. del.* 'and'
411.29 the] 'e' *ov.* 'is'; *aft. del. intrl.* 'th'
411.29 wh. I have read,] *intrl.*
411.36 boy] *final* 's' *del.*
411.38 you] *final* 'r' *del.*

To Francis Boott 27 April 1893

412.4 see] *aft. del.* 'get'
412.15 feet,] *bef. del.* 'and,'
412.20 better] *bef. del.* 'that'
412.21 pure] *ab. del.* 'his'
412.24 there] *alt. fr.* 'they'

412.26 that] *final* 't' *ov.* 'n'
412.30 meanness] *aft. del.* 'yelping'
413.1 innocent] *aft. del.* 'early a'
413.5 lacks] *alt. fr.* 'lakes'
413.6 which] *aft. del.* 'here I am'
413.14 hither] *alt. fr.* 'here'

To William James, Jr. 27 April 1893

413.6 like] *bef. del.* 'to'
414.2 write] *aft. del.* 'I'

To William James, Jr. 2 May [1893]

414.1 May] *aft. del.* 'Schweitz'
414.7 Tweedy] *bef. del.* 'is'

To Théodore Flournoy 5 May 1893

416.3 came] *bef. del.* 'yesterday'
416.27 Carl . . . name] *intrl.*
416.30 The book is] *intrl.*

To Eliza Putnam Webb Gibbens [8] May 1893

417.4 maternal] *aft. del.* 'pare'
417.5 resolved] *aft. del.* 'did it'
417.8 journeys,] *bef. del.* 'and'
417.10 Ideal] 'I' *ov.* 'T'
417.21 Sept.] *aft. del.* 'Spet'
417.27 sail] *bef. del.* '['later' *del.*] early'
417.30 aimlessness] 'ness' *aft. del.* 'less'
417.31 till that date] *intrl.*
417.31 ²the] *final* 'se' *del.*
417.32 have] *intrl.*
417.32 been] 'en' *insrtd.*
417.35 must have been] *ab. del.* 'was'
417.38 Billy,] *bef. del.* 'and'
418.1 house] *aft. del.* 'Cambridge'
418.3 will be to me] *intrl. w. caret ov. comma*
418.4 ³of] *intrl.*
418.6 and . . . day,] *intrl.*
418.8 almost] *aft. del.* 'have a'
418.12 me)] *paren ov. comma*
418.14 latter] *bef. del.* 'half or'
418.14 September] 'S' *ov.* 's'
418.19 poetical] *ab. del.* 'abstract'
418.24 But] *bef. del.* 'I'

418.29 we are] *ab. del.* 'we['re' *del.*] were'
418.30 truest] *intrl.*
418.31 don't] *intrl.*
418.32 required] *bef. del.* 'so imperfectly,'
418.39 continuous] *insrtd.*
419.3 ²to] *intrl.*
419.8 next] 'xt' *ov.* 'ar'
419.14 Mack] *bef. del.* 'as'
419.19 ²the] *intrl.*

To Mary Sherwin Gibbens Salter 11 May 1893

420.19 blackness] *ab. del.* 'frown'
421.15 constantly] *intrl.*
421.15–16 was . . . hands.] *intrl.*
421.19 Peggy] 'P' *ov.* 'p'
421.20 me.] *bef. del.* 'You will'
421.37 country] *intrl.*
421.38 into] *intrl.*

From Carl Stumpf 17 May 1893

423.41 gleiche] *bef. del.* 'Em'

To Henry Rutgers Marshall 24 May [1893]

424.4 ground] *bef. del.* 'greatly'
424.7 by] *aft. del.* 'well'

To Carl Stumpf 26 May 1893

425.13 who expect entertainment] *intrl.*
425.17 the thought of] *intrl.*
425.17 possibilities] *aft. del.* 'suspicious'
425.18 most] *aft. del.* 'it'
425.30 Soul] *insrtd. for del.* 'Heart'
425.30 soul] *ab. del.* 'heart'
426.1 that] *bef. del.* 'your'
426.6 Physiologie] *aft. del.* 'Psycholog'
426.7 wives] *aft. del.* 'wif'
426.10 Wundt] *bef. del.* 'on'
426.14 creative] *intrl.*
426.17 attempts] *bef. del.* 'to m'
426.20 sense] *ab. del.* 'feeling for truth'
426.21 "strenge"] *bef. del.* 'the in'
426.22 which] *ab. del.* 'that'
426.27 possibly] *intrl.*
426.28 for the truth] *intrl.*
426.29 treated] 'r' *ov.* 'e'; *bef. del.* 'of'

426.29 technical] *aft. del.* 'humbug'
426.32 disguises] *aft. del.* 'surrounds'
426.35 coexistent] *intrl.*
426.36 consciousness] *bef. del.* 'coex-
isting'
426.39 been] *bef. del.* 'talking all then'

To William Wilberforce Baldwin 4 June 1893

427.7 but] *aft. del.* 'but'
427.11 being] *bef. del.* 'n'
427.20–21 to morrow] *ab. del.* 'to day'
428.2 invalid] *aft. del. hyphen*
428.12 ²that] *intrl.*

To Margaret Mary James [11 June 1893]

428.6 sipping] *aft. del.* 'dr'
428.10–11 for me] *intrl.*

To François Pillon 17 June [1893]

429.6 3 young] *intrl.*

To Charles Ritter 22 June [1893]

429.4 Stuttgart] *bef. del. intrl.* 'or'
429.5 (or from Bern?)] *intrl.*
429.8 & my wife] *intrl.*
429.9 what] *aft. del.* 'I'
429.16 your] *aft. del.* 'you rep'
430.1 strong &] *intrl.*
430.12 I] *aft. del.* 'an'

To Shadworth Hollway Hodgson 23 June 1893

430.4 kinds)] *bef. del.* 'more often'
430.8 because] *aft. del.* 'all'
430.13 week] *bef. del.* 'and'
430.15 a] *intrl.*
430.17 in] *ab. del.* 'wi'
431.1 open] *aft. del.* 'bright and'
431.15 quartering] 'ing' *insrtd.*
431.20 over] *aft. del.* 'of'
431.21 till] *aft. del.* 'til'

To Théodore Flournoy 26 June [1893]

431.1 June] *aft. del.* 'May'
432.1 both] *intrl.*

To Hugo Münsterberg 6 July 1893

432.15 prophylactic] *aft. del.* 'ph'
432.19 what] *bef. del.* 'y'
433.4 courses] *aft. del.* 'couses'
433.4 yet] *bef. del.* 'the'
433.5 for] *ab. del.* 'to'
433.5 the] *intrl.*
433.6 now] *bef. del.* '; however'
433.9 so far as] *ab. del.* 'in'
433.16 just] *intrl.*
433.17 opinion] *bef. del.* 'it'
433.23 Harvard] *ab. del.* 'was'
433.28 Journal] *aft. del.* 'Jur'
433.32–33 better. Only] *period ov. comma;* 'O' *ov.* 'o'
433.33 that] *bef. del.* 'it m'
433.33–34 all special] *intrl.*
433.37 do,] *bef. del.* 'which'
433.37 duplication] *bef. del.* 'and'
434.1 sake] *aft. del.* '['gr' *del.*] interest of'
434.1 be sure of] *ab. del.* 'have'
434.4 for their articles.] *intrl. w. caret ov. period*
434.10 makes] *bef. del.* 'g'
434.11 behind] *intrl.*
434.12 our] *bef. del.* 'pro'

To James Bryce 8 July 1893

434.3 Academy] 'a' *ov.* 'd'
435.1 of] *bef. del.* 'us'

To Frederic William Henry Myers 9 July 1893

437.19 never] *bef. del.* 'go'
437.20 ²the] *intrl.*
437.20 am] *aft. del.* 'fe'
438.5 such] *ab. del.* 'sush'

To Frederic William Henry Myers 16 July [1893]

438.13 ¹I . . . but] *intrl.*
438.13 the boys.] *alt. fr.* 'them, though.'
439.1 Thélin,] *aft. del.* 'or'; *bef. del.* 'Thelin'
439.5 light] *aft. del.* 'and'
439.7 be] *bef. del.* 'to'
439.11 et al.] *intrl.*
439.11 had] *intrl.*

439.14 Farms,] *intrl. w. comma repeated in error*
439.19 Wendell] *ab. del.* 'Barrett'
439.19 professes] *aft. del.* 'profer'

From Alice Howe Gibbens James 17 July [1893]

440.11 a] *intrl.*

To Alice Howe Gibbens James 19 July [1893]

442.25 so,] *bef. del.* 'I'
443.1 will] *aft. del.* 'may do'

From Henry Holt 24 July 1893

443.6 though that] *intrl.*
443.7 perhaps] *bef. del.* 'limit my'
444.1 later] *bef. del.* 'days'
444.8 Whenever] *aft. del. illeg.*
444.16 yet] *ab. del.* 'though'
444.17 coherency] *aft. del.* 'and'
444.32 (i.e. at Stowe)] *intrl.*
444.38 I] *aft. del.* 'Just'

To Henry James III [26 July 1893]

445.5 my] *aft. del.* 'th'
445.13 I] *aft. del.* 'They'

From George Herbert Palmer 26 July 1893

446.32 $250,] *comma insrtd.*

To Hugo Münsterberg 29 July 1893

447.5 the general] *intrl.*
447.7 psychological] *aft. del.* 'periodical'
447.13 been] *aft. del.* 'mo'
448.8 shall] *ab. del.* 'may'
448.13 chief-] *intrl.*
448.16 be] *intrl.*
448.16–17 continuous] *alt. fr.* 'continue'
448.17 with] *intrl.*
448.17 journal,] *intrl.*
448.17 need] *bef. del.* 'bear'
448.23 several] *bef. del.* 'partial'
448.28 of . . . thing] *intrl.*
448.31 1st] *intrl.*

448.33 2nd.] *aft. del.* 'se'
448.34 on this programme,] *intrl.*
448.36 can] *bef. del.* 'then'
448.39 absolutely] *intrl.*
449.2 heartily] *aft. del.* 's'
449.2 the] *intrl.*
449.7 fit] *aft. del.* 'can'
449.15 be] *ab. del.* 'were'
449.16 are] *ab. del.* 'were'
449.19 ²it] *intrl.*
449.21 then . . . be] *ab. del.* 'seemed'
449.21 or] *bef. del.* 'un'
449.22 some] *ab. del.* 'a'
449.29 &] *intrl.*
449.36–37 & vague] *intrl.*
449.37 knowledge,] *bef. del.* 'confer'
449.38 which] *bef. del.* 'cl'
449.39 power,] *comma alt. fr. exclm. mk.*

To Hugo Münsterberg 11 August 1893

451.1 11] ¹'1' *ov.* '2'
451.3 you,] *bef. del.* 'and'
451.13 & do] *intrl.*
451.14 connected] *ab. del.* 'mixed'
451.15 when . . . acting,] *ab. del.* 'as an actor'
451.16 journal] *bef. del.* 'ha'
451.20 any kind of] *intrl.*
451.21 worse] 'e' *ov.* 't'
451.33 9] *bef. del.* '10'

To William Wilberforce Baldwin 12 August [1893]

452.3 might] *aft. del.* 'may'
452.7 vulgar] *bef. del.* 'denom'
452.11 keep] *aft. del.* 'go'
452.12 fellow] *bef. del.* 'gra'
452.17 chief] *intrl.*
452.19 graciousness] *ab. del.* 'sweetness'
452.21 God] 'Go' *ov.* 'go'
452.23 our] *ab. del.* 'my'
452.26 Aug.] *aft. del.* 'Sep'

To Josiah Royce 14 August 1893

453.5 at] *aft. del.* 'all'
453.8 Being] 'B' *ov.* 'b'
453.8–9 letter] *intrl.*
453.19 you] *aft. del.* 'of'
453.23 superfetation] 'fetation' *aft. del.* 'feat'

453.25 Do] 'o' *ov.* 'id'
453.33 all round] 'll' *ov.* 'n'; *bef. del.*
'['og' *del.*] organization of Publications'

To Lionel Dauriac 15 August 1893

454.6 You] *bef. del.* 'have'
454.12 reacted] *aft. del.* 'worked that'
455.17 upon] *intrl.*

To Alice Howe Gibbens James 15 August 1893

455.1 Aug.] *aft. del.* 'Sept 14'
456.11 dragged] *aft. del.* 'j'
456.16 to see] *intrl.*
456.17 me] *bef. del.* 'good'
456.18 daily] *aft. del. intrl.* 'H'
456.39 just] *intrl.*

To Charles Ritter 18 August 1893

457.14 say] *aft. del.* 'do'
457.21 saw] *aft. del.* 'dr'

To Parke Godwin 4 September 1893

458.6 extraordinary] *aft. del.* 'an'; *bef.
del.* 'thing'
459.6 are starting] *intrl.*

To Carl Stumpf 12 September 1893

460.5 hotels] *bef. del.* 'w'
460.5 most] *ab. del.* 'very'
460.6 costly] *aft. del.* 'very'
460.6 profitable] *aft. del.* 'very'
460.17 all] *intrl.*
460.22 request] *ab. del.* 'write'
461.2 to other Germans] *intrl.*
461.3 capacity] *aft. del.* 'editors'
461.8 Reviews] *bef. del.* 'of'
461.9 of] *intrl.*
461.10 etc.] *aft. del.* 'of'
461.11 Items] *aft. del.* 'Possibly'
461.13 either] *aft. del.* 'to'
461.14 long] *aft. del.* 'which'

To James McKeen Cattell 16 October [1893]

463.4 complete] *aft. del.* 'pretty'
464.1–2 "hallucinations,"] *bef. del.* 'and'
464.2 & "sleep,] *intrl.*

To Harald Höffding 23 October 1893

464.8 motor] *aft. del.* 'the'

To George Holmes Howison 28 October [1893]

465.5 How] *ab. del.* 'You'
465.16 all] *intrl.*
465.21 ²with] *intrl.*
466.4 psychologizing and] *intrl.*
466.6 a man's] *ab. del.* 'the'
466.6 intellectual] *intrl.*
466.7 never] *bef. del.* 'be called'
466.8 than] *bef. del.* 'that of'
466.15 really] *intrl.*
466.15 pages] *bef. del.* 'ga'

To Katharine Outram Rodgers 30 October 1893

466.10 days] *bef. del.* 'for'
467.1 altho'] *aft. del.* 'altho'
467.2 wanted] *bef. del.* 't'
467.9 here] *intrl.*
467.10 seriousness] *ab. del.* 'and jerky
tension'
467.12 below] *ab. del.* 'betow'
467.17–18 (I . . . man)] *parens ov.
commas*
467.20 &] *ov.* 'I'

To James Ward 19 November 1893

470.3–4 and . . . revokable] *intrl.*
471.7 did)] *paren ov. comma*
471.7 this] *bef. del.* 'p'

To Richard Hodgson 8 December 1893

472.13 ought] *bef. del.* 'to'
473.3 bad] *aft. del.* 'p'
473.3 so] *bef. del. comma*
473.4 failed to] *ab. del.* 'not'
473.4 connect] *final* 'ing' *del.*

473.5–6 confuse] *bef. del.* 'th'
473.7 ²and] *intrl.*
473.11 were] *ab. del.* 'was'
473.17 names] *bef. del.* 'which'
473.18 to Marie] *intrl.*
473.22 Eugenie, Charles] *intrl.*
473.25 grave] *intrl.*
473.29 possible] *intrl.*
473.33 servants] *aft. del.* 'who'
473.35 servant] *bef. del.* 'My im'

To Frederic William Henry Myers 17 December 1893

474.4 being] *intrl.*
474.9 I] *intrl.*
474.14 yesterday] *ab. del.* 'this'
474.17 lie] *aft. del.* 'be'
474.18 which] *bef. del.* 'I'
474.25 so] *aft. del.* 'som'
474.25 had] *aft. del.* 'tho't'
474.27 only] *aft. del.* 'own'
475.1 into] *ab. del.* 'in'
475.2 in the house] *intrl.*
475.3 *have*] *aft. del.* 'have'
475.8 Piper] *aft. del.* 'Pipp'

To Alice Howe Gibbens James 24 December 1893

475.5 (no] *paren ov. comma*
475.5 being] *intrl.*

To Alice Howe Gibbens James [28 December 1893]

477.9 —] *bel. del. intrl.* 'will arrive I'

To James Mark Baldwin 30 December 1893

478.8 yourself] *intrl.*
478.9 Treiben] *ab. del.* 'Trieben'
478.13 own] *intrl.*

To James McKeen Cattell 30 December 1893

478.7 towards] *aft. del.* 'for'
478.12 generous] 'ous' *ab. del.* 'al'
479.5 copies] *ab. del.* 'the names'
479.5–6 Thos. W. Ward,] *aft. del.* 'and'; *bef. del.* 'in N.Y.'
479.7 of 18] ('8' *ov.* '2'); *aft. del.* 'in'

From Charles Sanders Peirce 1 January 1894

481.20–482.1 Substitutions] *ab. del.* 'Functions'

To Charles Sanders Peirce 24 January 1894

483.7 creating] *ab. del.* 'fixing [alt. fr. 'fixed']'
484.6 the circular] *ab. del.* 'it'
484.17 a] *intrl.*

To Carl Stumpf 24 January 1894

484.3 myself] *ab. del.* 'you'
484.4 but] *bef. del.* 'o'
484.4 found me] *ab. del.* 'I was'
484.5 I] *intrl.*
484.5 regained] *bef. del.* 'myself'
485.7 America] 'A' *ov.* 'a'
485.16 But] *aft. del.* '['B' *ov.* 'I' *del.*] I'
485.18 nothing,] *bef. del.* 'the subject of'
485.19 however,] *intrl.*
485.21 vacation] *aft. del.* 'f'
485.24 3 + 2] *ab. del.* '5'
485.26 which] *bef. del.* 'the'
485.38 ravages] *bef. del.* 'of'
485.39 From] *ab. del.* 'With'
486.3 in importance] *intrl.*
486.3 "exact"] *intrl.*
486.3 laboratory] *bef. del.* 're'
486.4 For] *aft. del.* 'W'
486.5 opened] *aft. del.* 'thrown an entire'
486.5 human] *aft. del.* 'the sh'
486.13 here] *intrl.*
486.16 the pictures] *intrl.*
486.17 there] *intrl.*
486.20 Parts] *aft. del.* 'Pra'

From Charles Sanders Peirce 28 January 1894

487.13 his . . . himself] *ab. del.* 'being'
487.13 uncommitted] 'un' *insrtd.*
487.21 a little] *intrl.*
487.24 a positively] *ab. del.* 'an'
487.37–38 Shall . . . apteroent?] *insrtd.*
488.1 well] *aft. del.* 'not'
488.5 senses] *aft. del.* 'wh'

To Charles Sanders Peirce 27 February 1894

489.4 real] *aft. del.* 'a'

To James McKeen Cattell 1 March [1894]

489.5 the] *intrl.*
489.11 by] *intrl.*

To George Holmes Howison 3 March 1894

490.14 of] *aft. del.* 'f'
490.14 theoretical] *aft. del.* 'theote'
490.18 man] *aft. del.* 'many'
490.20 helpfulness] *aft. del.* 'and'
490.28 teaching,] *bef. del.* '['of p' *del.*]
   from'
490.35 if] *aft. del.* '—not respon'
491.1 what] *aft. del.* 'the'
491.1–2 is . . . to] *ab. del.* 'will'
491.3 now] *intrl.*
491.5 freely:] *bef. del.* 'and'

To William Dean Howells 19 March 1894

492.7 from] *intrl.*
492.14 the] *ab. del.* 'your'
492.18 his] *ab. del.* 'our'
492.21 by] *ab. del.* 'but'

To Katharine Peabody Loring 20 March [1894]

495.4 Course] *intrl.*
495.7 Outlines of] *intrl.*

To Henry Pickering Walcott 1 April 1894

496.5 you] *aft. del.* 'I'
496.6 whilst] *aft. del.* 'with'
496.7 against] *aft. del.* 'about'
496.9 and verbiage] *intrl.*
496.11 able] *aft. del.* 'of'
496.13 then] *aft. del.* 'would'
496.16 the existence of] *intrl.*
496.16 in my turn] *ab. del.* 'also'

To George Holmes Howison 2 April 1894

497.12 already] *aft. del.* 'all'
497.30 America] 'A' *ov.* 'am'
497.34 there] *aft. del.* 'that'
497.36 now] *intrl.*
498.3 basis] *insrtd.*
498.3–4 fashionable.] *period insrtd. bef.*
   del. 'basis.'
498.4 any] *aft. del.* 'the an'
498.9 or find] ('find' *alt. fr.* 'found'); *ab.*
   del. 'that I had'
498.9 carry] *aft. del.* 'cary'
498.9 them] *intrl.*
498.15 always] *bef. del.* 'go'
498.26 ½] *intrl.*

To Josiah Royce 3 April 1894

499.1 April] *ab. del.* 'March'
499.4 M——g] *ab. del.* 'he'
499.6 Schop.] *aft. del.* 'Ka'
499.6 himself] *intrl.*
499.7 he] *bef. del.* 'neither me'
499.15 not] *intrl.*
499.15 our] *bef. del.* '['s' *del.*] sep'
499.18 11] *bef. del.* 'ho or t'

To Frederic William Henry Myers 4 May 1894

500.3 for] *ab. del.* 'of'
500.5 accept] *aft. undel. false start* 'a'
500.14 left] 'l' *alt. fr.* 'b'

To Alice Howe Gibbens James 16 May 1894

501.3 go] *bef. del.* 'again'
501.8 Tweedy's] *ab. del.* 'Billy's'

To Alice Howe Gibbens James 17 May 1894

501.1 Thursday] 'Thurs' *ab. del.*
   'Wednes'
501.1 May 17] *ab. del.* 'Mar'
501.7 better] *bef. del.* 'when'
501.9 says] *bef. del.* 'you'
501.11 had] 'd' *ov.* 've'

To Alice Howe Gibbens James [21 May 1894]

504.6 babys] *alt. fr.* 'babies'
504.7 and] *aft. del.* 'so I'; *bef. del.* 'h'
504.13 shabby] *aft. del.* 'sa'

To Alice Howe Gibbens James 23 May 1894

505.5 your] *intrl.*
505.6 place] *bef. del.* 'still'
505.6 make] *aft. del.* 'let'
505.8 Chocorua] *ab. del.* 'it'
505.14 father-] *ab. del.* 'mother-'
505.20 ever] *final* 'y' *del.*
505.21 this morning] *ab. del.* 'th'
505.22 ²the] *intrl.*
505.23 sorellar] *aft. del.* 'fratellar sol'
505.27 Ames] *ov.* 'ames'
505.29 over] *ab. del.* 'with'
505.30 account] *aft. del.* 'ag'
505.33 laboratory] *bef. del.* 'as'
505.39 leaves] *ab. del.* 'makes it'
506.1 or] *insrtd. bef. del.* 'and'
506.2 so] *bef. del.* 'f'
506.3 it] *ab. del.* 'this'

To Richard Hodgson 24 May [1894]

506.4 How] *bef. del.* 'he'll w'
506.8 Let] *bef. del.* 'that be'
506.9 Did] *aft. del.* 'Have'

To Alice Howe Gibbens James 24 May 1894

507.9 Palmer's] 'P' *ov.* 'B'
507.11 to day] *intrl.*

To Granville Stanley Hall 27 May [1894]

507.9 power,] *aft. del.* 'or direct mind-reading'; *comma ov. period*
507.9 and] *intrl. bef.* 'So [*cap. in MS retained in error*]'
508.2 Sit] *aft. del.* 'Bring'
508.3 names] *bef. del.* 'as f'
508.4 closely] *intrl. bef. del. intrl.* 'and recently'
508.5 give] *aft. del.* 'and'
508.6 she] *bef. del.* 'recently'

508.7 (strangers] *aft. del.* '(Hodgson'
508.7 failed] *aft. del.* 'only'
508.8 forgot] *ab. del.* 'didn't know'
508.8 that] *bef. del.* 'she alread'
508.11 ¹of . . . gives,] *intrl.*

To Alice Howe Gibbens James 27 May 1894

508.7 all] *aft. del.* 'All'
508.18 including . . . architect] *intrl.*
508.19 in] *ab. del.* 'with'
509.3–4 the extent of] *intrl.*
509.11 performance,] *bef. del.* 'though'
509.11 ³the] *ab. del.* 'its'
509.13 was] *intrl.*
509.16–17 amongst . . . etc.] *intrl. w. caret ov. period*
509.18 Mary] *aft. del. opening paren*
509.21 call] *bef. del.* 'her'
509.22 also] *intrl.*
509.25 Brimmers,] *bef. del.* 'to London &'
509.29 be] 'e' *ov.* 'y'
509.36 have] *insrtd.*
509.36 stopped] 'ped' *insrtd.*
509.37 of my bedroom] *intrl.*
510.4 or] *bef. del.* 'an'

To Sarah Wyman Whitman 28 May [1894]

510.6 beside] *final* 's' *del.*
510.12–13 Not . . . her.] *intrl.*
511.3 (also . . . acquisition)] *opening paren ov. dash; closing paren ov. comma*

To Alice Howe Gibbens James 28 May [1894]

511.27 sheet] *aft. del.* 'glossy'
512.3 much of] *intrl.*
512.12 A] *ov.* 'I'

To Alice Howe Gibbens James 29 May 1894

512.4 back] *aft. del.* 'p'
512.5–6 you can,] *ab. del.* 'possible' *w. comma repeated in error*
512.11 proud] *intrl.*
512.18 stolen] *aft. del.* 'so'
513.6 can] *final* "t' *del.*

513.7 neither] *aft. del.* 'on Friday at the'
513.7 the morning train] *ab. del.* 'that train'

To Margaret Mary James 5 June 1894

514.8 and] *aft. del.* 'ad'
514.10 Julie] *aft. del.* 'Ja'

To George Holmes Howison 11 June 1894

515.4 to Leipzig] *ab. del.* 'there'
515.5 only] *intrl.*
515.6 all that] *ab. del.* '['they' *del.*] what'

To Alice Howe Gibbens James 11 June 1894

515.12 such] *bef. del.* 'I'
516.2 more] *ab. del.* 'too'

To Alice Howe Gibbens James 13 June [1894]

516.6 but] *aft. del.* 'and'
516.6 got] *alt. fr.* 'good'
516.7 journey] *aft. del.* 'jouney'; *bef. del.* 'to Lenoir'
516.19 horse cow & man] *intrl.*

To Alice Howe Gibbens James 15 June 1894

517.1 Friday] *intrl.*
517.1 15] '5' *ov.* '6'
517.7 Tuesday] *aft. del.* 'Wednesday'
517.13 and] *alt. fr.* 'I s'
517.20 foreground] *aft. del.* 'forgg'
517.21 whitey] *aft. del.* 'wa'
517.23 cool] *intrl.*
517.24 sits] *aft. del.* 'still'

To Alice Howe Gibbens James 18 June 1894

518.3 me] *bef. del.* 'a while a'
518.10 really] *bef. del.* 'wants'
518.21 all] *bef. del.* 'by'

To Alice Howe Gibbens James 24 June 1894

519.8 We] 'W' *ov.* 'I'

To Alice Howe Gibbens James [25] June 1894

520.7 and is] *intrl.*
520.10 B.D.'s] 's' *aft. del.* '& his'
520.18 house] *aft. del.* 'was'

To James Mark Baldwin [26] June 1894

521.10 discern] *ab. del.* 'feel'
521.11 is] *ab. del.* 'was'

To James McKeen Cattell 26 June 1894

522.13 matter] *aft. del.* 'theory'

To Alice Howe Gibbens James 26 June [1894]

523.6 misdated] *aft. del.* 'mist'; *bef. del.* 'a'
523.10 have] *aft. del.* 'f'
523.10 $267.77] '77' *ov.* 'oo'
523.15 Henry's] 'H' *ov.* 'he'
523.17 with] *bef. del.* 'an a'
523.17 volume] *bef. del.* 'contai'
523.22 an] *final* 'd' *del.*
523.24 bring] *aft. del.* 'pr'
523.27 ¹her] *final* 'e' *del.*
523.27 She] *aft. del.* 'Th'
523.28 *10 P.M.*] *insrtd.*
523.30 of] *insrtd.*
524.4 so] *bef. del.* 'fast'
524.11 bo't] *ab. del.* 'sent'

To Alice Howe Gibbens James 27 June 1894

524.11 Thayer,] *bef. del.* 'and'
524.17 well,] *comma ov. closing paren*
524.18 Grace Norton,] *intrl.*
525.5 our . . . Estate] *intrl.*
525.6 ²We] *aft. del.* 'Wh'

To Henry Rutgers Marshall 5 July 1894

525.8 what was] *ab. del.* 'my'
525.10 candid] *aft. del.* 'im sale'
526.5 having] *aft. del.* 'ha'
526.7 writing] *intrl.*

526.9 blown] *aft. del.* 'glo'
526.16 glasses] *intrl.*

To Alice Howe Gibbens James 20 July [1894]

527.3 we] *intrl.*
527.16 lightness] *aft. del.* 'littl'

To Alice Howe Gibbens James 23 July 1894

528.9 how] *bef. del.* 'tire'
528.9 he] *aft. del.* 'he['r' *del.*]'
528.12 give] *aft. del.* 'me'
528.18 Royce] 'R' *alt. fr.* 'r'
528.28 them] *bef. del.* 'except at'
528.30 of] *aft. del.* 'But'
529.1 over] *aft. del.* 'of'

To Alice Howe Gibbens James 25 July 1894

530.7 Grande] *aft. del.* 'play'
530.8 flat] *ab. del.* 'bad'
530.13 any] *aft. del.* 'anyt'
530.16 Marie] *bef. del.* 'all ov'
530.23 mere] *bef. del.* 'illum'
530.30 Shaler's] *bef. del.* 'to'

To Alice Howe Gibbens James 26 July 1894

531.6 Phil.] *aft. del.* 'young'
531.8 article] *bef. del.* 'to'
531.19 openings] *ab. del.* 'flues'
531.24 account] *aft. del.* 'balance'
531.27 my] *aft. del.* 'th'
532.1 In] *aft. del.* 'But if the sooner it does not a'
532.8–9 to Chocorua] *intrl.*

From Paul Bourget 27 July 1894

533.22 respects] *aft. del. illeg.*

To Sarah Wyman Whitman 31 July 1894

534.7 niggardly] *bef. del. qst. mk.*
534.22 Beside] *final* 's' *del.*
534.25 summer] *ab. del.* 'term'
534.26–27 conditions of] *aft. del.* 'winter'; *bef. del.* 'work'

534.31 now] *ab. del.* 'how'
534.33 write] *bef. del. comma*
534.35 awful] *insrtd.*
534.35 Book] 'B' *ov.* 'b'

To Théodore Flournoy August 1894

535.4 has] *intrl.*
535.4 brought] *bef. del.* 'up'
535.5 of] 'o' *ov.* 'f'
535.10 salubrity] *aft. del.* 'and'
535.14 ¹at . . . of] *ab. del.* 'from'
535.22 ¹had] *bef. del.* 'go'
535.26 off] *bef. del.* 'th'
535.27 with] *bef. del.* 'my'
536.9 professors] *ab. del.* 'teachers'
536.12 500] *aft. del.* 'f'
536.18 acute] *aft. del.* 'and'
536.20 delusion] *aft. del.* 'distinct'
536.23 a year] *aft. del.* 'las'
536.24 up] *ov.* 'on'

To Hugo Münsterberg 1 August 1894

537.1 Aug] *aft. del.* 'July'
537.5 of Cambridge] *intrl.*
537.6 barbarians] *aft. del. start of* 'f'
537.8 word] *aft. del.* 'f'
537.20 live] *ab. del.* 'life'
537.25 via . . . Mountains] *intrl.*

To Francis Boott 5 September 1894

539.3 letter,] *bef. del.* 'and'
539.4 for] *bef. del.* 'bu'
539.5 in . . . that] *intrl.*
539.18 Monday] *bef. del.* 'wi'
539.20 ¹as] *final illeg. letter del.; ab. del.* 'of your'
539.26 settling] 'ing' *aft. del.* 'ed'

To Thomas Davidson 13 September 1894

540.10 I] *aft. del.* 'The'
540.14 Pierre] *intrl.*
540.21 Janet] *aft. del.* 'If'
540.23 letters] *aft. del.* 'a'

To Alice Howe Gibbens James [13 September 1894]

541.3 Middleton] *aft. del.* 'the'
541.14 all] *intrl.*

To Alice Howe Gibbens James 14 September 1894

542.1 final] *intrl.*
542.2 sent] *aft. del.* 'paid'
542.4 a] *intrl.*
542.19 bairnies] *aft. del.* 'brats'

To Alice Howe Gibbens James 16 September 1894

542.4 last] *aft. del.* 'th'
543.9 at] *aft. del.* 'in' *and start of* 'B'
543.19 & . . . rest.] *intrl. w. caret ov. period*
543.21 would] *ab. del.* 'will'
543.25 after] *aft. del.* 'and hav'
543.26 the] *intrl.*
543.30 God] *bef. del.* 'bel'
543.32 dating] *aft. del.* 'Wil'
543.32 time—] *bef. del.* 'Wilk 18'
543.38 over] *ab. del.* 'in'

To Sarah Wyman Whitman 18 September 1894

545.7 a general] *ab. del.* 'generally tene-fitel'
545.7 condition] *final* 's' *del.*
545.7 "shape"] *ab. del.* 'condition'
546.10 C.W.E.] *bef. del.* 'talking of'
546.18 last] *aft. del.* 'letter'

To Alice Howe Gibbens James [19 September 1894]

546.11 Brooks] *aft. del.* 'Witmer'
546.12 account of] *ab. del.* 'character for'
547.7 with] *bef. del.* 'ag'

To Frank Thilly 20 September 1894

548.4 I congratulate] 'I co' *ov.* 'Suc'

To Alice Howe Gibbens James 26 September 1894

548.25 Please] *aft. del.* 'Pe'
549.10 only] *aft. del.* 'ju'
549.14 looks] *aft. del.* 'and'
549.17 answered] *bef. del.* 'Louise's'
549.27 once] *aft. del.* 'y'
549.30 run] *aft. del.* 'sh'

To Frederic William Henry Myers 29 September 1894

550.24 Nothing] 'N' *ov.* 'n'
551.6 (you say "Macmillan")] *intrl.*
551.7 copies] *aft. del.* '['some' *del.*] a'
551.8 ²of] *intrl.*
551.15 I] *aft. del.* 'Will'

To Oliver Wendell Holmes, Jr. 9 October 1894

554.9 now] *bef. del.* 'bu'

To Sarah Wyman Whitman 29 October 1894

555.3 called] *bef. del. comma*
555.6 with] *aft. del.* 'witth'
555.9 ¹and] *aft. del.* 'ch'

To William Wilberforce Baldwin 5 November 1894

556.5 in] *ab. del.* 'with'
556.6 creepy] *aft. del.* 'grisly'
556.9 know] *aft. del.* 'even'
556.14 as R.,] *intrl.*

To Ellen James Temple Emmet Hunter 18 November 1894

557.4 such] *intrl.*
557.15 were] *ab. del.* 'mere'
557.19 yesterday] *intrl.*
557.24 my incomparable] *intrl.*
557.28 we] *aft. del.* 'y'
558.5 lurid] *bef. del.* 'possibilities to which'

To James Mark Baldwin 1 December 1894

558.5 admiration] *aft. del.* 'ap'
558.10 have] *aft. del.* 'should at'

To Charles William Eliot 7 December 1894

559.6 material.] *ab. del.* 'matter.'

From Charles Montague Bakewell 23 December 1894

559.10 the] *intrl.*
560.3 to use] *intrl.*
560.39 Greek] 'G' *ov.* 'g'

561.18 a] *intrl.*
561.32 from him] *intrl.*
561.32 and] *bef. del.* 'he'

From Alice Howe Gibbens James 31 December 1894

562.28 to] *intrl.*
563.3 return] *ab. del.* 'do so'

Word Division

Each word is keyed by page and line number to the individual letter. The line numbers begin anew with each letter and include all elements in the letter except the editorial heading that precedes each letter and the notes that follow. If there is more than one letter on a page to which the page-line number might refer, a prefixed [1] or [2] indicates which of the two letters is intended.

The following is a list of compound words divided at the ends of lines in the manuscripts that could be read either as one word or as a hyphenated compound. In a sense, then, the hyphenation or the nonhyphenation of possible compounds in the present list is in the nature of editorial emendation.

[1]6.1 a-days
12.29 woodcuts
[2]34.14 non-mathematical
68.22 overworking
71.15 bank-book
[1]106.5 re-writing
291.15 overburdened
363.13 handmaids

370.13 nonprofessional
385.26 over-work
417.4 first-born
[2]443.6 stand-points
497.30 overstocked
540.19 ultra-scrupulous
561.9 self-satisfied

The following is a list of words divided at the ends of lines in the present edition that are authentic hyphenated compounds as found within the lines of the manuscripts. Except for this list, all other hyphenations at the ends of lines in the present edition are the modern printer's and are not hyphenated forms in the manuscripts.

3.27 reaction-|times
19.3 long-|suffering
26.37 brain-|states
27.29 wide-|awake
[2]31.3 rose-|water
[2]34.14 non-|higher
38.38 book-|proofs
78.5 silence-|business
78.13 moon-|hid
82.27 box-|tortoise
89.21 all-|importance
[2]104.6 self-|contempts

119.12 eye-|memories
119.22 eye-|movement
119.23 arm-|movement
140.15 self-|evisceration
144.7 Caird-|Young
[1]152.8 *apperception-*|*concept*
153.14 soul-|moving
158.5 *not-*|*deaf*
158.8 wolf-|children
162.23 one-|sided
169.3 hallucination-|
   correspondence

186.4 bed-|room
202.29 make-|believe
203.35 Augusta-|Victoria
²217.6 little-|known
256.37 B.-|Séquard
259.16 life-|time
¹299.5 cable-|connexion
317.12 ill-|kept
²324.8 over-|strained
325.16 nursery-|existence
339.10 sewing-|ridden
343.1 back-|rooms
343.23 most-|infernal
379.13 identity-|theory
²397.13 after-|consequences
417.14 all-|day

439.7 les-|Blanc
451.29 laboratory-|successes
452.11 over-|instigated
455.8 emotion-|theory
¹466.6 higgledy-|piggledyism
469.20 chicken-|professors
479.22 too-|burdensome
497.13 laboratory-|psychologist
²524.6 noon-|train
538.25 Brain-|review
543.26 *bon-*|*vivant*
549.8 3-|something
560.28 reading-|room
561.10 fair-|minded
561.20 Neo-|platonic

The following are actual or possible hyphenated compounds broken at the ends of lines in both the manuscripts and the present edition.

2.17 common-|sense (i.e., common-sense)
26.16 one-|sidedness (i.e., one-sidedness)
28.26 nerve-|cells (i.e., nerve-cells)
28.40 all-|pervasive (i.e., all-pervasive)
¹277.4 Congress-|time (i.e., Congress-time)

325.26 man-|cook (i.e., man-cook)
361.26 Along-|side (i.e., Alongside)
448.13 wide-|awake (i.e., wide-awake)
462.21 red-|letter (i.e., red-letter)
562.16 working-|men (i.e., workingmen)

Chronology of Letters

The following is a chronological list of the extant letters for the period 1890–94. Calendared letters are indicated by italics. The letters to and from Henry James may be found in volume 2 of the *Correspondence*.

1890

	From Charles-Robert	March 26	*From Phillips Brooks*
	Richet	March 29	From Granville Stanley
January 5	From Charles		Hall
	Augustus Strong	*March 29*	*From Henry Holt*
January 11	*To Henry Holt*	April 1	From Granville Stanley
January 13	*From Henry Holt*		Hall
January 15	To Henry Holt	April 2	To Alice James
January 22	*To William Mackintire*	April 2	To Henry James
	Salter	April 2	From Henry Holt
January 28	*To Henry Holt*	April 5	To Henry Holt
January 28	To William Mackintire	April 7	From Granville Stanley
	Salter		Hall
February 13	*To William Mackintire*	*April 7*	*From Henry Holt*
	Salter	April 8	To Henry Holt
February 14	To Samuel Burns	*April 14*	*From Henry Holt*
	Weston	*April 18*	*To J. Raymond Derby*
February 16	To William Mackintire	*April 25*	*From Henry Holt and Co.*
	Salter	April 29	*To Christine Ladd*
February 20	*To William Mackintire*		*Franklin*
	Salter	*May 5*	*From Henry Holt*
February 20	*From Alfred Binet*	May 7	To Henry Holt
February 27	To William Mackintire	May 7	To Katharine Peabody
	Salter		Loring
March 7	*To Charles William Eliot*	*May 8*	*From Henry Holt*
March 9	From Henry James	May 9	To Henry Holt
March 11	*From Robertson James*	*May 10*	*From Henry Holt*
March 12	*From Edward Appleton*	May 13	From Charles
	Bangs		Augustus Strong
March 16	To Charles Sanders	May 16	To Granville Stanley
	Peirce		Hall
March 16	From Alice James	May 16	To Alice Howe Gib-
March 21	To Henry Holt		bens James
March 23	From Pierre Janet	*May 16*	*To Alice Howe Gibbens*
March 26	To Harry Norman		*James*
	Gardiner	May 16	From Henry James
March 26	*To Katharine Hillard*		

1892

1894

Index

A., Sir (unidentified person), 438, 439n
Abbe, Cleveland, 54
Abbot (unidentified person), 186
Abbot, Edwin Hale, 187n
Abbot, Francis Ellingwood: and Royce, 82, 83n, 217, 218–19, 220–21, 222, 223–25, 227, 229, 230, 231, 589, 594; his writings, 217n, 224, 228n, 575; and *Principles*, 575; mentioned, 102n, 187n, 273n
—letters: calendared, to, 588; calendared, from, 575
Abbott, Holker, 51, 52n
Action, 329–30
Adams, Henry, 51, 52n
Adams House, 570
Adamson, Robert, 603
Adler, Felix, 5, 6n, 218, 219n, 565
Aesthetics, 334, 526
Agassiz, Alexander, 114, 524, 525n
Agassiz, Elizabeth Cary, 525n
Agassiz, Louis, 265–66, 303, 502n
Aïdé, Hamilton, 114, 115n
Aikins, Herbert Austin, 528, 529n
Aksakov, Aleksandr Nikolaevich, 134, 135n
Albee, John, 167, 168n
Alcan, Félix, 429
Alcohol, 554–55, 608–9
Alexander VI, 355, 356n
Alexander, Samuel, 477, 478, 607
Alger, J. W., 271, 272n
Alinari (unidentified person), 409
Allen, Miss (unidentified person), 591
Allen, Joseph Henry, 571
Allori Cemetery, 405n
Altichierro, 332
American Academy of Arts and Sciences, 434–35

American Journal of Psychology, 433, 434n, 459, 460, 589
American Psychological Association: founding of, 309; and journals, 447, 448, 449; meetings of, 477, 478, 480, 481, 490n, 587, 594, 607, 618; WJ as president, 477n; minutes of, 489; presidential address, 558, 619; mentioned, 563n
Americans, 480
Ames, James Barr, 505
Ames family, 163
Amputation, 197
Anagnos, Michael: letter to, 263–64; calendared letter from, 590
Andrew (servant): and theft, 512; his sulks, 571; AGJ on, 611; mentioned, 39, 167, 507, 513n, 572, 576, 616
Andrews, Elisha Benjamin: calendared letter from, 581
Angell, Frank, 335, 407, 497, 596
Angell, James Burrill, 335
Angell, James Rowland: WJ on, 311, 312, 398, 401, 433, 599; on Nichols, 333–34; on attention, 335n; and Harvard, 434n, 446, 603; in Minnesota, 435–36; on Miller, 436; his studies, 596; and Howison, 609; mentioned, 346, 394, 399
—letters: from, 333–35; calendared, from, 596
Angell, Marion Isabel Watrous, 596
Animals, 467–68
Annie (servant), 582
Annie, Aunt (unidentified person), 584
Anthony (unidentified person), 610
Apperception, 151–52, 239
Arey, Mr. (unidentified person), 587

THE JAMES FAMILY

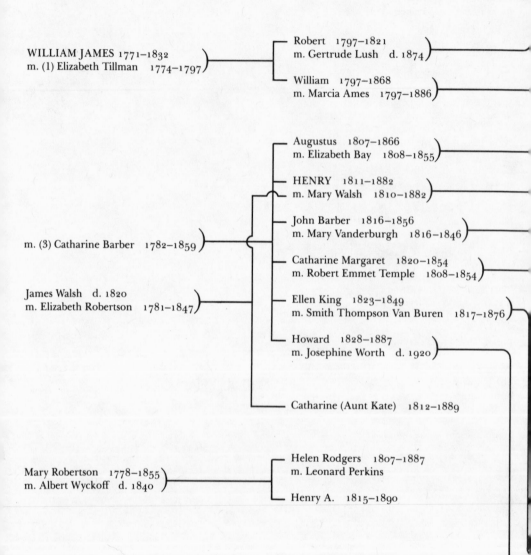

WILLIAM JAMES 1771–1832
m. (1) Elizabeth Tillman 1774–1797

> Robert 1797–1821
> m. Gertrude Lush d. 1874
>
> William 1797–1868
> m. Marcia Ames 1797–1886

m. (3) Catharine Barber 1782–1859

James Walsh d. 1820
m. Elizabeth Robertson 1781–1847

> Augustus 1807–1866
> m. Elizabeth Bay 1808–1855
>
> **HENRY** 1811–1882
> m. Mary Walsh 1810–1882
>
> John Barber 1816–1856
> m. Mary Vanderburgh 1816–1846
>
> Catharine Margaret 1820–1854
> m. Robert Emmet Temple 1808–1854
>
> Ellen King 1823–1849
> m. Smith Thompson Van Buren 1817–1876
>
> Howard 1828–1887
> m. Josephine Worth d. 1920
>
> Catharine (Aunt Kate) 1812–1889

Mary Robertson 1778–1855
m. Albert Wyckoff d. 1840

> Helen Rodgers 1807–1887
> m. Leonard Perkins
>
> Henry A. 1815–1890

Note: Stemmata are simplified to names often mentioned in the letters